MARRIAGE RECORDS

of

BERKELEY COUNTY, VIRGINIA

for the Period of

1781 - 1854

I0121624

located at

Berkeley County Court House

Martinsburg, W.Va.

Compiled and edited by

Guy L. Keesecker

CLEARFIELD

Originally published: Strasburg, Virginia, 1969
Reprinted: Genealogical Publishing Co., Inc.
Baltimore, 1983
Copyright © 1969 by Guy L. Keesecker
All Rights Reserved
Library of Congress Catalogue Card Number 83-80079
International Standard Book Number 0-8063-1023-5
Made in the United States of America

Reprinted for
Clearfield Company, Inc. by
Genealogical Publishing Co., Inc.
Baltimore, Maryland
1995, 1998, 2003

CONTENTS

*Compiled and edited at Martinsburg, Berkeley County, West Virginia during 1967 and 1968

A list of

ALL MARRIAGE BONDS, with their Suretors

and

ALL MARRIAGE CEREMONIES, performed by Certain Ministers

entered in

THE BERKELEY COUNTY, VIRGINIA RECORD BOOKS

during the period of

1781 - 1854

now stored in the Vaults in

BERKELEY COUNTY COURT HOUSE, MARTINSBURG, WEST VIRGINIA

Compiled and edited from the Originals

in

Seven Marriage Bond Books,

One Miscellaneous Marriage Record Book*,

One Combination Church and Court Record Book,

(three parts)

(Cross-indexed with both male and female names for your convenience)

by

© Guy L. Keesecker 1969

Martinsburg, W. Va.

FOREWORD

The purpose of the following pages is to preserve and organize for easy data retrieval valuable information located here in Berkeley County, West Virginia, for reference for present and future historians, genealogists and students who wish to study the families involved and the course of the Great Migration to the West. Since the settlement of the land beyond the "Blue Mountains", as the Blue Ridge was called, was the opening chapter in that important event and since little has been done to acquaint the reader of the out-standing part our West Virginia ancestors played in that early American drama, I thought it advisable to investigate and search out every fact or record that might tell us the true details of that story and make it usable for the enlightenment and enjoyment of our descendants. This volume is the first step in that project.

To do this properly it is necessary that the names of the families of the Eastern Panhandle, where much of this history occurred, should be catalogued according to the counties where they lived and married. Then, in order to save the many hours, days and months that can be wasted in searching for family details, each marriage should be set down in a cross-indexed form, whereby, in minutes, one can learn the basic families that lived in the area at a certain time and proceed with this information as a starting point. And finally, by a careful study of the Will, Deed, and other Court Record Books, a fairly rapid tracing of a Family's Ancestry can be made with less labor. My hope is that this tool, as this work might be called, will make it easier for our children to seek out and assemble facts and dates about their forebears, and, also, to enable compilers of history, as they read the records hidden in these ancient books in our Court House, our Churches and our Library, to appreciate and report the important contribution the people, here, made to the expansion and progress of our nation.

Much effort has been made to compile this record with as few errors as possible. The spelling of the names has been examined carefully. On one or more of the following pages various ways of spelling the names of ministers and families are shown so the reader may understand at first hand some forms of names he may not have been familiar with, and by following the leads given, may save himself mistakes and time. Then, too, the searcher should realise at this early time in our country's development few people had received an education. Many could neither read nor write their own language. It was considered an accomplishment to be able to sign properly your own name.

There, also, were the problems which occur when a number of different nationalities are thrown into the society of each other. The language barrier caused much confusion in the spelling of names. Countless times the Court Penman wrote what he thought he heard, however inaccurate, leaving with us the few facts , we now have laboriously garnered.

This, the result of that effort, is an account of each Berkeley County family and the Marriage Bond Books and the Church Record Books in which they are found from the years 1781 through 1854. The No. 8 Bond Book, which would have completed the annals up to 1865 and the Civil War has been lost.

Notice that each marriage is cross-indexed in both male and female names, followed by the date of the bond, if known, then the wedding date, and the suretor of the bond, then the minister's name, and finally, thirteen locations where the information may be found, are listed in the final columns. There are seven Bond Books with the page references, marked as shown, 1b100, which means it is to be found in #1 Bond Book on page 100. The other six Bond Books are listed in this same column, as 3b190, 6b137, etc. In the #4 Bond Book were found five bonds, unattached. These are shown as 4b LL, meaning they are Loose Leaves in the #4 Book, with no page number to each bond. Sixteen bonds are , also, seen in this column of symbols, which were found separated from all listed above. They are given as, 1b x, because the dates they bore were 1789, similar to the age of the #1 Bond Book. However, there was no place to store them properly, so they were placed in the front of a Marriage Book the D. A. R. Society was having restored at the time.

This restored Marriage Book was planned to be in three separate sections, that is, before the sixteen bonds were found and placed in the front of the book. This book was not to be a record of bonds, but instead, the first section of forty one pages comprised the Church Marriage records of a number of religious faiths and are listed as, cr 29, which indicates one is located on page 29 of this group. The second section included fifteen pages of marriages performed by the German Congregation, with the symbol, gc 1, meaning a marriage can be seen on page 1 of this part. The third section was of eighty eight pages shown as, mr100, giving page 100 as the location. This final part was composed of both marriage dates and, also, the dates the marriage certificates were filed in the Court House.

Together with these is a large Leather-bound book, sometimes referred to as the Miscellaneous Marriage Book. All marriages given in this book are in chronological order and are marked with an (*) in the last column.

The editor of this volume wishes to acknowledge, for their kind and helpful assistance and timely suggestions the following persons, namely: Mr. Eugene C. Dunham and his staff of the County Court, including Mr. John W. Small Jr., Mrs. Frye, Mrs. Denton, Mrs. Vickers, Mrs. Kershner; Mrs. Russell Bergen; Mrs. Harley Griffith; Mrs. Shewbridge and Mrs. Sendindiver of the library staff; and finally, Mr. Francis Silver, whose appreciation of the need of such an index gave me much encouragement, and his reviewing of the final product was extremely helpful. To all of these people and others I am very grateful.

Guy Leon Keesecker

Martinsburg, W. Va.
September, 1968.

VARIOUS FORMS OF SPELLING

MINISTER'S NAMES

Bragunier—Bragonier—Brazonier

Eglestone—Eaglestone—Azelstone

Hedtt—Hutt—Huth

Keepler—Kepler—Keppler

Lippeth—Lippelt—Lippett

Paynter—Pakmker—Raynker

Reebenack—Ravenack—Ravenaugh—Rabenach

Riser—Riser

Streit—Streik

Sturges—Sturgis

Two spelled their names "Charles P. Krauth" and three spelled "D or David Thomas".

(The dates of the service of these last two names give clues to this fact).

The first form of spelling appeared most often, but occasionally the others did also.

FAMILY'S AND SURETOR'S NAMES

Aart, Aout	Barrack, Barrett, Barrott	Blots, Bloys
Alabaugh, Alle-, Ally-, Aule-, Oll-	Bashore, Basore, Bayshore, Baysore	Boden, Bodine, Burdine
Anglous, English	Beal, Beales, Bell, Beall, Belle	Bogle, Vogle, Voigal
Athe, Athey, Athea	Beatty, Beaty	Bossell, Boxwell, Bozwell
Backenstats, Backenstos	Batliff, Bedliff	Bower Smith, Bowersmith
Baer, Bare, Bear	Bilmire, Bilmyer, Bilmyre, Billmire	Brather, Brother, Prather
Baggs, Boggs	Bitzer, Pitzer	Burkett, Burkhart
Balen, Baler, Bales	Blamer, Bleamer	Burnoff, Burnoss

Campbell, Cample
Canklin, K., Conklyn, Cunklin
Chrisman, Crisman
Chriswell, Criswell
Claycomb, Klaycomb, Kleicum
Comfee, Kumfee
Conaway, Conoway, Conway
Coons, Coontz, Kuntz
Copenhaver, Covenhaver
Conover, Cownover
Cramer, Creamer
Crem, Crim, Crum, Krum
Croesen, Kroesen
Cushwa, Gushwa
Dederick, Deiderick, Tederick
Devault, Devrall
Downes, Downs
Dunfee, Dunphy
Emberson, Emerson, Emmerson
Falk, Folck, Folk, Fouck, Foulke
Fernough, Fernow

Files, Philes
Fiser, Fizer
Flickinger, Fluckinger
Foran, Foren
Freize, Freize, Friese, Prize
Fullerton, Fullaton
Garard, Gerrard
Handshaw, Henshaw
Hamme, Hanna
Haselip, Haslip, Hazlett
Hawniker, Hanniker
Hedtt, Hett, Hitc, Hutt, Huth
Helferstay, -stine, Helphington
Hoffman, Hoofman, Huffman
Kain, Kaign, Kane
Karns, Kearns, Kerns
Kees, Keyes, Keys
Keesacre, -acker, Keysacker, -singer
Kennedy, Kennode
Keebler, -pler, -epler, -ibler, -up-
Klice, Klise, Clise

Kline, Cline
Kookus, Cookus
Kiser, Kyser, Keyser
Kiger, Kyger
Laman, Lamon, Lemen, Lemon
Laign, Lane
Liday, Lydy
McAllister, McAllister, McCollister
McGlaughlin, McLaughlin
McGowan, McKowan, McKown
Mallenaux, Malonex
Marchant, Merchant
Mayhew, Mayhugh, Mehu
Markle, Mericle
Metcalf, Midcalf, Mudcalf
Maxwell, Mixall, Moixwell, Marion
Moore, Murrer
Orick, Ororke, Orrick
Pain, Paine, Payne
Palmer, Pilmer
Panabaker, Pennybaker, Bennybaker

Parcels, Purcels	Saibert, Sey-, Sy-, Suber, Zuber	Waight, Waite
Parrell, Parrott	Seigler, Zeigler, Sigler	Vanarsdal, Vanorsdal
Pearce, Pierce	*Shimp, Stump	Vermilion, Vermilyea
Pearl, Perrel, Perrell	Siler, Syler, Ziler, Zyler, Seilor	Waggoner, Wagner, Wagoner
Pittlock, Pitturick	Snider, Snyder, Schneider	Warner, Wawner
Pitzer, Bitzer	Soister, Soyster, Syester	Waugh, Waw
Pisel, Poisal	Star, Starr, Starry, Stow	Wedse, Wise
Paulsgrove, Pottsgrove, Pultsgrove	Steelz, Stutz, Stuntz	Whitenaugh, Whiteneck, Whitney
Pulse, Pultz	Stookey, Stuckey	Wilson, Willson
Rainey, Raney	Strayer, Stayer, Streher	Windham, Windom
Ralphsnider, Refsnaider, Refsnyder	*Stump, Shimp	Wibly, Woibly
Rheinstine, Rightstine	Swaringen, Swearingen	Winecoop, Wynkoop
Riner, Ryner	Thruston, Thurston, Thirston	Yates, Yeates
Riser, Rizer	Ulum, Ulm, Wolham, Wollam	Yost, Youtz
*	*	*

Below is an example which explains the location of each item in the following cross-index.

Name of Marriage Participants	Date of bond	Date of marriage	Name of Suretor	Name of minister	Book and bond	Church Rec'ds	Cert. Court Rec'ds
Bartleson, James m. Parker, Barbara	Mar. 31,	Apr. 2, 1812	John Poisal	Rev. Reebenack	3b218	gc 12	*
VanMetre, Nancy m. Alburtis, John	Feb. 7,	Feb. 7, 1809	Robert Wilson	John Mathews	3b107	cr 17	mr 23 *

The * in the right-hand column indicates data can be found chronologically in the Leather-bound Miscellaneous Book.

Virginia—Berkeley County, to wit:

Know all men by these presents, That we, Rudolph Deere

and Jonathan Doe

are held and firmly bound unto the Commonwealth of Virginia in the sum of One Hundred and Fifty Dollars, to be paid to the said Commonwealth for the use of the Commonwealth; for the true payment whereof we bind ourselves, and our heirs, jointly and severally, firmly by these presents. Sealed with our seals, and dated this 1st day of May, one thousand eight hundred and one

THE CONDITION OF THE ABOVE OBLIGATION is—that whereas a License is desired for a marriage, intended to be had and solemnised, between the above bound Rudolph Deere

and Fanny Doe

of this County. Now, if there is no lawful cause to obstruct the said marriage, then the above obligation to be void else to remain in full force and virtue.

Sealed and Delivered }
in presence of

Don T. Waite
Clk.

his
Rudolph x Deere
mark
his
Jonathan J. Doe
mark

A fac-simile of a Berkeley County, Virginia Bond of the 1781-1854 Period.

The Institution of marriage as accepted in early Colonial America followed very closely the laws of matrimony as practiced in England, since England was the Mother Country. Even though there were some exceptions to this rule, in most cases the Crown and the Church performed in unison to enforce their doctrines. It was a plan in which they derived a mutual benefit, both in promoting military and religious control over their subjects and at the same time securing finances from the fees, required for each ceremony, and from the penalties, if these rules were not followed in their entirety.

(1) To secure this practice certain laws were drawn up. By present day standards many of them seem uncommonly severe. Even so, they formed the basis of our regulations to-day. Some of them may be reviewed here as follows: according to Hening's Statutes, "No minister shall celebrate matrimony betweene any persons without a facultie or lycense graunted by the Governor, except the baynes of matrimony have beene first published three severall Sundays or holy-days in the time of devyne service in the parish churches where the sayd persons dwell................."

(2) "The fees for the lycences to be as followeth (viz):

    to the Governor   200 pounds of tobacco or 20 shillings; to the clerke 50 pounds; to the secretarie 40;   to the minister   200 pounds or 20 shillings marrying with a lycence, if by baynes 50 pounds or 5 sh."

(3) "And if any minister shall contrary to this Act marry any persons, he shall be fined tenn thousand pounds of tobacco, and any pretended marriage hereafter made by any other than a minister be refuted null, and the children borne out of such marriage of the parents, be esteemed illegitimate, and the parents suffer such punishment as ..."

(4) "If a girl 12 to 16 years of age shall contrary to the consent of her parents or guardian and without public-ation of banns agree to a marriage, her lawful inheritance shall descend to the next of kin and her child disinherited."

(5) Even in 1775 a tax of 40 shillings was placed on every marriage, besides the necessity of the bond as security.

(6) The penalty on ministers for marrying servants without a certificate from their masters was 10,000 pds. of tob'o.

The severity of these laws gradually diminished as the 17th century merged with the 18th and the restless movement of the colonials began to surge westward. The mixture of people from various European ports arriving in this land caused a blending of thought and the English influence moderated to some degree. As the 19th century approached and the western civilization shrugged off the ruinous years of the Revolution, accepted the new feeling of "liberty" and faced the reality of their immediate problems they met head-on the danger of Indian massacre, the scarcity of food and medicines, and the need for social and religious advantages. The distances from the cities made it imperative that people congregate in meeting-places on the frontier. By this necessity the practice of circuit riding lawyers and preachers passing from one such community to another came into being. Even with this advance there were not enough lawyers and ministers to meet the situation, so a new law came into use:

(7) "An Act to authorize and confirm marriages in certain cases.

WHEREAS it has been represented to this present General Assembly, that many of the good people in the remote parts of the Commonwealth are destitute of any persons, authorized by law, to solemnize marriages among them; BE IT ENACTED, that where it shall appear to the Court of any County, in the western waters, that there is not a sufficient number of clergymen authorized to celebrate marriages therein, such Court is hereby empowered to nominate so many sober and discreet laymen as will supply the deficiency; and each of the persons so nominated, upon taken the Oath of allegiance to this state, shall receive a license to celebrate the rights of matrimony, according to the forms and customs of the church of which he is a reputed member,...............

AND BE IT ENACTED, that all publications of banns of matrimony, in the said western waters, shall be made in three several days, and not in less time than two weeks, in open public assemblies, convened for religious worship or other lawful purposes, within the bounds of the respective congregation or militia companies, in which the parties to be married severally reside......................................"

(8) As the population grew the Governor who was the only one authorized to certify a bond made a new ruling

whereby the eldest magistrate of the County was empowered to perform in place of the Governor. This responsibility fell on the Clerk of the Court and the secretary was ordered to list the names of the marriage participants, their surety and the tenor of the bond in the records.

The form of Bond used in Virginia up to 1805 required the posting of 50 pounds as security. After that time the amount was changed to 150 dollars. By then a stable form of monetary exchange had been adopted.

When one or both of the participants in a marriage were under the usual age and were refused a bond, the parent or guardian of this person was required to send a letter sanctioning the wedding. This was sent to the Clerk of the Court who had it recorded as his authority for issuing a certificate. For example this form of permit follows:

Mr. Waitts

    I do in form you That my daughter is of age and

    I am willing for John Sherer to Marry my daughter Sarah.

Robert Johnston   Ellender Johnson

                          (Berk. Co. Bond Book #6, p. 33—Feb. 26, 1835)
                          (Hezekiah Johnston, Suretor—6b33).

(9) Because of fraudulent tactics practiced by Clerks of neighboring counties a new Law was made as follows:"

IT IS ENACTED, that the Act for Lycences to issue certificates from clerkes of the county courts be declared to extend to noe other clerke but of the county, where the maid, her parents or guardian dwell...............
.... and every clerke that shall grant them otherwise than above expressed shall forfeit his place."

The Colonial influence was beginning to mellow the existing restrictions to the point that "Common Law" marriages were being accepted, especially among the Scottish immigrants and other nationalities that did not adher to British beliefs, before, and who wished to follow their own inherited doctrines. It was about this time around the year 1848 the Catholic faith arose to a position of prominence in Church affairs in Berkeley County, Virginia.

References: Hening's Statutes, (1)1 H 156; (2)2 H 54, 55; (3)2 H 51; (4)3 H 443, 444; (5)9 H 66; (6)2 H 114; (7)11 H 281(May 1783); (8)2 H 28; (9)2 H 281.

xi

MINISTERS

The various ministers who served in this community, during this period, and officiated at the wedding ceremonies performed in Berkeley County, Virginia and listed in the records are given here, together with the dates indicated.

They are printed alphabetically as follows:

Adam, Thomas	1807-
Allemong, John	1830-1837
Anardus, L. W.	1850-1854
Arnold, D. W.	1851-
Bailey, James	1825-
Baker, James	1847-1852
Baker, Joseph	1825-1853
Bansle, Jacob	1812-
Bauman, John	1850-
Beecher, Jacob	1827-1829
Bell, John	1784-
Belmain, Alex.	1813-1816
Berry, R. L.(T)	1850-1854
Bogg, John	1844-1847
Bond, Jacob	1804-1814
Boyd, A. H.	1853-
Boyd, John	1794-1806
Bragunier, D. F.(G)	1845-1854
Bromwell, Jacob L.	1823-1829
Brown, James M.	1824-1834
Brown, J. W.	1855-
Brown, Richard F.	1846-1850
Dunn, Seely	1813-
Cadden, Robert	1829-1831
Chenoweth, A. G.	1852-1853
Chisholm, James	1842-1849
Colloway, C.L.(M)	1833-1854
Cooper, Geo. W.	1833-1859
Deale, John S.	1853-
Dennis, J. M.	1853-
Duckwall, Lewis	1803-
Dulin, E. L.	1846-1847
Dutton, W. B.	1853-

Eglestone, W. G.	1854-
Ernest, J. W.	1851-
Fink, Reuben A.	1852-1853
Frary, J. L.	1855-
Frye, George M.	1812-1822
Furlong, Henry	1847-1851
Gardner, Elisha	1835-1837
Gibbons, John L.	1825-
Goheen, Mayberry	1842-1843
Graham, J. R.	1856-
Grove, John	1843-1854
Hall, William	1793-
Hamill, John	1835-
Hamilton, M. G.	1839-
Hamme, Jacob	1840-
Hanney, John	1851-
Harris, George W.	1851-1854
Harrison, James	1811-
Harrison, Peyton	1838-1842
Hawk(Hauk), W.	1832-1833
Hedges, John	1841-
Hedtt(Hutt), John	1797-1800
Herndon, R. N.	1835-1838
Hill, John	1793-1797
Hill, William	1793-1795
Hoge, John B.	1810-1822
Hoge, Moses	1781-1806
Howell, John	1834-1836
Hughes, James	1852-
Humphries, Geo. W.	1833-
Israel, F.	1854-
Jackson, J. E.	1827-1837
Jennings, James H.	1842-1858

Kearsley, John	1799-
Kehler, John	1818-1819
Keppler, Samuel	1834-
Krauth, Charles Jr.	1848-
Krauth, Chas. P.	1819-1827
Larken, J.	1837-
Light, John	1830-1854
Light, Joseph	1797-
Lippett, E. R.	1821-
Lipscomb, P.	1847-1850
Love, Wm.	1847-1850
Mathews, John	1806-1830
Mayer, Lewis	1808-1823
Medtart, Jacob	1828-1832
Mercer, W. F.	1843-
Mines, John	1802-1803
Monroe, T.H.W.	1828-1844
Page, Bernard	1794-
Paynter, James	1820-
Payton,Jos. Jas.	1820-
Phelps, E. P.	1837-
Plunkett, James	1848-1854
Potts, John	1797-1799
Proctor, John	1853-1855
Redmond, James	1820-
Reebenack, Rev.	1791-1816
Reily(Riley), Jas.	1825-1841
Riley, James	1827-
Reynolds, Benedict	1823-1828
Reynolds, J. S.	1845-1846
Reynoldsen, John	1844-
Rinehart, Jacob	1853-
Riser(-z-), Mathias	1816-1819

Robertson, S. S.	1821-
Rozell, Stephen	1841-
Samson, James	1822-1823
Schmucker, B. M.	1848-1851
Scott, W. N.	1811-1821
Shepherd, John	1825-
Smith, Samuel	1840-
Sprigg, D. Francis	1844-1854
Start, Nathan	1815-
Stephenson, G.	1853-
Stinger, Daniel	1781-1782
Stredt, Christian	1787-1809
Sturges, Daniel	1780-1782
Swift, Richard	1791-1806
Talbott, William	1799-
Talty, Andrew	1852-1853
Tebb, F. C.	1850-1851
Thomas, D.	1789-1795
Thomas, David	1832-
Thomas, David	1851-1853
Tibbett, Wm.	1797-
Tiffin, Edward	1785-1795
Vance, David	1793-1798
Vance, Hugh	1781-1793
Watts, James	1837-1855
Waugh, J. H.	1848-
Wilson, Jas. F.	1838-
Wilson, Lewis F.	1837-1854
Winter, John	1823-1849
Wolff, John W.	1849-
Young, J. David	1791-1804
Young, Nathan	1796-1837

Introduction to the Families

As we turn the page and meet for the first time the families represented here let us stop and reflect. These were the people who faced the wilderness with all its hardship, all its horror and all its uncertainty. They settled the land and made it fruitful, formed religious principles that have stood the test of years, conquered the tremendous problems of transportation and endured the ruin of many wars. Their mechanical genius surprised the rest of the world.

They have fought for the Rights of Common Man against the oppression of foreign influences. Theirs were the roots of western mankind which made America grow.

West Virginians of every nationality, every race and every creed, we salute you!

Name	(Date)	(Marriage)	(suretor)	(minister)	(bond)	
Aart, Solomon m. Harman, Elizabeth	Apr. 2,	May 18, 1815	Benoni Swingle	Rev. Reebemack	6b164	gc 14 *
Abbott, Elizabeth C. m. Wiley, James	June 3,	1839	Harrison Waite		6b107	
Abell, Joseph F. m. Good, Mary A.	Feb. 2,	1837	James Abernathy		1b166	
Abernathy, Ann m. Rankin, Samuel	Nov. 3,	1799	John Sharp		4b 49	mr 55 *
Abernathy, Clark m. Sharp, Rebecca	Jan. 10,	Nov. 6, 1817	Samuel Abernathy	Nathan Young	3b281	
Abernathy, Mary m. Johnson, Moses	Oct. 16,	1814	Daniel McKeever	Nathan Young	4b120	mr 56 *
Achey, Samuel m. McKeever, Jane	Aug. 14,	Oct 17, 1819	Aron Ralphsnider	Lewis Mayer	3b119	cr 16 mr 24 *
Achey, Michael m. Refschnider, Mary	May 23,	Sep 14, 1809	John Shepherd		5b 12	
Acres, George m. Shepherd, Margaret	May 1,	1825	Nathan Start		3b322	
Acres, Sarah m. Kalklacer, John C.		1815				
Adam, Samuel m. Cokenheas, Elizabeth		1798		David Young		gc 7 *
Adams, Jane m. Kiger, George Jr.	Apr. 8,	June 9, 1801	William Mackey	John Boyd	2b120	cr 35 mr 19 *
Adams, Mary Cath. m. Trowbridge, Wm.		Apr 3, 1854		John Grove	1b114	
Adams, Samuel m. Akinhead, Eliz.	June 8,	Feb 23, 1798	Robert Grimes			
Addams, Sarah m. Taylor, William		Nov 8, 1818		Nathan Young		mr 56 *
Addy, Robert m. Hughes, Elizabeth	Apr. 13,	Apr 14, 1798	George Snyder	Richard Swift	1b 98	cr 31 mr 15 *
Ady, Jessimina m. Pierce, William	Sep. 23,	1807	Thos. Blackburn		3b 71	
Aget, Abraham m. Zimmerman, Eliz.	Nov. 9,	1805	William Wheeler		3b 2	
Agent, Catherine m. Wheeler, Wm.	Apr. 10,	1806	Abraham Agent		3b 16	
Agre, John m. Sly, Catherine	Sept 8,	1798	Mathias Sly		1b130	
Agre, Robert m. Athy, Ann Harriet	Jan. 1,	Jan 2, 1798	Wilson Athy	Richard Swift	1b 77	cr 12 mr 16 *
Aiken, Alexander m. Kennedy, Margaret		Apr 17, 1783		Hugh Vance		mr 32 *
Aiken, John m. Hott, Ann	May 24,	1843	John Hott		6b298	
Aiken, Mary m. Hott, George	Jan. 16,	1843	John Aiken		6b287	
Aiken, Rachel m. Bell, Richard	Aug 10,	Aug 11, 1807	Robert Aiken	John Mathews	3b 66	cr 13 mr 23 *
Aiken, William m. Slaughter, Cath.	Feb 12,	1799	William Askew		1b170	
Ainsworth, Eliz. m. Eversole, Daniel	Apr 18,	1800	Wm. Ainsworth		2b 66	
Aldnhead, Eliz. m. Adams, Samuel	June 8,	1798	Robert Grimes		1b114	
Aky, Michael m. Ralfsnider, Mary	Aug. 14,	Sept 14, 1809	Aron Ralfsnider		3b119	or 16 mr 24 *
Alaman, Casper m. Dick, Christena	Mar 3,	Jan 25, 1818	John Shimp	Lewis Mayer	4b138	mr 29 *
Albright, Peter m. Shimp, Salome	July 15,	1820		Mathias Riser		
Albright, Peter m. Wilson, Sarah Ann	Dec 16,	1847	George M. Wilson		7b100	
Alburtis, Elizabeth m. Boyer, John		1813	Robert Wilson		3b279	
Alburtis, John m. Taylor, Cath. Eliz.	Dec 31,	Dec 31, 1805	Chet D. Wilson	Moses Hoge	3b 7	cr 17 mr 22 *
Alburtis, John m. Varmetre, Nancy	Feb 7,	1809	Robert Wilson	John Mathews	3b107	cr 17 mr 23 *
Alburtis, Josina m. Baker, J.L.W.	Apr 25,	Apr 25, 1848	Alfred Schnebly	James Chisholm	7b128	mr 78 *
Alburtis, J__ m. Mathews, Enoch	Nov 3,	1806	John Alburtis		3b 35	
Alburtis, Mary Ann m. Sutton, Daniel	Jan 17,	Jan 17, 1850	G.W. Miller	W. Love	7b175	mr 80 *
Alburtis, Samuel m. Showers, Susan M.	Mar 13,	Mar 13, 1847	Ezekiel Showers	John Winters	7b 91	mr 77 *
Alder, Marcus m. Swardgan, Priscilla	Jan 20,	1791		Moses Hoge		
Alder, Thomas m. Myers, Mary	Jan 23,	1837	John W. Daily		7b212	cr 5 mr 6 *
Ale, John m. Brown, Elizabeth	May 28,	1817	Valentine Ale	R. T. Berry	4b 36	mr 83 *
Alebaugh, Sally O. m. Houck, David	Apr 2,	1807	Jacob Houck		3b 54	

Name	(marriage)	(suretor)	(minister)	(bond)	ref	ref
Alexander, Elijah m. Hedges, Rebecca	Dec. 2, 1823	Josiah Hedges	Chas. P. Krauth	4b253		mr 46 *
Alexander, Mary m. Price, Daniel	Feb. 23, 1828	John Stanley	Nathan Young	5b 91		mr 59 *
Alexander, Rebecca m. Robinson, Sam'l	Jan. 27. 1840	Alex. Robinson		6b195		*
Allabaugh, Jacob m. Jeffries, Nancy	Oct. 6, 1810	Christn Mussetter	John Hedges	3b162		mr 72 *
Allabaugh, Amelia m. Phillips, Jason	Sept 25, 1841	Curtis Vermilyea	B. Reynolds	6b247		mr 52 *
Allebaugh, Eliz. m. Bowers, John	Apr. 9. 1828	Jacob Allebaugh		5b 98	gc 11	
Allebaugh, Jacob m. Jefferson, Nancy	Oct. 8, 1810		Rev. Reebenack			
Allebaugh, John m. Bowers, Mary	Apr. 18, 1825	John Bowers	Nathan Young	5b 8		mr 58 *
Allebaugh, Mary m. Spriggs, Robert	Mar. 23, 1826	James Beggs	Nathan Young	5b 38		mr 58 *
*Allemong, John m. Payne, Hannah	Jan. 17. 1823	John Payne	Nathan Young	4b232		
Allen, Elizabeth m. Collins, Thomas	May 3, 1785	William Allen	Hugh Vance			mr 33 *
Allen, Ruth m. Cresamor, Jacob	Mar. 3. 1800	Thomas Allender		2b 55		
Allender, Martha m. Devers, Joseph	Aug. 11. 1817			4b 42		
Aller, Eve m. Pitzer, Jacob	Mar. 30. 1788	Jacob Houke	Rev. Reebenack	3b317	gc 14	
Allison, Joshua m. Anford, Priscilla	Apr. 6, 1815		Moses Hoge	1b x		*
Allison, Mary m. Beton, John	Aug. 21. 1789	Henry Albright	Nathan Young	5b168		mr 36 *
Allott, Phebe m. Henderson, James	June 16, 1830	James McCouch	Nathan Young			mr 60
Allstadt, Susanna m. McPherson, Dan'l	Apr. 17, 1797	Isaac Allstadt	Nathan Young	1b 8	gc 14	mr 58 *
Allybaugh, John m. Bowers, Susannah	Apr. 18, 1825	John Bowers		5b 8		
Alt, William m. Darr, Susannah	July 19. 1800	John Rusler	Nathan Young	2b 76	cr 4	mr 5 *
Alway, Jane m. Britton, John	Mar. 30. 1790	Jacob Houke	Rev. Reebenack	3b317	gc 10	
Ambrose, Daniel m. Marquart, Sophia	Aug. 4, 1809	Nicholas Marquart	Rev. Reebenack	3b116		mr 29 *
Ambrose, Daniel m. Riser, Anna	Dec. 7, 1819	John Strother	Moses Hoge	4b 26		
Ambrose, David m. Waugh, Mary(Maria)	Jan. 25, 1818	William Waugh	Rev. Reebenack	4b 58	cr 15	mr 4 *
Ambrose, Margaret m. Riser, George	Dec. 1, 1789		Mathias Riser			
Ambrose, Mathias m. Clover, Rosanna	May 11, 1791		Christian Streit			
Ambrose, Polly m. Henry, Peter	Dec. 14, 1811	Nicholas Henry	David Young	3b203		
Ambrose, William m. Weller, Mary A.	Apr. 24, 1833	Harrison Waite		5b270		
Amey, George m. Winn, Elizabeth	June 24, 1797	Henry Fiser		1b 23		
Anderson, Amelia m. Varmeter, James	Oct. 28, 1829	Colbert Anderson	Nathan Young	5b144		mr 60 *
Anderson, Annabella m. Wilson, John	June 20, 1826	Charles D. Stewart	John Mathews	5b 44		mr 50 *
Anderson, Colbert m. Varmeter, Isab.	Apr. 22, 1833	Ab'm Varmeter	Nathan Young	5b268		mr 66 *
Anderson, Cornelius m. Troxwell, Eliz.	May 26, 1838	Robt. McIntire	James Watts	6b139		mr 69 *
Anderson, Elenor m. Kerney, John	Apr. 24, 1810	George Holliday		3b148		
Anderson, Eliz. m. Conover, Benj.	Dec. 12, 1827	Colb. Anderson	B. Reynolds	5b 85		mr 52 *
Anderson, Eliz. m. Hollinger, Geo	Jan. 17, 1803	Henry March		2b190		
Anderson, Harriet M. m. Ball, Alex.	Aug. 3, 1828	Benjamin Custer		5b104		
Anderson, Horace m. Tucker, Susan	June 21, 1832	Horace Anderson		5b232		
Anderson, Isabell m. Lettman, Peter	Mar. 15, 1827	John Shober	B. Reynolds	5b 63		mr 52 *
Anderson, Jabez m. Grimes, Margaret	July 29, 1811	William Anderson		3b192		
*Allemong, Jane m. Ellis, Leonard	Nov. 15, 1781	Robert Grimes	Daniel Sturges	3b 91		mr 42 *

Name	(marriage)	(surator)	(minister)	(bond)		
Anderson, Jacob m.Otton, Sarah	Sept 22, 1827	John Shober	Benedict Reynolds	5b 79		mr 52 *
Anderson, Jacob m. Roberts, Charity	Oct. 3, 1808	James Orrick		3b 97		
Anderson, James m. Creighton, Diana	Dec. 27, 1798	William Sterret	John Boyd	1b157	cr 37	mr 16 *
Anderson, James m. Gregory, Emily S.	Apr. 17, 1851	George Butler	D. F. Spriggs	7b222	cr 16	mr 84 *
Anderson, James m. Schoppert Chr'ena	Apr. 6, 1805	Nicholas Schoppert	Christian Streit	2b259	cr 25	mr 22 *
Anderson, John m. Culp, Elizabeth	May 28, 1794		Edward Tiffin		cr 38	mr 9 *
Anderson, John m. Duke, Sally(Polly)	July 23, 1799	Alex. Rogers	John Heitt(Hutt)	2b 11		mr 17 *
Anderson, John m. Murphy, Lydia	Mar. 8, 1837	Geo. W. Hensell	L. F. Wilson	6b101		
Anderson, John m. Stout, Rebecca	Mar. 9, 1804	Philip Stout		2b226		
Anderson, Jonathan m. Cornell, Willy	July 16, 1801	Basil Games		2b130		
Anderson, Joseph m. French, Nancy	Sept 2, 1833	George French		5b281		
Anderson, Lucy E. m. Dorsey, Wm.	Nov. 2, 1844	John S. Harrison	James Chisholm	7b 12		mr 75 *
Anderson, Mahala m. Stanley, Archel'd	Jan. 10, 1838	Isaac Stanley		6b130		
Anderson, Margaret m. Hodge, John	Jan. 13, 1840	David Hayes		6b193		
Anderson, Margaret m. Kidd, Chas.	Dec. 26, 1803	George Anderson		2b217		
Anderson, Mary m. Higgins, John	Sept 26, 1825	John Anderson	James Redley	5b 22		mr 49 *
Anderson, Mary m. Lewis, Franklin	Oct. 31, 1838	Wm. Anderson	James Watts	6b149		mr 69 *
Anderson, Mary m. McClure, Richard	Oct. 5, 1821	Joseph McFeely	Nathan Young	4b193		mr 57 *
Anderson, Mary A. m. Williams, W.F.	Sept 20, 1852		R. A. Fink			mr 86 *
Anderson, Nancy m. Deck, John	Jan. 5, 1825	Adam Chenoweth	Chas. P. Krauth	4b283		mr 48 *
Anderson, Nancy m. Dillon, Moses	May 6, 1818	John Kerney	Nathan Young	4b 70		mr 56 *
Anderson, Peggy m. Kneys, George	Jan. 8, 1808	Valentine Kneys		3b 82		
Anderson, Phebe m. Winning, John	June 22, 1812	Wm. Anderson	Rev. Reebenack	3b227	gc 13	
Anderson, Providence m. Cohagen, Nan	Dec. 19, 1801	Jas. Chenoweth		2b154		
Anderson, Providence m. Custer, Hanna	Dec. 21, 1815	Peter Custer	Nathan Young	3b351		mr 55 *
Anderson, Rebeca m. Morrison, John	Nov. 27, 1831	Colb't Collis	Nathan Young	5b209		mr 62 *
Anderson, Wm. m. Collis, Ann	Sept 20, 1837	Daniel Collis		6b112		
Anderson, Wm. m. Murphy, Nancy	June 27, 1809	John Winning		3b114		
Anderson, Wm.C. m.Harrison, Lucy E.	May 4, 1835	John S. Harrison		6b 43		
Andrews, Eliz. m. Campbell, Robert	Oct. 22, 1806	Wm. Campbell		3b 33		
Andrews, James m. Miller, Catherine	Jan. 16, 1850	John Points		7b175		
Andrews, James m. Rife, Polly	Nov. 8, 1804	Conrad Rife	John Bond	2b247	cr 13	mr 21 *
Andrews, Robert m. Veal, Sarah	Oct. 19, 1804	Wm. F. Campbell	John Bond	2b245	cr 13	mr 21 *
Angel, John m. McVey, Bridget	Aug. 10, 1784		Hugh Vance			mr 53 *
Anglous, Robert m. Hayson, Sarah	Jan. 17, 1793		David Young		go 2	
?Ariba, Isaiah D m. Shaffer, Martha	Mar. 12, 1851	Robert Nicely	John Iight	7b219		mr 86 *
?Ariba, Josiah D m. Shaffer, Martha	Mar. 7, 1824	Joseph Yarnell	Nathan Young	4b257	gc 4	mr 58 *
Ankrum, David m. Boak, Abigail	Mar. 5, 1795		David Young			
Ann, Mary m. Davidson, John B.	Nov. 30, 1822		Nathan Young			
Anmpister, Jacob m. Crowl, Margaret	Nov. 29, 1824	Jacob Crowl	Nathan Young	4b229		mr 58 *
Ansaln, Frederick m. Snider, Sarah	June 1800	Samuel Seibert	Chas. P. Krauth	4b267		mr 47 *
Anthony, Polly m. Irwin, John	Jan. 29, 1812	Zachariah Taylor		2b 50		
Aont, Philip m. Smith, Sarah	May 21, 1788	Edward Aris	Rev. Reebenack	3b226	gc 13	mr 36 *
*Anford, Priscilla m. Allison,Joshua	Aug. 21,		Moses Hoge			

Name	(marriage)		(suretor)	(minister)	(bond)	
Applegate, Hannah m. Riley, Thomas	Feb. 10,	1802	Nicholas Howard		2b160	*
Applegate, James m. Norman, Charley	May 15,	1792		David Young		gc 1 *
Applegate, Nancy m. Howard, Nicholas	Mar. 20,	1794		David Young		gc 4 *
Arachen, Jacob m. Seibert, Catherine	Mar. 20,	1810		Rev. Reebenack		gc 11 *
Ardinger, James m. Crowl, Eliza Ann	May 29,	1833	Peter Crowl	Nathan Young	5b275	mr 65 *
Ardinger, Mary Ann m. Cage, Andrew	Aug. 14,	1832	Chas. Ardinger	Nathan Young	5b238	*
Arick, George m. Moon, Hannah	Oct. 30,	1823	John Helferstay		4b251	*
Aris, Edward m. Smith, Barbara	Aug. 8,	1799	Philip Smith	Richard Swift	2b13	cr 34 mr 16 *
Aris, Polly m. Eaglestone, Richard	Mar. 1,	1821	Edward Aris	W. N. Scott	4b173	mr 41 *
Aris, Sarah m. Metcalf, Edward	Dec. 28,	1819	Edward Aris	W. N. Scott	4b27	mr 41 *
Arn, Mary m. Davidson, John B.	Mar. 3,	1795		David Young		gc 4 *
Ambrester, Michael m. Barnet, Mary	Sept 30,	1800	Philip Insuler	David Young	2b90	gc 9 *
Ambrester, Levina m. Parson, Tobias	Sept 30,	1834	Michael Armbrester	L. F. Wilson	6b290	*
Ambrester, Marcelina m. Dick, Peter	Feb. 23,	1843	Mich'l Armbrester	David Young	2b90	mr 74 *
Ambrester, Mich'l m. Barnett, Sally	Sept 30,	1800	Philip Insuler	Nathan Young	5b97	gc 9 *
Armpriest, Jacob m. Crowl, Margaret	Apr. 8,	1828	Mich'l Armbrester	Nathan Young	4b229	mr 60 *
Armsby, Nelly m. Joy, John	Nov. 30,	1822	John Haines	Nathan Young	2b52	mr 58 *
Armstrong, Cath. m. McKellop, John	Jan. 28,	1805	David Hunter	David Young	4b265	gc 5 *
Armstrong, Cath. m. Whisler, Isaac	May 15,	1824	Adam Shober		6b19	
Armstrong, Eliz. m. Stewart, Jacob	Sept 13,	1834	John Podsal		3b98	
Armstrong, George m. Podsal, Peggy	Oct. 7,	1808	Adam Stewart	Jacob Medtart	5b226	
Armstrong, Jacob m. Thompson, Nancy	Apr. 10,	1832	Peter Podsal		2b166	
Armstrong, James m. Podsal, Cath.	Mar. 26,	1802	James Starkey		1b84	
Armstrong, Nancy m. Kerin, Timothy	Feb. 3,	1798				mr 63 *
Armstrong, Thomas m. Lustre, Mary	Nov. 18,	1795				
Armstrong, Thomas D. m. Colvin, Endlyn	Jan. 15,	1852	John M. Colvin	Moses Hoge	7b243	cr 10 mr 11 *
Arnold, Eliz. A. m. Lupton, John W.	Oct. 11,	1853		Joseph Baker	5b240	
Arnoss, Barbara m. Lemen, Thomas	Sept 11,	1832	Arch'd Shearer	David Young	2b228	gc 3 *
Arp, John m. Kuhn, Eve	Apr. 6,	1794				
Artinger, John m. Wintersmith, Peggy	Mar. 17,	1804	Hor'o Wintersmith	William Hill	1b40	cr 30 mr 10 *
Artless, Ann m. Graous, Robert	Aug. 30,	1793				
Asenhurst, Eliz. m. Marshall, Benj.	Sept 12,	1797	Oliver Asenhurst	John Hedtt(Hutt)	2b75	cr 35 mr 19 *
Ashfield, Phebe m. Sheely(Theeby), S.	July 11,	1800	Benjamin Sheeley	William Hill		cr 30 mr 9 *
Ashfield, Rebecca m. Goldberg, Edw.	May 15,	1793		Daniel Sturges		mr 32 *
Ashley, Mary m. Sellers, William	Sept 19,	1781		Richard Swift		cr 26 mr 11 *
Athe, Eliz. m. Strode, Jeremiah	Feb. 6,	1796		Richard Swift		cr 34 mr 18 *
Athe, John m. Butt, Nancy	Mar. 5,	1800			2b105	
Athea, Elisha m. Cox, Ann	Dec. 24,	1800	Jacob Cox	Moses Hoge		cr 38 mr 20 *
Athy, Ann Harriet m. Agree, Robert	Jan. 1,	1798	Wilson Athy	Richard Swift	1b77	cr 12 mr 16 *
Athy, Wilson m. Comegys, Charlotte	Jan. 17,	1798	John Files	Richard Swift	1b102	cr 12 mr 16 *
Atkinson, John M. m. Harrison, Eliz.	May 10,	1843	Peyton Harrison		6b297	
Aubin, Geo. St. m. Kerner, Susan T.	Sept 25,	1816	James B. Kerney	John B. Hoge	4b12	*

Name		(marriage)	(surety)	(minister)	(bond)		
Augustus, David m. Hart, Anne	May 14,	July 21, 1798	Daniel Vanmetre		1b111		
Augustus, Enoch m. McIntire, Eliz.	Sept 19,	July 26, 1798	William Blue		1b133		
Aulebaugh, Nancy m. Porter, Jonathan	Feb. 20,	1835	Harrison Waite		6b 32		
Ault, Barbara m. Smith, Jonathan		1801					
Ault, Mary m. Sullivan, Thomas		1788					
Austin, Andrew m. Lemon, Jane	Jan. 4,	1831	Richard Brown	Moses Hoge	5b184	cr 38	mr 20 *
Austin, Mary m. McCleary, John	Oct. 18,	1849	Jacob VanDoren	Moses Hoge	7b166		mr 36 *
Austin, Mimay m. Billingsly, Robert	June 23,	1807	Thomas Barton	Nathan Young	3b 62		mr 61 *
Aver, Elira Ann m. Shoafstall, Geo.	June 5,	1845	Christian Aver	L.F. Wilson	7b 36		mr 83 *
Avis, Joseph m. Cage, Mary	Apr. 17,	1817	William Cage		4b 33		
Avis, Mary m. Shindler, Richard	Aug. 26,	1833	James Shane	Nathan Young	5b280		mr 66 *
Avis, Polly m. Eaglestone, Leonard	Dec. 4,	1820?		W. N. Scott			mr 41 *
Axe, Eliz. m. Johnston, William	Feb. 27,	1802	William Axe	Richard Swift	2b162	cr 32	mr 20 *
Aydelot, Benjamin m. Williams, Eliza	Dec. 9,	1817	John Strother	John Mathews	4b 58	cr 28	mr 23 *
Azlestone, Ann m. Johnstone, Henry	June 28,	1806	James Campbell	J. Bond	3b 23		

"B"

Name		(marriage)	(surety)	(minister)	(bond)		
Babb, Mary m. Hollingshead, Richard	Sept 5,	Dec. 13, 1796		David Young	2b 29	gc 6	*
Bacey, Joshua m. Ballard, Polly	Nov. 2,	Oct. 10, 1799	Thomas Rion	David Young	5b207	gc 9	*
?Backenstats, Jacob m. Toup, Evelina	Nov. 2,	Nov. 3, 1831	James S. Boyd	Jacob Medtart	5b207		mr 63 *
?Backenstos, Jacob H. m.Toup, Evelina	Nov. 1,	Nov. 3, 1831	James S. Boyd	Jacob Medtart	6b251		mr 63 *
Backhouse, Chas.m.McDaniel(Do-)Ellen	Nov. 27,	Nov. 1, 1841	Alex. McDaniel	John Hedges	3b277		mr 73 *
Bacon, Burwell m. Merchant, Priscilla	Jan. 16,	1813	William Merchant		2b111		
Bacon, Isaac m. Siler, Ruth	Jan. 22,	Jan. 22, 1801	Jacob Siler	John Boyd	5b169	cr 35	mr 19 *
Badley, Richard m. Ridenour, Eliza	June 21,	1830	George Ridenour		3b356		
Baer, Joseph m. Craglo, Catherine	Feb. 24,	1816	Peter Myers Jr.				
Bagge, James m. Chenoweth, Anne	Nov. 29,	1787	Adolph Shedg	Hugh Vance	7b208	cr 23	mr 2 *
Bahman, Adam m. Eisel, Elizabeth	Dec. 27,	1850		D. F. Spriggs	7b234		mr 83 *
Bailey, David m. Brannon, Mary Ann	Oct. 16,	1851	John Brannon	John Grove	4b237		mr 85 *
Bailey, David m. Ross, Margaret	Apr. 14,	1823	Nathan Ross	B. Reynolds	3b334		mr 49 *
Bailey, Elis. m. McFarland, John	Aug. 12,	1815	John Dawson	David Young			mr 55 *
Bailey, Elis. m. Standley, Joseph	Mar. 1,	1792		Mathias Riser			
Bailey, Elis. m. Unger, George		1817			4b 53	gc 1	*
Bailey, George m. Johnson, Charlotte	Dec. 20,	1836	Thomas Batley		6b 89		
Bailey, Ruth m. Miller, John	Dec. 21,	1782	John Strother	Daniel Sturges			
Bailey, Sarah m. Chenoweth, Isaac	Mar. 25,	1815	Barton Campbell	W. N. Scott	3b329		mr 42 *
Bailey, Wm. m. Bobrer(Bor-),Drusilla	July 21,	1818	George Whitmyre	Mathias Riser	4b 67		mr 26 *
Batley, William m. Boyd, Rachel	Apr. 7,	1793		David Young			mr 29 *
Bailiff, John m. Curtis, Mary	Apr. 11,	1798	Seth Curtis		1b 98		

Name	(marriage)	(suretor)	(minister)	(bond)		(mr)
Bailiff, Joshua m. Frye, Margaret	Dec. 24, 1801	Conrad Fry		2b154		
Bain, Abr'm B. m.Baker(Barker)Lydia	Mar. 13, 1845	Josiah H. Morgan	John Boggs	7b 29		mr 75 *
Bain, Barbara E. m. Crowl, William	Apr. 10, 1843	Joseph Bain		6b295		mr 45 *
Bain, Charles m. Shane, Fanny	Oct. 25, 1821	Nicholas Shanl Jr.	S.S.Robertson	4b104		
Baker, Ann R. m. Morgan, Wm. S.	Feb. 28, 1833	Alex. Cooper		5b259		*
Baird, Samuel m. Sigmund, Catherine	Dec. 1, 1791		David Young		gc 1	
Baker, Catherine m- Roberts, John	June 27, 1805	John Baker		2b265	cr 15	mr 4 *
Baker, Christian m. Slough, Sarah	Feb. 20, 1789		Christian Stredt			
Baker, Elias m. Billmyer,Mary Ann	Nov. 2, 1840	Solomon Billmyer		6b222		
Baker, Eliz. m. Dark, John	Dec. 21, 1789		Moses Hoge		cr 2	mr 3 *
Baker, Eliz. m. Riley, George	Feb. 7, 1792		Moses Hoge		cr 8	mr 7 *
Baker, Eliz. m. Shroad, William	Oct. 31, 1835	Jonathan Baker		6b 61	gc 9	
Baker, George m. Shriver, Eliz.	Feb. 8, 1800	Michael Beyerly	David Young	2b 52	cr 36	mr 12 *
Baker, Harriet m. Kemp, Christian	Apr. 28, 1796		Moses Hoge			
Baker, James A. m. Flemming, Cath.M.	Oct. 30, 1837	William A. Smith		6b122		
Baker, J.L.W.m. Alburtis, Josina T.	Apr. 25, 1848	Alfred Schnebly	James Chisholm	7b128		mr 78 *
Baker, John m. Brown, Eliz.	Sept 9, 1819	James Brown	John B. Hoge	4b114		mr 31 *
Baker, John m. Mark, Anna	Mar. 29, 1799	Mathew Ramone	Moses Hoge	1b176		mr 17 *
Baker, John m. Shearer(Schouer)Marg.	Aug. 30, 1799	Michael Cress	David Young	2b 23	cr 29	
Baker, Jonathan m. Schrode(Sh-)Mary	June 22, 1835	William Schrode	J.E. Jackson	6b 47	gc 9	
Baker, Juliet m. Hite, James	Feb. 20, 1798	Jacob H. Manning		1b 86		
Baker, Lydia m. Bain, Abraham B.	Mar. 13, 1845	Josiah H. Morgan	John Boggs	6b191		mr 75 *
Baker, Maria m. Wood, Edgar(Rev)	Sept 7, 1853		R.T.Berry	6b257		
Baker, Mary m. Barors, Joshua	Feb. 17, 1794		David Young		gc 3	
Baker, Mary E. m. Morrison, James	Dec. 30, 1839	Otho Baker		6b191		
Baker, Otho m. McCormack, Ellen	Dec. 13, 1841	Wm. McCormack	John Hedges	6b257		mr 73 *
Baker, Percdifor m. Custer, Margaret	Aug. 9, 1808	Peter Custer		5b 27		
Baker, Prudence m. Evans, Robert	Nov. 9, 1825	Joseph Shaw	John L. Gibbons	7b190		mr 49 *
Baker, Rachel Ann m. Collins, Albert	July 31, 1850	Robert M. Henderson	T.Berry	4b164		mr 83 *
Baker, Ruth m. Shaw, Joseph	Oct. 3, 1820	Redser Hudgel		3b250		
Baker, Samuel Jr. m. Reed, Eliza	Feb. 9, 1813	Cyrus Murray				
Baker, Susanna m. Wood, John	Oct. 8, 1781		Daniel Sturges	5b150		mr 42 *
Baker, Virginia H. m. Morrison, Wm.S	Jan. 28, 1830	Wm. C. Compton	W. Monroe	2b202		mr 54 *
Baker, William m. McIlvena, Hannah	June 7, 1803	James Sterrat		1b 62		
Baldwin, Amey m. Steele, George	Nov. 20, 1797	David Baldwin		2b141		
Baldwin, Hiram m. Lewis, Polly	Aug. 31, 1801	David Lewis		5b 51		
Baldwin, James m. Griffith, Amy	Sept 9, 1826	William Griffith		3b137		
Baldwin, James R. m. Mendenhall, Eliz	Feb. 21, 1810	Amos Mendenhall				
Baldwin, Jane m. Wilson, James	Aug. 13, 1789		Hugh Vance			
Baldwin, Joseph m. Wilson, Eliz.	Feb. 10, 1795		John Boyd			
Baldwin, Joshua m. Chenoweth, Elenor	Oct. 29, 1806	William Chenoweth		3b 34	cr 39	mr 4 *
Baldwin, Polly m. Daniel, John	July 8, 1804	David Baldwin		2b242	ce 10	mr 11 *
Baldwin, Rebecca m. Cawood, Thomas	Oct. 19, 1801	John Varmetre		2b144		

Name	Date	(marriage)		(suretor)	(minister)	(bond)		
Baldwin, William m. Mooney, Phebe	Dec. 8,		1798	Evan Rees	J. Larken	1b152		*
Balen, James m. Cock, Elizabeth	May 20,	Dec. 20,	1837		Rev. Reebenack			*
Bales, David m. Shober, Susanna	Sept 23,	May 21,	1815	John Shober	P. Lipscomb	3b325	gc 14	mr 81 *
Bales, Elenor M. m.Sheetz, Geo. W.	Dec. 4,	Sept 23,	1847	David Beales		7b107		*
Bales, Emily m. Kiger, Jacob	May 21,		1845	Jacob Bales		7b 50		*
Bales, John m. Bell, Geoge H.	Feb. 14,	May 21,	1847	David Beales	P. Lipscomb	7b 96		mr 81 *
Bales, Moses m. Helferstay, Mary A.	May 11,	Feb. 14,	1833	John Helferstay		5b257		*
Baley, Peggy m. Wright, James	Nov. 14,	May 11,	1849	Jacob Van Doren	W. Love	7b156		mr 80 *
Ball, Alex. m. Anderson, Harriet M.	June 21,	Nov. 15,	1812	William Wright	Lewis Mayer	3b241	cr 15	mr 25 *
Ball, Dabney m. Wysong, Mary D.	Oct. 29,		1832	Horace Anderson		5b232		*
Bell, Nathan m. Rollins, Mary		Oct. 20,	1845	Richard McGlathery		7b 47		*
Ballard, Polly m. Bacy, Joshua	Sept 5,	Oct. 10,	1792	Thomas Rion	Moses Hoge	2b 29	gc 9	mr 39 *
Bane, Abner m. Simmons, Rachel			1789		David Young			mr 37 *
Bane, Abraham S. m. Light, Peggy	Mar. 14,	Mar. 19,	1812	John Light	D. Thomas	3b217	cr 15	mr 25 *
Bane, Ann Eliz. m. Custer, Reuben C.	Feb. 5,	?	1848?	Charles A. Bane	Lewis Mayer	7b122		mr 78 *
Bane, Charles m. Shane, Fanny	Oct. 25,	Oct. 28,	1821	Nicholas Shaul	J.H.Waugh	4b104		mr 45 *
Bane, Margaret m. Mitchel, Wm. H.	June 23,	June 23,	1840	Jacob M Gouten	Jr.S.S.Robertson	6b214		mr 72 *
Bane, Nancy m. Spotts(Spa-), John H.	June 1,	June 14,	1840	Jacob Lemaster	James Reily	6b211		mr 71 *
Banks, John m. Stowers, Mary		Dec. 3,	1795		Samuel Smith		cr 10	mr 11 *
Banks, Mary m. Moler, Adam		May 25,	1790		Moses Hoge		cr 4	mr 5 *
Banks, Ruhanna m. Landis(Sandis)John		Sept 3,	1801		Moses Hoge		cr 17	mr 20 *
Banks, Vandevert m. Barns, Eliz.		Mar. 13,	1792		Moses Hoge			mr 38 *
Banner, Mary m. Sidnor, Philip		Oct. 2,	1791		Moses Hoge			mr 7 *
Banscott, Polly m. Swisher, George		Dec. 5,	1793		Christian Strett		cr 15	
Bansle, George m. Davis, Sally	Feb. 26,	Feb. 27,	1812	Jacob Bansle	David Young	3b213	gc 3	
Bansle, Jacob m.Wickham, Kitty	May 5,		1810	Jonas Hoover	Rev. Reebenack	3b150	gc 12	
Baobrest, Barbara m. Linton, John M.		Feb. 15,	1855		John O. Proctor			*
Barber, Cath. m. Thomas, James	Jan. 22,		1822	William Ray		4b205		
Barber, John m.Oller(Otter), Eliz.	Aug. 23,	Aug. 24,	1797	Jonathan Rust	David Young	1b 34	gc 6	mr 68 *
Barber, Sally m. Goings, George W.	Sept 9,		1833	Horace Anderson		5b282		
Barchus, Levi m. Hedges, Sarah K.	May 30,	June 2,	1835	Henry Myers	John Howell	6b 46	gc 3	
Bardmiss, Mary m. Custer, James		Oct. 27,	1793		David Young			mr 33 *
Bare, Adam m. Claycomb,Mary		Apr. 7,	1785		Hugh Vance			mr 76 *
Bare, Catherine m. Welsh, Maxwell	Feb. 1,	Feb. 4,	1845	Jeremiah Quinn	James Chisholm	7b 25		
Bare, Eliz. m. Quinn, Jeremiah	Feb. 17,		1840	William Hedges		6b197		mr 42 *
Bare, Henry m. Chambers, Sarah		May 9,	1786		Hugh Vance			mr 17 *
Bare, Jacob m. Steele, Mary	Sept 16,	Sept 17,	1799	Robert Hastings	John Boyd	2b 26	cr 34	mr 61 *
Bare, William m. Clark, Elizabeth		June 23,	1831		Nathan Young			
Bareford, Jenny m. Trigg, Samuel	Nov. 13,		1800	Horatio Hobbs		2b 99		
Bark, Jane m. Faris, Aron		Dec. 23,	1794		John Boyd	3b 25	cr 21	mr 8 *
Barkelow, Cornelius m. Blue, Fanny	Aug. 1,	Aug. 2,	1806	James Whitelock				
Barker, Elias m. Meek, Elizabeth	Apr. 13,		1812	John Robinson	John Bond	3b220	cr 28	mr 23 *

Name	(marriage)	(suretor)	(minister)	(bond)	ref
Barker, Lydia m. Bain, Abraham B.	Mar. 13, 1845	Josiah Morgan	John Boggs	7b 29	mr 75 *
Barker, Sarah m. Hume, James	June 10, 1817		Mathias Riser		*
Barket, Michael m. Stip, Mary	Feb. 2, 1796		David Young		*
Barklow, Cornelius m. Blue, Fanny	Aug. 1, 1806	James Whitelock	John Bond	3b 25	gc 5 mr 23 *
Barley, Nathaniel m. McClure, Mary E	Jan. 23, 1850	Richard McClure	P. Lipscomb	7b176	cr 28 mr 82 *
Barnard, Mrs. Eliz. m. McCoach, Jas.	Mar. 30, 1830	John Gallaher	Nathan Young	5b160	mr 60 *
Barnes, Archibald m. Cock, Eliz.	Mar. 30, 1794		David Young		gc 3
Barnes, Eliz. m. Cloninger, Thomas	Aug. 9, 1832	Henry Barnes	Nathan Young	5b235	mr 64 *
Barnes, Eliz. m. Connell, John	Feb. 21, 1803	Joshua Chew	Richard Swift	2b195	cr 27
Barnes, Eliz. m. Swisher, Henry	Oct. 7, 1837	John Helferstay		6b114	mr 21 *
Barnes, Eleinor m. Kitchen, Jas. M.	Dec. 22, 1846	Joseph D. Barnes		7b 81	
Barnes, George m. Pitzer, Margaret	Feb. 24, 1852	John Jordan		7b246	
Barnes, Henry m. Creamer, Charlotte	Nov. 4, 1806	George Creamer		3b 35	
Barnes, Ishmael m. Crown, Maria Horn	Dec. 29, 1817	Ehud Turner		4b 54	
Barnes, Ishmael m. Houk, Nancy	Feb. 14, 1854		John Light	1b172	cr 34 mr 16 *
Barnes, Jacob m. Tederick, Charlotte	Mar. 12, 1799	Jacob Tederick	John Boyd	6b 29	*
Barnes, Jacob m. Olinger, Catherine	Jan. 23, 1835	Christopher Ollinger		1b103	cr 32 mr 15 *
Barnes, John m. Tederick, Jane	Jan. 19, 1798	Robert Jones	John Boyd	7b172	mr 80 *
Barnes, Joseph D. m. Boher(Ro-Maria	Dec. 26, 1849	Martin Boher	John Light	6b317	
Barnes, Michael m. Strayer, Cath.	Apr. 1, 1844	Geo. W. Strayer	L.F.Wilson	3b 83	
Barnes, Michael m. Tabler, Phebe	Mar. 19, 1808	Adam Tabler		6b277	mr 73 *
Barnes, Phebe m. Basbore, Robert	Sept 12, 1842	Henry Barnes	Lewis F. Wilson	2b193	cr 27 mr 21 *
Barnes, Providence m. Chenoweth, A.	Feb. 11, 1803	John West	Richard Swift	2b193	cr 27 mr 21 *
Barnes, Prudence m. Chenoweth, Arch.	Feb. 11, 1803	John West	Richard Swift		mr 39
Barnes, Robert m. Cross, Mary A.	Oct. 12, 1793		Richard Swift		
Barnes, Ruth m. Osborne, David Jr.	Feb. 17, 1800	John Lafferty	Moses Hoge	2b 54	cr 29 mr 19 *
Barnes, Sarah Ann m. Harrison, Nathm	Oct. 17, 1840	Michael Barnes	John Light	6b221	mr 72 *
Barnes, Wm. E. m. Tabler, Eliza	June 2, 1841	Christian Tabler	Lewis F. Wilson	6b242	mr 72 *
Barnet, James m. Menghird, Joidal	May 23, 1838	Thomas G. Flagg	Peyton Harrison	6b139	mr 69 *
Barnet, John m-Gothard, Rebecca	Mar. 29, 1814		Rev. Reebenack		gc 14
Barnet, Susan m. Santman, Joseph H.	Oct. 1, 1840	James Mathews	James Relly	6b218	mr 72 *
Barnett, Drusilla m. Welsh, Benj.	Dec. 7, 1797	George Emmers	Richard Swift	1b 71	cr 12 mr 14 *
Barnett, George m. Moles, Eliz.	Dec. 11, 1815	Z. Moles	W.N. Scott	3b350	mr 26 *
Barnett, John m. Garden, Rebecca	Mar. 28, 1814	Mary Garden	Rev. Reebenack	3b291	gc 14
Barnett, Jonathan m. Crayson, Annie	Sept 29, 1787		Hugh Vance		cr 23
Barnett, Margaret m. Dorset, Wm.	1789		D. Thomas		
Barnett, Martha J. m. McDonald, Robt	Mar. 12, 1832	Joseph Severns	Nathan Young	5b219	mr 2 *
*Barnett, Mary m. Brown, Elias	Mar. 4, 1801	John Barnett		2b116	mr 38 *
?Barnett, Sally m. Ambrester, Mich'l	Sept 30, 1800	Philip Inswiler	David Young	2b 90	gc 9 mr 64 *
Barnett, William m. Blecum, Deborah	June 25, 1798	Henry Flemming		1b120	
Barney, John D. m. Hagaman, Antoinet	Sept 7, 1844	Thomas S. Gain		7b 5	*
Barney, William m. Hagaman, Ann	Mar. 26, 1832	Jacob Severns		5b222	
Barney, Wm. Jr. m. Stuckey, Hannah	Oct. 13, 1852		J.H.Jennings		mr 86 *
?*Barnett, Mary m. Ambrester, MichaelSept 30, 1800		Philip Inswiler	David Young	2b 90	gc 9 *

Name		(marriage)	(surety)	(minister)	(bond)		
Barnhart, Eliz.Mary m. Gerling,Ferd	May 1,	Oct. 20, 185-	Simon Shunk	R. A. Fink	1b 14	gc 6	mr 88 *
Barnhart, Henry m.Shunk(Shirok),Mary	Apr. 24,	May 2, 1797	Henry Nace	David Young	1b 11	gc 6	*
Barnhart, Philip m. Nace, Mary		Dec. 1, 1796		David Young	3b320	gc 8	*
Barnhart, Sarah m. Paskell, Isaac	Apr. 20,	1815	Robert Grimes		1b161		mr 38 *
Barnhouse, Caty m. Gilmore, Arch'd	Jan. 11,	Jan. 16, 1799	Mathew Ramone	David Young	5b 86		mr 59 *
Barnhouse, Richard m. Evans, Martha		Mar. 13, 1792		Moses Hoge	1b172	or 34	mr 16 *
Barns, Eliz. m. Banks, Vandevort	Dec. 26,	Dec. 27, 1827	Daniel Kyser	Nathan Young	6b 37		
Barns, Henry m. Kyser(Hy-), Susan	Mar. 9,	Mar. 12, 1799	Jacob Tederick	John Boyd	1b103	or 32	mr 15 *
Barns, Jacob m. Tederick, Charlotte	Mar. 24,	1835	Jacob Swisher		7b172		mr 80 *
Barns, John m. Compton, Sarah Ann	Jan. 19,	1798	Robert Jones	John Boyd	5b126		mr 60 *
Barns, John m. Tederick, Jane	Dec. 26,	Dec. 30, 1849	Martin Rohrer	John Light	6b277	or 29	mr 73 *
Barns, Joseph D. m. Rohrer, Maria	Apr. 15,	Apr. 18, 1829	Henry Barns	Nathan Young	2b 54		mr 19 *
Barns, Mary m. Clodinger, Philip C.	Sept 12,	Sept 15, 1842	Henry Barns	Lewis F. Wilson	6b242		mr 72 *
Barns, Phebe m. Bashore, Robert	Feb. 17,	Feb. 18, 1800	John Lafferty	Moses Hoge			
Barns, Ruth m. Osburn, David Jr.	June 2,	June 5, 1841	Christian Tabler	Lewis F. Wilson			
Barns, William m. Tabler, Eliza		Feb. 17, 1794		David Young		gc 3	
Barors, Joshua m. Baker, Mary	Oct. 26,	1821	Stephen Gano			gc 12	
Barr, Benj. Ross m. Gano, Mary	Oct. 25,	Oct. 25, 1811	John Powell	Rev. Reebenack			mr 61 *
Barr, Rachel m. Stitely, Solomon		1831		Nathan Young			mr 69 *
Barr, William m. Clark, Eliz.		1831		James Watts	4b195		mr 52 *
Barrack(-ick),Samuel m. Myers, Sarah	June 5,	June 5, 1838	Harrison Waite	B. Reynolds	3b196		mr 84 *
Barrett(-ott),Delia m. Toland, David	Jan. 5,	Jan. 6, 1828	John Shober		6b140		mr 1
Barrett, Lydia m. Mercer, John	Apr. 20,	1789	Edward Mercer		5b 87		mr 72 *
Barrett, Nancy E. m.Hoffman, Michael	Mar. 24,	Mar. 27, 1851	Wm. A. Cushwa	D. F. Bragunier	1b x	cr 18	mr 80 *
Barrett, Rachel m. Hutton, John		Sept 12, 1787		Hugh Vance	7b220		mr 58 *
Barrett, William m. Collins, Cath.	Sept 27,	Sept 27, 1841	Joseph Collins	John Hedges	6b247		mr 64 *
Barrett, William m. Inhuret, Rebecca	Mar. 7,	Mar. 2, 1850	William Crabb	W. Love	7b179		
Barrett, William m. Rainey, Eliz.	Aug. 2,	Aug. 27, 1825	Samuel Rainey	Nathan Young	5b 17		
Barrow, James m. Bell, Margaret	June 27,	June 27, 1832	Zebulon Bell	Nathan Young	5b232		
Berry, Patrick m. Driskel, Johannah	May 16,	1840	Harrison Waite	John Light	6b209	go 12	mr 86 *
Bartleson, Elijah m. Spencer, Martha	Apr. 27,	Apr. 27, 1852	Jacob VanDoren	Rev. Reebenack	7b253		
Bartleson, James m. Parker, Barbara	Mar. 31,	Apr. 2, 1812	John Poisal	John Light	3b218		mr 80 *
Bartleson, Virginia m. Thurston, Wm.	Apr. 24,	Apr. 25, 1850	Elijah Bartleson		7b183		
Bartleston, Marg. m. Emerson, John	Jan. 29,	1838	Thomas Jordan		6b117		
Bartley, Mary m. Haley, John	Nov. 12,	1839	Patrick Smith		6b184		
Bartley, Wm. m. Chaffin, Susannah	July 17,	1800	Uriah Blue		2b 76		
Bartolomew, Jacob m. Farr,Christiana	July 17,	1797	John Merritt		1b 25		
Barton, Eliz. m. Barton, Thomas	June 16,	June 17, 1798	John Thurston	David Young	1b117	gc 7	*
Barton, James m. Ward, Rachel	Mar. 26,	1822	Joshua Ward		4b209		
Barton, Thomas m. Barton, Eliz.	June 16,	June 17, 1798	John Thurston	David Young	1b117	gc 7	*
Barton, Thomas m. Thurston, John	Feb. 14,	1826			18117		
Bashore, Mary m. Keller, Henry	Feb.	1842	Henry Bashore		5b 36		mr 50 *
Bashore, Robert m. Barns, Phebe	Sept 12,	Sept 15, 1842	Henry Barns	Chas. P. Krauth	6b277		mr 73 *
Bashore, Samuel m. Snyder, Cath.	Mar. 18,	1839	Thomas Powell	Lewis F. Wilson	6b163		

Name	(bond date)	(marriage)	(suretor)	(minister)	(bond)		
Basket, Sarah m. Panter, Benjamin		Dec. 4, 1794	John Hite	Edward Tiffin	3b 4	cr 25	mr 9 *
Basil, Mary m. Devenport, Anthony		Mar. 21, 1785		Edward Tiffin		cr 38	mr 1 *
Basore, Barnard m. Hite, Eliz.	Nov. 25,	1805	Edw. P. Foreman	Seely Bunn	3b280	cr 41	mr 25 *
Basore, David m. Filson, Rachel	Dec. 30,	Dec. 30, 1813	Jacob Basore	John Light	6b313		mr 76 *
Basore, Eliz. m. Emberson, Warner	Feb. 6,	Feb. 8, 1844	James Bartleson	Rev. Reebenack	3b306	gc 14	
Basore, Jacob m. Parker, Nelly	Oct. 28,	Nov. 1, 1814	William Basore	John Light	7b 34		mr 76 *
Basore, Mary Ann m. Harrison, Jacob	May 13,	May 15, 1845	Jacob Sherard		6b 67		
Basore, Michael m. Westenhaver, Mary	Dec. 23,	Dec. 23, 1835					
Basswick, Susan m. Creighton,		June 26, 1788		Hugh Vance			mr 35 *
Baswell, Nancy m. Black, William		May 9, 1786		Hugh Vance			mr 42 *
Batt, Aaron m. Catlett, Eveline		Dec. 17, 1818		Mathias Riser			mr 30 *
Batt, Catherine m. Ray, Swearingen	Sept 23,	Sept 23, 1820	John Batt	Nathan Young	4b162		mr 57 *
Batt, Eliz. m. Kirkwood, Jacob	June 28,	1799	Henry Crowl		2b 10		
Batt, Mary m. Spurr, John	Sept 9,	1826	Elizabeth Batt		5b 51		
Batte, Catherine m. Wager, John Jr.	June 4,	1799	James Ferguson		2b 9		
Bauner, David m. Wedsgeben, John		Apr. 1, 1792		David Young		gc 1	*
Bauman, David m. Riser, Maria		Nov. 4, 1811		Rev. Reebenack		gc 12	*
Bauman, Hannah m. Kitzmiller, John		Apr. 5, 1793		David Young		gc 2	*
Bausel, George m. Davis, Sally	Feb. 26,	Feb. 27, 1812	Jacob Bansle	Rev. Reebenack	3b213	gc 12	*
Bauser, Frederick m. Boyd, Maria		Aug. 13, 1793		David Young		gc 3	
Bayles, Quentin m. Cannon, Eliz.		Dec. 14, 1787		Hugh Vance		cr 23	mr 2 *
Bayles, Tarply m. Throckmorton, Mary	Mar. 12,	Mar. 2, 1789		Hugh Vance	2b102		mr 37 *
Baylor, Cath. m. Tapscott, Wm.	Jan. 14,	1801	Richard Baylor		1b163		
Baylor, Frances m. Washington, John	Aug. 20,	1799	John Dixon		7b 34		
Bayshore, Mary Ann m. Harrison, Jacob		May 15, 1845	Wm. Basore	John Light	2b208		mr 76 *
Baysore, Barney m. Crothers, Eliz.	Feb. 6,	1803	George Baysore		6b313		
Baysore, Eliz. m. Emerson, Warner		Feb. 8, 1844	Jacob Basore	John Light	1b 35		mr 76 *
Baysore, John m. Riner, Susannah	Aug. 25,	1797	Henry Riner		2b174		
Baysore, Mary m. Jack, James	June 7,	1802	George Baysore				
Beach, Alexander m. Elliott, Sarah	Aug. 7,	1815	Ralph Durham		3b332		mr 59 *
Beach, Linda m. Noland, Obed	July 31,	July 2, 1827	Alexander Beach	Nathan Young	5b 73		mr 66 *
Beady, Chas. m. Kiger, Mary Ann	Nov. 9,	Nov. 10, 1833	Jacob Roads	Nathan Young	5b290		mr 30 *
Beal, Elinor m. Williams, Samuel	Nov. 16,	Nov. 26, 1818	Moses Beal	W. N. Scott	4b 87		mr 81 *
Beales, Elenor M. m. Sheets, Geo. W.	Sept 23,	Sept 23, 1847	David Beales	P. Lipscomb	7b107		
Beales, Emily E. m. Bell, Geo. H.	May 21,	May 21, 1847	David Beales	P.D. Lipscomb	7b 96		mr 81 *
Beales, Mary K. m. MacInnis, John W.	Dec. 23,	1837	David Beales		6b127		
Beales, Rosanna m. Bowman, Chas. H.	Oct. 7,	1846	David Beales		7b 75		
Beales, Susannah m. Brady, John E.	Mar. 10,	1841	Adam Shober		6b236		
Beall, Anna m. Silver, Francis		1802	Zephardiah Beall		2b182		mr 55 *
Beall(Bell),Elenor m.Worley,Welling	Sept 21,	Aug. 24, 1815	Jeremiah Beall	Nathan Young	3b335		mr 75 *
Beall, Jeremiah m. Miller, Rosanna	Aug. 21,	Aug. 31, 1843	James McSherry	T.H.W.Monroe	6b303	cr 26	
Beall, John m. Taylor, Mary	Aug. 30,	May 1795		Richard Swift			mr 10 *
Beall, John R. m. Watson, Mary Ann	Feb. 23,	Feb. 26, 1839	Daniel Watson	Lewis F. Wilson	6b160		mr 70 *

	(marriage)	(suretor)	(minister)	(bond)		
Beall, Joseph m. Faris, Catherine	Mar. 1B, 1841	John Faris	John Hedges	6b237		mr 72 *
Beall, Joseph m. Gartsell, Harriet	Jan. 2, 1799	Richard Gartsell	David Young	1b159	gc 8	mr 24 *
Beall, Lucy m. Wagoner, James	Dec. 1810	Edmund Wagoner	John B. Hoge	3b170	cr 14	mr 46 *
Beall, Richard m. Blake, Jane	July 15, 1823	Jacob Clise	Chas. P. Krauth	4b243		*
Beall, Vincent m. Chenoweth, Rachel	Jan. 13, 1813	James Chenoweth		3b248		
Beall, Wm. m. Green, Sarah	Dec. 10, 1793		Moses Hoge	1b168	cr 22	mr 8 *
Beally, John m. Sutherland(Sou)Diana	Feb. 14, 1799	George Sutherland	John Hutt(Heitt)	3b325	cr 12	mr 18 *
Beals, David m. Shober, Susannah	May 20, 1815	John Shober	Rev. Reebenack	4b 87	gc 14	*
Beals, Elinor m. Williams, Samuel	Nov. 16, 1818	Moses Beal	Wm. N. Scott	3b318		mr 30 *
Beals, Jacob m. Gallaher, Eliz.	Apr. 5, 1815	Robert Gallaher				
Beam, Eliz. m. Vanarsdale, James	Nov. 20, 1786	John Strother	Hugh Vance	4b123		mr 43 *
Bear, Ann Cath. m. Butt, Archibald	Nov. 16, 1819	Jeremiah Quinn	W.N. Scott	7b 25		mr 40 *
Bear, Catherine m. Welsh, Maxwell	Feb. 1, 1845	Robert Wilson	James Chisholm	3b152		mr 76 *
Bear, Jacob m. Chenoweth, Charlotte	May 22, 1810	Isaac Eversole	Lewis Mayer	6b 66	cr 14	mr 24 *
Bear, Jane m. Eversole, John	Jan. 6, 1836					
Bear, John m. Hldt, Eliza	July 19, 1825	George Hldt	James Relley	5b 16		mr 48 *
Bear, John C. m. Stuckey, Mary Eliz.	July 27, 1846	Samuel Stuckey	J.H. Jennings	7b 70		mr 82 *
Bear, Joseph m. Kragels, Catherine	Feb. 25, 1815		Rev. Reebenack			*
Bear, Michael m. Seneker, Catherine	May 2, 1798	Joseph Bear	David Young		gc 15	*
Bear, Sarah m. Kennedy, Daniel	July 4, 1836				gc 7	
Bear, Sarah m. Gerrard, Thomas R.	May 1, 1843	George W. Strayer	James Chisholm	6b 82		mr 75 *
Beard, Eliz. S. m. Horn, William	Oct. 30, 1848	James Beard		6b296		
Beard, John m. Helt, Nancy	Dec. 4, 1792		David Young	7b138		
Beard, Justice m. Leary, Johanna	Feb. 19, 1785		Hugh Vance		gc 2	
Beard, Margaret m. Bell, Launcelot	Mar. 14, 1810	Robert Wilson	John Mathews	3b141		mr 33 *
Beard, Mary Jane m. Heavy, Henry	Oct. 15, 1852		D. Thomas			mr 40 *
Beard, Sarah G. m. Schoppert, Samuel	Mar. 22, 1841	James Beard	John Hedges	6b238		mr 86 *
Beard, Thomas m. Wilkinson, Mary B.	May 10, 1796		John Boyd		cr 11	mr 72 *
Bearsore(Bas-),Cath.m.Cromwell,Hugh	Aug. 29, 1800	Robert Filson		2b 83		mr 12 *
Beatty, Amanda m. McCleary, Andrew	Mar. 23, 1830	Jacob F. Light	W. Monroe	5b159		mr 54 *
Beatty, Ann m. Hammond, George W.	Jan. 30, 1849	James Ijams		7b146		
Beatty, David m. Manor, Enid	Mar. 10, 1807	Benjamin Manor		3b 50		
Beatty, John m. Southerland, Diana	Feb. 14, 1799	George Southland	John Heitt(Hutt)	1b166	cr 12	mr 18 *
Beatty, Maria m. Seibert, Jacob M.	Mar. 23, 1840	Wm. Pendleton	John Light	6b202		mr 71 *
Beatty, Mary m. McClure, William	Jan. 24, 1826	John Porterfield	James M. Brown	5b 33		mr 50 *
Beatty, Melissa m. Speck, David	Jan. 18, 1845	Wm. Pendleton	Lewis F. Wilson	7b 22		
Beatty, William m. Soper, Eliz.	Sept 19, 1806	Robert Owen		3b 30		
Beaty, Margaret m. Smith, Jacob	May 19, 1823	Anthony Rosenbgr	Chas. P. Krauth	4b239		mr 46 *
Becket, Parker m. Smith, Martha A.	May 4, 1845	Jacob Smith	John Light	7b 42		mr 76 *
Becket, William m. Sprinkle, Eliz.	Sept 3, 1792		Moses Hoge			mr 39 *
Beckett, Eliz. m. Wallingsford, Rchd	Oct. 8, 1793		Moses Hoge			mr 7 *
Beckett, John m. Potts, Hannah	June 25, 1794		Richard Swift		cr 22	mr 40 *
Bedeman, Eve m. Spangler, Mathias	May 20, 1789		Hugh Vance		cr 39	mr 3 *

Name		(marriage)	(suretor)	(minister)	(bond)			
Bedinger, Adam m. Wigle, Catherine		Nov. 11, 1794	John Beall	David Young	1b 89	gc 4		*
Bedinger, Christian m. Taylor, Sophia	Mar. 12	Mar. 13, 1830	James Swearingen	Richard Swift	5b174	cr 31	mr 15	*
Bedinger, Elis. m. Davenport,Braxton	Aug. 31							*
Bedinger, Elis. m. Hughey, Isaac	Apr. 17	Apr. 18, 1797	Philip Bedinger	John Boyd	1b 8	cr 32	mr 13	*
Bedinger, Fred. m. Hoover, Catherine		Oct. 6, 1795		David Young		gc 5		*
Bedinger, Henry m. Strode, Rachel		Dec. 22, 1784?		Hugh Vance			mr 32	*
Bedinger, Maria m. Miller, Samuel	Mar. 27	Mar. 27, 1816	Henry Bedinger	Alex. Belmain	4b 16		mr 26	*
Bedinger, Mary m. Kibler, William	Feb. 22	Feb. 22, 1803	Philip Bedinger	David Young	2b195	gc 10		*
Bedinger, Nancy m. Swearingen,Jas.S.	Nov. 2	Nov. 3, 1811	Henry Bedinger	John B. Hoge	3b198	cr 14	mr 24	*
Bedinger, Peter m. Lechman, Nancy		Apr. 19, 1785		Hugh Vance			mr 33	*
Beech, Alexander m. Noland, Mary	Sept 2	Sept 2, 1820	Thomas Noland	John Mathews	4b159			*
Beems, Wm. J. m. Marshall, Jane	Aug. 27	Aug. 27, 1817	William Marshall	David Young	4b 44	gc 4		*
Beeson, David m. Goodman, Rebecca								*
Beeson, Edw. m.Stribling,Dulcebella	Sept 17	Sept 17, 1817	John Strother	John B. Hoge	4b 46			*
Beeson, George m. Menser, Sarah	Nov. 15	Sept 18, 1832	George Menser		5b246			
Beeson, Hiram m. Bishop, Susan	Aug. 7	Aug. 9, 1827	Exekial Showers	Nathan Young	5b 74		mr 59	*
Beeson, Hiram m. Helferstay, Marg.	June 5	June 1830	John Helferstay		5b166			
Beeson, Jesse m. Swearingen, Julia A.		Dec. 31, 1791		Christian Streit		cr 15		*
Beeson, Julia A. m. Heffner, Benj.	Dec. 21	Dec. 23, 1825	Thomas Crawford	Benedict Reynolds	5b 30		mr 7	*
Beeson, Juliett m. Haslett, Jackson	Sept 14	Sept 14, 1840	Lewis R. Beeson		6b217		mr 49	*
Beeson, Lewis R. m. Cunningham,Lydia	Nov. 15	Nov. 18, 1847	Robert Cunningham	Richard T. Brown	7b113		mr 79	*
Beeson, Lewis R. m. Roberts, Elis.	Dec. 16		Boyd Roberts		6b187			*
Beeson, Rebecca m. Crawford, Thomas	Aug. 13	Aug. 14, 1808	Moses Collins	Lewis Mayer	3b 94	cr 16	me 23	*
Begole, John m. Covenhaver, Nancy		Feb. 1, 1797	Wm. Covenhaver	David Young		gc 1		*
Beilers, Elis. m. Fisher, John	Oct. 17	Oct. 17, 1797	Henry Nicely	David Young	1b 56	gc 6		*
Belliff, Joshua m. Fregen, Margaret	Apr. 30	Apr. 4, 1797		David Young	1b 3	gc 9		*
Bell, Benj. m. Southwood, Margaret	Sept 2	Dec. 24, 1801	John Roberts		2b 24	gc 13		
Bell, Elis L. m. Roberts, Wm. Jr.	Nov. 24	Sept 2, 1799	Alfred Ross		7b 49			
Bell, Elis. m. Coleman, Jacob	Nov. 11	Nov. 24, 1845	Christian Silver	Rev. Reebensack	3b240	cr 17		*
Bell, Fanny m. Roberts, A. D. Dr.	Dec. 6	Nov. 12, 1812	William Bell	Moses Hoge	3b 5		mr 22	*
Bell, George H. m. Beales, Emily E.	May 21	Dec. 6, 1805	David Beales	P. Lipscomb	7b 96		mr 81	*
Bell, Hannah m. Miller, John	Jan. 25	May 21, 1847	William Bell		4b131			*
Bell, Hugh m. Lee, Jane		Jan. 25, 1820		David Young		gc 4		*
Bell, Jacob m. Grubb, Sarah	Sept 13	Dec. 30, 1794	Harrison Waite	John Howell	6b 19		mr 68	*
Bell, James m. Fulton, Margaret		Sept 16, 1834		John Boyd		cr 33	mr 11	*
Bell, John Jr. m. Kidd, Jane	Oct. 6	July 23, 1795	Michael Contchman	John Howell	6b 21		mr 68	*
Bell, John m. Maslin, Martha	Mar. 20	Oct. 9, 1834	John Griffith		5b 94			
•Bell, John m. Roberts, Elis.	Dec. 21		Benj. Lockhart		6b259			
Bell, Joseph E. m. Kownslar, Marg.	Mar. 22	Mar. 26, 1823	Conrad Kownslar	John Mathews	4b235		mr 45	*
Bell, Julianna m. Evans, Hezekiah W.	Nov. 13	Nov. 13, 1828	John Bell	W. Monroe	5b112		mr 53	*
Bell, Lancelot G. m. Beard, Marg.	Mar. 14	Mar. 15, 1810	Robert Wilson	John Mathews	3b141		mr 40	*
Bell, Lucy m. Prather, William		Feb. 6, 1797		Richard Swift		cr 26	mr 13	*
*Bell(Beall), John m. Talor, Mary		May 21, 1795		Richard Swift		cr 26	mr 10	*

	(marriage)	(surety)	(minister)	(bond)		
Bell, Lucy Ann m. Hett, Levi	Sept 20, 1837	Henry Payne	Nathan Young	9b232		mr 64 *
Bell, Margaret m. Barrow, James	June 27, 1832	Zebulun Bell	B. Reynolds	9b 82		mr 52 *
Bell, Mary m. Evans, John V.	Oct. 31, 1827	John Bell		9b 53		
Bell, Mary R. m. Roberts, James L.	Aug. 7, 1835	Isaac V. Burns		9b 96		
Bell, Polly m. Roberts, John	Apr. 7, 1796	John Bell		1b 96		
Bell, Rachel m. Stephens, Dennis	1791		Moses Hoge		cr 6	mr 6 *
Bell, Rebecca, m. Masters, Henry	Feb. 3, 1785 ?		Hugh Vance			mr 33 *
Bell, Richard m. Aiken, Rachel	Apr. 24, 1807	Robert Aiken	John Mathews	3b 66	cr 13	mr 23 *
Bell, Thomas m. Lyle, Nancy	Aug. 11, 1835	William Lyle		6b 48		
Bell, William m. Dunn, Hannah	July 1, 1815	Thomas Dunn		3b336		
Bell, William m. Painter, Eliz.	Aug. 28, 1808	George Painter		3b 85		
Bell, William m. Robinson, Emelia	Apr. 13, 1807	John Robinson		3b 77		
Bell, Zebulun m. Swingley, Rachel	Nov. 19, 1821	Benjamin Swingley		4b190		
Bellar, Abraham m. Deirdine, Mary	Sept 20, 1807	Abraham Varmetre		3b 80		
Bellar, Eli m. Burnes, Johanna	Dec. 21, 1804	William Burnes		2b219		
Bellar, Iiddy m. Croeson, William	Jan. 7, 1802	James Harrison		2b184		
Bellar, Naomi m. Sagaty, Jacob	Dec. 24, 1798	Jacob Bellar	David Young	1b137	gc 8	*
Belle, Fanny m. Roberts, Dr. A.D.	Oct. 9, 1805	William Belle	Moses Hoge	3b 5	cr 17	mr 82 *
Bellensly, James m. Esther, Barbary	Dec. 6, 1792		David Young		gc 1	*
Beller, Eliz. m. Edwards, Joseph	Nov. 24, 1840	Abisha Beller		6b225	gc 15	*
Beller, Eliz. m. Morlatt, Abraham	Aug. 8, 1816	Henry Seibert	Rev. Reebenack	4b 7		*
Beller, Evelina m. Hensel, William	Dec. 9, 1820	Abraham Morlatt		4b168		
Beller, Jacob m. Sagathy, Catherine	Mar. 13, 1794		David Young		gc 3	mr 5 *
Beller, Jacob m. Rush, Ann	Mar. 29, 1790		Moses Hoge		cr 3	mr 51 *
Beller, Julia Ann m. Underdunk, Henry	Aug. 1, 1826	Wm. Coffenberger	Chas. P. Krauth	5b 45		mr 33 *
Beller, Iiddy m. Morlatt, Richard	Mar. 29, 1786		Hugh Vance			mr 21 *
Beller, Lydia m. Kroeson, Wm.	Dec. 16, 1802		Moses Hoge		cr 17	mr 86 *
Beller, Mary A. m. Copenhaver, J.D.	Sept 16, 1852		D. Thomas		gc 8	mr 43 *
Beller, Naomi m. Sagaty, Jacob	Oct. 11, 1798	Jacob Beller	David Young	1b137		
Beller, Peter m. Sagaty, Emelia	Nov. 8, 1786		Hugh Vance		cr 10	mr 11 *
Beller, Rachel m. Harper, John	Dec. 30, 1795		Moses Hoge			
Belt, Maslin m. Burns, Ellender	June 8, 1794		Richard Swift			mr 40 *
Beltz, Daniel m. Fouke, Sarah	Jan. 3, 1843	Newland Byers	Rev. Reebenack	6b286	gc 10	
Bender, George m. Smith, Sarah	Apr. 11, 1809		John Boyd	1b 26	cr 32	mr 13 *
Bencher, Catherine m. Philips, Wm.	July 27, 1801	Nicholas Orrick		2b110		
Bender, Cath. m. Braidy,Benjamin	Jan. 16, 1798	Samuel B. Harris				
Bender, Cath. m. Walters, John	Sept 11, 1810		David Young		gc 8	
Bender, Eliz. m. Helferstay, John	May 17, 1853		Rev. Reebenack		gc 11	
Bender, Eliz. m. Pitzer, James S.	Feb. 8, 1793		A.G. Chenowith			mr 87 *
Bender, Magdalena m. Mong, John	Aug. 20, 1797		David Young		gc 3	
Bender, Rachel m. Davis, Lewis	Dec. 14, 1852	George Painter	David Young	1b 72	gc 7	
Bender, Samuel m. Smith, Sarah E.	Dec. 6, 1852		A.G.Chenowith			mr 87 *
Bender, Washington m. Pitzer,Rebecca	May 24, 1853		Geo. M. Cooper			mr 87 *

Name	Date	(marriage)	(surety)	(minister)	(bond)		
Benegar, George m. Matlock, Mary	Aug. 6,	Aug. 8, 1816	Joel Reed	Nathan Young	4b 8		mr 55 *
Bener, Eliz. m. Bowers, Jacob	Aug. 29,	Aug. 29, 1808	Michael Billmyre	Lewis Mayer	3b 95	cr 16	mr 24 *
Benner, Christmas m. Snider, Henry		Apr. 5, 1791		David Young		go 1	
Bennett, Ann m. Holliday, Allsworth	Apr. 23,	1789	Robert Bennett		1b x		
Bennett, Drusilla m. Welsh, Benjamin	Dec. 7,	Dec. 7, 1797	George Emmers	Richard Swift	1b 71	cr 12	mr 14 *
Bennett, James m. McCormick, Jane		Dec. 30, 1785		Hugh Vance			mr 34 *
*Bennett, Kitty m. Jones, Isaac	Aug. 27,	1803			2b208		
Bennett, Lurenah m. Magruder, Thos.	Apr. 4,	Apr. 5, 1842	John Bennett	Peyton Harrison	6b268		mr 73 *
Bennett, Mason m. Clark, Sarah Susan		Oct. 15, 1790	Jacob Vandoren	Moses Hoge		cr 5	mr 5 *
Bennett, Rees m. Simmons, Ann	July 3,	1800	Jonas Chamberlain		2b 75		
Bennett, Thomas m. Magnus, Susannah		Nov. 25, 1783					mr 32 *
Bennett, Van m. Vandoren, Phebe	Apr. 22,	Apr. 30, 1801	Thos. Swearingen	Moses Hoge	2b122	cr 38	mr 20 *
Bennybaker(Pe-).Marg't m Howe, Edward		Aug. 31, 1793		David Young		go 3	
Benoe, Betsy m. Bowers, Jacob	Aug. 29,	Aug. 29, 1806	Michael Billmire	Lewis Mayer	3b 95	cr 16	mr 24 *
Bentley, Jeremiah m. Muck, Caty		July 22, 1792		David Young		go 2	
Bentley, William m. Evans, Rosanna		Aug. 12, 1795		David Young		go 5	
Bentness, Mary m. Maxwell, James		Oct. 4, 1794		David Young		go 4	
Bentz, Eliz. m. Jamison, Sylvester		Feb. 1, 1853		J.H.Plunkett			mr 88 *
Berlin, George m. Vanmetre, Margaret	Nov. 24,	Nov. 25, 1851	William McDonald	Joseph Baker	7b237		mr 85 *
Bernard, Kephart m. Faulk, Sarah	May 2,	1803	Christopher Folk		2b201		
Bernhart, Christina m. Hill, Christ'r		Sept 27, 1795		David Young		go 5	*
Bernhard, Sarah m. Klein, Jacob		Nov. 15, 1791		David Young		go 1	*
Berry, Ann Eliz. m. Bowman, Samuel	Feb. 26,	1852	Norman Miller		7b247		
Berry, John m. Evan, Sarah	July 27,	1801	Robert Jones		2b132		
†Berry, John m. Fraize, Margaret	Apr. 24,	1797	John Fraize		1b 12		
Berry, John m. Oldfield, Agnes Ann	Apr. 24,	1818	Wm. Griffith		4b 62		
Berry, Joseph E. m. Hoke, Ann Maria	July 21,	1847	John Hoke		7b101		
†Berry, Joshua m.Fraize,Margaret		July 21, 1822		P. Lipscomb		go 6	mr 81 *
Berry, Peter m. Sellers, Catherine	Oct. 21,	May 4, 1797		David Young			
Berryman, Ann m. Clayton, Benj.	Jan. 30,	Oct. 1822	John Sellers	Chas. P. Krauth	4b225		mr 45 *
Berryman, John m. Clayton, Nelly	July 23,	1805	Thos. Clayton		2b253		
Berryman, Polly m. Oldfield, Joseph	Dec. 21,	1801	Frederick Blue		2b131		
Berryman, Wm. m. Clawson, Rachel	Aug. 21,	1801	Frederick Blue		2b153		
Betgraff, Henrietta m. Lechler, Mich	Jan. 22,	1797	Thomas Clawson		1b 33		
Beton, John m. Allison, Mary	Apr. 28,	1849	Michael Creamer		7b144		
Bett, Elender m. Faris, John	Apr. 17,	1789	Henry Albright	Richard Swift	1b x		mr 40 *
Bettice, James m. Kilmer, Catherine	Dec. 20,	1832	David Kilmer	William Monroe	5b249		mr 65 *
Betts, Adam m. Cook, Mary	Sept 18,	1829	Peter Cook	Nathan Young	5b141		mr 60 *
Beva, Charles m. Orick, Violet	Apr. 19,	1796		David Young		go 5	
Bexeley, David m. Brown, Rachel	June 4,	1788		Moses Hoge			
Beyerly, Michael m. Miller, Anna	Sept 6,	1800	Jacob Miller	David Young	2b 86	go 9	mr 35 *
Beasler, George m. Rife, Susannah	Oct. 3,	1815	Conrad Rife	W.N.Scott	3b342		mr 26 *
Biddle, Geo. m.Maxwell(Marion),Isabel	Oct. 10,	1830	John Helferstay	Nathan Young	5b176		mr 61 *
†*Bennett, Lurena m. Magruder, I.W.B.	Apr. 5,	1842		Peyton Harrison			mr 73 *

(marriage)			(surety)	(minister)	(bond)		
Biddle, Margaret m. Rigsby, David	Nov. 23,	1813	Patrick Duffy	John Mathews	3b276		mr 25 *
Biddle, Mary m. Shell, Jacob	Apr. 27,	1815	Francis Biddle	Rev. Reebenack	3b321	ge 14	*
Blecum, Deborah m. Barnett, William	June 25,	1798	Henry Fleming		1b120		*
Bierley, Michael m. Miller, Ann	Sept 6,	1800	Jacob Miller	David Young	2b 86	ge 9	mr 30 *
Biggerstaff, Wm. m. Williams, Marg't	Apr. 18,	1819		Mathias Riser			mr 35 *
Biggs, William m. Burr, Sarah	Apr. 2,	1788		Moses Hoge			*
Billingsly, Elis. m.Steal(Stool),Wm.	Dec. 15,	1798	John Thruston	David Young	1b154	ge 8	*
Billingsly, Nancy m. Thruston, Joseph	Apr. 1,	1794		David Young		ge 3	*
Billingsly, Robert m. Austin, Mimay	June 23,	1807	Thomas Barton		3b 62		
Billins, Newman m. Roberts, Jane	Oct. 1,	1802	Daniel Roberts		2b182		
Bilmire, Conrad m. Vorhees, Maria V.	Sept 7,	1839	Ganet Vorhees		6b174		
Bilmire, Mary m. Harris, John A.	Sept 20,	1826	Jacob Billmire	Charles P. Krauth	5b 52		mr 51 *
Bilmyer, Rosamah m. Swartz, Geo.W.	Oct. 1,	1840	Wm. Billmire		6b218		
Bilmyer, Cath. m. Curtis, Wm.	Apr. 7,	1825	Jacob Billmyer	Chas. P. Krauth	5b 7		mr 48 *
Bilmyer, Conrad m. Mason, Sarah A.	Oct. 14,	1833	James Mason	W. Hawk	5b287		mr 65 *
Bilmyer, Conrad m. Williamson,Soph	Aug. 11,	1823	John Williamson	John Mathews	4b244		mr 46 *
Bilmyer, Jacob m.Deale(ee,ed).Peggy	Nov. 8,	1800	Peter Deale	David Young	2b 97	ge 9	
Bilmyre, Mary m. Harris, John	Sept 20,	1826	Jacob B. Billmyre	Chas. P. Krauth	5b 52		mr 51 *
Bilmyre, Mary Ann m. Baker, Elias	Nov. 2,	1840	Solomon Bilmire		6b222		
Bilmire, Polly m. Ebberts, Jacob	May 2,	1801	Michael Bilmire		2b125		
Billum, Sarah m. Patterson, Thos.	Apr. 16,	1801	Israel Clawson		2b122		
Bingam, Nicholas m. Smith, Mary	Nov. 18,	1795	John Pickering	Richard Swift	5b 56	cr 26	mr 10 *
*Bishop, Arey m.Dellinger, Reuben	?	1826	Jacob Bishop	James Reily	3b229	ge 13	mr 50 *
Bishop, Catherine m. Horn, Jacob	June 26,	1812	James Merchant	Rev. Reebenack	4b 56		mr 29 *
Bishop, Elias m. Merchant(Ma-).Loud.	Jan. 6,	1818	Zachariah Sanks	Mathias Riser	3b286		mr 54 *
Bishop, Eliza m. McCarty, Peter	Mar. 3,	1814	Ezekial Showers	Nathan Young	5b 68		mr 52 *
Bishop, Eliz. m. Brown, Milton J.	Apr. 14,	1827	John Bishop	B. Reynolds	2b 78		*
Bishop, Eliz. m. Moore, John	July 25,	1800		David Young		ge 9	*
Bishop, George m. Moore, Nancy		1797		David Young		gc 6	*
Bishop, Jacob m. Jud, Nancy	Jan. 11,	1810	John Fisher	Rev. Reebenack	3b133	go 11	*
Bishop, Jacob m. Polsal, Eve	Apr. 3,	1794		David Young		go 3	*
Bishop, Joel m. Hout, Angelina P.M.	Jan. 12,	1836	John L. Rasler	Nathan Young	6b 63		mr 64 *
Bishop, Josephus m. Stookey,Margaret	Mar. 28,	1832	Henry J. Seibert	Rev. Reebenack	5b223		*
Bishop, Kitty m. Horn, Jacob	June 26,	1812	Jacob Bishop	James M. Brown	3b229	gc 13	*
Bishop, Margaret m. McIntire, Robt.	Apr. 12,	1830	Adam Stewart	David Young	5b177		mr 54 *
Bishop, Margaret m. Moore, Richard	Nov. 15,	1797	Valentine Grace	Jacob Medtart	1b 61	gc 7	*
Bishop, Maria m. Davis, Thomas	July 14,	1831	Milton J. Brown	David Young	5b198		mr 63 *
Bishop, Mary m. Stagner, Peter	Aug. 28,	1798	Henry Bishop	David Young	1b126	ge 8	*
Bishop, Mary Ellen m. Stuckey, John	Feb. 14,	1854		John O. Proctor			*
Bishop, Michael m. Smith, Elis.	Feb. 16,	1793		David Young		go 2	*
Bishop, Polly m. Patton, William	June 30,	1821		Chas. P. Krauth	4b185		mr 42 *
Bishop, Reason m. Kitchen, Margaret	Mar. 18,	1824	Joseph Kitchen Jr.	Nathan Young	4b258		mr 58 *
Bishop, Susan m. Beeson, Hiram	Aug. 9,	1827	Ezekial Showers	Nathan Young	5b 74		mr 59 *
*Bingham, Ann m. Lemon, Nathan	Nov. 15,	1792	?	Moses Hoge			mr 39 *

Name	(marriage)	(suretor)	(minister)	(bond)	Ref.
Bishop, Thomas m. Everhart, Eliz.	Feb. 5, 1833	Harrison Waite	Nathan Young	9b296	mr 66 *
Bittle, Mary m. Shell, Jacob	Apr. 27, 1815	Francis Bittle	Rev. Reebeneck	3b321	ge 14 / mr 64 *
Bitzer, Mary m. Perrell, John	May 29, 1832		Nathan Young		ge 3
Bitzer, Michael m. Shaffer, Maria	Mar. 11, 1794		David Young		
Bivens, Thomas m. Watson, Ellen S.	Mar. 16, / Mar. 19, 1845	Norman Miller	James Chisholm	7b 29	mr 76 *
Biseler, George m. Rife, Susannah	Oct. 3, / Oct. 5, 1815	Conrad Rife	W.N.Scott	3b342	mr 26 *
Black, Daniel m. Gardner, Mary	June 23, 1805	Jacob Gardner		2b264	cr 36 / mr 13 *
Black, Eliz. m. King, Mathew	Aug. 14, 1797	William Boyd	Moses Hoge	1b 30	ge 14
Black, Jacob m. Painter, Eve	Dec. 25, / Dec. 26, 1813	Jacob Painter	Rev. Reebeneck	3b280	mr 66 *
Black, John m. Campbell, Ann R.	Dec. 11, 1833	John Black	Nathan Young	4b 52	ge 12
Black, Polly m. Menser, George	Dec. 11, 1817	Robert Spriggs	W.N.Scott	3b200	mr 42 *
Black, Samuel m. Mingle, Margaret	Nov. 10, / Nov. 9, 1811		Rev. Reebeneck		mr 42 *
Blackburn, Joseph m. Boswell(Bas)Nancy	May 9, 1786		Hugh Vance		cr 7 / mr 6 *
Blackburn, Joseph m. Hendrick, Olive	Apr. 16, 1782		Daniel Sturges		
Blackford, Ebeneser m. Sewel, Sarah	June 15, 1791	John Gooding	Moses Hoge	1b 29	mr 55 *
Blackford, John m. Swearingen, Sarah	Aug. 17, 1797	Henry Job		4b 4	ge 5
Blackmore, Mary m. Job, Jacob	June 3, / June 4, 1815	Francis Silver	Nathan Young	4b130	mr 46 *
Blackmore, Nancy m. Clise, Jacob	Jan. 18, 1820				
Blade, Martha m. Riley, John	July 15, 1796	Jacob Clise	David Young	4b243	cr 3 / mr 5 *
Blake, Jane m. Beall, Richard	July 7, 1823	Seaman Garard	C.P.Krauth	5b293	cr 4
Blake, John m. Canfield, Ann Rebecca	Dec. 7, 1833				
Blake, Mary m.Huffman, John	May 9, 1790		Moses Hoge		mr 50 *
Blake, Patty m. Risley, John	Apr. 29, 1794		David Young		ge 12
Blakeney, Andrew J. m. Shoafstall, E.	Dec. 2, / Dec. 3, 1826	Seth Shoafstall	John Mathews	5b 58	cr 32 / mr 20 *
Blakeney, Edward m.Shoafstall, Mary	Jan. 15, 1825	Seth Shoafstall		4b285	mr 84 *
Blakeney, Juliet m.Zimmerman,Jacob	Nov. 28, / Nov. 26, 1811	Andrew Blakeney	Rev. Reebeneck	3b202	cr 11 / mr 12 *
Blamer, Zadock m.Butt, Susannah S.	May 24, / May 27, 1802	Richard Butt	Richard Swift	2b173	mr 84 *
Blamer, Mary m. Carroll, George	Jan. 21, / Jan. 27, 1851	Jacob French	Henry Furlong	7b211	mr 75 *
Bleads, Eliz. m. Yerkes, Joshua Jr.	Nov. 19, 1801	Martha Riley		2b149	
Bleamer, Mary m. Keith, Walter	May 5, 1796				
Blessing, Geo. W. m.Homerick,Minerva	Sept 15, / Sept 16, 1851	Joshua Homerick	John Boyd	7b232	cr 37 / mr 14 *
Blinco, Ann m. Riner, Daniel	Apr. 23, / Apr. 23, 1845	Joseph Blinco	David Thomas	7b 32	cr 37 / mr 1 *
Blinco, Mary Cath. m. Morrington,Jas	Aug. 19, 1848	William Downs	John Boggs	7b134	
Blogs, William m. Rankins, Frances	Dec. 31, 1797			1b 76	
Blois, Mary m. Lott, Anthony	Jan. 15, 1785		John Hill		
Blondel, John H. m. Young, Caroline	May 29, 1839	Adam Young	Edward Tiffin	6b170	
Blondel, Lydia m. Helferstay, John	July 27, 1839	Joseph Schoppert		6b173	
Blondel, Richard A. m. Helferstay, S.	Aug. 10, 1840	John Helferstay		6b215	
Blondel, Rosella m. Davis, John	Aug. 23, 1836	Anthony Chambers		6b 88	
Bloomer, Philip m. Smith, Eliz.	Oct. 12, 1819	John Lowe	W.N.Scott	4b118	cr 26 / mr 30 *
Bloomfield, John m. Gales, Sarah	Mar. 15, 1806	Peter Bellar	John Bond	3b 14	mr 22 *
Bloxeck, Eliz. m. King, Mathew	Sept 14, 1797	William Boyd	Moses Hoge	1b 30	cr 36 / mr 13 *
Bloys, William m. Rankin, Frances	Dec. 31, 1797	William Downs	John Hill	1b 76	cr 37 / mr 14 *

Name	(marriage)	(suretor)	(minister)	(bond)	cr/gc	mr
Blue, Catherine m. Grantham, John	Jan. 20, 1824	George Pulse	B. Reynolds	4b255		mr 49 *
Blue, Cornelius m. Jeans, Nancy	Dec. 14, 1790		Moses Hoge		cr 5	mr 5 *
Blue, Eliz. m. Grafton, Ambrose	Dec. 20, 1796		Moses Hoge		cr 36	mr 12 *
Blue, Eliz. m. Heath, Israel	July 25, 1799	Richard Blue	John Hutt(Hedtt)	2b 11	cr 38	mr 17 *
Blue, Eliz. m. McKee, Alexander	Feb. 2, 1802	David Blue		2b159		
Blue, Ezekiel m. Reed, Sarah	Jan. 11, 1799	James Watson	Moses Hoge	1b153	cr 29	mr 17 *
Blue, Ezekiel m. Robinson, Martha	June 12, 1798	Nathan Kennedy		1b115		
Blue, Fanny m. Barklow, Cornelius	Aug. 1, 1806	James Whitelock	John Bond	3b 25	cr 28	mr 23 *
Blue, Henry m. Garrett, Mary	Aug. 2, 1793		Christian Streit		cr 15	mr 8 *
Blue, Jacob m. Yerky, Peggy	Aug. 27, 1793		Moses Hoge		cr 36	mr 12 *
Blue, James m. Kerney, Jane	Nov. 19, 1796		Moses Hoge		cr 36	mr 25 *
Blue, Jesse m. Yerkey, Peggy	Nov. 10, 1813	William Kerney	John Mathews	3b275	cr 22	mr 12 *
Blue, John m. Blue, Mary	Oct. 22, 1793		Moses Hoge			mr 8 *
Blue, John m. Shoafstall, Margaret E	Jan. 10, 1832	Morgan Vancleve	Hugh Vance	5b213	cr 20	mr 3 *
Blue, John S. m. Wallingsford,Marg't	May 7, 1789	Jacob Gorrell		3b 70		
Blue, Lotta m. Curtis, Jonathan	Sept 19, 1807	M.A.Vancleve		6b 72		
Blue, Margaret m. Bowen, Jesse	Mar. 1, 1836					
Blue, Martha m. Blue, Samuel	Mar. 14, 1791		Moses Hoge		cr 6	mr 6 *
Blue, Mary m. Blue, John	Oct. 22, 1793		Moses Hoge		cr 22	mr 8 *
Blue, Mary m. Rogers, John	Apr. 9, 1789		Hugh Vance		cr 20	mr 3 *
Blue, Michael m. Cleary, Ann	Dec. 31, 1789	Frederick Blue	Moses Hoge	3b 46	cr 3	mr 3 *
Blue, Nancy m. Slater, James	Jan. 7, 1807	John Calvert		6b 8		
Blue, Nathaniel m. Walker, Cath.	Apr. 18, 1834	William Burnes Jr.		2b231		
Blue, Peter m. Clayton, Eliz.	Mar. 31, 1804			2b158		
Blue, Peter m. Robinson, Polly	Jan. 27, 1802	Frederick Blue				
Blue, Rebecca m. Trigg, Samuel	Feb. 17, 1793		Moses Hoge		cr 21	mr 7 *
Blue, Samuel m. Blue, Martha	Mar. 14, 1791		Moses Hoge		cr 6	mr 6 *
Blue, Susannah m. Lewis, Thomas	May 27, 1790		Moses Hoge		cr 4	mr 5 *
Blue, William m. McIntire, Mary	Mar. 15, 1788		Moses Hoge		gc 2	mr 35 *
Blume, Jacob m. Hart, Margaret	Mar. 4, 1793	John Lowe	David Young	4b118		mr 30 *
Blume, Philip m. Smith, Eliz.	Oct. 12, 1819	Joseph Yarnell	W.N.Scott	4b257		mr 58 *
Boak, Abigail m. Ankrum, David	Mar. 5, 1824	Rees Branson	Nathan Young	2b242	cr 13	mr 21 *
Boak, John m. Downing, Mary	Aug. 30, 1804	William Boak	John Bond	5b118		mr 53 *
Boak, Margaret J. m. Payne, Henry Jr	Feb. 12, 1829	Paul Taylor	William Monroe	4b151		
Boak, Mrs. Mary m. Fletcher, Peter	June 9, 1820	Alex. Miller		2b 37		
Boak, Robert m. Lee, Eleanor	Dec. 4, 1799	Jacob Seibert		5b165		
Boak, Wm. L. m. Seibert, Rachael E.	May 6, 1830	Philip Board	W. Monroe	2b 87	cr 29	mr 54 *
Board, Thomas m. Hart, Rebecca	Sept 15, 1800	Robert Gallaher	Moses Hoge	1b 59	gc 7	mr 19 *
Boarland, Alex. m. Smith, Jean	Oct. 31, 1797	Charles Boarman	David Young	6b273		
Boarman, Eliz. R. m. Brown, Thomas	July 19, 1842	Charles Boarman		7b 60		
Boarman, Sally A. m. Bryarly, Robt.P.	Mar. 2, 1846	Charles Boarman		7b216		
Boarman, Susan M. m. Harris, Jesse	Feb. 25, 1851			4b 44		
Bockey, John P. m. Snowdeal, Cath.	Aug. 24, 1817	Henry Rousch	W.N.Scott			

Name	(marriage)	(surety)	(minister)	(bond)	
Bockins, Daniel m. Smith, Eliz.	Sept 3, 1823	?	Chas. P. Krauth	4b247	mr 46 *
Bockins, David m. Smith, Eliz.	Sept 3, 1823	?			
Bocock, Thomas S. m. Faulkner, Annie	Oct. 4, 1853		A.H.Boyd		*
Boden, James m. Cooke, Eliz.	Dec. 20, 1837	Samuel Cooke		6b127	
Boden, William m. Briley, Nancy	Apr. 10, 1807	Garret Wynkoop		3b 55	
Bodine, Hannah m. Miller, Jacob	Dec. 23, 1809	John Bodine	Rev. Reebenack	3b129	ge 11
Bodine, John m. McManus, Cath.	Aug. 21, 1816	John Bodine	Rev. Reebenack	4b 6	ge 15
Bodine, Nancy m. Conaway, Isaac	Aug. 3, 1813	John Burdine	Rev. Reebenack	3b255	ge 13
Bodine, Richard m. Lee, Mary Ann	Dec. 17, 1849	Conrad Robbins	Lewis F. Wilson	7b170	
Bodine, William m. Morlatt, Rebecca	Nov. 19, 1816	George Morlatt		4b 22	mr 83 *
Bodley, Charles m. Kiger, Mary Ann	Nov. 9, 1833	Jacob Roads	Nathan Young	5b290	mr 66 *
Boerkapp, Adam m. Sellers, Eliz.	May 5, 1788		Hugh Vance		mr 34 *
Boggers, Bennet m. Grantham, Mary	July 1789		D. Thomas		mr 37 *
Boggs, Robert m. Rion, Cloe	Sept 23, 1788		Moses Hoge		mr 36 *
Boggs, Ann m. Marshall, Thos.	Mar. 1788		Chas. P. Krauth		mr 46 *
Boggs, Jane m. Harper, Thomas	Mar. 17, 1823	Boyd Roberts	D. Thomas	4b234	mr 37 *
Boggs, Thomas m. Stilwell, Nancy	Jan. 22, 1839	James Robinson	Hugh Vance	6b156	mr 42 *
Bogle, Ruth m. Gist(Gust), Joshua	Sept 27, 1815	Levi Cunningham		3b341	
Bogvell, Nancy m. Black, William	May 9, 1786				
Boher, Maria m. Barnes, Joseph D.	Dec. 26, 1849	Martin Boher		7b172	
Bohman, Adam m. Essl, Eliz.	Dec. 27, 1850	Adolph Sheig	John Light	7b208	mr 80 *
Bohrer, Abraham m. Widmire, Eliz.	June 26, 1802	Wm. Bailey	D. Francis Sprigg	2b176	mr 83 *
Bohrer, Barbara m. Bohrer, George	May 29, 1818	George Bohrer	Mathias Riser	4b 72	mr 29 *
Bohrer, Cath. m. Yost, Peter	June 7, 1799			2b 7	
Bohrer, Drusilla m. Bailey, Wm.	Apr. 7, 1818	George Whitmyre	Mathias Riser	4b 67	mr 29 *
Bohrer, George m. Bohrer, Barbara	May 29, 1818	Wm. Bailey	Mathias Riser	4b 72	mr 29 *
Bols, Nancy m. Royer, Samuel	Oct. 2, 1848	Samuel Henshaw		7b135	
Bokey, Peter m. Snowdeal, Cath.	Aug. 24, 1817	Henry Rousch	W.N.Scott	4b 44	mr 68 *
Boland, Eliz. m. Hess, John	Aug. 19, 1834	David Hess		6b 15	
Boland, Eliz. m. McGonagle, Patrick	Oct. 13, 1798	John Mulhall	James M. Brown	1b139	
Boley, Benj. m. Gorrell, Isabella	Aug. 19, 1847	Benjamin Boley Jr	Henry Furlong	7b104	mr 78 *
Boley, Benj. m. Gorrell, Isabella	May 12, 1840	Wm. B. Gorrell		6b208	
Boley, Dan1el m. Maxwell, Peggy	Nov. 19, 1795	Benj. Boley	David Young	2b 66	go 5
Boley, Eliz. m. Smith, Seth	Apr. 18, 1800	Jacob V, Gerrard		6b 30	
*Boley, Tholemiah m. Tabb, Ann V.	Feb. 2, 1835	Harrison Waite		6b 40	
Bolin, George m. McIlwaine, Marg't	Apr. 15, 1835	Geo. W. Bolin		6b 36	
Bolin, Thos. m. Donaldson, Margaret	Mar. 9, 1835	Michael Seibert		5b262	
Bolin, John G. m. Brannon, Mary Ann	Mar. 16, 1833	Harrison Waite		6b 19	
Boll, Jacob m. Grubb, Sarah	Sept 13, 1834	Joseph Snyder	John Howell	4b107	mr 68 *
Bolton, William m. Peck, Sarah	May 26, 1819	Harrison Waite		5b295	
Boltz, Eliz. Ann m. Sendiniver, J.	Dec. 13, 1833	John Pulse		3b 32	
Boltz, George m. Pulse, Cath.	Oct. 10, 1806		Rev. Reebenack		ge 11
Boltz, George m. Schall, Mary	Apr. 26, 1810				cr 15
*Boley, Peggy m. Wright, James	Nov. 14, 1812	William Wright	Lewis Mayer	3b241	mr 25 *

Name	(marriage)		(surety)	(minister)	(bond)			
Boltz, Matilda m. Ludwig, Geo. F.	Nov. 26,	1832	Harrison Waite	Rev. Reebemack	5b248	gc 10		*
Boltz, Susannah m. Shall, James	Jan. 19,	1809	William Wright	Lewis Mayer	3b241	cr 15	mr 25	**
Bolz, Peggy m. Wright, James	Nov. 15,	1812	Jacob Bonawitz	David Young	2b 63	gc 9		*
Bonawitz, Juliann m. Ralfsnider, L.	Apr. 10,	1800	Joel Reed		4b239			
Bond, George m. Matlock, Margaret	May 19,	1823	Chas. Henderson		3b249			
Bond, Geo. W. m. Duvall, Eliz.	Jan. 28,	1813	Lewis B. Willis		3b218			
Bond, Mary m. Fearman, Henry Jr.	Apr. 8,	1812	Walter Bond	Chas. P. Krauth	4b247		mr 46	*
Bond, Sarah m. Deck, Jacob	Aug. 26,	1823	Seth Bonham		3b270			
Bonham, Mary m. Rainey, Thos.	Aug. 11,	1813	Edmond Chismond	Nathan Young	3b354		mr 55	*
Bonham, Sarah m. Jeffreys, Joseph	Feb. 15,	1816	John Dupp		2b136			
Bonner, Cath. m. Swisher, Jacob	Aug. 13,	1801						
Bonner, Eliz. m. Keys, Frederick	Oct. 11,	1785		Hugh Vance			mr 34	*
Bonner, Eliz. m. Swisher, Solomon	Nov. 9,	1811	Frederick Shawhan	John B. Hoge	3b199	cr 14	mr 24	*
Bonner, Kath. m. Sturne(Starne),John	July 18,	1786		Hugh Vance			mr 43	*
Bonner, Mary m. Stacy, Thomas	Dec. 12,	1802	Samuel Hedges	Richard Swift	2b185	cr 32	mr 21	*
Bons, Polly m. Harrison, Alex.	Nov. 4,	1815	John Lindsey		3b346			
Booth, Eliz. m. Meanor, Samuel	Aug. 11,	1804	Caleb Booth		2b240			
Booth, Hannah m. Radney, William	Mar. 22,	1821	Caleb Booth		4b178			
Booth, Isaac m. Crumley, Eliz.	Apr. 24,	1809	Thomas Crumley		3b112			
Booth, Jane m. McCausland, Frances	Nov. 26,	1796	Frederick Gilbert	John Boyd	4b152	cr 11	mr 12	*
Booth, John m. Pane(Paul), Hannah	June 23,	1820	Jonathan Booth	Nathan Young	3b125	gc 10	mr 57	*
Booth, Nancy m. Shrode, George	Nov. 23,	1809	Thomas Butler	Rev. Reebemack	4b166		mr 57	*
Booth, Rebecca m. Dailey, John L.	Nov. 8,	1820	Richard Davidson	Nathan Young			mr 36	*
Boothe, Samuel m. Cathaway, Rodey	Dec. 12,	1788	Wm. Murphy	Hugh Vance	2b 25			
Boothe, Caleb m. Davidson, Ann	Sept 4,	1799	Samuel Meanor	Moses Hoge	2b294	cr 17	mr 22	*
Boothe, Easter m. Kennedy, John	Feb. 20,	1805	Robert Gallaher		2b266	gc 7		*
Boothe, Hannah m. Tate, John	Aug. 1,	1805	Jacob Borer	David Young	1b 59			
Boreland, Alex. m. Smith, Jane	Oct. 31,	1797	Geo. Whitayre		3b216			
Borer, Anna m. Siler, George	Mar. 12,	1812	Jane Hully	Mathias Riser	4b 67		mr 29	*
Borer, Drusilla m. Sellers, Wm.	Apr. 7,	1818	Barney Borock	Hugh Vance	3b 62		mr 34	**
Borerkopp, Adam m. Sellers, Eliz.	May 5,	1788	Michael Fiser		3b106			
Boring, Greenberry m.Holly, Cath.	June 20,	1807	William Hite		3b156			
Borock, Nancy m. Leamon, David	Jan. 13,	1809		Rev. Reebemack	6b 46	gc 11		
Boroff, Henry m. Fiser, Sarah	July 31,	1810		Elisha Gardner			mr 68	*
Boroff, Samuel m. Hite, Hannah	June 10,	1835		Hugh Vance	1b131		mr 32	*
Bossell, Eliz. m. Connell, Arthur		1781						
Bostick, James m. Vance, Jane	Sept 11,	1798	James Vance	David Young		gc 8		*
Bottere, Eliz. m. Veal, Samuel	Apr. 2,	1793		David Young		go 2		*
Bottwick, James m. Coons, Katherine	June 4,	1789	John Eydon	Hugh Vance	1b176	cr 39		*
Bough, Eliz. m. Jolly, Samuel	Mar. 30,	1799	Baker Wolham		1b 49			
Bough, Henry m. Wolham, Eliz.	Sept 28,	1797						
Bough, Mary m. Wolham, Henry	Dec. 14,	1801	Henry Bough Jr.		2b152			
Boughough, John m. Cury, Eliz.	Apr.	1804	James McLaughlin		2b232		mr 3	

Name		(marriage)		(surety)	(minister)	(bond)		
Bowling, Charlotte m. Clark, James	Aug. 28.	Aug. 26,	1833	Thos. J. Bowling	Nathan Young	5b281		mr 66 *
Bovey, Philip m. Meyer, Catherine		Mar. 31,	1793		David Young		gc 2	*
Bovy, Mary m. Manning(Roney),James		Sept 6,	1797		David Young		gc 6	*
Bowden, Maria m. Courtney, Michael	Jan. 7,		1820	Samuel Bowden		4b129		
Boudoin, Richard m. Lee, Mary Ann	Dec. 17,	Dec.	1849	Conrad Robbins	L.F.Wilson	7b170		mr 83 *
Bowen, Eliz. m. Lewis, Fielding	Apr. 20,		1802	Thomas Stilwell		2b171		
Bowen, Hiram m. Morrow, Ann Rabocca	Dec. 18.	Dec. 18.	1828	James Morrow	W. Monroe	5b115		mr 53 *
Bowell, Jesse m. Blue, Margaret	Mar. 1,		1836	M.A.VanClere		6b 72		
Bowen, Mary Ann m. Stoffer, Alfred L.	Oct. 28,	Oct.	1847	Hiram Bowen	P. Lipscomb	7b110		mr 81 *
Bowen, Rachel m. Pitzer, Martin	Nov. 3,	Nov. 4,	1813	Henry Bowers	Rev. Reebenack	3b274	gc 13	
Bowen, William m. Smh, Barbara	Feb. 23,		1833	Solomon Smh		5b27		
Bower, Adam m.Swingle, Catherine	Oct. 25,		1830	?		5b179		
Bower, Joseph m. Francaway, Carolina	Apr. 11,		1834			6b 5		
Bower, Mary m. Allebaugh(Alv), John	Apr. 18,	Apr. 19,	1825	John Bowers	Nathan Young	5b 8		mr 58 *
Bowers, Amelia T. m. Bowers, John W.	?	July 31,	1850	James Bowers	R.T.Berry	7b191		mr 83 *
Bowers, Ann A. m. Swartz, John F.	May 27,	May	1844	Ephraim Alburtis		7b 2		
Bowers, Catherine m. Burk, William	June 14,	June	1804	Thos. Donaway		2b236		
Bowers, Catherine m. Seibert, John	Dec. 31,	Dec.	1806	Henry Bowers		3b 40		
Bowers, Eliz. m. Fries, William	Apr. 4,		1846	William Bowers		7b 63		
Bowers, Eliz. m. Groff, Emanuel	Apr. 30,		1851	Joshua Gallaher		7b224		
Bowers, Eliz. m. Walker, William	Nov. 6,		1824	Henry Bowers		4b276		
Bowers, Ellen E. m. Turner, James H.	Nov. 23,		1844	Bennett Franceway		7b 18		
Bowers, George m. Lemon, Eleanor	Dec. 4,		1821	George Lemon		4b199		
Bowers, George m. Naff, Polly	Feb. 23,	Feb.	1825	John Naff	Chas. P. Krauth	5b 1		mr 48 *
Bowers, George m. Pitzer, Eve	Nov. 2,	Nov. 4,	1824	Jacob Pitzer	J.L.Bromwell	4b276		mr 47 *
Bowers, Harriett m. Conchman, Michael	Dec.23,	Dec.	1828	Henry Bowers		5b116		
Bowers, Henry m. Gill, Ann	Nov. 17,		1818	Thomas Gill		4b 88		
Bowers, Henry Jr. m. Young, Eliz.		Dec. 13,	1787		Hugh Vance		cr 23	
Bowers, Hiram m. Morrison, Amr R.		Dec. 18,	1828		W. Monroe		cr 16	mr 2 *
Bowers, Jacob m. Beman(~noe), Betsy	Aug. 29,	Aug. 29,	1808	Michael Bilmire	Lewis Mayer	3b 95	cr 39	mr 53 *
Bowers, Jacob m. Martin, Eliz.	June 23,	June 23,	1789	Jacob Allebaugh	Hugh Vance	5b 98		mr 24 *
Bowers, John m. Allebaugh, Eliz.	Apr. 9,	Apr. 12,	1828	John Ebberts	B. Reynolds	5b137		mr 3 *
Bowers, John m. Wareham, Mary Ann	Aug. 10,	Aug. 11,	1889	Hezekiah Kerns	W. Monroe	6b157		mr 52 *
Bowers, John Jr. m.Kerns, Mary E.	Jan. 16,	Jan.	1839	James Bowers		6b157		mr 53 *
Bowers, John W. m. Bowers, Amelia T.	?	July 31,	1850	John Bowers	R.T.Berry	7b191		mr 83 *
Bowers, Lurenah m. Miles, John	July 26,	July 27,	1852	John Bowers	R.A.Fink	7b257		mr 86 *
Bowers, Mary m. Price, Geo. L.	Nov. 30,		1840	Lewis Davis		6b226		
Bowers, Philip m. Grove, Shepherd B.	June 17,		1818	John Doll		4b 74		
Bowers, Polly m. Grove, Shepherd B.	Oct. 20,		1817	Samuel L. Rees		4b 48		
Bowers, Rachel A. m. Martin, Squire	Oct. 16,	Oct.	1851			7b229		
Bowers, Samuel m. Swisher, Ann	Aug. 11,	June 14,	1838	George Swisher	James Watts	6b117		mr 69 *
Bowers, Susanna m. Miles, John	June 11,	June 27,	1852	John Bowers	R.A.Fink	7b257		mr 86 *
Bowers, Susannah m. Shower(over)John	July 26,	Dec. 22,	1785		Hugh Vance	7b257		mr 34 *

Name	(marriage)		(suretor)	(minister)	(bond)		
Bowers, William m. Grove, Cath.	May 24,	1815	Peter Grove	Lewis Mayer	3b325		mr 26 *
Bowers, William m. Miller, Susannah	Sept 10,	1836	Samuel Miller		6b 84		
Bowersmith, Mary m. Zeigler, Martin	May 29,	1811	James Harrison	John B. Hoge	3b188	cr 14	mr 24 *
Bowling, Charlotte m. Clarke, James	Aug. 26,	1833	Thos. J. Bowling	Nathan Young	5b281		mr 66 *
Bowls, Sarah m. Jeffings, John	Oct. 15,	1788		Hugh Vance			mr 35 *
Bowman, Andrew m. Maxwell, Elis.	Aug. 23,	1820	John Strother		4b157		
Bowman, Catherine m. Moles, Daniel	Jan. 16,	1819	Peter Howard		4b 97		
Bowman, Chas. H. m. Beales, Rosanna	Oct. 7,	1846	David Beales		7b 75		
Bowman, Christena m. Bowman, Jacob Jr	May 14,	1804	Jacob Bowman Sr.		2b234		
Bowman, David m. Riser, Mary	Nov. 2,	1811	Magdalena Riser		3b199		
Bowman, Elenor m. Kernes, John	Dec. 11,	1810	George Peterman	Rev. Reebenack	3b167	gc 11	*
Bowman, Elis. m. Pitzer, James	June 25,	1822	Henry Burns	Chas. P. Krauth	4b218		mr 45 *
Bowman, George m. Potts, Elis.	Mar. 10,	1810	John Beckett	Lewis Mayer	3b140	cr 14	mr 24 *
Bowman, Isaac m. French, Hannah	Mar. 10,	1847	Conrad Crumbaugh		7b 91		
Bowman, Jacob Jr. m. Bowman, Chr't'a	May 14,	1804	Jacob Bowman Sr.		2b234		
Bowman, James m. Wright, Nancy	Mar. 29,	1815	John Wright	John Mathews	3b316		mr 25 *
Bowman, John m. Brouse, Rachel	Aug. 18,	1804	John Bronse		2b240		
Bowman, John m. Waight(Waite), Elis.	Jan. 4,	1799	John Ellis		1b159		
Bowman, Jonathan m. Stutsman, Sarah	Nov. 27,	1807	John Stutsman		3b 78		
Bowman, Julia A. m.Palmer(Palmer),Wm	Sept 27,	1828	S. Gerrard	B. Reynolds	5b107		mr 52 *
Bowman, Mary m. Lynn, Elijah	Apr. 10,	1798	Joseph Vance		1b 97		
Bowman, Mary m. Layers, Jacob	July 22,	1797	John Bowman		1b 25		
Bowman, Mrs. Jean m. Kroeson, Isaac	July 23,	1804	Charles Orrick		2b238		
Bowman, Sally m. Riser(Riger), Sam'l	June 12,	1815	David Bowman	Rev. Reebenack	3b328	gc 14	*
Bowman, Samuel m. Berry, A n Elis.	Feb. 26,	1852	Norman Miller		7b247		
Bown, James m. McIntire, E.M.	Jan. 24,	1844	Andrew McIntire	James Chisholm	6b312		mr 75 *
Boyd, Ann Maria m. Hagmire, Conrad	Feb. 5,	1818	James P. Erskine	John B. Hoge	4b 60		mr 46 *
Boyd, Anne R.H. m. Powell, Humphrey	Oct. 30,	1823	Philip C. Pendleton	John Mathews	4b251	cr 40	mr 4 *
Boyd, Elijah m. Hays, Phebe O.	Aug. 21,	1789		Hugh Vance			
Boyd, Isabell K. m. Compton, Wm. T.	Sept 8,	1829	Conrad Hogmire	Chas. P. Krauth	5b140	cr 24	mr 47 *
Boyd, James m. Turner, Lucinda	Dec. 27,	1845	William Turner	Hugh Vance	7b 51		mr 2 *
Boyd, James S. m. Wilson, Eliza K.	Oct. 21,	1824	John K. Wilson	John B. Hoge	4b274		mr 41 *
Boyd, John m. Corbin, Sarah	Oct. 28,	1788					
Boyd, John m. Horn, Elis.	Feb. 12,	1821	Maj. Geo. Horn	David Young	4b172	gc 1	*
Boyd, John m. Marlin, Ann	Sept 7,	1791					
Boyd, John m. Stephenson, Isabella	Oct. 10,	1803	Benj. Stephenson	David Young	2b209		*
Boyd, Maria m. Bawser, Frederick	Aug. 13,	1793		Rev. Reebenack		gc 3	
Boyd, Mary m. Houck, Samuel	Jan. 18,	1786					
Boyd, Mary m. Manford, William	Jan. 20,	1814	Wm. Thurston	Hugh Vance	3b282	gc 14	mr 33 *
Boyd, Mary m. McWhorter, Robert	Apr. 6,	1821	Robert Boyd	John B. Hoge	4b176		mr 41 *
Boyd, Mary W. m. Faulkner, Chas. J.	Mar. 12,	1833	Elsha Boyd	Jas. M. Brown	5b286	gc 3	mr 67 *
Boyd, Rachel m. Bailey, William	Sept 26,	1793		David Young			
Boyd, Samuel m. Stephenson, Maria	Oct. 26,	1798	James Kennedy	John Boyd	1b142	cr 37	mr 16 *

Name	(marriage)	(surety)	(minister)	(bond)		
Boyd, Sarah Ann m. Pendleton, Philip	Nov. 25, 1813	Elisha Boyd	John Mathews	3b277		mr 25 *
Boyd, William m. Grey, Alice	Apr. 1,	Andrew Yeates		1b108		
Boyd, William m. Parks, Jane	Nov. 10, 1798		John Boyd	1b 69	cr 11	mr 12 *
Boydstone, Ann m. Talbutt, William	Dec. 12, 1796				cr 12	mr 14 *
Boyer(Boyle), James m.McSherry,Polly	Jan. 29, 1797	Presley Boydstone	Richard Swift	1b165	gc 8	
Boyer, John m. Alburtis, Eliz.	Dec. 16, 1799	William Mackey Jr	David Young	3b279		
Boyer, Katherine m. Wise, Jacob	1813	Robert Wilson				
Boyle, Chas. A.m.McClintock,Rebecca	Feb. 27, 1787		Hugh Vance	7b207		mr 44 *
Boyle, James m. Hammond, Eliza	Aug. 11, 1782		Hugh Vance	7b241	cr 9	mr 1 *
Boyle, John m. Broderick, Cath.	Dec. 25, 1850	Joseph Duckwall		7b242		
Boyle, Patrick m. McBride, Katy	Jan. 5, 1852	Pat'k Cunningham	D. Thomas			mr 85 *
Boyle(Bay-),Quentin m.Cannon, Eliz.	Jan. 8, 1852	Joseph VanDoren	Hugh Vance		cr 23	mr 2 *
Boswell, George m. Taylor, Anne	Dec. 14, 1787		Hugh Vance			mr 43 *
Boswell, Nancy m. Black, William	Jan. 2, 1787		Hugh Vance			mr 42 *
Bozzell, Eliz. m. McKinney, Thomas	May 9, 1786	Cornelius Kelly	Hugh Vance	4b195		mr 44 *
Brabson, Eliz. m. Collins, Patrick	Oct. 25, 1821	Evan Reese	John B. Hoge	1b 23		
Brabson, Thomas m. Miller, Jane	June 20, 1797					
Brackenridge,Thos. m.Worthington,Eppy	Dec. 4, 1795	Richard Ranson	John Boyd	2b 37	cr 33	mr 10 *
Brackfiss, Cath. m. Herman, Michael	Feb. 13, 1799					*
Bradford, Mary m. Ray, Robert	Feb. 20, 1793		David Young		gc 2	
Bradley, Chas. m. Kiger, Mary Ann	Apr. 11, 1793		Christian Streit		cr 15	mr 8 *
Bradley, Jancy m. Clarns, Frances	Nov. 10, 1833	Jacob Roads	Nathan Young	5b290		mr 66 *
Bradley, Wm. m. Fowler, Eliz.	June 29, 1786		Hugh Vance			mr 43 *
	Apr. 30, 1783?		Hugh Vance			mr 32 *
Bradshaw, Harrison m.Lohr, Sarah C.	Feb. 17, 1847	Samuel Lohr	John Edtt(Butt)	7b 86		
Bradshaw, Joseph m. Jackson, Sarah	Jan. 19, 1799	John Vestall	W. Love	1b164	cr 12	mr 18 *
Brady, Benj. m. Pitzer, Harriet	Jan. 15, 1849	Jacob Pitzer	J. W. Bond	7b166		mr 80 *
Brady, Hannah m. Pendleton, Wm.	Oct. 15, 1806	David Hunter	Rev. Reebenack	3b 11	cr 28	mr 22 *
Brady, James m. Shober, Catherine	Feb. 14, 1813	John Shober		3b261	gc 13	
Brady, John E. m. Beales, Susannah	May 8, 1841	John Beavon		6b236		
Brady, Martha m. McCormick, Wm.	Mar. 10, 1801			2b134		
Brady, Mary Ann m. Menser, John C.	May 14, 1840	Adam Shober	Peyton Harrison	6b209		mr 71 *
*Braidy, Benj. m. Bender, Cath.	Aug. 3, 1840	Adam Shober		6b199		
Brakefield, John m. Smith, Eliz.	Mar. 5, 1801	Samuel B. Harris		2b110		
	Jan. 16, 1821	Jacob Zimmerman		4b185		
Braman, Wm. m.Pitwick, Geruay	June 26,				cr 2	mr 3 *
Bramble, Sarah m. Walker, John	Aug. 27, 1789		Moses Hoge		cr 1	mr 2 *
Bramhall, James m. Mahon, Jane	Mar. 23, 1789		Moses Hoge		cr 38	mr 1 *
Bramhall, John m. Current, Eliza	Feb. 24, 1785	John Current	Edward Tiffin	1b 87		
Bramhall, Margaret m. Wilson, James	Aug. 1, 1798				cr 38	mr 1 *
Bramhall, Peter m. Burns, Margaret	Mar. —, 1792		Edward Tiffin		cr 38	mr 38 *
Brandinger, Andrew m. Young, Eliz.	June 22, 1799	Peter Zinn	Moses Hoge	2b. 9	gc 8	
Brannen, John m. Hudson, Mary	Sept. 8, 1821	Robert Kennedy	David Young	4b189		mr 57 *
Brannen, Cath. m. Daw, Lorenzo	June 11, 1840	Abner Snyder	Nathan Young	6b212		
*braqunier, Jacob m. Palmer, Eliz.	June 7, 1798	James Harlan	David Young	1b114	gc 7	*

	(marriage)		(suretor)	(minister)	(bond)		
Brannon, Isaac m. Jett, Melinda	Apr. 16,	1814	William Britton	David Young	3b293		*
Brannon, James m. Fry, Susannah	Apr. 24,	1800	Jacob Fry		2b 68	gc 9	*
Brannon, John m. Ganoe, Pamela	Aug. 25,	1802	James Ganoe		2b178		*
Brannon, John m. Hudson, Mary	Sept 8,	1821	Robert Kennedy	Nathan Young	4b189		mr 57 *
Brannon, Levy m. Gray, Ruth	June 4,	1827	Hannans Gray		5b 71		*
Brannon, Mary m. Stanley, Arch'd	Jan. 18,	1803	John Brannon		2b190		*
Brannon, Mary Ann m. Bailey, David	Oct. 14,	1851	John Brannon	John Grove	7b234		mr 85 *
Brannon, Mary Ann m. Bolin, John C.	Mar. 16,	1833	Michael Seibert		5b262		*
Brannon, Melinda m.Unger, Daniel	Mar. 30,	1833	John W. Wolff	Nathan Young	5b265		mr 66 *
Brannon, Rachel m. Thatcher, Evans	Sept 13,	1817	Stephen Gano		4b 46		*
Brannon, Rebecca m. Williams, James	Dec. 31,	1821	Levi Brannon		4b203		*
Brannon, Rebecca J. m. Dunham, Benj.	Mar. 30,	1847	Stephen Gano		7b 93		*
Brannon, Thos. m. Strouse, Lydia	Feb. 5,	1852	Jacob Van Doren		7b244		*
Brannon, Virginia H. m. Mudge, Wm.R.	Sept 9,	1850	Jacob A. Shepherd		7b194		*
Brannon, William m. Keller, Sally	Jan. 2,	1807	Jesse Curry		3b 41		*
Brantner, Wm. H. m. Groff, Eliz.	Sept 9,	1847	Daniel Groff	P. Lipscomb	7b106		mr 81 *
Brashore, Reason m. Waters, Elinor		1792		Moses Hoge			mr 39 *
Brather, John m. Cross, Easter		1791		Moses Hoge		cr 6	mr 6 *
Brathers, Philip m. Dennahaw, Dolly		1796		Richard Swift		cr 26	mr 11 *
Bray, Samuel m. Lyle, Nancy		1796		John Boyd		cr 10	mr 12 *
Brazorier, Jacob m. Palmer, Eliz.	June 7,	1798		David Young	1b114	gc 7	
Bready, Nancy m. Taylor, George	Oct. 3,	1806			3b 97		
Bready, Rebecca m. Rankin, Samuel	Mar. 30,	1804			2b230		
Breast, Katherine m. Lemar, Chas.		1785					
Breckfield, Barbara m. Strigler, Geo.	Oct. 28,	1818	John Breckfield	Hugh Vance	4b 84		mr 33 *
Brennan, Fred. m. Refsnider, Susan	Mar. 10,	1821	Aron Refsnider		4b175		
Brenner, Fred. m. Felter, Cath.	Apr. 17,	1824	Lemuel Felter	Chas. P. Krauth	4b262		mr 42 *
Brenner, Mary m. Armbrester,Michael	Sept 30,	1800	Philip Inswler	David Young	2b 90	gc 9	*
Brewer, Chas. m. Gerrard, Polly	Mar. 3,	1807	James Burk		3b 48		*
Brewer, Mary m. Kyle, John	Jan. 20,	1803	John Mulhall	David Young	2b191	gc 10	*
Brewer, Mary E. m. Smith, John R.	Jan. 21,	1853		G. Stephenson			mr 88 *
Brewer, Sally m. Williams, James	Nov. 23,	1814	William Spence	Rev. Reebenack	3b300	gc 14	*
Bricker, Mary E. m. Stevens, Thos.	Aug. 13,	1838?	Richard W. Buckle	Peyton Harrison	6b137		mr 69 *
Bridenhart, Christi'r m. Verdier, Jane	Mar. 21,	1792		Moses Hoge			mr 39 *
†Bridgemen, Francis m. Hall, Mary	Dec. 22,	1799	William Adams	John Heitt(hutt)	2b 6	cr 13	mr 18 *
†Bridgemen, Francis m. Hall, MaryJane	May 25,	1799	William Adams	John Heitt(hutt)	2b 6	cr 13	mr 18 *
Bridgeman, Francis Jr. m. Dinarine	May 25,	1801	William Adams		2b133		*
Bridgeman, Uriah, m. Wheatly, Nancy	Aug. 1,	1825	John Wheatly	J.L.Bromwell	5b 6		mr 47 *
Bright, Susanna m. Parker, John	Apr. 2,	1804	Jephtha Martin		2b230		
Brley, Nancy m. Boden, Wm.	Mar. 30,	1807	Garret Wynkoop		3b 55		
Brill, Phebe m. Johnston, John	Apr. 10,	1818		Mathias Riser			mr 29 *
Brillhart, Jesse m. Sardker, Eliz.	Sept 16,	1852		David Thomas			mr 86 *
Brindenall, Anthony m. Leeper, Eliz.	Jan. 25,	1788		Hugh Vance		cr 24	mr 2 *

23

Name	Date	(marriage)	(suretor)	(minister)	(bond)		
Bringham, Margaret m. Lenox, Nathan	June 22,	Nov. 15, 1792	Peter Zimm	Moses Hoge	2b 9	gc 8	mr 39 *
Brimdger, Andrew m. Young, Eliz.	Nov. 5,	June 24, 1799	John O'Ferrall	David Young	1b144	cr 30	mr 15 *
Briscoe, Eliz. m. Hedges, Joseph Jr.		Nov. 24, 1798		John Hedt(Hatt)			mr 31 *
Briscoe, Fanny m. Davis, Ignatius		Jan. 30, 1781		Daniel Sturges			mr 99 *
Briscoe, John m. Williamson, Margt.		Jan. 10, 1793		Moses Hoge			
Brittain, Mary Ann m. Carper, Fred.	May 25,	May 27, 1844	John W. McDermott	Lewis F. Wilson	7b 2	cr 4	mr 5 *
Britton, John m. Alway, Jane		Apr. 22, 1790		Moses Hoge			
Britton, Rebecca m.Hoyle(Hoge-)Joseph	Feb. 22,	Feb. 25, 1851	Nathaniel Britton	Henry Furlong	7b215		mr 84 *
Britton, Wm. m. Cunningham, Jane	July 31,	July 31, 1809	Anthony Jett	Rev. Reebenack	3b115	gc 10	
Britton, Wm.Jr. m. Mericle, Mary	Feb. 12,	Feb. 13, 1820	Wm. Mericle	Nathan Young	4b135		mr 57 *
Broad, Thomas m. Hart, Rebecca	Sept 11,	Feb. 15, 1800	Philip Board	Moses Hoge	2b 87	cr 29	mr 19 *
Broderick, Catherine m. Boyle, John	Jan. 5,	Sept 11, 1852	Patr'k Cunningham		7b241		
Broderick, Michael m. Hilard, Ellen	Dec. 9,	Jan. 5, 1846	Patr'k Reynolds		7b 80		
Broderick, Michael m. Kerney, Ellen	June 5,	1840	Morris Slattery		6b211		
Brome(Burns),Marg. m. Bramhall, Peter							
Bronce, Ann m. Turner, John	Mar. 4,	Mar. 4, 1792		Moses Hoge			mr 38 *
Brook, Benj. m. Thompson, Martha	Mar. 2,	Mar. 2, 1790		Hugh Vance	4b 39		mr 38 *
Brooke, John m. Hunter, Rebecca L.	June 24,	June 26, 1817	Jacob R. Ripley	Mathias Riser	9b 69	cr 30	mr 9 *
Brooks, Elinor m. Lerer(Le—), Isaac	May 8,	May 29, 1827	John Strother	J.E.Jackson	4b 75		
Brooks, Eliz. m. Waggoner, Daniel	June 25,	1818	George Brooks	William Hill			
Brophy, Mary M. - LingamFelter,W H.	Apr. 5,	Apr. 5, 1854				gc 14	
Brosius, Eliz. m. Stoddart, James	Nov. 30,	Nov. 30, 1813		D.F.Spriggs			
Brother, Mary Ann m. Clark, Thos.	Dec. 20,	Dec. 20, 1791		Rev. Reebenack		cr 8	mr 6 *
Brothers, Mary Ann m. Cluke, Thos.	Mar. 29,	Mar. 29, 1796		Moses Hoge		cr 8	mr 6 *
Brothers, Philip m. Denna haw, Dolly		1822		Moses Hoge		cr 26	mr 11 *
Brotherton, Wm. m. Ross, Mary	May 11,	1812	Nathan Ross	Richard Swift	4b212		
Brouse, Lewis m. Riner, Mary	Mar. 2,	1804	Henry Riner		3b213		
Brouse, Rachel m. Bowman, John	Aug. 18,	1829	John Brouse		2b240		
Brown, Abel m. Dunn, Ann	June 23	1800	?		5b134		
Brown, Adam m. Miller, Mary	Oct. 29,	Oct. 12, 1797	Henry Miller		2b 95		
Brown, Andrew m. Smith, Jean	Oct. 6,	1789	Henry Small		1b 52	gc 7	mr 37 *
Brown, Anna m. Hair, Abraham		1807					
Brown, Benj. m.Yeardly, Phebe	Jan. 2,		Peter Gardner	David Young	3b 41		
Brown, B.N. m. Small, Ellen	Oct. 4,	Oct. 4, 1837	John M. Wolff	D. Thomas	6b113		mr 69 *
Brown, Ben. m. Lane, Catherine		Dec. 10, 1793					
Brown, Chas. H. m. Snickers, Eliz.F.	Feb. 17,	1835	Robert T. Brown	E.P.Phelps	6b 31	gc 3	
Brown, David m. McCoy, Milly	June 5,	June 5, 1796		David Young			
Brown, David m. Wilson, Margaret	Feb. 14,	Feb. 14, 1794					
Brown, Dennis m. Manning(Mans-)Sarah	Dec. 23,	Dec. 23, 1850	Robert Stewart	Richard Swift	7b207	cr 26	mr 11 *
Brown, Elias m. Barnett, Mary	Mar. 4,	1801	John Barnett	David Young	2b16	gc 3	mr 83 *
Brown, Eliz. m. Ale, John	May 28,	1817	Valentine Ale	F.C.Tebbs	4b 36		
Brown, Eliz. m. Baker, John	Sept 9,	Sept 14, 1819	James Brown	John B. Hoge	4b114		mr 31 *
Brown, Eliz. m. Gageby, Allen	Aug. 21,	Aug. 22, 1819	John Brown	Nathan Young	4b115		mr 56 *

	(marriage)	(surety)	(minister)	(bond)	
Brown, Eliz. m. Harris, Goerge	Jan. 12, 1792		David Young		gc 1 *
Brown, Eliz. m. Jarifer, James	Apr. 1, 1794		David Young		gc 3 **
Brown, George m. Goddard, Mary	Oct. 30, 1781		Daniel Sturges		mr 42 **
Brown, James m. McIntire, Eliz.M.	Jan. 24, 1844	Andrew McIntire	James Chisholm	6b312	mr 75 *
Brown, James m. Reed, Margaret K.	Jan. 13, 1812	Talif'o Stribling		3b208	
Brown, James m. Rife, Deborah	Apr. 26, 1797	Conrad Rife		1b 13	
Brown, James m. Rutherford, Elnor	Feb. 5, 1799		John Heit(Hatt)	7b 37	mr 18 *
Brown, James S. m.Burkhart, Margaret	July 2, 1845	Daniel Burkhart	James Chisholm	3b 5	mr 76 *
Brown, Jesse m. Cunningham, Rhody	Dec. 21, 1805	Geo. Cunningham		3b137	
Brown, Jesse m. Toole, Rosanna	Feb. 24, 1810	Magnus Tate	Rev. Reebenack	3b137	*
Brown, John m. Rife, Eliz.	Mar. 31, 1796		David Young		gc 11 **
Brown, John m. Waite, Eliz.	Jan. 4, 1799	John Ellis	John Boyd	1b159	gc 5 *
Brown, John Wm. m. Kirkhart, Cath.	Jan. 29, 1827	John Kirkhart	B. Reynolds	5b 60	cr 34
Brown, Joseph m. Henshaw, Ann W.	Oct. 9, 1848	Henry Henshaw		7b137	
Brown, Joseph m. Lemon, Esther G.	July 25, 1808	George Lemon		3b 92	
Brown, Jos. W. m. Gill, Mary E.	Nov. 20, 1837	John Gill	J.E.Jackson	6b125	
Brown, Loiner I. m. Burgess, Eliz.	Dec. 1, 1809	Nicholas Orrick		3b126	*
Brown, Margaret m. Kelly, Samson	Aug. 2, 1799		Moses Hoge	3b103	cr 29 *
Brown, Margaret m. Sommerville, Wm.	Dec. 23, 1808	David Hunter	Rev. Reebenack	3b164	gc 10 **
Brown, Martha m. Brown, Robert	Oct. 1810	Samuel Raney		4b 11	
Brown, Martha m. Chrisman (Chi)Edmund	Aug. 29, 1816	Samuel Lane	Nathan Young	2b 82	mr 55 *
Brown, Mary m. Fenner, James	Aug. 26, 1800	Adam Brown		2b191	
Brown, Mary m. Kyle, John	Aug. 18, 1803	John Mulhall	David Young	4b110	gc 10 *
Brown, Mary m. Odenwald, George	Jan. 20, 1819	John Wolff	John B. Hoge	4b 21	mr 31 *
Brown, Mary m. Thompson, James	June 26, 1816	Joseph Thompson	Nathan Young	1b 94	mr 55 *
Brown, Mary m. Watson, John	Nov. 19, 1798	Richard Ranson		5b 51	
Brown, Mary A. m. Keeves, Anthony	Feb. 5, 1830	John Brown	John Mathews	2b169	mr 53 *
Brown, Michael m. Whips, Nancy	Jan. 30, 1802	James Wright		5b 68	
Brown, Milton J. m. Bishop, Eliz.	Apr. 14, 1827	Ezekiel Showers	B. Reynolds	3b103	mr 52 *
Brown, Peggy m. Sommerville, Wm.	Apr. 7, 1808	David Hunter	Rev. Reebenack	3b180	gc 10 *
Brown, Peter m. Hannah, Nancy	Dec. 23, 1811	Collin Carroll		2b157	
Brown, Polly m. Chalfin, William	Mar. 12, 1802	Wm. Grantham			
Brown, Rachael m. Bexley, David	Jan. 4, 1788		Moses Hoge	5b153	mr 35 *
Brown, Richard m. Lemon, Eliz.(Mrs)	Feb. 19, 1830	Michael Umberhaur	W. Monroe	3b164	mr 54 *
Brown, Robert m. Brown, Martha	Oct. 21, 1810	Samuel Raney			
Brown, Robert m. Harper, Jennett	June 24, 1783		Hugh Vance		gc 11 *
Brown, Robert m. Raney, Martha	Oct. 25, 1810		Rev. Reebenack		cr 23 *
Brown, Sarah m. Grimes, Wm.	Oct. 23, 1787		Hugh Vance		
Brown, Sarah m. Rutherford, Wm.	Jan. 31, 1828	John Brown		5b 90	mr 32 *
Brown, Sarah m. Wilmouth, George	Apr. 15, 1800	Jos. H. Brown		2b 65	mr 2 *
Brown, Thomas m. Boarman, Els. R.	July 19, 1842	Chas. Boarman		6b273	mr 52 *
Brown, Timothy m. Ferguson, Cath.	Nov. 7, 1803	Fred. Rorabaugh	B. Reynolds	2b211	
Brown, Wm. m. Carper, Martha Jane	Oct. 23, 1849	Samuel Carper	W. Love	7b167	mr 80 *

Name	Date	(marriage)	(surety)	(minister)	(bond)		
Brown, William m. Felts(Felts), Mary	Feb. 3,	Feb. 3, 1848	John Dalwick	D.F.Bragunier	7b121		mr 78 *
Broy, Samuel m. Lyle, Nancy		Mar. 4, 1796	Ignts O'Ferrall	John Boyd	3b195	cr 10	mr 12 *
Bruce, James m. Cross, Ann B.	Sept 6,	1811					mr 33 *
Bruer, Henry m. Hawke, Sarah		Feb. 14, 1786		Hugh Vance		gc 1	
Bruer, Sophia m. Cameron, Alex.		Jan. 14, 1792		David Young			
Brunner, Margaret m. Jones, David	Oct. 27,	1800	Isaac McIntire	Nathan Young	2b 95		mr 64 *
Bryan, Enoch m. Crowl, Evelina	July 14,	July 15, 1832	Jacob Crowl	D.F.Bragunier	5b234		mr 78 *
Bryan, James m. Patton, Sarah Ann	Jan. 26,	Jan. 27, 1848	Chas. Ridenour		7b121		
Bryan, Joseph m. Walker, Prudence	Jan. 17,	1806	Robert Grimes		3b 9		
Bryan, Sarah m. Duval, Denton	May 2,	1805	Lewis B. Willis	John Bond	2b261	cr 28	mr 22 *
Bryan, Sarah R. m. Long, Wm. S.	Nov. 14,	1840	John Strother		6b224	cr 27	mr 20 *
Bryant, Chas. m. Hazlett, Elenor		Feb. 4, 1802		John Mines			mr 39 *
Bryant, Jane m. Wales, George		Oct. 19, 1792		Moses Hoge			
Bryarly, Robt. P. m. Bearman, Sally	Mar. 2,	1846	Chas. Bearman	Richard T. Brown	7b 60		mr 79 *
Bryarly, Sarah L. m. Glass, Robt. I.	Jan. 12,	Jan. 16, 1850	Robt. P. Bryarly	Mathias Riser	7b172		mr 30 *
Buck, Isaiah m. Waugh(Waw), Cath.	June 1,	June 11, 1819	James Waugh		4b109		
Buck, Margaret m. Henderson, John	Apr. 28,	1796	Robert Buck		1b109		
Buck, Margaret m. Snowdeal, Mich's	Feb. 9,	1819	Peter Snodgrass		4b100		
Buckels, Eliza m. Osborne, Wm.	Dec. 23,	1833	Aaron Buckels		5b297		mr 35 *
Buckels, Wm. m. Kyles, Mary		Feb. 5, 1788?		Moses Hoge			
Buckhammer, Cath. m. Dunham, David	Dec. 9,	1798	Samuel Dunham		1b152		
Buckhannon, James m. Stern, Mary	Dec. 31,	1797	James Stern		1b 76		mr 32 *
Buckhannon, Mary m. Wilson, James		Oct. 7, 1783?		Hugh Vance			
Buckingham, Nelly m. Dawson, Ephraim	Mar. 8,	1814	Isaac Conaway		3b287	gc 2	
Buckins, Daniel m. Diel, Mary		Aug. 9, 1792		David Young		gc 15	
Buckins, Mary Ann m. Wolff, Joseph	Sept 25,	1815	John Poisal	Rev. Reebenack	3b340		mr 37 *
Buckler, Wm. m. Seaman, Elinor		Sept 26, 1789		D. Thomas			
Buckles, Abigail m. Chipley, Jonathan	Nov. 29,	1798	William Buckles	Moses Hoge	1b150	cr 29	mr 15 *
Buckles, Abraham m. Buckles, Rachel	Apr. 27,	Apr. 28, 1801	William Buckles	Moses Hoge	2b123	cr 38	mr 20 *
Buckles, Abraham m. Wallingsford, E.	Jan. 31,	1801	Mich's Wallingsford		2b113		
Buckles, Ann m. McGard, Andrew		Jan. 26, 1791				cr 6	mr 6 *
Buckles, James m. Osborne, Ann		Feb. 3, 1789		Moses Hoge		cr 1	mr 2 *
Buckles, John m. Wallingsford, Fran's		Mar. 7, 1797		Moses Hoge		cr 36	mr 13 *
Buckles(Butler),Lucy m.Lenhart,Mich'l	May 19,	Mar. 28, 1799	John G. Fleek	Moses Hoge	2b 5	gc 8	
Buckles, Maria m. Lucas, Henderson	May 12,	1831	Jacob Sumpion	David Young	5b194		
Buckles, Phebe m. Osborne, David	Oct. 26,	1835	Aaron Buckles		6b 60		
Buckles, Rachel m. Buckles, Abr'm	Apr. 27,	1801	Wm. Buckles		2b123		
Buckles, Robert m. Lucas, Susanna		May 20, 1793		Moses Hoge			
Buckmaster, Alex. m. Offutt, Rachel	June 20,	1797	Zach'h Buckmaster	William Hill	1b 22	cr 38	mr 20 *
Buckmaster, Zach'h m. Stone, Polly	Apr. 2,	Apr. 6, 1800	Vincent Moore	John Heitt(Matt)	2b 62	cr 30	mr 9 *
Buckwalter, Anthony m. Buzzard, Mary		May 29, 1818		Mathias Riser			
Bulger, Nancy m. Mitchel, David	Dec. 11,	1838	John McCleary		6b153	cr 33	mr 18 *
Bull, John m. Caswell, Kitty	Mar. 19,	1798	William Little		1b 91		mr 29 *

Name	(marriage)		(suretor)	(minister)	(bond)		
Bull, Nathan m. Lilbourne, Frances	May 30,	1797	Thomas Mattock		1b 19		
Bull, Thomas m. Roberts, Polly	Oct. 17,	1803	Robert Roberts	Daniel Sturges	2b210		mr 31 *
Bull, Usomen m. Smith, John		1781					
Bumgardner, John m. Smith, Mary	Oct. 22,	1804	Zachary Murray		2b245	cr 7	mr 6 *
Bun, Jane m. Melvin, John	Aug. 2,	1791		Mosses Hoge			
Buncutter, Geo. W. m. Grimes, Rebecca	Jan. 10,	1842	William Grimes		6b261		mr 37 *
Bunn, Peter m. Lewis, Mary		1789					
Bunner, Daniel m. Custard, Elenor	Feb. 2,	1817		D. Thomas			
Burch, Barnet m. Smith, Mary	Nov. 1,	1827	Joseph Henderson	Mathias Riser	5b 83		
Burches, Cath. m. Phillips, Wm.	July 27,	1797	Nicholas Orrick	John Boyd	1b 26	cr 32	mr 13 *
Burckhart, Harry m. Weaver, Eliz.	May 15,	1827	Jacob Billmyer	Nathan Young	5b 70		mr 99 *
Burdine, Abraham m. Cross, Polly, Mrs	May 17,	1811	Isaac Morlatt		3b191		
Burdine, John, m. McManus, Catherine	Aug. 21,	1816	John McManus	Rev. Reebenack	4b 6	gc 15	*
Burdine, Nancy m. Conoway, Isaac	Mar. 4,	1813	John Burdine	Rev. Reebenack	3b255	gc 13	*
Buren, Nicholas m. Stilwell, Epha	Sept 22,	1803	Thomas Stilwell		2b209		
Burewell, Marg't A. m. Stauber, T.J.	Oct. 26,	1854					
Burg, Marg't m. Houseman, David	Mar. 21,	1797	Martin Houseman	G.W.Cooper	1b 5	gc 6	*
Burgess, Eliz. m. Brown, Loiner Isom	Mar. 18,	1809	Nicholas Orrick	David Young	3b126	cr 40	mr 67 *
Burk, Cath. H. m. Jack, William	Jan. 1,	1833	Alex. Boling Jr.	John Light	5b255	cr 17	mr 4 *
Burk, Henry m. McCollister, Eliz.	Aug. 26,	1789					
Burk, James m. Downing, Susanna	Jan. 12,	1813	Robert Daniel	Hugh Vance	3b247		mr 25 *
Burk, Libby m. Gray, George	Aug. 11,	1810	Arch'd Williams	Geo. M. Frye	5b157		
Burk, Mahitabel m. Gordon, Abraham	Sept 21,	1829	Ellis Rees		5b142		
Burk, Nellie m. Freshour, Mathias	June 16,	1819	George Freshour		4b110		
Burk, William m. Bowers, Catherine	June 14,	1804	Thomas Donoway		2b236		
Burk, William m. Hully(Kully), E.is.	Feb. 16,	1811	John Hully	Rev. Reebenack	3b175	gc 12	mr 29 *
Burke, Eliz. m. Freshour, George	Mar. 17,	1818?	James Burke	Mathias Riser	3b 46		
Burke, Elvira B. m. Hendrixon, John	Jan. 25,	1807	Adam Eyre		2b187		
Burke, James m. Demoss, Mary, Mrs.	Jan. 10,	1802	Wm. McCormick	F.C.Tebbs	7b205		mr 83 *
Burke, James m. McCormick, Mary C.	Dec. 7,	1850	David Garard Jr.	Hugh Vance	2b157		mr 32 *
Burke, John m. Vance, Jane	Dec. 7,	1782	James Burke		5b131		
Burke, Mary m. Smith, Charles	Jan. 13,	1802	Arch'd Williams		3b147		
Burke, Mary Mrs. m. Campbell, Andrew	June 1,	1829	James Burke		3b 38		
Burke, Polly m. Butler, Thomas	Apr. 18,	1810					
Burke, Rebecca m. Williamson, Arch'd	Dec. 22,	1806	Robert Daniels	Geo. M. Frye	4b206		
Burke, Sarah m. Grove(Groff), John	Jan. 25,	1822		David Young	4b 19	gc 6	mr 44 *
Burke, Thomas m. Thompson, Nancy	Feb. 23,	1797		John B. Hoge	6b 42		*
Burkett, John m. Poisal, Polly	Oct. 10,	1816	P.Jacob Poisal		4b192		
Burkett, Mary Ann m. Poisal, Geo.	Oct. 9,	1835	Jacob Hamme				
Burkett, Marg't Mrs. m. Lemon, Jacob	Sept 26,	1821	Robert Grimes				
Burkett, Parker m. Smith, Marg't A.	Sept 3,	1845	Jacob Smith	John Light	3b226		
Burkhart, Daniel m. Flagg, Ruth K.	Sept 27,	1812	Robert Wilson		7b 42		mr 76 *
Burkhart, Francis m. Rosenberger,C.A.	Dec. 11,	1829	Anthony Rosenberg	Jacob Medtart	5b147		mr 63 *

Name	Marriage Date	Year	Suretor	Minister	(bond)	Ref.	Ref.
Burkhart, Francis m. Stewart, Ann E.	Apr. 1,	1836	Harrison Waite	James Chisholm	6b 76		mr 76 *
Burkhart, Margaret m. Brown, James S.	July 2,	1845	Daniel Burkhart		7b 37		
Burkhart, Susan D. m. Rust, Robt. B.	May 7,	1833	Daniel Burkhart		5b273		
Burkhart, Wm. D. m. Sommers, Ann M.		1852		D. F. Spriggs			mr 86 *
Burkhouse, Chas. m. McDaniel, Ellen	Nov. 1,	1861	Alex. McDaniel	John Hedges	6b251		mr 73 *
Burkmaxon, Zachariah m. Stone, Polly	Apr. 2,	1800	Vincent Moore	John Hutt(Hedtt)	2b 62	or 33	mr 18 *
Burks, Elis. m. Gouter, John W.	July 31,	1847	William Jack		7b103		
Burnes, Ailsy m. Shartle, Jacob	Aug. 29,	1812	John Whiteneck		3b235		
Burnes, Elis. m. Hite, John	Feb. 8,	1813	George Burnes		3b250		
Burnes, Harnah m. Gorrell, Jacob	Dec. 4,	1817	Abraham Gorrell		4b 51		
Burnes, Isabel m. Gorrell, Jacob	Oct. 19,	1801	William Burns Jr.		2b144		
Burnes, John m. Lemon, Sally	Jan. 6,	1801	Robert Lemon		2b107		
Burnes, Johanna m. Bellar, Eli	Jan. 7,	1804	Wm. Burnes		2b219		
Burnes, Rebecca m. Hedges, Joseph	May 1,	1820	John Burnes		4b146		
Burney, Polly m. Varmetre, Asahel	May 14,	1808	Thomas Tabb		3b 89		
Burnoss, George m. Douglas, Sarah	June 11,	1789		Moses Hoge		cr 2	mr 2 *
Burns, Benj. F. m. Gorrell, Ruth	June 6,	1831	Abraham Gorrell	Jacob Mediart	5b197		mr 63 *
Burns, Caleb m. Williamson, Sidney	Nov. 15,	1830	John Williamson	W. Monroe	5b181		mr 61 *
Burns, Elender m. Belt, Maslin	June 18,	1794		Richard Swift			mr 40 *
Burns, Elisa m. Gorrell, Joseph	Sept 14,	1825	John Burns	Joseph Baker	5b 22		mr 49 *
Burns, Elis. m. Dust, Joseph E.	May 8,	1823	Joseph Gorrell	John Mathews	4b238		mr 46 *
Burns, Ely m. Wolford, Eliz.	Nov. 1,	1789		Christian Streit		cr 15	mr 4 *
Burns, Esther m. Flaggs, Thos. G.	Dec. 20,	1825	John Burns Jr.	Chas. P. Krauth	5b 30		mr 49 *
Burns, George m. Hedges, Agnes	July 10,	1795		John Boyd		cr 33	mr 11 *
Burns, Geo. W. m. Harrison, Nannie H	Aug. 11,	1852		D.F.Spriggs			mr 86 *
Burns, Hanna m. Varmetre, Abraham	Nov. 24,	1791		David Young		gc 1	
Burns, Jacob m. Marker, Eliz.	May 22,	1823	Daniel Marker	Chas. P. Krauth	4b240		mr 46 *
Burns, John m. Collins(Collis), Eliza	Apr. 2,	1841	Harrison Waite	James Reley	6b204		mr 72 *
Burns, John m. Southwood, Frances	Dec. 25,	1794		Moses Hoge		cr 19	mr 9 *
Burns, Jonathan m. Williamson, Nancy	Jan. 8,	1821	John Williamson	John Mathews	4b170		mr 44 *
Burns, Marg't m. Bramhall, Peter	Mar. 4,	1792		Moses Hoge			mr 38 *
Burns, Maria m. Fisher, Jacob	June 19,	1796		David Young		gc 5	
Burns, Mark m. Palmer, Charlotte	May 27,	1822	Thomas Patton	John B. Hoge	4b214		mr 44 *
Burns, Mary m. Miles, Thomas	Aug. 12,	1841	Joseph Bowers		6b245		
Burns, Mary m. Roberts, Josiah	May 22,	1822	John Burns Jr.		4b214		
Burns, Nancy m. Light, John S.	May 31,	1824	Wm. Geo. Burns		4b266		
Burns, Rebecca m. Dust, John E.	Apr. 2,	1821	John Strother	J.L.Bromwell	4b180		mr 47 *
Burns, Ruth m. Glenn, James	June 2,	1823	John Strother		4b241		
Burns, Wm. C. m. Kownslar, Eliz.	Apr. 1,	1824	Edward C. Southwood	John Mathews	4b260		mr 46 *
Burns, Wm. Jr. m. Marshall, Jane	Aug. 27,	1817	William Marshall	John Mathews	4b 44		*
Buroff, Christena m. Carber, Jonas	Feb. 2,	1819	Fred. Buroff		4b 99		
*Burr, Anna m. Megary, John		1801		Moses Hoge		cr 38	
*Burr, James m. McGerry, Nancy	Jan. 12,	1799	Mathew McGerry	Moses Hoge	1b162		mr 20 *
*Burr, Eliz. m. Reed, Samuel	Jan. 23,	1797		Moses Hoge		cr 36	mr 13 *

Name	(marriage)	(suretor)	(minister)	(bond)		
Burr, Jane m. Melvin, John	Aug. 2, 1791		Moses Hoge		cr 7	mr 6 *
Burr, Mary m. Smith, Daniel	June 29, 1784		Hugh Vance			mr 52 *
Burr, Miriam m. Conklin, John	Jan. 24, 1793		Moses Hoge	7b 33		mr 39 *
Burr, Moses W. m. Porterfield, Mary	Apr. 28, 1845	Abner Williamson			cr 3	mr 5 *
Burr, Peter m. Sewell, Hannah Ilsema	Feb. 9, 1790		Moses Hoge			mr 35 *
Burris, Sarah m. Biggs, William	Apr. 2, 1788		Moses Hoge			
Burtie, Thomas m. Hamman, Margaret	Sept 10, 1807	Wm. Jordan				
Burton, Andrew m. Purcell, Susanna	Aug. 6, 1793		David Young	3b 69	gc 3	*
Burwell, Bacon m. Merchant, Priscilla	Nov. 27, 1830	Wm. Merchant		3b277		
Burwell, Priscilla m. Gilbert, Isaac	May 4, 1788	Joseph Larkins		5b165		
Busby, Nancy m. Casey, Alexander	Dec. 22, 1817		Hugh Vance			mr 36 *
Busey, Benj. m. Rousch, Mary,Mrs.	Aug. 14, 1849	John Strother		4b 43		
Busey, Benj. T. m. Pitzer, Rachel S.	July 9, 1846	James Pitzer	R.F.Brown	7b 159		mr 77 *
Busey, Marg't J. m. Henshaw, A.F.	Oct. 25, 1842	Samuel Busey		7b 75		
Busey, Martha A. m. Cage, Andrew J.	Aug. 16, 1849	Lewis Minicken	L.F.Wilson	6b276		mr 83 *
Busey, Samuel m. McKown, Evelina	Feb. 26, 1789	Samuel McKown	Hugh Vance	7b147	cr 40	mr 4 *
Bush, Henry m. McCollister, Eliz.	Aug. 26, 1789					
Bushman, Isaac m. Marshall, Martha	Sept 23, 1845	George Roberts	Jacob Medtart	7b 44		mr 63 *
Bushman, Isaac m. Roberts, Mary Naomi	Jan. 2, 1832	Boyd Roberts	Jas. H. Jennings	5b213		mr 82 *
Bussard, Emily m. French, John K.	Jan. 21, 1846	Norman Miller		7b 55		
Bussear, Martin m. Callahan, Sarah	May 13, 1815	Joel Ward		3b323		
Butler, Douglas m. Hobbs, Eliz.	Feb. 25, 1801	Horatio Hobbs		2b115		
Butler, Elisha m. Melvin, Mary	Dec. 24, 1793		Moses Hoge		cr 22	mr 8 *
Butler, Geo. H. m. Leathers, Martha	June 20, 1853		Geo. W. Cooper			mr 87 *
Butler, Harriet M. m. Neer, John W.	Mar. 5, 1852	Joel Fulton	David Thomas	7b248		mr 86 *
Butler, Henrietta m. Owings, Beall	Mar. 13, 1810	Chas. Orrick	Rev. Reebenack	3b141	gc 11	mr 81 *
Butler, James W. m. Likens, Cath.	Jan. 25, 1848	Joseph Likens	P. Lipscomb	7b120		
Butler(Buckles),Lucy m. Lenhart,Mich'l	May 19, 1799	John G. Fleek	David Young	2b 5	gc 8	
Butler, Rachel A. m. Roberts, Sam'l	Sept 19, 1839	Thomas White		6b176		mr 84 *
Butler, Rebecca A. m. Hoyle, Jos. C	Feb. 22, 1851	Nathaniel Britton	Henry Furlong	7b215	cr 38	mr 20 *
Butler, Sarah m. Mathews, Levi	Jan. 7, 1801	C. Vanorsdale	Moses Hoge	2b107		mr 79 *
Butler, Sarah E. m. Cockrell, Jos.	May 13, 1847	David Farnsworth	R.T.Brown	7b127		
Butler, Susan m. Farnsworth, David	Mar. 4, 1844	Jeremiah Butler		6b315		
Butler, Susan A. m. Johnson, Francis	Feb. 13, 1829	Israel Butler		5b119		
Butler, Thomas m. Burke, Polly	Apr. 18, 1810	Arch'd Williams		3b147		
Butler, Thomas m. Seibert, Cath. E.	Dec. 2, 1848	Michael Seibert		7b140		
Butler, William m. Moore, Nancy	Mar. 17, 1800	Vincent Moore		2b 57		
Butler, Wm. G. m. Garry, Eliz.	Feb. 14, 1846	Benj. R. Boyd		7b 58		
Butler, Wm. G. m. Kerney, Salomy	Nov. 6, 1840	James A. Kerney		6b223		
Butt, Adah m. Snyder, Jacob	Jan. 9, 1823	Benjamin Thomas	Nathan Young	4b231	cr 34	mr 98 *
Butt, Ally m. Eade, James	Dec. 20, 1799	Richard Butt	Richard Swift	2b 41		mr 16 *
Butt, Arch'd m. Bear, Ann Cath.	Nov. 16, 1819		W.N.Scott	4b123		mr 40 *
Butt, Arch'd m. Franceway, Rebecca	Feb. 19, 1768	John Strother	Hugh Vance		cr 24	mr 2 *

Name	(marriage)	(suretor)	(minister)	(bond)		
Butt, Arch'd m. Harris, Drusilla	May 18, 1790	George Swinley	Moses Hoge	6b 11	cr 4	mr 5 *
Butt, Arch'd m. Salshammer, Sarah	May 8, / May 11, 1834		John Howell			mr 68 *
Butt, Arch'd m. Southern, Sarah	Jan. 20, 1789		Moses Hoge		cr 1	mr 2 *
Butt, Bazell m. Wilson, Susan Savana	Dec. 24, 1789		Moses Hoge		cr 3	mr 3 *
Butt, Catherine m. Hoe, George	Mar. 22, / Mar. 1824	Peter Myers	Chas. P. Krauth	4b259		mr 47 *
Butt, Catherine m. Needler, Peter	Sept 13, / Sept 15, 1831	Jacob Eaty	Nathan Young	5b206		mr 62 *
Butt, Cath. m. Ray, Swearingen	Sept 23, / Sept 23, 1820	John Butt	Nathan Young	4b162		mr 57 *
Butt, Charles m. Duncan, Catherine	May 25, / May 25, 1850	Michael Smeltzer	W. Love	7b186		mr 80 *
Butt, Charles m. Ray, Nancy	July 24, / July 16, 1810	William Butt	Rev. Reebenack	3b154	gc 11	mr 73 *
Butt, Charles m. Stilwell, Sarah	Nov. 25, / Nov. 29, 1841	Swearingen Butt	Peyton Harrison	6b254		
Butt, Charlot m. Sullivan, Hartley	May 7, 1817	?		4b 34		
Butt, Christena m. Caruthers, Wm.	Aug. 7, 1837	Benjamin Butt		6b 93		
Butt, Darky m. Butt, William	Apr. 9, / Apr. 20, 1786		Hugh Vance	2b121		mr 42 *
Butt, Diana m. Haines, Joseph	Apr. 23, / Apr. 11, 1801	John Butt	Richard Swift	6b 45	cr 31	mr 19 *
Butt, Dorcas A. m. Smeltzer, Michael	May 28, 1835	Charles Butt	Elisha Gardner	3b243	gc 13	mr 68 *
Butt, Edward m. Mitchel, Susanna	Nov. 21, / Dec. 24, 1812	John Richardson	Rev. Reebenack			
Butt, Elis. m. Stilwell, Sarah	Aug. 2, / Aug. 5, 1830	Cornellus Stilwell	Nathan Young	5b171		mr 61 *
Butt, Elis. m. Clarke, Solomon	Dec. / Dec. 4, 1843	Elisha Butt	Lewis F. Wilson	6b309		mr 74 *
Butt, Elis. m. Jack, Andrew	Aug. 27, / Aug. 26, 1798	James Maxwell	Richard Swift	1b124	cr 31	mr 15 *
Butt, Elis. m. Orr, William	Feb. 1, 1826	Joseph Butt		5b 35		
Butt, Ellen m. Cutwaltz, Jacob	May 18, 1839	Nathan Hutchinson		6b169		
Butt, Ellen m. Lucas, Jacob	Jan. 27, 1845	Stephen Mansfield		7b 24		
Butt, Evelina m. Hawk(Harlck), Harvey	Mar. 12, / Mar. 12, 1851	Samuel D. Beess	D.W.Arnold	7b218		mr 86 *
Butt, Fanny m. Litteral, John	May 30, / May 1797	Edward Beeson		1b 15		
Butt, Geo. W. m. Pitzer, Mary Ann	Sept 29, / Sept 16, 1847	Michael Pitzer	J.H.Jennings	7b106		mr 82 *
Butt, Hannah m. Harrison, John S.	Feb. 29, / Feb. 2, 1844	Benjamin Butt		6b314		
Butt, Hannah m. Snyder, Wm.	Mar. 31, / Apr. 2, 1846	Charles Butt	J.H.Jennings	7b 63	gc 11	mr 82 *
Butt, Henry m. Ray, Nelly	Aug. 8, / Aug. 8, 1810	Robert Collins	Rev. Reebenack	3b157		mr 36 *
Butt, Isaac m. Butt, Vealanda	Nov. 25, 1788		Hugh Vance	3b257		
Butt, jemima m. Richardson, John	Mar. 23, / Mar. 30, 1813		Rev. Reebenack	2b 6	gc 13	
Butt, jemima m. Filson, John	May 22, / May 21, 1799	William Butt	Richard Swift		cr 34	mr 16 *
Butt, John m. Green, Mary	Apr. 2, 1795	Arch'd Butt	David Young	3b340	gc 4	
Butt, John m. Morlay(Mar-), Gracy	Sept 16, / Sept 16, 1815	John Morlay		7b 87		
*Butt, John m. Sherard, Eliz.	Feb. 16, / Feb. 16, 1847	John Sherard		3b282		
Butt, Joseph m. G een, Eliz.	Jan. 13, / Jan. 17, 1814	Swearingen Ray		4b 96		
Butt, Mary m. Horn, Philip	? / 1818?	Samuel Butt	John Kehler	6b268		mr 31 *
Butt, Mary m. Raney, Jacob	Mar. 23, / Mar. 24, 1842	Elisha Butt	Peyton Harrison	6b305		mr 73 *
Butt, Mary m. Smith, Aaron	Oct. 9, / Mar. 23, 1843	Benjamin Butt				
Butt, Mary m. Spencer, John	Aug. 12, 1826					
Butt, Mary Ann m. Gageby, David	Feb. 8, 1854		Nathan Young			mr 58 *
Butt, Maxde(Masse) m. Green, Chas.	Feb. 14, 1793		F. Israel			
Butt, Mercy m. Butt, Thos. G.	Mar. 9, / Mar. 10, 1850	Joseph Ray	Moses Hoge	5b261	cr 21	mr 7 *
Butt, Michael m. Hess, Lane	Mar. 26, / Mar. 9, 1833	Peter Hess	Nathan Young	7b180		mr 66 *
*Butt, John m. Wigle, Christina	Sept 17, / Sept 17, 1804	Philip Wigle	John Bond	2b243	cr 13	mr 21 *

Name	Date	(marriage) Mar. 6, 1800	(surety)	(minister)	(bond)	
Butt, Nancy m. Athe, John	Feb. 9,	1800	Barrack Butts	Richard Swift	4b134	cr 34 *
Butt, Nancy m. McLean, John	Dec. 22,	1820	Barrack Butts		3b 80	*
Butt, Patsy m. Green, George	Jan. 12,	1807	Michael Hout	David Young	1b 81	gc 7
Butt, Polly m. Green, Joseph	July 20,	1798	John Butt	Richard Swift	2b206	cr 27 mr 21 *
Butt, Priscilla m. Wilson, Richard	July 30,	1803	Isaac Butt		3b303	
Butt, Rachel m. Collins, Robert	Sept 16,	1814	John Fist		4b 94	
Butt, Reginal m. Fist, Rebecca	Dec. 15,	1818	Swearingen Ray		3b200	
Butt, Richard m. Ray, Delilah	Nov. 8,	1811	Henry Stephens		6b311	
Butt, Sally m. Shaffer, Peter	Dec. 28,	1843				mr 1 *
Butt, Sally m. Souder, Christopher	Dec. 16,	1788	Peter Gardner	Moses Hoge	5b275	mr 66 *
Butt, Sally m. Tripp, Solomon	June 8,	1833		Nathan Young		mr 2 *
Butt, Sarah m. Green, Reginal	Jan. 15,	1788		Hugh Vance		mr 20 *
Butt, Susan Savanna m. Blamer, Zadok	May 24,	1802	Richard Butt	Richard Swift	2b173	cr 24 mr 57 *
Butt, Susannah m. Eaty, Jacob	Dec. 3,	1805	William Green		3b 4	cr 32 mr 66 *
Butt, Susannah m. Mansfield, Stephen	Mar. 15,	1822	Joseph Ray	Nathan Young	5b261	mr 57 *
Butt, Thos. G. m. Butt, Mercy	Mar. 9,	1833	Christopher Souther	Nathan Young	3b147	mr 66 *
Butt, V.Swearingen m. Souther, Ellen	Apr. 20,	1810				
Butt, Veelanda m. Butt, Isaac	Nov. 25,	1788		Hugh Vance		mr 36 *
Butt, William m. Butt, Darky	Apr. 20,	1786		Hugh Vance		mr 42 *
Butt, William m. Everhart, Margaret	Feb. 21,	1837	Henry Butt	R.N.Herndon	6b 97	mr 69 *
Butt, William m. Lawson, Mary	Aug. 25,	1853		G.W.Cooper		
Butt, William m. Ludwig, Pegky	May 18,	1807	John Ludwig		3b 59	
Butt, William m. Pain, Sally	Nov. 19,	1812		Rev. Reebenack	2b220	gc 13 mr 21 *
Butterfield, Mary m. Lemon, Thomas	Jan. 11,	1804	Thomas Butterfield	Moses Hoge	3b231	cr 17 mr 25 *
Butterfield, Sarah m.Keldow(Kil-) John	July 25,	1812	James Butterfield	Geo. M. Frye		cr 17 mr 43 *
Butterfield,Thomas m. Collins, Mary	Nov. 21,	1786		Hugh Vance		mr 21 *
Butts, John m. Wigle, Christena	Sept 17,	1804	Philip Wigle	John Bond	2b243	cr 13 mr 21 *
Butts, Thomas m. Butt, Mercy	Mar. 9,	1833	Joseph Ray	Nathan Young	5b261	mr 66 *
Butts, William m. Houseworth, Marg't	Aug. 10,	1816	Isaac Houseworth	Nathan Young	4b 17	mr 55 *
Burton, Bazil m. Weddell, Mary	Nov. 30,	1847	John M. Wolff	John Winter	7b114	mr 78 *
Buzzard, Eliz. J. m. Fury, Wm. A.	July 13,	1837	Harrison Waite	Lewis F. Wilson	6b110	*
Buzzard, Emily m. French, John K.	Jan. 21,	1846	Norman Miller	James H. Jennings	7b 55	mr 82 *
Buzzard, Geo. m. Lewis, Eliz.	July 31,	1830	William Lewis		5b170	
Buzzard, Margaret m. Grantham, John	Apr. 4,	1845	Bethuel Kitchen	J.H.Jennings	7b 30	mr 82 *
Buzzard, Mary m. Buckwalter, Anthony	May 29,	1818		Mathias Riser	6b 69	mr 29 *
Buzzard, Mary m. Kitchen, Bethuel	Jan. 14,	1836	John Buzzard			
Byant, Chas. m. Hazlett, Elenor	Feb. 4,	1802		John Mines	1b 3	cr 27 mr 20 *
Byers, Eliz. m. Fisher, John	Apr. 30,	1797	Henry Nicely	David Young	7b247	gc 6 *
Byers, Eliz. m. Cofferberger, Wm. Jr.-Feb. 24,	1852	Jacob Byers			
Byers, John m. Graham, Mary	Jan. 10,	1782		Hugh Vance		mr 32 *
Byers, Joseph m. Smith, Margaret	Apr. 8,	1798	Jacob Tinsell	David Young	1b106	gc 7 *
Byers, Newland m. Gwilliams, Maria	Aug. 17,	1825	Reason Gwilliams		5b 20	
Byers, Rebecca m. Elder, Ely	Dec. 6,	1803	Edward Graham	David Young	2b215	gc 10 *

(marriage)	Date	(suretor)	(minister)	(bond)	
Byers, William H. m. Daily, Sarah A	Mar. 11, 1846	John Daily	J.S.Reynoldson	7b 61	mr 76 *
Byrne, Henry A. m. Goulding, Marg't	Aug. 13, 1819	John Strother		4b113	
Byrne, Lawrence m. McSherry, Mary	July 3, 1827	Richard McSherry		5b 72	
Byrnes, Thomas m. Ridgeway, Eliz.	Feb. 10, 1794		William Hill		cr 29 cr 7
B_____, Hercules m.Powers, Mary	Apr. 23, 1791		Moses Hoge		mr 9 * mr 6

"C"

(marriage)	Date	(suretor)	(minister)	(bond)	
Cable, Margaret m. Egan, John	Apr. 27, 1847	John O'Brien	Nathan Young	7b 95	
Cage, Andrew m. Ardinger, Mary Ann	Aug. 14, 1832	Chas. Ardinger	Moses Hoge	5b238	mr 65 *
Cage, Andrew, Eaty, Rachel	Dec. 10, 1788				mr 36 *
Cage, Andrew J. m. Busey, Martha A.	Aug. 16, 1842	Lewis Minicken		6b276	mr 64 *
Cage, Elenor m. Shoafstall, Eli	Oct. 4, 1832	A.S.Chambers	Jacob Medtart	5b241	mr 56 *
Cage, Eliz. m. Crem, John	Apr. 3, 1819	Andrew Cage	Nathan Young	4b104	
Cage, James m. Chambers, Nancy	Sept 15, 1813	Abraham Hooper	Rev. Reebenack	3b271	ge 13
Cage, John m. Haines, Eliz.	May 22, 1799	John Moore	John Heit(Hutt)	2b 5	cr 13
Cage, Jos. E. m. Shoafstall, Margaret	Apr. 2, 1836	Michael Grover		6b 77	mr 18 *
Cage, Lucy M. m. Young, John R.	June 30, 1851	Wm. H. VanDoren	David Thomas	7b227	mr 84 *
Cage, Margaret m. Payne, Henson	Aug. 5, 1834	Harrison Waite		6b 15	mr 12 *
Cage, Martin m. McKinney, Cath.	Apr. 26, 1796				
Cage, Mary m. Avis, Joseph	Apr. 17, 1817	William Cage	Moses Hoge	4b 33	cr 36 *
Cage, Rachel A. m. Fisher, Thos. C.	June 14, 1838	Joseph Cage	James Watts	6b141	mr 69 *
Cage, Sarah m. Waldeck, John	July 28, 1823	Andrew Cage	Chas. P. Krauth	4b243	mr 46 *
Cage, William m. Games, Sarah	Aug. 16, 1820	Andrew Cage	W.N.Scott	4b156	mr 41 *
Cahill, Cath. m. Field, Philip	Sept 25, 1805	Dennis Cahill		3b 1	
Cahill, Dennis m. McCartney, Letitia	Apr. 30, 1805	Cornelius Kelly		2b260	
Cain, Cary m. Ward, James	Jan. 24, 1801	Mathew Mayhew		2b111	
Cain, Lydia m. Housworth, Valentine	Apr. 27, 1833	George Vanaker	Nathan Young	5b272	mr 66 *
Calhoun, Wm. m. Rigsby, Ann M.	Aug. 23, 1845	John A. Boyers		7b 40	
Callahan, Cath. m. Kavenaugh, Mathew	July 15, 1841	James McSherry		6b244	
Callahan, James W. m. Varmetre, Ann	Aug. 1, 1850	Colbert Anderson	R.T.Berry	7b191	mr 83 *
Callahan, Joshua S. m. Smith, Ann E.	Mar. 25, 1852	Wm. VanDoren		7b250	
Callahan, Sarah m. Bussear, Martin	May 13, 1815	Joel Ward		3b323	
Callahan, Sarah m. Robinson, Israel	Nov. 24, 1853	Harvey Boothe	G.W.Cooper	2b189	ge 9
Callahan, Tho. m.Marlin(Martin),Eliz.	Jan. 6, 1803	Colbert Anderson	David Young	7b191	mr 83 *
Callahan, James M. m. Varmetre, Ann	Aug. 1, 1850		R.T.Berry		
Callatin, Cath. m. Largent, Richard	June 14, 1796		David Young	2b119	gc 5
Calmes, Henry m. Griggs, Elira	Mar. 26, 1801	Thomas Griggs			
Calvert, John A. m. Manford, Jane	Mar. 13, 1834	Wm. Wilson Jr.		5b306	mr 73 *
Calvert, Robert m. Dennison, Letha	Oct. 27, 1841	Wm. Manford	John Hedges	6b249	
Calvin, John m. Wright, Polly B.	Feb. 29, 1816	John Wright	W.N.Scott	3b357	mr 26 *

Name	(marriage)	(suretor)	(minister)	(bond)		
Calvin, Robert m. Weidman, Mary	Feb. 20, 1822	John Colvin	James M. Brown	4b208		mr 51 *
Calvin, Sarah A. m. Kerney, Wm. P.	Jan. 24, 1828	John Colvin	P. Lipscomb	5b 88		mr 81 *
Calvin, Sarah M. m. Schoppert, Geo.	Jan. 26, 1848	John Colvin	David Young	7b120	gc 1	
Cameron, Alex. m. Bruer, Sophia	Jan. 14, 1792		David Young			
Cameron, Dariel m. Clinton, Susannah	Nov. 6, 1788		Moses Hoge			mr 36 *
Cameron, Joseph m. Marchant, Frances	June 23, 1798	Richard Marchant		1b119		
Cameron, Joseph m. Snyder, Jenny	Oct. 12, 1807	Levi Cunningham		3b 74		
Campbell, Andrew m. Burke,Mary,Mrs.	June 1, 1829	James Burke		5b131		
Campbell, Andrew S. m. Dusk, Sarah	Sept 11, 1798	Edward Mercer		1b132		
Campbell, Ann m. Orrick, Chas.	June 11, 1806	Geo. Porterfield		3b 22		
Campbell, Ann R. m. Black, John	Dec. 8, 1833		Nathan Young	4b LL		mr 66 *
Campbell, Barton m. Orrick, Marg't	Mar. 7, 1816	Chas. Orrick	W.N.Scott	2b255	cr 17	mr 26 *
Campbell,Douglas(Dugal m Lyle, Sarah	Feb. 10, 1805	James Campbell	Moses Hoge	2b167		mr 22 *
Campbell, Elenor m. Lackey, Hugh	Mar. 30, 1802	Benson Lackey		7b177		
Campbell, Hugh L. m. Varmetre, Mary	Feb. 11, 1850	William Maslin		7b221		
Campbell, Isabel M. m. McKown, Hiram	Apr. 8, 1851	Geo. W. Hoke		5b121		
Campbell, James m. Hodges, Rebecca	Mar. 5, 1829	Thomas Miller	James M. Brown	3b 29		mr 53 *
Campbell, James W. m. Lyle, Polly	Sept 9, 1806	John Lyle				
Campbell, John m. Futlaton, Sarah	Nov. 14, 1791		David Young		gc 1	*
Campbell, John m. Johnston, Eliz.	Aug. 1, 1785		Edward Tiffin		cr 38	
?Campbell, John m. Love, Mary	Mar. 18, 1797	Thos. Shepherd	Moses Hoge	1b 5	cr 36	mr 1 *
?Campbell, John m. Lowe, Mary	Mar. 18, 1797	Thomas Shepherd	Moses Hoge	1b 5	cr 36	mr 13 *
Campbell, John m. Rodgers, Mary	Apr. 18, 1794		David Young		gc 3	mr 13 *
Campbell, Joseph m. Demoss, Cath.	June 24, 1795		David Young		gc 5	*
Campbell, Lemuel m. McKown, Isabel	Feb. 8, 1847	Samuel McKown	Moses Hoge	7b 84	cr 22	mr 9 *
Campbell, Marg't m. Francis, James	Oct. 30, 1794	Wm. Campbell	John B. Hoge	3b181	cr 14	mr 24 *
Campbell, Marg't m. McFarland, Dugal	Mar. 21, 1811	Robert Campbell		2b147		
Campbell, Mary m. McCannon, Wm.	Nov. 9, 1801	Thos. Miller	John Winters	5b 20	cr 10	mr 50 *
?Campbell, Mary m. McDonald, Robert	Aug. 23, 1825		John Boyd			mr 12 *
Campbell, Mary m. Pollock, Alex.	Feb. 11, 1796	Walter Turner		2b237		
Campbell, Mary R. m. Wilcox, Robert	June 25, 1804		Joseph Baker		gc 4	mr 87 *
Campbell, Mary R. m. McKown, F.S.S.	Apr. 6, 1853	Thomas Miller	John Winters	5b 20	cr 11	mr 50 *
‡Campbell,Mary,Mrs. m. McDonald,Robt.	Aug. 25, 1825		David Young			
Campbell, Patrick m. Davis, ?	Oct. 23, 1794		John Heitt(Hutt)			mr 14 *
Campbell, Polly m.Perrell(Perll)Basil	Nov. 25, 1797	John Campbell		1b 64		
Campbell, Robert m. Andrews, Eliz.	Oct. 22, 1806	William Campbell		3b 33		
Campbell, Robert m. McCleary, Jane	Oct. 29, 1808	William McCannon		3b 99		
Campbell, Robert m. Whiteneck, Sarah	June 6, 1817	John Whiteneck	Nathan Young	4b 37	gc 7	mr 55 *
Campbell, Sarah Ann m. Smith, William	Sept 16, 1797	Cath. Campbell	David Young	1b 40		
Campbell, Sarah Ann m. Tabb, Bailey	Mar. 17, 1825	Douglas Campbell	James M. Brown	5b 4		mr 48 *
Campbell, Walter P. m. Pendleton, E.	Mar. 16, 1841	Wm. Pendleton		?6b246		
Campbell, Wm. m.Pendleton, Fanny C.	Aug. 20, 1811	Wm. Pendleton	John B. Hoge	3b177	cr 14	mr 24 *
Campbell, Wm. F. m. Kiff, Cath.	Feb. 5, 1807	Isaac Cilmer	John Mathews	3b 67	cr 13	mr 23 *
*Campbell, Nathan m. Pendleton, Ellen	Sept 1, 1841	Wm. Pendleton		6b246		

Name	(marriage)	(suretor)	(minister)	(bond)	ref
Cample, John m. Kheyle, Elvy	Feb. 25, 1793		David Young		gc 2
Canby, Anna m. Watkins, James	Dec. 10, 1789		Hugh Vance		
Canby, Beulah m. Siler, Jacob	Oct. 31, / Nov. 4, 1843	Elias Siler	Lewis F. Wilson	6b306	mr 38 *
Canby, David m. Weddle, Susanna	Nov. 14, 1835	Jacob Weddle		6b 62	mr 74 *
Canby, Margaret m. Siler, Jacob	Oct. 31, / Nov. 4, 1789	Elias Siler	Lewis F. Wilson	6b306	mr 38 *
Canby, Phebe m. Johnson(Jon-), Thos.	1789		D. Thomas		
Canby, Thomas m. Kissinger, Sybilla	Oct. 31, / Oct. 31, 1809	William Runner	Rev. Reebenack	3b122	ge 10
Candle, Margaret m. Hess(Hughes),Geo.	Apr. 26, / Apr. 26, 1828	Thomas Wolford	Benedict Reynolds	5b100	mr 52 *
Canfield, Ann R. m. Blake, John	Dec. 7, 1833	Seaman Garard		5b293	
Carine, Marg't m. Turner, Alex.	Dec. 22, 1838?	Henry Deck	Peyton Harrison	6b155	mr 69 *
Carine,Philip m. Rush, Rebecca			Moses Hoge		cr 7
Carine, Sarah m. Rush,William	Mar. 24, 1791		Moses Hoge		cr 7
Canklin, Jacob m. Ierky, Mary	Mar. 22, 1791		Moses Hoge		mr 6 *
Canklin, John m. Sewell, Abigail	Jan. 7, 1796		Moses Hoge	1b112	mr 11 *
Cann, Sarah m. Harley, Conrad	May 20, / May 29, 1798	James Burr			mr 14 *
Cannon, Eliz. m. Cumpston, Thomas	Apr. 13, 1852	Patrick Harley		7b253	mr 35 *
Carber, Jonas m. Buroff, Christena	Feb. 2, 1819	Fred. Buroff	Hugh Vance	4b 99	mr 2 *
Carden, George m. Davis, Tabitha	1791		Hugh Vance		cr 23
Carey, Henry m. Dixon(Doxan), Nancy	Nov. 15, 1833	Joshua Cline	Moses Hoge	5b291	cr 5
Carey, John m. Shilton, Eliz.	1795		Nathan Young		mr 66 *
Carothers, Jane m. McGowen, John	Aug. 5, 1799	John Ravenaugh	John Boyd	2b 16	mr 11 *
Carothers, Sarah m. Cowan, David	1791		John Heitt(Hutt)		cr 33
Carothers, Wm. m. Buttn, Christena	Aug. 7, 1837	Benjamin Butt	Moses Hoge	6b 93	cr 38
Carper, Fred. m. Brittain, Mary Ann	May 27, 1844	John McDermott		7b 2	mr 17 *
Carper, Isabel m. Gregory, James	Nov. 12, 1842	Jonas Carper	Lewis F. Wilson	6b283	mr 74 *
Carper, Jacob m. Roney(Raney),Maria	Aug. 11, 1849	Mr. Collins	Mayberry Goheen	7b162	mr 79 *
Carper, John m. Markle, Eliz.	Apr. 22, 1829	Wm. Marckel	B.M.Schumacker	5b127	mr 53 *
Carper, Martha J. m. Brown, Wm.	Oct. 23, 1849	Samuel Carper	W. Monroe	7b167	mr 80 *
Carper, Mary Ann m. Stilwell, John H.	Sept 17, 1839	Jonas Carper	W. Love	6b174	mr 70 *
Carper, Philip m. Walters, Eve	Apr. 19, 1822	John Walters	Lewis F. Wilson	4b210	mr 45 *
Carper, Samuel m. Hite, Margaret	Feb. ? 1834	William Hite	Chas. P. Krauth	9b303	
Carr, Sarah m. Gregory, G.W.	Oct. 13, / Oct. 6, 1847	James R. Gregory	P. Lipscomb	7b108	mr 81 *
Carr, John m. Turner, Mary	Nov. 13, 1828	Van Brashear		5b112	
Carr, Mary m. Kerns, Jacob	Dec. 15, 1821	Jesse Turner		4b201	
Carr, Robert m. Shull, ?	Mar. 6, 1805	John Shull		2b256	
Carr, Samuel m. Green, Sarah	Aug. 31, 1799	George Green		2b 23	
Carr, Thomas m. Lucas, Ellen	Aug. 5, 1829	Wm. McDonald		5b135	
Carrier, Geo. W. m. Thompson, Sarah	May 28, 1842	Jacob Armstrong	Nathan Young	6b271	mr 60 *
Carroll, Geo. m. Elamer,Mary	Jan. 21, 1851	Jacob French	Mayberry Goheen	7b211	mr 74 *
Carroll, Mary Ann m. Whitenaugh, John	Sept 17, 1823	Wm. G. Burns	Henry Furlong	4b249	mr 84 *
Carroll, Mary M. m. Moler, Robert	June 11, 1849	Geo. A. Carroll	B. Reynolds	7b160	mr 49 *
Carson, Margaret m.McClain(-Clure),J.	Sept 6, 1797	Chas. McGarran	David Young	1b 39	gc 6
Carothers, Rebecca m. Johnson, James	Feb. 9, 1796		David Young		gc 5

Name		(marriage)	(surety)	(minister)	(bond)		
Carson, Elinor m. Small, Henry	July 5,	June 9, 1795	John Morlatt	John Boyd	3b299	cr 33	mr 10 *
Carson, Robert m. Holliday, Milly	Jan. 21,	July 10, 1814	Robert Carter	John Mathews	1b165	cr 12	mr 25 *
?Carter, Eliz. m. English(Ingl-),John	Jan. 25,	Jan. 24, 1799	Thomas Carter	John Potts	4b 29		mr 18 *
Carter, Eliz. m. Kildow, Jacob		1817					mr 37 *
Carter, Thomas m. Ellis, Susanna		1789		D. Thomas			mr 29 *
Carts, Jacob m. Rockwell, Nancy	Dec. 7,	? 1818	Jesse Rockwell	Mathias Riser	1b 91		mr 74 *
Carver, Geo. W. m. Thompson, Sarah	May 28,	May 29, 1842	Jacob Armstrong	Mayberry Goheen	6b271		mr 36 *
Casey, Alex. m. Busby, Nancy		Dec. 22, 1788		Hugh Vance			
Casey, Daniel m. Mahoney, Ellen	June 15,	1842	James McSherry		6b212		mr 30 *
Cashman, Eliz. m. Kyser, John	Oct. 28,	1816	Christian Cashman		4b 19		mr 58 *
Cashman, John m. Murphy, Catherine	Oct. 13,	Oct. 14, 1819	Jacob Murphy	W.N.Scott	4b119		mr 62 *
Cashman, Marg't m. Starry, Nicholas	June 26,	June 29, 1823	John Cashman	Nathan Young	4b242		mr 80 *
Caskey, Eliz. m. Hollis, Washington	Aug. 25,	Aug. 25, 1831	Hiram Beeson	Nathan Young	5b204		mr 9 *
Caskey, Mary E. m Garner(Laman),Rich	Apr. 4,	Apr. 4, 1849	William Caskey	W. Love	7b152		
Caskey, Sarah m. Grimes, Robert		Feb. 27, 1794		Moses Hoge			
Caskey, William m. Palmer, Mary	Oct. 28,	1843	Geo. Dougherty		6b306	cr 22	mr 32 *
Caskey, Wm. m. Shoafstall, Ann	Jan. 3,	1822	Joseph Chambers		4b203		mr 74 *
*Caslett, Mary m. Reily, John		Feb. 25, 1783		Hugh Vance			mr 70 *
Casper, Isabel m. Gregory, James	Nov. 9,	Nov. 12, 1842	Jonas Carper	Mayberry Goheen	6b283		mr 59 *
Casper, Mary Ann m. Stilwell, John	Nov. 13,	Sept 17, 1839	Sarah Smart	Lewis F. Wilson	5b 55		mr 60 *
Castle, Elijah m. Smart, Sarah Ann	Nov. 8,	Nov. 14, 1826	Adam Leopard	Nathan Young	6b 22		
Castle, Elijah m. Wilson, Eliz.	Apr. 12,	Apr. 15, 1834	John Castle	Nathan Young	5b161		
Castle, Eliz. m. Stler, Jacob	Sept 8,	1830	John Castle		6b 18		
Castle, Mary Ann m. Sprigg, James	Mar. 9,	1834	John Castle		6b 35		
Castle, Melinda m. Winding, Israel		1835					
CastAick(Botwick), Jas. m. Coons,Kath.	Mar. 19,	June 4, 1789	William Little	Hugh Vance	1b 91	cr 39	mr 3 *
Caswell, Kitty m. Bull, John		Dec. 12, 1798	Conrad Miller	Hugh Vance			
Cathaway, Rodey m. Booth, Samuel	Aug. 29,	1788	William Catlett	Mathias Riser	2b140		mr 36 *
Catlett, Eliz. m. Miller, Christian		Dec. 17, 1818	William Catlett				mr 30 *
Catlett, Eveline m. Batt, Aaron	Apr. 6,	1815	Fred. Householder		3b319		
Catlett, Marg't m. Gaither, Elias	Aug. 22,	1797	James Wright		1b 34		
Catlett, Sarah m. Miller, Conrad	Sept 30,	Oct. 1, 1815	Daniel Ambrose	Nathan Young	3b341		mr 55 *
Catlett, Strother m. Shearer, Sarah	Jan. 2,	1835	John Beach		6b 27		
Catrow, Samuel m. Williams, Eliz.	Jan. 31,	Feb. 2, 1817	John Varmetre	Mathias Riser	4b 31		
Caw, Isaac m. Michael, Martha	Oct. 26,	1833			5b288		
Caw, Peter m. Thomas, Rosanna	Oct. 19,	1801			2b144		*
Cawood, Thomas m. Baldwin, Rebecca		Apr. 27, 1807?					
Cedous, Eliz. m. Snider, John	Aug. 14,	Aug. 17, 1799	Basil Games	John Mathews	2b 20	cr 13	mr 23 *
Cenwell, Loveless m. Hall, Eliz.		1789		John Heitt(Hutt)		cr 38	mr 17 *
Ceny, Eva Rose m. Steed, Jesse		1789		D. Thomas			mr 37 *
Ceole, Abraham m. Green, Matty	Nov. 18,	Nov. 19, 1801	William Green	Richard Swift	2b148	cr 32	mr 20 *
Cerby, Mary m. Close, John		June 19, 1788	John Fry	Hugh Vance			mr 35 *
Chaffin, Eliz. m. Shaffer, Aaron	Dec. 2,	1816			4b 24		
?*Casler, Eliz. m. English(Ing-)John	Jan. 21,	Jan. 24, 1799	Robert Carter	John Potts	1b165	cr 12	mr 18 *

Entry	Date	(marriage)	(suretor)	(minister)	(bond)	
Chaffin, Solomon m. McCoy(K-)Isabell	Nov. 21,	1803	Daniel McCoy		2b214	
Chaffin, Susanna m. Bartley, Wm.	July 17,	1800	Uriah Blue		2b 76	
Chaffin, Aaron m. Kennedy, Mary	Aug. 9,	1797	Daniel Kennedy		1b 28	
Chalfin, John m. Thornton, Nancy	June 26,	1797	Aaron Chalfin		1b 24	
Chalfin, William m. Brown, Polly	Jan. 4,	1802	Wm. Grantham		2b157	
Chamberlain, Abigail m. Farr, Joseph	Mar. 27,	1798	Benj. Beeler		1b 92	
Chamberlain, Eliz. m. Hunsecker, Hen	Mar. 1,	1838	Simon Minghini		6b135	
Chamberlain, Jane W. m. Hamell, Geo.	May 28,	1847	A.W.McCleary	Lewis F. Wilson	7b 97	mr 82 *
Chamberlain, Joseph m. Daniel, Susan	Dec. 30, June 1,	1811	Ellis Rees		3b206	
Chamberlain, Joseph m. Miller, Mary	May 30,	1815	Joshua Miller	Nathan Young	3b327	mr 55 *
Chamberlain, Joseph B. m. Morgan,E.S.	May 10, May 27,	1845	Morgan Morgan	James Chisholm	7b 34	mr 76 *
Chamberlain, Mary m. Morgan Morgan	Nov. 17,	1819	Ellis Rees		4b123	
Chamberlain, Sarah A. m. Fisher, John	Oct. 4,	1834	James Lashorn		6b 20	
Chambers, Ann R. m. Swartz, John T.	July 13,	1837	A.S. Chambers		6b110	
Chambers, Anthony m. Faris, Rebecca	Oct. 18,	1815	William Faris		3b344	
Chambers, Anthy S. m.Frances,Rebecca	Oct. 3,	1836	Samuel W.Catlin		6b 86	
Chambers, Cath. m. Fisher, Peter	May 13,	1788		Hugh Vance	3b217	gc 12 mr 35 *
Chambers, Cath. m. Hooper, Abr'm	Mar. 26,	1812	Joseph Chambers	Rev. Reebenack	5b152	* *
Chambers, Eliza m. Fogle(Fough),Geo.	Feb. 11,	1830	Ezekiel Showers	Jacob Medtart	3b205	gc 12 mr 63 *
Chambers, Eliz. m. Sprigg, Thomas	Dec. 25,	1811	Jacob Zimmerman	Rev. Reebenack	5b 82	
Chambers, Eliz. m. Tritch, Wm.	Nov. 1,	1827	Jas. Maxwell Jr.		4b238	
Chambers, Emily m. Maxwell, Jas. Jr.	May 8,	1823	Seaman Garard	Chas. P. Krauth	3b188	mr 46 *
Chambers, Esther m. Fisher, Peter	May 13,	1788	Robert Wilson	Hugh Vance	5b298	mr 35 *
Chambers, Hetty m. Hedges, Robert	May 26,	1811	Seaman Garard	John B. Hoge	6b 99	cr 14 mr 24 *
Chambers, Jacob m. Tabler, Sarah A.	Dec. 25,	1823	A.S.Chambers		7b141	
Chambers, Jas. H. m. Davis, Christena	Feb. 23,	1837	William Reed	P. Lipscomb	6b103	
Chambers, John M. m. Reed, Emily	Dec. 4,	1848	Garard McDonald	Hugh Vance	3b271	mr 82 *
Chambers, Joseph m. Snider, Nelly	Dec. 31,	1789	Abraham Hooper	Rev. Reebenack	4b 32	mr 38 *
Chambers, Jos. S. m. McDonald, Cath.	Mar. 30,	1837	Abraham Hooper	Hugh Vance	6b 62	gc 13 mr 2 *
Chambers, Nancy m. Cage, James	Sept 16,	1813	Bailey Hedges	Hugh Vance	1b 69	cr 24
Chambers, Robert m. McAlister, Mary	Jan. 17,	1788	Ellis Chapman	John Howell	2b225	
Chambers, Sally m. Winfield, Lawrenc	Mar. 27,	1817	James Doyle		2b268	
Chambers, Sarah m. Bare, Henry	May 9,	1786	Edward Chapman			mr 42 *
Chambers, Wesley m. Hedges, Mercy T.	Nov. 17,	1835	Jesse Payne			mr 68 *
Chapman, Abraham m. Cox, Eliz.	Nov. 14,	1797	Daniel H. Conrad			
Chapman, Edward m. Edmonds, Rebecca	Dec. 6,	1804	Abraham Mays			
Chapman, Francy m. Hall, William	Mar. 7,	1805				
Chapman, Hannah m. Johnson, Mathew	Aug. 15,	1786				
Chapman, John m. Payne, Eliz. Mrs.	Feb. 8,	1829		Hugh Vance	5b132	mr 33 *
Chapman, John G. m. Luckett, Mary E.	June 2,	1832			5b247	
Chapman, Joseph m. Ebberts, Phebe	Nov. 20,	1837		James Watts	6b124	
Chapman, Jost m. Mallenaux, Sarah	Nov. 16,	1794		David Young		gc 4 *
Charinger,David m. Smith, Eliz.	Dec. 27, Oct. 27,	1795		David Young		gc 5 *

Name (m. spouse)	(marriage) date		year	(suretor)	(minister)	(bond)	ref
Chaston, Sarah m. Ward, Archibald	Oct. 25,	Sept 25,	1842	James Barton	E.R.Lippett	4b192	cr 23 · mr 45 *
Checks, George m. Vorhees, Kitty	Sept 26.		1821	?		6b281	cr 27 · mr 2 *
Chenoweth, Annie m. Baggs, James		Nov. 29,	1787		Hugh Vance		mr 21 *
Chenoweth, Arch'd m. Barnes,Provid'ce	Feb. 11,	Feb. 19,	1803	John West	Richard Swift	2b193	cr 14 · mr 24 *
Chenoweth, Arthur m.Wlake, Catherine	Jan. 12,		1807	Jacob Weaver		3b 42	mr 44 *
Chenoweth, Charlotte m. Bear, Jacob	May 22,		1810	Robert Wilson	Lewis Mayer	3b152	
Chenoweth, Chloe m. Strode, James		Mar. 29,	1787		Hugh Vance		
Chenoweth, Edward m. Wilson, Mary	Sept 23,		1806	Zachariah Wilson		1b 44	mr 53 *
Chenoweth, Elenor m. Baldwin, Joshua	Oct. 29,	Apr. 16,	1829	Wm. Chenoweth		3b 34	mr 15 *
Chenoweth, Emily m. Kerney, John	Apr. 13,	Oct. 23,	1798	Philip Chenoweth	Jas. M. Brown	5b125	cr 31 · mr 53 *
Chenoweth, Hannah m. Harris, George	Oct.	Mar. 19,	1829	John Chenoweth	Richard Swift	1b140	
Chenoweth, Harriet m. Curtis, Jacob	Mar. 18,		1810	Philip Chenoweth	Jas. M. Brown	5b124	
Chenoweth, Henrietta m. Wilson, Robt	Oct. 23,	July 23,	1815	William Long	William Long	3b164	mr 26 *
Chenoweth, Isaac m. Bailey, Sarah	July 21,	Nov. 8.	1832	Barton Campbell	W.N.Scott	3b329	mr 64 *
Chenoweth, Jas. W. m. Walker, Ann B.	Nov. 7,		1806	James Walker	Jas. M. Brown	5b246	cr 31 · mr 15 *
Chenoweth, Jane m. Jennings, George	Sept 6.	Nov. 22,	1798	Absalom Chenoweth		3b 96	
Chenoweth, John m. Davenport, Mary	Nov. 14,		1817	George Harris	Richard Swift	1b146	
Chenoweth, John m. Gorrell, Martha	Sept 22,		1823	Robert Wilson		4b 47	
Chenoweth, John m. Varmetre, Isabel	Mar. 17,		1807	Washington Evans		4b235	cr 16 · mr 23 *
Chenoweth, Joseph m. Gorrell, Rachel	Dec. 2,	Dec. 21,	1809	Joseph Gorrell		3b 81	
Chenoweth, Julia m. Stephen, Alex.	Dec. 20,		1835	Robert Wilson	Christian Streit	3b128	
Chenoweth, Julian m. Kerney, William	Mar. 4,		1829	Samuel Chenoweth		6b 34	
Chenoweth, Levina m. Couchman, Geo.	Feb. 24,	May 13,	1830	Samuel Chenoweth		5b120	mr 54 *
Chenoweth, Mary P. m. Miller, Thos.	May 10,		1802	Joseph Chenoweth	Jas. M. Brown	5b166	
Chenoweth, Philemon m. Lyle, Sally	Jan. 1,		1813	Hugh Lyle		2b156	
Chenoweth, Rachel m. Beall, Vincent	Jan. 13,	Mar. 24,	1783?	James Chenoweth		3b248	mr 32 *
Chenoweth, Rachel m. Gorrell, Robert	Mar. 13,		1800	William Gorrell	Hugh Vance	2b 98	
Chenoweth, Richard m. Gorrell, Mary	Nov. 10,		1811	James Chenoweth		3b172	
Chenoweth, Ruth m. Lemon, John	Jan. 3,		1799	Joseph Miller		2b 17	
Chenoweth, Samuel m. Miller, Polly	Aug. 6,	Aug. 8,	1797	Edward Chenoweth	John Boyd	1b 50	cr 34 · mr 16 *
Chenoweth, Susan m. Wilson, Zach'h	Sept 29,		1801	Henry Watson		2b118	
Chenoweth, Thos. m. Watson, Eliz.	Mar. 22,		1796				
Cherry, Eliz. m. Patton, David	Oct. 17,	Oct. 17,	1801		David Young		go 6 · *
Chestnut, Eliz. m. May, George	Mar. 9,		1799	John Chestnut	David Young	2b117	go 8
Chestnut, William m. Errick, Jane	Jan. 19,	Jan. 24,	1838	George Errick	David Young	1b164	mr 69 *
Chew, Amy m. Light, Samuel	Apr. 21,	Apr. 26,	1813	Addison McKee	James Watts	6b118	
Chew, Henry m. Gustine, Amelia	Apr. 19,		1804	Thomas Young		3b259	
Chew, Joshua m. Marquart, Polly	Mar. 19,		1817	John Marquart		2b228	
Chew, Joshua m. McNealy, Eliz.	May 12,		1804	Robert Snodgrass		4b 35	
Chew, Mary m. Daniel, James	Oct. 6,	Nov.	1825	Hugh Davidson	John Winters	2b244	mr 50 *
Chew, Morris R. m. Crumley, Matilda	Nov. 7,		1846	Joel Rees		5b 26	
Chew, Ruth m. Crowl, William	Feb. 25,		1802	H.M.Chew		7b 59	
Chidester, Charlotte m. Ledman, Henry	Feb. 16,		1803	William Lowry		2b160	
Chenoweth, Arch'd m. Barnes,Prudence	Feb. 11,	Feb. 19,	1803	John West	Richard Swift	2b193	cr 27 · mr 21 *

Name	Marriage Date	Year	(suretor) Eliphlet Chidestr	(minister)	(bond)		
Chidester, Sarah m. Snyder, Abraham	June 10,	1797	Eliphlet Chidestr		1b 21		
Childs, Eliz. m. Mason, Jeptha	Apr. 28,	1801	Isaac Childs		2b124		
Childs, Sarah m. Johnston, John	Aug. 13, 16,	1822	John Childs	Nathan Young	4b221		mr 57 *
Childs, William m. Hite, Susanna	Jan. 3, 5,	1843	William Hite	Mayberry Goheen	6b287		mr 74 *
Chiles, John m. Siler, Eliz.	Oct. 12,	1818	Philip Siler		4b 82		
Chipley, Jonathan m.Buckles, Abigail	Nov. 29, 29,	1798	Wm. Buckles	Moses Hoge	1b150	cr 29	mr 15 *
Chisman, Edmond m. Brown, Martha	Aug. 26,	1816	Samuel Lane	Nathan Young	4b 11		mr 55 *
Chovald, Agness m. McGinnis, Felix	Apr. 17,	1793		David Young			gc 3
Chrisman, Edmund m. Brown, Martha	Aug. 26,	1816	Samuel Lane	Nathan Young	4b 11		mr 55 *
Chrisman, Geo. m. Porterfield, Nancy	Aug. 10, 11,	1829	Archibald Oden	Jas. M. Brown	5b136		mr 53 *
Chrisman, James m. Grubb, Beulah	Nov. 11, 13,	1817	James Sterrit	Nathan Young	4b 49		mr 56 *
Chrisman, Magdalena m. Eckhart, Elias	Nov. 4, 5,	1797	Philip Shutt	David Young	1b101		gc 7
Christian, Lucinda m. Morrow, James	Oct. 18,	1827	Israel Hoge	B. Reynolds	9b 80	gc 10	mr 52 *
Christie, Eliz. m. Patterson, Hugh	Oct. 19,	1803	Robert Christie	David Young	2b210		
Christie, Peter m. Wilson, Polly	Feb. 9,	1804	James Wilson		2b221		
Chriswell, Abraham m. Keesecker, Eliz	May 9, 16,	1833	Geo. H. Dugan	J.M.Brown	5b274		mr 67 *
Chriswell, James m. Seibert, Mary	Feb. 13, 16,	1837	Jacob Seibert	Lewis F. Wilson	6b 95	cr 10	
Chriswell, John m. Roberts, Agness	Mar. 12,	1795		Moses Hoge			mr 11 *
Church, Truman m. Palmer, Melinda	Oct. 14, 14,	1851	Edw. B. Hooper	D. Thomas	7b234		mr 85 *
Cister, Peter m. Freshour, Mary	June 5,	1818	George Freshour	Mathias Riser	4b 73		mr 29 *
Clanson, Anna m. Mortal, Abraham	Jan. 22,	1788		Moses Hoge			mr 35 *
Clapton, Fred. m. Poisal(Pisel), Eve	June 28, 30,	1805	Joseph Chambers	Christian Streit	2b266	cr 16	mr 22 *
Clapton, John m. Manning, A.	Oct. 19,	1796		David Young			gc 6
Clark, Anthony m. Quaid, Anna	Jan. 10,	1813	John Harrison		3b246		
Clark, Arch'd m. Grove, Lucy(Susanna)	Aug. 22, 23,	1804	Abraham Grove	John Bond	2b241	cr 13	
Clark, Ebenezer m. Kildow, Susanna	Sept 23, 25,	1826	Peter Hess	Nathan Young	5b 53		mr 21 *
?Clark, Eliz. m. Barr, William	June 23, 23,	1831		Nathan Young			mr 59 *
?Clark, Eliz. m. Penn, William	Dec. 4,	1833			5b198		mr 61 *
Clark, Frances m. Miller, Daniel	June 23,	1831	James Clark		5b292		
Clark, James m. Bowling, Charlotte	Aug. 28, 26,	1833	John Clark		5b281		
Clark, John m. Collins, Eliz.	Nov. 15, 18,	1847	Thos. J. Bowling	Nathan Young	7b113		mr 66 *
Clark, John m. Flagg, Eliz.	Aug. 3,	1810	Joseph Collins	P. Lipscomb	3b156		mr 81 *
Clark, John m. Loudon, Sarah	Aug. 7,	1794	Josiah Flagg				
Clark(Clerk)Jos-John m.Holliday,Mary	Sept 22, Oct. 4,	1809	Phil. Nadenbousch	Edward Tiffin	3b120	cr 25	mr 9 *
Clark, Margaret m. Naff, Jacob	Nov. 21, 22,	1829	James Clark	John Mathews	5b145		mr 40 **
Clark, Mary m. Johnson, Samuel	Jan.	1854		Nathan Young			mr 60 *
Clark, Mary m. Kerns, John	Oct. 18, 18,	1827	James Clark	James Watts			mr 59 *
Clark, Mary m. Light, William	Aug. 30, 30,	1838	Solomon Clark	Nathan Young	5b 80		mr 69 *
Clark, Mary m. LittleJohn, Joseph	Oct. 7,	1809	John Clark	James Watts	6b 91		
Clark, Nancy m. Light, Fred.	Nov. 11,	1836	Solomon Clark		3b120		
Clark, Peter m. Turner, Ann	June 16,	1845	Michael Grove	R.N.Herndon	6b 87		mr 69 *
Clark, Teresa m. Harrison, John	Nov. 27,	1815	Dennis Clark		7b 37		
Clark, Walter m. Gird, Harriet	Oct. 23,	1804	John Catlett		2b247		

Name (marriage)	(marriage)		(suretor)	(minister)	(bond)		
Clarke, Ann m. Johnston, Joseph	Apr. 17,	1835	John Clarke		6b 41		
Clarke, Anna m. Peters, Isaac	Mar. 4,	1799	Conrad Fultz		1b171		mr 14 *
Clarke, Charity m. Hess, Peter	Oct. 20,	1818	Solomon Clarke		4b 82		mr 29 *
Clarke, Eliz. m.MacGill, Carroll N.	May 11,	1829	Mathew J. Clarke		5b129		*
Clarke, Eliz. Powell, John	Mar. 5,	1798	Robert Powell		1b 87		
Clarke, Esther m. Lashels, John	Dec. 6,	1797	Richard Ranson	John Hill	1b 70	cr 37	mr 14 *
Clarke, Henry m. Smith, Nancy	Apr. 2,	1819?	Joseph Coltman	John B. Hoge	4b104		mr 29 *
Clarke, Isaac m. Price, Jane	Oct. 31,	1811	Isaac Crabb		3b197		
Clarke, John m. Polsal, Catherine	June 21,	1812	Bastion Potsal	Rev. Reebenack	3b228	gc 13	*
Clarke, Margaret m. French, Jacob	Nov. 4,	1833	John Stephens		5b288		
Clarke, Samuel m. Devour, Phebe	Sept 28,	1785		Hugh Vance			mr 34 *
Clarke, Solomon m. Butt, Eliz.	Dec. 4,	1843	Elisha Butt	Lewis F. Wilson	6b309		mr 74 *
Clarke, Solomon m. Fisher, Mary	Nov. 14,	1799	Caleb Boothe		2b 35		
Clarke, Wm. m. Robertson, Susanna	Apr. 17,	1782		Daniel Sturges			mr 42 *
Clarns, Francis m. Bradley, Jancy	June 29,	1786		Hugh Vance			mr 43 *
Clary, Daniel J. m. Curtis, Dorothy	Nov. 13,	1842	Thomas Harper	Peyton Harrison	6b252		mr 73 *
Clasby, Polly m. Murphy, Philip	Sept 6,	1804	Robert Grimes	John Bond	2b244	cr 13	mr 21 *
Clasby, Robert m. Cross, Mary	Dec. 6,	1798	Basil Cross	Richard Swift	1b151	cr 31	mr 15 *
Claspy, Joseph m. Faris, Mary	Apr. 16,	1799	James Faris	Richard Swift	2b 2	cr 28	mr 16 *
Claton, John m. Philips, Charity	July 29,	1802	William Hawk	Richard Swift	2b177	cr 32	mr 20 *
Clawson, Azariah m. Lawson, Nancy	Feb. 27,	1789		Hugh Vance			mr 37 *
Clawson, Eliz. m. Clawson, John	Mar. 23,	1792		David Young		gc 1	
Clawson, Hasumpy m. Conner, Joseph	Nov. 29,	1797	Bergan Covert		1b 66		
Clawson, Iram m. Sharp, Mary	Dec. 8,	1819	Thomas Sharp	Nathan Young	4b126		mr 56 *
Clawson, Isaac m. Sharp, Mary	Dec. 8,	1819	Thomas Sharp	Nathan Young	4b126		mr 56 *
Clawson, John m. Clawson, Mary	Mar. 23,	1792		David Young		gc 1	
Clawson, Okey m. Middleton, Mary	Oct. 31,	1826	John Shober	Nathan Young	5b 54		mr 59 *
Clawson, Peggy m. Oglin, James	Feb. 22,	1791		Moses Hoge		cr 6	mr 6 *
Clawson, Phebe m. Orrick(Quick),John	Nov. 12,	1810	John Clawson		3b165		
Clawson, Polly m. Harris, James	Jan. 10,	1829	David Miller	Nathan Young	5b116		mr 60 *
Clawson, Rachel m. Berryman, Wm.	Aug. 21,	1797	Thomas Clawson		1b 33		
Clawson, Sarah m. Rothwell, Thomas	Oct. 10,	1797	Brant Clawson		1b 53		
Clawson, Thos. m. Rawlings, Hannah	Oct. 27,	1794	Christ'r Widmire	David Young	3b293	gc 4	*
Clawson, William m. Widmire, Eliz.	Apr. 12,	1814	Conrad Claycomb		3b183	cr 14	mr 24 *
Claycomb, Barbara m. Myers, Jacob	Apr. 3,	1811?	Conrad Claycomb	John B. Hoge	3b 29		
Claycomb, Cath. m.Robbins, Job	Sept 13,	1806	John Ridenour		2b115		
Claycomb, Conrad m. Ridenour, Eliz.	June 9,	1802	Harvey A.Hedges		6b162		
Claycomb, Conrad m. Sutton, Susanna	Mar. 6,	1839	Conrad Claycomb	Rev. Reebenack	3b145	gc 11	*
Claycomb, Eliz. m. Green, John	Apr. 10,	1810	John Burk	John B. Hoge	3b189	cr 14	mr 24 *
Claycomb, Fred. m. Lowman(So-),Elisa	June 9,	1811?	Adam Tabler	W.N.Scott	4b 5		mr 26 *
Claycomb, Fred. m. Tabler, Cath.	June 13,	1816		John Boyd		cr 11	mr 13 *
Claycomb, John m. James, Drusilla	Dec. 13,	1796		Hugh Vance			mr 33 *
Claycomb, Mary m. Bare, Adam	Apr. 7,	1785					

Name	(marriage)	(suretor)	(minister)	(bond)	
Claycomb, Mary m. Myers, John Jr.	Dec. 8, 1801	Conrad Claycomb		2b151	
Clayton, Benj. m. Berryman, Ann	Jan. 30, 1805	Thomas Clayton		2b253	
Clayton, Eliz. m. Blue, Peter	Mar. 31, 1804	William Burns		2b231	
Clayton, Ellen m. Hudgel, Thomas	Aug. 24, 1835	Henry Gedilliams		6b 55	
Clayton, Henry m. Fulton, Eliz.	May 4, 1819	James Bell		4b106	
Clayton, John m. Fulton, Margaret	Feb. 22, 1819	James Bell			
Clayton, John m. Philips, Charity	July 27, July 29. 1802	William Hawke	Richard Swift	2b177	cr 32 mr 20 *
Clayton, John m. Thompson, Rhua	Aug. 22, 1804	David Gerrard		2b241	
Clayton, Nelly m. Berryman, John	July 23, 1801	Frederick Blue		2b131	
Clayton, Polly m. Rooney(Koney), Geo.	Apr. 12, Apr. 13, 1820	Isaac Bacon	W.N.Scott	4b144	mr 41 *
Cleamons, Leonard m. Davis, Marg't	Nov. 29, Nov. 30, 1809	Bastion Poisal	Rev. Reebenack	3b126	gc 10
Cleary, Ann m. Blue, Michael	Dec. 31, 1789		Moses Hope		cr 3 mr 3 *
Cleary, Daniel J. m. Curtis, Dorothy	Nov. 13, Nov. 16, 1842	Thos. S. Harper	Peyton Harrison	6b252	mr 73 *
Cleghorn, ? m. ?	Mar. 2, 1792		Moses Hope		mr 38 *
Clemmons, Marg't m. Throckmorton, Ri'd	May 7, 1816		Rev. Reebenack	4b191	gc 15
Cleon, Martha B. m. Shanks, Mich'l	Sept 20, 1821	John Strother			cr 5 mr 5 *
Clerk, Elenor m. Donaldson, John	Nov. 11, 1790		Moses Hope		mr 40 *
Clerk(Clark),Jos.John m.Holliday,Mary	Sept 22, Oct. 4, 1809	Phil. Madenbousch	John Mathews	3b120	cr 1 mr 2 *
Clerk, Marg't m. Frogle, George	Mar. 3, 1789		Moses Hope		cr 5 mr 5 *
Clerk, Sarah(Susan) m. Bennet, Mason	Oct. 17, 1790		Moses Hope		cr 8 mr 6 *
Clerk, Thos. m. Brother, Mary Ann	Dec. 20, 1791		Moses Hope		
Clice, Mary m. Hoke, Peter	Aug. 12, Aug. 13, 1811	George Clice	Rev. Reebenack	3b193	gc 12
Cline, Barbara m. Williams, John	June 13, 1803	John Cline	Richard Swift	2b203	cr 27 mr 21 *
Cline, Catherine m. Snowdeal, Jacob	Dec. 23, Dec. 26, 1811	James Brady	Rev. Reebenack	3b204	gc 12
Cline, Eve m. Horn, William	Aug. 29, 1818	David Cline		4b 77	
Cline, Hannah m. French, John	Jan. 19, 1818	Swearingen Ray		4b 57	
Cline, Hiram m. Kildow, Ann	Mar. 28, 1820	Jos. L. Kildow	W.N.Scott	4b142	mr 41 *
Cline, Isabel(Eve) m. Poisal, Peter	Aug. 25, Aug. 1824	David Cline	Chas. P. Krauth	4b?70	mr 47 *
Cline, Jacob m. Refsnider, Rachel	Sept 30, 1818	Aaron Refsnider		4b 81	
Cline, Jacob m. Wilson, Abigail	Apr. 12, Apr. 16, 1820	William Wilson	Nathan Young	4b144	mr 57 *
Cline, John m. Piper, Lucy	Dec. 20, 1811	?	John Howell	6b 25	gc 12
Cline, Kitty m. Snowdeal, Jacob	Dec. 23, Dec. 26. 1811	James Brady	Rev. Reebenack	3b204	mr 68 *
Cline, Margaret m. Davis, Daniel	Aug. 10, 1804	John Shober		2b239	
Cline, Mary Jane m. Hess, David H.	Dec. 12, 1839	Wm. T. Seibert		6b186	
Cline, Peggy m. Rutherford, Geo.	Nov. 14, Nov. 15, 1810	Jacob Snowdeal	Rev. Reebenack	3b166	gc 11 mr 16 *
Cline, Philip m. Newman, Jacob	? 8, May 12, 1799	Thomas Manlkin	Richard Swift	1b179	cr 28
Cline, Sophia m. Crowl, Jacob	July 20, July 31, 1803	Marg't Cline	David Young	2b206	gc 10
Clinton, Susanna m. Cameron, Daniel	Nov. 6, 1788		Moses Hope		gc 10 mr 36 *
Clse, Ann m. Godman, Richard	Apr. 5, 1820	Peter Hoke		4b143	
Clse, Henry m. Francis, Rebecca	May 10, 1810	William Francis	Rev. Reebenack	3b151	gc 11
Clse, Jacob m. Blackmore, Nancy	Jan. 18, 1820	Francis Silver		4b130	
Clse, John m. Locke, Sophia	Dec. 24, 1829				
Clse, Rebecca m. Refsnider, Aron	Aug. 2, 1821		Nathan Young	4b186	mr 60 *

	(marriage)	(suretor)	(minister)	(bond)		
Cloninger, Henry m. Crook, Catherine	Dec. 16, 1801	Jacob Crook	David Young	2b152	gc 9	mr 71 *
Cloninger, Mary Ann m. Swisher, Geo.	Oct. 5, 1839	John Clarke	M.G. Hamilton	6b178		mr 84 *
Cloninger, Mary E. m. Deck, Peter W.	Mar. 1, 1851	Philip Cloninger	F.C.Tebbs	7b216	cr 28	mr 22 *
Cloninger, Philip m. Siling, Mildred	May 30, 1805	Henry Cloninger	John Bond	2b262		mr 60 *
Cloninger, Philip C. m. Barns, Mary	Apr. 15, 1829	Henry Barns	Nathan Young	5b126		mr 64 *
Cloninger, Thomas m. Barns, Eliz.	Aug. 7, 1832	Henry Barns	Nathan Young	5b235	cr 28	mr 23 *
Clonis, Eliz. m. Steele, John	Aug. 30, 1806	John Clouse	John Bond	3b 27		mr 35 *
Close, John m. Cerby, Mary	June 19, 1788		David Young			
Close, John m. McDade, Nancy	Aug. 12, 1795		David Young		gc 5	
Close, Joseph m. Moffett, Rachel	Nov. 21, 1793		Hugh Vance		gc 3	
Clough, Wm. m. Elliott, Mary	Aug. 3, 1824	Edward A. Gibbs	David Young	4b269	cr 28	mr 47 *
Clouse, Eliz. m. Steele, John	Aug. 30, 1806	John Clouse	Chas. P. Krauth	3b 27	cr 28	mr 23 *
Clover, Amelia m. Duckwall, Isaac	Oct. 24, 1815	Daniel Duckwall	John Bond	3b345		mr 6 *
Clover, Rosanna m. Ambrose, Mathias	May 11, 1791		David Young			
Cluke, Geo. m. Brother, May Ann	Dec. 20, 1791		Moses Hoge		cr 8	mr 64 *
Cluke, Thomas m. Brother, Mary	Dec. 20, 1791		Moses Hoge		cr 8	mr 69 *
*Coal, Joseph m. Painter, Mary	Apr. 16, 1832	George Painter	Jacob Medtart	5b226		mr 77 *
Coalman, Michael m. Swingle, Mary	Aug. 20, 1838	James L. Maslin	Lewis F. Wilson	6b144		mr 85 *
Coats, Jesse J. m. Crim, Harriet C.	May 12, 1846	Abraham Crim	E.L.Dulin	7b 65		
Cobert, Barbara E. m. Kiser, Henry	Dec. 31, 1851		David Thomas		gc 3	
Cock, Eliz. m. Balen, James	Dec. 20, 1837		J. Larkin			
Cock, Eliz. m. Barnes, Arch'd	Mar. 30, 1794		David Young			
Cockburn, Robt. m. Williams, Kath.	Feb. 7, 1785		Hugh Vance			mr 33 *
Cocke, John m. Cocke, Rebecca	Sept. 2, 1800	Edward Howe	David Young	1b 68		
Cocke, Mary m. Howe, William	Dec. 2, 1797		David Young		gc 7	
Cocke, Peter m. Poisal, Susannah	June 8, 1794		David Young		gc 4	
Cocke, Rebecca m. Cocke, John	Sept. 2, 1800		David Young			
Cockran, Geo. m. Reichard, Cath. Mrs	Aug. 2, 1824	George Hoe	Chas. P. Krauth	4b268	cr 29	mr 47 *
Cockran, Hannah m. Newell, Wm.	Oct. 2, 1799	Andrew Davis	Moses Hoge	2b 28		mr 17 *
Cockrane, Rachel m. McCormick, Ed.	Feb. 9, 1799	Mathew Ramone		1b166		
Cockwell, Joseph m. Butler, Sarah E.	May 13, 1847	David Farnsworth	Richard T. Brown	7b127	cr 15	mr 79 *
Coe, Ebenezer m. Wilson, Mary M.	Nov. 9, 1824	Samuel K. Wilson		4b277	gc 13	mr 4 *
Coffenberg, Mary m. Rombo, Wm.	Apr. 13, 1789		Christian Streit	3b253		mr 88 *
Coffenberger, Cath. m. Weddle, Jacob	Feb. 25, 1813	Geo. Coffenberger	Rev. Reebenack			
Coffenberger, Ellen m. Varmetre, Jas.	?, 185-?		R.A.Fink			
Coffenberger, Geo. m. Rumbo, Susan	Dec. 25, 1793		David Young		gc 3	
Coffenberger, Jacob m. Lee, Eliza	?, 1848?	Wm. Coffenberger	Chas. P. Krauth	7b126		mr 78 *
Coffenberger, John m. White, Susan	Apr. 4, 1848	Geo. W. Burns	Jas. H. Jennings	7b127		mr 82 *
Coffenberger, John m. Wood, Mary	Mar. 14, 1834	Robert Wood		6b 26		
Coffenberger, Mary m. Weddle, Michl	Apr. 3, 1816	Geo. Coffenberger	Rev. Reebenack	4b 16	gc 15	
Coffenberger, Michl m. Delaplan, Hetty	Aug. 8, 1831	Geo. Coffenberger	Jas. M. Brown	5b200		mr 62 *
Coffenberger, Samuel m. Myers, Sarah	Mar. 16, 1818		J.H.Jennings			
Coffenberger, Wm. m. Underdunk, Maria	Oct. 20, ?	Henry Underdunk	John Kehler	4b 83		mr 31 *
*Coal, Elinor m. Pulse, Joseph	Nov. 3, 1832	Samuel Cole	Nathan Young	5b245		mr 65 *

Entry	(marriage)	(suretor)	(minister)	(bond)		
Coffenberger, Wm. Jr. m. Byers, Eliz.	Feb. 24, 1852	Jacob Byers	Hugh Vance	7b247		mr 52 *
Coffenberry, Frances m. Stipp, Fred.	Dec. 5, 1784		Hugh Vance			mr 43 *
Coffenberry, Geo. L. m. little, Eliz.	1786					mr 20 *
Coflin, James m. Potts, Nelly	July 18, 1801	John Potts	Richard Swift	2b131	cr 31	mr 20 *
Cofry, John m. Daily, Abia	Apr. 15, 1789		Hugh Vance	2b154	cr 20	mr 3 *
Cohagen, Nancy m. Anderson, Prov'dle	Dec. 22, 1801	James Cheroweth				
Cokenheas, Eliz. m. Adam, Samuel	June 9, 1798		David Young		gc 7	*
Colbert, Ann m. Hoffman, David W.	Aug. 1, 1847	Joseph Hoffman	William Love	7b103		mr 78 *
Colbert, Barbara m. Kisner, Wm. Henry	Dec. 31, 1851	Jas. M. Manford	D. Thomas	7b117		mr 85 *
Colbert, Fielding m. Nipe, Martha	May 18, 1894	George Nipe	John Light	6b 12		mr 67 *
Colbert, Jean m. Mortal, Peter	Oct. 2, 1788		Moses Hoge			mr 36 *
Cole, Abraham m. Green, Matty	Nov. 19, 1801	William Green	Richard Swift	2b148	cr 32	mr 20 *
Cole, Barbara m. Miles, William	Oct. 10, 1806	Barney Cole	Nathan Young	3b 33		
Cole, Elenor Ann m. Pulse, Joseph	Nov. 8, 1832	Samuel Cole	Nathan Young	5b245		mr 65 *
?Cole, Elenor m. Pulse, John	Nov. 3, 1832					
Cole, George m. Cox, Catherine	Oct. 4, 1832	William Cox	Richard Swift	2b 29	cr 34	mr 16 *
Cole, Joseph m. Painter, Mary	Oct. 5, 1799	George Painter	Jacob Medtart	5b226		mr 64 *
Cole, Mary A. m. Huff, John	Apr. 19, 1832	Barney Cole		1b178		
Cole, Samuel m. Wilson, Sarah	Apr. 7, 1799	Jacob Kroesen		4b132		
Cole, Wm. m. McNeal, Polly	Jan. 26, 1820					
Cole, Wm. m. Lewis, Catherine	Aug. 10, 1825	Levi Austin	James Reilly	5b 19		mr 48 *
Coleman, Jacob m. Bell, Eliz.	Oct. 6, 1837	Joseph Lewis		6b114	gc 13	
Coleman, Michael m. Swingle, Mary	Nov. 12, 1812	Christian Silver	Rev. Reebenack	3b240		mr 69 *
College, James m. Hill, Cath.	Aug. 22, 1838	Jas. L. Maslin	Lewis F. Wilson	6b144		mr 30 *
College, John m. Meeks, Phebe	Jan. 14, 1819		Mathias Riser			
Collet, Daniel m. Hanes, Mary	Dec. 26, 1808	William Bell		3b104		
Colliflower, John m. Webb, Elinor	Feb. 28, 1781		Daniel Sturges			mr 31 *
Collins, Albert m. Baker, Rachel Ann	Mar. 2, 1847	James M. Newkirk	John Light	3b 88		mr 79 *
Collins, Cath. m. Barrett, Wm.	Aug. 7, 1826	William Webb	Chas. P. Krauth	5b 48		mr 51 *
Collins, Cath. m. Jones, Wm.	July 31, 1850	Robt. M.Henderson	R.T.Berry	7b190		mr 83 *
Collins, Cath. m. Thomas, John	Sept 29, 1841	Joseph Collins	John Hedges	6b247		mr 72 *
Collins, Daniel m. Ellis, Eliz. Ann	Jan. 12, 1799	Thos. Butterfield	David Young	1b161	gc 8	mr 2 *
Collins, Elinor m. Nadenboush, Fred.	Sept 13, 1787		Hugh Vance		cr 18	mr 79 **
Collins, Eliza m. Burns, John	Feb. 26, 1847	Jas. M. Newkirk	John Light	7b 88		mr 25 **
Collins, Eliz. m. Clark, John	Apr. 6, 1815	Ignat's O'Ferrall	John Mathews	3b318		mr 72 *
Collins, Eliz. m. Garard, Seaman	May 4, 1826	Harrison Waite	James Redley	6b204		mr 81 *
Collins, Harriet m. Crabb, Wm.	Apr. 10, 1847	Joseph Collins	P. Lipscomb	7b113		mr 50 *
Collins, Joseph m. Raney, Agnes	Aug. 20, 1840	John Snodgrass	John Mathews	5b 41		mr 82 *
Collins, Marg't m. Oak, Silas	Nov. 15, 1815	Joseph Collins	Jas. H. Jennings	7b 94		
Collins, Mary m. Butterfield, Thos.	Nov. 21, 1786	William Barrett	John Mathews	6b216		mr 25 *
Collins, Mary n. Myers, James	Jan. 2, 1845	Robert Wilson	Hugh Vance	3b347		mr 43 *
Collins, Moses m. Maxwell, Jane	Dec. 8, 1789	Joseph Collins	Lewis F. Wilson / Hugh Vance	7b 19	cr 25	mr 4 *

		(marriage)		(suretor)	(minister)	(bond)			
Collins, Patrick m. Brabson, Eliz.	June 20,		1797	Evan Rees		1b 23			
Collins, Robert m. Butt, Rachel	Sept 16,		1814	Isaac Butt		3b303			
Collin, Solomon m. _______, _______		Oct. 20,	1788		Hugh Vance			mr 35	
Collins, Thomas m. Allen, Eliz.		May 3,	1785		Hugh Vance			mr 33	*
Collins, Timothy m. Lowe, Phebe	Sept 22,	Sept 27,	1800	Richard Lowe	David Young	2b 88	gc 9		*
Collins, Wm. m. Cookus(Kookus),Mary	Mar. 24,	Mar. 24,	1800	Jacob Cookus	Moses Hoge	2b 59	cr 29	mr 19	*
Collis, Ann m. Anderson, Wm.	Sept 20,		1837	Daniel Collis		6b112			
Collis, Eliza m. Burns, John	Apr. 2,	Apr. 2,	1841	Harrison Waite	James Reiley	6b204		mr 72	*
Collis, Hannah m. Thompson, Wm.	May 2,		1837	Daniel Collis		6b106			
Collis, Lucy m. Custer, John	Sept 13,	Sept 14,	1850	Jonathan Custer	D.F. Bragunier	7b195		mr 80	*
Colston, Eliz. m. Williams, R. A.	May 23,		1849	Edward Colston		7b158			
Colston, Mary I. m. Thomas, John H.	Oct. 5,		1809	Rawleigh Colston		3b121			
Colston, Susan m. Leigh, Benj. W.	Nov. 28,	Nov. 30,	1813	Philip Pendleton	Alex. Belmain	3b278	cr 41	mr 25	*
Colter, Betsy m. Littlejohn, Edward	Apr. 27,		1812	Corbin Colter		3b223			
Colter, John m. Gano, Rebecca	June 27,	June 30,	1812	Joseph Henderson	Rev. Reebenack	3b229	gc 13		*
Colter, Mathew m. Lynch, Mary	Sept 18,		1839	James Lynch		6b176			
Coltman, Joseph m. Shepherd, Polly	Jan. 11,	Jan. 11,	1816	James Shepherd	Rev. Reebenack	3b352	gc 15		*
Colvin, Emily m. Armstrong, Thos. D.	Jan. 15,		1852	John M. Colvin		7b243			
Colvin, John m. Wright, Polly B.	Feb. 29,	Feb. 29,	1816	John Wright	W.N.Scott	3b357		mr 26	*
Colvin, Sarah A. m. Kerney, Wm. P.	Jan. 23,	Jan. 24,	1828	John Colvin	James M. Brown	5b 88		mr 51	*
Colvin, Sarah M. m. Schoppert, Geo.	Jan. 26,	Jan. 27,	1848	John M. Colvin	P. Lipscomb	7b120		mr 81	*
Colyen, William m. Long, Elenor		Mar. 19,	1782		Hugh Vance			mr 32	*
Comegys, Benj. m. Thompson, Demaris	Apr. 8,	Apr. 8,	1811	John Thompson	John Mathews	3b183		mr 40	*
Comegys, Charlotte m. Athy, Wilson	Jan. 17,	Jan. 18,	1798	John Files	Richard Swift	1b102	cr 12	mr 16	*
Comegys, Deborleigh m. Cross, John	Feb. 12,		1807	Benj. Comegys		3b 47			
Comegys, Hannah m. Warner, Wm.	Mar. 23,		1810	Benj. Comegys		3b143			
Comegys, John m. Marshall, Eliz.	Apr. 26,		1810	Wm. Marshall		3b149			
Comegys, Mary E. m. Taylor, Isaac C.	Apr. 2,		1851	Benj. Comegys		7b221			
Comegys, Nancy m. Cross, Joseph	Aug. 3,		1803	Jacob Comegys		2b207			
Comegys, William m. Morgan, Sarah	June 21,	June 21,	1800	James Foreman	Richard Swift	2b 74	cr 34	mr 18	*
Comfee, Conrad m. Confar, Eliz.	Dec. 31,	Jan. 2,	1817	Jacob Wagoner	Nathan Young	4b 28		mr 55	*
Compston, Eliz. m. Delaplane, Isaac		Nov. 15,	1785		Hugh Vance			mr 34	*
Compston, Mary m. Park, Amos(Ebenezer		Mar. 23,	1789		Hugh Vance		cr 20	mr 3	*
Compton, Ann m. Myers, George	June 11,	?	1818	Ezekiel Compton	Mathias Riser	4b 73		mr 29	*
Compton, Cath. m. Murphy, Abraham	Mar. 4,	Feb. 7,	1833	Ezekiel Compton	Nathan Young	5b260		mr 66	*
Compton, Deborah m. Ford, David	Apr. 18,		1835	Edward Winning		6b 41			
Compton, Elijah m. Pinkerton, Mary	July 31,	Aug. 6,	1799	Robert Pinkerton	David Young	6b 13	gc 8		*
Compton, Eliz. m. Smith, Joseph	July 24,	July 27,	1843	Philip Siler	Lewis F. Wilson	6b302		mr 74	*
Compton, Henry m. Delaplane, Esther		July 31,	1787		Hugh Vance		cr 18	mr 1	*
Compton, Henry m. Hill, Mary	Sept 10,	Sept	1822	Robert Hill	Chas. P. Krauth	4b223		mr 45	*
Compton, Isaac m. Kizer, Eliz.	Sept 16,		1799	George Kizer		2b 26			
Compton, Isaac m. Miller, Nancy	Dec. 9,	Dec. 19,	1799	Elijah Compton	David Young	2b 40	gc 9		*
Compton, Sarah A. m. Barns, John	Mar. 24,		1835	Jacob Swisher		6b 37			

Name	(marriage)	(suretor)	(minister)	(bond)	ref
Compton, Wm. T. m. Boyd, Isabel K.	Sept 8, 1829	Conrad Hogmire	Moses Hoge	5b140 26 47	cr 29 / mr 19 *
Condear, John m. Neal, Eliz.	Jan. 10, 1800	Basil Williamson	Moses Hoge		mr 35 *
Condon, Easter m. Grafton, Thomas	Mar. 13, 1788				mr 55 *
Confar, Eliz. m. Lompa(Comfee)Conrad	Dec. 31, 1817	Jacob Wagoner	Nathan Young	4b 28	cr 36 / mr 14 *
Conklyn, James m. Sewell, Abigail	May 20, 1798	James Burr	Moses Hoge	1b12	mr 39 *
Conklyn, John m. Burr, Miriam	Jan. 24, 1793				mr 21 *
Conwell, Anna m. Murray, Wm. m.	Mar. 21, 1803	John Conwell	Richard Swift	2b198	cr 27 / mr 32 *
Conwell, Arthur m. Bossell, Eliz.	Mar. 24, 1811		Hugh Vance		
Conwell, Benjamin m. Rhodes, Kitty	May 22, 1811	Jacob Rhodes	Richard Swift	3b176	mr 21 *
Conwell, John m. Barnes, Eliz.	Feb. 20, 1803	Joshua Chew	J.H. Plunkett	2b195	cr 27 / mr 88 *
Conwell, Patrick m. Reedy, Hannah	Feb. 21, 1851	Michael Conwell	Rev. Reebenack	7b198	gc 11
Connelly, Benj. V. m. Rhodes, Cath.	Mar. 25, 1811		Henry Furlong		mr 79 *
Connelly, Cath. m. Spriggs, Robert	Apr. 1, 1849	John E. Hogeland	John Winters	7b151	mr 50 *
Connelly, Matilda m. Chew, Morris R.	Nov. 7, 1825	Joel Rees		5b 26	
Conner, Ann m. Page, Nathaniel	Sept 15, 1815	Joseph Conner		3b339	
Conner, Anna m. Rorke, Barney	Dec. 19, 1799	William Reed	David Young	2b 40	gc 9 / mr 88 *
Conner, Eliz. O. m. Walsh, Thomas	Dec. 7, 1852		J.H.Plunkett		mr 62 *
Conner, George m. Needler, Maria	Aug. 24, 1831	George Biddle	Nathan Young	5b203	
Conner, Joseph m. Clawson, Hasumpy	Nov. 29, 1797	Bergon Covert		1b 66	
Conner, Nancy m. Demoss, Throckmorton	Apr. 7, 1802	David Conner		2b169	
Conner, Patrick m. Quinn, Bridget	Jan. 11, 1840	Nicholas Dumfee		6b192	
Conner, Peter m. Cookens, Cath.	Mar. 29, 1797	John Jameson		1b 2	
Conner, Sarah m. Matson, Daniel	Mar. 21, 1807	Abraham Howe		3b 51	
Conover, Benjamin m. Anderson, Eliz.	Dec. 12, 1827	Colbert Anderson	B. Reynolds	5b 85	mr 52 *
Conoway, Eliza m. Thomas, Isaac(John	Mar. 23, 1820	Samuel Conoway	John B. Hoge	4b141	mr 31 *
Conoway, Isaac m. Burdine(Bo-),Nancy	Mar. 3, 1813	John Burdine	Rev. Reebenack	3b255	gc 13
Conoway, James m. Sagathy, Isabel	Feb. 1, 1812	Peter Sagathy	Rev. Reebenack	3b210	gc 12
Conoway, John m. Hamilton, Susanna	Jan. 31, 1818	Samuel Conoway		4b 59	
Conoway, John m. Varnes, Eliz.	Apr. 24, 1799	William Harris		2b 3	
Conoway, Joseph m. Thatcher, Nancy	Aug. 27, 1827	Washington Boling	Nathan Young	5b 76	mr 59 *
Conoway, Mary m. Curtis, James	Apr. 9, 1825	Isaac Thomas	Jas. M. Brown	5b 7	mr 48 *
Conrad, Betty C. m. Harrison, Edw. J.	Oct. 8, 1850		D. Francis Sprigg	7b199	mr 81 *
Conrad, Eliz. m. Davis, Joseph W.	Jan. 1, 1799	David H. Conrad	John Heitt(Hutt)		cr 12 / mr 18 *
Conrad, Rebecca m. Harrison, Geo. F.	June 10, 1851	David H. Conrad	D. Francis Sprigg	7b227	mr 84 *
Constant, Jane m. Newcomb, Wm.	Jan. 12, 1790		Hugh Vance		mr 38 *
Conwell, Ann m. Murray, Wm.	Mar. 21, 1803	John Conwell	Richard Swift	2b198	cr 22 / mr 21 *
Conwell, Eleanor m. Tillis(Ta-)John	Apr. 25, 1799	John Bull	John Heitt(Hutt)	2b 4	cr 13 / mr 18 *
Conwell, John m. Barnes, Eliz.	Feb. 24, 1803	Joshua Chew	Richard Swift	2b195	mr 21 *
Conwell, Loveless m. Hall, Eliz.	Aug. 14, 1799	Basil Games	John Hutt(Heitt)	2b 20	cr 38 / mr 17 *
Conwell, Willy m. Anderson, Jonathan	July 16, 1801	Basil Games		2b130	
Conwell, Wm. m. Thomas, Mary	Feb. 6, 1803	Evan Rees		2b193	
Coogler, Benj. m. Pitzer, Susannah	Dec. 10, 1799	John Pitzer	David Young	2b 38	gc 9
Cook, Adam m. Jones, Emily	Aug. 28, 1843	Robert Jones	Lewis F. Wilson	6b303	mr 74 *

Name	(marriage)		(suretor)	(minister)	(bond)	Ref.
Cook, Benj. m. Sprigg, Mary Ann	Aug. 26,	1845	Robert Sprigg		7b 41	cr 9 mr 10 *
Cook, Catherine m. Rhodes, Jacob	Aug. 23,	1834	Peter Cook		6b 16	cr 22 mr 8 *
Cook, Eliza m. Evans, Thomas B.	Dec. 20,	1794		B. Fages	6b127	gc 3 *
Cook, Eliz. m. Boden, James	Jan. 9,	1837	Samuel Cook			*
Cook, Eliz. m. Gibbons, Morris	Aug. 29,	1793		Moses Hoge		
Cook, Jacob m. Moffett, Wm.	Dec. 5,	1793		David Young		mr 81 *
Cook, Jacob m. Gladden, Christiana	July 6,	1848	George Smith	P. Lipscomb	7b133	
Cook, Jacob m. Miller, Ann	Feb. 19,	1817	John Fuller	W.N.Scott	4b 31	
Cook, Jane m. Gephart, George G.	Aug. 3,	1830	Bernard C. Wolff		5b171	gc 9
Cook, John m. Cook, Rebecca	Sept 2,	1800	William Howe	David Young	2b 84	mr 25 *
Cook, John R. m. Pendleton, Maria W.	Nov. 17,	1813	Robert Wilson	John Mathews	3b276	mr 36 *
Cook, Lucy m. Davenport, Samuel	Dec. 23,	1788		Hugh Vance		
Cook, Margaret m. Grimes, Alex.	Mar. 14,	1836	Jacob Rhodes	Nathan Young	6b 73	mr 60 *
Cook, Mary m. Betts, Adam	Sept 17,	1829	Peter Cook	David Young	5b141	gc 7
Cook, Mary m. Howe, Wm.	Dec. 2,	1797	Edward Howe		1b 68	
Cook, Mary m. Watt, John	May 29,	1821	John Hildt		4b184	
Cook, Peggy m. Lountis, Samuel	Nov. 1,	1793	Daniel Doll	David Young	7b 96	gc 3 mr 78 *
Cook, Peter m. Gladden, Martha	May 23,	1847	William Howe	John Winter	2b 84	mr 85 *
Cook, Rebecca m. Cook, John	Sept 2,	1800	George Smith	David Young		gc 9
Cook, Sarah Ann m. Roach, Edward	Dec. 27,	1851	Jacob Cook	J.W. Ernest	7b240	
Cook, Susan m. Smith, George A.	Oct. 30,	1838	John S. Light		6b148	
Cook, Thomas m. Light, Susan	Jan. 6,	1834	John Jameson		5b299	
Cookens, Catherine m. Conner, Peter	Mar. 29,	1797		David Young	1b 2	cr 29 mr 19 *
Cookus, Mary m. Collins, William	Mar. 24,	1800	Jacob Cookus	Moses Hoge	2b 59	
Cookus, Peter H. m. McCleary, Angel'apr.	Mar. 9,	1832	Andrew McCleary		5b225	
Coon, Eve m. Gottshall, Jacob	Aug. 19,	1797	Jacob Coon		1b 32	gc 1 *
Coomet, Peter m. Leonard, Eliz.	May 1,	1792	Peter Imnes	David Young		
Cooney, Alice m. McIntire, Owen	July 21,	1836			6b 83	
Coons, Cath. m. Jones, Jonathan	July 30,	1813	Nathaniel Jones		3b268	mr 23 *
Coons, Cath. m. Miller, Henry	Aug. 30,	1798	Jacob Coons		1b127	mr 37 *
Coons, Eliz. m. Snider, John	Apr. 22,	1807	David Coons		3b 57	cr 13
Coons, Henry m. Howe, Mary	Feb. 19,	1789		Hugh Vance		
Coons, Jacob Jr. m. Geiger, Eliz.	Mar. 15,	1800	Jonathan Rust	David Young	2b 56	gc 9 mr 3 *
Coons, Kath. m. Botbick(Castbick)Jas.	June 16,	1789				cr 39
Coons, Mary m. Engle, John	May 19,	1800	Jacob Coons	Hugh Vance	2b 70	cr 34 mr 18 *
Coons, Philip m. Starr(Stow)Christina	May 22,	1812	Frederick Starr	Richard Swift	3b210	gc 12
Coons, Polly m. Hlyard, John	Jan. 30,	1803	Jacob Coons	Rev. Reebenack	2b205	gc 10
Coontz, Abraham m. Lucas, Eliz.	July 7,	1790		David Young		cr 4
Coontz, Samuel m. Perrell, Emily	Dec. 23,	1840	Thomas Perrell	Moses Hoge	6b228	mr 5 *
Cooper, Adam m. Griste(Guste), Ruth	Jan. 27,	1838	Jesse Nesmith	John Light	6b131	mr 72 *
Cooper, Alex. m. Reed, Maria K.	Nov. 21,	1805	David Hunter	R.N.Herndon	3b 3	mr 69 *
Cooper, Ann m. Hall, John	June 4,	1795		John Boyd		mr 10 *
Cooper, Israel m. Proctor(Prather)Ann	Aug. 5,	1831	Nathan Davis	John Light	5b200	cr 33 mr 62 *

Name	Date	Year	(suretor)	(minister)	(bond)	Ref.	mr
Cooper, Jane m. Smith, Thomas C.	Nov. 25,	1819	James Stephenson	John B. Hoge	4b124		mr 31 *
Cooper, Joseph m. Riner, Kitty	July 14,	1814	John Harden		3b299		mr 19 *
Cooper, Margaret m. Stanford, John	Sept 4,	1800	John Crasmuck	John Reitt(Rutt)	2b 85	cr 35	
Cooper, Mary m. McDade, Daniel	Sept 4,	1797	Richard Ransom		1b 37		
Cooper, Merry m. Lewis, John	Dec. 27,	1803	Jonathan Gerrard		2b218		
Cooper, Marg't Mrs. m. Mellon, Patrk	Feb. 22,	1823	Geo. McLaughlin		4b234		
Cooper, Robert m. Crook, Mary	Mar. 22,	1803	Jacob Crook	David Young	2b198	gc 10	mr 8 **
Cooper, Thomas m. Hamell, Mary	Nov. 24,	1793		Edward Tiffin		cr 9	mr 8 *
Coover, Gideon m. Downes, Jean	Mar. 14,	1798	Wm. Downes		1b 90		
Copas, Eliz. m. Dellon, William	Apr. 15,	1790		Moses Hoge		cr 4	mr 5 *
Copas, Mary m. Satterfield, James	Sept 8,	1793		William Hill		cr 30	mr 10 *
Copas, Robert m. Crook, Mary	Mar. 22,	1803	Jacob Crook	David Young	2b198	gc 10	
Copelan, Sarah(Sally) m. Shrode,David	Mar. 4,	1813	William Copelan	Rev. Reebenack	3b254	gc 13	
Copelan, Wm. m. Snyder, Sarah	Mar. 4,	1813	David Shrode	Rev. Reebenack	3b254	gc 13	
*Copeland, Nancy m. Fry, Jacob	Feb. 11,	1790		Hugh Vance			mr 38 **
Copeland, Phebe m. Paskell, Jerry	Apr. 15,	1796		David Young		gc 5	
Copeland, Sally m. Midanda, Francis	Apr. 28,	1806	Phebe Copeland		3b 17		
Copenhaver, Cath. m. Shuh, Jacob	Nov. 12,	1798	Charles Myers	David Young	1b146	gc 8	
Copenhaver, Eliz. m. Kerns, Cyrus	Apr. 29,	1852	Wm. M. Kiser	David Thomas	7b254		mr 86 **
Copenhaver, Eliz. m. Welshans, Henry	Jan. 4,	1801	Daniel Welshans		2b114		
Coplan, Jacob m. Foster, Mary	Sept 23,	1799	George Lemon		2b 27		
Coplin, James m. Potts, Nelly	July 18,	1801	John Potts	Richard Swift	2b131	cr 31	mr 20 *
Coplin, Mary m. Sergeant, Nathan	Feb. 25,	1788		Moses Hoge		cr 20	mr 35 *
Coply, John m. Dally, Abia	Apr. 15,	1789		Hugh Vance		cr 24	mr 3 *
Corbin, Sarah m. Boyd, John	Feb. 28,	1788		Hugh Vance		cr 29	mr 2 *
Cordeary, John m. Neal, Elis.	Jan. 10,	1800	Basil Williamson	Moses Hoge	2b 47	cr 20	mr 19 *
Core, Christian m. Spirling, Fanny		1789		Hugh Vance			mr 3 *
Cornelius, Jos. W. m. Elliott, Mary	May 26,	1832	Christ'r McAlister	Nathan Young	5b230		mr 64 **
Correll, Martha m. Griffith, Wm.	Feb. 5,	1821	John Light		4b171		
Cosgrove, Patrick m. Morgan, Martha	Dec. 16,	1844	Mathias Kyne		7b 15		
Cosley, Wm. m. Kitchen, Hannah	Apr. 20,	1833	Harrison Waite		5b267		
Cotter, John m. Starkley, Cath.	Nov. 17,	1796					
Cou, Christian m. Spirling, Fanny	Mar. 31,	1789		J.M.Brown		gc 6	mr 67 *
Couchman, Ann E. m. Small, Wm. C.	Feb. 25,	1851	John Couchman	David Young	7b215	cr 20	mr 3 *
Couchman, Benj. m. Small, Mary Ellen	Dec. 22,	1847	John C. Small	B.M.Schmucker	7b117		mr 84 *
Couchman, Cath. m. Motter, John		1795					
Couchman, Cornelius m. Dubble, Sarah	May 11,	1840	John Waite	David Young	6b208	gc 4	mr 71 *
Couchman, Corn's m. Pitzer, Mary A.C.	May 26,	1832	Martin Pitzer	P. Harrison	5b251		mr 65 *
Couchman, Eliz. m. Riner, Henry	Dec. 27,	1836	Henry J.Couchman	Wm. Monroe	6b 78		
Couchman, Eliz. m. Hageman, Marenes	Apr. 19,	1844	Henry Couchman		6b315		
Couchman, Geo. m.Chenoweth, Lavina	Mar. 4,	1829	Samuel Chenoweth		5b120		
Couchman, Geo. m. Rush, Susan	May 8,	1832	Jacob Rush	Jacob Medtart	5b229		mr 64 *
Couchman, Geo. m. Strayer, Susanna	Oct. 17,	1827	John Davis	David Young	1b 55	gc 7	
*Copeland, Jacob m. Beller, Mary E.	Sept 16,	1852		David Thomas			mr 86 *

Name	(marriage)	(suretor)	(minister)	(bond)	ref
Couchman, Henry m. Hansell, Mary	June 11, 1801	Laurence Hansell		2b129	
Couchman, Henry J. m. Myers, Sarah A	Mar. 25, 1840	Henry Myers		6b203	mr 69 **
Couchman, James m. Stip, Eliz.	May 20, 1838	Jas. Hutchinson	Lewis F. Wilson	6b140	mr 63 **
Couchman, John G. m. Myers, Eliz.	Nov. 19, 1831	Henry Myers	Jacob Medtart	5b208	
Couchman, Magdalena m. Thompson, C.	Apr. 30, 1792		David Young		gc 1
Couchman, Mary E. m. McWilliams, Geo.	Sept. 17, 1851	William Rush	Geo. W. Harris	7b232	mr 85 **
Couchman, Michael m. Small, Mary	Dec. 3, 1828	William Small	Jacob Medtart	5b114	mr 63 **
Couchman, Mich'l m. Bowers, Harriet	Dec. 23, 1828	Henry Bowers		5b116	
Couchman, Polly m. Small, Wm.	Mar. 23, 1825	Geo. Couchman	Chas. P. Krauth	5b 5	mr 48 *
Couchman, Rebecca m. Vanaker, Geo.	June 16, 1830	Henry Couchman		5b168	
Couchman, Wm. m. Pitzer, Cath.	Oct. 26, 1842	Jacob Pitzer	Lewis F. Wilson	6b282	mr 73 **
Couglan, Timothy m. Mahony, Joanna	Oct. 22, 1850		Joseph Plunkett		mr 84 *
Coulter, John m. Magill, Nelly	Dec. 5, 1806	James Eakin		3b 34	
Coupe, Cath. m. Ray, Nicholas	Mar. 4, 1809	Andrew Shewinder	Rev. Reebeneck	3b127	go 10 *
Courtney, Barbara m. Stinson, Samuel	May 19, 1809	Enoch Mathews		3b109	
Courtney, David m. Kerns, Mary	May 31, 1817	Jacob Kerns		4b 35	
Courtney, Geo. H. m. Norrington, Lany	Oct. 22, 1852	Wm. H. VanDoren	W.N.Scott	7b255	
Courtney, Jacob m. Rowe, Nancy	June 14, 1818	Jacob Murphy		4b 83	
Courtney, Jas. H. m. Norrington, Nancy	Dec. 20, 1851	Jacob VanDoren		7b226	
Courtney, John m. Kerns, Sarah J.	Nov. 7, 1842	Jacob Kerns	Lewis F. Wilson	6b285	?mr 73 *
Courtney, Mary m. Pitzer, Conrad	Jan. 7, 1797	Jas. Robinson		1b 60	
Courtney, Michael m. Bowden, Maria	Jan. 20, 1820	Samuel Bowden		4b129	
Courtney, Michael m. Shepherd, Cath.	Mar. 6, 1836	Henry Swisher		6b 70	
?Cove, Christian m. Spirling, Fanny	Mar. 31, 1789			3b139	cr 20; mr 3 *
Covenhaver, Joseph m. Morlatt, Mary	Aug. 3, 1810	Josiah Varmetre	Hugh Vance		
Covenhaver, Lydia m. Prather, Richard	Feb. 26, 1782		Hugh Vance	2b196	cr 9; mr 1 **
Covenhaver, Lydia m. Varmetre, Josiah	Oct. 17, 1803	Wm. Covenhaver	David Young	1b 56	ge 10 *
Covenhaver, Nancy m. Begole, John	Dec. 23, 1797	Wm. Covenhaver		1b 73	
Covert, John m. Yates, Eliz.	Sept. 8, 1797	Peter Morlatt			
Covey, Mary m. Nnef(Naff), George	Apr. 3, 1789				cr 40; mr 4 *
Cowan, David m. Carothers, Sarah	Nov. 17, 1791	Francis Dutton	Hugh Vance	4b197	cr 7; mr 6 *
Cowarden, James m. Dutton, Susan	Dec. 12, 1821	Colbert Anderson	Moses Hoge	5b 85	mr 44 **
Cownover, Benj. m. Anderson, Eliz.	Dec. 24, 1827	Jacob Cox	George Frye	2b105	mr 52 **
Cox, Ann m. Eaty (Athea), Elisha	June 13, 1800		Benedict Reynolds		cr 38; mr 20 **
Cox, Anna m. Love, John	Dec. 4, 1793	William Cox	Moses Hoge		cr 9; mr 8 *
Cox, Anna m. Forens(Fon-), Samuel	Oct. 5, 1784	Ellis Chapman	Edward Tiffin		mr 32 *
Cox, Cath. m. Cole, George	Oct. 4, 1799	John Groves	Hugh Vance	2b 29	cr 34; mr 16 *
Cox, Elis. m. Chapman, Abraham	Dec. 6, 1797		Richard Swift	1b 69	
Cox, Eliz. m. Miles, Jacob	Apr. 12, 1813			3b258	
Cox, Frances E. m. Wandling, Geo. I.	May 31, 1847	James Cox	James Chisholm	7b 97	mr 78 *
Cox, Henry m. Miles, Mary	Dec. 25, 1832	John Floyd	William Hawk	5b251	mr 65 *
Cox, Horace m. Lefevre, Nancy	Oct. 18, 1838	Daniel Lefevre	Lewis F. Wilson	6b147	mr 69 **
Cox, Isaac m. Prather, Eliz.	Sept. 16, 1790		Moses Hoge		cr 5; mr 5 *

Name	(marriage)	(suretor)	(minister)	(bond)		
Cox, Jacob m. Ropp, Elis.	Oct. 6, 1824	Solomon Ropp	J.L.Bromwell	4b274		mr 47 *
Cox, James m. Robinson, Susan	Dec. 22, 1819	James Robinson		4b127		
Cox, John m. Grove, Elis.	Mar. 13, 1804	Elijah Miles		2b227		
Cox, John J. m. Morgan, Margaret	May 20, 1835	Henry Miller	John Light	6b 44		mr 67 *
Cox, Lena m. Downs, Theophilus	Sept 18, 1809	Elisha Athy	John Mathews	3b119		mr 40 *
Cox, Mary m. Horner, John	May 31, 1820	Abraham Cox	W.N.Scott	4b150		mr 41 *
Cox, Samuel m. Croney, Sarah	Feb. 13, 1841	Harrison Waite		6b232		
Cox, Samuel m. Putman, Cath.	Jan. 16, 1816					mr 26 *
Cox, Samuel m. Ward, Hannah	Feb. 7, 1833	William Ward	Mathias Riser	5b256		mr 67 *
Cox, Thomas m. Mercer, Margaret	Oct. 25, 1786					mr 43 *
?Cox, William m. Williams, Elis.	Mar. 9, 1799	John Williams	John Light	1b172		
?Cox, William m. Williams, Elis.	Dec. 26, 1800	John Williams	Hugh Vance	2b 44	cr 34	mr 18 *
Coyle, James m. Howard, Elis.	May 22, 1797	James Powell	Richard Swift	1b 18		mr 56 *
Coyle, John m. Powell, Cath.	Apr. 13, 1818	William Coyle		4b 68		
Coyle, Mary m. Moore, Peter	Sept 28, 1797	Peter Shaffer	Nathan Young	1b 49		mr 56 *
Crabb, Isaac m. Hdr, Rachel	Apr. 6, 1810	John Strother		3b145		
Crabb, Jacob m. Swan(Givan), Hannah	Aug. 12, 1819	Edward Crabb	Nathan Young	4b112		
Crabb, John m. Talman, Hannah	Sept 23, 1800	John Porter		2b 89		
Crabb, Mary m. Hicke, James	June 8, 1807			3b 50		
Crabb, Mary m. Nolan, William	Dec. 24, 1851	John P. Walters	David Thomas	7b240		mr 85 *
Crabb, Nancy m. Gossett, John	Mar. 9, 1812	Peter Shaffer	Rev. Reebenack	3b215		
Crabb, Nancy m. Hess, Peter Jr.	Nov. 21, 1837	Peter Hess Sr.		6b125	go 12	
Crabb, Phebe m. Roe, James	Dec. 19, 1810	Isaac Crabb		3b168		
Crabb, Priscilla m. Shockey, John	1789		D. Thomas			mr 37 *
Crabb, Wm. m. Collins, Harriet	Apr. 10, 1847	Joseph Collins	Jas. H. Jennings	7b 94		mr 82 *
Craghill, Harry m. Hannah, Margaret	Sept 21, 1792	Benj. Harrison	David Young		go 2	
Craghill, Julia m. Wilkinson, Beverly	Mar. 31, 1824	William Maxwell	Chas. P. Krauth	4b260		mr 47 *
Craghill, Wm. m. Griffith, Mary	Jan. 23, 1815	Teter Myers Jr.		3b309		
Craglo, Catherine m. Baser, Joseph	Feb. 24, 1816	Jacob Seibert		3b356		
Craglo, George m. Seibert, Peggy	Mar. 4, 1814	Maxwell Welsh	Rev. Reebenack	3b286	go 14	
Craglow, George m. Welsh, Marg't Ann	Feb. 10, 1845	William Pitzer	Lewis F. Wilson	7b 26		
Craglow, Peter m. Ladgner, Elis.	Sept 28, 1818		W.N.Scott	4b 80		
Cram, Samuel m. Roberts, Mary	Aug. 23, 1787		Hugh Vance			mr 1 *
Cramer, John m. Richardson, Micka Ann	Sept 2, 1812	Joseph Richardson		3b235	cr 18	
Crason, Mary m. Gooden, Patrick	Mar. 21, 1782		Daniel Sturges			mr 42 *
Crass, Margaret m. Moore, Charles	Sept 19, 1795		Richard Swift		cr 26	mr 10 *
Crawford, Augustine m. Paine, Elis.	Dec. 8, 1854		L.M.Callaway			
Crawford, Elis. m. Lockery, Charles	Sept 4, 1786		Hugh Vance			mr 43 *
Crawford, James m. Godman, Elis.	June 17, 1813	Thomas Crawford		3b265		
Crawford, Matilda m. Firth, Wm.	Aug. 12, 1826	Thomas Crawford		5b 47		
Crawford, Thomas m. Beeson, Rebecca	Aug. 13, 1808	Moses Collins	Lewis Mayer	3b 94	cr 16	mr 23 *
Cray, Samuel m. Douglas, Rebecca	Apr. 13, 1793		Moses Hoge		cr 21	mr 7 *
Crayson, Annie m. Barnett, Jonathan	Sept 29, 1787		Hugh Vance		cr 23	mr 3 *

Names		(marriage)	(suretor)	(minister)	(bond)		
Creamer, Benjamin m. Klice, Sally	Dec. 3,	Dec. 4, 1817	Jacob Klice	Nathan Young	4b 50		mr 56 *
Creamer, Charlotte m. Barnes, Henry	Nov. 4,	1806	George Creamer		3b 35		*
Creamer, George m. Moore, Eliz.	Dec. 24,	Dec. 27, 1810	Johnson Moore	Rev. Reebenack	3b169	gc 11	mr 12 *
Creamer, Jacob m. Allen, Ruth	Mar. 3,	1800	William Allen		2b 55	cr 11	
Creamer, Mary m. Keith, Walter		May 5, 1796					
Creamer, Polly m. Pitzer, Michael	Sept 3,	1810	George Creamer	John Boyd	3b160		mr 12 *
Credons, Eliz. m. Snider, John		1807?					
Creighton, Dianna m. Anderson, James	Dec. 27,	Apr. 22, 1807	Wm. M. Sterret	John Mathews	1b157	cr 13	mr 23 *
Creighton, Isabel m. Lyle, Hugh		Dec. 27, 1798		John Boyd		cr 37	mr 16 *
Creighton, Margaret m. Hard, John		Dec. 23, 1784		Hugh Vance			mr 32 *
Creighton, Polly m. Sterret(Stin),Wm	Feb. 14,	Apr. 17, 1793	Wm. Creighton	Moses Hoge	1b167	cr 21	mr 7 *
Creighton, m. Basswick, Susan		Feb. 14, 1799		John Boyd		cr 34	mr 16 *
Crem, John m. Cage, Eliz.		June 26, 1788		Hugh Vance			mr 35 *
Crem, Mary m. Wolford, Martin	Apr. 3,	Apr. 4, 1819	Andrew Cage	Nathan Young	4b104		mr 56 *
Crem, Rosanna m. Smithy, James	July 31,	Aug. 3, 1815	John Crem	Nathan Young	3b331		mr 55 *
Cresinger, John m. Markle, Mary	Nov. 25,	1828	Philip Seckman		5b113		
Cress, Philip m. Pitzer, Nancy	Sept 22,	1810	Philip Wright		3b161		
Crim, Deborah m. Myers, Abraham	Aug. 8,	1808	Michael Pitzer		3b 93		
Crim, George m. Sencindiver, Cath. C	May 24,	1852	Richard Crim		7b254		
Crim, Harriet m. Coats, Jesse J.	Nov. 13,	1850	Martin Sencindiver		7b202		
Crim, Henry m. Moles, Eliz.	May 12,	May 14, 1846	Abraham Crim	E. L. Dulin	7b 65		mr 77 *
Crim, John P. m. Hetterly, Eliz. B.	Apr. 25,	Apr. 25, 1850	Daniel Moles	Henry Furlong	7b183		mr 81 *
Crim, John S. m. Morrison, Mary	Jan. 12,	Jan. 12, 1854	John Fearls	L. M. Colloway	7b 69		
Crim, John W. m. Sencindiver, Lydia	June 8,	1846	Martin Sencindivr		7b 90		mr 77 *
Crim, Mary m. Custer, Samuel	Mar. 8,	Mar. 11, 1847	John Knipe	Richard F. Brown	4b241		mr 46 *
Crim, Peter m. Lewis, Ann Rebecca	June 9,	June 1823	Jacob Custer	Chas. P. Krauth	7b151		
Crim, Peter m. Shrode, Susannah	Mar. 31,	1849	Solomon Shrode		2b104		
Crim, Polly m. Wolford, Martin	Dec. 22,	1800	John Crim	Nathan Young	3b331		mr 55 *
Crim, Susan m. Smith, John F.	July 31,	1815	John Sencindiver	Chas. P. Krauth	5b 57		mr 51 *
Criswell, Eliz. m. Keesacre, Mathias	Nov. 29,	1826	James Waugh		3b301		
Criswell, Eliz. m. Sellers, Samuel	Aug. 18,	1842	Wm. D. Wilson	John Light	6b264		mr 74 *
Criswell, Elvira m. Robbins, John K.	Feb. 14,	1843	Samuel Hedges	James Chisholm	6b291		mr 75 *
Criswell, James m. McCleary, Marg't	Feb. 27,	1807	Robert Grimes		3b 63		
Criswell, John m. Hedges, Elvina	July 22,	1832	Harrison Waite		5b250		
Criswell, Joseph m. Myers, Louisa	Dec. 24,	1847	Aaron Myers	James Chisholm	7b 85		mr 77 *
Crockwell, Betsy m. Hiett(Hutt),John	Feb. 8,	1799	William Wood	John Potts	2b 14	cr 12	mr 18 *
Croeson, Jacob m. Harris, Susannah	Mar. 3,	1799	James Harrison		2b184		mr 17 *
Croeson, William m. Bellar, Liddy	Aug. 2,	1802	William Green	John Hiett(Hutt)	2b148	cr 38	
Crole, Abraham m. Green, Matty	Dec. 24,	1801	Evan Rees	Richard Swift	2b140	cr 32	mr 20 *
Cromsley, Henry m. Rees, Mary	Nov. 18,	1801	John Lamon				
Cromwell, Edward A. m. Lamon, Rebecca	Aug. 30,	1832	Nicholas Orrick		5b242		
Cromwell, Hannah m. Taylor, Thomas	Oct. 8,	Oct. 9, 1798	Nicholas Orrick	John Boyd	1b136	cr 32	mr 15 *

Name	(marriage)	(suretor)	(minister)	(bond)		
Cromwell, Hugh m. Basore, Cath. Mrs.	Aug. 29, 1800	Robert Filson	John Boyd	2b 83	cr 32	mr 15 *
Cromwell, Ruth m. Mackey, Wm.Jr.	Sept 8, 1798	James Faulkner	John B. Hoge	1b128	cr 14	mr 24 *
Crone, Mary M. m.Palmer, Henry	Oct. 28, 1811	Samuel Cunningham	John Reilly	3b197		mr 70 *
Croney, Charlotte m. Gardner, John S	Dec 26, 1839	Thomas Widdy		6b191		
Croney, Eliz. m. Kinard, William	Aug. 24, 1835	Harrison Waite	J.L.Bromwell	6b 55		mr 47 *
Croney, Margaret m. Ebberts, John	Apr. 16, 1825	Thos. S. Croney		5b 8		
Croney, Maria m. Snyder, Geo.	July 10, 1838	John P. Strayer		6b142		
Croney, Sarah m. Cox, Samuel	Feb. 13, 1841	Harrison Waite		6b232		
Crook, Andrew m. Martin, Mary	Jan. 25, 1793		David Young		go 2	*
Crook, Cath. m. Cloninger, Henry	Dec. 12, 1801	Jacob Crook	David Young	2b152	go 9	*
Crook, John m. Patterson, Ann	Feb. 18, 1794		David Young		go 3	*
Crook, Mary m. Copas(Cooper),Robert	Mar. 22, 1803	Jacob Crook	David Young	2b198	gc 10	*
Crook, Sarah m. McDonald, Cleburg	Oct. 6, 1815	Edward Beeson Jr.		3b342		
Crosen, Mary m. Vance, John	June 16, 1789		Hugh Vance		cr 39	mr 3 *
Cross, Ann B. m. Bruce, James	Sept 6, 1811	Ignatius O'Ferral		3b195		
Cross, Basil m. Seaborn, Mary	Feb. 11, 1800	David Seaborn	Richard Swift	2b 53	cr 34	mr 18 *
Cross, Cath. m. Jett(Sett),Anthony	Apr. 12, 1800	George Boston	John Heitt(Hutt)	2b 64	cr 33	mr 18 *
Cross, Cenea m. Evans, Richard	Mar. 23, 1824	Walter Evans		4b259		
Cross, Easter m. Brather, John	Mar. 17, 1791		Moses Hoge	3b114	cr 6	mr 6 *
Cross, Elenor m. Evans, Walter	June 3, 1809	Basil Cross		4b 81		
Cross, Elinor m. Taylor, Samuel	Sept 30, 1818	Basil Cross				
Cross, Eliz. m. Philes, John	Jan. 14, 1795		Richard Swift	4b174	cr 26	mr 10 *
Cross, James m. McCausland, Fanny	Mar. 5, 1821	John Fertor	Nathan Young	3b 47		mr 57 *
Cross, John m. Comegys, Deborleigh	Feb. 12, 1807	Benj. Comegys			cr 1	mr 2 *
Cross, John m. Hardwick, Eliz.	Jan. 20, 1789					
Cross, Joseph m. Comegys, Nancy	Aug. 3, 1803	Jacob Comegys	Moses Hoge	2b207	cr 26	mr 10 *
Cross, Margaret m. Moore, Chas.	Sept 19, 1795	John Files	Richard Swift	4b275		mr 50 *
Cross, Margaret m. Williamson, Leon'd	Nov. 1, 1824	Basil Cross	John Mathews	1b151	cr 31	mr 15 *
Cross, Mary m. Clasby(Glasby),Robt.	Dec. 6, 1798		Richard Swift			mr 39 *
Cross, Mary A. m. Barnes, Robert	Oct. 12, 1793		Richard Swift			
Cross, Polly Mrs. m. Burdine, Abr'm	July 15, 1811	Isaac Morlatt		3b191		
Cross, Sarah m. Miller, Samuel	Dec. 27, 1837	Conrad Billmire		6b128		
Crothers, Eliz. m. Baysore, Barney	Aug. 20, 1803	Geo. Baysore		2b208		*
Crothers, Henry m. Payne, Eliz.	Dec. 10, 1816	Thomas Payne	John B. Hoge	4b 26		
Crothers, James m. Job, Mary B.	Jan. 15, 1811	William Long		3b172		
Crowl, Cath. m. Keller, Jonas	Aug. 9, 1800	Henry Crowl	David Young	2b 81	gc 9	
Crouse, Cath. m. Shade, Jacob	Feb. 4, 1816		Mathias Riser			
Crouse, Charles m. Milburn, Eliz.	Feb. 18, 1843	Jesse Gain	John Grove	6b290		mr 26 *
Crouse, Christian m. Shockey, Susan	Aug. 23, 1811	John Shockey		3b194		mr 75 *
Crouse, Jacob m. Tyson, Belinda	Jan. 17, 1837	John Waite		6b 94		
Crout, Daniel m. Snider, Eliz.	Apr. 28, 1797	Jacob Snider		1b 13		
Crow, Benj. m. Green, Sarah Ann	Feb. 22, 1825	William Green	Chas. P. Krauth	5b 1		mr 48 *
Crow, Catherine m. Ray, Joseph	Mar. 15, 1830	John Crow		5b158		

Name		(marriage)		(suretor)	(minister)	(bond)	
Crow, David m. Keyes, Mary	Aug. 25,		1845	John Keyes	Chas. P. Krauth	7b 40	mr 48 *
Crow, John Jr. m. Houte, Sarah	Jan. 10,	Jan.	1825	Michael Houte		4b284	
Crow, Sophia m. Ray, William	Aug. 27,		1822	Jacob Crow		4b222	gc 9 *
Crowl, Betsy m. Davis, Nathaniel	Jan. 30,		1828	Ishmael Barnes		5b 89	
Crowl, Cath. m. Keller, John	Aug. 9,	Aug. 10,	1800	Henry Crowl	David Young	2b 81	
Crowl, Cath. m. Stout, Philip	Feb. 17,		1815	Robert Wilson		3b311	
Crowl, Eliza Ann m. Ardinger, James	May 29,		1833	Peter Crowl		5b275	
Crowl, Ellen m. Lemaster, David	Feb. 9,	July 15,	1852	Wm. H.C.Crowl	Nathan Young	7b245	mr 64 *
Crowl, Evelina m. Bryan, Enoch	July 14,		1832	Jacob Crowl		5b234	
Crowl, George m. Myers, Betsy	Aug. 10,		1815	John Myers		3b333	
Crowl, Henry m. Plotner, Sally	Dec. 22,		1809	Manus Plotner		3b129	
Crowl, Isabella m. Jones, Hiram H.	Oct. 10,		1837	Henry Stevens		6b115	gc 10 *
Crowl, Jacob m. Cline, Sophia	July 20,	July 31,	1803	Margaret Cline	David Young	2b206	mr 79 *
Crowl, Jacob m. Daylong, Emily	Feb. 25,	Feb. 16,	1850	Lewis Inbody	Henry Furlong	7b177	mr 68 *
Crowl, Jacob m. Pool(Paol),Mary J.	Sept 22,	Sept 22,	1835	Harrison Waite	John Howell	6b 58	mr 74 *
Crowl, John F. m. Randall, Eliz. B.	Aug. 17,	Aug.	1842	Geo. S. Randall	John Light	6b275	mr 58 *
Crowl, Marg't m. Ambrester(prl.)Jacob	Nov. 30,	Nov. 30,	1822	Jacob Crowl	Nathan Young	4b229	mr 17 *
Crowl, Marg't m. Miller, Joshua	Oct. 28,	Oct. 31,	1799	Thos. Thompson	John Heitt(Hutt)	2b 32	mr 68 *
Crowl, Mary Ann m. Gregory, John	Jan. 17,	Jan. 19,	1835	Jacob A. Crowl	John Howell	6b 28	cr 33
Crowl, Mary Mrs. m. Flemming, Wm.	Dec. 31,		1827	Richard Higgins		5b 86	
Crowl, Sarah m. Elliott, Wm.	May 21,	May	1825	William Cole	Chas. P. Krauth	5b 11	mr 48 *
Crowl, Sarah m. Plotner, Daniel	May 11,		1807	Henry Crowl		3b 58	
Crowl, Susan Ann m. Gregory, Thom. R	Dec. 20,	Dec. 13,	1842	John M. Gregory	Mayberry Goheen	6b286	mr 74 *
Crowl, Susan m. Hensell, Parker H.	July 30,	Dec. 23,	1852	Ebenezer Tally	John Light	7b 39	mr 88 *
Crowl, Thos. J. m. Gregory, Jane	Apr. 10,		1845	Joseph Bain		6b295	
Crowl, William m. Bain, Barbara E.	Feb. 25,		1843	H.M.Chew		7b 59	
Crowl, Wm. m. Chew, Ruth	July 30,	Aug. 2,	1846	Andrew Mc Intire	Wm. Monroe	5b234	mr 65 *
Crown, Belinda m. Syester, Jacob	July 30,		1632	Enud Turner		4b 54	
Crown, Maria Horn m. Barnes, Ishmael	Dec. 29,	Apr. 25,	1817	Daniel Moles	Henry Furlong	7b183	mr 81 *
Crum, Henry m. Moles, Eliz.	Apr. 25,		1850	George Eagle		3b173	
Crum, Lewis m. Eagle, Sally	Feb. 4,	Aug. 3,	1811	John Crim	Nathan Young	3b331	mr 55 *
Crum, Mary m. Wolford, Martin	July 31,		1815	Thomas Crumley		3b112	
Crumley, Eliz. m. Booth, Isaac	Apr. 24,		1809	Morris Rees		3b292	
Crumley, Henry m. Flowers, Eliz.	Apr. 11,		1814	Joel Rees		5b 26	
Crumley, Matilda m. Chew, Morris R.	Nov. 7,	Nov. 4,	1825	Thomas Wright	John Winters	3b274	mr 50 *
Crumley, Rebecca m. Stewart, Wm.	Oct. 28,		1813	Robt. Pinkerton	Rev. Reebenack		gc 13
Crumpton, Elijah m. Pinkerton, Mary	July 31,	Aug. 6,	1799	Ezekiel Crumpton	David Young	2b 13	gc 8
Crumpton, Evelina m. Swisher, Jacob	Jan. 13,	Jan. 16,	1825		Nathan Young	5b285	mr 58 *
Cruson, Eliz. m. Messor, Wm.	Nov. 13,	Nov. 16,	1786		Hugh Vance		mr 43 *
Cudd, Hannah m. Lee, Thomas			1789		D. Thomas		mr 37 *
Cullaber, Patty m. Sipe, Michael	Mar. 9,	May 28,	1794	James Callahan	Edward Tiffin	3b214	cr 25
Culp, Eliz. m. Anderson, John			1812		Hugh Vance		mr 9 *
Cumpston, Thos. m. Cannon, Ann		Oct. 15,	1788		Hugh Vance		mr 35 *

(name / marriage)	(marriage date)	(surety)	(minister)	(bond)		(ref)
Compton, Evelina m. Swisher, Jacob	Jan. 13, 1825	Ezekiel Compton	Nathan Young	4b285		mr 58 *
Cumklin, Jacob m. Yerkey, Mary	Jan. 7, 1796		Moses Hoge		cr 35	mr 11 *
Cunningham, Ann m. McDade, John	Oct. 16, 1781		Daniel Sturges			mr 42 *
Cunningham, Ann m. Stephenson, James	May 17, 1792		David Young		gc 1	
Cunningham, Anna m. Knight, Benj.	Aug. 3, 1819		Mathias Riser			
Cunningham, Dolly m. Robinson, Alex.	Mar. 2, 1824	Wm. Cunningham	Chas. P. Krauth	4b257		mr 30 *
Cunningham, Elinor m. Locke, Jacob L	Oct. 13, 1845	F. M. Cunningham		7b 45		mr 47 *
Cunningham, Ellen m. Dunn, John	Feb. 13, 1843	Patr'k Cunningham		6b289		
Cunningham, Ellen m. Foran(--en)David	Aug. 23, 1822	James O'Donnell	John B. Hoge	4b222		mr 44 *
Cunningham, Geo. H. m. Richards, Jane	Dec. 29, 1813	Levi Cunningham		3b279		
Cunningham, Geo. H. m. Hedges, Angels	May 25, 1833	Josiah Hedges		5b274		
Cunningham, Hugh m. Hedges, Ann W.	Jan. 26, 1829	Henry Myers	W. Monroe	5b117		mr 53 *
Cunningham, Hugh m. Murphy, Eliza	Dec. 24, 1833	William Faris	J.M.Brown	5b297		mr 67 *
Cunningham, James m. Winning, Marg't	Sept 26, 1797	Wm. Cunningham	John Boyd	1b 43	or 32	mr 13 *
Cunningham, Jas. L. m. Kisinger, Susn	Apr. 9, 1832	Jas. S. Orrick	Jas. M. Brown	5b225		mr 64 *
Cunningham, Jas. L. m. Newkirk, Eliz.	Mar. 28, 1837	George Chrisman	Lewis F. Wilson	6b102		mr 47 *
Cunningham, Jane m. Britton, Wm.	July 31, 1809	Anthony Jett	Rev. Reebenack	3b115	gc 10	
Cunningham, John m. Kisinger, Cath.	Dec. 4, 1824	Alex. Robinson	Chas. P. Krauth	4b279		
Cunningham, John m. Pendleton, Eliz.	Dec. 22, 1800	Wm. Pendleton		2b102		
Cunningham, John m. Robinson, Hannah	Sept 17, 1795		John Boyd	7b 98	cr 33	mr 11 *
Cunningham, John P. m. Rogers, Hester	June 8, 1847	Ephraim Haslett	P. Lipscomb	5b155		mr 81 *
Cunningham, Kitty m. Tabb, Edw. F.	Mar. 8, 1830	Wm. Cunningham	Jas. M. Brown	3b355		mr 54 *
Cunningham, Levi m. Haslett, Ailse	Feb. 20, 1816	John Haslett		7b113		
Cunningham, Lydia m. Beeson, Lewis R	Nov. 18, 1847	Robt. Cunningham	Richard T. Brown	3b103		mr 79 *
Cunningham, Lydia m. Roberts, Boyd	Dec. 12, 1808	Levi Cunningham		3b 86		
Cunningham, Mary m. Shields, David	Apr. 20, 1808	Wm. Cunningham	John Mathews	5b176	cr 17	mr 23 *
Cunningham, Mary D. m. Payne, John	Oct. 14, 1830	Wm. Cunningham	John Allemong	2b184	cr 17	mr 54 *
Cunningham, Nancy m. Roberts, Daniel	Dec. 8, 1802	Wm. Cunningham	Moses Hoge	3b 5		mr 21 *
Cunningham, Rhody m. Brown, Jesse	Dec. 21, 1805	Geo. Cunningham		1b120	gc 7	
Cunningham, Robt. m. Winning, Agnes	June 25, 1798	Jas. Cunningham	David Young	2b246	cr 11	mr 74 *
Cunningham, Rosanna m. Duffield, Wm.	Oct. 22, 1804	Wm. Cunningham		oo309	cr 21	mr 12 *
Cunningham, Sam. O.m. Light, Mary A.	Dec. 1, 1843	Jas. Cunningham	John Light			mr 7 *
Cunningham, Saml. m. Shields, Charity			John Boyd			
Cunningham, Sarah m. Harper, Saml.	Apr. 17, 1793		Moses Hoge		cr 17	mr 70 *
Cunningham, Sarah E. m. Hammond,Allen	Nov. 24, 1838	John W. Waite	Lewis F. Wilson	6b152		mr 53 *
Cunningham, Wm.Hugh m. Hedges, Ann W.	Jan. 26, 1829	Henry Myers	William Monroe	5b117		mr 22 *
Cunningham, Wm. m. Long, Nancy	Dec. 24, 1805	Charles Orrick	Moses Hoge	3b 6		mr 71 *
Cunningham, Wm. m. Oden, Martha	Oct. 15, 1840	George Tabb	Lewis F. Wilson	6b221	cr 17	
Cunningham, Wm. m. Payne, Mary P.	Aug. 10, 1844	Samuel D. Rees		7b 5		
Cunningham, Wm. C. m. Newkirk, Margt	Oct. 29, 1847	Archibald Oden	Lewis F. Wilson	7b111		mr 82 *
Cunningham, Nancy m. Roberts, David	Dec. 4, 1802	William Cunningham	Moses Hoge	2b184	cr 17	mr 21 *
Cuny, Eliz. m. Boughhough, John	Apr. 1804	Jas. McLaughlin		2b232		
Curder, Geo. m. Davis, Tabitha	Jan. 13, 1791					
*Cunningham, Jas. L. m.Rhinestine,Eiz	Mar. 24, 1837	George Chrisman	Moses Hoge	6b102	cr 5	mr 6 *

Name	(marriage)	(surtor)	(minister)	(bond)		
*Current, Sarah m. James (Ga-)Absalom	Dec. 28, 1793		William Hill	2b 96	cr 30	mr 10 *
Current, Susan m. James (Ga-)Absalom	Dec. 28, 1793		William Hill	3b 55	cr 30	mr 10 *
Curry, John m. Shulton, Eliz.	July 31, 1795		John Boyd	6b252	cr 33	mr 11 *
Curry, Margt m. Stanford, Wm.	Nov. 7, 1800	John Curry				
Curtis, David m. Hedges, Eliz.	Apr. 14, 1807	Solomon Hedges	Peyton Harrison			
Curtis, Dorothy m. Cleary(Clar-)Paul	Nov. 13, 1842	Thos. S. Harden	Hugh Vance		cr 20	mr 73 *
Curtis, Edward m. Sharp(Shoas) Jane	May 1, 1789					mr 3 *
Curtis, Elenor m. Hutcheson, Nathan	Mar. 17, 1832	John Shober	Lewis F. Wilson	5b220		mr 73 *
Curtis, Eliz. m. Wandle, John	Nov. 17, 1842	John Burke	Nathan Young	6b253		mr 55 *
Curtis, Hannah m. Anderson, Prov'ce	Dec. 21, 1815	Peter Curtis	Lewis F. Wilson	3b351		mr 71 *
Curtis, Isaiah m.Seaman, Nancy D.	Mar. 18, 1840	Richard D. Seaman	Jas. M. Brown	6b201		mr 53 *
Curtis, Jacob m. Chenoweth, Harriet	Mar. 1E, 1929	Philip Chenoweth	W.N.Scott	5b124		mr 41 *
Curtis, Jacob m. Holly, Mary	Aug. 26, 1820	Jacob Shimp	Jas. M. Brown	4b158		mr 48 *
Curtis, James m. Conoway, Mary	Apr. 10, 1825	Isaac Thomas	Jas. M. Brown	5b 7		
Curtis, Jane m. Stewart, John	Apr. 22, 1844	Abner Mendenhall	Lewis F. Wilson	6b320		
Curtis, Jonathan m. Blue, Lotta	Sept 19, 1807	Jacob Gorrell		3b 70		
Curtis, Margt m. Pitzer, Conrad	Dec. 12, 1797		David Young	1b 98	gc 7	*
Curtis, Mary m. Bailiff, John	Apr. 11, 1798	Seth Curtis		7b131		mr 81 *
Curtis, Mary m. Daily(Dogley), John	June 12, 1848	Jacob VanDoren	P. Lipscomb		gc 14	mr 57 *
Curtis, Nancy m. Daily, John	Mar. 23, 1814	David Curtis	Rev. Reebenack	4b134		mr 48 *
Curtis, Pegy m. Greenwell. John	Feb. 11, 1820	Jacob Walter	Nathan Young	3b284		mr 29 *
Curtis, Rhuanna m. Thompson,Bennett	Feb. 10, 1814	David Curtis		5b 7		
Curtis, Wm. m. Billmyre, Cath.	Apr. 7, 1825	Jacob Billmyre	Chas. P. Krauth	4b 91		mr 58 *
Curtz, Jacob m. Rockwell, Nancy	Dec. 7, 1818	Jesse Rockwell	Mathias Riser	6b276		mr 54 *
Cushong, John W. m. Keyes, Mary Ann	Sept 1, 1842	James McSherry				mr 64 *
Cushman, Marg.m.Starry(Stang)Nich's	June 26, 1823	John Cashman(Cu-)	Nathan Young	6b 96		mr 46 *
Cushwa, Barnett m. Gehr, Cath.	Feb. 13, 1837	Daniel Gehr	Lewis F. Wilson	5b154		
Cushwa, Cath. m. Middlekauf, John	Mar. 8, 1830	David M. Cushwa	Jas. M. Brown	5b215		mr 51 *
Cushwa, David W. m. Noll, Mary	Jan. 30, 1832	George Noll	Jas. M. Brown	6b 39		
Cushwa, John D. m. Seibert, Susan	Mar. 30, 1835	Michael Seibert		4b236		
Cushwa, Marg't m. Emert, George	Mar. 27, 1823	?	Chas. P. Krauth	6b161		
Cushwa, Mary m. Kilmer, Eli	Mar. 5, 1839	John M. Small		5b 37		
Cushwa, Mary m. Small, Jacob A.	Mar. 14, 1826	John Strother	Chas. P. Krauth	6b267		
Cushwa, Wm. A. m. Staner, Eliz.	Mar. 21, 1842	William Seibert				
Cusick, Eliz. m. Pool, Henry	Jan. 20, 1795		Richard Swift		cr 26	mr 10 *
Custard, Elenor m. Bunner, Daniel	Feb. 2, 1817		Mathias Riser			
Custard, Hannah m. Holiday, Colbert	Aug. 10, 1830	Chas. B. Custard	Nathan Young	5b172		mr 61 *
Custer, Catherine m. Custer, Chas.	July 22, 1830	Hiram Merchant		5b169		
Custer, Cath. m. Grubb, John Madison	Aug. 30, 1848	Jonathan Custer		7b135		
Custer, Cath. E. m. Kines, Samuel	Jan. 24, 1820	Peter Custer	Nathan Young	4b131		mr 56 *
Custer, Chas. M. m. Custer, Cath.	July 22, 1830	Hiram Merchant		5b169		
Custer, Hannah m. Anderson, Prov'ce	Dec. 19, 1815	Peter Custer	Nathan Young	3b351		mr 55 *
Custer, Isaiah m. Salehamer, Eliz.	June 2, 1825	George Knup	Nathan Young	5b 13		mr 49 *
*Current, Eliza m. Bramhall, John	Feb. 24, 1798	John Current	B. Reynolds	1b 87		

Name	Date	(marriage)	(suretor)	(minister)	(bond)		
*Custer, Jacob m. Lewis, Catherine	Dec. 9,	Dec. 12, 1833	Lewis Lewis	W. Hawk	5b293	gc 3	mr 65 *
Custer, James m. Bardness, Mary		Oct. 27, 1793		David Young			*
Custer, John m. Collis, Lucy	Sept 13,	Sept 14, 1850		D.P.Bragunier	7b195		mr 80 *
Custer, Marg't m. Baker, Ferdifor	Aug. 9,	1808	Jonathan Custer		3b 93		
Custer, Mark m. Kimble, Mary	Oct. 8,	1810	Peter Custer		3b163		
Custer, Mary m. Seckman, Charles	Mar. 15,	1830	Richard Morrison		5b158		
Custer, Mary Mrs. m. Freshour, Geo.	Jan. 23,	1826	Benjamin Custer		5b 33		
Custer, Peter m. Fletcher, Eliz.	Oct. 19,	Oct. 19, 1848	Daniel Lemaster	Richard T. Brown	7b137		mr 79 *
Custer, Peter m. Lewis, Matilda	Dec. 8,	1846	John M. Grubb		7b 79		
Custer, Rachel m. Grubbs, Nathaniel	June 26,	1843	Lewis Lewis		6b301		
Custer, Reuben C. m. Bane, Ann Elis.	Feb. 5,	1848?	Colbert Holiday	J.H.Waugh	7b122		mr 78 *
Custer, Samuel m. Crim, Mary	June 9,	?	Charles Bane	Chas. F. Krauth	4b241		mr 46 *
Cutting, Nathaniel m. Wilson, Marg't	Jan. 8,	Jan. 7, 1851	John Knipe	B.M.Schmucker	7b210		mr 84 *
Otwaltz, Jacob m. Butt, Ellen		1839	William Wilson		6b169		mr 49 *
*Custer, Isaiah m. G.Williams, Elis.	May 18,	June 5, 1825	Nathan Hutchinson	Benedict Reynolds			

"D"

Name	Date	(marriage)	(suretor)	(minister)	(bond)		
Dabldeck, Mary m. Kiger, Henry	Jan. 10,	1804	John Smith		2b219		mr 74 *
Dack, Peter m. Armbrester, Marcelina	Feb. 20,	Feb. 23, 1843	Michael Armbrester	Lewis F. Wilson	6b290	cr 20	mr 3 *
Daily, Abia m. Copely(Cofry), John	Apr. 15,	1789					*
Daily, Daniel M. m. Steen, Mary	Aug. 9,	1849	John Gilbert	Hugh Vance	7b162		*
Daily, Eliz. m. Kearfott, Levi H.	Jan. 7,	1854		Geo. W. Harris			mr 88 *
Daily, Eliz. m. McDonald, Gerrard	Nov. 5,	Nov. 6, 1814	Robert Grimes	Rev. Reebenack	3b307	gc 14	*
Daily, James H.C. m. Gardner, Lizzie		Oct. 20, 1853		R.A.Fink			*
Daily, John m. Curtis, Nancy	Mar. 23,	Mar. 24, 1814	David Curtis	Rev. Reebenack	3b289	gc 14	mr 81 *
Daily, John m. Curtis, Mary	June 12,	June 13, 1848	Jacob VanDoren	P. Lipscomb	7b131		mr 57 *
Daily, John L. m. Booth, Rebecca	Nov. 8,	Nov. 8, 1820	Thomas Butler	Nathan Young	4b166		
Daily, John W. m. McQuilkin, Sarah	Feb. 3,	1851	Jacob Williamson		7b213		
Daily, Levi m. Thomas, Eliz.	Jan. 23,	1843	Jacob Thomas	Mayberry Goheen	6b288		mr 74 *
Daily, Marg't m. Swearingen, James	July 12,	1841	Benjamin Daily	John Hedges	6b243		mr 73 *
Daily, Rachel m. Faris, Henry Clay	Dec. 20,	1845	John Daily	J.S.Reynoldson	7b 50		mr 76 *
Daily, Sarah Ann m. Byers, Wm. H.	Mar. 11,	1846	John Daily	J.S.Reynoldson	7b 61		mr 76 *
Dandridge, Adam S. m. Pendleton,Sarah	Jan. 1,	1805	Philip C. Wilson		2b250	cr 17	mr 22 *
Dandridge, Ann m. Hunter, Moses	Apr. 26,	1787		Hugh Vance			mr 44 *
Daniel, Andrew m. Daniel, Hester E.	Feb. 28,	Feb. 28, 1833	Robert Daniel	Jas. M. Brown	5b258		mr 67 *
Daniel, Annabel m. Daniel, John H.	Dec. 2,	1835	William Daniel		6b 65		
Daniel, Eliz. m. Miller, David	Mar. 20,	1800	William Seaman		2b 58		
Daniel, Hester E. m. Daniel, Andrew	Feb. 27,	Feb. 28, 1833	Robert Daniel	Jas. M. Brown	5b258		mr 67 *
Daniel, James m. Chew, Mary	Oct. 6,	1804	Hugh Davidson		2b244		
Daniel, John m. Baldwin, Polly	July 8,	1804	David Baldwin		2b242		

Name	(marriage)	(suretor)	(minister)	(bond)	ref
Daniel, John H. m. Daniel, Annabella	Dec. 2, 1835	William Daniel		6b 65	
Daniel, Joseph H. m. Shaffer, Maria	June 13, 1837	George Shaffer		6b108	
Daniel, Lavina m. Sanks, Joshua	Jan. 28, 1812	Morgan Morgan		3b209	
Daniel, Robert m. Miller, Eliz.	Nov. 18, 1809	William Miller		3b124	
Daniel, Robert Jr. m. Houseworth, Eliz.	June 22, 1822	Isaac Houseworth		4b217	*
Daniel, Sarah m. Lyle, Robt. Glenn	May 31, 1853		John O. Proctor	3b206	
Daniel, Susan m. Chamberlein, Joseph	Dec. 30, 1811	Ellis Rees		3b 49	
Daniel, Susannah m. Rees, David	Mar. 4, 1807	John Dandel		6b243	
Darby(-by), Marg. m. Swearingen, James	July 12, 1841	Benj. Dalley	John Hedges	3b151	mr 73 *
Dare, Henry m. McKewan, Cath.	May 15, 1810	Lewis B. Willis			
Darke, Eliz. m. Holliday, James	Feb. 12, 1793		William Hill		cr 30; mr 10 *
Darke, John m. Baker, Eliz.	Dec. 21, 1789		Moses Hoge		cr 2; mr 3 *
Darke, Mary m. Kain, John	Feb. 28, 1797		Richard Swift		cr 12; mr 14 *
Darke, Mary m. Rutherford, Thomas	Nov. 30, 1792		Christian Streit		cr 15; mr 7 *
Darke, Nancy m. Welsh, Samuel I.	Mar. 29, 1798	Edward Bennett	Richard Swift	1b 93	cr 31; mr 15 *
Darke, Peter m. Ambrester, Marcelina	Feb. 23, 1843		Lewis F. Wilson		mr 74 *
Darke, Rebecca m. McCollough, Jos.	Apr. 2, 1789		Hugh Vance		cr 20; mr 3 *
Darky, Marg. m. Swearingen, Jas. H.	July 15, 1841	Benjamin Dalley	John Hedges	6b243	mr 73 *
Darnhafer, John m. Springle, Eliz.	July 12,	Casper Walper		2b 17	
Darr, Catherine m. Hugh, Joseph	Aug. 6, 1799	John Merritt		1b147	
Darr, Susannah m. Alt, William	Nov. 19, 1798	John Rusler		2b 76	
Darriel, Polly m. Hiatt, William	July 29, 1800	Samuel Darriel		2b 45	
Darriel, Samuel m. McDaniel, Eliz.	Dec. 27, 1799	Wm. McDaniel		2b 49	
Darriel, William m. Ellis, Rebecca	Aug. 4, 1800	George Bediger		2b 79	
Daugh, Michael m. Price, Mary	1789	William Iles	David Thomas	1b 94	mr 37 *
Daugherty, Eliz. m. Fry, Michael	Feb. 12, 1798	Abraham Varmetre		6b212	
Daugherty, Geo. m. Varmetre, Ann E.	June 8, 1840	John Daugherty Sr	Rev. Reebenack	3b207	
Daugherty, John m. Ward, Esther	Jan. 4, 1812	John Heining		6b220	gc 12 *
Daugherty, Rich'd m. Heining, Charlot	Oct. 3, 1840		Edward Tiffin		cr 38; mr 1 *
Davenport, Anthony m. Basil, Mary	Mar. 21, 1785	Jas. Swearingen		5b174	
Davenport, Braxton m. Bedinger, Eliz.	Aug. 31, 1830	Hezekiah Young		1b 82	
Davenport, Elenor m. Magruder, Daniel	Jan. 24, 1798	Norman Miller		7b 20	
Davenport, Jacob V. m. Locke, Rose	Jan. 8, 1845		James Chisholm		mr 76 *
Davenport, Kath. m. Orrick, Charles	Jan. 2, 1787	George Harris	Hugh Vance	1b146	mr 43 *
Davenport, Mary m. Chenoweth, John	Nov. 14, 1798		Richard Swift		cr 31; mr 15 *
Davenport, Samuel m. Cook, Lucy	Dec. 23, 1788		Hugh Vance		mr 36 *
Davenport, Susan m. Winning, James	Mar. 16, 1792		David Young		
David, Marg. m. Cleamons, Leonard	Nov. 30, 1809	Bastion Poisal		3b126	gc 1 *
Davidson, Ann m. Boothe, Caleb	Nov. 29, 1799	Richard Davidson	Rev. Reebenack	2b 25	gc 10; *
Davidson, Ann m. Sugar, Benjamin	Sept 4, 1790				
Davidson, John m. Arm(Ann), Mary	Feb. 4, 1795		Hugh Vance		mr 38 *
Davidson, Mary m. Wilson, Wm.	Mar. 3, 1820		David Young	4b155	gc 4 *
Davidson, Rees m. Lewis, Ann	July 27, 1797	Philip Hunter	John B. Hoge	1b 39	mr 41 *
Davies, Ephraim m. Oliver, Agnes	Sept 5, 1789	Thomas Lewis	Hugh Vance		mr 38 *

Name	(marriage)	(suretor)	(minister)	(bond)	
Davis, Ann m. Early, James	May 11, 1825	James Day		5b 10	
Davis, Ann m. Middleton, John	Mar. 26, 1821	Bethnel Middleton		4b178	
Davis, Ann m. Watts, Samuel	Aug. 20, 1816	Wm. Davis Jr.	W.N.Scott	4b 6	mr 6 *
Davis, Ann A. m. Kilmer, William	Jan. 15, 1842	William Wolford		6b261	
Davis, Ann E. m. Howard, Samuel S.	Jan. 29, 1849	Joseph Davis		7b145	
Davis, Benj. m. Miller, Mary Jane	June 16, 1835	Thomas Miller		6b 47	
Davis, Benj. m. Morlatt, Elinor	Mar. 30, 1818	Peter Morlatt	W.N.Scott	4b 67	*
Davis, Cath. m. Dutton, Francis	Sept 9, 1823	Edward Littlejohn		4b248	
Davis, Cath. m. Shaffer, John	July 24, 1821	Daniel Shaffer		4b186	
Davis, Christena m. Chambers, Jas.	H.Feb. 23, 1837	Anthony Chambers		6b 99	
Davis, Daniel m. Cline, Marg't	Aug. 10, 1804	John Shober		2b239	
Davis, David m. Kearns, Cath.	Jan. 25, 1810	Michael Kearns	Rev. Reebenack	3b135	gc 11 *
Davis, Drusilla m. Grove, George	June 6, 1798	Joseph Davis	David Young	1b113	gc 7 *
Davis, Eliz. m. Gilland, Daniel	Sept 23, 1797	Edmond Champion	David Young	1b 45	gc 7 *
Davis, Eliz. m. Kyser, Joseph	Feb. 8, 1827	Thomas Davis	Nathan Young	5b 61	mr 59 *
Davis, Eliz. m. Rippy(--sy), Joseph	Sept 1, 1798	David Gerrard	Moses Hoge	1b127	cr 29 mr 14 *
Davis, George m. Fearman, Kleanor	Dec. 14, 1841	Henry Fearman		6b258	
Davis, Henry m. Wilson, Hannah	Aug. 23, 1798		David Young	5b 77	gc 7 *
Davis, Ignatius m. Briscoe, Fanny	Jan. 30, 1781		Daniel Sturges	6b 88	gc 7
Davis, Jacob m. Goucher, Jane	Nov. 25, 1783		Hugh Vance		mr 31 *
Davis, Jeremiah m. Young, Susan	1827		Nathan Young		mr 32 *
Davis, John m. Blondell, Rosella	Aug. 28, 1836	Anthony Chambers			
Davis, John m. Quigley, Sarah	Nov. 23, 1789		Hugh Vance		cr 40
Davis, John Leml m. Shaffer, Ann B.	Mar. 30, 1846	George Shaffer	John Winter	7b 62	mr 4 *
Davis, Joseph m. Kennedy(--ey)Angelina	July 17, 1828	Seaman Garard	B. Reynolds	5b103	mr 76 *
Davis, Joseph m. Littlejohn, Mary A	June 17, 1833	Francis R. Dutton	Nathan Young	5b276	mr 52 *
Davis, Joseph m. Madden, Rachal	Oct. 19, 1793		William Hill		mr 66 *
Davis, Joseph W. m. Conrad, Eliz.	Jan. 1, 1799		John Heitt(Hutt)		cr 30 mr 10 *
Davis, Lewis m. Painter(Bender),Rachl	Dec. 14, 1797	George Painter	David Young	1b 72	cr 12 mr 18 *
Davis, Marg't m. Clemons, Leonard	Nov. 29, 1809	Bastian Poisal	Rev. Reebenack	7b126	gc 10
Davis, Mary m. Bowers, Philip	June 17, 1818	Lewis Davis		4b 74	
Davis, Mary m. Lonas, John	Nov. 3, 1801	Michael Byerly		2b146	
Davis, Mary Ann m. Greer, Jacob	July 23, 1828	Thomas Davis		5b103	
Davis, Mary Ann m. McNeal, Jacob	July 25, 1828				
Davis, Mary Eliz. m. Miller, G.W.	Sept 13, 1851	Elias Baker	B.Reynolds	7b231	mr 52 *
Davis, Nathaniel m. Crowl, Betsy A	Jan. 30, 1828	Ishmael Barnes	Geo.W. Harris	5b 89	mr 85 *
Davis, Phebe m. Hudson, James	May 16, 1814	Robert Hudson		3b297	
Davis, Phebe Mrs. m. Saunders, John	Apr. 20, 1809	George Payne		3b113	
Davis, Phebe Mrs. m. Hudson, Robert	May 16, 1814	James Hudson		3b297	
Davis, Polly m. Magowan, William	Oct. 10, 1799	Samuel Harrison		2b 30	
Davis, Rebecca m. Miller, Christian	Dec. 24, 1846	William Davis		7b 81	
Davis, Richard m. Sellers, Mary	July 2, 1804	Balser Sellers	John Light	2b238	mr 79 *
Davis, Ruth Mrs. m. Huggins, Michael	Aug. 3, 1801	David Baldwin		2b133	
Davis, Walter m. Tracey, Mary	June 11, 1785		Hugh Vance		mr 33 *

Name	Date	(marriage)	(surator)	(minister)	(bond)			
Davis, Sally m. Bansle(Bausel),Geo.	Feb. 26,	Feb. 27, 1812	Jacob Bansle	Rev. Reebenack	3b213	gc 12		*
Davis, Samuel Y. m. Waggoner, Sally	Jan. 4,	1847	Isaac V. Burnes		7b 82		mr 35	*
Davis, Sarah m. White, Daniel	Mar. 6,	1788		Moses Hoge			mr 88	*
Davis, Susan A. m. VanDoren, John P.	Jan. 5,	1854		Geo. W. Harris			mr 65	*
Davis, Susamah m. Penery, Robert	June 30,	July 4, 1832	Henry Myers	William Monroe	5b233		mr 6	*
Davis, Tabitha m. Carden(Carden), Geo	Jan. 13,	1791		Moses Hoge		cr 5		*
Davis. Thomas m. Bishop, Maria	July 14,	July 14, 1831	Milton J. Brown	Jacob Medtart	5b198		mr 63	*
Davis. Thomas m. Kerns, Margaret	Aug. 19,	Aug. 22, 1833	Jacob Kerns	Jas. M. Brown	5b279		mr 67	*
Davis. Thomas m. Ranson, Ann Eliz.	May 23,	1831	Mathew Ranson		5b196			*
Davis. Thomas m. Walgamott, Susanna	June 29,	June 30, 1799	Jonathan Sattle	David Young	2b 10	gc 8	mr 12	*
Davis. Thos. W. m. Moore, Sarah	Oct. 20,	1796		Moses Hoge		cr 36		*
Davis. ? m. Campbell, Patrick	Oct. 23,	1794		David Young		gc 4		*
Daw, Lorenzo m. Brannen, Cath.	June 11,	1840	Abner Snyder		6b212			*
Dawes, Isaac H. m. Young, Eliza F.	Apr. 23,	Apr. 23, 1850	John Young	Henry Furlong	7b182		mr 81	*
Dawson, Abraham m. Ingle, Eliz.	Apr. 27,	Oct. 5, 1819		Mathias Riser			mr 30	*
Dawson, Eleanor m. Rion, Thomas	Dec. 22,	Apr. 27, 1798	Timothy Collins	David Young	1b 99	gc 7		*
Dawson, Eliz. m. Hess, Jacob	Mar. 8,	1817	Swearingen Ray		4b 54			*
Dawson, Ephraim m. Buckingham,Nelly	Jan. 15,	1814	Isaac Conoway		3b287			*
Dawson, Isaac m. Michael, Mary	Feb. 23,	Jan. 16, 1816	Peter Michael	Mathias Riser	3b353		mr 26	*
Dawson, Isaac m. Ryan, Harriet	Jan. 15,	Mar. 1, 1818	Samuel Hill	Mathias Riser	4b 62		mr 29	*
Dawson, Israel m. Michael, Mary	Mar. 28,	1816	Peter Michael		3b353			*
Dawson, John m. Pierce, Eliz.	Jan. 31,	Mar. 31, 1831	Thomas Spencer	Jas. M. Brown	5b189		mr 62	*
Dawson, Illiana R. m. Evans, Isaac B.	Oct. 24,	Mar. 3, 1826	John Dawson	Benedick Reynolds	5b 34		mr 49	*
Dawson, Marg't m. Fauber, Nicholas	Aug. 9,	1812	Ephraim Dawson		3b238			*
Dawson, Nancy m. Spencer, Thomas	Sept 11,	1815	Samuel Christy	Rev. Reebenack	5b 34	gc 14		*
Dawson, Nelly m. Spencer, Henry		1820	Thomas Spencer		3b333			*
*Dawson, Thomas m. Kapp, Ann B.	Mar. 3,	1826		B. Reynolds	4b160		mr 49	*
Day, Anastasia m. Floyd, Wm.	Oct. 5,	1843	Bridget Day	Hugh Vance	6b304		mr 38	*
Day, James W. m. Hollis, Mary A.		Dec. 22, 1853	James Day	G.W.Cooper	6b165			*
Day, Jane m. McLaughlin, George	Apr. 3,	1839	John Miller		3b263			*
Day, Larkin m. Keys, Mary	Apr. 24,	1813	Lewis Inbody					*
Daylong, George m. Crowl, Jacob	Feb. 25,	Feb. 26, 1850	Christopher Thrasher	Henry Furlong	7b177		mr 79	*
Daylong, Elisa m. Thrasher,Susanna	Apr. 6,	1798	?		1b106			*
Daymond, Eliza m. Kennedy, Thomas	May 13,	May 13, 1851		J.H.Plunkett	7b224		mr 88	*
Dedenbaugh, Adam m. Krone, Christmas		Mar. 29, 1796		David Young				*
Deal, Rosanna m. Potsal, John	Nov. 6,	July 3, 1796		David Young	4b 20	gc 5		*
Deal, Susanna m. Thomas, John		1816	Robt. Cockburn Jr.			gc 6		*
Dean, Henry m. Johnson(Jon-), Mary	Jan. 13,	1785	Philip Stout	Hugh Vance				*
Dedrick(Tederick),Peter m Stout,Sally	June 23,	1803	Richard Morrison	David Young	2b204	gc 10	mr 33	*
Deberry, Rachel m. Snyder, Gasper	June 15,	1805	Henry C. Faris		2b265			*
Deck, Abraham m. Faris, Anne B.	Apr. 10,	1850		W. Love	7b180		mr 80	*
Deck, Elenor m. Waln, Joseph	Apr. 10,	1819		Mathias Riser			mr 30	*

(marriage)				(surety)	(minister)	(bond)		
Deck, Fred. D. m. Varmetre, Eliza M	Oct. 10,	1837		Abraham Varmetre		6b119		
Deck, Geo. Jr. m. McAllister, Marg't	Aug. 8,	1836		Chris'r McAllister		6b 83		
Deck, Henry m. Williamson, Sidney	Apr. 22,	1829		William Rush	Jacob Medtart	5b128		mr 63 *
Deck, Jacob m. Bond, Sarah	Aug. 26,	1823		Walter Bond	Chas. P. Krauth	4b247		mr 46 *
Deck, John m. Grimes, Marg't Jane	May 19,	1840		William Grimes		6b210		
Deck, Peter m. Anderson, Nancy	Jan. 5,	1825		Adam Shoppert	Chas. P. Krauth	4b283		mr 48 *
Deck, Peter m. Clodinger, Mary E.	Mar. 4,	1851		Philip Clodinger	F.C.Tebbs	7b216		mr 84 *
Dederick, Charlot m. Barnes, Jacob	Mar. 12,	1799		Jacob Dederick	John Boyd	1b172	cr 24	mr 16 *
Deel, Eliz. m. Devinney, Cornelius	Mar. 11,	1794			David Young		gc 3	
Deele, Peggy m. Billmire, Jacob	Nov. 9,	1800		Peter Deele	David Young	2b 97	gc 3	
Deevar, Isaac m. Hiser, Marg't	Nov. 18,	1794			David Young		gc 3	
Degroot, Sophia m. Seaborn, David	Mar. 22,	1792			Moses Hoge			mr 39 *
Dehaven, Job m. Littlejohn, Sarah	Mar. 18,	1815		Edw. Littlejohn	David Young	3b315		
Deiderick, Eliz. m. Grouk, Henry	Mar. 4,	1792		Peter Deale	David Young	2b 97	gc 1	
Dell, Rebecca(Peggy)m.Billmyre,Jacob	Nov. 6,	1800		Abraham Varmetre	David Young	3b 80	gc 9	
Deinine, Mary m. Bellar, Abraham	Dec. 21,	1807			Hugh Vance		cr 18	
Delaplane, Esther m. Compston, Henry	July 31,	1787		Geo. Coffenberger	Jas. M. Brown	5b200		mr 1 *
Delaplane, Hetty m. Coffenberger, N.	Aug. 18,	1831			Hugh Vance			mr 62 *
Delaplane, Isaac m. Compston, Eliz.	Nov. 15,	1785						mr 34 *
Delaplane, Jesse m. Fry, Jean	Nov. 21,	1798		Daniel Seaborn		1b148		
Delgard, John W. m. Thompson, Mary	Apr. 11,	1814		Joseph Thompson	Nathan Young	3b291		
Delgarm, Stephen m. Thompson, Nancy	July 28,	1817		Joseph Thompson	Francis Sprigg	4b 41		mr 55 *
Delinger, Fred. D. m. Locke, Sarah J	June 24,	1852		Jacob VanDoren	James Reily	7b298		mr 85 *
Dellinger, Reuben m. Bishop, Arey	Nov. 18,	1826		John Pickering	Moses Hoge	5b 56		mr 50 *
Dellon, William m. Copas, Eliz.	Apr. 15,	1790		Morris Rees		3b316	cr 4	mr 5 *
Demoss, Ann m. Willis, John	Mar. 21,	1815			David Young			
Demoss, Cath. m. Campbell, Joseph	June 24,	1795			David Young		gc 5	
Demoss, Eliz. m. McClure, Daniel	Sept 13,	1794			Richard Swift			mr 40 *
Demoss, Eloisa m. McKown, John	Nov. 16,	1830		William Wilson	Jas. M. Brown	5b180		mr 54 *
Demoss, Jane m. Mackey, James	Sept 7,	1795			David Young		gc 5	
Demoss, Jane m. Sagathy, Peter	Sept 16,	1768			Hugh Vance			mr 35 *
Demoss, Lewis m. Throckmorton,Jean	Aug. 29,	1797		Thomas Demoss		1b 36	cr 4	
Demoss, Margaret m. Tool, Moore	Apr. 1,	1790			Moses Hoge		cr 4	mr 5 *
Demoss, Mary Mrs. m. Burke, James	Dec. 22,	1802		Adam Eyre		2b187		
Demoss, Sarah m. Thompson, Wm.	July 29,	1799		William Seaman		2b 12		
Demoss, Thomas m. Gerrard, Mary	Apr. 10,	1797		Jonathan Gerrard		1b 11		
Demoss, Throckmorton m. Conner,Nancy	Apr. 7,	1802		David Conner		2b169		
Demoss, William m. Heaton, Ruth	Sept 15,	1797		Ebenezer Heaton		1b 41		
Denhifer, John m. Spangler, Eliz.	Aug. 8,	1799			David Young		gc 8	
Denahaw, Dolly m. Brothers(s),Philip	Mar. 29,	1796		James Hall	Richard Swift	1b x	cr 26	mr 11 *
Denney, John m. Hall, Martha	Mar. 29,	1789		James Hall		7b110		
Denney, Sarah J. m. Hollis, Joseph	Oct. 27,	1847		James Denney		7b110		
Dennis, Henry m. Price, Eliz.	Oct. 24,	1818		George Powell		4b 84		

(name)	(marriage)	(surety)	(minister)	(bond)		
Dennison, Eliz. m. Miller, David	Feb. 21, 1815	Samuel Cunningham	Rev. Reebenack	3b312	gc 14	*
Dennison, Jane m. Robinson, James	Sept 18, 1821	William Manford		4b190		*
Dennison, Letha m. Calvert, Robert	Oct. 26, 1841	William Waddeon	John Hedges	6b249	mr 73	*
Dennison, Thomas m. Manford, Leatha	May 27, 1826	Thomas Waddeon	Chas. P. Krauth	5b 43	mr 51	*
Dermott, James m. Harkin, Ailsy	July 2, 1820	Philip McGorran	James Redmond	4b153	mr 31	*
Derst, John m. Hill, Jane	Jan. 14, 1813		Rev. Reebenack			*
Devault, Daniel m. Green, Keziah	May 3, 1785		Hugh Vance		gc 13	*
Devers, Benj. m. Saunders, Elenor	Mar. 8, 1824	Ellis Rees		4b258		*
Devers, Joseph m. Allender, Martha	Aug. 11, 1817	Thomas Allender		4b 42		*
Devine, Mary m. Veal, William	Sept 15, 1835	Jas. R. Dugan		6b 57		*
Devinney, Cornelius m. Deel, Eliz.	Mar. 11, 1794		David Young		gc 3	*
Devinney, Eliz. Ann m. Miller, Jos.	Oct. 18, 1826	John Shober	Chas. P. Krauth	5b 54	mr 51	*
Devoure, Phebe m. Clarke, Samuel	Sept 28, 1785		Hugh Vance		mr 34	*
Dewall, Denton m. Bryan, Sarah	May 2, 1805	Lewis B. Willis	John Bond	2b261	cr 28 mr 22	*
Dick, Christena m. Alaman, Casper	Jan. 25, 1818		Mathias Riser		mr 29	*
Dick, Harriet m. McIntire, Patrick	Apr. 22, 1833	Jacob Shaffer		5b268		*
Dick, Mary m. McGarah, Robert	Sept 22, 1798	John Dick		1b134		*
Dick, Peter m. Ambrester, Marcelina	Feb. 20, 1843	Michael Ambrester	Lewis F. Wilson	6b290	mr 74	*
Dick, Philip m. Kees, Nancy			Mathias Riser		mr 29	*
Dick, Wm. S. m. Wilson, Hannah	Jan. 10, 1792	Samuel Manor	B. Reynolds	5b 32	mr 49	*
Diel, Mary m. Buckins, Daniel	Aug. 9, 1827		David Young		gc 2	*
Diffenderfer, Ann M. m. Poisal, Jacob	Nov. 8, 1827	Geo. Diffenderfer	Jacob Beecher	5b 84	mr 53	*
Diffenderfer, Cath. m. Kerns, Emanuel	Aug. 20, 1840	John Davis		6b215		*
Diffenderfer, Geo. m. McGonagle, Sally	Feb. 11, 1818	John Doll	John B. Hoge	4b 60	mr 29	*
Diffenderfer, Geo. B. m. Wleas, Cam	Aug. 12, 1826	Thos. Dennison		5b 48		*
Diffenderfer, Mary m. Poisal, Jacob	Nov. 9, 1827	Geo. Diffenderfer	J. Beecher	5b 84	mr 53	*
Diffenderfer, Philip m. Mong, Nancy	May 1, 1832	John Mong	Jacob Medtart	5b227	mr 64	*
Diffenderfer, Philip m. Walters, Sara	Apr. 30, 1837	Michael Walters		6b101		*
Dillon, Moses m. Anderson, Nancy	Mar. 7, 1818	John Kerney	Nathan Young	4b 70	mr 56	*
Dinarine, Jane m. Bridgman, Francis	Aug. 1, 1801	William Adams		2b133		*
Disor, George m. McDonald, Rebecca	Nov. 19, 1838	Wm. G. Butler		6b151		*
Ditzler, Jacob m. Starry, Eliz.	Sept 6, 1796		David Young		gc 6	*
Dix, Rebecca m. Ferrall, Thos.	Mar. 6, 1853		D. Francis Sprigg	6b200		*
Dixon, James m. Franceway, Evaline	Mar. 17, 1840	Joseph Bowers	P. Harrison	5b291	mr 86	*
Dixon, Nancy m. Carey, Henry	Nov. 15, 1833	Joshua Cline	Nathan Young		mr 71	*
'Dnoon, James m. Rig(Rinehart),Eliz.	Dec. 25, 1809?	Arch'd Butt	Rev. Reebenack	3b130	mr 66	*
Dobsin, Samuel m. Philips, Cath.	Mar. 10, 1796		Moses Hoge		go 11	*
Dodd, David m. Lefevre, Ann Eliza	Jan. 31, 1852	John M. Speck	Lewis F. Wilson	7b243	go 11 cr 35	*
Dodd, Rachel m. Roberts, Wm.	Mar. 8, 1802	James Chenoweth		2b164	mr 87	*
Doddewick, Molly m. Sanders, Christn	Dec. 16, 1792		David Young		gc 2	*
Dogley, John m. Curtis, Mary	June 12, 1848	Jacob VanDoren	P. Lipscomb	7b131	mr 81	*
Doll, Bernard m. Showers, Maria E.	Apr. 10, 1834	Ezekiel Showers	John Howell	6b 4	mr 68	*
Doll, Christn W. m. Harlan, Marg't A	Sept 10, 1845	Harrison Waite	Lewis F. Wilson	7b 43	mr 77	*

Name	(marriage)		(bond)	(minister)	(suretor)		
Doll, Daniel H. m. Wolff, Cath. E.	Feb. 25,	1833	9b258	D.F.Bragunier	George Wolff		mr 78 *
Doll, Eliz. C. m. White, Daniel S.	Apr. 9,	1845	7b 31	David Young	C.W.Doll		
Doll, George m. Heck, Eliz.	Nov. 6,	1792					
Doll, George m. McSherry, Cath. G.	Apr. 21,	1834	6b 9			gc 2	
Doll, John m. Wolff, Ann Maria	Apr. 6,	1820	4b143	Lewis Mayer	Harrison Waite		mr 40 *
Donacre, Joseph m. Livingston, Mary	Feb. 5,	1800 ?	2b 51		Bernard Wolff		
Donaldson, Eliza A. m. Householder, J.	Aug. 8,	1839	6b173	James Reily	Geo. Livingston		mr 70 *
Donaldson, Geo. F. m. Wilson, Sarah	Apr. 10,	1845	7b 31	John Boggs	Moses Grantham		mr 75 *
Donaldson, John m. Clark, Elenor	Nov. 11,	1890		Moses Hoge	James Wilson	cr 5	
Donaldson, Marg't m. Bolin, Thos. J	Mar. 9,	1835	6b 36		Geo. W. Bolin		
Donaldson, Sally m. Noland, Lazarus	Jan. 20,	1813	3b248		Job Kitchen		
Donaldson, Sarah m. Grove, Abr'm B.	Feb. 22,	1815	3b312		John Miller		
Dooley, Eliz. m. Miller, Abr'm	July 27,	1819	4b111		William Boden		
Dorney, Alex. m. Murphy, Elenor		1794		David Young		gc 4	
Dorney, Isaac M. m. Young, Eliza T.	Apr. 23,	1850	7b182	Henry Furlong	John Young		mr 81 *
Dorres, Wm. m. Barnett, Margaret		1789		D. Thomas			mr 38 *
Dorsey, Edw. m. Graves, Mary Ann	Aug. 31,	Sept 2, 1847	7b105	John Light	William Graves		mr 79 *
Dorsey, Wm. m. Anderson, Lucy E.	Nov. 2,	Nov. 5, 1844	7b 12	James Chisholm	John S. Harrison		mr 75 *
Dougherty, John Jr. m. Ward, Esther	Jan. 4,	Jan. 12, 1812	3b207	Rev. Reebenack	John Dougherty	gc 12	
Douglas, John m. Patch, Margaret	Oct. 29,	1801	2b145		Isaac Patch		
Douglas, Rachel m. English, David	Aug. 1,	1799	2b 14		Wm. Barnett		
Douglas, Rebecca m. Cray, Samuel M.	Apr. 13,	1793		Moses Hoge		cr 21	mr 7 *
Douglas, Sarah m. Burnop(Burnoss)Geo.	June 11,	1789		Moses Hoge		cr 2	mr 2 *
Douglas, Wm. m. Goddard, Mary	Oct. 10,	1815	3b343	Rev. Reebenack	Isaac Goddard	gc 15	mr 81 *
Dours, Isaac m. Young, Eliza T.	Apr. 23,	1850	7b182	Henry Furlong	John Young	cr 15	mr 1 *
Dousk,Adolph(Chr't'r) m.Halmbolt,Eliz	Apr. 11,	1787		Christian Stredt			
Dowden, Nancy m. Zimmerman, Jas.	Mar. 11,	1811	3b179		Wm. Mound		
Dowlan, Christian m. Hamilton, Ann	Aug. 12,	1807	3b 66		Wm. Hamilton		
Dowlan, John m. Grinnold, Polly	Feb. 25,	1804	2b223		Henry Clondinger		
Dowlan, Mary m. O'rorke, Felix	Aug. 21,	1816	4b 9		Bernard O'rorke		
Dowlan, Thomas m. Lowman, Rachel	July 2,	1807	3b 63		John Lee		
Downes, Jean m. Coover, Gideon	Mar. 14,	1798	1b 90		William Downes		
Downey, Jane m. Seaman, Jonas	Apr. 6,	1802	2b168		Mathias Urick		
Downey, Lydia m. Urick, Mathias	May 19,	1800	2b 70		Jesse Brown		
Downey, Susanna m. Rafferty, Wm. B.	Aug. 28,	1838	6b145		Joseph Bell		
Downing, Mary m. Boak, John	Aug. 30,	1804	2b242	John Bond	Rees Branson		mr 21 *
Downing, Samuel m. Johnson, Maria	Apr. 19,	1824	4b263	Chas. P. Krauth	Joel Rees		mr 47 *
Downing, Sarah(Susan) m. Burke, Jas.	Jan. 12,	1813	3b247	Geo. M. Frye	Robert Daniel		mr 25 *
Downs, Angeline m. Mayhugh, Warner W	Dec. 24,	1839	6b188	John Light	Andrew Criswell		mr 70 *
Downs, Ann Rebecca m. Shervin, Wm.	Jan. 28,	1845	7b 24		Christopher Downs		
Downs, Charles m. Parker, Ann	Feb. 28,	1822					
Downs, Hamilton m. Lefevre, Sarah	Oct. 30,	Nov. 2, 1847	7b138	John B. Hoge	Jacob Lefevre		mr 44 *
Downs, Mary m. Fiser, Michael	Aug. 31,	1832	9b238	John Light	Charles Downs		mr 79 *
*Dow, Lorenzo m. Brannen, Cath.	June 11,	1840	6b212		Abner Snyder		

Name	(marriage)	(surety)	(minister)	(bond)	ref
Downs, Theophilus m. Cox, Lena	Sept 18, 1809	Elisha Athy	John Mathews	3b119	mr 40 *
Doxan, Nancy m. Carey, Henry	Nov. 25, 1833	Joshua Cline	Nathan Young	3b291	mr 66 *
Doyle, Eliz. m. Doyle, John	Apr. 19, 1828	Thomas Sprigg	B. Reynolds	5b 99	mr 52 *
Doyle, Eliz. m. Loudon, William	Oct. 2, 1797	John Clarke	Richard Swift	1b 51	cr 12 mr 14 *
Doyle, Eliz. m. Ramety, John	Oct. 12, 1797		Richard Swift		
Doyle, James m. Edmonds, Susanna	Mar. 25, 1801	Simon Doyle		2b118	
Doyle, James m. Turner, Lucinda	Dec. 30, 1845		John Light		
Doyle, John m. Doyle, Eliz.	Apr. 20, 1828	Thomas Sprigg	B. Reynolds	5b 99	mr 76 *
Drinker, John m. Peppers, Eliz.	Apr. 12, 1797	Robt. W. Wood		1b 7	mr 52 *
Driskell, Johanna m. Barry, Patr'k	May 16, 1840	Harrison Waite		6b209	
Dubble, Sarah m. Coachman, Cornelius	May 14, 1840	John Waite	P. Harrison	6b208	mr 71 *
Dubble, Rebecca m. Sperow, Wm.	Aug. 11, 1835	Jacob Dubble		6b 53	
Ducker, Cath. m. Wilson, Wm.	Mar. 15, 1826	William Ducker	B. Reynolds	5b 37	mr 49 *
Duckwall, Henry m. Lingamfelter, Rose	Oct. 27, 1807	John Riner		3b 75	
Duckwall, Isaac m. Clover, Amelia	Oct. 24, 1815	Daniel Duckwall		3b345	
Duckwall, Joseph m. Dummell, Lydia	Jan. 28, 1800	Beal Dummell		2b 49	
Duckwall, Lewis m. Wagoner, Susan	Oct. 26, 1798	Jonas Grove		1b141	
Duffey, Cath. m. Severns, Joseph	Mar. 12, 1832	Robt. McDonald	Nathan Young	5b219	mr 64 *
Duffey, John W. m. Raimer, Cath.	Apr. 17, 1837	Fred. Raimer		6b105	gc 8
Duffield, John W. m. Stewart, Eliz.	Sept 4, 1834	Thomas Hite		6b 17	gc 6
Duffield, Rachel m. Myers, Henry	Nov. 17, 1798	Peter Hedges	David Young	1b147	
Duffield, Sarah m. Wollam, John	Apr. 24, 1797	Peter Hedges	David Young	1b 12	
Duffield, Wm. m. Cunningham, Rosanna	Oct. 22, 1804	Wm. Cunningham		2b246	
Dugan, Cath. Ann m. Lefevre, Henry	Nov. 12, 1847	Thomas Dugan		7b112	mr 67 *
Dugan, Geo. H. m. Leopard, Nancy	Dec. 9, 1833	Adam Brown	Jas. M. Brown	5b294	gc 11
Dugan, James m. Hous(Horn),Peggy	Jan. 13, 1810	George House	Revr. Reebenack	3b133	
Dugan, Marg't m. McAllister, Benj.	Aug. 18, 1849	Michael Leopard		7b163	
Dugan, Philip m. Leopard, Margaret	May 13, 1839	Jos. R. Criswell		6b169	
Dugan, Rebecca A. m. French, John A	Jan. 9, 1854		Jos. H. Plunkett		*
Dugan, Robinson m. Stonebraker, Jane	Apr. 8, 1837	John Stonebraker	Jas. M. Brown	6b104	or 38 mr 54 *
Dugan, Thomas m. Small, Marg't Mrs.	Feb. 1, 1830	Saml. Williamson	John Hutt(Hedtt)	5b151	or 20 mr 17 *
?Duke, Polly(Patty) m. Anderson, John	Aug. 1, 1789	Alex. Rodgers	Hugh Vance	2b 11	or 38 mr 17 *
Duke, Rebecca m. McCullough, Joseph	Apr. 1, 1799		John Hedtt(Hutt)		mr 3 *
?Duke, Sally m. Anderson, John	Aug. 1, 1800				
Dummell, Lydia m. Duckwall, Joseph	Jan. 28, 1844	Beal Dummell		2b 49	
Dunavan, Mary m. Maloney, Wm.	Apr. 11, 1850	Daniel Comkery	W. Love	6b318	mr 80 *
Duncan, Cath. m. Butt, Charles	May 25, 1818	Michael Smelser		7b186	
Duncan, James m. Spencer, Sally	Jan. 6, 1795	Peter Hess		4b 57	gc 5
Duncan, James m. Hamilton, Rebecca	June 29, 1795		David Young		
Duncan, Thomas m. Snodgrass, Eliz.	Feb. 12, 1782		Hugh Vance		
Dunden, Jean m. Wilkinson, John	Nov. 9, 1798	John Auten		1b145	
Dunham, Aaron m. Thatcher, Mary	Mar. 18, 1819	John Strother	Moses Hoge	4b102	mr 32 *
Dunham, Able m. Morlatt, Nancy	Dec. 24, 1795				cr 10 mr 11 *

Name	Date	(marriage)	(suretor)	(minister)	(bond)	(ref.)
Dunham, Benj. m. Brannon, Rebecca J.	Mar. 30,	1847	Stephen Gano		7b 93	mr 57 *
Dunham, Benj. m. Manor, Eliz.	Apr. 12,	1813	Samuel Dunham		3b259	
Dunham, David m. Buckhamer, Cath.	Dec. 9,	1798	Samuel Dunham		1b152	
Dunham, David m. Merchant, Rebecca	Apr. 25,	1806	Abr'm Merchant		3b 88	
Dunham, Dinah m. Gerrard, Mathew	July 28,	1806	Samuel Dunham		3b 24	
Dunham, Eliz. m. Parkinson, Wm. R.	Dec. 27,	1847	Benjamin Dunham		7b118	
Dunham, Hannah m. Ladley, George	Oct. 24,	Oct. 27, 1820	David Dunham	Nathan Young	4b165	
Dunham, Hannah m. Watson, Wm.	Dec. 15,	1797	Samuel Dunham		1b 72	mr 30 *
Dunham, Jacob m. Goodnight, Cath.	Sept 28,	Oct. 21, 1819	John Strother	Mathias Riser	4b116	mr 45 *
Dunham, Jas. C. m. Young, Eliz.	Jan. 24,	Jan. 1822	Adam Young	Chas. P. Krauth	4b206	mr 15 *
Dunham, Jane m. Wilkinson, John		Dec. 20, 1798		Richard Swift	3b 15	cr 31
Dunham, John m. Holiday, Polly	Apr. 9,	1806	James Harrison		7b248	
Dunham, Marg't m. Gilbert, Joseph	Mar. 10,	Dec. 26, 1852	Wm. Parkinson	John Grove	7b 19	cr 36
Dunham, Maria m. Tyson, Wm.	Dec. 24,	Apr. 26, 1844	Samuel Dunham	Moses Hoge	5b 3	
Dunham, Rachel m. Kyle, Joseph		1796			7b 75	mr 75 *
Dunham, Rosanna m. Roach, James	Mar. 2,	1825	Samuel Dunham		1b 85	cr 36
Dunham, Samuel m. Manor, Rosanna	Oct. 22,	1846	Joseph Manor		3b185	mr 14 *
Dunham, Sarah m. Fortney(Tarl-)Peter	Feb. 17,	Feb. 21, 1798	Paul Verdier	Moses Hoge	2b229	
Dunham, Thomas m. McNeal, Martha	Apr. 18,	Apr. 18, 1811	Jas. B. Small	Rev. Reebenack	5b134	gc 12
Dunlap, Sarah m. Sanks, Joshua	Mar. 20,	1804	Robert Dunlap		2b146	mr 34 *
Dunlap, Joseph m. Tingle, Jane	July 20,	July 20, 1785	?	Hugh Vance	3b336	
Dunn, Ann m. Brown, Abel	June 23,	1829	Cyrus Farr		3b207	
Dunn, Deborah m. Lee, Thomas	Nov. 4,	1801	Thomas Dunn		6b289	
Dunn, Hannah m. Bell, William	Aug. 28,	1815	David Dunn		2b109	cr 35 / mr 19 *
Dunn, Jane m. Mendenhall, Amos	Jan. 3,	1812	Patr'k Cunningham		1b 75	cr 37 / mr 14 *
Dunn, John m. Cunningham, Ellen	Feb. 13,	1843	George Baker	John Boyd	1b160	
Dunn, John m. Swisher(Sayher), Rachel	Jan. 14,	1801	Basil Games	John Hill	1b 66	cr 8 / mr 7 *
Dunn, Marg't m. Games, James	Dec. 27,	1797	George Payne		2b108	cr 37 / mr 14 *
Dunn, Martha m. Payne, Jesse	Jan. 8,	1799	Jonathan Moore	Moses Hoge	1b137	
Dunn, Mary m. Martin, Peter		1791	Ephraim Murphy	John Hill	4b202	cr 35 / mr 19 *
Dunn, Richard m. Wirmere(Wim-),Mary	Nov. 29,	1797	Robert Dunn	John Boyd	6b144	cr 32 / mr 15 *
Dunn, Robt. Jr.m. Murphy, Lydia	Jan. 13,	1801	Jacob Cline	John Boyd	2b109	mr 44 *
Dunn, Rosanna m.Kenny(Henry,Henly)Wm.	Oct. 8,	1798		Geo. M. Frye	3b185	cr 11 / mr 13 *
Dunn, Seth m. Throckmorton, Sarah	Dec. 18,	1821	Bartholomew Garney	John Boyd	1b 60	cr 35 / mr 19 *
Dunn. Wm. m. Johnston, Eliz.	Dec. 8,	1796	George Baker		1b132	gc 12
Dumphy, Nicholas m. Woods, Mary	Aug. 20,	1838	James B. Small	John Boyd	1b 90	
Dupp, John m. Swisher, Rachel	Jan. 14,	1801	Isaac Allstadt	Rev. Reebenack	3b247	
Durham, Thomas m. McNeal, Martha	Apr. 18,	1811	Edward Mercer		4b180	
Dusk, Mary m. Thatcher, Sylvester	Nov. 4,	1797	John Dust			
Dusk, Sarah m. Campbell, Andrew S.	Sept 11,	1798	Robert Hill			
Dust, Eliz. m.Ramsbaugh(Ramsberg),Geo	Mar. 19,	1798	John Strother			
Dust, John m. Hill, Fanny	Jan. 11,	1813		Robert Hill		
Dust, John E. m. Burns, Rebecca	Apr. 2,	1821		John Strother		

Name	(marriage)	(suretor)	(minister)	(bond)		
Dust, Joseph m. Burns, Eliz.	May 8, 1823	Joseph Gorrell	John Mathews	4b238		mr 46 *
Dust, Rebecca m. Markwood, John	Nov. 27, 1797	Paul Dust		1b 64		
Dutton, Francis m. Davis, Cath.	Sept 9, 1823	Edw. Littlejohn		4b248		
Dutton, Hannah m. Hensel, Daniel	Feb. 5, 1817	Benjamin Wilson	Nathan Young	4b 31		mr 55 *
Dutton, Nancy m. Mills, Josiah	Sept 17, 1821	David Dutton	Geo. M. Frye	4b189		mr 44 *
Dutton, Sarah m. Matson, Nehemiah	Jan. 30, 1807	Daniel Dutton		3b 45		
Dutton, Susan m. Cowarden, James	Nov. 17, 1821	Francis Dutton	Geo. M. Frye	4b197		mr 44 *
Duval, Denton m. Bryan, Sarah	May 2, 1805	Lewis B. Willis		2b261	cr 28	
Duvall, Eliz. m. Bond, Geo. W.	Jan. 28, 1813	Chas. Henderson	John Bond	3b249		mr 22 *
Dye, Sarah m. Noose, William	Jan. 20, 1800	Thos. Sullivan		2b 48		
Dyer, Zebulon m. Waggoner, Rebecca	Nov. 17, 1801	Elisha Boyd		2b148		
Dyhouse, Joseph m. Irwin, Sarah	Jan. 18, 1798	Robert Irwin		1b102		
Dyser, Jenny m. Leign, William	Jan. 30, 1808	Azel Fletcher		3b 83		
Dysert, Libby m. Sumption, Jacob	July 18, 1809	Jabez Anderson		3b115		

"E"

Name	(marriage)	(suretor)	(minister)	(bond)		
Eachus, David m. Mong, Eve	Aug. 20, 1828	Jacob Seibert	Jacob Mediart	5b106		mr 63 *
Eachus, Robert m. Thornburg, Phoebe	Dec. 20, 1789		D. Thomas			mr 37 *
Eade, James m. Butt, Alley	Dec. 29, 1799	Richard Butt	Richard Swift	2b 41	cr 34	mr 16 *
Eads, Eliz. m. Franceway, Joseph	Feb. 12, 1791				cr 6	mr 6 *
Eagle, Mary m. Melvin, John	May 30, 1799	John Engle	Moses Hoge	2b 8	cr 29	mr 17 *
Eagle, Sally m. Crum, Lewis	Feb. 4, 1811	George Eagle	Moses Hoge	3b173		
Eaglestone, James m. Jackson, Hannah	Jan. 29, 1818	Amos Nichols		4b 58		
Eaglestone, Richard m. Aris, Polly	Mar. 1, 1821	Edward Aris	W.N.Scott	4b173		mr 41 *
Eaglestone, Leonard m. Avis, Polly	Dec. 4, 1820?		W.N.Scott			mr 41 *?
Eakins,Esther(Easter) m. Patton,John	Jan. 6, 1818	Robert Eaken	W.N.Scott	4b 56		
Eakins, Mary m. Lucas, Dennis	Jan. 21, 1817	John Wright	W.N.Scott	4b 30		
Eaken, William m. Snodgrass, Sarah	June 7, 1781		Hugh Vance			mr 32 *
Earhart, Cath. m. Heffner, Jonathan	June 29, 1839	Patrk Cunningham		6b172		
Earls, Edward m. Smith, Barbara	Aug. 8, 1799	Philip Smith	Richard Swift	2b 13	cr 34	mr 16 *
Early, James m. Davis, Ann	May 11, 1825	James Day		5b 10		
Early, James m. Kiger, Mary	July 4, 1835	Harrison Waite		6b 49		
Earnest, Martin m. Grove, Christena	Apr. 13, 1789		Christian Streit		cr 15	
Earp, Ann m. Pitzer, James	May 21, 1839	Burgess Earp	John Light	6b170		mr 4 *
Earp, Burgess R. m. Myles, Marg't S	June 2, 1817	Jesse Turner	W.N.Scott	4b 37		mr 70 *
Earp, Cath. Ann m. Pitzer, James	May 21, 1839	Burgess Earp		6b170		
Earp, William m. Metcalf,Drusilla	Nov. 21, 1785		Hugh Vance			
Easterday, John m. Paul, Sarah	July 28, 1817	Robert Paul	John B. Hoge	4b 40		mr 34 *
Eaton, Eliz. m. McCormick, James	Feb. 28, 1801	Cornelius McCormick		2b116		

	(bond date)	(marriage)	(suretor)	(minister)	(bond)	(ref)
Eaton, James m. McDaniel, Emily	Feb. 3,	Feb. 14, 1847	A. McDaniel	William Love	7b 84	mr 78 *
Eaton, John M. m. Moles, Mary A.	Oct. 20,	1842	Daniel Moles		6b280	
Eaton, Sarah m. Worrell, John	Nov. 26,	1804	John Eaton		2b248	
Eaty, Elisha m. Cox, Anna	Dec. 24,	Dec. 27, 1800	Jacob Cox	Moses Hoge	2b105	cr 38 mr 20 *
Eaty, Jacob m. Butt, Susanna	Dec. 3,	1805	William Green		3b 4	
Eaty, Jacob m. Strider, Sarah	Feb. 15,	1799	Michael Houts		1b168	
Eaty, Rachel m. Cage, Andrew		Dec. 10, 1788				
Eaty, Sarah m. McDermott, James	Jan. 2,	1834	Harrison Waite	Moses Hoge	5b298	mr 36 *
Ebbert, Anna M. m. Hastings, John	May 5,	May 5, 1831	John Ebbert	Robert Cadden	5b193	mr 62 *
Ebbert, Eliz. m. Emberson, Daniel	Apr. 2,	Apr. 10, 1831	James Ardinger	Nathan Young	5b191	mr 61 *
Ebberts, Frederica m. Hastings, Danl.	Apr. 22,	1835	Margaret Ebberts		6b 43	
Ebberts, George m. Wood, Sarah	Feb. 8,	Feb. 8, 1789		Moses Hoge		cr 1 mr 2 *
Ebberts, Jacob m. Bilhdire, Polly	May 2,	1801	Michael Billmire	J.L.Bromwell	2b125	
Ebberts, John m. Croney, Marg't	Apr. 16,	Apr. 17, 1825	Thomas C.Croney		5b 8	mr 47 *
Ebberts, John m. Everly, Charlotte	Nov. 2,	Nov. 3, 1814	George Hill	John Bond	3b306	cr 41 mr 25 *
Ebberts, Marg't m. Mayer, Abraham	June 10,	1837	Esom E. Mayhew		6b109	
7Ebberts, Mary Ann m. Hastings, John	May 5,	May 5, 1831	John Ebberts	Robert Cadden	5b193	mr 62 *
Ebberts, Nancy m. Plotner, Benj.	Oct. 13,	1801	John Sherrard		5b 24	*
Ebberts, Phebe m. Chapman, Joseph	Nov. 16,	Nov. 16, 1837	Abraham Mays	James Watts	6b124	*
Ebberts, Phebe m. Landerkin, James	Apr. 9,	Apr. 10, 1812	Christian Ebberts	Rev. Reebensack	3b219	gc 12 mr 79 *
Eck, John T. m. Suber, Mary	Jan. 15,	Jan. 17, 1850	Weidman, Solomon	Richard Brown	7b173	mr 75 *
Eck, Theodore m. Grubb, Susanna	Feb. 12,	Feb. 15, 1844	Henry L. Grubb	T.H.W. Monroe	6b313	mr 67 *
Eckels, William m. Ray, Ann	Sept 14,	Sept 15, 1833	Jacob Sperow	John Light	5b283	*
Eckhart, Elias m. Chrisman,Magdalena	Nov. 4,	Nov. 5, 1797	Philip Shutt	David Young	1b101	gc 7 mr 17 *
Eckhart, Henry m. Sheetz(ortz),Julia	Apr. 17,	Apr. 18, 1797	Michael Yearly	David Young	1b 7	gc 6 mr 1 *
Eckels, Allen m. Fry, Mary	Sept 8,	Sept 12, 1799	James McLaughlin	John Boyd	2b 25	cr 34 mr 67 *
Eckles, Richard m. Oliver, Margaret		July 17, 1787		Hugh Vance		cr 18 mr 1 *
Eckles, William m. Ray, Ann	Sept 14,	Sept 15, 1833	Jacob Sperow	John Light	5b283	mr 67 *
Edleman, Caty m. Roberts, Thomas		Oct. 15, 1789	James Ford	Hugh Vance	2b101	cr 25 mr 4 *
Ellin, Charles m. Ford, Mary	Dec. 1,	1800	Daniel Harlan		2b260	
Ellin, Mary m. Ellis, Ellis	Apr. 22,	1805				
Edmond, Ann m. Green, Charles	Dec. 2,	Dec. 2, 1797	James Edmond	Richard Swift	1b 67	cr 12 mr 14 *
Edmonds, Rebecca m. Chapman, Edward	Dec. 7,	1804			2b225	
Edmonds, Susanna m. Doyle, James	Mar. 25,	1801	James Doyle		2b118	
Edmonds, Wm. m. Goddy(Gaudy),Nancy		Dec. 31, 1789	Simon Doyle	Moses Hoge		
Edmondson, Thos. m. Tate, Mary		Mar. 27, 1782		Daniel Sturges		
Edwards, Abraham m. McCormick,Patsy	May 28,	1807	Mathias Lightner		3b 60	cr 3 mr 3 *
Edwards, John m. Widdows, Eliz.		May 7, 1796		David Young	6b292	mr 42 *
Edwards, John m. Wright, Marg't Ann	Mar. 13,	Mar. 16, 1843	Levi Henshaw Jr	Lewis F. Wilson	6b225	gc 5 mr 74 *
Edwards, Joseph m. Beller, Eliz.	Mar. 24,	1840	Abisha Beller		3b268	
Edwards, Joseph m. Roberts, Lidy	Aug. 9,	1813	Levi Cunningham		5b 68	
Edwards, Joseph m. Silvers, Nancy	Apr. 20,	May 3, 1827	Zepnaniah Silver	J.E.Jackson		
Edwards, Mary m. Sheets, Wm.	Apr. 1,	Apr. 1, 1845	Joseph Edwards	John Boggs	7b 30	mr 75 *

(marriage)		(surety)	(minister)	(bond)		
Edwards, Wm. B. m. Sommerville, Eliza	June 24, 1833	Ezekiel Showers		5b277		
Egan, John m. Cable, Margaret	Apr. 27, 1847	John O'Brien		5b 95	cr 28	mr 23 *
Eglestone, Ann m. Johnston, Henry	June 28, 1806	James Campbell	J. Bond	3b 23	cr 14	mr 24 *
Eglestone, Ann m. Miller, Michael	June 28, 1811	John Porterfield	John B. Hoge	3b174		*
Eglestone, Eliz. m. Morlatt, Isaac	Feb. 13, 1818	Richard Morlatt	W.N. Scott	4b 55		mr 61
Eglestone, Hannah m. Moore(Moon), Geo.	Jan. 1, 1830	Henry Nichols	Nathan Young	5b172	gc 15	
Eglestone, Marg't m. Fuller, Stephen	Aug. 4, 1816	William Wilson	Rev. Reebenack	4b 11		mr 44 *
Eichelberger, David m. Slaughter, Amelia	Mar. 29, 1822	James Sterrett	Geo. M. Frye	4b207	cr 27	mr 83 *
Eisal, Eliz. m. Bowman(Balman), Adam	Jan. 31, 1850	Adolph Shedg	D. Francis Sprigg	7b208	gc 10	mr 13 *
Elbert, John m. Fickling, Eliz.	Dec. 27, 1797	Fielding Beall	William Tibbett	1b 63	cr 10	mr 12 *
Elder, Eli m. Byers, Rebecca	Nov. 21, 1803	Edward Graham	David Young	2b215	cr 33	mr 10 *
Eliason, Anna m. Tabb, George	Dec. 6, 1796		John Boyd	4b 43		
Eliason, Eliz. m. Harlan, George	Aug. 13, 1795		John Boyd	3b227		
Elkins, John m. Kemble, Eliz.	June 8, 1817	George Myers				
Elkins, Lucy H. m. Summers, John	Feb. 26, 1812	Jacob Fenner				
Ellen, Eliz. Ann m. Collier, Daniel	Mar. 2, 1847	James M. Newkirk	John Light	7b 88		mr 79 *
Ellenberger, Eliz. m. Free, George	July 22, 1815	Jacob Garinger		3b330		
Ellenberger, Mary Ann m. Pentony, Lake	Aug. 11, 1816	John Ellenberger	Mathias Riser	4b 2		*
Elliot, Eli Wm. m. Orrick, Mary	Feb. 8, 1815	Cromwell Orrick		3b310		
Elliot, James m. Ridenour, Sarah K.	May 19, 1831	Henry Rohrer	Chas. P. Krauth	5b195		mr 47 *
Elliot, Mary m. Clough, William	Aug. 3, 1824	Edw. A Gibbs	Nathan Young	4b269		mr 64 *
Elliot, Mary A. m. Cornelius, Jos. W.	May 26, 1832	Chris'r McAlister	John Light	5b230		mr 88 *
Elliot, Mary C. m. Leopard, G.W.	Jan. 6, 1852			2b 46		mr 1 *
Elliot, Patrick m. Maxwell, Mary	Mar. 6, 1785		Edward Tiffin	3b332	cr 38	
Elliott, Samuel m. Hoke, Mary	Jan. 6, 1800	Thomas Elliot		2b 47		
Elliot, Sarah m. Beach, Alexander	Aug. 7, 1815	Ralph Durham		6b 37		
Elliot, Thomas m. Miller, Peggy	Jan. 6, 1800	Samuel Elliot				
Elliot, Verlinda m. Ullum(Wm), Andrew	Mar. 16, 1835	Thomas Powell				mr 48 *
Elliot, William m. Crowl, Sarah	May 21, 1825	William Cole	Charles P. Krauth	5b 11		
Ellis, Abraham m. Riner, Eliz.	Jan. 24, 1801	Henry Riner		2b12		
Ellis, Ann m. Russell, John	Apr. 3, 1804	Thomas Carothers		2b231		
Ellis, Ann m. Strickle, Jacob	Sept 27, 1806	Abraham Ellis		3b 31		
Ellis, Eliz. Ann m. Collier, Daniel	Feb. 2, 1847	Jas. M. Newkirk	John Light	7b 88		mr 79 *
Ellis, Benj. m. Foreman, Eliz.	Oct. 11, 1810	George Newkirk		3b163		
Ellis, Ellen m. Seibert, Jacob	May 12, 1837	Ellis Ellis		6b107		
Ellis, Ellis m. Edlin, Mary	Apr. 22, 1805	Daniel Harlan		2b260		
Ellis, Leonard m. Allemong, Jane	Nov. 15, 1781	John Ellis	Daniel Sturges	6b239		mr 42 *
Ellis, Maria m. Williamson, David P	Mar. 25, 1841	George Bender	Lewis F. Wilson	2b 79		mr 72 *
Ellis, Rebecca m. Daniel, William	Aug. 4, 1800	Geo. Peterman	W.N. Scott	4b114		
Ellis, Rhuana m. McCoy, Moses	Sept 11, 1819		Hugh Vance			mr 30 *
Ellis, Rowland m. Judy, Frances	June 15, 1786	Amos Hoff				mr 43 *
Ellis, Sarah m. Thornburg, Thos.	May 28, 1806	Ellis Ellis	John Bond	3b 21	cr 28	mr 22 *
Ellis, Sarah Ann m. Jacques, Denton	Mar. 28, 1836			6b 75		

Name	(marriage)	(surety)	(minister)	(bond)	code
Ellis, Susanna m. Carter, Thomas	Mar. 9, 1789	Thos. Thompson	D. Thomas	6b200	mr 37 *
Ellis, Wesley m. Thompson, Rebecca	Mar. 12, 1840	Swearingen Ray	Lewis F. Wilson	3b323	mr 71 *
Ellison, Jacob m. Ray, Eliz.	May 13, 1815			4b 87	*
Emberson, Cath. L. m.Sappington, Wm.	Nov. 11, 1818	Leonard Emberson	W.N.Scott	5b191	mr 30 *
Emberson, Daniel m. Ebberts, Eliz.	Apr. 10, 1831	James Ardinger	Nathan Young	5b191	mr 61 *
Emberson, Eliz. m. Sellers, Geo.	June 1, 1829	Daniel Emberson	Nathan Young	5b131	mr 60 *
Emerson, Francis m. Pitzer, Cath.	Nov. 11, 1830	Mathias Pitzer	Nathan Young	5b180	mr 61 *
Emerson, John m. Bartleson, Marg't	Jan. 29, 1838	Thomas Jordan		6b117	
Emerson, Mary m. Newson, Abraham	Apr. 19, 1834	Charles Ardinger		6b 8	
Emerson, Noble m. Keesecker, Mary	Aug. 13, 1830	Fielding Colbert	John S. Light	5b173	mr 62 *
Emerson, Warner m. Basore(Bays-)Eliz.	Feb. 6, 1844	Jacob Basore	John Light	6b313	mr 76 *
Emert, George m. Cushwa, Marg't	Mar. 27, 1823	?	Chas. P. Krauth	4b236	mr 46 *
Emert, Geo. C. m. Noll,Susan Nicod's	Nov. 25, 1847	Gottlieb Noll	D. Bragunder	7b114	mr 78 *
Emert, Marg't m. Withrow, Joseph	May 7, 1832	Harrison Waite	Jas. M. Brown	5b228	mr 64 *
Emery, George m. Welsh, Marg't	Nov. 5, 1794		Richard Swift		mr 40 *
Emrick, Nicholas m. Upsalom,Hannah	Aug. 16, 1792		David Young		gc 2
Endler, Marg't m. Hummel, Geo.	Jan. 17, 1795		David Young		gc 4
England, Eliz. m. Smith, Charles	Jan. 24, 1810	Jacob England		3b134	*
Englatt, Joseph m. Mann, Catherine	Oct. 2, 1840	Andrew Mann		6b219	*
Englatt, Michael m. Mann, Marg't	Oct. 2, 1840	Andrew Mann		6b219	*
Engle, Cath. m. Freshour, George	Feb. 14, 1797		David Young		gc 6
Engle, John m. Coons, Mary	May 22, 1800	Jacob Coons	Richard Swift	2b 70	cr 34
Engle, Martha m.Hutchinson,John Isaac	Feb. 6, 1821	Wm. D. Engle	John B. Hoge	4b171	mr 41 *
Engle, Mary m. Melvin, John Jr.	May 30, 1799	John Engle	Moses Hoge	2b 8	cr 29 *
Engle, William m. Lemon, Mary	Oct. 29, 1798	Frederick Imhoff		1b142	mr 17 *
English, David m. Douglas, Rachel	Aug. 1, 1849	Wm. Barnett		2b 14	
English, Henry m. VanDoren, Eliz. V.	Apr. 9, 1799	Jacob VanDoren		7b153	
English, John m. Carter(Casler),Eliz.	Jan. 21, 1799	Robert Carter	John Potts	1b165	cr 12 *
English, Mary m. Murphy, John	June 24, 1788		Moses Hoge		mr 18 *
Erick, John m. Price, Susanna	Jan. 5, 1803	James Walker	John Mines	2b189	cr 27 *
Enriss, John m. Green, Molly	Feb. 24, 1830	William Green	Robert Cadden	5b153	mr 21 *
Ensminger, Christian m.Harmison,Matty	Dec. 14, 1812	Henry Schriver		3b243	mr 61 *
Ensminger, David m. Stripe, Hannah	Mar. 29, 1810	Mathias Keesacre	Rev. Reebenack	3b144	gc 11 *
Ensminger, Martha m.Rooney, Michael	Nov. 27, 1816	Cornelius Keely		4b 25	
Entler, Mary m. Yost, John	May 13, 1797	Jacob Entler	David Young	1b 16	gc 6 *
Entler, Solomon m. Faris, Sarah	Feb. 15, 1815	William Faris		3b310	
Errick, Eliz. m. Welshans, Daniel Jr	Nov. 10, 1807	*Danl Welshans Sr.		3b 76	
Errick, Jane m. Chestnut, William	Jan. 19, 1799	George Errick	David Young	1b164	gc 8 *
Errick, John m. Price, Susanna	Jan. 5, 1803	James Walker	John Mines	2b189	cr 27 *
Esidant, Charles m. Smith, Cath.	Aug. 20, 1827	John Murray	B. Reynolds	5b 75	mr 21 *
Essex, Joseph m. McClay, Nancy	Aug. 31, 1799	James McClay		2b 24	mr 51 *
Esthem, Barbara m. Bellensty, James	Jan. 10, 1792	*George Errick(also)	David Young		gc 1 *

*George Errick(also)

Name	Date	(marriage)	(suretor)	(minister)	(bond)			*
Evans, Chas. H. m. Middlekauff,Ann V.	Nov. 24,	Mar. 15, 1854	William Orrick	D.F.Braqunier	2b149			*
Evans, Eliz. m. McAllister, Benj.	Dec. 31,	1801	Elijah Williams	David Young	1b158			*
Evans, Eliz. m. McCormick, Moses	Jan. 4,	Dec. 31, 1798	*John Shoafstall		2b217			
Evans, Eliz. m. Shoafstall, Isaac	Aug. 23,	1804	Stephen Snodgrass		5b238			
Evans, Eliz. B. m. Larimore, Robert	Nov. 12,	Nov. 13, 1832	John Bell	W. Monroe	5b112		mr 53	*
Evans, Gabriel m. Hays, Charity		1789		D. Thomas			mr 38	*
Evans, Hezekiah W. m. Bell, Juliana	Nov. 12,	1828		W. Monroe	5b112	cr 16	mr 53	*
Evans, Isaac m. Myers, Susan (Sarah)	Jan. 16,	1828	John Bell	Thomas Adams	3b 42		mr 23	*
Evans, Isaac m. Dawson, Lillian Rose	Jan. 31,	1807	Teter Myers	B. Reynolds	5b 34		mr 49	*
Evans, Isaac W. m. Orrick, Sarah Ann	July 20,	1826	John Dawson		6b 82			
Evans, Isaac W. m. Silver, Lydia	Jan. 20,	1836	James Orrick		5b185			
Evans, Isabella J. m. Rees, John E.		1831	John Faris					
Evans, Jacob V. m. Walker, Eliza	Feb. 10,	1853	Jacob Poisal	R.G.Chenoweth	6b256		mr 87	*
Evans, James m. Wickersham, Maria	Dec. 7,	1841	Samuel Swingley	John Hedges	4b229		mr 73	*
Evans, Jefferson m. Snodgrass,Mary	Nov. 26,	1822	Jas. M. Brown	James Samson	5b 85		mr 45	*
Evans, Jeremiah m. Turner, Mary	T.Dec.	1828	Charles Orrick	Richard Swift	2b177	cr 32	mr 51	*
Evans, John m. Evans, Nancy	Aug. 14,	1802	Magnus Tate	Moses Hoge	3b 7	cr 17	mr 20	*
Evans, John m. McFadden, Eliz.	Dec. 31,	1806?		David Young		go 2	mr 22	*
Evans, John m. Tate, Eliz.	June 11,	1793	John Porterfield		4b216			
Evans, John m. Varmetre, Mary	Jan. 19,	1822		Moses Hoge		cr 36	mr 13	*
Evans, John T. m. Maxwell, Susan	Jan. 26,	1797	Washington Evans	W. Monroe	5b149		mr 54	*
Evans, John V. m. Bell, Mary	Oct. 31,	1830	John Bell	B. Reynolds	5b 82		mr 52	*
Evans, Joseph m. Snodgrass, Ann	Jan.	1827		Hugh Vance			mr 34	*
Evans, Joseph m. Thomas, Mary		1786	James Faulkner	D. Thomas	3b 10		mr 37	*
Evans, Kitty m. Snodgrass, Robert		1789	Isaac Evans		3b 57			
Evans, Margaret m. Harlan, Silas	Feb. 3,	1806	Mathew Ramone	John Mathews		cr 13	mr 23	*
Evans, Margaret m. Williams, Elijah	Apr. 22,	1807	Isaac Varmetre	David Young	1b161	go 6		
Evans, Martha m. Barnhouse,Richard	Jan. 12,	1797	Silas Harlan	David Young	3b124	go 8		
Evans, Martha m. Gorrell, Joseph	Jan. 16,	1799			6b 56			
Evans, Mary E. m. Harlan, Levi	Nov. 18,	1809	Magnus Tate		3b 7			
Evans, Mary S. m. Robbins, Geo. W.	Sept 14,	1835	Silas Harlan	D.F.Spriggs	4b173	cr 17	mr 22	*
Evans, Nancy m. Evans, John	Dec. 31,	1853	John McIver	Moses Hoge	2b181		mr 41	*
Evans, Nancy m. Harlan, Joshua(Jehu)	Feb. 26,	1806?		John B. Hoge				
Evans, Nancy m. Varmetre, Joseph	Sept 18,	1821						
Evans, Polly m. Varmetre, Isaac	Jan. 19,	1802		David Young		go 2		*
Evans, Rachel m. Hedges(Herges)Jos.	Jan. 15,	1793		David Young		go 3		*
Evans, Richard m. Cross, Cenea	Aug.	1793			4b259			
Evans, Robert m. Baker, Prudence	Mar. 23,	1824	Walter Evans	John L. Gibbons	5b 27		mr 49	*
Evans, Rosanna m. Bently, William	Nov. 9,	1825	Joseph Shaw	David Young		go 5		
Evans, Ruth M. m. Hutzler(Hutz-)Ruth	Aug. 12,	1795	Andrew Griffith					
Evans, Sarah m. Berry, John	Jan. 3,	1851	Robert Jones	Geo. W. Harris	7b209		mr 83	*
Evans, Susan M. m. Harrison, James	July 27,	1801	John Evans,		2b132			
	Sept 5,	1832	*Ephraim Evans(also)	Wm. Monroe	5b239		mr 65	*

Name	date	(marriage)	(suretor)	(minister)	(bond)		
Evans, Thomas m. Cooke, Eliza	Mar. 8,	Jan. 9, 1794	James Orr	B. Fages	7b125	cr 9	mr 10 *
Evans, Tillotson F m. Orr, Mary Ann	June 3,	1848	Basil Cross		3b114		mr 64 **
Evans, Walter m. Cross, Elenor	July 20,	1809	James Maxwell		3b230		mr 9 **
Evans, Washington m. Maxwell, Maria	Oct. 15,	1812	Stephen Snodgrass	Jas. M. Brown	5b244	cr 22	mr 82 **
Evans, Washington m. Snodgrass, Lavin	Oct. 16,	1832					
Evelin, Eliz. m. Martin, Peter	Nov. 4,	1794		Moses Hoge			
Everhart, Barbara m. Snyder, Geo.	Jan. 1,	1849	Teter Everhart	J.H.Jennings	7b143		
Everhart, Barbara E. m. Kees, John	Aug. 28,	1848	Teter Everhart	J.H.Jennings	7b134		mr 33 *
Everhart, Cath. m. Myers, John	Jan. 29,	1798	Geo. Everhart		1b 83		mr 64 **
Everhart, Christfr m. Miller, Sarah	June 1,	1785	Henry Miller	Hugh Vance	5b215		
Everhart, Clara m. Thompson, Thos.	Feb. 1,	1832	James Laughlin	Nathan Young	2b224		
Everhart, Daniel m. Foster, Eliz.	Mar. 2,	1804					mr 66 *
Everhart, Eliz. m. Bishop, Thomas	Feb. 5,	1833	Harrison Waite	Nathan Young	5b256		mr 82 **
Everhart, Ellen m. Kees, John	Aug. 28,	1848	Teter Everhart	J.H.Jennings	7b134		
Everhart, Henry m. Tharp, Abgail	Oct. 21,	1797	Nathan Tharp		1b 57		
Everhart, Hester m. Riner, Andrew	Mar. 9,	1842	Jacob Riner		6b266		
Everhart, John m. Kerns, Cath.	June 2,	1846	John Kerns		7b 67		
Everhart, John m. Tharp, Mary	Aug. 19,	1801	Nathaniel Tharp		2b137		
Everhart, Kitty m. Ogelvie, David	Apr. 12,	1819	Henry Everhart		4b105		
Everhart, Marg't m. Butt, William	Feb. 17,	1837	Henry Butt	R.N.Herndon	6b 97		mr 69 *
Everhart, Marg't m. Oxenrider, Henry	Aug. 23,	1825	John Walter	Chas. P. Krauth	5b 21		mr 49 **
Everhart, Martha Jane m. James, Walter	Jan. 22,	1858		J.H.Jennings			*
Everhart, Mary m. Riner, Jacob	Mar. 9,	1837	Natnan Everhart	Lewis F. Wilson	6b100		
Everhart, Nathan m. Siler, Sarah	Mar. 6,	1816	Philip Siler	Rev. Reebenack	4b 15	gc 15	
Everhart, Nathan Jr. m. Kees, Eliza	July 30,	1851	Jacob Kees		7b239		mr 82 *
Everhart, Peter m. Snyder, Hannah	Dec. 23,	1850	Jacob Kees	J.H.Jennings	7b185		mr 75 *
Everhart, Philip m. Satterfield, Sarah	May 21,	1844	Harrison Waite	James Chisholm	6b321		mr 86 *
Everhart, Sarah m. Kees, Jacob	Apr. 29,	1853		J.H.Jennings			mr 82 *
Everhart, Teter m. Snyder, Hannah	Jan. 6,	1850	Jacob Kees	J.H.Jennings	7b185	cr 41	mr 25 *
Everly, Charlotte m. Eberts, John	May 21,	1814	George Hill	John Bond	3b306	cr 29	mr 9 *
Eversole, Abraham m. Martin, Kath.	Nov. 2,	1794		W. Hill			
Eversole, Cath. m. Miles, Wm.	Dec. 23,	1835	Isaac Eversole		6b 68		
Eversole, Daniel m. Ainsworth, Eliz.	Apr. 1B,	1800	Wm. Ainsworth		2b 66		
Eversole, Eliza m. Eversole, Jacob	Feb. 17,	1852	Christian Eversole	Wm. Hill	7b246	cr 30	mr 9 *
Eversole, Eliz. m. Williams, Patrick		1821					
Eversole, Henry m. Loveless, Sally	Aug. 20,	1793	Thomas Taffe		4b187		
Eversole, Isaac m. Powell, Lydia	Aug. 15,	1831	John McFarland	W. Monroe	5b211		mr 62 *
Eversole, Jacob m. Eversole, Eliza	Dec. 13,	1852	Christian Eversole		7b246		
Eversole, Jacob m. Miller, Eliz.	Feb. 17,	1834	Henry M. Miller		6b 10		
Eversole, John m. Bear, Jane	Apr. 26,	1836	Isaac Eversole		6b 66		
Eversole, John m. Randall, Ellen	Jan. 6,	1851	John F. Crowl		7b217		
Eversole, John F. m. Crowl	Mar. 5,						
Eversole, Mary m. Miles, John	Mar. 19,	1833	Isaac Eversole		5b262		
Eversole, Nancy m. Weaver, Wm.	Jan. 5,	Jan. 8, 1833	Sanl Middlekauf	W. Monroe	5b252		mr 65 *

Name	Date	(marriage)	(surety)	(minister)	(bond)			
Eversole, Rosanna m. Perrel, Thos.	Apr. 8,	Apr. 9, 1839	James Pitzer	John Light	6b166		mr	70 *
?Evis, David m. Godhart, Eliz.		June 13, 1789		Moses Hoge		cr 2	mr	2 *
*Evis, Jane m. Godhart, John		Mar. 1, 1791		Moses Hoge	3b 64	cr 6	mr	6 *
Ewing, Ann m. Worthington, Samuel	July 30,		John Gray			gc 3		*
Ewing, John m. Gordon, Rachel		Apr. 11, 1793		David Young		cr 2		*
?*Evis, Richard m. Godhart, Elis.		June 13, 1789		Moses Hoge			mr	2 *

"F"

Name	Date	(marriage)	(surety)	(minister)	(bond)			
Faber, Eliza m. Marker, Leonard	Mar. 13,	Mar. 14, 1798	Adam Farber	David Young	1b 89	gc 7		*
Fackwell, Will m. Heller, Cath.		Oct. 22, 1793		David Young	6b318	gc 3		*
Fague, Solomon Jr m. Faris, Rebecca	Apr. 2,	Apr. 13, 1844	John Hoke	W. Monroe	5b137		mr	75 *
Faidley, Arch'd m. Young, Rosana	Aug. 13,	Aug. 13, 1829	Adam Young	Jacob Medtart	3b 73	cr 13	mr	63 *
Falk, Cath. m. Westenhaver, John	Sept 30,	Oct. 1, 1807	Christ'r Faulk	John Mathews	3b113	cr 10	mr	23 *
Falk, Jacob m. Small, Polly	May 17,	May 18, 1809	Jacob Small	*Rev. Reebenack	1b 74	gc 7		*
Falk, John m. Hensel, Eliz.	Dec. 26,	Dec. 26, 1797	Lawrence Hensell	David Young	3b283	gc 14		*
Falk, Rebecca m. Keefer, Joseph	Feb. 8,	Feb. 10, 1814	Abraham Folk	Rev. Reebenack		gc 21	mr	24 *
Faltom, Samuel m. Watson, Rebecca		Sept 8, 1794		John Boyd		cr 8	mr	8 *
Fanas, Patrick m. McCany, Cath.		Mar. 24, 1799		David Young		gc		*
Funglinder, Geo. m. Lay, Prudence	July 26,	July 26, 1826	Samuel Taylor	David Young	5b 44	gc 7		*
Far, Mary m. Noncum, George		Jan. 4, 1798		David Young			mr	30 *
Farber, Cath. m. Snyder, Wm.		Sept 21, 1819		Mathias Riser			mr	67 *
Farber, Christian m. McDonald, Sarah	Aug. 3,	Aug. 8, 1833	Chas. McDonald	Wm. Monroe	5b278		mr	53 *
Farber, Eliz. m. Noland, Thos.	Oct. 18,	Oct. 23, 1828	Christ'r Farber	Wm. Monroe	5b109			*
Farber, Henry m. Yost, Polly	Sept 23,	1799	William Yost		2b 27		mr	43 *
Farsacre, James m. Savely, Rosanna		Jan. 16, 1787		Hugh Vance			mr	30 *
Faris, Aaron m. Young, Hannah		Jan. 14, 1819		Mathias Riser			mr	8 *
Faris, Aaron m. Park(Bark), Jane		Dec. 23, 1794		John Boyd	7b180	cr 21	mr	80 *
Faris, Ann B. m. Deck, Abraham	Apr. 10,	Apr. 10, 1850	Henry C. Faris	W. Love	6b237		mr	72 *
Faris, Cath. m. Beall (Bell), Joseph	Mar. 18,	Mar. 1, 1841	John Faris	John Hedges			mr	43 *
Faris, Charity m. White, John		May 1786		Hugh Vance			mr	43 *
Faris, David Jr. m. Hendriek, Eliz.		June 8, 1786		Hugh Vance	3b278	gc 14	mr	76 *
Faris, Geo. m. McAlister, Eliz.	Nov. 27,	Dec. 2, 1813	Thos. C. Smith	Rev. Reebenack	7b 50		mr	40 *
Faris, Henry Clay m. Daily, Rachel A	Dec. 20,	Dec. 24, 1845	John Daily	J.S.Reynoldson				*
Faris, John m. Bett, Klender		Apr. 17, 1794		Richard Swift	4b281			*
Faris, John m. Pulse, Mary	Dec. 23,	Dec. 23, 1824	George I, Boltz		2b 2	cr 28	mr	16 *
Faris, Mary m. Claspy, Joseph	Apr. 13,	Apr. 16, 1799	James Faris	Richard Swift			mr	43 *
Faris, Nancy m. Harper, Wm.		May 9, 1786		Hugh Vance				*
Faris, Nancy m. Stern, Alex.	Feb. 21,	Feb. 1, 1803	Aaron Faris		2b194			*
Faris, Rachel m. O'Neal, Joseph	May 1,	May 15, 1826	Peter Hoke	Benedict Reynolds	5b 41		mr	49 *
Faris, Rebecca m. Chambers, Anthony	Oct. 18,	1816	Wm. Faris		3b344			*

Name	(marriage)		(surety)	(minister)	(bond)	Ref
Faris, Rebecca m. Wares(Waver),Andrew	Apr. 2,	1793	John Hoke	Richard Swift	6b318	mr 38 *
Faris, Rebecca Ann m. Fague,Solomon	Feb. 15,	1844	William Faris	W. Monroe	3b310	mr 75 *
Faris, Sarah m. Entler, Solomon	Mar. 8,	1815			4b139	
Faris, Wm. m. Rousch, Cath.	Mar. 9,	1820	Henry Rousch	John Hoge	1b 25	mr 31 *
*Farr, Christina m. Bartholomew,Jacob	July 17,	1797	John Merritt		1b 47	*
Farr, Edward m. Newlin, Mary	Sept 27,	1797	John St. Clair		1b 92	
Farr, Joseph m. Chamberlain,Abigail	Mar. 27,	1798	Benj. Beeler		1b 78	*
Farr, Mary m. Newcomb, George	Jan. 2,	1798	John Farr		2b251	
Farr, Mary m. Spear, Wm.	Jan. 3,	1805	Benjamin Lecky		1b174	
Farr, Patrick m. Kann, Cath. M.	Mar. 21,	1799	Patrick McGonegal		5b278	mr 67 *
Farrar(Farber),C.S. m.McDonald,Sarah	Aug. 8,	1832	Chas. McDonald	W. Monroe	1b100	cr 32
Farrell, Eliz. m. Truelock, Parker	Nov. 1,	1797	Robert Jack	John Boyd	2b 94	mr 13 *
Farrell, Mary m. Miles, John	Oct. 21,	1800	Joseph Farrell		2b 20	
Farrell, Peggy m. Steele, John	Aug. 14,	1799	Elsha Boyd			
Faschtwin, Metia m. Mixall, John	Jan. 25,	1791		David Young	1b 89	ge 1
Fauber, Eliz. m. Marker, Leonard	Mar. 13,	1798	Adam Fauber	David Young	3b238	ge 7
Fauber, Nicholas m. Dawson, Marg't	Oct. 24,	1812	Ephraim Dawson	Moses Hoge	7b 15	cr 7 / mr 6 *
Faulk, Charles m. Strider, Eliz.	Apr. 3,	1791	John Wysong	Lewis F. Wilson	2b201	gc 10
Faulk, John S. m. Mathews, Marg't	Dec. 11,	1844	Christ'r Folk	David Young	5b286	
Faulk, Salome m.Kephart, Bernard	May 4,	1803		A.H.Boyd	2b216	
Faulkner, Annie A. m. Bocock, Thos.8	Oct. 4,	1853	Elisha Boyd	Jas. M. Brown	5b 12	mr 67 *
?Faulkner, Chas. J. m. Boyd, Mary W.	Sept 26,	1833	William Mackey	Richard Swift	2b216	cr 27 / mr 21 *
?Faulkner, James m. Mackey, Sally	Dec. 15,	1803	Cornelius Kelly	A.H.Boyd		cr 27
Faulkner, James m. Minghini, Hannah	May 23,	1825		Richard Swift		cr 21
Faulkner, Sally P. m. Lott, Garrett	Oct. 4,	1853		Hugh Vance		cr 40
?Faulkner, Samuel m. Mackey, Sally	Dec. 15,	1803	William Mackey	Moses Hoge	2b216	cr 21
Faulkner, Thomas m. Hornbaker, Eliz.	Sept 24,	1789		John Boyd	2b 12	cr 34
Fawrence, Rebecca m. Morgan, John	Apr. 8,	1793				
Fauster, Nancy m. Laughlin, James	July 31,	1799	Charles Black		6b258	
Fearman, Eleanor m. Davis, Geo.	Dec. 14,	1841	Henry Fearman		3b218	
Fearman, Henry Jr. m. Bond, Mary	Apr. 8,	1812	Lewis B. Willis		3b348	
Fearman, Henry Jr. m. VanPelt, Anna	Nov. 28,	1815	Jacob VanPelt		6b 84	
Fearman, Maria m. Powell, Arch'd M.	Aug. 17,	1836	Thos. Friddle			
Fedder, Susanna m. Jones, Rob't Hiram	Dec.17,	1831	Fred. Brenner	Nathan Young	5b212	mr 62 *
Feller, Jane m. McMullen, Nimrod	Nov. 25,	1833	Henry Fellers	Nathan Young	5b291	mr 66 *
Fellers, Geo. R. m. Stephens, Mary J	Dec. 23,	1844	Benj. Stephens		7b 17	
Fellers, Lorixon m. Fiser, John	Aug. 17,	1829	Henry Fellers		5b138	
Fellers, Mary Ann m. Henry, Philip	Apr. 6,	1839	Henry Fellers	P. Harrison	6b165	mr 71 *
Fellers, Mary Jane m. Myers, Alfred	Mar. 22,	1855	Henry Fellows	J.L.Frary		
Fellows, Eliz. m. Myers, Benjamin	Mar. 3,	1836		John Howell	6b 73	mr 68 *
Felter, Cath. m. Bremner, Fred.	Mar. 2,	1824	Lemuel Dalrick		4b262	
Felts, Mary M. Brown, William	Apr. 17,	1848	John Dalrick	D.F.Bragunier	7b121	mr 78 *
Femensdahl, Cath.m. Spelman,Solomon	Feb. 3,	1816		Mathias Riser		
*Farnsworth, David m. Butler, Susan	Mar. 4,	1844	Jeremiah Butler		6b315	

(names)	(marriage)	(surety)	(minister)	(bond)			
Fendrick, Richard m. Gerringer, Eliz.	Feb. 18, 1802	Malachi Grove	Richard Swift	2b161	cr 32	mr 20	*
Fenner, Eliz.m. Fisher, John	Oct. 10, 1816		Mathias Riser	2b161			*
Fenner, James m. Brown, Mary	Aug. 18, 1800	Adam Brown		2b 82			
Fenster, Ellen m. Yaoban, Patrick	Aug. 12, 1841	Dominick O'Connel		6b245		mr 20	*
Fenwick, Richard m. Gerringer, Eliz.	Feb. 18, 1802	Malachi Grove	Richard Swift	2b161			
Ferby, Nancy m. Marchant, Abraham	Jan. 13, 1812	Weitman Ferby		3b208			
Ferguson, Cath. m. Brown, Timothy	Nov. 7, 1803	Fred. Rorebaugh		2b211	gc 5		*
Ferguson, Isaac m. Harns, Sarah	Feb. 8, 1796		David Young		gc 5		*
Ferguson, Rachel m. Postgale, Billy	Feb. 8, 1796		David Young				
Fernough, Matty m. Goodright, Leonard	Apr. 27, 1811	Daniel Fernough		3b185			
Fernow, Daniel m. Ridenour, Cath.	Sept 28, 1811	Leonard Goodnaugh		3b195			
Ferrell, Eliz. m. Hiser, Lewis	Sept 1, 1800	John Unseld		2b 83			
Ferrell, Effy m. Stuckey, Jacob S.	Mar. 19, 1844	Benj. Ferrell		6b316		mr 82	*
Ferrell, Jacob m. Robinson, Jane	Dec. 12, 1850		James Chisholm			mr 77	*
Ferrell, John m. Stuckey, Marg't Ann	Nov. 30, 1846	Chas. Stuckey	D.F.Spriggs	7b 78		mr 86	*
Ferrell, Thos. m. Dix, Rebecca	Mar. 6, 1853		Nathan Young			mr 60	*
Fetter, John m. Keesecker, Susanna	Oct. 22, 1828	Henry Keesecker	Wm. Tibbett	5b110			
Fickling, Eliz. m. Elbert, John	Nov. 23, 1797	Fielding Beall		1b 63	cr 27	mr 13	*
Fields, Philip m. Cahill, Catherine	Sept 25, 1805	Dennis Cahill		3b 1			
Flery, Bridget m. Vermilion, Curtis	Jan. 28, 1855		James Watts		cr 26	mr 7	*
Figg, John m. Mitchell, Eliz.	Mar. 15, 1792		Moses Hoge	3b146			
Files, Jacob m. Slonaker, Mary	Feb. 7, 1854	Joseph Haines	John O. Proctor	5b 97			
Files, John m. Hovermale, Marg't	Apr. 13, 1810	Abraham Vanmetre		4b112			
Files, John Jr. m. Vanmetre, Eliza	Apr. 8, 1828	John Files					
Files, Mary m. Martin, Levi	Aug. 4, 1819						
Files, Thos. A. m. Vanmetre, Rachel	Oct. 15, 1833	Arch'd Butt	G.W.Cooper	2b 6			
Filson, George m. Sack, Isabel	Apr. 29, 1795	Edw. Foreman	Richard Swift	3b280	cr 26	mr 10	*
Filson, Jane m. Miller, Jacob	May 26, 1795	Daniel Stoley	Richard Swift	3b 72	cr 26	mr 10	*
Filson, John m. Butt, Jemima	May 21, 1799		Seely Bunn		cr 34	mr 16	*
Filson, Rachel m. Basore, David	Dec. 30, 1813	John Finch		2b 60	cr 41	mr 25	*
Filson, Thomas m. Foreman, Mary	Oct. 1, 1807						
Finch, David m. Place, Mary	? 1818		Mathias Riser	5b177		mr 29	*
Finch, Thomas m. Hooke, Ruth	Mar. 29, 1800	William Long		5b273			
Finley, David m. Yeates, Mary	May 19, 1796	William Long	John Boyd	1b 22	cr 11	mr 12	*
Finley, Jas. W. m. Long, Eliz. Mary	Oct. 14, 1830	Wm. Gilbert	Jas. M. Brown			mr 54	*
Finley, Wm. Warren m. Long,Lucinda S	May 8, 1833			5b 47			
Finney, John m. Luke, Mary	June 20, 1797	Thos. Crawford		6b 97	cr 2		
Fipe, Sarah m. Myers, Thomas	Dec. 9, 1789	Wm. Robinson	Moses Hoge	3b336		mr 3	*
Firth, William m. Crawford, Matilda	Aug. 12, 1826	John Myers		5b138			
Fiser, Jacob m. Puffenberger, Maria	Feb. 11, 1837	Henry Fellers		3b255			
Fiser, James m. Myers, Nancy	Aug. 28, 1815	Michael Fiser					
Fiser, John m. Fellers, Lorixon	Aug. 17, 1829				gc 13		*
Fiser, Marg't m. Myers, John	Mar. 13, 1813		Rev. Reebenack				

Entry	(marriage)	(suretor)	(minister)	(bond)		
Fiser, Mary m. Jones, John	Sept 29, 1798	Michael Fiser		1b136		
Fiser, Michael M. m. Downs, Mary	Aug. 31, 1832	Chas. Downs		5b238		
Fiser, Peter m. McPherson, Marg't	Mar. 16, 1799	Hugh Black		1b173		
Fiser, Sarah m. Boroff, Susanna	July 31, 1810	Michael Fiser	Rev. Reebenack	3b156	gc 11	
Fish, James m. Snyder, Susanna	Feb. 1, 1827	Reginal Butt	B. Reynolds	5b 61		mr 51 *
Fish, John m. McCoy, Mary	Dec. 1, 1828	Henry Payne Jr.	W. Monroe	5b114		mr 53 *
Fishburn, John m. Showalter, Eliza	Dec. 12, 1815	Joseph Showalter	W.N.Scott	3b350		mr 26 *
Fisher, Cath. m. McCormick, Thomas	Dec 27, 1810	Peter Fisher	John B. Hoge	3b169	cr 14	mr 24 *
Fisher, Christina m. Nelsie, Henry	Sept 1, 1795		David Young		gc 5	
Fisher, Edward m. Goodman, Kesiah	Jan. 17, 1795		David Young		gc 4	
Fisher, Elisa m. Gardner, Jacob	Jan. 6, 1825	Michael Billmyre	Chas. P. Krauth	4b283		mr 48 *
Fisher, Elis. m. Lashorn, James	Jan. 15, 1828	Joseph Grubb	B. Reynolds	5b 88		mr 52 *
Fisher, Elis. m. Melius, Stephen	May 20, 1820	Andrew Tate		4b148		
Fisher, Fred. m. Miller, Susanna	Apr. 26, 1801	Mathew Ransome		2b123		
Fisher, George m. Houseman, Elis.	June 20, 1785		Hugh Vance			mr 34 *
Fisher, George m. Kensell, Mary	Aug. 29, 1794		Richard Swift			mr 40 *
Fisher, Jacob m. Burns, Maria	June 19, 1796		David Young		gc 5	
Fisher, Jacob m. Helferstay, Ann E.	Dec. 8, 1836	John Helferstay		6b 89		
Fisher, Jacob m. Shoafstall, Elenor	Nov. 26, 1835	Anthony S.Chambers		6b 64		
Fisher, James m. Ramsburg, Cath.	Jan. 25, 1830	John Ramsburg	W. Monroe	5b150		mr 54 *
Fisher, John m. Byers(Bei-), Elis.	Apr. 30, 1797	Henry Nicely	David Young	1b 3		
Fisher, John m. Chamberlain, Sarah A	Oct. 4, 1834	James Lashorn		6b 20	gc 6	
Fisher, John m. Fenner, Elis.	Oct. 10, 1816		Mathias Riser			
Fisher, John m. Judd, Elis.	May 24, 1800	Mathew Ranson	David Young	2b 71	gc 9	
Fisher, Kath. m. Redkart(Ru-), Adam	June 24, 1788		Moses Hoge			mr 36 *
Fisher, Marg't m. Wherritt, George	Sept 23, 1829	John Shober	Jacob Medtart	5b142		mr 63 *
Fisher, Mary m. Clarke, Solomon	Nov. 14, 1799	Caleb Boothe		2b 35		
Fisher, Mary m. Maxwell, John	Nov. 8, 1820	Peter Fisher		4b166		
Fisher, Mary m. Pittlock, John	Feb. 15, 1791		John B. Hoge		cr 6	mr 41 *
Fisher, Mary m. Vancellor, Ferd.	June 14, 1792		Moses Hoge			mr 6 *
Fisher, Nancy m. Welsh(Wlsh),James	Dec. 5, 1799	William Aikens	Moses Hoge	2b 36	cr 33	mr 39 *
Fisher, Peter m. Chambers,Cath(Esther)	May 13, 1788		John Hedtt(Hutt)			mr 17 *
Fisher, Peter m. Shilly, Davis	June 2, 1788		Hugh Vance			mr 35 *
Fisher, Rachel A. m. Hutcheson,Wm. E.	Dec. 26, 1845	Jas. Hutcheson		7b 51		
Fisher, Sally m. Grubb, Joseph	Dec. 3, 1821	Peter Fisher	John B. Hoge	4b199		mr 44 *
Fisher, Samuel m. McDonald(-Den)Alice	Feb. 17, 1836	Chas. McDonald	John Howell	6b 72		mr 68 *
Fisher, Thos. C.S. m. Cage, Rachel A	June 14, 1838	Joseph Cage	James Watts	6b141		mr 69 *
Fist, Charles m. Snider, Mary	Jan. 24, 1825	Martin Snider		4b287		
Fist, James m. Snyder, Susan	Feb. 1, 1827	Reginal Butt	B. Reynolds	5b 61		mr 51 *
Fist, John m. McCoy, Mary	Dec. 8, 1828	Henry Payne Jr.	W. Monroe	5b114		mr 53 *
Fist, Rebecca m. Butt, Reginal	Dec. 15, 1818	John Fist		4b 94		
Fitch, Jane m. Walker, Wm.	Mar. 21, 1789?	Anthony Turner	Wm. Talbott	1b173	cr 24	mr 18 *
Fitch, Peter m. Warner, Mary	Dec. 22, 1785		Hugh Vance			mr 34 *
Fitch, Samuel m. Bryan, Sarah	Dec. 8, 1790		Moses Hoge		cr 5	mr 5 *

Name	(marriage)	(surety)	(minister)	(bond)		
Fitzgerald, Mary m. Whets, John	June 28, 1838	Philip Fitzgerald	James Watts	6b141		mr 69 *
Fitzsimmons, Eve m. Lewis, Joseph	Dec. 18, 1792		David Young		gc 2	**
Fitzsimmons, Nich's m. Stump, Polly	Mar. 4, 1800	Henry Small		2b 56		
Fiser, Michael m. Myers, Cath.	Mar. 27, 1819	John Myers		4b103		
Fizz, Thomas m. Lindsey, Sarah	Nov. 5, 1801	Christ'r Perfetter		2b147		
Flack, Cath. m. Wilson, James	Aug. 5, 1794		John Boyd		cr 21	mr 8 *
Flagg, Elis. m. Clark, John	Aug. 3, 1810	Josiah Flagg		3b156		
Flagg, Frances C. m. Sampson, Wm.	Sept 22, 1824	Jacob Potsal	J.L.Bromwell	4b272		mr 47 *
Flagg, John M. m. Hughes, Eliz.	Nov. 6, 1822	John Faris	Chas. P. Krauth	4b227		mr 45 *
Flagg, Marg't M. m. Riner, David	Dec. 4, 1848	John M. Flagg	P. Lipscomb	7b140		mr 82 *
Flagg, Martha m. Hivner, Joseph	Feb. 18, 1813	Thomas Tabb	John Mathews	3b252		mr 25 *
Flagg, Mary M. m. Riner, David	Dec. 4, 1848	John M. Flagg	P. Lipscomb	7b140		mr 82 *
Flagg, Ruth K. m. Burkhart, Daniel	May 27, 1812	Robert Wilson		3b226		
Flagg, Thos. G. m. Burns, Esther	Dec. 20, 1825	John Burns	Chas. P. Krauth	3b 30		
Fleece, Mary m. McFenn(McFarm) David	Aug. 26, 1798	Robert Grimes	David Young	2b 22	gc 8	mr 49 *
Fleece, Rebecca m. Hayes, Daniel	Jan. 3, 1837	Alex. Catlett		1b 79		
Fleming, Cath. M. m. Baker, Jas. A.	Oct. 30, 1834	Wm. A. Smith	John Light	6b122		mr 67 *
Fleming, Eli m. Leopard, Hannah	Jan. 25, 1798	Adam Leopard		5b301		
Fleming, Henry m. Seaborn, Olive	Dec. 25, 1792	Daniel Seaborn		1b157		
Fleming, James m. Jamison, Mary	June 7, 1845		David Young		gc 2	*
Fleming, Joseph m. McAllister, Ann S.	May 8, 1834	Benj. McAllister	John Light	7b 33		mr 76 *
Fleming, Mary m. Ward, Joseph	Jan. 21, 1827	Jacob Harrison	John Light	5b300		mr 67 *
Fleming, We. m. Crowl, Mary Mrs.	Dec. 31, 1807	Richard Higgins		3b 86		
Fleming, We. m. Thatcher, Mary	July 27, 1807	Samuel Dunham		3b 64		
Fletcher, Axel m. Gardner, Jane	Feb. 23, 1848	Jacob Price		3b 48		
Fletcher, Elis. m. Custer, Peter	Oct. 19, 1828	John M. Grubb	Richard T. Brown	7b137		mr 79 *
Fletcher, Moses m. Gray, Lucy(Lacey)	Mar. 4, 1820	Hannam Gray	Nathan Young	5b 92		mr 59 *
Fletcher, Peter m. Boak, Mary Mrs.	June 19, 1799	Paul Taylor		4b151		
Flickinger,Magda m. Wolldim, Jos.	Dec. 10, 1820	Michl Flickinger	David Young	2b 39	gc 9	*
Flinn, Maidtabel m. Gano, John	Feb. 18, 1818	Abraham Levy		4b135		
Flinn, Nancy m. Shierly, Daniel	May 26, 1812	Joshua Robinson	Mathias Riser	4b 71	gc 13	mr 29 *
Floukee, Sally m. Hite, Wm.	Dec. 14, 1814	Jacob Houck	Rev. Reebenack	3b242		
Flowers, Elis. m. Crumley, Henry	Apr. 11, 1843	Morris Rees		3b292		
Floyd, Wm. m. Day, Anastasia	Oct. 5, 1799	Bridget Day		6b304		
Fluckinger, Magda Wollman, Joseph	Dec. 10, 1830	Michael Flickinger	David Young	2b 39	gc 9	*
Fogle, George F. m. Chambers, Eliza	Feb. 11, 1807	Ezekiel Showers	Jacob Medtart	5b152		
Folk, Cath. m. Westenhaver, John	Sept 30, 1835	Christ'r Folk	John Mathews	3b 73	or 13	mr 63 *
Folk, Elis. m. Lefevre, Daniel	Feb. 23, 1801	Henry Small		6b 32		mr 23 *
Folk, Elis. m. Reel, Peter	Jan. 12, 1809	Christ'r Folk		2b108		
Folk, Hannah m. Keefer, Joseph	Aug. 28, 1850	Christ'r Folk	Lewis Mayer	3b117	cr 16	mr 24 *
Folk, Jacob m. lingamfelter,Martha J	Dec. 4, 1809	W. H. Lingamfeltr	D.F. Spriggs	7b204		mr 82 *
Folk, Jacob m. Small, Polly	May 17, 1809	Jacob Small	Rev. Reebenack	3b113	go 10	**
Folk, John m. Hensell, Elis.	Dec. 26, 1797	Lawrence Hensell	David Young	1b 74	go 7	*

Name	Date	(marriage)	(surety)	(minister)	(bond)		
Folk, Magdala m. Lingamfelter, Abr'm	May 11,	May 14, 1799	Daniel Lefevre	David Young	6b207	ge 8	*
Folk, Mary Ann m. Bopp, Solomon	Jan. 23,	May 14, 1840	Hbbard	Lewis F. Wilson	6b 29		mr 71 *
Folk, Peter m. Hibbard, Barbara	Jan. 13,	1835	Hbbard		1b180		
Folk, Polly m. Lingamfelter, Abraham	May	1799	Christ'r Folk		3b283	ge 14	mr 24 *
Folk, Rebecca m. Keefer, Joseph	Feb. 8,	Feb. 10, 1814	Abraham Folk	Rev. Reebenack	2b201	ge 10	
Folk, Salome m. Kephart, Bernard	May 2,	May 3, 1803	Christ'r Folk	David Young			
?Fonens, Samuel m. Cox, Anna		Dec. 4, 1784		Hugh Vance			mr 32 *
Foran, David m. Cunningham, Ellen	Aug. 23,	Aug. 25, 1822	James O'Donnell	John B. Hoge	4b222		mr 44 *
Forbes, Eliz. m. Thornburg, Eli	Oct. 4,	Oct. 5, 1824	James Forbes	Nathan Young	4b273		mr 58 *
Forbes, John m. Harris, Maria	Apr. 23,	Apr. 23, 1821	Lazar s Noland	Nathan Young	4b182		mr 57 *
Ford, Ann m. Woke, David		Feb. 4, 1816		Mathias Riser			mr 26 *
Ford, David m. Compton, Deborah	Apr. 18,	Apr. 16, 1835	Edward Winning		6b 41	cr 15	mr 25 *
Ford, Henry m. Nichols, Elenor	Apr. 15,	Aug. 3, 1812	Amos Nichols Jr.	Lewis Mayer	3b221	cr 13	
Ford, Joseph m. Vermilion, Susan	July 24,	1813	John Lown	Rev. Reebenack	3b266	ge 13	
Ford, Mary m. Edelin, Charles	Dec. 1,	1800	James Ford		2b101		
Ford, Mary m. Newkirk, James	Jan. 28,	1833	Wm. P. Hammond		5b255		
Fordt, Joseph m. Vermilion, Susan	July 24,	Aug. 3, 1813	John Lown	Rev. Reebenack	3b266	cr 37	mr 16 *
Foreby, Waitman m. Luke(Luck), Jean	Jan. 22,	Aug. 25, 1798	Richard Blue	John Heit(fmtt)	1b103	cr 31	mr 15 *
Foreman, Edward m. Snodgrass, Pris'l	Apr. 9,	Apr. 10, 1798	Wm. Snodgrass	Richard Swift	1b 97	cr 26	mr 10 *
Foreman, Ellen m. Mason, Thornton W	Oct. 1,	1849	Samuel Mathews		7b165	cr 14	mr 24 *
Foreman, Eliz. m. Ellis, Benjamin	Oct. 11,	1810	George Newkirk		3b163		
Foreman, Eliz. m. Strode, John		Oct. 24, 1795		Richard Swift		cr 7	mr 6 *
Foreman, John m. Shawhan, Mary	Mar. 11,	Mar. 12, 1811	Fred. Shawhan	John B. Hoge	3b178		mr 76 *
Foreman, Mary m. Filson, Thomas	Oct. 1,	1807	Daniel Stoley		3b 72		
Foreman, Mary m. Strode, George		Aug. 23, 1791		Moses Hoge			
Foreman, Mary m. Kroesen, Wash'n	Aug. 4,	Aug. 4, 1846	Robt. P. Bryarly	John Winter	7b 71	cr 31	mr 15 *
Foreman, Nancy m. Mason, James	Apr. 5,	1836	Solomon Billmire		6b 77		mr 44 *
Foreman, Priscilla m. Saunders, Jas.	Jan. 1,	1817	Joseph Foreman		4b 29	ge 8	
Foreman, Rebecca m. Lyles, Ignatius	Oct. 25,	1830	Arch'd Oden		5b179	ge 1	mr 75 *
Foreman, Ruth m. Strode, William	Nov. 6,	Nov. 3, 1798	Joseph Foreman	Richard Swift	1b145		mr 14 *
*Foren, David m. Cunningham, Ellen		Aug. 25, 1822		John B. Hoge			
Forest, Hannah m. Mard, Stephen		Aug. 15, 1799		David Young			
Forrest, Sally m. Locke, Mervil	Sept 25,	Sept 15, 1844	R.P.Bryarly	James Chisholm	7b 6		
Fortney, Christian m. Wilson, Mary		Feb. 21, 1792		David Young			
Fortney, Peter m. Dunham, Sarah	Feb. 17,	Nov. 19, 1792	Paul Verdier	Moses Hoge	1b 85	cr 36	mr 68 *
Foster, Cath. m. Foster, John				David Young			
Foster, Eliz. m. Everhart, Daniel	Mar. 2,	Mar. 2, 1804	James Laughlin		2b224	go 2	
Foster, Isaac m. McMillen, Marg't	Apr. 23,	Apr. 23, 1808	George McMillen		3b 87	go 4	
Foster, James m. Gilbert, Jane		Jan. 3, 1795		David Young		go 2	
Foster, John m. Foster, Catherine		Nov. 19, 1792		David Young		gc 4	
Foster, Magdaline m-Walker, James	May 1,	1797	Jacob Foster		1b 14	gc 2	
Foster, Mary m. Coplan, Jacob	Sept 23,	1799	George Lemon		2b 27		mr 68 *
Foster, Mary m. Sterm(Steen)Stephen	Dec. 13,	Dec. 15, 1834	Jas.W. Gray	Jas. M. Brown	6b 24		mr 32 *
?*Forens, Samuel m. Cox, Anna		Dec. 4, 1784		Hugh Vance			

Name	(marriage)		(surety)	(minister)	(bond)			
Foster, Nancy m. Laughlin, Wm.James	July 31,	1799	Chas. Black	John Boyd	2b 12	cr 34		*
Foster, Rebecca m. Melix, David	Oct. 12,	1798	Jonas Baldwin		1b138		mr 17	*
Foster, Seth B. m. Williams, Jane C	Apr. 16,	1834	Christian D. Wolff		6b 7			
Fough, Geo. F. m. Chambers, Eliza	Feb. 11,	1830	Ezekiel Showers	Jacob Medtart	5b152		mr 63	*
Fouke, Christian m. Swearingen, Peggy	Nov. 2,	1799	Marcus Alder		2b 33			**
Fouke, Hugh m. Kister , Eliz.	Sept 22,	1817	Peter Kister	Mathias Riser	4b 47			**
Fouke, Jos. E. m. Showers, Naomi	Dec. 13,	1824	Seginmund Showers	J.L.Bromwell	4b280		mr 47	**
Fouke, Sarah m. Belts, Daniel	Jan. 3,	1843	Newland Myers		6b286			
Foulk, George m. Holiday, Sarah	Mar. 15,	1847	John W. Holiday		7b 92			
Foulk, John S. m. Mathews, Marg't S	Dec. 11,	1844	John Wysong		7b 15			
Fontch, Hugh m. Kister, Eliz.	Sept 22,	1817	Peter Kister	Mathias Riser	4b 47			**
Fowler, Eliz. m. Bradley, Wm.	Apr. 30,	17837		Hugh Vance			mr 32	**
Fox, Rebecca m. Giles, Wm.	Jan. 22,	1798	Paul Taylor		1b104			
Fox, Sarah m. O'Connor, Hugh	Mar. 5,	1804	William Patterson		2b225			
Foy, Patrick m. Sagathy, Sarah	Nov. 24,	1798	George Mason		1b149			
Foye, Mary m. Grooms, John	June 30,	1797	Robert Grooms		1b 24			
Fraize, John m. Shler, Charity	Jan. 16,	1787		Hugh Vance			mr 43	*
Fraize, Marg't m. Berry, John	Apr. 24,	1797	John Fraize		1b 12			
Frances, Eliz. m. Murphy, John	Oct. 20,	1795		David Young		go 5		*
Frances, Rebecca m. Chambers, Anthony	Oct. 3,	1836	Samuel W. Catlin		6b 86			
Franceway, Bennett m. Shull, Mary Va.	July 28,	1847	David Shull		7b102		mr 78	*
Franceway, Caroline m. Bowers, Jos.	Apr. 11,	1834	Henry Bowers	John Winter	6b 5			
Franceway, Eveline m. Dixon, James	Mar. 17,	1840	Joseph Bowers	P. Harrison	6b200		mr 71	*
Franceway, Joseph m. Eads, Eliz.	Feb. 12,	1791		Moses Hoge		cr 6	mr 6	*
Franceway, Mary m. Hogg, Thomas	Aug. 5,	1844	Wm. B. Welsh	John Light	7b 4		mr 76	*
Franceway, Rebecca m. Butt, Arch'd	Feb. 19,	1788		Hugh Vance		cr 24	mr 2	*
Francis, James m. Campbell, Marg't	Oct. 30,	1794		Moses Hoge		sr 22	mr 9	*
Francis, Rebecca m. Klice, Henry	May 10,	1810	William Francis	Rev. Reebemack	3b151	cr 11	mr 18	*
Francis, Sarah m. Hall(Hull), Wm.	Feb. 19,	1799	Samuel Wood	John Hett(Hutt)	1b169	cr 12		*
Frank, Barbara m. Freise, Frank	July 26,	1791		David Young		go 1		*
Frank, Geo. m. Klaycomb, Maria	Dec. 18,	1794		David Young		go 4		*
Fraser, Alex. m. Modley, Ella	Oct. 22,	1793		Moses Hoge		cr 22	mr 8	*
Frazier, Thomas m. Manor, Eliz.	Dec. 27,	1836	David Manor	Moses Hoge	6b 90			
Frealy, Adam m. Rumsey, Susanna	July 11,	1794		Moses Hoge		cr 22	mr 9	*
Free, Eliz. m. Huffman(Hoffman),John	Feb. 8,	1800	George Kiger	David Young	2b 52	go 9	mr 9	*
Free, George m. Ellenburg, Eliz.	July 22,	1815	Jacob Garinger		3b330			
Free, Peggy m. Harper, James	May 4,	1806	Frederick Free	J. Bond	3b 18	cr 28	mr 22	*
Frees, John m. Shrode, Hannah	Apr. 31,	1813	Solomon Shrode	Nathan Young	3b264		mr 28	*
Frees, Rebecca m. Inbody, George	July 22,	1810	Barney Friese	Rev. Reebemack	3b192	go 12	mr 22	*
Fregen, Marg't m. Bedliff, Joshua	Dec. 24,	1801		David Young		go 9	mr 54	**
Frein, John W. m. Grove, Mary	Jan. 8,	1846	Michael Grove		7b 54			
Freis, Cath. m. Inbody, Mathias	Feb. 11,	1804	Barney Freis		2b223			
Freise, Frank m. Frank, Barbara	July 26,	1791		David Young		go 1		*

Name	(marriage)	(surator)	(minister)	(bond)	
Freise, Hannah m. Smith, Jonas	Feb. 17, Sept. 7, 1836	Harrison Waite	Hugh Vance	6b 71	mr 34 *
Freise, Michael m. Kinder, Katherine	Jan. 26, 1785				mr 78 *
Freise, Peter m. Lucas, Matilda	Jan. 24, 1849	George Swinley	James Chisholm	7b145	
French, Barbara m. Lephart, Michael	Aug. 16, 1806	Jacob French		3b 26	mr 60 *
French, George m. Grantham, Maria	Apr. 12, Apr. 15, 1830	Wm. Grantham	Nathan Young	5b162	mr 4 *
French, George m. Savely, Molly	Oct. 10, 1789		Hugh Vance		cr 25
French, Hannah m. Bowman, Isaac	Mar. 10, 1847	Conrad Crumbaugh		7b 91	mr 82 *
French, Harrison m. Quigley, Cath.	July 19, July 21, 1847	Michael Quigley	Jas. H. Jennings	7b101	
French, Jacob m. Clarke, Marg't	Nov. 4, 1833	John Stephens		5b288	mr 56 *
French, Jacob m. Kitchen, Charity	Feb. 28, Mar. 1, 1818	Joseph Kitchen	Nathan Young	4b 64	
French, Jacob m. Strouse, Eliz.	Oct. 12, 1839	Thos. G. Evans		6b179	
French, John m. Cline, Hannah	Jan. 19, 1818	Swearingen Ray		4b 57	mr 45 *
French, John m. Myers, Sarah	Nov. 11, Nov. 1822	Peter Myers		4b227	
French, John m. Stacey, Sarah	Dec. 14, 1802	Conrad Keesecker		2b187	
French, John m. Strouse, Sarah E.	Mar. 16, 1850	Isaiah Strouse	Chas. P. Krauth	7b179	*
French, John A. m. Dugan, Rebecca A	Jan. 9, 1854				
French, John K. m. Buzzard, Emily	Jan. 21, Jan. 22, 1846	Norman Miller	Jos. H. Plunkett	7b 55	mr 82 *
French, Mary m. Miller, Henry	Apr. 22, 1835	Wm. A. Donaldson	Jas. H. Jennings	6b 42	
French, Mary m. Proctor, Robert	Mar. 14, Mar. 23, 1831	John French		5b188	mr 62 *
French, Mary Ann m. Strouse, Isaiah	Oct. 3, 1848	Conrad Crumbaugh	Jas. M. Brown	7b136	
French, Nancy m. Anderson, Joseph	Sept 2, 1833	George French		5b281	
French, Rachel m. Hout(Hanth),Henry	Apr. 14, Apr. 23, 1812	Henry Job		3b220	
French, Wm. m. Tabler, Rosanna	Mar. 28, 1835	Wash'n Tabler	Rev. Reebenack	6b 38	gc 12
Freshour, Barbara m. Slaine, Peter	Sept 1, 1789				cr 40 mr 4 *
Freshour, Cath. m. Hartman, Henry	Feb. 16, 1796		Hugh Vance		gc 5 mr 29 *
Freshour, George m. Burke, Eliz.	Jan. 25, 1818?		David Young		
Freshour, George m. Custer,Mary Mrs.	Jan. 23, 1826	Daniel Lemaster	Mathias Riser	5b 33	gc 6
Freshour, George m. Engle, Cath.	Feb. 14, 1797				
Freshour, Mary m. Kester, Peter	June 5, 1818	George Freshour	David Young	4b 73	mr 29 *
Freshour, Mathias m. Burk, Nelly	June 16, 1819	George Freshour	Mathias Riser	4b110	mr 29 *
Freshour, Sophia m. Williams, Wm.	Aug. 17, 1797	Alex. Catlett		1b 31	
Freshour, Susan m. Lord, George	Dec. 18, 1792				gc 2
Fricker, Rebecca m. Smith, Henry	Nov. 10, 1789		David Young		cr 15
Friddle, Mary Jane m. Page, Jas. N.	Aug. 25, 1853		Christian Streit		
Friddle, Nimrod m. Williams,Priscilla	July 20, 1846	Thos. S. Friddle	John Light	7b 70	mr 4 *
Friddle, Thos. M. m. Grove, Susan	Nov. 24, 1820	Thomas Grove		4b167	
Friend, Andrew m. Hayes, Harriet	May 8, 1828	Alexander Oden		5b101	
Friend, Elinor m. Jack, Jeremiah Jr.	Nov. 27, 1832	Nathan Davis		5b249	
Frier, Jas. G. m. Holiday, Ann	Jan. 10, 1832	Wm. Holiday		5b214	mr 86 *
Frier, Ruth m. Shirley, James	Mar. 5, 1793				cr 30
Fries, William m. Bowers, Eliz.	Apr. 11, 1846	William Bowers	William Hill	7b 63	mr 10 *
Friese,Peter m. Shoafstall, Sally	May 29, June 1, 1820	Solomon Shrode	W.N.Scott	4b149	
Friese, Rebecca m. Inbody, George	July 22, July 25, 1811	Barney Friese	Rev. Reebenack	3b192	gc 12

Name	(marriage)	(suretor)	(minister)	(bond)	
Frilman, Adeline m. Masch, John N.	May 20, 1846	Norman Miller	W.N.Scott	7b 66	mr 41 *
Fritz, Catherine m. Lynn, Edward	May 4, 1801	Caty Fritz		2b126	mr 78 *
Frize, Michael m. Shoafstall, Sally	May 29, 1820	Solomon Shrode	James Chisholm	4b149	go 4 · mr 2 *
Frize, Peter m. Lucas, Matilda	Jan. 26, 1849	George Swinley	David Young	7b145	cr 1
Frogle, Ruby m. Miller, John	1794		Moses Hoge		
Frogle, George m. Clerk, Marg't	Mar. 3, 1789				
Fry, Catherine m. McGuire, Robert	Nov. 2, 1802	Conrad Fry		2b183	
Fry, Isabel m. Packett, Jos. G.	Mar. 1, 1845	Moses Grantham		7b 28	mr 38 *
Fry, Jacob m. Copeland, Nancy	Feb. 11, 1790		Hugh Vance	2b103	
Fry, Jacob m. Miller, Judith	Dec. 22, 1800	Thomas Sharp		1b148	
Fry, Jean m. Delaplane, Jesse	? 1838?	Daniel Seaborn	Peyton Harrison	6b151	cr 34 · mr 69 *
Fry, John m. Stuckey(Stoo-), Mary	Nov. 21, 1798	John Stuckey	John Boyd	2b 25	mr 17 *
Fry, Mary m. Eckles, Allen	Sept 12, 1799	James McLaughlin		1b 94	
Fry, Michael m. Daugherty, Eliz.	Feb. 12, 1798	William Iles		2b134	
Fry, Nancy m. Hudson, Robert	Aug. 3, 1801	John McMillan			
Fry, Newton H m. Parkinson,Mary A.	Mar. 8, 1841	Wm. Parkinson	Lewis F. Wilson	6b236	go 9 · mr 72 *
Fry, Susanna m. Brannon, James	Apr. 24, 1800	Jacob Fry	David Young	2b 68	mr 61 *
Fryatt, Deborah m. Shoafstall, David	Apr. 25, 1830	John Gallaher	Robert Cadden	5b164	mr 37 *
Fryatt, Eliz. m. McCleary, John	Jan. 1, 1789	Conrad Rousch	Hugh Vance	6b 92	cr 32 · mr 15 *
Fryatt, James m. Rousch, Eliz.	Jan. 26, 1837	Philip Diffenderfr		6b280	mr 32 *
Fryatt, James m. Walters, Eliz. E.	Oct. 20, 1842	Abraham Hooper		6b 5	cr 9 · mr 1 *
Fryatt, John T. m. Hooper, Eleanor	Apr. 10, 1834	Jas. H. Schwartz		6b293	
Fryatt, Marg't Ann m. Seibert, Wm.T.	Mar. 14, 1843	Robert Snodgrass		1b113	
Fryatt, Nancy m. Snodgrass, Wm.	July 7, 1798		John Boyd		
Fryatt, Robert m. Chenoweth, Rachel	Mar. 24, 1783?	Arthur Chenoweth	Hugh Vance		cr 31 · mr 19 *
Fryatt, Sarah m. McConnell, Moses	Jan. 16, 1783		Hugh Vance	3b 38	
Fryatt, Sarah m. Thomas, Thos.	Dec. 23, 1806				
Frye, Barbara m. Hayes, Joseph	June 1, 1801	Thomas Henshaw	Richard Swift	5b 18	
Frye, Barbara m. Landbright, Jacob	June 1, 1801	Conrad Frye	Richard Swift	2b154	
Frye, Cath. m. Shook, Jacob	Aug. 8, 1825	John Trigg		1b 50	
Frye, Marg't m. Bailiff, Joshua	Dec. 24, 1801	William Gilbert		2b138	
Fryer, Mary m. Noland, William	Sept 28, 1797	Wm. H. Lemon		6b230	
Fryer, Mathew m. Rees, Ruth	Aug. 22, 1801	Jonathan Gerrard		1b 20	
Fulk, Jacob m. Lemon, Marg't M.	Jan. 20, 1841	Robert Grimes		1b 1	go 6
Fuller, Frances m. Lenox, John	June 7, 1797	William Wilson	David Young	4b 11	go 15
Fuller, Nathaniel m. Wells, Marg't	Mar. 27, 1797		Rev. Reebenack		mr 33 *
Fuller, Stephen m. Eglestone, Marg't	Mar. 5, 1836		Hugh Vance		mr 41 *
Fullerton, Ann m. McKnight, Robert	Jan. 9, 1786	Cornelius Kelly	W.N.Scott	4b152	
Fullerton, Jane m. McIntyre, Thos.	June 22, 1820			4b106	
Fulton, Eliz. m. Clayton, Henry	June 22, 1819	James Bell	John Boyd		cr 33
Fulton, Marg't m. Bell, James	July 23, 1795				mr 11 *
Fulton, Marg't m. Clayton, John	May 4, 1819	James Bell		4b100	cr 29
Fulton, Mary m. Middleton, Adam	Feb. 22, 1794		William Hill		mr 9 *

	(marriage)	(surety)	(minister)	(bond)		
Fulton, Mary m. Warner, Zebulon Dec. 5,	June 12, 1792	Henry Fulton	Moses Hoge	2b249		mr 39 *
Fulton, Rebecca Mrs. m. Spear, James	1804					mr 8 *
Fulton, Samuel m. Watson, Rebecca	Sept. 8, 1794		John Boyd	7b121	cr 21	mr 78 *
Fultz, Mary m. Brown, William Feb. 3,	Feb. 9, 1848	John Deidok	D.F.Braganier		cr 28	mr 23 *
Fultz, Mary m. Jackson, Francis Aug. 30.	Aug. 30, 1806	John Clouse	J. Bond	3b 28	cr 11	mr 12 *
Furley, David m. Yeates, Mary	May 19, 1796		John Boyd			mr 35 *
Fury, Henry m. Peter , Eliz.	June 10, 1768		Hugh Vance			
Fury, William A. m. Buzzard, Eliz. J July 13,	Aug. 9, 1837	Harrison Waite	Lewis F. Wilson	6b110		
Fuss, John G. m. Schwartz,Fredericka Apr. 17,	Apr. 18, 1839	Mathias Schwartz	P. Harrison	6b167	gc 1	mr 71 *
Fuslaton, Sarah m. Campbell, John	Nov. 14, 1791		David Young			

"G"

	(marriage)	(surety)	(minister)	(bond)		
Gaff, Mary m. McFerla, William	Dec. 22, 1800	John McFerla	Nathan Young	2b103		mr 56 *
Gageby, Allen m. Brown, Eliz.	Aug. 21, 1819	John Brown	F. Israel	4b115		
Gageby, David m. Butt, Mary Ann	Feb. 9, 1854					mr 66 *
Gadlett, Charles m. Lashorn, Rebecca July 27,	July 28, 1837	Ralph Lashorn	Nathan Young	2b278		
Gain, Christian m. Ross, Lydia Jan. 19,	1837	John A. Wolff		6b 92		
Gaines, Ann m. McFellin, Hugh Jan. 2,	Jan. 4, 1800	Mathew McGerry		2b 45	cr 33	
Gaither, Elias m. Catlett, Margaret Apr. 6,	1815	Wm. Catlett	John Heitt(Hutt)	3b319		mr 18 *
Gaither, Ephraim m. Taylor, Kath.	Feb. 2, 1792		Moses Hoge		cr 8	mr 7 *
Gaither, Richard R. m. Slusser,Sarah Apr. 27,	Apr. 28, 1850	David Boyer	Henry Furlong	7b184		mr 81 *
Gaither, Sally m. McPherrin, Thos. May 6,	May 6, 1812	Robert Wilson	Rev. Reebenack	3b224	ge 12	
Gaitrell, Chas. m. Lashorn,Rebecca July 27,	July 28, 1833	Ralph Lashorn	Nathan Young	5b278		mr 66 *
Gaitwell, Harriet m. Bell(-ea), Jos. Jan. 2,	Jan. 3, 1799	Richard Gartsell	David Young	1b159	gc 8	
Galbraith, Martha m. Heard, Joseph	Apr. 12, 1785		Hugh Vance			mr 33 *
Gales, Sarah m. Bloomfield, John Mar. 14,	Mar. 15, 1806	Peter Bellar	John Bond	3b 14	cr 28	
Gallaher, Ann, R. m. Mathews, Geo. Apr. 14,	1846	Harrison Waite		7b 64		mr 22 *
Gallaher, Eliz. m. Beals, Jacob Apr. 5,	1815	Robert Gallaher		3b318		
Gallaher, Eliz. m. McLaughlin, James	Mar. 5, 1793		David Young		gc 2	
Gallaher, James m. Hooper, Hannah Jan. 7,	1819	Jacob Hooper	W.N.Scott	4b 95		mr 30 *
Gallaher, John m. Shaw, Ann Apr. 30.	Apr. 30, 1819?	John Strother	John B. Hoge	4b106		mr 29 *
Gallaher, Joshua S. m. Smith, Ann E.	Mar. 25, 1852		David Thomas			mr 86 *
Gallaher, Marg't m. Gallaher, Sar'l Nov. 1,	1812	John Gallaher		3b239		
Gallaher, Marg't m. Householder, Wm. May 10,	1834	Harrison Waite		6b 12		
Gallaher, Mary m. Shafer, John F. Mar. 26.	1836	Charles Downs		6b 75		
Gallaher, Nancy m. Wintersmith, Chas.Dec. 31,	1810	Robert Gallaher		3b171		
Gallaher, Patrick m. McLaughlin,Susan June 6,	1848	Geo. McLaughlin		7b131		
Gallaher, Robert m. Miller, Rebecca Aug. 8,	1826	John Shober		5b 47		
Gallaher, Samuel m. Gallaher, Marg't Nov. 1,	1812	John Gallaher		3b239		

	(marriage)	(suretor)	(minister)	(bond)		
Gallaher, Samuel m. McCormick, Jane	July 11, 1822	James McCormick	Chas. P. Krauth	4b219		mr 45 *
Gallaway, Wm. m. Gray, Susanna	Aug. 12, 1800	Thomas Griggs		2b 81		
*Games, Anna m. McFellin, Hugh	Jan. 2, 1800	Mathew McGerry	John Hatt(Hettt)	2b 45	cr 33	mr 18 *
Games, James m. Dunn, Margaret	Dec. 27, 1797	Basil Games	John Hill	1b 75	cr 37	mr 14 *
Games, Sarah m. Cage, William	Aug. 16, 1820	Andrew Cage	W.N.Scott	4b156		mr 43 *
Gano, Amos m. Sharp, Eliza	Mar. 18, 1830	James Gano	Jas. M. Brown	5b159		mr 54 *
Gano, Amy m. Hartsook, Wm.	Apr. 6, 1828	Stephen Gano	Nathan Young	5b 95		mr 59 *
Gano, Amy m. Kitchen, Henry	Nov. 16, 1816	John Colter		4b 21		
Gano, Cath. m. Henderson, Joseph	Apr. 30, 1797	Stephen Gano		1b 6		*
Gano, Cath. m. Kitchen, Joseph H.	Feb. 2, 1854	John Gano	R.T.Berry	6b143		
Gano, Cath. m. O'Connell, Dominick	July 16, 1838	Stephen Gano		2b191		
Gano, Eliz. m. Young, Rhesa	Jan. 22, 1803	George Jones		4b270		mr 50 *
Gano, George m. Steel, Jane	Aug. 24, 1824	Joseph Kitchen	John Winter	3b338		
Gano, James m. Kitchen, Catherine	Sept 9, 1815	John Mussetter		5b101		mr 60 *
Gano, James Jr. m. Mussetter, Ruth	May 13, 1828	Abraham Levy	Nathan Young	4b135		
Gano, John m. Flinn, Mahitable	Feb. 18, 1820	Stephen Gano		5b 96		mr 59 *
Gano, John S. m. Hartsook, Mary	Mar. 26, 1828	Harrison Waite	Nathan Young	6b231		mr 71 *
Gano, Joseph m. Stilwell, Jane	Jan. 24, 1841	Oliver Armbrester	Lewis F. Wilson	6b 91		
Gano, Margaret m. Light, John	Dec. 1, 1838	Stephen Gano		4b195		
Gano, Mary m. Barr, Benj. Ross	Oct. 26, 1821	Bethuel Middleton		2b124		
Gano, Mary m. Thatcher, Isaac	Apr. 29, 1801	Stephen Gano		1b 51		
Gano, Naomi m. Middleton, Bethuel	Oct. 2, 1797	James Gano		2b178		
Gano, Pamela m. Brannon, John	Aug. 25, 1802	Joseph Henderson		3b229	gc 13	*
Gano, Rebecca m. Colter, John	June 27, 1812	Joseph Henderson	Rev. Reebenack	1b 6		
Gano, Stephen m. Middleton, Aby	Apr. 30, 1797					
Ganses, Absalom m. Current, Susan	Dec. 28, 1793	John Faris	William Hill	4b157	cr 30	mr 10 *
Garard, Caleb m. Murphy, Sally	Aug. 21, 1820	Thos. Robinson		4b 40		
Garard, John m. Robinson, Eliz.	July 28, 1817	Jas. R. Robinson	W.N.Scott	6b278		mr 75 *
Garard, Lucinda m. Kerns, Peter	Sept 29, 1842	John Snodgrass	James Chisholm	5b 41		mr 50 *
Garard, Seaman m. Collins, Eliz.	May 4, 1826	Christian Garber	John Mathews	5b 89		mr 59 *
Garber, Catherine m. McGee, John	Feb. 27, 1828	John Garber	Nathan Young	5b130		mr 60 *
Garber, Eliz. m. Syler, David	June 1, 1829	Abr'm Robinson	Nathan Young	4b234		mr 46 *
Garber, Jacob m. Robinson, Hannah	Mar. 17, 1822	Adam Mixell	Charles P. Krauth	4b263		mr 47 *
Gard, Eli m. Mixwell, Mary	Apr. 29, 1824	Mary Garden	J.L.Bromwell	3b291	gc 14	
Garden, Rebecca m. Barnett, John R.	Mar. 28, 1814	Ezekiel Showers	Rev. Reebenack	5b242		
Gardner, Abr'm m. Showers, Mary E.	Oct. 8, 1832	Michael Billmyre	Chas. P. Krauth	4b283		mr 48 *
Gardner, Jacob m. Fisher, Eliza	Jan. 1825	Jacob Price		3b 48		
Gardner, Jane m. Fletcher, Azel	Feb. 23, 1807	Thomas Widdy		6b191		mr 70 *
Gardner, John S. m. Croney, Charlotte	Dec. 26, 1839	Edward Tiffin	James Reily	1b 67	cr 37	mr 14 *
Gardner, Joseph m. Tiffin, Peggy	Dec. 7, 1797		John Potts			
Gardner, lizzie A. m. Daily, Jas.	Oct. 20, 1853		R.A.Fink			
Gardner, Mary m. Bales, Wm.	May 11, 1849	Jacob VanDoren	W. Love	7b156		mr 80 *
Gardner, Mary m. Black, Daniel	June 23, 1805	Jacob Gardner	Wm. Hill	2b264	cr 30	
*Games, Absalom m. Current, Sarah Sus	Dec. 28, 1793					mr 10 *

79

Name	(marriage)	(suretor)	(minister)	(bond)	ref
Gardner, Peter m. Koplinger, Eliza	Sept 28, 1833	Harrison Waite		5b285	mr 34 *
Gardner, Peter m. Morgan, Rebecca	Dec. 5, 1798	Jacob Gardner		1b151	mr 80 *
Gardner, Sarah m. Lucas, Gabriel	Feb. 25, 1799	Samuel Gardner		1b171	
Garner, Mary m. Gossett, Mathias	Jan. 17, 1788		Hugh Vance		
Garner, Richard m. Caskey, Mary	Apr. 4, 1849	William Caskey	William Love	7b152	cr 15
Garner, Samuel m. Lemen, Rachel	Aug. 10, 1799	John Mulhall		2b 19	
Garrett, Mary m. Blue, Henry	Aug. 27, 1793		Christian Streit		mr 8 *
Garrety, Mary m. McAlpin, John	Oct. 4, 1841	Bernard Fealey		6b248	mr 38 *
Garry, Eliz. m. Butler, Wm. G.	Feb. 14, 1846	Benj. R. Boyd		7b 58	gc 8
Garten, Delilah m. Hunter, John	Jan. 28, 1791		Richard Swift		
Gartsell, Harriet m. Beall, Joseph	Jan. 2, 1799	Richard Gartsell	David Young	1b159	mr 66 *
Gartsell, Chas. m. Lashorn, Rebecca	July 27, 1833	Ralph Lashorn	Nathan Young	5b278	
Gary, Mary D. m. Payne, John M.	Apr. 13, 1839	Jos. E. Payne		6b166	
Gary, Patrick F. m. Miller, Eliz.	July 4, 1832	Wm. Showalter		5b233	
Gary, Patrick W. m. Loftus, Cath.	Dec. 26, 1839	Thomas Higgins		6b189	
Gassaway, Hannah m. Lot, Richard	Dec. 11, 1780				
Gassaway, Nancy m. Shipman, Stephen	May 26, 1801	Benjamin Palmer	Daniel Sturges	2b127	mr 31 *
Gates, Richard m. Kerr, Mary	Aug. 7, 1787		Hugh Vance		cr 18 / mr 1 *
Gatig, Elenor m. Godman, Will	Dec. 9, 1792		David Young		gc 2 / mr 8 *
Gatrel, Richard m. Sheckles, Eliz.	Oct. 19, 1793		Moses Hoge		cr 22 / mr 32 *
Gaucher, Jane m. Davis, Henry Jacob	Nov. 25, 1783		Hugh Vance		mr 3 *
Gaudy, Nancy m. Edmonds, Wm.	Dec. 31, 1789		Moses Hoge		cr 3
Gaw, Joseph m. Nadenbousch, Eliza M	June 25, 1825		John Winter		
Gay, Michael m. Jones, Sarah	Apr. 27, 1789	Vincent Bell		5b 15	mr 50 *
Gehr, Catherine m. Cushwa, Barnett	Feb. 13, 1837	John Jones	Lewis F. Wilson	1b x	mr 70 *
Gehr, Susan m. Mason, John F.	Sept 14, 1839	Daniel Gehr	Lewis F. Wilson	6b 96	
Geiger, Anton m. Kerk, Maria	Sept 26, 1797	Daniel Gehr	David Young	6b175	gc 7 *
Geiger, Daniel m. Rodes, Polly	Jan. 12, 1815	John Beard	Rev. Reebenack	1b 46	gc 14 *
Gedger, Eliz. m. Coons(Koontz), Jacob	Mar. 16, 1800		David Young		gc 9 *
Gedger, Nancy m. Shober, Adam	Aug. 20, 1840	Jonathan Rust		2b 56	
Gedsendorff, G.W. m. Young, Hannah	Mar. 12, 1834	Peter Potsal		6b216	
Gedsendorff, Jacob C. m. Young, Margt	Feb. 16, 1832	George Young	Jacob Medtart	5b304	mr 63 *
Gerickson, Mary m. Smith, Zachariah	Apr. 15, 1816	Nathan Young		5b216	
Gephart, Geo. C. m. Cook, Jane	Aug. 3, 1830	William Palmer		4b 3	
Gerling, Ferd'd m. Barnhardt, Eliz.M	Oct. 20, 1857	Bernard C. Wolff	R.A. Link	5b171	mr 88 *
Gerrard, John m. Robinson, Eliz.	July 20, 1817	Thos. Robinson	W.N.Scott	4b 40	
Gerrard, Justus m. Marchant, Roady	Sept 16, 1797	David Lewis		1b 42	
Gerrard, Mary m. Demoss, Thomas	Apr. 10, 1797	Jonathan Gerrard		1b 11	
Gerrard, Mathew m. Dunham, Dinah	July 28, 1806	Samuel Dunham		3b 24	
Gerrard, Polly m. Brewer, Charles	Mar. 3, 1807	James Burk		3b 48	
Gerrard, Seaman m. Collins, Eliz.	May 4, 1826	John Snodgrass	John Mathews	5b 41	
Gerrard, Thos. R. m. Bear, Sarah C.	May 1, 1843	Geo. W. Strayer	James Chisholm	6b296	mr 50 *
Gerrard, William m. Miller, Nancy	May 23, 1808	David Miller		3b 89	mr 75 *

Marriage bond index (rotated table):

Name	(marriage)	(suretor)	(minister)	(bond)		
Gerringer, Eliz. m. Fenwick, Richard	Feb. 18, 1802	Malachi Grove	Richard Swift	2b161	cr 32	mr 20 *
Gerst, Magdaline m. Hackman, Geo. F.	Sept 28, 1794		David Young		gc 4	*
Gertman, Christ'r m. Starry, Barbara	Sept 26, 1795		David Young		gc 5	*
Gher, Joseph m. Light, Eliza V.	Oct. 13, 1852		John Light			mr 86 *
Gibbons, Giles C. m. Miller, Eliz.	Sept 30, 1839			6b177		*
Gibbs, Norris m. Cook, Eliz.	Aug. 29, 1793	Daniel Miller	Moses Hoge		cr 22	mr 8 *
Gibbs, Edw. A. m. Orrick, Betsy	June 22, 1813					
Gibson, Jeremiah S. m. Grantham,Rachl	Mar. 2, 1848	Nicholas Orrick	Henry Furlong	3b265		mr 78 *
Gibson, Sarah m. Montgomery, Geo.	Aug. 7, 1794	Remington L. Bell	Edward Tiffin	7b124	cr 25	mr 9 *
Gibson, Elenor m. Smith, Moses	Sept 1, 1815		Rev. Reebenack		gc 15	*
Gilbert, Eliz. H. m. Suhelm, Jacob B.	Dec. 1, 1853		G.W.Cooper			*
Gilbert, Henry m. Pultz, Elis.	Aug. 8, 1797	Peter Pultz		1b 27		
Gilbert, Isaac m. Burwell, Priscilla	May 4, 1830	Joseph Larkins		5b165		
Gilbert, Jane m. Foster, James	Jan. 3, 1795		David Young		gc 4	*
Gilbert, Jane m. Gray, John	May 10, 1805					
Gilbert, Joseph m. Dunham, Marg't	Mar. 20, 1852	D. Hunter		2b262		
Gilbert, Lucy m. Sherrard, John	Oct. 5, 1807	Wm. Parkinson		7b248		
Gilbert, Martha J. m. Gray, Jas. W.	Feb. 6, 1840	John Gray	J.P.Harrison	3b 75		mr 71 *
Gilbert, Mary Ann m. Manor, Warner	Feb. 23, 1841	Edward Gilbert	Lewis F. Wilson	6b195		mr 72 *
Gilbert, Mary A. m. Manor,Zebulam W.	Feb. 22, 1841	Edward Gilbert		6b235		
Gilbreth, Hannah m. Mainor(Ma-),John	Oct. 2, 1819	Fred. Gilbert				
Gilchrist, Henry m. Wilson, Sarah	Sept 1, 1785	Norman Miller	Hugh Vance	4b117		mr 34 *
Gildis, Cath. E. m. Speer, Mathew	Jan. 3, 1846	Paul Taylor		7b 53		
Giles, William m. Fox, Rebecca	Jan. 22, 1798	Joseph Cromwell		1b104		
?Gilkrest, Robert m. Graham, Anne	Nov. 22, 1797	Christ'r Hill	David Young	1b 63		
Gill, Absalom m. Hill, Catherine	June 2, 1827	Thomas Gill	J.B.Reynolds	5b 71	go 7	mr 52 *
Gill, Ann m. Bowers, Henry	Nov. 17, 1818	Thomas Gill	J.E.Jackson	4b 88	cr 33	mr 11 *
Gill, Hannah m. North, Wm. D.	Apr. 13, 1829	John Gill	John Boyd	5b125		
Gill, Joseph m. Hannah, Ann	Sept 24, 1795					
Gill, Mary E. m. Brown, Joseph W.	Nov. 23, 1837	John Gill	J.E.Jackson	6b125		
Gill, Sarah R. m. Smith, Eli	Nov. 20, 1834		J.E.Jackson	6b 25	cr 33	mr 11 *
Gill, Thomas m. Patterson, Hannah	Dec. 10, 1795		John Boyd			
Gill, William m. Payne, Martha	Mar. 29, 1834					
Gillard, Daniel m. Davis, Elis.	Sept 23, 1796	Jesse Payne	David Young	6b 1	go 7	*
Gillaspy, Nancy m. Henderson, John	Nov. 5, 1825	Edmond Champion	Chas. P. Krauth	1b 45	gc 7	mr 49 *
?Gillgrist, Robert m. Graham, Ann	Nov. 22, 1797	William Faris	David Young	5b 26	go 7	*
Gillmore, Arch'd m. Barnhouse, Caty	Apr. 20, 1815	Joseph Cromwell		1b 63		
Galney, Henry m. Johnson, Maria	Apr. 19, 1812	Robert Grimes	Rev. Reebenack	3b320		
Gilpin, Agnes m. Swisher, Henry	Aug. 1, 1798		David Young	1b124		
Gingerlck, Michael m. Young, Julia A.	Aug. 28, 1836	James Robinson		6b 76	gc 12	*
Ginham, Michael m. Sullivan, Ellen	Feb. 8, 1851	Wm. L. Boak	Andrew Tilty		gc 7	*
Gird, Harriet, Clark, Walter	Oct. 23, 1804	John Sullivan		7b 214		mr 84 *
*Gist, Joshua m. Bogle, Ruth	1789	John Catlett	D. Thomas	2b247		mr 37 *

*This could be Ruth Vogle ?

Name	(marriage)	(surety)	(minister)	(bond)		
Givan, Hannah m. Crabb, Jacob	Aug. 12, 1819	John Strother	Nathan Young	4b112		mr 56 *
Givan, James m. Lewis, Mary	Apr. 1, 1835	William Lewis	John Light	6b 39		mr 67 *
Gladden, Christiana m. Cooke, Jacob	July 6, 1848	George Smith	P. Lipscomb	7b133		mr 81 *
Gladden, Joseph m. Miller, Lucy	Oct. 23, 1828	John Miller Jr.	J.B.Reynolds	5b11		mr 52 *
Gladden, Martha m. Cook, Peter	Mat 21, 1847	Daniel H. Doll	John Winter	7b 96		mr 78 *
Gladden, Mary C. m. Pitzer, Elias M.	Sept 6, 1842	William Gladden		6b277		*
Gladden, Susan M. m. Grove, George	Feb. 12, 1852	William Gladden	James Hughes	7b246		mr 85 *
Gladden, William m. Mong, Marg't	Dec. 20, 1823	John Mong	Chas. P. Krauth	4b254		mr 46 *
Glass, Margaret m. McNutt(Natt).David	Apr. 22, 1797	Thomas Green	Richard Swift	1b 10	cr 27	mr 13 *
Glass, Robert I. m. Bryarly, Sarah L.	Jan. 12, 1850	Robert P. Bryarly	Richard T. Brown	7b172		mr 79 *
Glassby, Robert m. Cross, Mary	Dec. 6, 1798	Basil Cross	Richard Swift	1b151	cr 31	mr 15 *
Glassford, Dennis m. Prather, Ady	July 3, 1848	Norman Miller	Wm. Love	7b132		mr 80 *
Glassford, George m. Harper, Lydia	July 30, 1798	George Hazely		1b123		
Glaze, Thomas m. Hall, Rachel	Nov. 15, 1797	William Hall		1b 61		
Glenn, James m. Burns, Ruth	June 11, 1823	John Strother	John Mathews	4b241		mr 46 *
Gletner, David m. Harrison, Sarah	Jan. 25, 1842	Nathan Harrison		6b262		*
Godan, Sally m. Hogan, Daniel						*
Goddard, John m. Evis, Jane	Oct. 4, 1792		David Young		gc 2	mr 6 *
Goddard, Mary m. Brown, George	Mar. 1, 1791		Moses Hoge		cr 6	mr 42 *
Goddard, Mary(Nancy) m. Douglas, Wm.	Oct. 30, 1781		Daniel Sturges			
Goddard, Michael m. Grant, Catherine	Oct. 12, 1815	Isaac Goddard	Rev. Reebenack	3b343	gc 15	mr 7 *
Goddy, Nancy m. Edmonds, Wm.	Apr. 30, 1793		Moses Hoge		cr 21	mr 3 *
Godhart, Elis. m. Evis, Richard David	Dec. 31, 1789		Moses Hoge		cr 3	mr 2 *
Goding, Hester m. Swearingen, Benomi	June 13, 1789		Moses Hoge		cr 2	mr 2 *
Godman, Charlotte m. Shirley, Wm.	Jan. 24, 1793		Moses Hoge			mr 39 *
Godman, Eliz. m. Crawford, James	Dec. 30, 1801	Zachariah Godman		2b155		
Godman, Nancy m. VanPelt, Jacob	June 17, 1813	Thos. Crawford		3b265		
Godman, Richard m. Clise, Ann	Mar. 27, 1805	William Godman	John Bond	2b259	cr 28	mr 22 *
Godman, Will m. Gatig, Elenor	Apr. 5, 1820	Peter Hoke		4b143	gc 2	*
Godman, Wm. m. Harper, Hannah	Dec. 9, 1792		David Young			
Goheen, Michael m. Sullivan, Ellen	Feb. 8, 1851	John Sullivan	Andrew Talty	7b214		mr 84 *
Goings, Geo. W. m. Barber, Sally	Sept. 9, 1833	Horace Anderson		5b282		
Gold, Washington m. McKown, Jane	June 7, 1830	George McKown		5b167		
Goldburg, Edward m. Ashfield, Rebecca	May 15, 1793		William Hill			
Goldburg, Mary m. Wilson, Jesse	June 9, 1785		Edward Tiffin		cr 30	mr 9 *
Goldburg, Teddy m.Spencer(Spinner)M.	Feb. 2, 1800		John Hedt(Hutt)		cr 38	mr 1 *
Good, Alex. C. m. Tate, Rosanna B.	May 6, 1833	Stephen Snodgrass		5b272	cr 33	mr 18 *
Good, John m. Miller, Maria	Dec. 16, 1794		David Young			
Good, Margaret m. Lane, Barkley	May 14, 1797	Peter Shaffer	David Young	1b 16	gc 4	*
Good, Mary A. m. Abell, Joseph F.	June 3, 1837	Harrison Waite		6b107	gc 6	*
Gooden, John m. Leach, Harriet	Sept 2, 1817	Walter Leach	W.N.Scott	4b 45		
Gooden, Patrick m. Crason, Mary	Mar. 21, 1782		Daniel Sturges		cr 22	mr 42 *
Gooding, John m. Warner, Hannah	Jan. 2, 1794		Moses Hoge			mr 9 *

Name	(marriage)	(suretor)	(minister)	(bond)	cross-ref
Goodman, Keziah m. Fisher, Edward	Jan. 17, 1795		David Young	4b116	gc 4 *
Goodman, Rebecca m. Beeson, David	Sept. 13, 1794		David Young	3b185	gc 4 *
Goodman, Venelia m. Woke, Thomas	Aug. 24, 1794		David Young	2b143	gc 4 *
Goodnight, Cath. m. Dunham, Jacob	Sept. 28,	John Strother		5b142	mr 30 *
Goodnight, Leonard m. Fernough, Matty	Apr. 27, 1819	Dan'l Fernough	Mathias Riser		
Goodwin, Tabitha m. Watson, Henry	Oct. 17, 1811	Gabriel Goodwin			
Gordon, Abraham m. Burk, Mahitabel	Sept. 21, 1801	Ellis Rees			*
Gordon, Rachel m. Ewing, John	Apr. 11, 1829		David Young		gc 3
Gordon, Ruth m. Kennedy, Thomas	Dec. 15, 1793	Robert Hedges	Nathan Young	5b 29	mr 58 *
Gorgas, Cath. m. Main, Wm.	Aug. 17, 1825	Samuel Gorgas	James Reily	5b 19	mr 48 *
Gorman, Edward m. Vorhees, Matilda	Mar. 29, 1825	David Hoffman	John Winter	7b150	mr 79 *
Gorrell, Abr'm m. Miller, Cath. E.	May 19. 1849	John A. Miller		6b 13	cr 8
Gorrell, Abr'm m. Varmetre, Eliz.	Jan. 5, 1834	Abr'm Gorrell	Moses Hoge	4b282	mr 7 *
Gorrell, Abr'm V. m. Gorrell, Isabel	Jan. 3, 1825	Thomas Harley	Chas. P. Krauth	6b187	mr 48 *
Gorrell, Cath. m. Hedges, Harvey A.	Dec. 18. 1792				
Gorrell, David H. m. Varmetre, Mary	Nov. 3, 1825	Asahel Varmetre		6b251	mr 76 *
Gorrell, Eliz. V. m. Wright, Jas. B.	June 6, 1839	B.F.Burns	John Winter	7b 68	mr 83 *
Gorrell, G.W. m. Miller, Mary Ann	Aug ? 1841	Wm. S. Miller	Lewis F. Wilson	7b192	cr 40, mr 4 *
Gorrell, Hannah m. Quick, James	Sept. 23, 1846		Hugh Vance		
Gorrell, Isabel A. m. Boley, Benj.F.	Aug. 19, 1850	Benj. Boley Jr.		7b104	mr 78 *
Gorrell, Isabel m. Gorrell, Abr'm V.	Jan. 3, 1825	Abr'm Gorrell	Henry Furlong	4b282	mr 48 *
Gorrell, Isabel m. VanCleve, Morgan	Aug. 7, 1847	William Gorrell	Chas. P. Krauth	5b 74	mr 59 *
Gorrell, Isabal E. m. Boley, Benj.	May 12, 1827	Wm. B. Gorrell	Nathan Young	6b208	mr 62 *
Gorrell, Jacob m. Burnes, Hannah	Dec. 4, 1840	Abr'm Gorrell		4b 51	mr 88 *
Gorrell, Jacob m. Burnes, Isabella	Oct. 19, 1817	Wm. Burnes Jr.		2b144	
Gorrell, Jacob V. m. Tabb, Mary Mrs.	Sept. 13, 1801	John Shober		5b205	mr 49 *
Gorrell, John B. m. Miller, Rebecca			Nathan Young		
Gorrell, Joseph m. Burns, Eliza	Sept. 14, 1824	John Burns	Geo. W. Harris	5b 22	
Gorrell, Joseph m. Evans, Martha	Nov. 18, 1853	Isaac Varmetre	Joseph Baker	3b124	
Gorrell, Joseph m. Varmetre, Ruth	Aug. 7, 1807	Isaac Varmetre		2b 18	cr 29, mr 17 *
Gorrell, Martha m. Chenoweth, John	Sept. 22, 1831	Robert Wilson		4b 47	
Gorrell, Mary m. Chenoweth, Richard	Nov. 10, 1786	Wm. Gorrell	Moses Hoge	2b 98	
Gorrell, Mary A. m. Hunt, David B.	Feb. 2, 1834	John Alburtis		4b255	mr 46 *
Gorrell, Mary A. m. Hunt, David B.	Mar. 26. 1838		Chas. P. Krauth		
Gorrell, Rachel m. Chenoweth, Joseph	Dec. 2, 1847	Joseph Gorrell	C.M.Callaway	3b 81	
Gorrell, Ruth m. Burns, Benj. F.	June 6, 1799				
Gorrell, Ruth m. Quick, Turis	Feb. 1807	Abr'm Gorrell	Jacob Medtart	5b197	
Gorry, John m. Johnston, Mary Mrs.	Apr. 14, 1831	Levi Henshaw	Hugh Vance	6b 6	mr 63 *
Gosnell, Jas. L.B. m. McSherry, Sally	Dec. 15, 1786	Peter Cook	J.E.Jackson	6b154	mr 33 *
Gosnell, Mathew T. m.	Mar. 4, 1834	Mathew T. Gosnell		7b 89	
Gosner, John m. Sporr, Cath.	Mar. 25, 1838	Thomas Stilwell	James Chisholm	1b175	mr 77 *
Gossett, Betsy m. Mayhew, Percy	Aug. 29, 1847	Mathias Gossett		3b 67	ge 12 *
Gossett, John m. Crabb, Nancy	Mar. 9, 1812	Peter Shafer	Rev. Reebenack	3b215	*

Name (marriage)	(marriage)	(suretor)	(minister)	(bond)	Ref.
Gossett, Mathias m. Garner, Mary	Jan. 17, 1788		Hugh Vance		mr 34 *
Goth, James m. Wright, Mary	Aug. 25, 1794		David Young		gc 4 *
Gothard, Rebecca m. Barnett, John	Mar. 29, 1814		Rev. Reebenack		gc 14 *
Gotschall, Jacob m. Coon, Eve	Aug. 19, 1797	Jacob Coon			*
*Goulding, John m. Kyser(Kyor) Maria	Jan. 6, 1799		David Young	1b 32	gc 8 *
Gouter, John W. m. Burk, Eliz. Ann	Aug. 13, 1819	John Strother		4b113	
Govn, Cath. A. m. Hull, Henry	July 31, 1847	William Jack		7b103	
Grafton, Ambrose m. Blue, Eliz.	Jan. 22, 1851	John Zorn	James H. Jennings	7b212	mr 83 *
Grafton, Thomas m. Condon, Robert	Jan. 23, 1851		Moses Hoge		mr 12 *
Graham, Anne m. Gilgrist, Robert	Dec. 20, 1796		Moses Hoge		mr 35 *
Graham, Ann Swearingen m. Zinn, Dan'l	Mar. 13, 1788	Joseph Cromwell	David Young	1b 63	cr 36
Graham, David m. Hanner, Eve Eliz.	Nov. 22, 1797	Robert Wilson		3b230	gc 7
Graham, Edmund m. Swearingen, Mary	June 30, 1812	David Graham		2b200	
Graham, James m. Swearingen, Nancy	Apr. 16, 1803		Hugh Vance		mr 37 *
Graham, John m. Greenwalt, Cath.	Jan. 8, 1789		Hugh Vance		mr 43 *
Graham, Julia Ann m. Thistle, Arch'd	July 27, 1786	Jas. Richardson	David Young	2b203	gc 10
Graham, Mary m. Byers, John	June 16, 1803	Edmund Graham	W.N.Scott	4b 95	mr 30 *
Graham, Samuel m. O'Ferrall, Cath.	Dec. 22, 1818	Ignat's O'Ferrall	Hugh Vance	3b267	mr 32 *
Gramp, John m. Nonal, Catherine	Jan. 10, 1782		David Young		gc 2
Grant, Cath. m. Goddard, Michael	July 27, 1813		Moses Hoge		cr 21
Grant, Chas. S. m. Pine, Eliz. A.	Jan. 25, 1793	James Pine	P. Lipscomb	7b147	mr 7 *
Grantham, Cath. m. Winning, Edward	Apr. 30, 1793	William Grantham	W.N.Scott	4b141	mr 82 *
Grantham, David m. Lemaster, Sarah	Feb. 21, 1849	David Lemaster		7b203	mr 41 *
Grantham, Eliza m. Seibert, John S.	Mar. 22, 1820	Wm. Grantham	Nathan Young	5b129	mr 60 *
Grantham, Eliz. m. Stuckey, Daniel	Nov. 18, 1850	Lewis Grantham	Lewis F. Wilson	7b202	mr 87 *
Grantham, Hannah m. White, Uriah	May 4, 1829	Moses Smith		2b 42	mr 48 *
Grantham, Jemima m. Starry, Conrad	Nov. 16, 1850	Wm. Grantham		3b290	mr 49 *
Grantham, Jemima m. Weaver, John	Apr. 9, 1851	George Boltz		5b 4	mr 82 *
Grantham, John m. Blue, Cath.	Dec. 20, 1799	George Pulse	Chas. P. Krauth	4b255	mr 57 *
Grantham, John M. m. Buzzard, Marg't	Mar. 24, 1814	Bethuel Kitchen	B. Reynolds	7b 30	mr 69 *
Grantham, Joseph m. Rush(Rusk), Elenor	Jan. 20, 1824	William Rush	Jas. H. Jennings	4b 32	mr 37 *
Grantham, Lewis m. Jones, Catherine	Jan. 16, 1825	Peter Jones	W.N.Scott	4b216	mr 60 *
Grantham, Lydia F. m. Griffith, John	Mar. 14, 1825	Moses Grantham	Nathan Young	6b157	mr 37 *
Grantham, Marg't m. Shepherd, Gideon	Apr. 8, 1845	James Grantham	Lewis F. Wilson	5b 43	
Grantham, Marg't m. That, Simon	Apr. 17, 1817				
Grantham, Maria m. French, George	Apr. 14, 1822	William Grantham	D. Thomas	5b162	
Grantham, Mary m. Boggers, Bennett	Apr. 12, 1830		Nathan Young		
Grantham, Phebe m. Payne, George	July, 1798	Henry Payne	D. Thomas		
Grantham, Rachel Ann m. Gibson, Jermh	Feb. 29, 1848	Remington L. Bell	Henry Furlong	1b125	mr 78 *
Grantham, Susan m. Stuckey, David	Feb. 10, 1845	Lewis Grantham	James Chisholm	7b124	mr 76 *
Grantham, Jemima m. Weaver, John	Mar. 14, 1825	George Boltz	Chas. P. Krauth	7b 26	mr 48 *
*Goucher, Jane m. Davis, Jacob	Nov. 25, 1783		Hugh Vance	5b 4	mr 32 *

(name)	(marriage)	(suretor)	(minister)	(bond)		
Graous, Robert m. Artless, Ann	Aug. 30, 1793	Christian Grove	William Hill	2b211	cr 30	mr 10 *
Grave, Barbara m. Pugle(Pugh), Samuel	Oct. 20, 1803	John Doll	David Young	4b 94	gc 10	*
Graver, George m. McIlnsey, Mary	Dec. 17, 1818		John B. Hoge	7b156		mr 29 *
Graves, Chas. C. m. Shoafstall, Eliza	1849	Wm. Graves		7b105		*
Graves, Mary Ann m. Dorsey, Edward	Sept 2, 1847	Wm. Graves	John Light	7b105	cr 30	mr 79 *
Graves, Wm. m. Stuckey, Sarah	Nov. 27, 1851	Daniel K. Stuckey	Jas. H. Jennings	7b237		mr 85 *
Gravles, Robert m. Artless, Ann	Aug. 30, 1793		William Hill		cr 30	mr 10 *
Gray, Alice m. Boyd, Wm.	1798	Andrew Yeates		1b108		*
Gray, Andrew m. McKewan, Mary	Nov. 20, 1787		Hugh Vance		cr 23	mr 2 *
Gray, Eliz. m. Willis, Richard	May 24, 1798	John Craghill	David Young	1b112	gc 7	*
Gray, George m. Burk, Libby	1810	Arch'd Williams		3b157	cr 33	*
Gray, James m. Wilson, Sarah	June 25, 1795		John Boyd			mr 11 *
Gray, Jas. W. m. Gilbert, Martha J.	Feb. 6, 1840	Edward Gilbert	J.P.Harrison	6b195		mr 71 *
Gray, John m. Armbrester, Nancy	Apr. 11, 1828	Michael Ambrester	Nathan Young	5b 97		mr 60 *
Gray, John m. Gilbert, Jane	1805	D. Hunter		2b262		
?Gray, Lacey m. Fletcher, Moses	Mar. 9, 1828	Hannans Gray	Nathan Young	5b 92		mr 59 *
lilly m.Ranier(Ranson)Hezekiah	June 24, 1788		Moses Hoge			mr 36 *
?Gray, Lucy m. Fletcher, Moses	Mar. 3, 1825	Hannans Gray	Nathan Young	5b 92		mr 59 *
Gray, Mary Ann m. Miller, Smith	Mar. 4, 1816	Thomas Miller	Jas. M. Brown	5b 2		mr 48 *
Gray, Michael m. Kesler, Eliz.	Feb. 4, 1816		Mathias Riser			mr 26 *
Gray, Philip m. Hunt, Jane	1827		Mathias Riser			mr 26 *
Gray, Ruth m. Brannon, Levi	June 4, 1827	Hannons Gray	Mathias Riser	5b 71		mr 30 *
Gray, Susanna m. Gallaway, Wm.	May 27, 1819	Thomas Griggs	Richard Swift	2b 81	cr 34	mr 16 *
Gray, Susanna m. Grove, George	Oct. 22, 1799					
Green, Ann m. Metcalf, Vatchel	1800	William Green		5b 79		
Green, Catherine m. Haines, Henry	Oct. 1, 1827		Moses Hoge		cr 21	mr 7 *
Green, Charles m. Butt,Maxe(Masse)	1793	James Edmonds	Richard Swift	1b 67	cr 12	mr 14 *
Green, Charles m. Edmonds, Ann	Feb. 14, 1793	Swearingen Ray		3b282		
Green, Eliz. m. Butt, Joseph	Dec. 2, 1797	Barrick Butt		3b 80		
Green, George m. Butt, Patsy	1814	David Hunter		3b330		
Green, Jas. C. m. Hunter, Mary	1807					
Green, John m.Klaycomb(Clay-), Eliz.	1815	Conrad Claycomb	Rev. Reebenack	3b145	gc 11	*
Green, Johnson m. Ross, Mary	Apr. 12, 1810	Enoch Ross		3b 13		
Green, Joseph m. Butt, Polly	1806	Michael Hout	David Young	1b 81	gc 7	mr 33 *
Green, Kesiah m. Devrault, Daniel	Jan. 14, 1798		Hugh Vance		gc 4	
Green, Mary m. Butt, John	May 3, 1785		David Young			
Green, Mary Ann m. Miller, Jacob R.	Apr. 2, 1795	John Green	Jas. M. Brown	5b218		mr 64 *
Green, Matty m.Cole(Crole,Cecle)Abrm.	Feb. 9, 1832	William Green	Richard Swift	2b148	cr 32	mr 20 *
Green, Molly m. Ennbss, John	Nov. 19, 1801	William Green	Robert Cadden	5b153		mr 61 *
Green, Rebecca m. Heyatt, Wm.	Feb. 25, 1830		Moses Hoge		cr 22	mr 9 *
Green, Regnal m. Butt, Sarah	Feb. 12, 1794		Hugh Vance		cr 24	mr 2 *
Green, Sarah m. Beall(Bell), Wm.	Jan. 15, 1788		Moses Hoge		cr 22	mr 8 *
Green, Sarah m. Carr, Samuel	Dec. 10, 1793	George Green		2b 23		
	Aug. 31, 1799					

	(marriage)	(suretor)	(minister)	(bond)		
Green, Sarah Ann m. Crow, Benjamin	Feb. 22, 1825	William Green	Chas. P. Krauth	5b 1	cr 3	mr 48 *
Green, Thomas m. Highett, Eliz.	Mar. 4, 1790		Moses Hoge			mr 5 *
Green, Thomas m. Job, Peggy	Apr. 22, 1808	David Johnstone		3b 87		
Green, Thomas m. Morlay, Marg't	Apr. 17, 1812	John Morlay		3b221		
Greenwalt, Cath. m. Graham, John	June 16, 1803	Jas. Richardson	David Young	2b203	gc 10	*
Greenwalt, John W. m. Kesler, Eliz.	June 16, 1839	Andrew Criswell		6b175		
Greenwell, Jane Ann m. Saunders, Jas.	Sept 12, 1824		J.L.Bromwell			mr 47 *
Greenwell, Jane Ann m. Williams,John	Aug. 4, 1824	John M. Cleary Jr.		4b269		
Greenwell, John m. Curtis, Peggy	Feb. 13, 1820	Jacob Walter	Nathan Young	4b134		mr 57 *
Greenwell, Rebecca m. Walters, Jacob	May 16, 1816	John Strider	W.N.Scott	4b 1		mr 26 *
Greer, Cecelia m. Moran, Daniel	Dec. 22, 1852		J.H.Plunkett			mr 88 *
Greer, Jacob m. Davis, Mary Ann	July 23, 1828	Thomas Davis		5b103		
Gregg, Cath. S. m. Williams, John B.	June 1, 1848	Henry K. Gregg	W. Love	7b130		mr 80 *
Gregg, Henry H. m. Hill, Mary S.	Apr. 14, 1845	William Hill	John Light	7b 32		mr 76 *
Gregg, John m. Klinger, Mary Ann	Apr. 18, 1811	Thomas Shearer	John B. Hoge	3b184	cr 14	mr 24 *
Gregg, John m. Porterfield, Cath.	Apr. 11, 1809	John Porterfield	John Mathews	3b11	cr 17	mr 23 *
Gregory, Amelia m. Kennedy, Aaron	Mar. 30, 1807	Wm. Gregory		3b 52		
Gregory, Ellen M. m. Huston, Joseph	Mar. 7, 1837	Robert Gregory		6b100		
Gregory, Emily m. Anderson, James	Apr. 17, 1851	George Butler	D.Francis Spriggs	7b222		mr 84 *
Gregory, G.W. m. Carper, Susan Sarah	Oct. 2, 1847	Jas. R. Gregory	P. Lipscomb	7b108		mr 81 *
Gregory, James m. Carper(Cas),Isabal	Nov. 9, 1842	Jonas Carper	Mayberry Goheen	6b283		mr 74 *
Gregory, Jane m. Crowl, Thos. J.	July 30, 1845	Ebenezer Tally		7b 39		
Gregory, Jane m. Nesbitt, Isaac	Oct. 15, 1832	Robert Gregory		5b244		
Gregory, John m. Crowl, Mary Ann	Jan. 17, 1835	Jacob A. Crowl	John Howell	6b 28		mr 68 *
Gregory, Mary L. m. Kennedy, Robt. S	Oct. 25, 1825	William Gregory	John L. Gibbons	5b 25		mr 49 *
Gregory, Thos. R. m. Crowl, Sarah A.	Dec. 13, 1842	John M. Gregory	Mayberry Goheen	6b286		mr 74 *
Gregory, Thos. R. m. Hess, Sarah A.	Mar. 13, 1851	Jos. M. Hess	B.M.Schmucker	7b218		mr 84 *
Gregory, Thompson R. m. Crowl, Susan	Dec. 13, 1842		Mayberry Goheen			mr 74 *
Gregory, Wm. m. Kennedy, Jane	Nov. 15, 1800	Robert Kennedy		2b100		
Gresoker, Christina m.Hank(Hawk),Jos.	Mar. 31, 1793		David Young		gc 2	*
Gretinger, Solomon m. Kernlick, Cath.	Sept 2, 1794		David Young		gc 4	*
Griffins, Zachariah m. Hibban, Sarah	Nov. 11, 1785		Edward Tiffin		cr 38	mr 1 *
Griffith, Amy m. Baldwin, James	Sept 9, 1826	Wm. Griffith		5b 51		
Griffith, Ann m. Little, George	June 28, 1781		Daniel Sturges			mr 31 *
Griffith, Ann m. Russell, George	Nov. 30, 1818	Samuel K. Wilson		4b 91		
Griffith, Camelius m. William, Elenor	Apr. 26, 1814	Robert Mandeville		3b296		
Griffith, Elijah m.Seibert, Harriet	Aug. 25, 1831	John F. Smith	William Monroe	5b202		mr 62 *
Griffith, Frances m. Smith, Conrad	Oct. 11, 1850	Nicholas Smith	Henry Furlong	7b200		mr 81 *
Griffith, John m. Grantham, Lydia	Jan. 14, 1839	Moses Grantham	Lewis F. Wilson	6b157		mr 69 *
Griffith, John m. Thornberg, Hannah	Nov. 6, 1794		John Boyd		cr 21	mr 8 *
Griffith, Mary m. Craighill, Wm.	Jan. 23, 1815	Wm. Maxwell	Moses Hoge	3b309	cr 2	mr 2 *
Griffith, Mary m. Mickler, Michael	May 5, 1789		Moses Hoge		cr 6	mr 6 *
Griffith, Sarah m. Moler, John	Mar. 8, 1791					

(name)	(marriage)	(suretor)	(minister)	(bond)	
Griffith, Wm. m. Correll, Martha	Feb. 5, 1821	John Light	David Young	4b171	gc 1 *
Griffith, Zebulon m. Shimp, Sarah A	Mar. 31. 1849	Benj. G. Manor		7b152	
Grify, John m. Middleton, Eliz.	May 17, 1791			2b119	
Griggs, Elira m. Colmes(Ca-),Henry	Mar. 26, 1801	Thomas Griggs	John Heitt(Hutt)	1b 52	cr 11 *
Griggs, Elis. m. McClanihan, Wm.	Oct. 7, 1797	John Griggs		1b x	mr 14 *
Grigsby, John m. Ivell, Rebecca	Apr. 8. 1789	George Ron			gc 7 *
Grim, Eliz. m. Henegar, Martin	July 31. 1798		David Young		
Grimes, Alex. m. Cooke, Margaret	Mar. 14, 1836	Jacob Rhodes		6b 73	
Grimes, Eliz. m. Larin, Hiram	Mar. 6, 1819	Jonathan Roberts		4b101	
Grimes, Jane m. McCormick, Levi	Feb. 4, 1816	John Hawkins	Nathan Young	3b353	mr 55 *
Grimes, Jane m. Manor, Samuel	1798	William Grimes		1b119	
Grimes, John m. Rogers, Jenny	July 4, 1786		Hugh Vance		mr 43 *
Grimes, Marg't m. Anderson, Jabez	June 14, 1808	Robert Grimes		3b 91	
Grimes, Marg't Jane m. Deck, Jacob	May 19, 1840	William Grimes		6b210	
Grimes, Mary m. Naff, Michael	May 26, 1828	William Wolff		5b 94	
Grimes, Rebecca m. Buncutter, Geo.	W.Jan. 10. 1842	William Grimes		6b261	
Grimes, Robert m. Caskey, Sarah	Feb. 27, 1794	William Grimes	Moses Hoge	7b 72	cr 22 *
Grimes, Sarah m. Stimmel, Peter	Aug. 31. 1846	William Grimes		7b125	
Grimes, Tizzy A. m. Sumption, John	Mar. 3. 1848				
Grimes, William m. Brown, Sarah	June 18. 1787	John McIntire	Hugh Vance	3b 61	cr 23 *
Grimes, Wm. m. Hawes, Jane	1807		John Mathews		cr 13 *
Grimes, Wm. m. liken, Marg't	1797		Richard Swift		cr 26 *
Grimold, Polly m. Dowland, John	Feb. 25, 1804	Henry Clominger		2b223	
Griste, Ruth m. Cooper, Adam	Jan. 27, 1838	Jesse Nesmith	R.N. Herndon	6b131	mr 69 *
Groff, Eliz. m. Brantner, Wm.	Sept 9, 1847	Daniel Groff	P. Lipscomb	7b106	mr 81 *
Groff, Emanuel m. Bowers, Eliz.	Apr. 30, 1851	Joshua S, Gallaher		7b224	
Groff, John . Burke, Sarah	Jan. 25, 1822	Robert Daniels	Geo. M. Frye	4b206	mr 44 *
Gromes, Wm. m. Hauliss, Hanna	Oct. 2, 1800		John Heitt(Hutt)		mr 19 *
Grooms, John m. Foye, Mary	June 30, 1797	Robert Grooms		1b 24	
Grooms, John m. Haselip, Nancy	Apr. 22, 1800	Richard Haselip Jr		2b 67	cr 35 *
Grooms, Robert m. Artless, Ann	Aug. 30. 1793		William Hill		cr 30 *
Groover, Christian m. Mouser, Eliz.	Feb. 16, 1810	Jacob Mouser		3b136	gc 1 *
Gronk, Henry m. Deddrick, Eliz.	Mar. 4, 1792		David Young		mr 49 *
Grove, Ann m. Hess, David	Oct. 10, 1825	Jesse Myers	Chas. P. Krauth	5b 24	gc 10 *
Grove, Barbara m. Pugh, Samuel	Oct. 21, 1803	Christian Grove	David Young	2b211	
Groves, Abr'm B. m. Donaldson, Sarah	Feb. 22, 1815	John Miller		3b312	mr 26 *
Grove, Cath. m. Bowers, Wm.	May 24, 1815	Peter Grove	Lewis Mayer	3b325	
Grove, Cath. m. Miller, Abr'm	Feb. 25, 1814	Robt. V. Snodgrass		3b285	
Grove, Cath. m. Now, Abr'm	Nov. 27, 1792		Moses Hoge		mr 39 *
Grove, Christina m. Earnest, Martin	Apr. 13, 1789				mr 4 *
Grove, David m. Homerick(Horw-)Susan	Feb. 28, 1850	Joshua Homerick	Christian Streit	7b178	mr 83 *
Grove, Eliz. m. Cox, John	Feb. 28, 1804	Elijah Miles	B.M. Schmucker	2b227	
Grove, Eliz. m. Myers, Jesse	Mar. 23, 1822	?	Chas. P. Krauth	4b211	mr 45 *
*Grove, Abraham m. Steck, Maria	Apr. 22, 1796		David Young		gc 6 *

	(marriage)	(suretor)	(minister)	(bond)	
Grove, Eliza m. Stapleton, Clayton	June 12, 1833	Abr'm Grove	Nathan Young	5b276	mr 66 *
Grove, George m. Davis, Drusilla	June 6, 1798	Joseph Davis	David Young	1b113	go 7 mr 85 *
Grove, Geo. W. m. Gladden, Susan M.	Feb. 12, 1852	William Gladden	James Hughes	7b245	mr 30 *
Grove, George m. Gray, Susannah	May 27, 1819		Mathias Riser		mr 44 *
Grove, Jacob m. Pensil, Catherine	Dec. 23, 1799	Johan Pensil		2b 42	
Grove, John m. Burke, Sarah	Jan. 25, 1822	Robert Daniels	Geo. M. Frye	4b206	
Grove, John m. Jackson, Mary	Nov. 3, 1819	Henry Myers		4b122	
Grove, John m. Neff, Susannah	Mar. 7, 1827?	John Neff		5b 63	mr 50 *
Grove, Joseph R. m.Helferstay, Marg't	Jan. 30, 1851	Geo. Helferstay	James Relly	7b213	mr 84 *
Grove, Lucy m. Clark, Arch'd	Aug. 23, 1804	Abr'm Grove	Jos. Plunkett	2b241	cr 13 mr 21 *
Grove, Marg't m. Hammond, Philip	July 28, 1798	John Butt	John Bond	1b122	cr 31 mr 15 *
Grove, Marla m. Stuckey, Jacob	Oct. 26, 1837	Wm. S. Grove	Richard Swift	6b122	
Grove, Mary m. Frein, John W.	Jan. 8, 1846	Michael Grove		7b 54	
Grove, Mary m. Miller, John	Nov. 18, 1812	John Grove		3b241	
Grove, Mary m. Small, George	May 29, 1822	Peter Grove	Rev. Reebenack	4b215	go 13 mr 45 *
Grove, Michael m. Shoafstall, Pris'l	Apr. 27, 1822	Seth Shoafstall	Chas. P. Krauth	4b211	
Grove, Nancy m. Peltz, Jos. M.	May 26, 1852	Michael Grove	A. Talty	7b255	mr 88 *
Grove, Shepherd B. m. Bower, Polly	Oct. 20, 1817	John Noll		4b 48	
Grove, Stephen m. Hammond, Rachel	May 9, 1818	Edw. D. Foreman		4b 70	
Grove, Susan m. Friddle, Thos. M.	Nov. 24, 1820	Thomas Grove		4b167	
Grove, Susan m. Marker, Daniel	July 10, 1851	Wm. L. Selbert	David Thomas	7b228	mr 84 *
?Grove, Susannah m. Clark, Arch'd	Aug. 22, 1804	Abraham Grove	John Bond	2b241	cr 13 mr 21 *
Grove, Wm. Y. m. Miller, Sarah(Susan)?	Oct. 4, 1846	John Kearfott	Joseph Baker	7b 74	cr 1 mr 77 *
Grovine, Mary m. Satterfield, Benj.	Feb. 19, 1789		Moses Hoge		mr 2 *
Groving, John m. Hauliss, Nancy	Apr. 29, 1800		John Heitt(Hutt)		mr 19 *
Grubb, Adam m. McBride, Eliz.	May 8, 1800	James Johnson	David Young	2b 69	ge 9
Grubb, Adam m. Mercer, Phoebe	Jan. 16, 1798	John Stuart		1b101	
Grubb, Bula m. Chrisman, James	Nov. 11, 1817	James Sterrett	Nathan Young	4b 49	mr 56 *
Grubb, Jefferson m. Payne, Frances	Dec. 17, 1849	Hanson Payne		7b170	
Grubb, John m. Ryner, Marg't	Sept 27, 1820	Daniel Ryner	James Paynter	4b163	mr 40 *
Grubb, John M. m. Custer, Cath.	Aug. 30, 1848	Jonathan Custer		7b135	
Grubb, Joseph m. Fisher, Sally	Dec. 3, 1821	Peter Fisher	John B. Hoge	4b199	mr 44 *
Grubb, Marg't m. Mathews, John	May 4, 1797	Andrew Grubb	Wm. Tibbett	1b 15	cr 27 mr 13 *
Grubb, Sarah m. Bell(Boll), Jacob	Sept. 13, 1834	Harrison Waite	John Howell	6b 19	mr 68 *
Grubb, Susannah m. Eck, Theodore	Feb. 15, 1844	Henry L. Grubb	T.H.W.Monroe	6b313	mr 75 *
Grubb, William m. Smith, Olly	Feb. 27, 1804	William Smith		2b224	
Gruber, Jacob m. Robinson, Hannah	Mar. 17, 1823	Abr'm Robinson	Chas. P. Krauth	4b234	mr 46 *
Gruber, John G. m. Staub, Leonora P.	Jan. 15, 1850	Andrew Bowman	John Light	7b173	mr 80 *
Grubs, Nathaniel m. Custer, Rachel	June 26, 1843	Colbert Holiday		6b301	
Grumm, Eliz. m. Harriser, Martin	July 30, 1798	Daniel Lumprick		1b123	
Guber, Eliza m. Syler, David	June 1, 1829	John Garber	Nathan Young	5b130	mr 60 *
Gudnm, Jeremiah m. Bare, Eliz.	Feb. 17, 1840	William Hedges		6b197	
Gudnm, John m. Myers, Eliz.	Feb. 8, 1847	Conrad Robbins		7b 85	

Name (marriage)	(date)	(marriage) year	(suretor)	(minister)	(bond)	
Gunder, Nancy m. Leedman, James P.	Feb. 22,	1837	John Waite		6b 98	mr 31 *
Guseman, John m. Strayer, Eliz.	Jan. 26,	1814	George Shaffer		3b283	*
Gushwa, Eliz. m. Seibert, George	Mar. 7,	1820	Jonathan Gushwa	Lewis Mayer	4b138	*
Gusman, Abr'm m. Refsnyder, Eliz.	July 8,	1795		David Young		gc 5
Gusman, John m. Storm, Eliz.	Jan. 27,	1814		Rev. Reebenack		gc 14
Gust, Joshua m. Bogle, Ruth		1789		D. Thomas		
Guste, Ruth m. Cooper, Adam	Jan. 27,	1838	Jesse Nesmith	R.N.Herndon	6b131	mr 37 *
Gustine, Amelia m. Chew, Henry	Apr. 19,	1813	Thomas Young		3b259	mr 69 *
Gustine, Mary m. Throckmorton, James	Jan. 21,	1813	Thomas Young		3b249	
Gustis, Delilah m. Hunter, John	June 28,	1791		Richard Swift		mr 38 *
Gwilliams, Eliza m. Light, Hamilton	Feb. 17,	1853		A. G. Chenoweth		mr 87 *
*Gwilliams, Henry m. Staley, Susan	Feb. 9,	1832	Solomon Staley	Wm. Monroe	5b216	mr 62 *
Gwilliams, Maria m. Byers, Newland	Aug. 17,	1825	Reason Gwilliams		5b 20	
Gwilliams, Mary E. m. Jacques, Wm.	Nov. 25,	1852		A. G. Chenoweth	6b 39	mr 87 *
Gwinn, James m. Lewis, Mary	Apr. 1,	1835	William Lewis	John Light	4b265	mr 67 *
Gwinn, James m. Sterrett, Nancy	May 3,	1824	James Sterrett		1b 45	
Gylland, Dardel m. David, Elis.	Sept 23,	1797	Edmund Champion	David Young		go 7
*Gwilliams, Elis. m. Custer, Isaiah	June 5,	1825		Benedict Reynolds		mr 49 *

"H"

Name (marriage)	(date)	(marriage) year	(suretor)	(minister)	(bond)	
Hackman, Geo. F. m. Gerst, Madeline	Apr. 16, / Sept 28,	1794	Adam Shober	David Young	6b206	gc 4 *
Haddox, John P. m. Shober, Mary Ann	Dec. 23,	1840	Adam Shober		5b222	
Hagaman, Ann m. Barney, William	May 22,	1832	Jacob Severns		7b 5	
Hagaman, Antoinette m. Barney, John	Oct. 1,	1844	Thomas S. Gadin		6b315	
Hagaman, Marenes m. Couchman, Eliz.	Apr. 26,	1844	Henry Couchman		4b107	
†Hage, John B. m. Hunter, Ann K.	Jan. 6,	1819	John Strother			
Hagaley, Marg't m. Marriot, John	May 6,	1788		John Mathews		
Hager, George m. Waugh, Elenor	May 21,	1814	James Waugh	Moses Hoge	3b298	mr 44 *
Hagerty, John m. Thelford, Nancy	July 20,	1784		Rev. Reebenack		gc 14
Hagler, Joseph m. Young, Eliz.	Aug. 10,	1799		Hugh Vance		mr 36 *
Hagmere, Conrad m. Boyd, Ann Maria	Feb. 5,	1818	John Cooke	John Hutt(Hedtt)	2b 18	cr 38
Hahn, Jacob m.Hanniker(Hawn-), Susan	Nov. 13,	1792	James P. Erskine	John B. Hoge	4b 60	
Hahn, Mary m. Myers, William	Dec. 8,	1831	James Kidwell		5b210	mr 53 *
Hahn, Sally m. Hedrick, John	May 1,	1814		David Young		gc 2
Hall, Susannah m. Murphy, Wm.	June 10,	1797	Thomas Murphy	Nathan Young	1b 20	mr 17 *
Hain, Thos. Rosel m. Staley, Cath.	Dec. 23,	1811	Jacob Staley	Rev. Reebenack	3b205	gc 14
Haines, Elis. m. Cage, John	May 22,	1799	John Moore		2b 5	mr 62 *
Haines, Henry m. Green, Cath.	Oct. 1,	1827	William Green	John Hutt(Hedtt)	5b 79	or 13
Haines, Henry m. Miller, Evalina	Apr. 26,	1833	Nancy Miller		5b271	
Haines, John m.Stuntz(-em-ut),Marg.	Jan. 6,	1835	Harrison Waite			mr 18 *
*Haines, Sarah m. Spitznogle, Michael	Apr. 8, / Jan. 6,	1835		Christian Stredt	6b 40	cr 15
Haines, Sarah E.M. m. Kipe, George	Nov. 8,	1847	Henry Haines	John Light		cr 6 *
*Haines, Joseph m. Butt, Diana	Apr. 9, / Apr. 11,	1801	John Butt	Richard Swift	7b111 / 2b121	mr 79 * cr 31 mr 19 *

	(marriage)	(surety)	(minister)	(bond)	
Hainey, Thomas m. Bonham, Mary	Aug. 11, 1813	Smith Bonham	D. Thomas	3b270	mr 37 *
Hair, Abraham m. Brown, Anna	1789				mr 58 *
Hair, Henry m. Steen, Sarah	Jan. 31, 1826	Aaron Dunham	Nathan Young	5b 34	mr 36 *
Hair, Mary m. McDonald, Andrew	Oct. 2, 1788		Moses Boge	3b145	*
Hair, Rachel m. Crabb, Isaac	Apr. 6, 1810	Peter Shaffer			gc 4
Hale, Christina m. Pilmer, Wm.	Feb. 11, 1795		David Young		mr 34 *
Hale, Thomas m. Hanlin, Mary	Dec. 19, 1785		Hugh Vance		
Haley, John m. Bartley, Mary	Nov. 12, 1839	Patrick Smith		6b184	cr 19
Haley, Thomas m. Wheeland, Mary	1789		Hugh Vance		mr 3 *
Hall, Catherine m. Hall, James	July 31, 1798	Edward Chapman		1b125	
Hall, Cynthia m. Locke, Thomas	Dec. 27, 1809	Reuben Hall		3b131	
Hall, Elis. m. Cenwell(Cen-)oveless	Aug. 14, 1799	Basil Games	John Hutt(Hett)	2b 20	cr 38
Hall, Elis. m. Potts, John	Oct. 15, 1800	Robert McKnight		2b 93	
Hall, Elis. m. Wood, Samuel	Feb. 19, 1799	William Hall	John Hett(Hutt)	1b170	cr 13
Hall, Elis. G. m. Hedges, Benj.	Jan. 14, 1817	James Preston	Nathan Young	4b 30	mr 18 *
Hall, James m. Hall, Cath.	July 31, 1798	Edward Chapman		1b125	mr 55 *
Hall, James m. Kain, Keziah	Sept 22, 1798	William Hall	John Hutt(Hett)	1b134	cr 11
Hall, John m. Cooper, Ann	June 4, 1795		John Boyd		cr 33
Hall, John m. Hayes, Mary	Sept 13, 1797	Philip Strider		1b 41	
Hall, Lorenda m. Maynugh(Mayburg)Amos	Aug. 5, 1817	Peter Kreps	Nathan Young	4b 42	mr 55 *
Hall, Marg't m. McKown, John	Sept 28, 1818	Morgan Morgan		4b 80	
Hall, Maria m. Laufen, Frederick	Mar. 3, 1795		David Young		gc 4
Hall, Martha m. Denny, John	Mar. 29, 1789	James Hall		1b x	
Hall, Mary m. Bridgeman, Francis	May 25, May 27, 1799	Wm. Adams	John Hett(Hutt)	2b 6	cr 13 mr 18 *
Hall, Rachel m. Glaze, Thomas	Nov. 15, 1797	William Hall		1b 61	
Hall, Thomas m. Stephen, Sophia	Mar. 27, 1797	John Hall		1b 2	
Hall, William m. Chapman, Francy	Aug. 15, 1805	Edward Chapman		2b268	
Hall, William m. Francis, Sarah	Feb. 19, Feb. 21, 1799	Samuel Wood	John Hett(Hutt)	1b169	cr 12 mr 18 *
Halpin, Thomas m. Seery, Bridget	May 24, 1848	Cornelius McDermot		7b129	
Haman, Cath. m.Zimmerman,Daniel David	Feb. 22, 1814	Geo. Peterman	Rev. Reebensack	3b285	gc 14
Hamell, Mary m. Cooper, Thomas	Nov. 24, 1793		Edward Tiffin		cr 9
Hamer, Elis. m. Short, George	Oct. 5, 1802	Andrew Yates	Richard Swift	2b183	cr 32
Hamilton, Ann m. Dowlan, Christian	Oct. 2, 1807	Wm. Hamilton		3b 66	mr 8 *
Hamilton, Francis m. Lee, Sarah Ann	Aug. 12, Feb. 28, 1818	Joseph Adams		4b 64	mr 21 *
Hamilton, Hannah m. Mills, Wm.	Mar. 5, 1818		Mathias Riser		
Hamilton, Isabel m. Hartness, James	Apr. 26, 1793		Edward Tiffin		mr 29 *
Hamilton, Marg't m. Miller, Joseph	Dec. 25, 1821	Thomas Miller	Geo. M. Frye	4b202	cr 9 mr 8 *
Hamilton, Matilda m. Lee, William	Oct. 18, 1808	Alex. Miller		3b 99	mr 44 *
Hamilton, Rebecca m. Duncan, James	July 3, 1817		Mathias Riser		
Hamilton, Sarah m. Spence, William	June 29, 1795		David Young		gc 5
Hamilton, Susan m. Conoway, John	Mar. 27, Apr. 28, 1833	David H. Brunner	Jas. M. Brown	5b263	mr 67 *
Hamme, Cath. m. Keplinger, John	Jan. 31, 1818	Samuel Conoway		4b 59	
Hamme, Louisa m. Towson, Wm.	Jan. 8, 1840	Jacob Hamme		6b192	
	Oct. 4, 1824	Jacob Hamme	Chas. P. Krauth	4b273	mr 47 *

Name	(date)	(marriage)	(suretor)	(minister)	(bond)		
Hamme, Lydia m. Stephen, Albert	July 5,	July 5, 1810	Jacob Hamme Jr.	Rev. Reebenack	3b153	gc 11	*
*Hammell, Geo. A. m. Chamberlain,Jane	May 28,	June 1, 1847	A.W.McCleary	Lewis F. Wilson	7b 97	mr 82	*
Hammon, Marg't m. Burris, Thomas	Sept 10,	Sept 10, 1807	William Jordan		3b 69		*
Hammon, Mary m. Miller, George	Dec. 5,	Dec. 6, 1808	Richard Hammond	Rev. Reebenack	3b102	gc 10	*
†Hammon, Susan m. Peterman, John	Aug. 17,	Aug. 17, 1820	?	W.N.Scott	4b156	mr 41	*
Hammond, Allen C. m. Cunningham,Sarah	Nov. 24,	Nov. 24, 1838	John W. Waite	Lewis F. Wilson	6b152	mr 70	*
Hammond, Allen C. m. Newkirk,Marg't	Apr. 24,	Apr. 29, 1830	Jas. M. Newkirk	Jas. M. Brown	5b164	mr 54	*
Hammond, Charles m. Martin(Mor-)Sarah	Aug. 23,	1801	Magnus Tate Jr.		2b138		
Hammond, Eliza m. Boyle, James	Dec. 25,	1850	Joseph Duckwall		7b207		
Hammond, Geo. W. m. Beatty, Ann E.	Jan. 30,	1849	James Ijams		7b146		
†Hammond, Mary m. Miller, George	Dec. 5,	Dec. 6, 1808	Michael Hammond	Rev. Reebenack	3b102	gc 10	*
Hammond, Philip m. Grove, Marg't	July 28,	July 31, 1798	John Butt	Richard Swift	1b122	cr 31	*
Hammond, Rachel m. Grove, Stephen	Mar. 9,	1818	Edw. D. Foreman		4b 70	mr 15	*
Hammond, Rebecca m.Kearns, G. Henry	Aug. 17,	1850	?	Lewis F. Wilson	4b156	mr 83	*
†Hammond, Susan m. Peterman, John	Aug. 19,	Aug. 17, 1820		W.N.Scott	1b 9	mr 41	*
Hammond, Thomas m. Washington,Mildred	Apr.19,	1797	Joseph Crane		4b179		
Handler, Wentworth m. Schaffer, Mary	Mar. 28,	1821	Daniel Schaffer		2b178		
Handshaw, Adam S. m. McKenny, Marg't	Aug. 25,	1802	Daniel McKenny		5b178		
Handshew, Hiram m. Saunders, Dorothy	Oct. 18,	Oct. 21, 1830	John Payne	William Monroe	4b278	mr 61	*
Handshew, Thomas m. Light, Hannah	Nov. 22,	1824	John Hancher		6b201		
Henery, John m. Knags, Eliz.	Mar. 23,	Mar. 25, 1840	John W. Waite	Lewis F. Wilson	3b 84	mr 71	*
Hanes, Mary m. Collet, Daniel	Feb. 28,	Feb. 28, 1781		Daniel Sturges	2b226	mr 31	*
Hanlin, Mary m. Hale, Thomas	Dec. 19,	Dec. 19, 1785		Hugh Vance	4b 31	mr 34	*
†Hanly, Mary m. Sheely, Wm.	Feb. 1,	Feb. 1, 1793		William Hill	3b153	mr 10	*
Hanna, Eliz. m. Long, Abr'm D.	May 22,	May 22, 1817		W.N.Scott	2b216	cr 30	
Hanna, Eliz. m. Parker, John	Apr. 12,	1808	Wallace Hanna		2b 90		
Hanna, James m. Parker, Anna	Mar. 12,	1804	William Hanna		3b180		
Hanna, James m. Pitzer, Mary	Mar. 22,	1817	Martin Pitzer		2b200		
Hanna, Lydia m. Stephens, Albert	July 5,	July 5, 1810	Jacob Hamme Jr.	Nathan Young	6b201	gc 11	*
Hanna, Mary m.Scott, William	Feb. 23,	1785	William Hanna	Rev. Reebenack	2b216	mr 55	*
Hannah, Ann m. Gill, Joseph	July 5,	1810		Hugh Vance	2b129	mr 34	*
Hannah, David m. Vance, Mary	Dec. 14,	Dec. 15, 1803	William Williamson	Moses Hoge	6b146	mr 21	*
Hannah, Marg't m. Craighill, Harry	Sept 24,	1795	Harry Craighill	John Boyd		mr 11	*
Hannah, Nancy m. Brown, Peter	Mar. 12,	1800					
Hanniker, Eve Eliz. m. Graham, David	Apr. 16,	1811	Collin Carroll	David Young		gc 2	
Hanriker, Susan m. Hahn, Jacob		1792	David Graham				
Hanris, David m. Wood, Nancy	Nov. 13,	1803					
Hanny, John m. Scott, Eliz.	July 28,	1792		David Young		gc 2	
Hanny, Mary m. Scott, William	Mar. 25,	1795	John W. Waite	Richard Swift	6b201	cr 26	
Hansell, Mary m. Conteman, Henry	Dec. 15,	1840	Wm. Hanna	Lewis F. Wilson	2b216	cr 17	*
Hanson, Thomas m. Noland, Marg't	June 11,	1802	Laurence Hansell	Moses Hoge	2b129	cr 17	*
Hanth, Henry m. French, Rachel	Oct. 6,	1801	John Williamson		6b146		
	Apr. 14,	1838	Henry Job	Rev. Reebenack	3b220	gc 12	*
*Hammell, Elenor m.Whigdon, Richard	Apr. 23,	1812	Geo. H. Hammell	Lewis F. Wilson	7b229	mr 87	*

Name	(marriage)	(suretor)	(minister)	(bond)		
Hard, John m. Creighton, Marg't	Apr. 17, 1793	Andrew Ulm	Moses Hoge	5b 3	cr 21	mr 7 *
Harden, Christian m. Shorts, Cath.	Mar. 1, 1825	John Harden	Chas. P. Krauth	5b 81		mr 48 *
Harden, Elena m. Hess, Joseph	Oct. 27, 1827	John Harden	B. Reynolds	5b 81		mr 52 *
Harden, Eliz. m. Lewis, David	Mar. 28, 1833	John Harden	Nathan Young	5b265		mr 66 *
Harden, Ellinor m. Hess, Joseph	Oct. 27, 1827	John Harden	Benedict Reynolds	5b 81		mr 52 *
Harden, Harriet m. Lyeth, Benj. S.	Nov. 28, 1850	Wm. H. VanDoren	D.Francis Spriggs	7b204		mr 82 *
Harden, John m. Malone, Casey(Cassy)	Apr. 14, 1803	Thomas Malone	David Young	2b200	gc 10	
Harden, John A. m. Kiser, Mary	Mar. 12, 1839	John Merry		6b163		
Harden, Susanna m. Smith, Jonas	Sept 12, 1818	William Tabler		4b 78		
Harding, Richard m. McManus, Polly	Dec. 14, 1786					
Hardwick, Eliz. m. Cross, John	Jan. 27, 1807	Luke McManus	Hugh Vance	3b 44		mr 43 *
Hardy, Eliz. J. m. Hess, Elisha	Jan. 20, 1789		Moses Hoge		cr 1	mr 2 *
Hardy, John C. m. Thompson, Rachel	Aug. 4, 1827	Lewis Hardy	Nathan Young	5b 73		mr 99 *
Hardy, Lewis m. Wilson, Mary	Mar. 12, 1834	John Ramsburg	Jas. M. Brown	5b305		mr 67 *
Hardy, Mary m. Sheely, William	Jan. 20, 1826	William Orr	James Redly	5b 32		mr 49 *
Hardy, Rebecca J. m. Sirbaugh, Henry	Feb. 1, 1793	Joseph Hardy	William Hill	7b 43	cr 30	mr 10 *
Hare, Hannah m. White, Bately	Sept 10, 1845	Joseph Hare		3b284		
Harick, Harry m. Butt, Eveline	Feb. 22, 1814	Samuel D. Beess	D.W.Arnold	7b218		mr 86 *
Harlan, Alice(Alcy) m. Dermott, Jas.	Mar. 12, 1851	Philip McCorren	James Redmond	4b153		mr 31 *
Harlan, Elijah m. Porterfield, Mary	July 2, 1820	Mathew Porterfield	John Mathews	3b339		mr 25 *
Harlan, George m. Eliason, Eliz.	Sept 14, 1815	John Vance	John Boyd		cr 33	mr 10 *
Harlan, George m. Vance, Sarah	May 4, 1795	Charles Orrick	John Mathews	2b165		mr 40 *
Harlan, James m. Orrick, Mary	Mar. 18, 1802		David Young	3b215	gc 3	
Harlan, James m. Palmer, Rachel	Mar. 11, 1812	Silas Harlan	John B. Hoge	4b173		mr 41 *
Harlan, Joshua m. Evans, Nancy	Oct. 2, 1793	Silas Harlan	John B. Hoge	4b173		mr 41 *
Harlan, John(Jehu) m. Evans, Nancy E.	Feb. 26, 1821			6b 56		
Harlan, Levi m. Evans, Mary E.	Feb. 26, 1821					
Harlan, Marg't A. m. Doll, Christian	Sept 14, 1835	Harrison Waite	Lewis F. Wilson	7b 43		mr 77 *
Harlan, Silas m. Evans, Marg't	Sept 10, 1845				cr 13	
Harlan, Stephen m. Phelps, Mary	Apr. 22, 1807	Isaac Evans	John Mathews	3b 57	cr 26	mr 23 *
Harley, Conrad m. Cann, Sarah	June 11, 1795	Patrick Harley	Richard Swift	7b253		mr 10 *
Harley, Thos. J. m. Robinson, Ann E.	Apr. 13, 1852	Jas. H. Robinson		6b297		
Harman, Eliz. m. Aart, Solomon	May 16, 1843		Rev. Reebeneack	3b243	go 14	*
Harmison, Martha m. Ensminger,Chris'n	May 18, 1815	Henry Shriver				
Harmison, Samuel m. Harper, Sarah	Dec. 14, 1812	Joseph Harper		6b 79		
Harmon, Eliz. m. Start, Solomon	May 23, 1836	Michael Harmon		3b324		
Harns, Sarah m. Ferguson, Isaac	May 16, 1815					*
Harnsworth, David m. Butler, Susan A	Feb. 8, 1796	Jeremiah Butler	David Young	6b315	gc 5	mr 63 *
Haron, Rachel m. Kidwell, James	Oct. 4, 1844	George Hawn	Jacob Medtart	5b108		mr 7 *
Harp, Ruth m. Varmetre, Daniel	Oct. 5, 1828		Moses Hoge		cr 21	
Harper, Alex. m. Slater, Mary	Apr. 17, 1793				cr 21	
Harper, Hannah m. Godman, William	Mar. 27, 1805	Thos. Blackburn	John Boyd	2b258		mr 8 *

Name	date	(marriage)	(suretor)	(minister)	(bond)		
Harper, James m. Free, Peggy	May 3,	May 4, 1806	Frederick Free	J. Bond	3b 18	cr 28 *	mr 22 *
Harper, James m. Murray, Sarah		Nov. 13, 1794		David Young		gc 4	mr 59 *
Harper, Jane m. Johnston, Joseph	Nov. 28,	Nov. 30, 1826	Joseph Harper	Nathan Young	5b 57		mr 32 *
Harper, Jennett m. Brown, Robert		June 24, 1783		Hugh Vance			mr 11 *
Harper, John m. Beller, Rachel		Dec. 30, 1795		Moses Hoge		cr 10	mr 60 *
Harper, Joseph m. Shield, Eliz.	May 6,	May 8, 1828	Alex. Robinson	Nathan Young	5b100		
Harper, Lydia m. Glassford, George	July 30,	1798	George Hazeley		1b123		
Harper, Meazy m. Shimp, Jacob	Aug. 26,	Aug. 31, 1820	Jacob Curtis	James Paynter	4b158		mr 40 *
Harper, Polly m. Wandling, Jonathan	Dec. 27,	Dec. 28, 1824		J.L.Bromwell	4b282		mr 47 *
Harper, Samuel m. Cunningham, Sarah		Apr. 17, 1793		Moses Hoge		cr 21	mr 7 *
Harper, Sarah m. Harmison, Samuel	May 23,	1836	Joseph Harper		6b 79		
Harper, Thomas m. Boggs, Jane	Jan. 22,	1839	James Robinson		6b156		
Harper, William m. Faris, Nancy		May 9, 1786		Hugh Vance		cr 26	mr 43 *
Harris, David m. Wood, Nancy		July 28, 1795		Richard Swift		cr 4	mr 10 *
Harris, Drusilla m. Butt, Arch'd		May 18, 1790		Moses Hoge			mr 5 *
Harris, Emily m. Myers, Henry	Dec. 9,	Dec. 12, 1820	Samuel Hedges	James Paynter	4b169		mr 40 *
Harris, George m. Brown, Eliz.		Jan. 12, 1792		David Young		gc 1	mr 15 *
Harris, George m. Chenoweth, Hannah	Oct.	Oct. 23, 1798	John Chenoweth	Richard Swift	1b140	cr 31	
?Harris, Geo. S. m. Strode, Sarah		Dec. 26, 1799		John Heitt(Hutt)		cr 33	mr 17 *
Harris, Geo. S. m. Strider, Sarah	Dec. 23,	1799	Henry Harris		2b 43		
Harris, Geo. W. m. Miller, Ann Maria	Aug. 17,	Aug. 10, 1846	Samuel Miller	Joseph Baker	7b 71		mr 77 *
Harris, James m. Clawson, Polly	Jan. 10,	Jan. 11, 1829	David Miller	Nathan Young	5b116		mr 60 *
Harris, Jane m. Mulhall, John		Dec. 30, 1796		David Young		gc 6	
Harris, Jesse m. Boarman, Susan M.	Feb. 25,	1851	Charles Boarman	Chas. P. Krauth	7b216		mr 51 *
Harris, John R. m. Billmire, Mary	Sept 20,	Sept 1826	Jacob B. Billmyre	David Thomas	5b 52		mr 85 *
Harris, Marg't A. m. Nadenbousch, Moses	Dec. 15,	Dec. 1851	Thomas Harris	Nathan Young	7b239		mr 57 *
Harris, Maria m. Forbes, John	Apr. 23,	Apr. 23, 1821	Lazarus Noland	Hugh Vance	4b182		mr 37 *
Harris, Mary m. Hedges, Aaron		Jan. 22, 1789		David Young			
Harris, Michael m. Roshmier, Susan		Oct. 30, 1795					
Harris, Nancy m. Hedges, Samuel	Sept 23,	1807	Joseph Hedges	John Heitt(Hutt)	3b 70	cr 38	mr 17 *
Harris, Nancy m. Wood, Wm.	Aug. 2,	1799	Jacob Croeson	Moses Hoge	2b 15	cr 3	mr 5 *
Harris, Rebecca m. Maroning, John		Mar. 23, 1790		John Hutt(Heitt)		cr 38	mr 17 *
Harris, Susannah m. Croeson, Jacob	Aug. 2,	Aug. 8, 1799	William Wood	Wm. Monroe	2b 14		mr 65 *
Harris, Thomas m. Polsal, Mary	Apr. 19,	Apr. 19, 1832	Jacob Polsal		5b227		
Harris, Wm. H. m. Paine, Betsy	Apr. 1,	1809	Samuel Harris		3b110		
Harrison, Alex. m. Bons, Polly	Nov. 4,	1815	John Lindsey		3b346		
Harrison, B.F. m. Star, Christiana	Sept 8,	Sept 1814	Fred. Star	John Bond	3b302	cr 41	mr 25 *
Harrison, Dennis W. m. Mason, Mary Cath		Oct. 25, 1853	James Mason	John S. Deale	7b 9		
Harrison, Edw. J. m. Conrad, Betty C.	Oct. 21,	Oct. 8, 1844	David H. Conrad	Lewis F. Wilson	7b199		mr 81 *
Harrison, Eliz. C. m. Atkinson, John	Oct. 8,	1850	Peyton Harrison	D. Francis Sprigg	6b297		
Harrison, Geo. F. m. Conrad, Rebecca	May 10,	1843	David H. Conrad	D. Francis Sprigg	7b227		mr 84 *
Harrison, Jacob m. Basore, Mary A.	June 10,	May 13, 1845	William Basore	John Light	7b 34		mr 76 *

Name	(marriage)		(surety)	(minister)	(bond)	
Harrison, Jacob m. Porterfield, Eliz.	Sept 5,	Dec. 22, 1853	John Evans	G.W.Cooper	5b239	mr 65 *
Harrison, James m. Evans, Susan M.	Aug. 22,	Sept 13, 1832	Jacob Harrison	Wm. Monroe	3b335	gc 15 *
Harrison, Jane m. Ward, Joshua	Nov. 27,	Aug. 24, 1815	Jacob Harrison	Rev. Reebenack	3b348	*
Harrison, John m. Clarke, Teressa	Sept 21,	1815	Dennis Clark		3b237	*
Harrison, John m. Palmer, Polly		1812	Wm. Palmer			
Harrison, John F. m. Tabb, Lucinda		Nov. 6, 1852		Lewis F. Wilson		mr 87 *
Harrison, John S. m. Butt, Hannah	Feb. 29,	1844	Benjamin Butt		6b314	
Harrison, John S. m. Locke, Mary	Nov. 6,	1838	Harrison Waite		6b149	
Harrison, Lucy m. Anderson, Wm. C.	Mar. 4,	1835	John Harrison Jr.		6b 43	
Harrison, Mahala m. Hooper, Thomas	Apr. 17,	1834	William Palmer		6b 7	
Harrison, Mary Jane m. Wolff, Amos	Dec. 25,	1848	Wm. L. Buzzard		7b142	
Harrison, Mercy L. m. Hunter, David	Mar. 6,	1828	*Ferdinand Fairfax		5b 93	
Harrison, Nannie H. m.Burns, Geo. W.	Aug. 11,	1852		D.Francis Spriggs		mr 86 *
Harrison, Nathan m. Barnes, Sarah A.	Oct. 17,	Oct. 22, 1840	Michael Barnes	John Light	6b221	mr 72 *
Harrison, Samuel B. m. Hunter, Eliz.	Feb. 2,	1846	Wm. Hunter		7b 56	
Harrison, Sarah m. Gletner, David	Jan. 25,	1842	Nathan Harrison		6b262	
Harrison, Sarah A m. Waite,Harrison	Oct. 31,	1837	Philip Pendleton		6b123	
Harrison, Susan m. Peterman, John	Aug. 17,	1820		W.N.Scott		mr 41 *
Harsch, Mary m. Grumm, Elis.	July 30,	1798	Daniel Lumprick		1b123	mr 88 *
Hart, Anne m. Poisier, Frans		Dec. 30, 1853		J.H.Plunkett		
Hart, Anne m. Augustus, David	May 14,	1798	Dariel Varmetre		1b111	mr 12 *
Hart, David m. Kenner, Matilda		Sept 29, 1796		John Boyd		cr 11
Hart, Marg't m. Blume, Jacob		Mar. 4, 1793		David Young		gc 2
Hart, Marg't m. Robinson, Joseph	June 13,	1798	Thomas Hart		1b116	
Hart, Rebecca m.Board(Broad), Thos.	Sept 11,	Sept 15, 1800	Philip Board	Moses Hoge	2b 87	cr 29 mr 19 *
Hartley, John m. Williams, Eliz.		Dec. 3, 1819		Mathias Riser		mr 30 *
Hartman, Eliz. m. Tederick, John	Feb. 4,	1806	Christian Hartman		3b 10	
Hartman, Henry m. Freshour, Cath.		Feb. 16, 1796		David Young		gc 5
Hartness, James m. Hamilton, Isabel	Dec. 25,	Dec. 25, 1821	Thomas Miller	Geo. M. Frye	4b202	mr 44 *
Hartsook, Elijah m. Steddley, Eliz.	May 27,	May 29, 1820	Solomon Steddley	Nathan Young	4b149	mr 57 *
Hartsook, Elis. m. Lowry, James M.	Feb. 6,	1836	Joseph Hartsook		6b 70	
Hartsook, Elis. m. Noll, Jacob	Mar. 27,	1835	Harrison Waite		6b 38	
Hartsook, Mary m. Gano, John S.	Mar. 26,	1828	Stephan Gano		5b 96	
Hartsook, Sarah m. Middleton, Thos.	Oct. 22,	1827	Enoch Hartsook		5b 81	
Hartsook, Wm. m. Gano, Amy	Apr. 6,	1828	Stephan Gano		5b 95	
Haslip, Nancy m. Grooms, John	Apr. 22,	1800	Richard Haslip Jr		2b 67	
Haslett, Ailse m. Cunningham, Levi	Feb. 20,	1816	John Haslett		3b355	
Haslett, Hannah m. Swinley, John	Mar. 14,	1820	John Haslett		4b140	
Haslett, Jackson m. Beeson, Juliet	Sept 14,	1840	Lewis R. Beeson	Nathan Young	6b217	mr 57 *
Haslip, Robert m. Pultz, Eliz.	Nov.	1833	Jacob Shaull		5b290	
Haslip, John m. Satterfield, Eliz.	Sept 2,	1797	Joseph Dillon		1b 37	
Hassell, Thomas m. Turner, Susan	Nov. 12,	1838	William Turner		6b150	
Hastings, Amanda m. McDaniel,Michael	Sept 29,	Oct. 30, 1851	John Hastings	F.C.Tebbs	7b235	mr 85 *

*Edmund Hunter also signed as suretor.

Name	(marriage)	(suretor)	(minister)	(bond)	ref.
Hastings, Daniel m. Ebberts, Frederic	Apr. 22, 1835	Marg't Ebberts		6b 43	
Hastings, Frances m. Tully, Isaac	June 1, 1843	John Hastings		6b299	
Hastings, John m. Ebberts, Mary Ann	May 5, 1831	John Ebberts	Robert Cadden	5b193	mr 62 *
Hastings, John m. Iikens, Harriet	July 14, 1839	Joseph Iikens	James Redly	6b172	mr 70 *
Hastings, Robert m. McKeever, Nancy	Aug. 24, 1797	Wm. McCausland		1b 35	
Hauliss, Hannah m. Grimes, Wm.	Oct. 2, 1800		John Hedtt(Hutt)		cr 35
Hauliss, Nancy m. Groving, John	Apr. 29, 1800		John Hedtt(Hutt)		or 24
Haw, Eliz. m. Watson, John	Feb. 13, 1788		Hugh Vance		
Haw, George m. Weaver, Barbara	Feb. 14, 1811	Jonathan Thatcher	Rev. Reebenack	3b174	mr 19 *
Hawk, Harriet m. Sumption, Franklin	Oct. 17, 1844	Wm. H. Mong		7b 8	mr 19 *
Hawk, Harvey(Harry) m. Butt, Evelina	Mar. 12, 1851	Samuel D. Beess		7b218	mr 2 *
?Hawk, Isaac m. Sargeant, Sarah	Sept 25, 1800		D.W.Arnold		
?Hawk, Jesse m. Sargeant, Sarah	Sept 23, 1800	John Shaffer	David Young	2b 89	mr 86 *
Hawk, Jacob m. Gresoker, Christiana	Mar. 31, 1793		David Young		gc 9
Hawk, Marg't m. Leopard(Lippet)Mich'l	Apr. 9, 1798	Jacob Hawk	David Young	1b107	gc 2
Hawk, Michael m. Mong, Eliz.	Sept 16, 1816	John Mong	David Young	4b 14	gc 7
Hawk, Sarah m. Bruer, Henry	Feb. 14, 1786		Lewis Mayor		
Hawk, William m. Stewart, Susanna	May 11, 1804	Isaac Hawk	Hugh Vance	2b235	
Hawniker, Susan m. Hahn, Jacob	Nov. 13, 1792		David Young		gc 2
Hawnes, Jane m. Grimes, Wm.	June 18, 1807	John McIntire	John Mathews	3b 61	cr 13
Hawker, Barbara m. McMahon, Richard	Feb. 27, 1787		Hugh Vance		
Hawkins, James m. Orr, Sarah	Oct. 15, 1801	Wm. Mitchell		2b143	mr 23 *
Hawkins, Rebecca m. Mowles, Adam	Sept 8, 1798	Wm. McDaniel		1b129	mr 44 *
Hawns, Rachel m. Kidwell, James	Oct. 4, 1828	George Hawns	Jacob Medtart	5b108	mr 63 *
Hay, Jane m. Grimes, William	June 18, 1807	John McIntire	John Mathews	3b 61	or 13
Hay, Eliz. m. Ingman(Ingram), Luke	Jan. 14, 1801	Adam Hay	Richard Swift	2b109	or 31
Hay, Gabriel m. Quigley, Jane	Mar. 17, 1789		Hugh Vance		or 40
Hayden, Teresa Ann m. Johnson, Sam'l	Apr. 24, 1836	Jesse Hayden		6b 74	
Hayden, Wm. H. m. Levy, Sarah Ann	Dec. 2, 1833	Abraham Levy	D.Francis Spriggs	5b270	
Bayes, Anthony R. m. Payne, Marg't A	Sept 16, 1788?		Hugh Vance		gc 2
Hays, Barbara m. Herton, Henry	1789		D. Thomas		
Hays, Charity m. Evans, Gabriel	Jan. 3, 1798	Alex. Catlett		1b 79	mr 35 *
Hays, Daniel m. Fleece, Rebecca	July 22, 1830	Barnett Gilbert	Nathan Young	5b170	mr 38 *
Hays, David m. Merchant, Hannah	June 3, 1799	Thos. Swearingen		2b 7	mr 61 *
Hays, Eleanor m. West, John	June 11, 1825	Joseph Hays	Richard Swift	5b 14	cr 34
Hays, Eliz. m. Kime, Isaac	May 8, 1828	Alexander Oden		5b101	mr 16 *
Hays, Harriet m. Friend, Andrew	Dec. 1823		Chas. P. Krauth		mr 46 *
Hays, Jacob m. Hays, Marg't	July 22, 1800	George Hoops		2b 77	
Hays, John m. Hoops, Mary	Nov. 3, 1845	Andrew J. Johnson		7b 47	
Hays, John F. m. Mayhugh, Rachel C.	June 1, 1801				
Hays, Joseph m. Frye, Barbara	Nov. 28, 1823				*
Hays, Joseph m. Hays, Mary, Mrs.	Mar. 2, 1802	John Houseman	Richard Swift	4b252	
Hays, Justice m. Patterson, Elenor	1793				
*Haymond, John m. Houtt(Hoa-),Dorcas	Dec. 4, 1793	Thomas Gill	Edward Tiffin	2b163	cr 9 mr 8 *

Name	(marriage)	(surety)	(minister)	(bond)		
Hays, Margaret m. Hays, Jacob	Sept 13, 1823	Philip Strider	Chas. P. Krauth	1b 41		mr 46 *
Hays, Mary m. Hall, John	Nov. 28, 1797	John Houseman		4b252		
Hays, Mary Mrs. m. Hays, Joseph	May 1, 1823	Joseph Sander		2b173		
Hays, Nathan m. Shane, Mary	Oct. 22, 1802	Andrew Hays		4b120	cr 40	
Hays, Phebe m. Johnston, William	Oct. 24, 1819		Nathan Young			mr 56 *
Hays, Phebe O. m. Boyd, Elijah	Aug. 21, 1789		Hugh Vance			mr 4 *
Hays, Phebe R. m. Lewis, Lewis	Dec. 22, 1853		D.Francis Spriggs			
Hays, Rebecca m. Jenkins, George	Apr. 25, 1850	David Hays	Richard T. Brown	7b184		mr 80 *
Hays, Sally m. Whaley, Benjamin	June 25, 1818	William Brown	W.N.Scott	4b 75		
Hays, Sarah m. Riser, Anthony	Mar. 29, 1787		Hugh Vance			mr 44 *
Hays, Sarah m. Whittington, Richard	Aug. 5, 1829	Joseph Hays	W. Monroe	5b135	cr 35	mr 53 *
Hays, Susanna m. Newkirk, Turds(Thos)Apr.	Apr. 9, 1801	Adam Hays	John Boyd	2b120	cr 11	mr 19 *
Hays, Thomas m. McKoy(McKay),Mary	Dec. 22, 1796		John Boyd			mr 13 *
Hayson, Sarah m. Anglous, Robert	Jan. 17, 1793	David Stewart	David Young		gc 2	mr 20 *
Hazlett, Elenor m. Bryant(By-), Chas.	Feb. 4, 1802		John Mines		cr 27	
Hazlett, Elis. m. Roberts, Nathan	Aug. 8, 1816		John B. Hoge	4b 7		
Hazlett, Hannah m. Swinley, John	Mar. 14, 1820	John Hazlett	Nathan Young	4b140		mr 57 *
Hazlett, Mary m. Swinley, Henry	Oct. 16, 1834	John Swinley		6b 14		
Hazlett, Robert m. Shepherd, Marg't	Oct. 12, 1837	Lewis R. Beeson		6b119		
Harlewood, William m. Swinley, Dorothy	Feb. 10, 1825	John Swinley	John Winter	4b289		mr 50 *
Harlewood, Evelina m. Hill, Samuel	Feb. 11, 1830	James Collett	Wm. Monroe	5b152		mr 54 *
Harlewood, Jas. T. m. Hughes, Eliza	Sept 28, 1846	Jas. J. Kenney		7b 74		
Harlewood, Jesse m. Thompson, Kitty	Mar. 17, 1807	Abraham Howe		3b 50		
Harlewood, Thomas m. Luke, Cath.	Oct. 7, 1806	Thos. Harlewood	J. Bond	3b 32	cr 28	mr 23 *
Heard, Joseph m. Galbraith, Martha	Apr. 12, 1785		Hugh Vance			mr 33 *
Heard, William m. Hanna, Marg't	June 30, 1785		Hugh Vance			mr 34 *
Hearse, Philip m. Spencer, Nancy	Jan. 22, 1805	Thomas Spencer		2b252		
Heath, Hannah m. Shennebere, Geo.	Dec. 23, 1788		Hugh Vance			mr 36 *
Heath, Israel m. Blue, Elis.	July 25, 1799	Richard Blue	John Hutt(Hatt)	2b 11	cr 38	mr 17 *
Heath, James m. Slocum, Betsy	May 11, 1803		David Young		gc 10	
Heaton, Rachel m. Varley, Thomas	Aug. 8, 1797		David Young		gc 6	
Heaton, Ruth m. Demoss, William	Sept 15, 1797	Ebenezer Heaton		1b 41		
Heavy, Henry m. Beard, Mary Jane	Oct. 4, 1852		D. Thomas			mr 86 *
Hebrigle, Cresse m. Sheckles, Hezekiah	Mar. 28, 1799	Richard Gartrell	David Young	1b175	gc 8	
Heck, Catherine m. Shaffer, Henry	May 1, 1798	George Doll	David Young	1b 99	gc 7	
Heck, Elis. m. Doll, George	Nov. 6, 1792		David Young		gc 2	
Heck, Sarah R.R. m. Stewart, Thos. W	Nov. 7, 1844		D.Francis Spriggs			
Hecken, Barbara m. Huffman, Henry	Feb. 3, 1789		Moses Hoge			
Hedges, Aaron m. Harris, Mary	Jan. 22, 1789		Hugh Vance		cr 1	mr 2 *
Hedges, Agnes m. Burns, George	July 10, 1795		John Boyd		cr 33	mr 37 *
Hedges, Agnes m. Pain(Pair), Wm.	Mar. 11, 1811	Samuel Hedges		3b178	gc 11	mr 11 *
Hedges, Angelina m.Cunningham, Geo.H.	May 29, 1833	Josiah Hedges	Rev. Reebenack	5b274		

Name	(marriage)	(suretor)	(minister)	(bond)	
Hedges, Ann Maria m. Mathews, John T	Mar. 22, 1832	Anthony Chambers		50.221	
Hedges, Anna m. Robinson, Alexander	Jan. 26, 1785	Hugh Vance			mr 33 *
Hedges, Ann W. m. Cunningham, W. Hugh	Jan. 14, 1829	Henry Myers	W. Monroe	5b117	mr 53 **
Hedges, Benjamin F. m. Hall, Eliz. G.	Jan. 1, 1817	James Preston	Nathan Young	4b 30	mr 55 **
Hedges, Benj. m. Ropp, Marg't	Oct. 1840	Jacob Ropp		6b217	
Hedges, Benj. m. Wigle, Elis.	Jan. 7, 1784		Hugh Vance		mr 32 *
Hedges, Cath. Va. m.Seibert, Harrism	Feb. 8, 1848	Wm. L. Seibert	James Chisholm	7b122	mr 78 **
Hedges, Elinor m. Hood, George	Mar. 11, 1790		Hugh Vance		mr 38 *
Hedges, Elis. m. Curtis, David	Apr. 14, 1807	Solomon Hedges		3b 55	
Hedges, Elvina m. Criswell, John	Dec. 24, 1832	Harrison Waite		5b250	
Hedges, Enoch m. Perkins, Mary	June 10, 1793		William Hill		cr 30
Hedges, Enoch G. m. Robinson, Jane	Apr. 13, 1840	Bailey T. Hedges	Lewis F. Wilson	6b205	mr 10 *
Hedges, Harriet m. Hedges, Joseph	Aug. 15, 1831	Henry Myers		5b201	mr 71 *
Hedges, Harvey A. m. Gorrell, Cath.	Dec. 18, 1839	Thomas Harley		6b187	
Hedges, Heseklah m. Snodgrass, Elis.	Nov. 20, 1824	Seaman Garard		4b278	
Hedges, Isabel m. Thatcher, Absalom	Feb. 20, 1828	Henry Myers	Nathan Young	5b 90	mr 59 *
Hedges, James m. Kennedy, Elis.	Feb. 4, 1783?		Hugh Vance		mr 32 *
Hedges, Jane m. Patton, Samuel	Apr. 19, 1821	Robert Hedges		4b181	
Hedges, John P.m.Keesecker, Barbara	Oct. 18, 1825	George Keesecker	Nathan Young	5b 25	mr 58 *
Hedges, John m. Philipy, Eleanor	Dec. 2, 1824	Alex. Stephens	Jacob L. Bromwell	4b279	mr 47 *
Hedges, John m. Robinson, Elis.	Nov. 11, 1812	John Robinson		3b240	
Hedges, John m. Sutton, Amy	Jan. 16, 1790		Hugh Vance		mr 38 *
Hedges, John m. Turner, Elis.	Nov. 29, 1821	William Burns	John B. Hoge	4b198	mr 44 *
Hedges, Jonas m. Plotner, Eve	Apr. 4, 1799	Jesse Hedges	David Young	1b177	gc 8
Hedges,Jonas K. m. Shimp, Barbara	Dec. 6, 1847	Jonas Shimp		7b115	
Hedges, Joseph Jr, m. Briscoe, Eliz.	Nov. 5, 1798	John O'Ferrall	John Hett(Hutt)	1b144	cr 30 mr 15 *
Hedges, Joseph m. Burns, Rebecca	May 1, 1820	John Burns		4b146	
Hedges, Joseph m. Hedges, Harriet	Aug. 13, 1831	Henry Myers		5b201	
Hedges, Joshua m. Miller, Mary	Apr. 13, 1804	Jonas Miller		2b233	
Hedges, Joshua m. Southwood, Ruth	June 11, 1804	Edward Southwood		2b236	
Hedges, Josiah m. Morgan, Cath.	Oct. 21, 1800	Morgan Morgan		2b 94	
Hedges, Josiah m. Robinson, Susan	Nov. 26, 1801	John Stevens		5b239	
Hedges, Mary m. Lingamfelter, John	Aug. 22, 1826	Josiah Hedges		5b 49	
Hedges, Mary m. Myers, Aaron	May 14, 1822	Josiah Hedges	Chas. P. Krauth	4b213	mr 45 *
Hedges, Mary m. Norrington, Wm.	Nov. 11, 1844	Jonas Hedges	Lewis F. Wilson	7b 13	
Hedges, Mary E. m. Robinson,Geo. W.	Feb. 1, 1843	Bailey T. Hedges	James Chisholm	6b 289	mr 75 **
Hedges, Mary E. m.Mussetter,Plummer	Sept 13, 1847	Israel Robinson	John Winter	7b107	mr 78 **
Hedges, Mary J. m. Kerns, John A.	Nov. 15, 1847	John P. Hedges		7b112	
Hedges, Mary O. m. Shawhan, David	Jan. 18, 1810	Jonas Hedges	John Mathews	3b134	mr 40 **
Hedges, Mercy T. m. Chambers, Wesley	Jan. 15, 1835	Bailey Hedges	John Howell	6b 62	mr 68 **
Hedges, Morgan m. Snodgrass,Ludnda	Nov. 14, 1831	Paul V. Snodgrass	Nathan Young	5b211	mr 62 **
Hedges, Nancy m. Parr, John	Dec. 8, 1817	Peter Myers	W.N.Scott	4b 36	
Hedges, Phebe m. Lesee, William	June 1, 1820	Solomon Hedges	John B. Hoge	4b169	mr 41 **
*Hedges, Joseph m. Evans, Rachel	Aug. 15, 1793		David Young		gc 3

*

97

Name	(marriage)	(surety)	(minister)	(bond)	Ref
Hedges, Phebe m. Vincent, Robert	Jan. 17, 1825	Hesekiah Hedges	Chas. P. Krauth	4b286	mr 48 *
Hedges, Rebecca m. Alexander, Elijah	Dec. 2, 1823	Josiah Hedges	Chas. P. Krauth	4b253	mr 46 *
Hedges, Rebecca m. Campbell, Jas. L.	Feb. 28, 1829	Thomas Miller	Jas. M. Brown	5b121	mr 53 *
Hedges, Rebecca m. Robinson, Abr'm	Mar. 27, 1793		David Young		gc 3
Hedges, Robert m. Chambers, Hetty	May 26, 1811	Robert Wilson	John B. Hoge	3b188	cr 14 / mr 24 *
Hedges, Ruth m. Manor, Benj. G.	Apr. 21, 1849	Jonas Hedges		7b155	
Hedges, Ruth m. Robinson, James	Sept 28, 1814	Hesekiah Hedges		3b305	
Hedges, Samuel m. Harris, Nancy	Sept 23, 1807	Joseph Hedges		3b 70	
Hedges, Samuel m. Manor, Klenor Cath.	Jan. 18, 1847	William Hedges	E.L.Dulin	7b 83	mr 77 *
Hedges, Samuel m. Shields, Charity	Mar. 30, 1807	John Shields		3b 52	
Hedges, Samuel m. Tabb, Mary	June 26, 1783		Hugh Vance		mr 32 *
Hedges, Sarah m. Reed, Wm. Jr.	Sept 5, 1810	Wm. Reed Sr.	John Mathews	3b161	mr 40 *
Hedges, Sarah K. m. Barchus, Levi H.	May 30, 1835	Henry Myers	John Howell	6b 46	mr 68 *
Hedges, Solomon m. Shaffer, Eliz.	Apr. 20, 1820	Henry Shaffer	John B. Hoge	4b145	mr 31 *
Hedges, Solomon m. Wincenheller, Sarah	July 28, 1789		Hugh Vance		cr 39 / mr 3 *
Hedges, Wm. m. Light, Eliz.	Feb. 4, 1822	John Light	John B. Hoge	4b207	mr 44 *
Hedges, William m. Weller, Eve Ann	Apr. 19, 1841	George Weller	John Hedges	6b240	mr 72 *
Hedson, Rachel m. Vacley, Thomas	July 30, 1797	Johnson Moore		1b 26	
Hedrick, George m. Tyson, Peggy	Oct. 8, 1809				
Hedrick, John m. Hahn, Sally	May 1, 1814				
Heffner, Benj. m. Besson, Julia Ann	Dec. 21, 1825		Rev. Reebeenack	5b 30	gc 10 *
Heffner, Jonathan m. Earhart, Cath.	June 29, 1839		Rev. Reebenack	6b172	gc 14 *
Haddenrick, Mary m. Kinkle, Caleb		Thos. Crawford	Benedict Reynolds		*
Heding, Charlotte M. m. Daugherty, R'd	Oct. 3, 1824	Patr'k Cunningham	Chas. P. Krauth		mr 49 *
Heironimus, Geo. m. Shink, Eliz.	Nov.				*
Heironimus, Sarah m. McDonald, Garard	Jan. 9, 1793	John Heining		6b220	*
*Heitt, Peter m. Slomacre, Catherine	Apr. 16, 1840	Michael Couchman	David Young	5b254	gc 3 *
Helferstay, Ann E. m. Fisher, Jacob	Dec. 8, 1836	John Helferstay	David Young	6b 89	gc 4 *
Helferstay, George m. Tully, Marg't	Mar. 31, 1821	Samuel Blake		4b180	
Helferstay, Henry Jr. m. Whetston, Sarah	Jan. 20, 1829	Isaac Whisler	Jacob Medtart	5b17	mr 63 *
Helferstay, John m. Bender, Eliz.	Mar. 17, 1810	Joseph Schoppert	Rev. Reebenack	6b173	gc 11 *
Helferstay, John m. Blondel, Lydia	July 27, 1839	Jacob Painter		3b152	
Helferstay, John m. Painter, Eliz.	May 17, 1810	Adam Stewart	Jacob Medtart	5b239	mr 64 *
Helferstay, John m. Tabler, Susan	Sept 3, 1832	Jacob VanDoren		7b 98	
Helferstay, Lydia m. Murphy, Michael	June 7, 1847	John Helferstay		5b166	
Helferstay, Marg't m. Beeson, Hiram	June 5, 1830	John Helferstay		5b257	
Helferstay, Mary Ann m. Bales, Moses	Feb. 14, 1833	Geo. Helferstay	Jos. Plunkett	7b213	mr 84 *
Helferstay, Marg't Ann m. Grove, Jos.	Jan. 30, 1851	John Helferstay		6b215	
Helferstay, Sarah m. Blondel, Rich'd	Aug. 10, 1840			7b 69	
Helferstay, Wm. m. Poisal, Cath.	June 18, 1846	Jacob Poisal	John Winter	5b178	mr 76 *
Helferstine, Henry m. Poisal, Eliz. Mrs	Oct. 17, 1830	John Shober	Nathan Young		mr 61 *
Heller, Cath. m. Fackwell, Will	Oct. 22, 1793		David Young		
Helm. Barbara m. McAllister, Christ'r	Dec. 13, 1810	Patr'k Duffy	Rev. Reebenack	3b168	gc 3 *
*Hedtt(Hutt), John m. Crockwell, Betsy	Mar. 3, 1799		John Potts		gc 11 / cr 12 / mr 18 *

Name	(license)	(marriage)	(suretor)	(minister)	(bond)		
Helm, Mary m. Ott, John(Jacob)	June 21,	June 22, 1800	Mathew Ranson	David Young	2b 74	gc 9	mr 1 *
Helmbolt, Eliz. m. Dousk, Christ'r		Apr. 11, 1787		Christian Streit		cr 15	mr 36 *
Helphington, Henry m. Pysle,Rebecca		Dec. 4, 1788		Hugh Vance		gc 2	mr 15 *
Holt, Nancy m. Beard, John		Dec. 5, 1792		David Young		cr 31	mr 60 *
Homer, Richard m. Linch, Sarah		Apr. 5, 1798		Richard Swift			
Henderson, David m. Steddley, Hannah	Oct. 6,	Oct. 8, 1829	Solomon Steddley	Nathan Young	5b143		
Henderson, Eliza L. m. Jones, Rhys	June 12,	1844	James McSherry		7b 3		mr 60 *
Henderson, James m.Allott(-stadt)Phebe	June 16,	June 17, 1830	James McCouch	Nathan Young	5b168		mr 45 *
Henderson, James m. Severns, Eliz.	Jan. 27,	Jan. 30, 1823	Richard Severns	James Samson	4b233		
Henderson, John m. Buck, Margaret	Apr. 28,	1798	Robert Buck		1b109		
Henderson, John m. Gillaspy, Nancy	Nov. 5,	Nov. 29, 1825	William Faris	Chas. P. Krauth	5b 26		mr 49 *
Henderson, John m. Steddley, Cath.	Mar. 27,	Mar. 29, 1827	John Steddley	Nathan Young	5b 65		mr 59 *
Henderson, Joseph m. Gano, Cath.	Apr. 30,	1797	Stephen Gano		1b 6		
Henderson, Mary m. Hinkle, George	Mar. 7,	1834	Joseph Henderson		5b304		
Henderson, Rachel m. Hinkle, Henry	Jan. 14,	1837	Harrison Waite		6b 90		
Hendre, Mary m. Jones, Samuel	Mar. 19,	1793		Moses Hoge		cr 21	mr 7 *
Hendrick, Abigail m. Ingle, John	May 10,	1793		William Hill		cr 30	mr 9 *
Hendrick, Eliz. m. Faris, David Jr.	June 8,	1786		Hugh Vance			mr 43 *
Hendrick, Olive m. Blackburn, Joseph	Apr. 16,	1782		Daniel Sturges			mr 42 *
Hendrick, Mary m. Jones, Samuel	Mar. 19,	1793		Moses Hoge		cr 21	mr 7 *
Hendrick, Nathan m. Wynkoop, Marg't	Mar. 12,	Mar. 15, 1821	Adrian Wynkoop	John Mathews	4b176	cr 21	mr 44 *
Hendrick, Priscilla m. Sewel, John	Apr. 22,	1793		Moses Hoge		cr 2	mr 7 *
Hendrick, Rebecca m. Sewell, Aaron	Apr. 3,	1798	John Ingle		1b 96	cr 2	mr 2 *
Hendrick, Tobias m. Wright, Peggy	May 13,	1789		Moses Hoge			
Hendrixon, John m. Burke, Elvira B.	Jan. 10,	1807	James Burke		3b 46		
Henegar, Martin m. Grim, Elis.						gc 7	
Henley, Wm. m. Dunn, Rosanna	July 31,	1798	Robert Dunn	David Young	1b137	cr 32	mr 15 *
Henry, George m. Myers, Polly	Oct. 8,	Oct. 25, 1798	Adam Myers	John Boyd	3b 9		
Henry, George m. Waggener, Sally	Jan. 30,	1806	Nicholas Henry		3b211		
Henry, Michael m. Pinkerton, Cath.	Feb. 1,	1812	Robert Pinkerton		3b219		
Henry, Peter m. Ambrose, Polly	Apr. 13,	1812	Nicholas Henry		3b203		
Henry, Philip m. Feller, Mary Ann	Dec. 14,	1811	Henry Feller	P. Harrison	6b165		mr 71 *
Henry, Susannah m. Jacques, Arthur	Apr. 6,	Apr. 10, 1839	Alexander Henry	John Boyd	9b254	cr 32	mr 15 *
Henry, Wm. m. Dunn, Rosanna	Jan. 8,	1833	Robert Dunn		1b137		
Henry, Wm. m. Horn, Mary Ellen	Oct. 8,	Oct. 25, 1845	John R. Crow		7b 39		
Henry, Wm. m. Myers, Sally	Aug. 5,	1798	Richard Henry		4b 66		
Hensel, Daniel m. Detton, Hannah	Mar. 19,	Mar. 22, 1818	Benjamin Wilson	Nathan Young	4b 31		mr 56 *
Hensel, David m. Miller, Nancy C.	Feb. 6,	1817	Wm. D. Miller	Nathan Young	3b295		mr 55 *
Hensel, Eliz. m.Folk(Folck), John	Apr. 5,	Apr. 21, 1814	Lawrence Hensel	Nathan Young	1b 74		mr 54 *
Hensel, Geo. W. m. Robinson, Sarah	Dec. 20,	Dec. 26, 1797	Aaron Chaffin	David Young	6b 94	gc 7	
Hensel, Jacob m. Robinson, Jane	Jan. 31,	1837			7b205		
Hensel, Jas. W. m. Zorn, Harriet A.	Oct. 9,	Oct. 10, 1850	John Zorn	Henry Furlong	7b200		mr 81 *
Hensel, Joseph m. Lamar, Mary Jane	Dec. 9,	Dec. 23, 1843	William Lamar	T.H.W.Monroe	6b310		mr 75 *

(name)	(marriage)	(suretor)	(minister)	(bond)	
Hensel, Michael m. Myers, Eliz.	Apr. 27, 1808	John Myers	John Light	3b 88	mr 88 *
Hensel, Parker H. m. Crowl, Susan	Dec. 23, 1852				mr 24 *
Hensel, Sally m. Miller, William	Jan. 3, 1811	Henry Coutchman	John B. Hoge	3b170	cr 14
Hensel, Wm. m. Beller, Evelina	Dec. 9, 1820	Abraham Morlatt		4b168	
Henshaw, Anderson m.Busey,Marg't J.	Oct. 25, 1846	Samuel Busey	R.F.Brown	7b 75	mr 77 *
Henshaw, Ann M. m. Brown, Joseph	Oct. 9, 1848	Henry Henshaw		7b137	
Henshaw, Barton m. Hyett, Rachel	Apr. 14, 1829	Ezekiel Neff		5b126	
Henshaw, Elenor m. Lyle, Hugh M.	Nov. 27, 1820	Levi Henshaw		4b167	*
Henshaw, Evelina m. McKown, George	Feb. 3, 1825	Hiram Henshaw	Jas. M. Brown	4b288	mr 48 *
Henshaw, Hiram m. McConnell, Mary	Feb. 24, 1802	Wm. McConnell		2b162	
Henshaw, Isabel J. m. Gorrell, Wm B.	Apr. 17, 1834	Levi Henshaw	J.E.Jackson	6b 6	*
Henshaw, Isabel L. m. Swearingen,H.H.	Feb. 15, 1836	Bailey Tabb		6b 71	
Henshaw, James m. McConnell, Marg't	Nov. 23, 1818	Levi Henshaw		4b 90	
Henshaw, Jas. W. m. Miller, Nancy	Dec. 14, 1837	Jas. H. Miller	Lewis F. Wilson	6b126	*
Henshaw, Jonathan S. m. Mounts, Eliz.	Feb.18, 1799	Seth Duncan		1b169	
Henshaw, Levi m. McConnell, Anna	Apr. 29, 1805	Wm. McConnell		3b 18	
Henshaw, Levi m. Snodgrass, Annie S.	Dec. 11, 1851	Robt. V. Snodgrass	J.H.Jennings	7b238	mr 85 *
Henshaw, Marg't D. m. Moon,Valentine	Nov. 4, 1850	Jas. W. Henshaw		7b201	
Henshaw, Martha J. m. Silver,Zephan'h	Apr. 14, 1834	Hiram Henshaw	Jas. M. Brown	6b 6	mr 68 *
Henshaw, Mary C. m. Morgan, Wm. G.	Feb. 25, 1839	Hiram Henshaw	Lewis F. Wilson	6b161	mr 70 *
Henshaw, Thornton m. Snodgrass,Susan	Apr. 26, 1844	Wm. T. Snodgrass	Lewis F. Wilson	6b320	*
Henshaw, Uriah m. McDonald, Eliz.	Sept 29, 1807	John McDonald		3b 72	
Henshaw, Wash't'n m. Mallok,Charlott	Apr. 10, 1802	John Barckley		2b170	
Henshaw, Wm.S. Jr. m. Lyle, Harriet	Sept 17, 1816	Robert ?	John B. Hoge	4b 13	mr 72 *
Herbert, Hilary m. Houck, Maria	May 1, 1841	William Ripple	John Light	6b240	mr 36 *
Herd, Susanna m. Hopkins, James	Sept 4, 1788		Moses Hoge		gc 3
Herges, Joseph m. Evans, Rachel	Aug. 15, 1793		David Young		
Herley, Mary m. Hole, James	Jan. 25, 1840	Thomas Herley		6b194	
Herley, Thomas m. Murphy, Hannah	Feb. 13, 1840	Daniel Mullins		6b196	gc 2
Herman, Michael m. Brackfise, Cath.	Feb. 20, 1793		David Young		
Herring, Wm. T. m. Myers, Harriet	Mar. 27, 1849	Jacob Myers	B.M.Schmucker	7b149	mr 79 *
Herton, Henry m. Hays, Barbara	Sept 16, 1788?		Hugh Vance		or 36
Heson, Christena m. Watts, Charles	Oct. 20, 1796		Moses Hoge		gc 4
Hess, Benj. m. McCollough, Nancy	Jan. 6, 1795		David Young		
Hess, Charlotte m. Raney, Samuel	July 30, 1804	Luke Pentony		2b239	
Hess, David m. Grove, Ann	Oct. 10, 1825	Jesse Myers	Chas. P. Krauth	5b 24	mr 49 *
Hess, David H. m. Cline, Mary Jane	Dec. 12, 1839	Wm. T. Seibert		6b186	
Hess, Elisha m. Hardy, Eliz. J.	Aug. 4, 1827	Lewis Hardy	Nathan Young	5b 73	mr 99 *
Hess, Eliza m. Trigg, Samuel	Apr. 18, 1833	Charlotte Hess	Nathan Young	5b267	mr 66 *
Hess, Eliz. m. Kerns (Kearns),Joseph	May 30, 1849	Peter Hess	B.M.Schmucker	7b159	mr 79 *
Hess, Eliz. m. Leather, Wm.	Mar. 17, 1828	Daniel Brunner	B. Reynolds	5b 93	mr 52 *
Hess, George m. Candle, Margaret	Apr. 26, 1828	Thos. Wolford	B. Reynolds	5b100	mr 52 *
Hess, Harriet m. Hubbard, Conrad	Dec. 19, 1849	Peter Hess	B.M.Schmucker	7b171	mr 79 *

	(marriage)	(suretor)	(minister)	(bond)		
Hess, Jacob m. Dawson, Eliz.	Dec. 22, 1817	Swearingen Ray		4b 54		mr 68 *
Hess, John m. Bolan, Eliz.	Aug. 19, 1834	David Hess	Jas. M. Brown	6b 15		mr 52 *
Hess, Joseph m. Harden, Elena(Elinor)	Oct. 27, 1827	John Harden	B. Reynolds	5b 81		
Hess, Lane m. Butt, Michael	Mar. 26, 1850	Peter Hess		7b180		
Hess, Maria m. Maddox(-ttox),Lorenzo	Mar. 3, 1832	John Hess		5b21B		
Hess, Maria m. Mitchell, Samuel	Nov. 15, 1825	Peter Hess	Chas. P. Krauth	5b 27		mr 49 *
Hess, Mary m. Maddox(Madden),Aquilla	Mar. 24, 1844	Lorenzo D. Maddox	James Chisholm	6b316		mr 75 *
Hess, Mary m. Podsal, Henry	May 28, 1835	Wm. W. Walker		6b 45		
Hess, Peter m. Clarke, Charity	Oct. 20, 1818	Solomon Clarke		4b 82		
Hess, Peter m. Mathews, Nancy					gc 4	*
Hess, Peter Jr. m. Crab, Nancy	Nov. 21, 1837	Peter Hess Sr.	David Young	6b125		
Hess, Polly m. Smith, Nicholas	May 16, 1848	Jacob Gapman		7b128		
Hess, Sarah Ann m. Gregory, Thos. R.	Mar. 10, 1851	Joseph M. Hess	B.M.Schmucker	7b218		mr 84 *
Hess, Sarah Ann m.Sharff(Sharp),Henry	Jan. 8, 1846	Norman Miller	Lewis F. Wilson	7b 53		mr 77 *
Hess, Solomon m. Triggs, Sarah E.	Jan. 25, 1854		G.W.Cooper			
Hessey, Mary m. Rightstine, Adam	May 11, 1837	Abraham Harris		6b106		
Hetherington, Lydia m. Saffell, Jesse	Sept 23, 1854	Thos. Hetherington		1b 43		
Hetterley, Eliz. B. m. Crim, John P.						*
Hew, John m. Robinson, Sarah	Jan. 2, 1806		L.M.Collaway	3b 8		
Hewitt, Thomas m. Miller, Eliz.	Sept 18, 1837	Thomas Smart		6b111		mr 52 *
Hews, George m. Candle, Margaret	Apr. 26, 1828	David Miller	Lewis F. Wilson	5b100		mr 9 *
Hoyatt, William m. Green, Rebecca	Feb. 12, 1794	Thos. Wolford	B. Reynolds		cr 22	
Hatt, William m. Darriel, Polly	Dec. 29, 1799	Samuel Darriel	Moses Hoge	2b 45		
Hibban, Sarah m. Griffins, Zachariah	Nov. 11, 1785		Edward Tiffin		cr 38	mr 1 *
Hibban, Susan m. Potts, John	Mar. 14, 1782		Daniel Sturges			mr 42 *
Hibban, William m. Sheeley, Margaret	Feb. 4, 1790		Moses Hoge		cr 3	mr 5 *
Hibbard, Barbara m. Folk, Peter	Jan. 23, 1835	? Hibbard		6b 29		
Hibbard, Conrad m. Hess, Harriet	Dec. 19, 1849	Peter Hess	B.M.Schmucker	7b171		mr 79 *
Hibler, Susannah m.Kidinger, John	Apr. 26, 1796		John Boyd		cr 11	mr 12 *
Hicks, James m. Crabb, Mary	June 8, 1807	John Porter		3b 60		
Hiele, Rebecca m. Watson, Thomas	Jan. 1, 1798	Joseph Bell		1b 81		
Hiett, John m. Crockwell, Betsy					cr 12	mr 18 *
Hett, Levi m. Bell, Lucy Ann	Mar. 3, 1799	Henry Payne	John Potts			
Higgins, Eliz. m. Sybole, Presley B.	Sept 20, 1837	John Shull		6b113		
Higgins, John m. Anderson, Mary	Feb. 22, 1838	John Anderson	James Watts	6b132		mr 49 *
Higgins, Joseph m. Wisenberger, Eliz.	Sept 26, 1825	Stephen Gano	James Reiley	5b 22		
Higgins, Marg't m. Murray,Patrick	Apr. 5, 1810			3b149		
Higgins, Thomas m. Loftus, Marg't	Oct. 14, 1852	Michael Loftus	J.H.Plunkett	6b179		mr 88 *
Hlgh, Esther m. Lover(Loran), Henry	Aug. 15, 1839	Daniel Hlgh		3b334		
Highett, Eliz. m. Green, Thomas	Aug. 22, 1815		Rev. Reebenack		gc 15	mr 5 *
Hildt, Eliza m. Bear, John	Mar. 4, 1790	George Hildt	Moses Hoge	5b 16	cr 3	
Hill, Ann m. Small, Jacob A.	July 19, 1825	David Hill		6b206		mr 48 *
Hill, Benjamin m. Pitzer, Jane	Apr. 28, 1840		James Reiley	6b319		
	Apr. 17, 1844	Michael Pitzer				

Name	Date	(marriage)	(suretor)	(minister)	(bond)	Ref
Hill, Catherine m. College, James	June 2,	1819	Christopher Hill	Mathias Riser	3b247	mr 30 *
Hill, Catherine m. Gill, Absalom	Sept 4,	1827	Christopher Hill	J.B.Reynolds	1b 38	mr 52 *
Hill, Christiana m. Syers, Alex.		1797				*
Hill, Christopher m.Bernhart,Christ'a	Sept 27,	1795		David Young		gc 5 *
Hill, Fanny m. Dust, John	Jan. 11,	1813	Robert Hill		3b247	
Hill, George m. Miller, Margaret	Dec. 20,	1817	John Miller		4b 53	
Hill, George m. Porterfield, Rachel	Mar. 9,	1829	John Shober	Jas. M. Brown	5b122	mr 53 *
Hill, George m. Rush, Susannah	Oct. 19,	1815	Samuel Hill	Nathan Young	3b344	mr 55 *
Hill, Jacob m. Miller, Sophia	May 2,	1822	John Miller	Chas. P. Krauth	4b212	mr 45 *
Hill, Jacob m. Randall, Eliz.	Oct. 30,	1839	John Waite		6b182	
?Hill, James E. m. Hill, Margaret	July 30,	1849	Geo. L. Hill	P.D.Lipscomb	6b182	mr 82 *
?Hill, James E. m. Hill, Mary	July 30,	1849		P.D.Lipscomb	7b161	mr 82 *
Hill, Jane m. Derst, John	Jan. 14,	1813		Rev. Reebenack		gc 13
Hill, Jane m. Reed, Isaac	Feb. 27,	1809	John Hill		3b108	
Hill, Job C. m. Miller, Mary	June 27,	1849	Henry S. Seibert		7b161	mr 82 *
Hill, John m. Walgamott, Mary E.	Apr. 19,	1846	Thos. S. Hooper		7b 65	mr 45 *
Hill, John W. m. Rusler, Sarah	Nov. 2,	1839	John L. Rusler		6b183	mr 76 *
Hill, Mary(Marg't) m. Hill, James E.	July 17,	1849	John Hill	P.D.Lipscomb	7b161	mr 82 *
Hill, Mary m. Compton, Henry	Sept 17,	1822	Robert Hill	Chas. P. Krauth	4b223	mr 45 *
Hill, Mary E. m. O'Neal, John R.	May 25,	1846	John Schaffer	John Winter	7b 67	mr 76 *
Hill, Mary M. m. Hodge,Jennifer	Nov. 14,	1844	Jacob A. Small		7b 14	
Hill, Mary S. m. Gregg, Henry	Apr. 14,	1845	William Hill	John Light	7b 32	mr 76 *
Hill, Moses m. McIntire, Mary	Apr. 13,	1831	John McIntire		5b192	
Hill, Nancy m. Lefevre, John	Dec. 6,	1819	George Hill		4b125	
Hill, Polly m. Stilwell, Thomas	Jan. 1,	1811	Thomas Sharp		3b171	
Hill, Robert m. Young, Mary	June 13,	1836	Michael Roney		6b 81	
Hill, Sally m. McWarms, John	Dec. 10,	1818	Robert Hill	W.N.Scott	4b 93	mr 30 *
Hill, Samuel m. Harlewood, Evelina	Feb. 11,	1830	James Collett	Wm. Monroe	5b152	mr 54 *
Hill, Samuel m. Whisler, Cath.	Apr. 24,	1821	Isaac Whisler		4b182	
Hill, Samuel m. Wilson, Isabella	Feb. 24,	1816	John P. Porterfield	Nathan Young	4b 63	mr 56 *
Hill, Wm. m. Keesecker, Mary Ann	Sept 17,	1827	Jacob Keesecker	Jas. M. Brown	5b 78	mr 51 *
Hill, Wm. m. Winebrenner, Ellen	Dec. 23,	1861	Israel Cooper	John Light	6b260	mr 72 *
Hillard, Cath. m. Windom, Nicholas	June 14,	1829	John Shober	Nathan Young	5b133	mr 60 *
Hillard, Ellen m. Broderick, Michael	Dec. 9,	1846	Patrick Reynolds		7b 80	
Hillard, John m. Coons, Polly	July 7,	1803	Jacob Coons	David Young	2b205	gc 10 *
Hinkle, George m. Henderson, Mary	Mar. 7,	1834	Jos. Henderson		5b304	
Hinkle, Henry m. Henderson, Rachel	Jan. 14,	1837	Harrison Waite		6b 90	
Hiser, Cath. m. Nolehans, Frederick		1793				*
Hiser, Lewis m. Ferrall, Eliz.	Sept 1,	1800	John Unseld	David Young	2b 83	gc 3 *
Hite, Margaret m. Deevar, Isaac	Mar. 18,	1794		David Young		gc 3 *
Hite, Eliz. m. Basore, Bernard	Nov. 25,	1805	John Hite		3b 4	*
Hite, Eliz. m. Violet, Edward	Dec. 29,	1799	?Joseph Hite	John Heitt(Hutt)	1b158	cr 12 mr 18 *
Hite, Frances M. m. Willis, Carver	Dec. 16,	1798	Richard Willis	John Heitt(Hutt)	1b153	cr 12 mr 16 *

Name	(marriage)	(surator)	(minister)	(bond)	
Hite, Hannah m. Boroff, Samuel	June 10, 1835	William Hite	Elisha Gardner	6b 46	mr 68 *
Hite, Jacob m. Houck, Eliz.	Apr. 14, 1807	Jacob Houck		3b 55	
Hite, Jacob m. Johnstone, Hannah	Mar. 22, 1813	Abr'm Johnstone		3b 257	
Hite, James m. Baker, Juliet	Feb. 20, 1798	Jacob H. Manning		1b 86	
Hite, John m. Burns, Eliz.	Feb. 8, 1813	George Burns		3b 250	mr 70 *
Hite, John m. Roberts, Prudence M.	June 7, 1839	Samuel Roberts	Lewis F. Wilson	6b 171	
Hite, Margaret m. Carper, Samuel	Feb. ? 1834	William Hite		5b 303	mr 20 *
Hite, John m. Southwood, Susannah	Dec. 13, 1802	George Smithers	John Mines	2b 186	cr 27
Hite, Sarah m. Kemp, Henry	Sept 25, 1797	Reuben Newkirk		1b 46	
Hite, Susanna m. Childs, William	Jan. 3, 1843	William Hite	Mayberry Goheen	6b 287	mr 74 *
Hite, William m.Houck(Flook), Sally	Dec. 14, 1812	Jacob Houck	Rev. Reebenack	5b 242	gc 13
Hite, William m. Kees, Mary Ann	Aug. 23, 1847	Calender Wibeley	Jas. H. Jennings	7b 104	mr 82 *
Hite, William m. Zeckman, Sarah	Aug. 20, 1818	Abraham Weidman		4b 77	
Hitz, Frederick m. Holbert, Nancy	Nov. 7, 1844	Levi Spitznegle		7b 13	
Hively, Abr'm m. Shell, Susannah	Oct. 8, 1799	James Lane		2b 30	*
Hiveley, Susannah m. Snider, Wm.	Dec. 23, 1809	Solomon Shrodes	Rev. Reebenack	3b 130	gc 11
Hivner, Joseph m. Flagg, Martha	Feb. 18, 1813	Thomas Tabb	John Mathews	3b 252	mr 25 *
Hoake, Polly m. Houck,George	Dec. 12, 1811	Jacob Houck	Rev. Reebenack	3b 202	gc 12
Hoatt, Dorcas m. Haymond, John	Dec. 4,		Edward Tiffin	2b 115	cr 9 · mr 8 *
Hobbs, Eliz. m. Butler, Douglass	Feb. 25, 1801	Horatio Hobbs		2b 197	
Hobday, William m. Widmire,Christ's	Mar. 15, 1803	Wm. Widmire		6b 193	
Hodge, John m. Anderson, Margaret	Jan. 15, 1840	David Hays		2b 194	
Hodge, John m. McConnell, Jane	Feb. 15, 1803	Wm. McConnell		4b 210	
Hoe, Catherine m. Richards, Fred.	? 1822	George Hoe	Chas. P. Krauth	4b 299	mr 47 *
Hoe, George m. Butt, Catherine	Mar. 22, 1824	Peter Myers	Chas. P. Krauth	4b 228	mr 45 *
Hoff, Elienor m. Sellers, Jacob	Nov. 13, 1822	John Sellers	Chas. P. Krauth	4b 228	mr 45 *
Hoff, Eliz. m. Sellers, Jacob	Nov. 13, 1822	John Sellers		5b 70	
Hoffman, Abraham m. Perry, Polly	May 31, 1827		D.F.Bragunier	7b 88	mr 78 *
Hoffman, David m. Ropp, Hannah	Mar. 1, 1847	Daniel Ropp	Wm. Love	7b 103	mr 78 *
Hoffman, David W. m. Colbert, Ann	July 31, 1847	Joseph Hoffman	David Young	2b 52	gc 9
Hoffman, John m. Free, Eliz.	Feb. 8, 1800	George Kiger	Nathan Young	4b 97	mr 56 *
Hoffman, John m. Marckel, Kitty	Jan. 16, 1819	Wm. Marckel	Peyton Harrison	6b 130	mr 69 *
Hoffman, Joseph m. Wilson, Eliz. P.	Jan. 15, 1838?	William Wilson	John Mathews	5b 6	mr 50 *
Hoffman, Mary m. Martin, Manning	Apr. 25, 1825	Levi Martin		6b 288	
Hoffman, Mary m. Mounts, Geo. W.	Jan. 25, 1843	Joseph Randall		7b 189	
Hoffman, Michael m. Sigler, Rhuanna	July 20, 1850		D.F.Bragunier	7b 220	mr 80 *
Hoffman, Michael m. Barrett, Nancy E	Mar. 24, 1851	Wm. A. Cushwa	D.F.Bragunier	2b 73	mr 84 *
Hoffman, Susan m. Seibert, Henry	June 17, 1800	Wendle Seibert	David Winter	5b 35	gc 9
Hoffman, Valentine m. Seibert, Eliz.	Feb. 1, 1826	John Seibert	John Winter	7b 73	mr 50 *
Hoffman, Wm. m. Miller, Eliz.	Sept 21, 1846	Jacob Spero	John Light		mr 79 *
Hogan, Bridget m. Shelby, William	Aug. 10, 1853		J.H.Plunkett		mr 88 *
Hogan, Daniel m. Godan, Sally	Oct. 4, 1792				
Hoge, John m. Rippy, Eliz.	June 1, 1808	Mathew Rippy	David Young	3b 90	gc 6

	(marriage)		(surety)	(minister)	(bond)	
Hoge, John Blair m. Wilson, Anna C.	Nov. 1,	1848	David H. Strother	Wm. Love	7b139	mr 80 *
Hogeland, John m. Hogeland, Massie	May 10,	1813	Jas. Hogeland		3b262	
Hogeland, Massie m. Rhodes, Susannah	Mar. 29,	1834	Benj. Connelly		6b 2	
Hogeland, Massie m. Hogeland, John	May 10,	1813	James Hogeland		3b262	
Hoges, John B. m. Hunter, Ann R.	May 6,	1819	John Strother	John Mathews	4b107	mr 44 *
Hogg, Thomas m. Franceway, Mary	Aug. 7,	1844	Wm. B. Walsh	John Light	7b 4	mr 76 *
Hoggens, Richard m. Payne, Sarah	Oct. 22,	1816	Jacpb Payne		4b 18	
Hogle, Joseph m. Britton, Rebecca A	Feb. 22,	1851	Nathaniel Britton	Henry Furlong	7b215	mr 84 *
Hogmire, Conrad m. Boyd, Ann Maria	Feb. 5,	1818	Jas. P. Erskine	John B. Hoge	4b 60	
Holle, James m. Harley, Mary	Jan. 25,	1840	Thomas Harley		6b194	
Holle, Sarah m. Leonard, Nicholas	Oct. 21,	1797	John Holle		1b 56	
Hoke, Ann Maria m. Berry, Joseph E,	July 21,	1847	John Hoke		7b101	mr 81 *
Hoke, Catherine m. Pearce, Lewis B.	Aug. 1,	1818	Joseph Morlatt	P. Lipscomb	4b 76	
Hoke, George m. McKown, Maria	Oct. 20,	1847	Morgan McKown		7b109	
Hoke, Jacob m. Thatcher, Abigail (Marg Oct.	3,	1825	Jonathan Thatcher	James Redley	5b 23	gc 14
Hoke, Mary m. Elliott, Samuel	Jan. 6,	1800	Thomas Elliott		2b 46	gc 12
Hoke, Nancy m. Morlatt, Joseph	Sept 28,	1814	Peter Hoke	Rev. Reebenack	3b305	**
Hoke, Peter m. Clice, Mary	Aug. 12,	1811	George Clice	Rev. Reebenack	3b193	
Hoke, Susan m. Shanks, John	Dec. 13,	1841	Peter Crowl	John Light	6b258	mr 72 *
Holaney, Gertrude E. m. Moss, Wm.	Sept 24,	1807	Elisha Boyd		3b 71	
Holbert, Nancy m. Hite, Frederick	Nov. 7,	1844	Levi Spitznogle		7b 13	
Holden, Jane m. Madden, Patrick	Apr. 26,	1786		Hugh Vance	3b299	mr 42 *
Holderman, Cath. m. Smith, Andrew	Oct. 7,	1792		David Young	6b143	gc 2
Holland, Wm.m. Carson, Robert	July 5,	1814	John Morlatt	John Mathews	3b299	mr 25 *
Holland, Joseph m. Ray, Margaret	Aug. 7,	1836	Harvey E. Foreman		6b143	
Hollenberger, Cath. m. Speck, Geo. F. June	15,	1811	Jonathan Hoover	John B. Hoge	3b190	cr 14
Holliday, Alsworth m. Bennett, Ann	Apr. 23,	1789	Robert Bennett		1b x	
Holliday, Amelia m. Williams, David	Aug. 5,	1822	George Bennett	Nathan Young	4b220	mr 57 *
Holliday, Ann m. Frier, James G.	Jan. 10,	1832	Wm. Holliday		5b214	
Holliday, Colbert m. Custard, Hannah	Aug. 10,	1830	Chas. B. Custard	Nathan Young	5b172	mr 61 *
Holliday, Geo. W. m. Lyle, Sarah M.	Aug. 29,	1850	Wm. H. VanDoren		7b193	
Holliday, Geo. W. m. Seibert, Harriet	Sept	8,	1831	Jacob F. Seibert	5b205	
Holliday, James m. Darke, Eliz.	Feb. 12,	1793		William Hill	3b120	cr 30
Holliday, Mary m. Clark, Joseph	Oct. 4,	1809		John Mathews	3b299	mr 10 *
Holliday, Mary Cath. m. Harrison, B.	Sept 22,	1853	Philip Nadenbousch	John S. Deale	3b120	mr 40 *
Holliday, Milly m. Carson, Robert	Oct. 26,	1814	John Morlatt	John Mathews	3b299	mr 25 *
Holliday, Polly m. Dunham, John	July 10,	1806	James Harrison		3b 15	
Holliday, Rachel m. Ward, Nicholas	Apr. 9,	1818	George Holliday		4b 59	
Holliday, Sarah m. Foulk, George	Feb. 3,	1847	John H. Holliday		7b 92	
Holliday, Thomas m. Swaim, Eliz.	Mar. 15,	1801	John Swaim		2b114	
Hollimback, Cath. m. Young, Peter	Feb. 5,	1801	George Leps		2b132	
Hollinger, George m. Anderson, Eliz.	July 27,	1803	Henry March		2b190	
Hollinger, John m. March, Hannah	Dec. 21,	1799	Henry March		2b 41	

Name	date	(marriage)	(suretor)	(minister)	(bond)	ref.	
Hollinger, Mary m. March, Henry	Apr. 5,	Dec. 13, 1800	John Hollinger	David Young	2b 62	ge 6	*
Hollinghead, Richard m. Babb, Mary	Sept 8,	Sept 10, 1796		Rev. Reebenack		ge 10	*
Hollingworth, Wm. m. Moore, Marg't	Mar. 17,	Mar. 17, 1809		Nathan Young		mr 61	
Hollis, James J. m. Paskell, Eliza		1831	Jeremiah Jack		3b118		
Hollis, John J. m. Thornburg,Rebecca		1845	John Boglin		5b188		*
Hollis, Joseph m. Denney, Sarah Jane		1847	Joseph M. Hollis		7b 46		*
Hollis, Mary A. m. Day, James W.	Oct. 27,	Dec. 22, 1853	Jas. H. Denny	G.W.Cooper	7b110	mr 79	*
Hollis, Thos. P. m. Mathews, Mary	Oct. 27,	Feb. 26, 1850		Henry Furlong		mr 62	*
Hollis, Washington m. Caskey, Elis.	Feb. 25,	Aug. 25, 1831	William Mathews	Nathan Young	7b178		
Holloway, Ann m. Ryan, James		1823	Hiram Beeson		5b204	mr 41	*
Hollowbaugh, Eliz. m. Tully,John	Aug. 25,	Sept 28, 1797	Seaman Gerard	W.N.Scott	4b253		
Holly, Mary m. Curtis, Jacob	Dec. 19,	Aug. 26, 1820	Walter Shirley		1b 18		
Holmes, Christian m. Ward, Nancy	May 27,	Mar. 28, 1810	Jacob Shimp	Elisha Gardner	4b158		*
Holt, Cath. m. Stinecley, Amos	Aug. 26,	Oct. 10, 1837	Jacob Hamme	David Thomas	3b144	mr 84	*
Homer, John m. Cox, Mary		1820		B.M.Schmucker		mr 83	*
Homerick, Minerva m. Blessing, Geo.	May 31,	Sept 16, 1851	Abraham Cox	David Young	4b150	gc 1	*
Homerick, Susanna m. Grove, David	Sept 15,	Feb. 28, 1850	Joshua Homerick		7b232		
Homas, William m. Russell, Elis.	Feb. 28,	June 13, 1791	Joshua Homerick	Hugh Vance	7b178	mr 38	*
Homn, Elis. m. Kennedy, Joseph	Aug. 7,	Mar. 11, 1800	James Kennedy	John Boyd		mr 12; cr 11	*
Hood, George m. Hedges, Elinor	Mar. 11,	Oct. 13, 1790	Wendle Seibert	David Young	2b 80	gc 9	*
Hood, James m. Norwood, Elis.	Oct. 13,	June 19, 1796	John Finch			gc 12	*
Hoofman, Susannah m. Seibert, Henry		1800		Rev. Reebenack			
Hooke, Ruth m. Finch, Thomas	June 17,	Mar. 26, 1800	Joseph Chambers	M.G.Hamilton	2b 73		
Hooper, Abraham m. Chambers, Cath.	Mar. 29,	Apr. 18, 1812	John M. Wolff	Benedict Reynolds	2b 60	mr 71	*
Hooper, Alfred m. Salehauer, Phebe	Mar. 20,	Nov. 15, 1839	Jacob Hooper	W.F.Mercer	3b217	mr 52	*
Hooper, Cath. m. Klout(Krout),Henry	Apr. 18,	June 23, 1827	William Palmer	Henry Furlong	6b157	mr 74	*
Hooper, Edmund m. Palmer, Charlotte	Nov. 15,	June 7, 1843	Robert Maxwell		5b 84	mr 79	*
Hooper, Edward B. m. Maxwell, Ellen		1849		James Watts			
Hooper, Eleanor m. Fryatt, John T.	June 7,	Dec. 14, 1834	Abraham Hooper	W.N.Scott	6b272	mr 30	*
Hooper, Evelina m. Polsal, Sebastion	Apr. 10,	Jan. 7, 1837	Abraham Hooper	Richard Swift	7b160	mr 39	*
Hooper, Hannah m. Gallaher, James	Dec. 14,	Oct. 14, 1819	Jacob Hooper	W.N.Scott	6b 5	mr 40	*
Hooper, John P. m. Hoskins, Mary	Jan. 7,	Dec. 2, 1793	John Gallaher	W.N.Scott	6b126	mr 41	*
Hooper, John P. m. McGaughlin,Marg't	Oct. 14,	May 18, 1819	Jacob Polsal	Mayberry Goheen	4b 95	mr 74	*
Hooper, Mary E. m. Ott, Michael	Dec. 2,	Oct. 24, 1820	Wm. McDonald		4b125		
Hooper, Mary E. m. Sybole, James	May 18,	Apr. 17, 1842	William Palmer		4b147		
Hooper, Thomas m. Harrison, Mahala	Oct. 22,	Mar. 4, 1834	Adam Schoppert		6b281		
Hooper, Thomas m. Schoppert, Cath.	Apr. 17,	Nov. 7, 1833	Everhart Bunnell		6b 7		
Hooper, Thos. B. m. Schaffer, Marg't	Mar. 4,	July 22, 1846	George Boops		5b260	mr 77	*
Hoops, Mary m. Hays, John	Nov. 7,	1800	Robert Filson		7b 76		
Hoover, Cath. m. Bedinger, Fred.		Oct. 6, 1795		John Winter	2b 77		
Hoover, Henry m. Ray, Mildred	Feb. 2,	1802	Daniel Welshans		2b159		
Hoover, Jonas m. Welshans, Magdalena	Dec. 1,	1801	John Keesecker		2b150		
Hoover, Joseph m. Keesecker, Mary	June 4,	1808		David Young	3b 90	gc 5	*

Name	(marriage)	(suretor)	(minister)	(bond)		
Hoover, Polly m. Lindsey, John	Dec. 27, 1803		Richard Swift	4b172	cr 27	mr 21 *
Hopkins, James m. Herd, Susanna	Sept 4, 1788		Moses Hoge	7b217		mr 36 *
Horn, Eliz. m. Boyd, John	Feb. 13, 1821		John B. Hoge	3b 6		mr 41 *
Horn, Emily m. Miller, Harrison W.	Feb. 12, 1851	Maj. Geo. Horn		3b229		*
Horn, George m. Painter, Mary	Mar. 8, 1805	Joshua S.Gallaher		4b174	gc 13	
Horn, Jacob m. Bishop, Kitty(Cathy)	Dec. 23, 1805	George Painter	Rev. Reebenack	3b138		mr 41 *
Horn, Jesse m. Whisler, Eliza	June 26, 1812	Jacob Bishop	W.N.Scott	7b139	gc 11	
Horn, John m. Lashorn, Cath.	Mar. 1, 1821	Isaac Whisler	Rev. Reebenack	7b 39		mr 79 *
Horn, Marg't Jane m. Sigler, Wm.	Mar. 3, 1810	John Lashorn	B.M.Schmucker	3b133		
Horn, Mary Ellen m. Henry, Wm.	Nov. 6, 1848	Jeptha Hansell		4b 96	gc 11	
Horn, Peggy m. Dugan, James	Aug. 15, 1845	John R. Crow	Rev. Reebenack	4b188		mr 31 *
Horn, Philip m. Butt, Mary	Jan. 16, 1810	George House	John Kehler	7b138		mr 42 *
Horn, Thomas m. Bout(Hous), Mary	Jan. 13, 1818?	Samuel Butt	Chas. P. Krauth	4b 77		
Horn, Wm. m. Beard, Eliz. S.	Aug. 22, 1821	John Gelbricks				
Horn, Wm. m. Cline, Eve	Oct. 30, 1848	James Beard				
Hornb, John m. McCarty, Susanna	May 18, 1800	David Cline	John Hett(Hatt)	7b 57	cr 35	mr 19 *
Hornbaker, Eliz. m. Faulkner, Thomas	Sept 24, 1789		Hugh Vance	5b224	cr 40	mr 4 *
Hornell, Mary m. Cooper, Thomas	Nov. 24, 1793		Edward Tiffin	2b183	cr 9	mr 8 *
Horner, Abraham m. Kennedy, Nancy	Feb. 4, 1846	James Lamaster	Lewis F. Wilson	6b 36		mr 77 *
Horner, Dorsey m. Perrell, Mary	Apr. 3, 1832	John Perrell	William Monroe	4b150		mr 65 *
Horner, Eliz. m. Short, George	Oct. 2, 1802	Andrew Yates	Richard Swift	1b105	cr 32	mr 21 *
Horner, Evelina m.Householder, Jacob	Mar. 11, 1835	Henry M. Nichols	John Light	7b178		mr 67 *
Horner, John m. Cox, Mary	May 31, 1820	Abraham Cox	W.N.Scott	6b298		mr 41 *
Horner, Richard m. Lynch, Sarah	Apr. 5, 1798	Cornel's Thompson		6b115		
Horvdok, Susannah m. Grove, David	Feb. 28, 1850	Joshua Homerick	B.M.Schmucker	6b287		mr 83 *
Hoskins, Mary m. Hooper, John P.	Oct. 14, 1793		Richard Swift	7b 78		mr 39 *
Hott, Ann m. Aiken, John	May 24, 1843	John Hott		7b236		
Hott, Cath. m. Steddley, Amos	Oct. 9, 1837	Jacob Hott		2b199		
Hott, George m. Aiken, Mary	Jan. 16, 1843	John Aikens				
Hott, Jane m. Rowland, Samuel J.	Dec. 3, 1846	Jacob Hott	John Winter			mr 77 *
Hott, Mary Ann m. Willett,David	Oct. 29, 1851	Jacob Hott				
Hott, Peter m. Wright, Marg't	Apr. 1, 1803	James Sterratt				
Houck, Cath. m. Keesecker, Andrew	Dec. 6, 1796	Dan'l McGlaughlin	David Young	4b159	gc 6	
Houck, Christina m. McKimney, James	Aug. 31, 1820	Jacob Houck		3b 54		
Houck, David m. Alebaugh, Sally O.	Apr. 2, 1807	Jacob Houck		3b 56		
Houck, Eliz. m. Hite, Jacob	Apr. 14, 1807	Jacob Houck				
Houck, George m. Houck, Polly	Dec. 12, 1811	Jacob Houck	Rev. Reebenack	3b202		
Houck, George m. Weaver, Barbara	Feb. 13, 1811	Jonathan Thatcher	Rev. Reebenack	3b174	gc 12	mr 72 *
Houck, Maria m. Herbert, Hilary	May 2, 1841	William Ripple	John Light	6b240	gc 11	
Houck, Nancy m. Barnes, Ishmael	Feb. 14, 1854		John Light			
Houck, Polly m. Houck, George	Dec. 9, 1811	Jacob Houck	Rev. Reebenack	3b202	gc 12	
Houck, Sally m. Hite, William	Dec. 14, 1812	Jacob Houck	Rev. Reebenack	3b242	ge 13	
Houck, Samuel m. Boyd, Mary	Jan. 18, 1814	Wm. Thurston	Rev. Reebenack	3b282	ge 14	*

Name	(marriage)		(suretor)	(minister)	(bond)		
House, Mary m. Horn, Thomas	Aug. 22,	1821	John Gelwicks	Chas. P. Krauth	4b188		mr 42 *
House, Peggy m. Dugan, James	Jan. 13,	1810	George House	Rev. Reebenack	3b133	gc 11	*
House, Sarah m. Sunsford, Nicholas	Nov. 10,	1800	Henry Vollum		2b 98		*
Householder, Elis. m. Livingston,John	Oct. 30,	1832	Jonathan Householder	Marthan Young	5b245		mr 65 *
Householder, Jacob m. Horner,Evelina	Mar. 11,	1835	Henry M. Nichols	John Light	6b 36		mr 67 *
Householder, Jonathan m.Donaldsn,Eliz	Aug. 8,	1839	Moses Grantham	James Rely	6b173		mr 70 *
Householder, Wm.m. Gallaher, Marg't	May 8,	1834	Harrison Waite		6b 12		*
Houseman, Christian m. Reichert, Eve	June 11,	1795		David Young		gc 5	*
Houseman, David m. Burg, Margaret	Mar. 18,	1797		David Young	1b 5	gc 6	*
Houseman, David m. Krmp, Fanny	July 27,	1812	Martin Houseman		3b231		*
Houseman, Elis. m. Fisher, George	June 20,	1785	Valentine Krmp				*
Houseman, Peter m. Risert, Cath.	Mar. 18,	1794		Hugh Vance			mr 34 *
Houseman, Rachel m. Merchant, Justice	Sept. 2,	1808		David Young		gc 3	*
Houser, Isaac m. Mason, Mary Jane	Apr. 24,	1851	Martin Housaman		3b 96		*
Housworth, Elis. m. Daniel,Robt.Jr.	June 22,	1822	Jacob Miller	D.F.Bragunier	7b223		mr 84 *
Housworth, Isaac m. Reimer, Sarah	Apr. 25,	1831	Isaac Housworth		4b217		*
Housworth, Marg't m. Butts, Wm.	Apr. 10,	1816	Frederick Raimer	Jacob Medtart	5b193		mr 63 *
Housworth, Mary m. Moon, Jacob	Sept 1,	1847	Isaac Housworth	Nathan Young	4b 17		mr 55 *
Housworth, Nancy m. Riley, Alex.	Dec. 6,	1816	Hiram Bowen	J. Boggs	7b105		mr 78 *
Housworth, Valentine m. Cain, Lydia	Apr. 27,	1833	Isaac Housworth	Nathan Young	3b349		mr 55 *
Housworth, Valentine m. Suber, Elis.	Sept 28,	1829	George Vanaker	Nathan Young	5b272		mr 66 *
Hout, Adam B.M. m. Angel B.M.	Oct. 21,	1822	Robert Danriel	Jas. M. Brown	5b143		mr 53 *
Hout, Angel B.M. m. Hout, Adam	Nov. 21,	1822	Michael Hout	Chas. P. Krauth	4b228		mr 45 *
Hout, Angel B.M. m. Bishop, Joel P.	Jan. 12,	1822	Michael Hout	Chas. P. Krauth	4b228		mr 45 *
Hout, Cath. m. Hmaldorf(Wom—),John	Sept 22,	1836	John L. Rusler		6b 63		*
Hout, Dorcas m. Haymond, John	Dec. 4,	1810	Michael Houte	Rev. Reebenack	5b162	gc 11	*
Hout, Elis. m. Russell(Rusler),John	Dec. 22,	1793	Henry Job	Edward Tiffin	4b126	cr 9	*
Hout, Henry m. French, Rachel	Apr. 14,	1819	John Gelwicks	Chas. P. Krauth	3b220		mr 8 *
Hout, Mary m. Horn, Thomas	Aug. 22,	1812		Rev. Reebenack	4b188	gc 12	mr 40 *
Hout, Peter m. Miller, Rosanna	Jan. 10,	1821	Michael Hout	Hugh Vance			mr 42 *
Hout, Sarah m. Crow, John	May 7,	1786	Jacob Miller	Chas. P. Krauth			mr 43 *
Hoveralle, Christian m. Miller, Elis.	Oct. 29,	1825			4b284		mr 48 *
Hoveralle, Elis. m. Seilor, Peter	Apr. 13,	1801	Joseph Haines	David Young	2b125	gc 9	*
Hoveralle, Margaret m. Files, John	May 22,	1799	Martin Howard		3b146		*
Howard, Elis. m. Coyle, James	Apr. 15,	1810	Robert Stewart	Wm. Monroe	1b 18		mr 53 *
Howard, James m. McCoy, Nancy	Apr. 10,	1797	John How		5b127		*
Howard, John m. McCarty, Savannah	May 15,	1829		David Young	2b 64	gc 4	*
Howard, Nicholas m. Applegate, Nancy	Jan. 29,	1800	Joseph Davis	David Young	7b145		*
Howard, Samuel S. m. Davis, Ann K.	May 22,	1794	Martin Howard		1b 17		*
Howard, Sarah m. Thomas, Joseph	Apr. 15,	1849	John Moore	John Hedt(Hutt)	2b 43	gr 33	mr 17 *
Howard, Susarmah m. Offutt(-ord),Jos.	Dec. 26,	1799		David Young		gc 3	*
Howe, Andrew m. Severs(Si-), Eliz.	Dec. 27,	1793		David Young		gc 3	*
Howe, Edward m.Pennybaker(Be-),Marg't	Aug. 31,	1793					

Name	(marriage)		(surtor)	(minister)	(bond)		mr
Howe, Elis. m. Porter, John	Mar. 21,	1799	John Howe	David Young	1b174	gc 8	mr 79 *
Howe, Margaret m. Sigler, William	Nov. 6,	1848	Jephtha Hensell	B.M.Schmucker	7b139		mr 37 *
Howe, Mary m. Coon, Henry	Feb. 19,	1789		Hugh Vance			mr 54 *
Howe, Mary m. Yarnell, Joseph	July 26,	1813	Abraham Bell	Nathan Young	3b266		mr 54 *
Howe, William m. Cooke(Cook), Mary	Dec. 2,	1797	Edward Howe	David Young	1b 68	gc 7	
Howe, Rachel m. Kidwell, James	Oct. 5,	1828	George Hawn	Jacob Medtart	5b108		mr 63 *
Howell, Chas. G. m. McCormick,Isabel	Dec. 17,	1844	John M. Holmes		7b 16		
Howell, Chas. G. m. McCormick,Isabel	Dec. 13,	1841	Wm. McCormick		6b257		
Boyle, Jos. m.Britton, Rebecca Ann	Feb. 22,	1851	Nathaniel Britton	Henry Furlong	7b215		mr 84 *
Boyle, Mary E. m. Wilson, David	Dec. 18,	1830	Samuel Malnor	Jas. M. Brown	5b183		mr 54 *
Boyle, Rachel m. Shockey, David	Mar. 30,	1797	Mathias Riser		1b 3		
Bebbard, Conrad m. Hess, Harriet	Dec. 20,	1849	Peter Hess	B.M. Schmucker	7b171		mr 79 *
Budgel, Jesse, Lucas, Elis.	Aug. 24,	1830	Barton Henshaw		5b173		
Budgel, Elis. m. Walsh, John J.	July 5,	1836	Harrison Waite	W. Monroe	6b 81		mr 68 *
Budgel, Jennifer m. Hill, Mary M.	Nov. 12,	1844	Jacob A. Small		7b 14		
Budgel, John(Joshua) m. Taylor, Elis.	Nov. 17,	1835	Jonas Smith	Nathan Young	5b181		mr 61 *
Budgel, Thomas m. Clayton, Ellen	Aug. 24,	1830	Henry Gwilliams		6b 55		
Hudson, Cath. m. Myers, Isaac	Aug. 16,	1821	John Brennan	Nathan Young	4b187		mr 57 *
Hudson, Elis. m. Rumbaugh, Nicholas	July 31,	1826	Isaac Myers	Nathan Young	5b 45		mr 58 *
Hudson, James m. Davis, Phebe	May 16,	1814	Robert Hudson		3b297		
Hudson, James m. Rambaugh, Susan	June 13,	1825	Wm. Grantham	Nathan Young	5b 14		mr 58 *
Hudson, Mahala m. Stanley, Archelaus	Jan. 10,	1838	Isaac Stanley	James Watts	6b130		mr 57 *
Hudson, Mary m. Brannon(-en), John	Sept 8,	1822	Robert Kennedy	Nathan Young	4b189		mr 58 *
Hudson, Mary m. Myers, Philip	Aug. 8,	1826	Isaac Myers,	Nathan Young	5b 46		
Hudson, Robert m. Davis, Phebe	May 16,	1814	James Hudson		3b297		
Hudson, Robert m. Fry, Nancy	Aug. 3,	1801	John McMillan		2b134		
Huff, John m. Cole, Mary A.	Apr. 7,	1799	Barney Cole		1b178		
Huff, John m. Knadler, Leah Ann	Sept 5,	1829	Andrew Knadler	Nathan Young	5b139		mr 60 *
Huffman, Cath. m. Riner, John	Jan. 26,	1807	Henry Riner		3b 43	cr 1	mr 2 *
Huffman, Henry m. Hecken, Barbara							
Huffman, Henry m. Shepherd, Lydia	Feb. 3,	1805	David Rees	Moses Hoge	2b257	cr 1	
Huffman, John m. Blake, Mary	Mar. 19,	1789					
Huffman, John m. Free, Elis.	Feb. 8,	1800	George Kiger	Moses Hoge	2b 52	cr 3	mr 5 *
Huffman, Mary m. Martin, Manning	Apr. 4,	1825	Levi Martin	David Young	5b 6	gc 9	
Huffman, Michael m.Lingamfelter,Mary	Apr. 10,	1802	Valentine Lingamfelter	John Mathews	2b171		mr 50 *
Huffman, Susanna m. Sharff, Peter	Dec. 15,	1830	Philip Carper	Nathan Young	5b183		
Huffman, Wm. D. m. Kimble, Sarah	Dec. 11,	1815	Richard Morrison	W.N.Scott	3b349		mr 61 *
Huffman, Wm. m. Miller, Elis.	Sept 21,	1846	Jacob Sperow	John Light	7b 73		mr 26 *
Huggins, Michael m. Davis, Ruth Mrs.	Aug. 3,	1801	David Baldwin		2b133		mr 79 *
Bughes, Elisa jane m.Haslewood,Jas.T.	Sept 28,	1846	Jas. J. Kenney		7b 74		
Bughes, Elis. m. Addy, Robert	Apr. 14,	1798	George Snyder	Richard Swift	1b 98	cr 31	mr 15 *
Bughes, Elis. m. Flagg, John H.	Nov. 6,	1822	John Faris	Chas. P. Krauth	4b227		mr 45 *
Bughes, Elis. m. Phelps, Elisha	Apr. 21,	1789	John Stead		1b x		

Name	(Marriage)		(suretor)	(minister)	(bond)		
Bughes, George m. Candle, Margaret	Apr. 26, Apr. 26,	1828	Thomas Wolford	Benedict Reynolds	5b100		mr 52 *
Bughes, Joseph m. Darr, Catherine	Nov. 14,	1798	John Merritt		1b147		
Bughes, Jas. E. m. Stephen, Charlotta	Apr. 23,	1851	T.D.Scott		7b223		
Bughes, Rebecca m. Reitsell(Re-Jacob	Mar. 8, Mar. 9,	1830	Christian Conrad	Jacob Hedtart	5b156		mr 63 *
Bughes, Thomas m. Lemon, Nancy	June 10,	1801	Fred. Imhoff		2b128		
Bughey, Isaac m. Bedinge., Elis.	Apr. 17, Apr. 18,	1797	Philip Bedinger	John Boyd	1b 8	cr 32	mr 13 *
Bugly, John m. Young, Elis.	Aug. 10, Aug. 16,	1799	John Cooke	John Hedt(Hutt)	2b 18	cr 38	mr 17 *
Bakehart, Ann m. Smith, Joseph	Mar. 5, Mar. 8,	1798	Joseph Thomas	Moses Hoge	1b 88	cr 36	mr 14 *
Bolett, Ann m. Mace, Francis	Apr. 22,	1789	John Brady		1b x		
Bull, Henry m. Zorn(Gorn), Cath. A.	Jan. 22, Jan. 23,	1851	John Zorn	Jas. H. Jennings	7b212		mr 83 *
Bull, Jacob m. Selbert, Elis.	Mar. 7, Mar. 9,	1837	Michael Seibert	Lewis F. Wilson	6b 99	cr 11	mr 16 *
Bull, James m. Kein, Kesiah	Sept 22, Sept 22,	1798	William Hall	John Hedt(Hutt)	1b134	cr 33	mr 17 *
Bull, Louisa m. Thompson, Philip	Oct. 29,	1799		John Hedt(Hutt)		cr 12	mr 18 *
Bull, William m. Frands. Sarah	Feb. 19, Feb. 21,	1799	Samuel Wood		1b169		
Bully, Cath. m. Boring, Greenberry	June 20,	1807	Jane Holly		3b 62	gc 12	
Bully, Elis. m. Burk, William	Feb. 16,	1811	John Holly	Rev. Reebemack	3b175		
Home, Beersheba m. Smith, James	Apr. 23,	1799	Hubbard Hume		2b 3		*
Home, James m. Barker, Sarah	June 10,	1817		Mathias Riser			mr 77 *
Humaldorf, Cath. m. Price, George	Apr. 8,	1847	Jacob VanDoren Jn.	John Winter	7b 93	go 11	
Humaldorf, John m. Houte, Cath.	Sept 22, Sept 23,	1810	Michael Houte	Rev. Reebemack	3b162		
*Humphries, Cath. m. Kiger, John	May 22,	1797	Daniel Humphries		1b 17		
Humphries, David m. Keyes, Cath.	Aug. 7,	1797	Robert McKnight		1b 27		
Humphries, Hannah m. Lucas, Joseph	Apr. 23, Feb. 14,	1792	Arch'd Magill	Moses Hoge	1b x	cr 8	mr 7 *
Humphries, Sally m. Stribling, Wm.		1789	Simon Minghini		6b135		
Hunteker, Henry m. Chamberlain, Elis	Mar. 1,	1838					
Hunt, David B. m. Gorrell, Mary A.	Dec. 26,	1833	Jacob Switzer	C.M.Calloway	3b 51		mr 26 *
Hunt, Jane m. Grey, Philip	Feb. 4,	1816	John Heaton	Mathias Riser	1b 44		
Hunt, Stewart m. Switzer, Sally	Mar. 18,	1807	Philip Wilson		3b 31		
Banb, William m. Shine, Phebe	Sept 23,	1797	John Strother		4b107		
Hunter, Evelina m. Tucker,Henry St.G.	Sept 23, May 6,	1819	Enoch Mathews	John Mathews	6b 64		mr 44 *
Hunter, Ann K. m. Hoge, John B.	May 18,	1835	*Edmund Hunter	David Young		go 1	
Hunter, David m. Mathias, Maria W.	Nov. 18, Nov. 19,	1791	William Hunter		5b 93		
Hunter, David m. Pendleton, Elis.		1828			7b 56		
Hunter, David Jr.m-Harrison, Mercy L.	Mar. 6,	1846	John Gallaher	Wm. Monroe	5b257		mr 65 *
Hunter, Elis.m. Harrison, Samuel B.	Feb. 2,	1833	Robert Wilson	John Mathews	7b337		mr 25 *
Hunter, Elis. m. Roe, James	Feb. 17,	1815		Richard Swift			mr 38 *
Hunter, Elis. m. Strother, John	Sept 7,	1791		Edward R. Lippett			mr 45 *
Hunter, John m.Gastie(Garten),Delila	June 28,	1821	John G. Wilson		4b200		
Hunter, John m. Robinson, Sarah	Dec. 10,	1815	David Hunter		3b330		
Hunter, Mary m. Green, James C.	Dec. 20,	1793					
Hunter, Mary m.Straith(Strewk), Alex.	July 30,	1831	Alex. Cooper	Moses Hoge	5b203		mr 39 *
Hunter, Mary Susan m.Mathews, Wm. C.	Jan. 22,	1840	Silas Oaks	Lewis F. Wilson	6b199		mr 70 *
Hunter, Mathias m. Oaks, Mary E.	Aug. 23, Mar. 3,	1795	David Young	David Young		gc 4	
*Hummel, Geo. m. Endler, Marg't	Feb. 29, Jan. 17,	1795					

*Ferd. Fairfax also signed as suretor.

Name	(marriage)	(suretor)	(minister)	(bond)		
Hunter, Moses m. Dandridge, Ann	Apr. 26, 1787	John Strother	Hugh Vance	4b242		mr 44 *
Hunter, Philip P. m. Smith, Ann Amelia	June 26, 1823	John Strother	John Mathews	5b 69		mr 46 *
Hunter, Rebecca L. m. Brooke, John T.	May 8, 1827	Smith Miller	J.E.Jackson	6b 78		
Hunter, Robert m. Kidd, Margaret	Apr. 20, 1836	Patr'k Cummingham		6b262		
Hunter, Wm. C. m. Ro , Eliz.	Jan. 27, 1842	George Price		7b 38		
Huntsburg, Emalina m. Price, Jacob	July 19, 1845	Samuel Morehead	B.M.Schmucker	7b220		mr 84 *
Hurdle, Geo. W. m. Morehead, Eliz.	Apr. 1, 1851	John Porter		6b224		
Hurley, Samuel m. Porter, Eleanor	Nov. 23, 1840		David Young		gc 1	*
Husband, James m. Beevis, Sarah	Feb. 1, 1792			6b100		
Huston, Joseph m. Gregory, Ellen Mary	Mar. 7, 1837	Robert Gregory	David Young	1b 88	gc 4	*
Huston, Margaret m.McGlaughlin, Geo.	Dec. 23, 1794	Joseph Thomas	Moses Hoge	5b220	cr 36	*
Hutchcraft, Ann m. Smith, Joseph	Mar. 8, 1798	John Shober		7b 51		mr 14 *
Hutcheson, Nathan m. Curtis, Elenor	Mar. 5, 1845	Jas. Hutcheson		4b171		mr 41 *
Hutcheson, Wm.E. m. Fisher, Rachel A	Dec. 26, 1821	Wm. D. Engle	John B. Hoge	4b233		mr 58 *
Hutchinson, Isaac m. Engle, Martha	Feb. 6, 1823	Abraham Stipp	Nathan Young			mr 37 *
Hutchinson, James m. Stipp, Fanny	Feb. 11, 1789		D. Thomas			mr 41 *
Hutchinson, Jane m. Reed, John	?					
Hutchinson, John m. Engle, Martha	Feb. 8, 1821	William D. Engle	John B. Hoge	4b171		mr 83 *
Hutaler, John m. Evans, Ruth M.	Jan. 3, 1851	Andrew E.Griffith	George W. Harris	7b209		mr 74 *
Hutaler, Joseph m. Mainor, Mary Ann	Nov. 5, 1842	John Mainor	Mayberry Goheen	6b283		mr 16 *
Hutaler, Mary m. Pine, James	Feb. 22, 1847	Alfred Hutaler		7b 87		mr 18 *
Hutson, John m. Walters, Eliza F.	May 7, 1834	Jas. W. Walters		6b 11	cr 37	
Hutson, Nancy m. Jackson, John	Aug. 25, 1798	Alex. Eckhart	John Hett(Hutt)	1b121	cr 12	
Hutt, John m. Crockwell, Betsy	Mar. 3, 1799		John Potts			mr 51 *
Huttle, Henry m. Markel(-kle)Rosanna	Dec. 27, 1826	Isaac Eversole	B. Reynolds	5b 99		mr 83 *
Hutzler, Henry m. Evans, Ruth M.	Jan. 6, 1851	Andrew Griffith	Geo. W. Harris	7b209		mr 74 *
Hutzler, Joseph m. Mainor, Mary A.	Nov. 5, 1842	John Mainor	Mayberry Goheen	6b283		mr 47 *
Hydemrick, Fanny m. Zeekman, Samuel	Sept 13, 1824	Ebenezer Hydemr'k	Chas. P. Krauth	4b272		mr 47 *
Hydemrick, Marg't m. Kimble, Caleb	Nov. 19, 1824	Expritus Hydemr'k	Chas. P. Krauth	4b277		
Hyeth, Rachel m. Henshaw, Barton	Apr. 14, 1829	Ezekiel Neff		5b126		mr 38 *
Hyett, Milly m. Metcalf, Amos	Aug. 3, 1793		Richard Swift			mr 59 *
Hyser, Susan m. Barms, Henry	Dec. 27, 1827	Daniel Hyser	Nathan Young	5b 86	cr 18	
*Hutton, John m. Barrett, Rachel	Sept 12, 1787		Hugh Vance			mr 1 *

"I"

Name	(marriage)	(suretor)	(minister)	(bond)		
Ijams, James m. Tabb, Dorcas S.M.	Dec. 4, 1849	Geo. P. Morrison	Lewis F. Wilson	7b169		mr 83 *87
Inbody, George m. Friese(ees),Rebecca	July 22, 1811	Barney Friese	Rev. Reebenack	3b192	gc 12	*
Inbody, Jacob m. Shaffer, Cath.	Dec. 13, 1810	Jacob Shaffer	Rev. Reebenack	3b167	gc 11	*
Inbody, John m. Thompson, Jane	Sept 8, 1814	Jos. Thompson	Nathan Young	3b303		mr 55 *
Inbody, Lewis m. Long, Susan	Oct. 28, 1841	Wm. McDonald	John Hedges	6b250		mr 73 *

Name	(marriage)	(surety)	(minister)	(bond)			
Inbody, Mathias m. Friese, Cath.	Feb. 11, 1804	Barney Friese	John Hedtt(Butt)	2b223	or 33	mr 17	*
Inge, Elis. m. Wycoff, Cornelius	Dec. 8, 1799	Jacob Kroesen	Mathias Riser	2b 39	or 30	mr 30	*
Ingle, Elis. m. Dawson, Abraham	1819		William Hill		or 30	mr 9	*
Ingle, John m. Hendricks, Abigail	1793						
Ingle, Samuel P. m. Snyder, Marg't	Feb. 17, 1838	Wm. Karley	John Potts	6b132	or 12	mr 18	*
Inglish, John m. Carter(Casler),Elis.	Jan. 21, 1799	Robert Carter	Richard Swift	1b165	or 32	mr 21	*
Ingram(Ingram)Henry m.Rigsby,Henr'ta	Dec. 11, 1802	William Rigby	Richard Swift	2b186	or 31	mr 19	*
Ingman(Ingram),Luke m. Hay, Elis.	Jan. 14, 1801	Adam Hay	W. Love	2b109	or 31	mr 80	*
Inhurst, Rebecca m. Barrett, Wm.	Mar. 7, 1850	William Crabb	John Boyd	7b179	or 34	mr 17	*
Irvin, Sarah m. Taylor, Zachariah	Nov. 13, 1799	Jonathan Tritt	Hugh Vance	2b 35	or 34	mr 34	*
Irvine, John m. Reed, Francis	1785		Moses Hoge		or 35	mr 11	*
Irvine, Francis m. Terkey, Rachel	1796						
Irwin, John m. Anthony, Polly	Jan. 29, 1800	Zachariah Taylor		2b 50	or 38		
Irwin, John m. McAlister, Elis.	Aug. 31, 1785		Edward Tiffin	1b 10	gc 6	mr 1	*
Irwin, John m. Weaver, Catherine	Apr. 20, 1797	William Irwin	David Young	2b214	gc 10		
Irwin, Robert m. Malone, Cath.	Nov. 22, 1803	John Cunningham	David Young	1b102			
Irwin, Sarah m. Dyhouse, Joseph	Jan. 18, 1798	Robert Irwin		1b108			
Irwin, Thomas m. Jeans, Martha	Apr. 14, 1798	John Grantham		1b x			
Ivell, Rebecca m. Grigsby, John	Apr. 8, 1789	George Ron					

"J"

Name	(marriage)	(surety)	(minister)	(bond)			
Jack, Andrew m. Butt, Elis.	Aug. 27, 1798	James Maxwell	Richard Swift	1b124	or 31	mr 15	*
Jack, Ann m. Ranley, Frederick	Jan. 12, 1797		Richard Swift		or 26	mr 13	*
Jack, Anne m. Paul, William	May 10, 1796		John Boyd		or 11	mr 12	*
Jack, Ann R. m. Porterfield, James	July 1, 1820	Arch'd Porterfield	John B. Hoge	4b154		mr 41	*
Jack, Catherine m. Stewart, James	Sept 20, 1838	William H. Dagan		6b 49			
Jack, James m. Baymore, Mary	June 7, 1802	George Baymore		2b174			
Jack, Jeremiah Jr. m. Friend, Kliner	Nov. 27, 1832	Nathan Davis		5b249			
Jack, Robert m. Truelock, Charlotte	Nov. 2, 1797	Parker Truelock	John Boyd	1b100	or 32	mr 13	*
Jack, William m. Burk, Cath. El.	Jan. 17, 1833	Alex. Boling Jr.	John Light	5b255		mr 67	*
Jackson, Charles m.Thornberry, Polly	Aug. 23, 1797	Joseph Light	John Boyd	1b 33	or 32	mr 13	*
Jackson, Francis m. Fults, Mary	Aug. 30, 1806	John Clouse	J. Bond	3b 28	or 28	mr 23	*
Jackson, George m. Mounts, Elis.	Feb. 7, 1798	Alex. Eckhart		3b 84			
Jackson, Hannah m. Eaglestone, James	Jan. 29, 1818	Amos Nichols		4b 98			
Jackson, John m. Hutson, Nancy	July 25, 1798	Alex. Eckhart	John Hedtt(Butt)	1b121	or 37	mr 16	*
Jackson, Margaret m. Roush, John	Sept 28, 1830	John Grove	Nathan Young	5b175		mr 61	*
Jackson, Mary m. Grove, John	Nov. 3, 1819	Henry Myers		4b122			
Jackson, Nancy C. m. Kline, Henry	Oct. 21, 1836	Mary Jackson		6b 86			
Jackson, Rachel m. Meracle, Daniel	Dec. 25, 1793		Moses Hoge		or 22	mr 8	*
Jackson, Sarah m. Brudshaw, Joseph	Jan. 19, 1799	John Vestal	John Hedtt(Butt)	1b164	or 12	mr 1B	*

	(marriage)	(suretor)	(minister)	(bond)		
Jackson, Thomas m. Smith, Nancy	Apr. 23, 1789	Wm. Stribling				
Jacques, Arthur m. Henry, Susannah	Jan. 8, 1833	Alexander Henry				
Jacques, Arthur m. Silvers, Harriet	Feb. 26, 1841	John Miles	John Light	1b x		mr 72 *
Jacques, Denton m. Ellis, Sarah Ann	Mar. 28, 183f	Ellis Ellis		5b254		
James, Wm. m. Gedlliams, Mary E.	Nov. 25, 1852		A.G.Chenoweth	6b235		mr 87 *
James, Absalom m. Current, Sarah Sue	Dec. 28, 1793		Wm. Hill	6b 75	cr 30	mr 10 *
James, Drusilla m. Claycomb, John	Dec. 13, 1796		John Boyd		cr 11	mr 13 *
James , Elis. m. Tate, Andrew	Mar. 29, 1818	Solomon Offutt	Nathan Young	4b 66		mr 56 *
James, John m. Johnston, Sidney	Oct. 15, 1800	Abr'm Johnston		2b 92		
James, Reuben m. Shoafstall, Mary	Jan. 18, 1825	Adam Strayer	Chas. P. Krauth	4b286		mr 48 *
James, Walter m. Everhart, Martha J.	Jan. 22, 1858		J.H.Jennings		gc 6	*
Jameson, Martha m. Wolff, Henry	Aug. 9, 1796		David Young		gc 2	*
Jamison, Mary m. Fleming, James	June 7, 1792		David Young			*
Jamison, Sylvester m. Bents, Elis.	Feb. 1, 1853		J.H.Plunkett			mr 88 *
Janney, James m. Brown, Elis.	Apr. 1, 1794		David Young		gc 3	
Janney, Israel R. m.Tabb, Mary Ev'a	May 19, 1831	William Long		5b195		
Jeans, Martha m. Irwin, Thomas	Apr. 14, 1798	John Grantham		1b108		
Jeans, Nancy m. Blue, Cornelius	Dec. 14, 1790		Moses Hoge		cr 5	mr 5 *
Jeans, Rassey m. Merchant, Wm.	Nov. 23, 1806	Richard Merchant		3b 36		
Jefferson, Hamilton m.Whiting,Judith	June 22, 1798	Joseph Gardner	John Hedtt(Hatt)	1b121	cr 37	mr 16 *
Jefferson, James m. Jones, Mary	Nov. 2, 1799	Joseph Newman		2b 34		
Jefferson, John m. Whiting, Susanna	Apr. 3, 1793		Edward Tiffin		cr 9	mr 8 *
Jefferson, Nancy m. Alebaugh, Jacob	Oct. 8, 1810		Rev. Reebenack		gc 11	
Jeffings, John m. Bowls, Sarah	Oct. 15, 1788		Hugh Vance	6b 10		mr 35 *
Jeffries, Jacob m. Kennedy, Ann E.	Apr. 24, 1834	Alex. Stephen	John Howell			mr 68 *
Jeffries, Jervis m. Snider, Elis.	Mar. 9, 1790		Hugh Vance			mr 38 *
Jeffries, Joseph m. Bonham, Sarah	Feb. 12, 1816	Edmond Chismond				mr 55 *
Jeffries, Nancy m. Alebaugh, Jacob	Oct. 6, 1810	Christn Mussetter	Nathan Young	3b354		
Jeffries, Rebecca m. Shimmafelt, Wm.	Mar. 25, 1801	Peter Williamson	Richard Swift	3b162	cr 31	mr 19 *
Jeffries, Sally m. Watts, William	Dec. 28, 1808	James Catlett		2b119		
Jenkins, Elis. m. Linton, David	May 16, 1850	George Jenkins	John Light	3b105		mr 80 *
Jenkins, George m. Hays, Rebecca E.	Apr. 25, 1850	David Hays	Richard T. Brown	7b185		mr 80 *
Jenkins, Wm. m. Williams, Polly	Oct. 11, 1799	George Verraka		7b184		
Jennings, George m. Chenoweth, Jane	Sept 6, 1808	Absalom Chenoweth		2b 31		
Jennings, Jas. H. m. Robinson, Elis.	Jan. 2, 1848	B.M.Kitchen	Lewis F. Wilson	3b 96		mr 83 *
Jennings, Sarah m. Quick, James	Oct. 17, 1807	William Maslin		7b144		
Jett, Ann m. Thompson, Thomas	Jan. 10, 1820	John Strother		3b 74		
Jett, Anthony m. Cross, Catherine	Apr. 12, 1800	George Boston	John Hatt(Hedtt)	4b130	cr 33	mr 18 *
Jett, Malinda m. Brannon, Isaac	Apr. 16, 1814	Wm. Britton		2b 64		
Jett, Wm. m. Rees, Elis.	Oct. 8, 1800	John Rees		3b293		
*Job, Henry m. Miller, Elis.	May 14, 1807	Adam Miller		2b 91		
Job, Jacob m. Blackmore, Mary	June 3, 1815	Henry Job	Nathan Young	3b 58		mr 55 *
Job, Lydia m. Moon, Thomas	June 4, 1806	John Shober		4b 4		
Job, Mary B. m. Carothers, James	Jan. 15, 1811	William Long		3b 22		
*Job, Andrew m. Miller, Abigail	Jan. 31, 1786		Hugh Vance	3b172		mr 33 *

(name)	(marriage)	(surety)	(minister)	(bond)	ref
Job, Peggy m. Green, Thomas	Apr. 22, 1808	David Johnston		3b 87	*
Job, Sarah m. Sellers, Bolser	Jan. 29, 1807	Daniel Rees		3b 44	*
John, Anne m. Williamson, Samuel	Apr. 18, 1808	David John		3b 85	*
John, Cath. m. McBride, Thomas	Sept 28, 1789	Robert Jones		1b 48	gc 7 *
Johnson, Abby m. Payne, Wm.	Sept 28, 1797		David Young		gc 7
Johnson, Andrew m.Shimp, Eliz. Rachel	Nov. 22, 1841	Casper Shimp	Hugh Vance	6b254	cr 19 mr 3 *
Johnson, Ann m. Stephen, Robert	Apr. 15, 1792		John Hedges / Christian Stredt		cr 15 mr 7 *
Johnson, Cath. m. Wood, Robert	Apr. 2, 1838	Thos. C. Harper		5b138	
Johnson, Cath. Elis. m. Murphy,Philip	May 31, 1845	William Abel	Lewis F. Wilson	7b 36	mr 77 *
Johnson, Charlotte m. Beiley, George	Dec. 21, 1836	John Strother		6b 89	
Johnson, Debrick m. O'Brien, James	Nov. 21, 1819		Mathias Riser		mr 30 *
Johnson, Francis m. Butler, Susan	Feb. 13, 1829	Ismael Butler		5b119	
Johnson, Frances m. Steele, B.F.	Apr. 15, 1851	John W. Lemon	F.C.Tebbs	7b222	mr 84 *
Johnson, Isaac m. Sencindiver,Marg't	Dec. 23, 1850	Martin Sencindiver	F.C.Tebbs	7b206	mr 83 *
Johnson, James m. Carothers, Rebecca	Feb. 9, 1796		David Young		gc 5
Johnson, James m. Rankin, Abigail	June 17, 1800	Wm. Murphy		2b 72 / 5b251	
Johnson, Jane m. Miller, Daniel	Jan. 20, 1833	Harrison Waite	John Heitt(Hatt)	2b 73	cr 35 mr 19 *
Johnson, John m. McGerman, Mary	June 20, 1800	John Conoway		4b 89	
Johnson, John m. Prill, Phebe	Nov. 23, 1818	John Robinson		5b228	mr 64 *
Johnson, John m. Wells, Harriet	May 10, 1832	Daniel Price	Nathan Young	3b269	gc 13 mr 43 *
Johnson, Joseph m. Murphy, Eliz.	Aug. 26, 1813	Wm. Anderson	Rev. Reebenack		
Johnson, Lucretia m. Seppey, Joseph	Feb. 20, 1847	Jos.H.Plunkett	Hugh Vance	7b 99 / 6b 35	
Johnson, Lucretia E. m. Johnson,Wm.	June 11, 1835	Joseph Johnson			
Johnson, Lydia m. Murphy, Samuel	Mar. 6, 1819				mr 30 *
Johnson, Margaret m. Morgan, Joncy	Nov. 21, 1824		Mathias Riser	4b263	mr 47 *
Johnson, Maria m. Downing, Samuel	Apr. 19, 1812	Joel Rees	Chas. P. Krauth		
Johnson, Maria m. Gilney, Henry	June 19, 1811		Rev. Reebenack	3b187	gc 12 mr 33 *
Johnson, Mary m. McDaniel, Alex.	May 18, 1786	Daniel Gavin	Rev. Reebenack		gc 12
Johnson, Mathew m. Chapman, Hannah	Feb. 8, 1814		Hugh Vance		
Johnson, Moses m. Abernathy, Mary	Jan. 10, 1841	Samuel Abernathy		3b281	
Johnson, Nancy m. Windham, Alfred H.	Nov. 15, 1815	John D. Jones	John Hedges	6b253	gc 15 mr 73 *
Johnson, Rachel. Martin, James	Dec. 26, 1838	Alex. McDonald	Rev. Reebenack	3b351	
Johnson, Rosanna m. Teele, Wm.	Jan. 8, 1854	Hezekiah Hedges		6b129	
Johnson, Samuel m. Clark, Mary	Jan. 4, 1836		James Watts		*
Johnson, Samuel H. m. Hayden,Teresa	Mar. 17, 1847	Jesse Hayden		6b 74 / 7b 99 / 4b245	
Johnson, Wm. W. m. Johnson, Lucretia	June 11, 1823	Jos. H. Plunkett			
Johnston, Amy m. Lane, Samuel	Aug. 12, 1792	Joel Rees			cr 15 mr 7 *
Johnston, Ann m. Stephen, Robert	Apr. 23, 1833		Christian Stredt	5b259	
Johnston, Cath. m. McCleary,Ephraim	Apr. 23, 1785	Lemuel Johnston			cr 38 mr 1 *
Johnston, Elis. m. Campbell, John	Aug. 1, 1796		Edward Tiffin		cr 11 mr 13 *
Johnston, Elis. m. Dunn, William	Dec. 8, 1851		John Boyd		mr 84 *
Johnston, Frances Amanda m.Steel,B.F.	Apr. 15, 1813	Johnston W. Lemon	F.C.Tebbs	7b222	
Johnston, Hannah m. Hite, Jacob	Mar. 22, 1789	Abraham Johnston		3b257	
*Johnston, Thos. m. Canby, Phebe			D. Thomas		mr 38 *

Name	(marriage)	(suretor)	(minister)	(bond)		
Johnston, Henry m. Aslestone(Egl-)Ann	June 28, 1806	James Campbell	J. Bond	3b 23	cr 28	mr 23 *
Johnston, James m. Olinger, Sarah	Oct. 19, 1836	Christ'r Olinger		6b 85		mr 29 *
Johnston, John m. Brill, Phebe	? 1818					mr 57 *
Johnston, John m. Childs, Sarah	Aug. 13, 1822	John Childs	Mathias Riser	4b221		
Johnston, John m. Long, Jane	Mar. 22, 1805	John Hixon	Nathan Young	2b257		
Johnston, John W. m. Morrington, Mary	Aug. 7, 1787		Hugh Vance	7b 3	cr 18	
Johnston, John W. m. Keesacre, Cath.	June 8, 1844	Henry Keesacre		6b 41		mr 1 *
Johnston, Joseph m. Clarke, Ann	Apr. 17, 1835	John Clarke		5b 57		
Johnston, Joseph m. Harper, Jane	Nov. 28, 1826	Joseph Harper	Nathan Young	3b187	gc 12	mr 59 *
Johnston, Mary m. McDaniel, Alex.	Nov. 16, 1811	Daniel Gavin	Rev. Reebenack	2b161	cr 32	mr 20 *
Johnston, Mary m. Woodring, John	Feb. 19, 1802	Henry Clayaomb	Richard Swift	5b166		mr 54 *
Johnston, Milton m. Kennedy, Jane E.	May 7, 1830	Robert Kennedy	Wm. Monroe	6b154		
Johnston, Mary Mrs. m. Gorry, John	Dec. 15, 1838	Peter Cook		2b185		
Johnston, Richard m. Keating, Sarah	Dec. 9, 1802	Thos. Sappington	Richard Swift	3b140	cr 32	mr 21 *
Johnston, Robert m. Miller, Nancy	Mar. 12, 1810	James Miller		4b172		
Johnston, Robert m. Shane, Sarah	Feb. 15, 1821	John Downing		5b 23		
Johnston, Robert m. Taylor, Rebecca	Oct. 3, 1825	Jesse Payne		6b 18		
Johnston, Ruth m. Miller, Jacob	Sept 6, 1834	John H. Palmer				
Johnston, Samuel m. Mormouth, Louisa	Aug. 9, 1833	William Wilson	Geo. W. Humphries	5b279		mr 67 *
Johnston, Sarah m. Shearer, John	Feb. 26, 1835	Hezekiah Johnston		6b 33		
Johnston, Sidney m. James, John	Oct. 15, 1800	Abr'm Johnston		2b 92		
Johnston, Wm. m. Axe, Eliz.	Feb. 27, 1802	William Axe	Richard Swift	2b162	cr 32	mr 20 *
Johnston, Wm. m. Hays, Phebe	Oct. 22, 1819	Andrew Hays	Nathan Young	4b120		mr 56 *
Johnston, Wm. m. Shirley, Eliz.	May 2, 1792		Moses Hoge			mr 39 *
Jolly, Samuel m. Bough, Eliz.	Mar. 30, 1799	John Eydon		1b176		*
Jones, Adrian m. Lemen, Mary	Feb. 4, 1839	James Lemen		6b158	gc 4	
Jones, Ann m. Recob, Joseph	Jan. 6, 1795		David Young			mr 57 *
Jones, Cath. m. Grantham, Lewis	June 8, 1822	Peter Jones	Nathan Young	4b216		
Jones, David m. Brunner, Margaret	Oct. 27, 1800	Isaac McIntire		2b 95	cr 5	mr 5 *
Jones, Edward m. Offutt, Clarisse	Nov. 4, 1790	Solomon Offutt	Moses Hoge	4b 66		mr 56 *
Jones, Eliz. m. Tate, Andrew	Mar. 28, 1818	Robert Jones	Nathan Young	6b303		mr 74 *
Jones, Emily m. Cook, Adam	Aug. 29, 1843	John Randall	Lewis F. Wilson	3b186	cr 5	
Jones, Francis m. Randall, Susannah	May 13, 1811	Adrian Wynkoop	Richard Swift	2b156	cr 32	mr 20 *
Jones, Francis m. Wynkoop, Susanna	Jan. 2, 1802?		Moses Hoge		cr 38	mr 20 *
Jones, George m. Longbright, Eve	Dec. 18, 1800?	Henry Stevens		6b115		
Jones, Hiram H. m. Crowl, Isabella	Oct. 10, 1837	Frederick Bremner	Nathan Young	5b212		mr 62 *
Jones, Hiram m. Fedder, Susanna	Dec. 17, 1831	John Bennett		2b208		
Jones, Isaac m. Bennett, Kitty	Aug. 27, 1803	Michael Fiser		1b136		
Jones, John m. Fiser, Mary	Sept 29, 1798		David Young		gc 4	
Jones, John m. Manken, Mary	Nov. 25, 1794		Richard Swift	2b139	cr 32	mr 20 *
Jones, John M. Stripe (Sh-), Hannah	Aug. 29, 1801	John Brakefield	Samuel Smith	6b227		
Jones, John D. m. Kreglow, Mary	Dec. 14, 1840	George Kreglow		3b268		mr 71 *
Jones, Jonathan m. Coons, Cath.	July 30, 1813	Nathaniel Jones				

(marriage)	(surety)	(minister)	(bond)		
Jones, Jonathan m. Scanlyn, Barbara — Jan. 14, 1799	Jacob Etty	Richard Swift	1b163	cr 28	mr 16 *
Jones, Mary m. Jefferson, James — Nov. 2, 1799	Joseph Newman		2b 34		mr 58 *
Jones, James m. Noland, Obed — Sept 23, 1826	Robert Jones	Nathan Young	5b 53		mr 70 *
Jones, Mary m. Washington,James M. — Dec. 19, 1839	Warner Mayhugh	Lewis F. Wilson	6b 189		mr 25 *
Jones, Mathew m. Williamson, Eliz. — Jan. 6, 1813	Robert Wilson	John Mathews	3b245		mr 62 *
Jones, Robert m. Fedder, Susanna — Dec. 17, 1831	Fred. Brenner	Nathan Young	5b212		
Jones, Rhys m. Henderson, Eliza L. — June 12, 1844	James McSherry	Nathan Young	7b 3		
Jones, Samuel m. Hendricks(-dre)Mary — Mar. 19, 1793	John Jones	Moses Hoge	1b x	cr 21	mr 7 *
Jones, Sarah m. Gay, Michael — Apr. 27, 1789	Garrett Wynkoop		4b136		*
Jones, Sarah m. Kerney, Wm. — Feb. 15, 1820					
Jones, Wm. m. Collins, Catherine — Jan. 12, 1799	Thos. Butterfield	David Young		ge 8	mr 33 *
Jonson, Mary m. Dean, Henry — Jan. 13, 1785		Hugh Vance			mr 38 *
Jonson, Thomas m. Canoy, Phebe — Feb. 27, 1789		D. Thomas			
Jordan, Ann E. m. Silver, Thomas — Sept 23, 1838	Thomas Jordan	James M. Brown	6b134		mr 67 *
Jordan, Hannah m. Pitzer, Wm. — Dec. 15, 1833	Thomas Silver	Nathan Young	5b284		mr 58 *
Jordan, Ruth m. Kennedy, Thomas — Jan. 31, 1825	Robert Hedges	Hugh Vance	5b 29		mr 33 *
Joslin, Jeremiah m. Sewell, Ann — 1786	John Haines		2b252		
Joy, John m. Armsby, Nelly — Jan. 28, 1805	Joseph Haines	John Light	5b223		
Joy, Peter m. Oldfield, Eliz. — Apr. 5, 1812	Thomas Powell	Nathan Young	5b204		mr 62 *
?Joy, Stephen m. VanZant, Sarah Ann — Aug. 27, 1831		John Light			
Joy, Stephen m. Wells, Harriet — May 10, 1832					
?Joy, Stephen m. Sargeant, Sarah Ann — Aug. 28, 1831	Mathew Ranson	David Young			
Judd, Eliz. m. Fisher, John — May 24, 1800	John Fisher	Rev. Reebenack	2b 71	ge 9	mr 63 *
Judd, Nancy m. Bishop, Jacob — Jan. 11, 1810		Hugh Vance	3b133	ge 11	mr 64 *
Judy, Frances m. Ellis, Rowland — June 15, 1786					mr 43 *

"K"

(marriage)	(surety)	(minister)	(bond)		
Kaign, Susanna m. Myers, Henry — Nov. 11, 1783	Stephen Heard	Hugh Vance	2b 99		mr 32 *
Kain, Eliz. m. Vance(Warn), Alex. — Nov. 11, 1800		David Young		gc 9	
Kain, John m. Darke, Mary — Feb. 28, 1797		Richard Swift	1b134	cr 12	mr 14 *
Kain, Kesiah m. Hall(Hull),James — Sept 22, 1798	William Hall	John Heitt(Hatt)	2b 34	cr 11	mr 16 *
Kain, Mary m. Nichols, Robert — Nov. 9, 1799	Henry Myers	John Boyd	3b322	cr 34	mr 17 *
Kalklacer, John C. m. Acres, Sarah — May 1, 1815	Nathan Start				
Kane, James m. Miller, Eliz. — Feb. 5, 1810	Henry Myers	Rev. Reebenack	3b135	gc 11	mr 62 *
Kane, Nancy m. Sellers, William — July 31, 1831	Jacob Smith	John Light	5b199		mr 35 *
Kanfer, Anna m. Kerns(Kearns),Jesse — Feb. 11, 1788		Moses Hoge			
Kanifer, John m. Reed, Sarah — Feb. 17, 1797		David Young		gc 6	
Kaum, Cath. M. m. Farra, Patrick — Mar. 21, 1799	Patr'k McGonagle		1b174		
Kapp, Ann B. m. Dawson, Thomas — Jan. 18, 1790		Hugh Vance			mr 38 *

Name	(marriage)	(suretor)	(minister)	(bond)	
Karinger, Jacob m. Moore, Patsy	Nov. 19, 1806	Johnstone Moore		3b 36	
Kase, Betsy m. Kephart, Anthony	Sept 3, 1807	Isaac Paschal		3b 68	
Kavenaugh, Mathew m. Callahan, Cath.	July 15, 1841	James McSherry		6b244	
Kay, Anne m. Ray, Van	Aug. 14, 1820	Jacob Kay		4b155	
Kear, Margaret m. Lee, John	Aug. 13, 1832	John Kearn	Nathan Young	5b237	mr 65 *
Kearfott, George m. Trout, Dorcas	Jan. 1, 1846	David Seibert		7b 52	
Kearfott, Levi H. m. Dailey, Eliz.	1854				mr 88 *
Kearns, Anna m. Kiser, Wm. M.	Jan. 8, 1853	Cyrus M. Kerns	George W. Harris	7b242	mr 85 *
Kearns, Cath. m. Davis, David	Jan. 25, 1810	Michael Kearns	David Thomas	3b135	go 11
Kearns, Cyrus M. m. Copenhaver, Eliz.	Apr. 29, 1952	William M. Kiser	Rev. Reebenack	7b254	
Kearns, Eliz. m. Lashorn, James	Sept 27, 1850	Jacob VanDoren	David Thomas	7b197	mr 86 *
Kearns, G. Henry m. Hammond, Rebecca	1850				mr 83 *
Kearns, James m. Riner, Sarah	Dec. 21, 1841	Jacob Riner	Lewis F. Wilson	6b259	
Kearns, Jesse m. Kanier, Anna	Feb. 11, 1788		Moses Hoge		mr 35 *
Kearns, John J. m. Levy, Virginia R.	Mar. 31, 1853		Jas. H. Jennings		mr 86 *
Kearns, Joseph m. Hess, Eliz.	May 31, 1849		B.M.Schmucker		mr 79 *
Kearns, Joseph m. Spencer, Susanna	May 30, 1802	Peter Hess		2b159	
Kearns, Marg't. m. Lee, John	Apr. 28, 1832	Thomas Spencer	Nathan Young	2b172	mr 65 *
Kearns, Michael m. Ray, Eliz.	Aug. 13, 1832	John Kearn	Rev. Reebenack	5b237	
Tkearns, Rebecca m. Stuckey, John	Sept 3, 1815	Abraham Levy	W.N.Scott	3b337	gc 15
Kearns, Sarah m. Courtney, John	Dec. 20, 1842	Jacob Kerns	Lewis F. Wilson	6b285	mr 26 *
Kearns, Sarah Cath. m. Miller, Henry	Dec. 4, 1830	Jacob Kerns	Nathan Young	5b182	mr 73 *
Kearns, Saran m. Wolford, William	Aug. 4, 1831	Abraham Hooper	Nathan Young	5b199	mr 61 *
Kearsley, Betsy m. Michael, Alex.Dr.	June 17, 1790		Moses Hoge		mr 62 *
Kearsley, Jane m. Sanderson, Alex.	Feb. 1, 1793		Moses Hoge		mr 5 * cr 4
Tkearsley, Marg't m. Mines, John	Apr. 22, 1799	John Kearsley	Moses Hoge	2b 2	mr 39 * cr 29
Tkearsley, Peggy m. Mines, John	Apr. 22, 1799	John Kearsley	Moses Hoge	2b 2	mr 17 * cr 29
Keath, Zacharias m. Wright, Richard	Apr. 7, 1791	Thos. Sappington	Moses Hoge	2b185	mr 17 * cr 7
Keating, Sarah m. Johnston, Richard	Dec. 9, 1802	John Throckmorton	Richard Swift	2b 68	mr 6 * cr 32
Keating, Wm. m. Mitchell, Hannah	Apr. 23, 1800	Jacob Keebler	John Winter	5b 67	mr 21 *
Keebler, Eliz. m. White, Thomas	Apr. 10, 1827	Isaac Crab	Nathan Young	4b221	mr 51 *
Keef, John m. Sharp, Eliz.	Apr. 12, 1822				mr 58 *
Keef, John W. m. Leathers, Sarah F.	Aug. 15, 1852	Wm. Leathers	David Thomas	7b250	mr 86 *
Keefer, Joseph m. Folk, Hannah	Mar. 29, 1809	Christ'r Folk	Lewis Mayer	3b117	mr 24 * cr 16
Keefer, Joseph m. Folk (Falk),Rebecca	Aug. 28, 1814	Abraham Folk	Rev. Reebenack	3b283	mr 24 * go 14
Keefer, Joseph m. Stuckey, Mary	Feb. 8, 1822	Jacob Stuckey	Chas. P. Krauth	4b223	mr 45 *
Keen, Susan m. Watson, Thomas	Sept 14, 1791		Moses Hoge		mr 6 * cr 6
Keepler, John,Rev. m. Shearer, Mary	Apr. 4, 1834	Archibald Shearer	Samuel Keepler	6b 3	mr 67 *
Keersley, Sally m. Riddle, Joseph	Sept 12, 1789		Moses Hoge		mr 3 * cr 2
Kees, Dariel m. Rumbo, Catherine	May 7, 1816	John Kees		4b 3	
Kees, Eliza Jane m. Everhart, Nathan	Dec. 23, 1851	Jacob Kees		7b239	
Kees, Jacob m. Everhart, Sarah	Jan. 6, 1853				
Kees, Jane m. Kees, John	Apr. 23, 1850	Nathan Everhart	Jas. H. Jennings	7b182	mr 86 *

Name	(marriage)	(suretor)	(minister)	(bond)			
Kees, John m. Everhart,Barbara Ellen	Aug. 28, 1848	Teter Everhart	J. H. Jennings	7b134		mr 82	*
Kees, John m. Kees, Jane	Apr. 23, 1850	Nathan Everhart		7b182			*
Kees, John m. Lashorn, Margaret	Dec. 21, 1816	John Lashorn	W. N. Scott	4b 27		mr 82	*
Kees, Mary Ann m. Hite, Wm.	Aug. 26, 1847	Calender Wibeley	Jas. H. Jennings	7b104		mr 29	*
Kees, Nancy n. Dick, Philip	Feb. 12, 1818		Mathias Riser			mr 60	*
Kees, Peter m. Riner, Hannah	Feb. 6, 1829	Wm. Myers	Nathan Young	5b118			*
Keesacre, Cath. m. Johnston, John W.	June 8, 1844	Henry Keesacre		7b 3			*
Keesacre, Eliz. m. Criswell, Abraham	May 9, 1833	George H. Dugan	James M. Brown	5b274		mr 67	*
Keesacre, George m. Potter, Drusilla	Oct. 16, 1844	John Riser		7b 8			*
Keesacre, Jane m. Wilson, Wm. Darke	Dec. 9, 1833	James Criswell	John Light	5b294		mr 67	*
Keesacre, Mathias m. Criswell, Eliz.	Aug. 18, 1814	James Waugh		3b301			*
Keesacre, Michael m. Keesacre, Susan	May 26, 1815	John Bitzer	Rev. Reebenack	3b326	gc 14		*
Keesacre, Susan m. Keesacre, Michael	May 26, 1815	John Bitzer	Rev. Reebenack	3b326	gc 14		*
Keesacre, Aaron Wesley m.Welsh, Ann	Apr. 19, 1855		James Watts				*
Keesecker, Andrew m. Houck, Cath.	Dec. 6, 1796		David Young		gc 6		*
Keesecker, Barbara m. Hedges, John P	Oct. 20, 1825	George Keesecker	Nathan Young	5b 25		mr 58	*
Keesecker, Cath. m. Keesecker, Geo.	July 19, 1794		David Young		gc 4		*
Keesecker, Cath. m. Shaffer, Martin	Sept 19, 1795		David Young		gc 5		*
Keesecker, El1 m. Miller, Ann	Feb. 14, 1854		John Light				*
Keesecker, Eliz. m. Criswell, Abr'm	May 16, 1833	George Dugan	James M. Brown	5b274		mr 67	*
Keesecker, Eliz. m. McManne, James	Feb. 8, 1853		J. H. Plunkett			mr 88	*
Keesecker, Fanny Mrs. m. Smith, Jacob	Aug. 13, 1828	?		5b105			*
Keesecker, George m. Keesecker, Cath.	July 19, 1794	Daniel Riner	David Young	5b 42	gc 4		*
Keesecker, George m. Riner, Eliz.	May 11, 1826	Fielding Colbert	Nathan Young	6b173		mr 58	*
Keesecker, Mary m. Emberson, Noble	Aug. 13, 1830	John Keesecker	John Light	3b 90		mr 62	*
Keesecker, Mary m. Hoover, Joseph	June 4, 1808						*
Keesecker, Mary m. Pitzer, John	May 11, 1799	Andrew Keesecker	David Young	1b180	gc 8		*
Keesecker, Mary Ann m. Hill, William	Sept 12, 1827	Jacob Keesecker	James M. Brown	5b 78		mr 51	*
Keesecker, Mich'l m. Keesecker, SusanMay	Sept 20, 1815	John Bitzer	Rev. Reebenack	3b326	gc 14		*
Keesecker, Rachel m. Shook(Shu),John	June 30, 1817	John Pitzer Jr.	W. N. Scott	4b 39			*
Keesecker, Rosanna m. Shuh, Henry	Mar. 2, 1833	Eli Fleming		5b259			*
Keesecker, Susan m. Keesecker, Mich'lMay	Mar. 26, 1815	John Bitzer	Rev. Reebenack	3b326	gc 14		*
Keesecker, Susanna m. Fetter, John	Oct. 23, 1828	Henry Keesecker	Nathan Young	5b110		mr 60	*
Keeves, Anthony m. Brown, Mary Ann	Feb. 22, 1830	John Brown	John Mathews	5b151		mr 53	*
Keith, Jacob m. Moses, Eliz.	Jan. 30, 1793		William Hill			mr 10	*
Keith, Walter m. Creamer(Blea—),Mary	Mar. 30, 1796		John Boyd		cr 30	mr 12	*
Keldow, John m. Butterfield, Sarah	July 25, 1812	Thos. Butterfield	George M. Frye	3b231	cr 11	mr 25	*
Kellenberger, Cath. m. Speck, Geo. F	June 15, 1811	Jonathan Hoover	John B. Hoge	3b190	cr 17	mr 24	*
Keller, Eliz. m. Turner, Joseph	Sept 16, 1833	Jacob Spero		5b282	cr 14		*
Keller, George m. Shaffer, Mary	Sept 18, 1813	Peter Kress	Rev. Reebenack	3b271	gc 13		*
Keller, Henry m. Bashore, Mary	Feb. 14, 1826	Henry Bashore	Chas. P. Kreuth	5b 36			*
Keller, John m. Crowl, Cath.	Aug. 9, 1800	Henry Crowl	David Young	2b 81	gc 9	mr 50	*
Keller, Sally m. Brannon, William	Jan. 2, 1807	Jesse Curry		3b 41			*

Name	(marriage) date	(marriage) year	(suretor)	(minister)	(bond)	ref.
Keller, Samuel m. Smith, Sarah	Oct. 17,	1820	Jesse Smith	William Hill	4b165	cr 30 mr 9 *
Kelley, Eliz. m. Wilmuth, Joseph	Dec. 28,	1793		Moses Hoge		cr 29 mr 17 *
Kelley, Samson m. Brown, Margaret	Aug. 2,	1799			6b 22	
Kelley, Thomas m. Showalter, Ann R.	Oct. 22,	1834	John McCleary		4b 43	*
Kemble, Eliz. m. Elkins, John	Aug. 13,	1817	George Myers	W.N.Scott	4b 48	
Kemble, Mina m. Turner, Jesse	Oct. 6,	1817	John Perel			cr 36 mr 12 *
Kemp, Christian m. Baker, Harriet	Apr. 28,	1796	Reuben Newkirk	Moses Hoge	1b 46	
Kemp, Henry m. Hite, Sarah	Sept 25,	1797	Henry Kemp	Moses Hoge	1b 45	cr 36 mr 13 *
Kemp, Mary m. Newkirk, Reuben	Sept 25,	1798		Moses Hoge		cr 29 mr 14 *
Kankle, m. Lemon, Mary		1807	Wm. Gregory		3b 52	
Kennedy, Aaron m. Gregory, Amelia	Mar. 30,	1828	Seaman Garard	Benedict Reynolds	5b103	mr 52 *
Kennedy, Angelina m. Davis, Joseph	July 17,	1834	Alex. Stephen	John Howell	6b 10	mr 68 *
Kennedy, Ann E. m. Jeffry, Jacob	Apr. 24,	1820	Edward Kennedy	W.N.Scott	4b150	mr 41 *
Kennedy, Cath. m. Winning, James	June 8,	1836	Joseph Bear		6b 82	
Kennedy, Dardel m. Bear, Sarah E.	July 4,	1800	Samuel Kennedy		2b 53	
Kennedy, Dardel m. Lowry, Jane	Feb. 10,	1783?		Hugh Vance		mr 32 *
Kennedy, Eliz. m. Hedges, James	Apr. 10,	1788		Hugh Vance		mr 34 *
Kennedy, Eliz. m. Loyd, James		1797	Daniel Kennedy		1b 73	
Kennedy, Eliz. m. McGovran, Charles	Dec. 19,	1849	Hugh Kennedy		7b148	
Kennedy, Eliz. m. Norrington, John	Mar. 20,	1847	Geo. W. Murphy		7b 92	
Kennedy, Eveline m. Murphy,Harrison	Mar. 22,	1800	James Kennedy		2b 46	
Kennedy, George m. Melick, Marg't	Jan. 4,	1833	Harrison Waite	Hugh Vance	5b266	
Kennedy, James m. Pear, Nancy	Apr. 9,					cr 25 mr 4 *
Kennedy, James m. Relly, Mary	Nov. 3,	1789	Robert Kennedy	Hugh Vance	2b100	
Kennedy, Jane m. Gregory, Wm.	Nov. 15,	1800	Samuel Roney		6b140	
Kennedy, Jane m. Murphy, Geo. W.	June 11,	1838	Samuel Kennedy		2b212	
Kennedy, Jane m. Murphy, William	Nov. 8,	1803	Robert Kennedy	Wm. Monroe	5b166	mr 54 *
Kennedy, Jane E. m. Johnston, Milton	May 7,	1830	Wm Murphy	Moses Hoge	2b254	cr 17 mr 22 *
Kennedy, John m. Boothe, Easter	Feb. 20,	1805	Wm. Gordon		1b 65	
Kennedy, John m. Ledman, Peggy	Nov. 28,	1797	John Lyle		3b236	
Kennedy, John m. Lyle, Anna	Sept 16,	1812				
Kennedy, John m. Pendleton, Ann	Oct. 2,	1794	James Kennedy	John Boyd	2b 80	cr 21 mr 8 *
Kennedy, Joseph m. Horn, Eliz.	Aug. 7,	1800				
Kennedy, Kath. m. Vincenheller,Thos.	Jan. 8,	1789		Hugh Vance		mr 37 *
Kennedy, Marg't m. Aiken, Alex.	Apr. 17,	1783	Daniel Kennedy	Hugh Vance	1b 28	mr 32 *
Kennedy, Mary m. Chalfin, Aaron	Aug. 9,	1797	Nicholas Marquart	John Bond	2b267	cr 28 mr 22 *
Kennedy, Mathias m. Marquart, Anne	Aug. 11,	1805	James Lemaster	Lewis F. Wilson	7b 57	mr 77 *
Kennedy, Nancy m. Horner, Abraham	Feb. 4,	1846	John Rainey Jr.		3b272	
Kennedy, Robert m. Rainey, Polly	Sept 22,	1813	Wm. Gregory	John L. Gibbons	5b 25	mr 49 *
Kennedy, Robert S. m. Gregory, Mary	Oct. 25,	1825		Hugh Vance		cr 13 mr 37 *
Kennedy, Ruth m. Robinson,Thomas	Jan. 8,	1789	Josiah Hedges		5b175	
Kennedy, Samuel m. Robinson,Christ'a	Sept 27,	1830	John Kennedy	John Mathews	3b 43	cr 13 mr 23 *
Kennedy, Sarah m. Oburn, Daniel	Jan. 24,	1807				

(name)	(date)	(marriage)	(suretor)	(minister)	(bond)		
Kennedy, Sarah E. m. Weller, Geo. B.	May 27,	May 30, 1850	John T. Kerney	Henry Furlong	7b186		mr 81 *
Kennedy, Stephen m. Reed(Reese),Jane	Apr. 9,	Apr. 10, 1798	Wm. Snodgrass	Richard Swift	1b107	cr 31	mr 15 *
Kennedy, Thos. m. Jordan(Gordon),Eliza	May 13,	May 13, 1851	?	J.H. Plunkett	7b224		mr 88 *
Kennedy, Thos. m. Jordan(Gordon),Ruth	Dec. 15,	Dec. 18, 1825	Robert Hedges	Nathan Young	5b 29		mr 56 *
Kenneford, John m. Wasson, Cath.	Dec. 29,	Dec. 30, 1819	Thomas Simpson	Nathan Young	4b128		mr 12 *
Kenner, Matilda m. Hart, David	Sept 29,	Sept 29, 1796		John Boyd			
Kenney, Angelina m. David, Joseph	July 17,	July 17, 1828	Seaman Gerard	B. Reynolds	5b103	cr 11	mr 52 *
Kenney, Samuel m. Poisal, Rose	Nov. 25,	Nov. 25, 1850	Jacob VanDoren	Lewis F. Wilson	7b203		mr 87 *
Kenney, Susan T. m. Aubin, Geo. St.	Sept 15,	Sept 26, 1816	James B. Kerney	John B. Hoge	4b 12		mr **
Kennede, James m. Stephenson, Sarah		Dec. 29, 1792		David Young			
Kenry, Mathias m. Marquart, Ann	Aug. 24,	Aug. 11, 1805	Nicholas Marquart	John Bond	2b267	gc 2	mr 22 *
Kenry, Wm. m. Dunn, Rosanna	Oct. 8,	Oct. 25, 1798	Robert Dunn	John Boyd	1b137	cr 28	mr 15 *
Kensel, John S. m. Turner, Mary Eliz.	Jan. 30,	Jan. 25, 1850	John D. Turner		7b176	cr 32	
Kensley, Mary m. Fisher, George	Aug. 29,	Aug. 29, 1794		Richard Swift		cr 2	mr 40 *
Kensley, Sally m. Riddle, Joseph	Sept 12,	Sept 12, 1789		Moses Hoge			mr 3 *
Kenter, Jacob m. Pendry, Eliz.	Oct. 22,	Oct. 1804	James Shearer		2b246		
Kephart, Anthony m. Kase, Betsy	Sept 3,	Sept 1807	Isaac Paschal		3b 68		
Kephart, Bernard m.Folk(Fanik)Salome	May 2,	May 3, 1803	Christ'r Folk	David Young	2b201		
Kepler,Rev.J.m.Shearer(Shriver),Mary	Apr. 4,	Apr. 8, 1834	Arch'd Shearer	Samuel Kepler	6b 3	gc 10	mr 67 **
Keplinger, John m. Hamme, Cath.	Jan. 8,	1840	Jacob Hamme		6b192		
Kercheval, Jas. m. Lemon, Christiana	Mar. 17,	Mar. 1810	Wm. Engle		3b142		
Kercheval, Samuel m. Young, Lydia	Feb. 25,	Feb. 1812	Nathan Young		3b212		
Kerin, Timothy m. Armstrong, Nancy	Feb. 2,	1798	James Starky	David Young	1b 84	gc 7	mr 6 *
Kerk, Maria m. Geiger, Anton	Sept 26,	Sept 26, 1796	John Beard	Moses Hoge	1b 46	cr 7	mr 39 *
Kerney, Alex. m. Neuques, Abby(Auly)	May 18,	May 20, 1841		Moses Hoge			mr 72 *
Kerney, Edward m. Williamson, Olly	Mar. 8,	Mar. 11, 1830		Lewis F. Wilson			mr 54 *
Kerney, Eldergirt M. m.Kilmer,Isaac	June 8,	June 1846	Thomas Patton	J.M.Brown	6b241		mr 78 *
Kerney, Eliza m. Seibert, David	Apr. 28,	Apr. 30, 1820	Thomas Patton	D.F.Bragunier	5b156		mr 31 *
Kerney, Eliza Mrs. m. Kerney, Wm.	June 5,	1840	Jacob Myers	John B. Hoge	7b 68		
Kerney, Eliz. m. Patton, Thomas	Sept 15,	Sept 1829	John Strother		4b146		
Kerney, Ellen m. Broderick, Michael	Nov. 10,	Nov. 10, 1813	Morris Slattery		6b211		
Kerney, Jane B. m.O'Ferral, Francis	Apr. 24,	Apr. 16, 1810	Jacob VanDoren	John Mathews	5b141		mr 25 *
Kerney, Jane m. Blue, James	Apr. 13,	Apr. 1829	William Kerney		3b275		
Kerney, John m. Anderson, Elenor	Dec. 23,	Dec. 24, 1839	George Holliday		3b148		
Kerney, John m. Chenoweth, Emily	May 27,	May 30, 1850	Philip Chenoweth	Jas. M. Brown	5b125		mr 53 *
Kerney, Julia Ann m. Rameburg, John	Sept 25,	Sept 26, 1816	Jas. Chenoweth	Lewis F. Wilson	6b190		mr 70 *
Kerney, Sarah E. m. Weller, Geo. B.	Mar. 21,	1829	John T. Kerney	Henry Furlong	7b186		mr 81 *
Kerney, Susan T. m. Aubin, Geo. St.	Mar. 4,	1835	Jas. B. Kerney	John B. Hoge	4b 12		
Kerney, Uriah m. Bowen, Marg't K.	Feb. 15,	1820	Wm. S. Kerney		5b124		
Kerney, Wm. m. Chenoweth, Julia Ann			Samuel Chenoweth		6b 34		
Kerney, Wm. m. Jones, Sarah	June 8,	June 8, 1846	Garrett Wynkoop	D.F.Bragunier	4b136		mr 78 *
Kerney, Wm. m. Lemon, Mary Ann	Sept 16,	Sept 17, 1850	Jacob Myers	C.W.Andrews	7b 68	cr 8	mr 80 *
Kerney, Wm. m. McColister, Martha		Dec. 31, 1791	Hiram Lemon	Moses Hoge	7b196		mr 7 *

Name	(marriage)	(suretor)	(minister)	(bond)		
*Kerney, Wm. m. VanDoren, Katy	Feb. 14, 1801		Moses Hoge		cr 38	mr 20 *
Kerney, Wm. m. Young, Polly	May 14, 1795		Richard Swift		cr 26	mr 10 *
Kerney, Wm. P. m. Calvin(Col-),Sarah Jan. 23,	Jan. 24, 1828		Jas. M. Brown	5b 88		mr 51 *
Kermlick, Cath. m. Gretinger, Solomon	Sept 2, 1794	John Colvin	David Young		gc 4	
Kerns, Ann Rebecca m. Kiser, Wm.	Jan. 8, 1852	Cyrus M. Kerns	David Thomas	7b242		mr 85 *
Kerns, Barbara m. Stuckey(Stoo-John June 13,	June 13, 1816	Jacob Kerns	W.N.Scott	4b 5		mr 26 *
Kerns, Cyrus M. m. Everhart, John	June 2, 1846	John Kerns		7b 67		
Kerns, Cath. m. Copenhaver, Elis.	Apr. 29, 1852	Wm. M. Kiser	David Thomas	7b254		mr 86 *
Kerns, Elis. m. Shimp, Jonas	Sept 20, 1813	Jacob Kerns		3b272		
Kerns, Emanuel m.Diffenderfer, Cath.	Aug. 20, 1840	John David		6b215		
Kerns, Ezra m. Toup, Elis.	July 14, 1820	?		4b154		
Kerns, George m. Robinson, Jane	Mar. 21, 1811	John Robinson	Rev. Reebenack	3b180	gc 12	*
Kerns, Geo. B. m. Keys, Nancy E.	Sept 24, 1845	Jacob Kerns		7b 44		
Kerns, Henry m. Riner, Margaret	Sept 27, 1814	Henry Riner		3b304		
Kerns, Jacob m. Carr, Mary	Dec. 15, 1821	Jesse Turner		4b201		
Kerns, Jacob m. Thompson, Mary Marg.	Feb. 21, 1803	John Thompson	David Young	2b196	gc 10	*
Kerns, Jacob m. Wigle, Cath.	Dec. 26, 1840	John Wigle		6b228		
Kems, John m. Clark, Mary	Oct. 18, 1827	James Clark	Nathan Young	5b 80		mr 59 *
Kerns, John m. Bowman, Elenor	Dec. 11, 1810	George Peterman	Rev. Reebenack	3b167	gc 11	*
Kerns, John A. m. Hedges, Mary J.	Nov. 15, 1847	John P. Hedges		7b112		
Kerns, John J. m. Levy, Virginia R.	Mar. 31, 1853		Jas. H. Jennings	5b279		mr 86 *
Kerns, Marg't m. David, Thomas	Aug. 19, 1833	Jacob Kerns	Jas. M. Brown	4b 35		mr 67 *
Kerns, Mary m. Courtney, David	May 19, 1817	Jacob Kerns	W.N.Scott	6b157		
Kerns, Mary E. m. Bowers, John Jr.	Jan. 16, 1839	Hezekiah Kerns		3b290		
Kerns, Michael m. Keys, Nancy	Mar. 24, 1814	John Keys				
Kerns, Michael m. Ray, Elis.	Sept 3, 1815	Abraham Levy	Rev. Reebenack	3b337	gc 15	*
Kerns, Peter m. Garard, Lucinda	Sept 29, 1842	Jas. M. Robinson	James Chisholm	6b278	gc 2	mr 75 *
Kerns, Philip m. Kerr, Eliz.	Mar. 11, 1793		David Young			
Kerns, Philip m. Lee, Jane	Aug. 13, 1849	Jesse Lee		7b163		
Kerns, Sarah m. Watson, Thomas	Feb. 1, 1791		Moses Hoge		cr 6	mr 6 *
Kerns, Sarah Cath. m. Miller, Henry	Dec. 4, 1830	Jacob Kerns	Nathan Young	5b182		mr 61 *
Kerns, Sarah J. m. Courtney, John	Dec. 20, 1842?	Jacob Kerns	Lewis F. Wilson	6b285		mr 73 *
Kerns, Susan m. Wilson, Geo. M.	Apr. 6, 1826	Samuel Lowry	Nathan Young	5b 39		mr 58 *
Kerns, Susan m. Wolford, Wm.	Aug. 4, 1831	Abr'm Hooper	Nathan Young	5b199		mr 62 *
Kerns, Wm. m. Shull, Mary Ann	Apr. 21, 1834	John Shull	John Howell	6b 9		mr 68 *
Kerns, Wm. m. Weaver, Susan	Mar. 17, 1813	Robert Wilson	Rev. Reebenack	3b256		
Kerr, Elis. m. Kerns, Philip	Mar. 11, 1793		David Young		gc 13	
Kerr, John m. Lewins, Ruth	Dec. 28, 1791		Moses Hoge		gc 2	
Kerr, Mary m. Gates, Richard	Aug. 7, 1787		Hugh Vance		or 8	mr 7 *
Kerring, Sabilla m. Canby, Thomas	Oct. 31, 1809	Wm. Runner	Rev. Reebenack	3b122	or 18	mr 1 *
Kerahner, Laura Cath. m.Tearry, John Jan. 28,	Jan. 28, 1845	Robert Lewis		7b 23	gc 10	
Kerahner, Samuel m. Williamson,Ann A.Jan. 10,	Jan. 10, 1846	William Cole		7b 54		
*Kerney, Salome m. Butler, Wm. G.	Nov. 6, 1840	Jas. A. Kerney	John Light	6b223		mr 76 *

Name	(marriage)		(suretor)	(minister)	(bond)		
Kerney, Wm. P. m. Calvin, Sarah A.	Jan. 23,	1828	John Colvin	Jas. M. Brown	5b 88	mr 51	*
Kerdin, Elis. m. Lane, Andrew	Sept 12,	1853		D.Francis Spriggs		mr 26	*
Kesler, Elis. m. Gray, Michael	Oct. 27,	1816		Mathias Riser			*
Kesler, Elis. m. Greenawalt, John W.	Apr. 1B,	1839	Andrew Criswell		6b175	mr 69	*
Kesler, Wm. m. Thatcher, Hester	June 5,	1838	Jonathan Thatcher	James Watts	6b148		*
Kessler, Mary Ann m.Mccodemus, Fred.	Aug. 7,	1833	Harrison Waite		5b266		*
Kestner, Peter m. Freshour, Mary	May 10,	1818	George Freshour	Mathias Riser	4b 73	mr 29	**
Kestner, Henry m. Lodmaw, Cath.	Dec. 21,	1792		David Young			**
Keyes, Cath. m. Humphreys, David	June 8,	1797	Robert McKnight		1b 27	gc 2	
Keys, Elis. m. Pate, Thomas	Oct. ?	1818	John Keys		3b262		
Keys, Fred. m. Bonner, Elis.	Aug. 25,	1785		Hugh Vance	4b 27	mr 34	*
Keys, John m. Lashorn, Margaret	May 24,	1816	John Lashorn	W.N.Scott	3b189		**
Keys, John m. Podsal, Margaret	Sept 1.	1811	Jacob Podsal	Rev. Reebensck	6b305	gc 12	
Keys, John m. Raney, Eve	Mar. 24,	1843	Samuel Raney		7b 40		
Keys, Mary m. Crow, David	Sept 24,	1845	John Keyes		3b263		
Keys, Mary m. Day, Larkin	Jan. 23,	1813	John Miller		6b276		
Keys, Mary Ann m. Cushong, John W.	Aug. 13,	1842	James McSherry		3b290		
Keys, Nancy m. Kerns, Michael	Jan. 28,	1814	John Keyes		7b 44		
Keys, Nancy E. Kerns, Geo. B.	Apr. 10,	1845	Jacob Kerns		1b 82		
Keys, Thomas m. Rodgers, Margaret	Feb. 21,	1798	George North		5b173		
Koysacker, Mary m. Emerson, Noble	Dec. 26,	1830	Fielding Colbert	John S. Light	2b 50	mr 62	*
Kheyle, Elvy m. Cample, John	May 11,	1793		David Young	5b 67	gc 2	
Kibler, Elis. m. Sheets, Daniel	Oct. 6,	1800	Gabriel Hayes		2b195		*
Kibler, Elis. m. White, Thomas	Apr. 20,	1827	Jacob Kibler	John Winter	2b217	mr 51	*
Kibler, John m. Rife, Mary	Oct. 4,	1796		David Young	5b 42	gc 5	
Kibler, Wm. m. Bedinger, Mary	Sept 1,	1803	Philip Bedinger	David Young	6b 21	gc 10	
Kidd, Charles m. Anderson, Margaret	Jan. 12,	1803	Geo. Anderson		6b 78		
Kidd, Elis. m. Pearson, Solomon	May 20,	1826	Thos. Thornburg	James Reily	5b108	mr 49	*
Kidd, Jane m. Bell, John Jr.	Apr. 8,	1834	Mich'l H.Contchman	John Howell	3b 67	mr 68	*
Kidd, Mary't m. Hunter, Robert	Jan. 10,	1836	Smith Miller		3b308		
Kidwell, James m.Hawn(Haron),Rachel	Dec. 4,	1826	George Hawn	Jacob Medtart	2b 71	mr 63	*
Kiff, Cath. m. Campbell, Wm. F.	May 22,	1828	Isaac Climer	John Mathews	2b120	mr 23	*
Kiger, Daniel m. Rhodes, Mary	July 4,	1807	Jacob Rhodes		2b219	cr 13	
Kiger, Elis. m. McKenny, Wm.	Nov. 9,	1815	George Kiger	David Young	7b 50	gc 9	
Kiger, Geo. Jr. m. Adams, Jane	Mar. 28,	1800	Wm. Mackey	John Boyd	1b 17	cr 35	
Kiger, Henry m. Dabldeck, Mary	Nov. 7,	1801	John Smith		6b 49		*
Kiger, Jacob m. Bales, Elis. Ellen		1804	Jacob Bales		5b290	mr 19	*
Kiger, John m. Humphries, Cath.		1845	Daniel Humphries	Hugh Vance	4b142		
Kiger, Kath. m. Harden, Wm.		1797		Nathan Young	4b 18	mr 43	*
Kiger, Mary m. Early, James		1786	Harrison Waite	W.N.Scott		mr 66	*
Kiger, Mary Ann m. Bradley(Beady)Chas		1835	Jacob Reads			mr 41	*
Kildow, Ann m. Cline, Hiram		1833	Joseph Kildow				
Kildow, Elis. m. Worley, Silas		1816	Jacob Kildow				

	(marriage)		(surety)	(minister)	(bond)		
Kildow, Jacob m. Carter, Eliz.	Jan. 25,	1817	Thomas Carter		4b 29		
Kildow, John m. Butterfield, Sarah	July 25,	1812	James Butterfield	Geo. M. Frye	3b231	cr 17	mr 25 *
Kildow, Susanna m. Clarke, Ebeneser	Sept 23,	1826	Peter Hess	Nathan Young	5b 53		mr 99 *
Kilhown, Eliz. m. Porter, John	June 29,	1808	Collin Carroll		3b 92		
Kilmer, Cath. m. Bettice, Mary	Dec. 19,	1832	David Kilmer	Wm. Monroe	5b249		mr 65 *
Kilmer, Eliz. m. Cushwa, Mary	Mar. 5,	1839	John M. Small		6b161		
Kilmer, Eliz. m. Small, John	Mar. 28,	1825	David Kilmer	Chas. P. Krauth	5b 5		mr 48 *
Kilmer, Isaac m. Kermey, Eldergirt	May 18,	1841	Thomas Patton	Lewis F. Wilson	6b241		mr 72 *
Kilmer, John m. Walters, Cath.	Apr. 3,	1830	John Walters		5b161		
Kilmer, Mary m. Walters, John P.	Mar. 15,	1841	Isaac Kilmer		6b 237		
Kilmer, Nancy E. m. Walters, Harriet	Dec. 2,	1851	Isaac Kilmer		7b238		
Kilmer, Wm. m. Davis, Anna A.	Jan. 15,	1842	Wm. Wolford		6b261		
Kimberling, Fred. m. Rickers, Rake	May 19,	1851	?	David Thomas	7b225		mr 84 *
Kimble, Caleb m. Rydenrick, Marg't	Nov. 19,	1824	Eberitus Rydenr'k	Chas. P. Krauth	4b277		mr 47 *
Kimble, Margaret m. Custer, Mark	Oct. 8,	1810	Richard Morrison		3b163		
Kimble, Margaret m. Palmer, Joseph	Aug. 11,	1801	Jacob Kimble		2b135		
Kimble, Mary m. Morrison, Richard	Aug. 8,	1801	Richard Merchant		2b135		
Kimble, Mina m. Turner, Jesse	Oct. 6,	1817	John Perrel	W.N.Scott	4b 48		*
Kimble, Rebecca m. Ott, John	Nov. 28,	1801	Jacob Kimble	W.N.Scott	2b150		mr 26 *
Kimble, Sarah m. Huffman, Wm. D.	Dec. 11,	1815	Richard Morrison		3b349		
Kime, Isaac m. Hayes, Eliz.	June 11,	1825	Joseph Hayes		5b 14		
Kimes, Samuel m. Custer, Cath. E.	Jan. 24,	1820	Peter Custer	Nathan Young	4b131		mr 56 *
Kinard, Wm. m. Croney, Eliz.	Aug. 24,	1835	Harrison Waite		6b 55		
Kinder, John m. Swingley, Cath.	Aug. 24,	1799	John Bashore		2b 22		
Kinder, Kath. m. Freize, Michael	Sept 7,	1785		Hugh Vance			mr 34 *
Kine, Mathias m. Myers, Margaret A.	July 4,	1843	Jacob Myers	Lewis F. Wilson	6b301		mr 74 *
King, Polly m. Weisenbaugh, Jacob	Oct. 29,	1805		Lewis Duckwall		cr 17	mr 22 *
King, James m. McGlaughlin, Nancy	May 18,	1798	Israel Crow		1b111		
King, Margaret m. Wilson, Jacob	Feb. 14,	1801	William Boyd	Moses Hoge	1b 30	cr 38	mr 20 *
King, Mathew m. Black(Blozeck), Eliz.	Aug. 8,	1797	Amos Tallice	Moses Hoge	2b101	cr 36	mr 13 *
King, Samuel m. McKinney, Margaret	Dec. 4,	1800	Philip Wigle	David Young	2b 79	gc 9	
King, Samuel m. Wigle, Margaret	Aug. 5,	1806	Abealom Miller	Moses Hoge	3b 12	cr 17	mr 22 *
King, Wm. B. m. Miller, Nancy	Feb. 20,	1806	George Boltz		3b 8		
Kiripp, Cath. m. Shaul, George	Jan. 13,	1824		Chas. P. Krauth			*
Kinkle, Caleb m. Rydenrick, Margaret	Nov.	1835	Harrison Waite	Lewis F. Wilson	6b 65		mr 87 *
Kinney, Ann m. Seibert, Jacob	Dec. 1,	1850	Jacob VanDoren	G.W.Cooper	7b203		
Kinsey, Samuel m. Pdsal, Rose	Nov. 25,	1854					
Kinsey, Samuel m. Young, Elis. S.	Jan. 15,	1827	Jacob Hooper	B. Reynolds	5b 84		mr 52 *
Klout, Henry m. Hooper, Cath.	Nov. 15,	1797	Robert Boggess		1b 1		
Kirby, Susannah E. m. Lovejoy, John	Mar. 13,	1801		David Young	1b 46	gc 7	
Kirk, Mary m. Geiger, Anthony	Sept 26,	1797	John Beard	B. Reynolds	5b 60	gc 1	
Kirkhart, Cath. m. Brown, John Wm.	Feb. 1,	1827	John Kirkhart	David Young			mr 51 *
Kirkhart, Cath. m. McWert, Daniel	Dec. 27,	1791		David Young			*
King, Samuel m. Volgal, Magda	Aug. 5,	1800					

Name	(marriage)	(surety)	(minister)	(bond)	Ref
Kirkhart, Jacob m. Batt, Elis.	June 28, 1799	Henry Crowl	Benedict Reynolds	2b 10	nr 52 *
Kirkhart, John m. Wageley, Elis.	Apr. 16, 1828	Wm. Wageley	B. Reynolds	5b 98	nr 52 *
Kirkhart, Marg't m. Wageley, David	Mar. 26, 1828	John Kirkhart		5b 95	*
Kiser, Mary m. Harden, John A.	Mar. 12, 1839	John Merry		6b163	*
Kiser, W. Henry m.Cobert, Barbara E.	Jan. 8, 1851	Cyrus M. Kerns	David Thomas	7b242	nr 85 *
Kiser, Wm. M. m. Kerns, Ann Rebecca	Dec. 4, 1852	Alex. Robinson	David Thomas	4b279	nr 85 *
Kislnger, Cath. m. Cunningham, John	Dec. 20, 1824		Chas. P. Krauth		nr 47 *
Kislnger, Geo. m. McCormack, Nancy	Nov. 1, 1814		Rev. Reebenack		*
Kislnger, James m. Myers, Catherine	Feb. 25, 1837	Peter Myers Jr.	Lewis F. Wilson	6b 98	ge 14 *
Kislnger, John m. Bibler, Susannah	Apr. 26, 1796		John Boyd		or 11 *
Kislnger, Otho m. Speck, Elis.	Feb. 15, 1831	Jonathan Cushma	Jas. M. Brown	5b186	nr 12 *
Kislnger, Samuel H. m. Nichols,Susan	Jan. 27, 1834	James Criswell		5b301	nr 62 *
Kislnger, Susan m. Cunningham,Jas. L.	Apr. 9, 1832	James S. Orrick	Jas. M. Brown	5b225	nr 64 *
Kisner, Susan D. m. Robinson, Wm.	Dec. 8, 1853		G.W.Cooper		nr 85 *
Kisner, Wm. Henry m. Colbert,Barbary	Oct. 31, 1851		D. Thomas	7b117	ge 10 *
Kistler, Elis. m. Fontch(Fouck),Hugh	Sept. 22, 1809	Jas. M. Manford	Rev. Reebenack	3b122	nr 53 *
Kitchen,Alma(Alena)m.Thatcher,Hesek'h	Feb. 26, 1817	Wm. Runner	Mathias Kiser	4b 47	*
Kitchen, Bethuel m. Buzzard, Mary	Jan. 14, 1829	Peter Kister	Jas. M. Brown	5b120	*
Kitchen, Cath. m. Gano, James	Sept. 9, 1836	Henry G. Kitchen		6b 69	nr 56 *
Kitchen, Charity m. French, Jacob	Feb. 28, 1815	John Buzzard	Nathan Young	3b338	nr 57 *
Kitchen, Hannah m. Cosley, Wm.	Apr. 20, 1818	Joseph Kitchen		4b 64	*
Kitchen, Henry m. Gano, Amy	Nov. 16, 1833	Joseph Kitchen	Jas. M. Brown	5b267	*
Kitchen, Jas. M. m. Barnes, Elsinor	Dec. 22, 1816	Harrison Waite		4b 21	*
Kitchen, Job m. Noland, Rachel	July 2, 1846	John Coulter		7b 81	*
Kitchen, John J. m. Myers, Prudence	Feb. 19, 1810	Jos. D. Barnes		3b153	*
Kitchen, Joseph H. m. Gano, Cath.	Feb. 2, 1844	Thomas Noland		6b314	*
Kitchen, Julia m. Richards, Thomas	Mar. 10, 1854	Henry Kitchen	R.T.Berry	5b157	nr 60 *
Kitchen, Marg't m. Bishop, Resin (Rea	Mar. 15, 1830		Nathan Young	4b258	nr 58 *
Kitchen, Thomas m. Middleton,Leonley	Feb. 5, 1824	Henry G. Kitchen	Nathan Young Jr.	2b192	*
Kiter, Easter W. m. Miller, Ephraim	Feb. 19, 1803	Joseph Kitchen Jr.	Mathias Kiser		*
Kithhart, Jane m. Shane, Frank	1818	Stephen Gano	D. Thomas		nr 29 *
Kitsmiller, John m. Bateman, Hannah	Apr. 5, 1789		David Young		nr 38 *
Kitsmiller, Martha m. Moore, Johnson	Nov. 25, 1793		Hugh Vance		nr 36 *
Kizer, Elis. M. m. Compton, Isaac	Sept. 16, 1788	George Kizer		2b 26	go 2 *
Klaycomb, Cath. m. Streithoff,Francis	Nov. 1, 1799		David Young		go 6 *
Klaycomb, Elis. m. Green, John	Apr. 12, 1796	Conrad Clayton	Rev. Reebenack	3b145	go 11 nr 24 *
Klaycomb, Fred. m. Lowman, Elisa	June 9, 1810	John Burk	John B. Boge	3b189	cr 14 nr 26 *
Klaycomb, Fred. m. Tabler, Cath.	June 6, 1811?	Adam Tabler	W.N.Scott	4b 5	*
Klaycomb, Maria m. Frank, George	Dec. 18, 1816		David Young		go 4 *
Klein, Christian m. McQuint, Esther	Nov. 22, 1794		David Young		go 1 *
Klein, Jacob m. Bernhart, Sarah	Nov. 15, 1791		David Young		go 1 *
Klice, Henry m. Francis, Rebecca	May 10, 1810	Wm. Francis	Rev. Reebenack	3b151	go 11 *

Name	(marriage)			(surety)	(minister)	(bond)		
Kine, Sally m. Creamer, Benjamin	Dec. 3,	Dec. 4,	1817	Jacob Kine	Nathan Young	4b 50		mr 56 *
Kline, Eve m. Polsal, Peter	Aug. 25,	Aug.	1824	David Cline	Chas. P. Krauth	4b270		mr 47 *
Kline, Henry m. Jackson, Nancy	Oct. 21,		1836	Mary Jackson		6b 86		
Kline, Philip m. Newman, Elis.	?, 8,	May 12,	1799	Thomas Hamlain	Richard Swift	1b179	cr 28	mr 16 *
Kline, Sophia m. Crowl, Jacob	July 20,	July 31,	1803	Margaret Kline	David Young	2b206	gc 10	
Klinger, Mary Ann m. Gregg, John	Apr. 16,	Apr. 18,	1811	Thomas Shearer	John B. Hoge	3b184	cr 14	mr 24 *
Klinger, Sarah m. Mason, Wm.	Apr. 18,	Apr. 19,	1821	John Gregg	John B. Hoge	4b181		mr 41 *
Knadler, Leah Ann m. Huff, John	Sept 5,	Sept 6,	1829	Andrew Knadler	Nathan Young	5b139		mr 60 *
Knadler, Mary M. m. Murman, Michael	Sept 2,		1845	David Knadler		7b 42		
Knags, Elis. m. Hanny(Henery), John	Mar. 23,	Mar. 25,	1840	John W. Waite	Lewis F. Wilson	6b201		mr 71 *
Knave, Nancy m. Sellers, Wm.	July 29,	July 31,	1831	Jacob Smith	John Light	5b199		mr 62 *
Kneedler, David m. Wilhelm, Elis. A.	Aug. 7,	Aug. 5,	1837	Philip Wilhelm		6b 93		
Kneedler,Jacob Jos. m. Tabler, Eliza	Jan. 5,	Jan. 5,	1833	John Badgel	Nathan Young	5b253		mr 65 *
Kneys, George m. Anderson, Peggy	Jan. 8,		1806	Valentine Kneys		3b 82		
Knight, Benjamin m. Cunningham, Anna		Aug. 3,	1819	John Faris	Mathias Riser			mr 30 *
Knor, James m. Morgan, Rebecca	Sept 16,		1837	Valentine Knupp	Nathan Young	6b111		
Knupp, Elis. m. Moore, John	Nov. 21,	Nov. 22,	1818	Valentine Knupp		4b 89		mr 56 *
Knupp, Fanny m. Houseman, David	July 27,		1812			3b231		
Koney, George m. Clayton, Polly	Apr. 12,	Apr. 13,	1820	Isaac Bacon	W.N.Scott	4b144		mr 41 *
Kookus, Mary m. Collins, Wm.	Mar. 24,	Mar. 24,	1800	Jacob Cookus	Moses Hoge	2b 59	cr 29	mr 19 *
Koontz, Jacob m. Gedger, Elis.	Mar. 15,	Mar. 16,	1800	Jonathan Rusk	David Young	2b 56	go 9	
Koplinger, Eliza m. Gardner, Peter	Sept 28,		1833	Harrison Rusk		5b285		
Kopp, Joseph m. Maine, Cath.	Dec. 8,		1799	George Grove		2b 38		
Koughlyns, Hannah m. Welsh, Wm.		Feb. 12,	1788		Moses Hoge			mr 35 *
Koutsman, Cath. m. Motter, John		May 19,	1795		David Young		go 4	
Kownslar, Elenor m. Showalter,Jos.Jr.	Nov. 13,	Nov. 14,	1826	John Shober	John Winter	5b 56		mr 51 *
Kownslar, Elinor m. Showalter, Jos.	Nov. 13,	Nov. 14,	1826	John Shober	John Winter	5b 56		mr 51 *
Kownslar, Eliza m. Rupert, Gideon H.	Sept 29,	Oct. 1,	1828	Thomas Walker	J.E.Jackson	5b107		
Kownslar, Eliz. m. Burns, Wm. C.	Apr. 1,		1824	Edward C. Southwood		4b260		
Kownslar, Lydia Ann m. Nelson,Mann P	Sept 22,	Sept 27,	1832	Gideon Rupert	J.E.Jackson	5b241		mr 45 *
Kownslar, Margaret m. Bell, Jos. E.	Mar. 22,	Mar. 26,	1823	Conrad Kownslar	John Mathews	4b235		
Kownslar, Randolph m.McCleary, Mary	Jan. 5,		1836	John Harrison Jr.	John Harrison Jr.	6b 68		
Kragels, Cath. m. Bear, Joseph		Feb. 25,	1815		Rev. Reebenack			
Kraunk, Mary m. Sowers, Henry		Mar. 20,	1787		Hugh Vance		go 15	mr 44 *
Kreglow, Adam m. Strayer, Mary	Feb. 10,		1838	Addison McKee		6b131		
Kreglow, Eliz. m. Tabler, Wm. W.	Oct. 23,		1839	George Kreglow		6b181		
Kreglow, Fred. m. Westenhaver, Sophia	May 17,	May 19,	1847	John Guinn	John Winter	7b 95		mr 78 *
Kreglow, Mary m. Jones, John D.	Dec. 14,	Dec. 15,	1840	George Kreglow	Samuel Smith	6b227		mr 71 *
Kressen, Cornelius m.Philips, Hannah	Mar. 12,	Mar. 24,	1800	Isaac Kressen	John Hedtt(Hett)	2b 58	cr 33	mr 18 *
Kressen, Elis. m. Ray, Hazel	Oct. 21,		1834	John Hedges		6b 21		
Kressen, Isaac m. Bowman,Jean Mrs.	July 23,		1804	Charles Orrick		2b238		
Kressen, Isaac m. Wilson, Sarah	May 10,	May 10,	1806	Charles Orrick	John Bond	3b 19	cr 28	mr 22 *
Kressen, Richard m.Welsh(Wolick),Eliz.	Nov. 9,	Nov. 9,	1803	John Welsh	David Young	2b212	go 10	

Name	(marriage)	(suretor)	(minister)	(bond)		
Kroesen, Washington m.Foreman,Mary	Aug. 4, 1846	Robert Bryarly Jr	John Winter	7b 71		mr 76 *
Kroesen, Wm. m. Bellar, Lydia	Dec. 10, 1802		Moses Hoge		cr 17	mr 21 *
Kroh, Margaret m. Myers, Jacob	Apr. 17, 1820	Henry Kroh	Lewis Mayer	4b145		mr 40 *
Krone, Christmas m.Deafenbaugh, Adam	Mar. 29, 1796		David Young		gc 5	
Krout, Henry m. Hooper, Cath.	Nov. 15, 1827	Jacob Hooper	Benedict Reynolds	5b 84	gc 11	mr 52 *
Kruber, Christian m. Mansen, Eliz.	Feb. 16, 1810		Rev. Reebenack		gc 11	mr 77 *
Krum, John W. m.Sendindiver,Lydia	Mar. 8, 1847	Martin Sendindiver	Richard T. Brown	7b 90		
Kuhn, Eve m. Arp. John	Apr. 6, 1794		David Young		gc 3	*
Kully, Eliz. m. Burke, Wm.	Feb. 16, 1811	John Hully	Rev. Reebenack	3b175	gc 12	*
Kuntz, Sarah m. Summer, Abraham	Nov. 1, 1791		David Young		gc 1	*
Kupler, Benj. m. Pitzer, Susan	Dec. 7, 1799	John Pitzer	David Young	2b 38	gc 9	*
Kyer, Elis. m. Spong, David	July 20, 1811	Patrick Duffy	Rev. Reebenack	3b191	gc 12	*
Kyer, John m. Thompson, Mary	July 27, 1810	Penny Thompson		3b155		
Kvori, Maria m. Gotshall, John	Jan. 6, 1799		David Young		gc 8	*
Kyle, John m. Brewer(Brown), Mary	Jan. 21, 1803	John Kyle	David Young	2b191	gc 10	*
Kyle, Joseph m. Dunham, Rachel	Apr. 26, 1796	John Podsal	David Young		cr 36	*
Kyle, Mary m. Buckel, Wm.	Feb. 5, 1788?		Moses Hoge			
Kyle, Mary m. Smock, Wm.	Nov. 11, 1809		Moses Hoge			
Kyle, Mathew m. Podsal, Elis.	Nov. 7, 1807	John Podsal	Rev. Reebenack	3b123	gc 10	
Kyne, Mathias m. Myers, Marg't Ann	July 3, 1843	Jacob Myers	Lewis F. Wilson	3b 76		mr 74 *
Kyser, David m. Smart, Elisa	Aug. 21, 1833	Zachariah Smart	Nathan Young	6b301		mr 66 *
Kyser, Elis. m. Spong, David	July 20, 1811	Patrick Duffy	Rev. Reebenack	5b280	gc 12	
Kyser, John m. Cashman, Eliz.	Oct. 28, 1816	Christian Cashman		3b191		
Kyser, John M. m. Lambert, Cath.	June 1, 1797		David Young	4b 19	gc 6	
Kyser, John m. Smart, Amelia	Apr. 29, 1825	Daniel Smart		5b 9		
Kyser, Joseph m. Davis, Elis.	Feb. 8, 1827	Thomas Davis	Nathan Young	5b 61		mr 99 *
Kyser, Susan m. Barns, Henry	Dec. 27, 1827	Daniel Kyser	Nathan Young	5b 86		mr 99 *
*Kyser, Agnes m. Mayer, George	Nov. 14, 1793		David Young		gc 3	*
*Kyser, Maria m. Gotshall, John	Jan. 6, 1799		David Young		gc 8	*

"L"

Name	(marriage)	(suretor)	(minister)	(bond)		
Lackey, Hugh m. Campbell, Eleanor	Mar. 30, 1802	Benson Lackey	Nathan Young	2b167		mr 57 *
Ladley, George m. Dunham, Hannah	Oct. 24, 1820	David Dunham	Richard Swift	4b165		mr 40 *
Lafferty, Esther m. Taylor, Lewis(Wm)	Jan. 7, 1794		Moses Hoge		cr 29	mr 19 *
Lafferty, John m. Osborne, Sarah	Sept. 6, 1800	David Osborne	Moses Hoge	2b 86		
Laign, John m. Thompson, Polly	Aug. 9, 1800	Peter Williamson		2b 80		
Laign, Wm. m. Dyser, Jenny	Jan. 30, 1808	Asel Fletcher		3b 83		
*Laman, Richard m. Caskey, Mary E.	Apr. 30, 1849	Wm. Caskey	W. Love	7b152		mr 80 *
Lamar, Wm. L. m. Hong, Margaret	Apr. 8, 1842	Harrison Waite	Peyton Harrison	6b266		mr 73 *
Lamar, Mary Jane m. Hensell, Joseph	Dec. 23, 1843	William Lamar	T.H.W.Monroe	6b310		mr 75 *
*Lake, Cath. m. Chenoweth, Arthur	Jan. 12, 1807	Jacob Weaver	David Young	3b 42	gc 8	

Name	(marriage)	(surety)	(minister)	(bond)			
Lambert, Cath. m. Kyser, John	June 1, 1797	George Lamon	David Young	7b233	go 6	mr 87	*
Lamon, Ann W. m. Morgan, Wm.	Sept 18, 1851	Jacob Ward	Lewis F. Wilson	4b264		mr 49	*
Lamon, George m. Ward, Eliz.	May 2, 1824	John Lamon	John Winter	5b242			
Lamon, Rebecca m. Cromwell, Edward	Oct. 8, 1832	Richard Brown		5b184			
Lamon Jane H. m. Austin, Andrew	Jan. 4, 1831		Nathan Young		cr 31	mr 61	*
Landbright, Jacob m. Frye, Barbara	June 1, 1801	Christian Ebberts	Richard Swift	3b219	go 12	mr 19	*
Landerkin, James m. Ebberts, Phebe	Apr. 10, 1812	Jacob VanDoren	Rev. Reebenack	7b150	cr 17	mr 79	*
Landerkin, Mary m. Stipes, Benj.	Mar. 29, 1849		John Winter			mr 20	*
Landis, John m. Banks, Rhuanna	Sept 3, 1801		Moses Hoge				
Landis, Andrew m. Kerdin, Eliz.	Sept 27, 1853		D.Francis Spriggs				
Lane, Barkley m. Good, Margaret	May 14, 1797	Peter Shaffer	David Young	1b 16	ge 6	mr 36	*
Lane, Cath. m.Brown.Benj.(Benont)	Dec. 10, 1793		David Young		go 3		
Lane, Lewis m. Pennybaker, Sarah	Nov. 18, 1788						
Lane, Martin m. Vance, Rebecca	Sept 16, 1820	William Orr	Hugh Vance	4b161			
Lane, Samuel m. Johnston, Amy	Aug. 12, 1823	Joel Rees		4b245			
Lang, James m. Linthecum, Sarah	Dec. 26, 1792						
Larew, Isaac m. Brook, Elinor	May 29, 1793		Richard Swift	5b238	cr 30	mr 38	*
Largent, Richard m. Callatin, Cath.	June 14, 1796	Stephen Snodgrass	William Hill	4b101	ge 5	mr 9	*
Larimore, Robert m. Evans, Elis. B.	Aug. 23, 1832	Jonathan Roberts	David Young	2b126			
Larin, Hiram m. Grimes, Eliz.	Mar. 6, 1819	Jacob Rees					
Larken, Joseph m. Rees, Rachel	May 20, 1801						
Lashells, John m. Clarke, Esther	Dec. 6, 1797	Richard Ranson	John Hill	1b 70	cr 37	mr 14	*
Lashorn, Cath. m. Horn, John	Mar. 1, 1810	John Lashorn	Rev. Reebenack	3b138	ge 11		
Lashorn, Elis. m. Peisal, Sebastion	Mar. 4, 1816	John Lashorn	Rev. Reebenack	4b 11	ge 15		
Lashorn, Harriet m. Walters, Wm.	Nov. 25, 1841	Jos. M. Higgins	Stephen Roxmell	6b255		mr 73	*
Lashorn, James m. Fisher, Eliz.	Jan. 15, 1828	Joseph Grubb	B. Reynolds	5b 88		mr 52	*
Lashorn, James m. Kearns, Eliz.	Sept 27, 1850	Jacob VanDoren		7b197			*
Lashorn, Jas. H. m. Sampson, Mary I.	Jan. 3, 1854						*
Lashorn, Margaret m. Kees, John	Dec. 21, 1816	John Lashorn	G.W.Cooper	4b 27			
Lashorn, Ralph m. Page, Elis.	June 10, 1830	Adam Schoppert	W.N.Scott	5b167		mr 63	*
Lashorn, Rebecca m. Gaitrell, Chas.	July 27, 1833	Ralph Lashorn	Jacob Medtart	5b278		mr 66	*
Laufen, Fred. m. Hall, Mariah	Mar. 3, 1795		Nathan Young				
Laughlin, James m. Foster(Fau-)Nancy	July 31, 1799	Charles Black	David Young	2b 12	go 4	mr 17	*
Law, Ann m. Waters, Wm.	Aug. 13, 1794		John Boyd		cr 34		
Lawson, Mary m. Butt, Wm.	Nov. 25, 1853		David Young		go 4		
Lawson, Nancy m. Clawson, Asariah	Feb. 27, 1801		G.W.Cooper				
Lawyer, Mary m. Ward, Joseph	Aug. 19, 1801	Stephen Ward	Hugh Vance	2b137	cr 31	mr 37	*
Lawyer, Mary m. Leeard, Joseph	July 20, 1823						
Lay, Lydia m. Taylor, Samuel	Aug. 23, 1826	Resen Hudgel	Richard Swift	4b246		mr 19	*
Lay, Prudence m. Fanglinder, George	July 26, 1853	Samuel Taylor		5b 44			
Laymaster, Jacob m. Strode, Mary E.	May 31, 1853						
Leach, Harriet m. Gooden, John	Sept 2, 1817	Walter Leach	John Light	4b 45		mr 88	*
Leamon, David m. Brook, Nancy	Jan. 13, 1809	Barney Borock	W.N.Scott	7b106			

Name	(marriage)	(surator)	(minister)	(bond)		
Lackman, Jas. P. m. Gander, Nancy	Feb. 22, 1837	John Waite		6b 98		mr 33 *
Leary, Johanna m. Beard, Justice	Feb. 19, 1785		Hugh Vance			mr 87 *
Leathers, Martha m. Butler, Geo. H.	June 20, 1853		Geo. W. Cooper			mr 86 *
Leathers, Sarah F. m. Keef, John Wm.	Mar. 29, 1852	Wm. Leathers	David Thomas	7b250		mr 52 *
Leathers, Wm. m. Hess, Elis.	Mar. 17, 1828	Daniel Brunner	B. Reynolds	9b 93		*
Lecklar, Michael m. Belgraff,Henrietta	Mar. 22, 1849	Michael Creamer		7b144		
Lecker, John m. Rife, Magdalina	Jan. 11, 1791		David Young		gc 1	
Leckner, Peggy m. Shepherd, Mathew	Aug. 26, 1812	John Leckner	Rev. Reebemack	3b234	gc 13	
Leckner, Susan m. Miller, Jacob	Sept 30, 1816	John Mulhall	John B. Hoge	4b 10		
Lectron, Michael m. Redgrave,Henrietta	Jan. 22, 1849		B.M.Schmecker			
Ledge, Elis. m. Wycoff, Cornelius	Dec. 8, 1799	Jacob Krossen	John Bedt(Butt)	2b39	or 33	mr 79 *
Ledge, Henry m. Chidester, Charlott	Feb. 16, 1802	Wm. Lowry		2b160		mr 17 *
Ledman, Henry m. Bedinger, Peter	Apr. 19, 1785		Hugh Vance			mr 33 *
Ledman, Nancy m. Kennedy, John	Nov. 28, 1797	William Gordon		1b 65		mr 65 *
Ledman, Peggy m. Stookey, Sarah	Oct. 15, 1832	Jacob Stookey	W. Monroe	9b243		mr 51 *
Lee, Alfred m. McClure, Isabella	Mar. 20, 1827	James McClure	John Mathews	9b 64		
Lee, Eleanor m. Boak, Robert	Dec. 4, 1799	Alex. Miller		2b 37		mr 78 *
Lee, Elisa m. Coffenberger, Jacob	Mar. 14, 1848 ?	Wm. Coffenberger	Chas P. Krauth	7b126		mr 61 *
Lee, Elis. m. McDonald, John	Mar. 14, 1831	Anthony Lee Jr.	Nathan Young	9b187		mr 49 *
Lee, Elis. m. Walters, Jonathan E.	Apr. 22, 1826	Jeremiah Lee	B. Reynolds	9b 40		mr 76 *
Lee, Hannah m. Weddle, George	Apr. 16, 1846	Jacob Coffenberg	John Winter	7b 64		
Lee, James m. Morlatt, Elis.	Mar. 13, 1813	Joseph Morlatt	Rev. Reebemack	3b295		mr 60 *
Lee, James m. Myers, Nancy	Dec. 21, 1829		Nathan Young		gc 13	
Lee, Jane m. Bell, Hugh	Dec. 30, 1794		David Young		gc 4	
Lee, Jane m. Karns, Philip	Aug. 13, 1849	Jesse Lee	Nathan Young	7b163		mr 58 *
Lee, Jesse m. Neal, Polly	Oct. 14, 1822	Aaron Chaffin	Nathan Young	4b225		mr 65 *
Lee, John m. Kearn(Kear), Margaret	Aug. 13, 1832	John Kearn	Nathan Young	9b237		mr 61 *
Lee, Leah m. Throckmorten, Job	May 18, 1831	John Lee	Lewis F. Wilson	9b194		mr 83 *
Lee, Mary Ann m. Bodine(Bowd-),Rich'd	Dec. 17, 1849	Conrad K. Robbins	Mathias Riser	7b170		mr 29 *
Lee, Sarah Ann m. Hamilton,Francis	Feb. 28, 1818	Joseph Adams	D. Thomas	4b 64		mr 37 *
Lee, Thomas m. Cudd, Hannah	? 1789					
Lee, Thomas m. Dunn, Deborah	Nov. 4, 1801	Cyrus Farr	Mathias Riser	2b146		
Lee, Wm. m. Hamilton, Mary	July 3, 1817		Richard Swift		or 31	
Leonard, Joseph m. Leyrer, Mary	July 20, 1801		Hugh Vance		or 24	
Leeper, Eliz. m.Brindenhall,Anthony	Jan. 25, 1788		Lewis F. Wilson			mr 19 *
Lefevre, Ann Elisa m. Dodd, David	Jan. 31, 1852	John M. Speck	Lewis F. Wilson	7b243		mr 2 *
Lefevre, Daniel m. Folk, Elis.	Feb. 23, 1835	Henry Small		6b 32		mr 87 *
Lefevre, Daniel m. Speck, Margaret	Nov. 20, 1844	John M. Speck	Lewis F. Wilson	7b 14		
Lefevre, Elis. m. Solster, John	Jan. 15, 1822	Henry Lefevre	John B. Hoge	4b204		mr 44 *
Lefevre, Henry m. Dugan, Cath. Ann	Nov. 12, 1847	Thomas Dugan		7b112		
Lefevre, Jacob m. Spero, Maria	Aug. 27, Aug. 30, 1827	George Spero	Jas. M. Brown	9b 76		mr 51 *
Lefevre, John m. Hill, Nancy	Dec. 6, 1819	George Hill		4b125		
Lefevre, Nancy m. Cox, Horace	Oct. 16,Oct. 18, 1838	Daniel Lefevre	James F. Wilson	6b147		mr 69 *

Name	Date	(marriage)	(surety)	(minister)	(bond)		mr
Lefevre, Sarah m. Downs, Hamilton	Oct. 30,	Nov. 2, 1847	Jacob Lefevre	John Light	7b138		mr 79 *
Legg, Mary A. m. Snyder, Samuel R.	Sept 24,	Sept 24, 1850	Jacob VanDoren	Henry Furlong	7b197		mr 81 *
Leglar, Martin m. Stover, Frances	May 3,	May 5, 1803	Robert Filson	Richard Swift	2b201	cr 27	mr 21 *
Lehman, Charlotte m. Perry, John	Jan. 12,	Jan. 12, 1809	Peter Snowdeal	Rev. Reebemack	3b106	gc 10	
Leiby, Jonathan m. Seith, Cath.	Mar. 4,	Mar. 4, 1818	Jacob Wagner		4b 65		
Leidy, Valentine m. Thornberg, Susan	Nov. 28,	Apr. 7, 1789		Hugh Vance		cr 20	mr 3 *
Leigh, Benj.W. m. Colston, Susan	Nov. 30,	Nov. 30, 1813	Phil. C.Pendleton	Alex. Belmain	3b278	cr 41	mr 25 *
Leighner, Eliz. m. Craiglow, Peter	Sept 28,	Sept 29, 1818	William Pitzer	W.N.Scott	4b 80		
Leighner, Mary m. Pitzer, Samuel	June 15,	June 15, 1817	Jacob Miller	W.N.Scott	4b 38		
Leighner, Nancy m. Pitzer, Wm.	Apr. 26,	Apr. 29, 1817	Elijah Wilson	W.N.Scott	4b 33		
Leighmer, Philip m. Wolff, Sarah Ann	Mar. 22,	Apr. 26, 1834	James Criswell	Jas. M. Brown	6b 1		
Leikins, Eliz. M. m. Mathews, Chas.	Mar. 25,	Mar. 27, 1840	Harrison Waite	Lewis F. Wilson	6b202		mr 67 *
Leman, Ann Ward m. Morgan, Wm.	Sept 18,	Sept 18, 1851	George Lemon	Lewis F. Wilson	7b233		mr 71 *
Leman, Mary Ann m. Kerney, Wm. F.	Sept 16,	Sept 17, 1850	Hiram Leman	C.W.Andrews	7b196		mr 84 *
Lemar, Charles m. Breast, Kath.	Feb. 25,	Jan. 25, 1785	W. Snider	Hugh Vance	4b 63		mr 80 *
Lemaster, Dardel m. Snider, Mary	Feb. 29,	Feb. 25, 1818	Wm. H C.Crowl		7b245		mr 33 *
Lemaster, David m. Crowl, Ellen		Feb. 29, 1852	Samuel Taylor	John Bauman	7b194		
Lemaster, James m. Taylor, Susan M.	Sept 3,	Sept 5, 1850	Joshua Tabler	John Light	6b233		mr 80 *
Lemaster, John m. Tabler, Rhoanna	Feb. 15,	Feb. 16, 1841	John H. Wilson	John Light	6b180		mr 72 *
Lemaster, Margaret m. Nichols,Henry	Oct. 21,	Oct. 22, 1839	David Lemaster		7b203		mr 70 *
Lemaster, Sarah m. Grantham, David	Nov. 18,	Nov. 18, 1850	Jacob Ward	Richard Swift	4b264		
Lemen, Alex. m. Morgan, Mary		Aug. 24, 1793	Wm. M. Lemen	John Winter	5b257		mr 39 *
Lemen, Geo. Jr. m. Ward, Eliz.	May 1,	May 2, 1824	Alex. Lemen	Wm. Hawk	1b 54	cr 12	mr 49 *
Lemen, James m. Lemen, Sarah Elinor	Feb. 19,	Feb. 21, 1833	James Lemen	Richard Swift	6b158		mr 65 *
Lemen, Jane m. Reynolds, John	Oct. 15,	Nov. 8, 1797	John Mulhall		2b 19		mr 14 *
Lemen, Mary m. Jones, Adrian	Feb. 4,	1839	Wm. M. Lemen		5b257		
Lemen, Rachel m. Garner, Samuel	Aug. 10,	Aug. 10, 1799	Arch'd Shearer		5b240		
Lemen, Sarah m. Lemen, James	Feb. 19,	Feb. 19, 1833	Solomon Hedges	Wm. Hawk	4b169		mr 65 *
Lemen, Thomas m. Amoss, Barbara	Sept 11,	Sept 11, 1832	James Lemin		3b146		
Lemin, Wm. m. Hedges, Phebe	Dec. 18,	Dec. 18, 1820		John B. Hoge			mr 41 *
Lemin, Wm. M. m. Wyncoop, Hannah	Apr. 14,	Apr. 14, 1810	George Lemon				
Lemins, Ruth m. Kerr, John	Dec. 28,	Dec. 28, 1791	Peter Snowdeal	Moses Hoge	3b117	cr 8	mr 7 *
Lemmon, George m. McDonald, Mary	Nov. 17,	Nov. 17, 1785	Wm. Engle	Hugh Vance	3b106		mr 34 *
Lemmon, Robert m. McKewan, Mary	Jan. 31,	Jan. 31, 1788	James Shane	Hugh Vance	3b142	cr 24	mr 2 *
Lemon, Aurra m. Maslin, Joseph	Sept 4,	Sept 4, 1809	George Lemon	Rev. Reebemack	6b 13	gc 10	
Lemon, Charlotte m. Perry, John	Jan. 12,	Jan. 12, 1809	Michael Umberbaugh	W. Monroe	4b199		
Lemon, Christiana m. Kercheval,James	Mar. 17,	Mar. 17, 1810	George Lemon		5b153		
Lemon, Edwin M. m. Shane, Marg't Ann	June 6,	June 6, 1834	John V. Lemon		3b 92		
Lemon, Eleanor m. Bowers, George	Dec. 4,	Dec. 4, 1821	Robert Grimes	Chas. P. Krauth	4b236		mr 54 *
Lemon, Elis. m. Brown, Richard	Feb. 19,	Feb. 21, 1830	John Lemaster		4b192		
Lemon, Esther G. m. Brown, Joseph	July 25,	1808			6b133		mr 46 *
Lemon, Harriet m. Stedman(Strod)Lowry	Mar. 29,	Mar. 1823					
Lemon, Jacob M. m. Burkett,Martha Mr	Sept 26,	1821					
*Lemaster, Eliz. m. Myers, David	Feb. 26,	1838					

Name	(marriage)		(suretor)	(minister)	(bond)		
Lemon, Jane m. Austin, Andrew	Jan. 4,	1831	Alex. Lemon	Nathan Young	5b184		mr 61 *
Lemon, Jane m. Reynolds, John	Oct. 15, Nov. 8,	1797	James Chenoweth	Richard Swift	1b 54	cr 12	mr 14 *
Lemon, John m. Chenoweth, Ruth	Jan. 3,	1811	Wm. H. Lemon		3b172		
Lemon, Marg't M. m. Falk, Jacob	Jan. 20,	1841	Fred. Imhoff		6b230		
Lemon, Mary m. Engle, Wm.	Oct. 29,	1798			1b142		
Lemon, Mary m. Kehle, ?		1798					
Lemon, Mary A. m. Kerney, Wm. F.	Sept 16,	1850	Hiram Lemon	Moses Hoge	7b196	cr 29	mr 14 *
Lemon, Eliz. Mrs. m. Brown, Richard	Feb. 19,	1830	Michael Umberhaur	C.W. Andrews	5b153		mr 80 *
Lemon, Nancy m. Hughes, Thomas	June 10,	1801	Fred. Imhoff	W. Monroe	2b128		mr 54 *
Lemon, Rhuana m. Sybert, Jacob F.	Nov. 17,	1813	George Holiday		3b275		
Lemon, Robert m. Light, Sarah E.	Nov. 11,	1839	Samuel N. Light		6b183		
Lemon, Sally m. Burnes, John	Jan. 6,	1801	Robert Lemon		2b107		
Lemon, Sarah Elinor m. Lemon, James	Feb. 19,	1833	Wm. M. Lemon	Wm. Hawk	5b257		mr 65
Lemon, Thomas m. Butterfield, Mary	Jan. 11,	1804	Thos. Butterfield	Moses Hoge	2b220	ur 17	mr 21 *
Lemon, Wm. m. Hedges, Phebe	Dec. 18,	1820	Solomon Hedges	John B. Hoge	4b169		mr 41 *
Lemon, Wm. m. Maslin, Margaret		1781		Daniel Sturges			mr 31 *
Lemon, W.L. m. Mong, Marg't	Mar. 8,	1842	Harrison Waite	Peyton Harrison	6b266		mr 73 *
Lenhart, Mich'l m. Butler(Buckles)Lucy	May 19,	1799	John G. Fleek	David Young	2b 5	gc 8	mr 34 *
Lenmor, Eliz. m. Willet, James	Nov. 21,	1785?		Hugh Vance			mr 36 *
Lenox, James m. Williams, Marg't	July 29,	1788		Moses Hoge			
Lenox, John m. Fuller, Frances	June 7,	1797	Jonathan Gerrard		1b 20		
Lenox, Nathan m. Bringham, Marg't	Nov. 15,	1792		Moses Hoge			mr 39 *
Leonard, Eliz. m. Coomer, Peter	May 1,	1792		David Young	1b 56	gc 1	
Leonard, Nichols m. Hodle, Sarah		1844	John Hodle		7b 11		
Leonard, Sarah m. Stephens, Benj.	Oct. 21,	1796	John Gallaher				
Leonard, Abr'm m. Seiser, Maria	Oct. 30,	1814		David Young	3b289	gc 5	
Leopard, Daniel m. Miller, Eliz.	Mar. 21,	1852	Wm. Miller	Rev. Reebenack		gc 14	
Leopard, G.W. m. Elliott, Mary C.		1834	Adam Leopard	John Light	5b301		mr 88 *
Leopard, Hannah m. Flemming, Kis	Jan. 25,	1839	Jos. R. Criswell	John Light	6b169		mr 67 *
Leopard, Marg't m. Dugan, Philip H.	May 13,	1837	Michael Leopard		6b 96		
Leopard, Marg't m. Lowman, Daniel	Feb. 14,	1789					
Leopard, Mary m. Miller, Jacob	Feb. 16,	1844	John Zorn	Lewis F. Wilson	6b317	cr 15	mr 4 *
Leopard, Mary m. Points, John H.	June 11,	1798	Jacob Hawke	Christian Streit	1b107		
Leopard, Michael m. Hawke, Marg't	Apr. 23,	1833	Adam Leopard	Lewis F. Wilson	5b294	gc 7	
Leopard, Nancy m. Dugan, Geo. H.	Apr. 9,	1806	Jacob French	David Young	3b 26		mr 67 *
Lophart, Michael m. French, Barbara	Dec. 9,			Jas. M. Brown			
Lorew, Isaac m. Brooks, Elinor	Aug. 16,	1793		William Bill		cr 30	mr 9 *
Lotham, John m. Saveley, Cath.	May 29,	1795		David Young		gc 4	
Lott, Anthony m. Blois, Mary	Jan. 13,	1785		Edward Tiffin		gc 37	mr 1 *
Lotel, Henry m. Thompson, Eliz.	Jan. 15,	1795		David Young		gc 5	
Lotham, Peter m. Anderson, Isabel	Sept 19,	1811	Wm. Anderson		3b192		
Lotton, Wm. m. Milbatton, Kis.	July 29,			David Young		gc 2	mr 8 *
Lovick, Caleb m. Taylor, Rachel	Dec. 26,	1792		Christian Streit		cr 15	mr 39 *
*Lemon, Nathan m. Bingham, Ann	Jan. 13,	1793		Moses Hoge			
	Nov. 15,	1792					

Name (marriage)	Date	(marriage)	(suretor)	(minister)	(bond)	
Levy, John J. m. McIntire, Mary't	June 26,	1834	John McIntire		6b 14	
Levy, Sarah Ann m. Hayden, Wm. H.	Apr. 24,	1833	Abraham Levy		5b270	
Levy, Virginia R. m. Kerns, John J.	Mar. 31,	1853		Jas. H. Jennings		mr 86 *
Lewis, Ann m. Davidson, Rees	Sept 5,	1797			1b 39	
Lewis, Ann Rebecca m. Crim, Peter	Mar. 31,	1849	Thomas Lewis		7b151	
Lewis, Cath. m. Cole, Wm.	Oct. 6,	1837	Jacob Custer		6b114	
Lewis, Cath. m. Custer, Jacob	Dec. 9,	1833	Joseph Lewis		5b293	mr 65 *
Lewis, David m. Harden, Elis.	Mar. 28,	1833	Lewis Lewis		5b265	mr 66 *
Lewis, David m. Snider, Elis.	Apr. 10,	1802	John Harden	William Hawk	2b170	
Lewis, Elis. m. Buzzard, George	July 31,	1830	John Grantham	Nathan Young	5b170	mr 66 *
Lewis, Elis. m. Sendindiver, Elisha	Jan. 10,	1833	William Lewis		5b253	
Lewis, Fielding m. Bower, Elis.	Apr. 20,	1802	Lewis Lewis	Nathan Young	2b171	
Lewis, Franklin m. Anderson, Mary	Oct. 31,	1838	Thomas Stilwell		6b149	mr 69 *
Lewis, John m. Cooper, Merry	Dec. 27,	1803	Wm. Anderson	James Watts	2b218	
Lewis, Joseph m. Fitzsimmons, Eve	Dec. 18,	1792	Jonathan Gerrard			go 2
Lewis, Lewis m. Hays, Phoebe R.	Dec. 22,	1853		David Young		**
Lewis, Lewis m. Sackman, Polly	Aug. 17,	1812	Charles Keel	D.Francis Spriggs	3b232	
Lewis, Mary m. Bunn, Peter		1789				
Lewis, Mary m. Glvan(Gwinn), James	Apr. 1,	1835	William Lewis	D. Thomas	6b 39	mr 37 *
Lewis, Mary m. Ridgeway, Jonas J.	Nov. 25,	1843		John Light	7b 79	mr 67 *
Lewis, Matilda m. Custer, Peter	Dec. 8,	1846	Lewis Lewis	D.Francis Spriggs	6b116	mr 86 *
Lewis, Nancy m. Ripples, John	Jan. 9,	1838	Joseph Lewis			
Lewis, Nicholas m. Sanderson, Elenor	Oct. 25,	1797	Thos. Armstrong	David Young	1b 58	gc 7 *
Lewis, Polly m. Baldwin, Hiram	Aug. 31,	1801	David Lewis		2b141	
Lewis, Polly m. Sumpsion, Joseph	May 22,	1810		Rev. Reebenack		gc 11 *
Lewis, Priscilla m. McDonald, Robert	Aug. 22,	1808	David Lewis		3b 95	
Lewis, Sally m. Sumpsion(tion), Jos.	Mar. 19,	1810	Jacob Sumpsion		3b143	
Lewis, Samuel m. McFeeley, Mary Ann	Mar. 5,	1838	Elijah Sendindiver		6b136	
Lewis, Susan m. Nichodemus, John	Nov. 20,	1832	William Lewis		5b247	
Lewis, Thomas m. Blue, Susannah	May 27,	1790		Moses Hoge		cr 4 *
Lewis, Thomas m. Morgan, Mary	Nov.	1789		D. Thomas		mr 5 *
Lewis, Walter m. Mayhew, Harriet A.	Aug. 26,	1852		David Thomas		mr 37 *
Lewis, William m. Williams, Ann	Mar. 16,	1790		Moses Hoge		mr 86 *
Lida, James m. Stotlmeyer, Mary A.	Dec. 23,	1817		Mathias Riser		mr 5 *
Light, Samuel m. McKeever, Sarah	Oct. 30,	1798	Robert Hastings	David Young	1b143	
Light, Ann m. Thornberry, Will	Feb. 6,	1800	Wm. Orrick	David Young	2b 51	cr 3 *
Light, B. B. m. Weddle, Cath.	Jan. 18,	1848	George Weddle		7b119	gc 8 *
Light, Cath. Ann m. Ward, James T.	May 19,	1845	Jacob F. Light		7b 35	gc 9 *
Light, David, m. Soper, Elis.	Mar. 11,	1815	Wm. Beatty		3b314	
Light, Elinor m. Wilson, Robert	May 29,	1815	Peter Light Jr.	John Light	3b326	mr 76 *
Light, Elisa V. m. Gher, Joseph		1853				
Light, Elis. m. Hedges, William	Feb. 4,	1822	John Light	John Light	4b207	mr 86 *
Light, Elis. m. Lumon, William	Jan. 14,	1801	Winn Winship	John B. Hoge	2b110	mr 44 *

Name	(marriage)		(surety)	(minister)	(bond)		
Light, Eliz. M. m. Shepherd, Geo.A.	June 24,	1850	Jacob F. Light	R.N.Herndon	7b189		mr 69 *
Light, Fred. m. Clark, Nancy	Nov. 11,	1836	Solomon Clark	D.Francis Spriggs	6b 87		mr 86 *
Light, Fred. m. Seckman, Mary Ann	Feb. 10,	1853		A.G.Chenoweth			mr 87 *
Light, Hamilton m. Gwilliams, Eliza	Feb. 17,	1852					
Light, Hannah m. Hanshew, Thomas	Nov. 22	1824	John Handshew		4b278		nr 84 *
Light, Jacob m. Polsal, Charlotte E	Sept 11,	1851	Jacob Polsal	David Thomas	7b231		nr 23 *
Light, Jacob m. Porterf'd,Sarah,Sally	Mar. 20,	1809	Arch'd Shearer	John Mathews	3b110	cr 17	
Light, Jacob m. Soper, Ruth	Nov. 18,	1817	Thomas Soper		4b 50		
Light, John m. Gano, Margaret	Dec. 1,	1838	Oliver Armbrester		6b 91		
Light, John m. Strode, Nancy	May 15,	1786		Hugh Vance			nr 43 *
Light, John S. m. Burns, Nancy	June 3,	1824	Wm. Geo. Burns	J.L.Bromwell	4b266		nr 47 *
Light, Joseph m. Payne, Ann Jane	Jan. 30,	1839	Thomas Payne	Lewis F. Wilson	6b158		nr 70 *
Light, Mary A. m. Cunningham, Samuel	Dec. 1,	1843	Jas. Cunningham	John Light	6b309		mr 74 *
Light, Peggy m. Bane, Abr'm S.	Mar. 14,	1812	John Light	Lewis Mayer	3b217	cr 15	nr 25 *
Light, Peter m. Rooney, Milly	Oct. 16,	1819	James Saunders		4b119		
Light, Polly m. Smith, John H.	Jan. 10,	1825	Peter Light	Chas. P. Krauth	4b284		nr 48 *
Light, Rebecca m. Smith, John H.	Jan. 10,	1825	Peter Light	Chas.P. Krauth	4b284		nr 48 *
Light, Samuel m. Chew, Amy	Apr. 21,	1838	Addison McKee	James Watts	6b118		nr 69 *
Light, Samuel H. m. Tabb, Ann W.	Feb. 14,	1842	Wm. Cunningham	Lewis F. Wilson	6b264		nr 73 *
Light, Sarah E. m. Lemon, Robert	Nov. 11,	1839	Samuel H. Light		3b183		
Light, Susan m. Cooke, Thomas	Jan. 6,	1834	John S. Light		3b299		
Light, Wm. m. Clark, Mary	Aug. 30,	1838	Solomon Clarke	James Watts	6b 91		nr 69 *
Lighter, Mathias m. McCormick, Elis.	Aug. 30,	1803	Corn's McCormick		2b213		
Likam, Ann m. Ridgeway, Josiah	Apr. 13,	1789	Johas Likam		1b x		
Likens, Cath. m. Butler, James W.	Jan. 27,	1848	Joseph Likens	P. Lipscomb	7b120		mr 81 *
Likens, Elis. m. Mathews, Chas. H.	Mar. 27,	1840	Harrison Waite	Lewis F. Wilson	6b202		mr 71 *
Likens, Harriet m. Hastings, John	July 14,	1839	Joseph Likens	James Reily	6b172		mr 70 *
Likens, Joseph m. Merehant, Sarah	Apr. 18,	1818	Bacon Burwell	Nathan Young	4b 69	cr 26	mr 56 *
Likens, Margaret m. Grimes, Wm.	Mar. 28,	1833	Christian Wolff	Richard Swift	5b264		mp 13 *
Likens, Wm. R. m. McCleary, Elis.	May 30,	1797	Thomas Mattock		1b 19		
Lilbourne, Frances m. Bull, Nathan	Aug. 19,	1797	Jarvis Jeffries		1b 32		
Lincle, Nancy m. Snyder, Conrad		1797					
Linch, Sarah m. Hamer, Richard	Apr. 5,	1798	John Lindsey	Richard Swift	3b253	cr 31	mr 15 *
Linden, Ann m. Morlatt, Abr'm	Aug. 2,	1785		Hugh Vance			mr 34 *
Lindsey, Anna m.Shupe(Shoop),Daniel	Feb. 24,	1813	David Rees	Rev. Reebenack	3b 3	ge 13	mr 21 *
Lindsey, John m. Hoover, Polly	Feb. 25,	1803	Christian Perfetter	Richard Swift	2b147	cr 27	
Lindsey, Mary m. Marchant, Nathan	Dec. 27,	1805					*
Lindsey, Sarah m. Fizs, Thomas	Nov. 18,	1801				ge 10	
Line, Cath. m. Myers, Lewis	Nov. 5,	1809					
Line, Daniel m. Rousch, Elis.	Apr. 28,	1814	Nicholas Roush Jr.	Rev. Reebenack	3b296	ge 14	
Line, Daniel m. Rousch, Elis.	Apr. 27,	1817?		Rev. Reebenack			*
Line, Elis. m. Stewart, Robert	Sept 10,	1829	William Faris	Jacob Mediart	5b140		mr 63 *
Line, Henry m. Snively, Mary	Sept 10,	1807	Jacob Snyder		3b 69		

Name	(marriage)	(surety)	(minister)	(bond)		
Lingenfelter, Abr'm m. Folk, Magdala	May 13, / May 14, 1799	Christ'r Folk	David Young	1b180	gc 8	*
Lingenfelter, Abr'm m. Folk, Polly	May 26, 1799					
Lingenfelter, Jacob m. Ropp, Cath.	May 28, 1829	Solomon Ropp	Jas. M. Brown	5b130		mr 53 *
Lingenfelter, John m. Hedges, Mary	Aug. 22, 1826	Josiah Hedges		5c 49		
Lingenfelter, Martha J. m. Folk,Jacob	Dec. 4, / Dec. 5, 1850	Walter Lingenfelt.	D.Francis Spriggs	7b204		mr 82 *
Lingenfelter, Mary m. Hufman,Mich'l	Apr. 10, 1802	Valentine "		2b171		
Lang'f't'r, Mary m. Riner, Peter	Dec. 5, / Dec. 7, 1817	Jonathan Gushwa	Lewis Mayer	4b 51		*
Lang'f't'r, Rosanna m.Duckwall,Henry	Oct. 27, 1807	John Riner		3b 75		
Lang'f't'r, Walter m.Nadenb'sh,Marg't	Mar. 18, / Mar. 28, 1851	M.C.Nadenbousch	Lewis F. Wilson	7b219		mr 87 *
Lang'f't'r, Walter m. Brophy, Mary	Apr. 5, 1854		D.Francis Spriggs			
Rankin, Wm. m. Williams, Polly	Oct. 11, / Oct. 15, 1799	George Verraka	John Hedtt(Butt)	2b 31	cr 33	*
Ram, Diana m. Vance, John	Oct. 20, 1793		Moses Hoge		cr 22	
Ranthecum, Sarah m. Lang, James	Dec. 26, 1792		Richard Swift			
Linton, Ann E. m. Myers, Henry W.	Sept 1, / Sept 7, 1843	Zachariah Linton	T.H.W. Monroe	6b304		mr 17 *
Linton, David m. Jenkins, Eliza	May 16, / May 23, 1850	George Jenkins	John Light	7b185		mr 8 *
Linton, Geo. W. m. Brady, Susan	Mar. 5, 1840	Adam Shober		6b199		mr 36 *
Linton, Henrietta m. Powell, Samuel	Sept 23, / Sept 24, 1850	Zachariah Linton	B.M.Schmucker	7b196		mr 75 *
Linton, James F. m. Walker, Marg't	Nov. 7, 1855	Jacob Potsal	F.C.Tabbs	7b201		mr 80 *
Linton, John M. m. Baobrast, Barbara	Feb. 15, 1855		John O. Procter			mr 84 *
Linvil, Elisha m. Moore, Sarah	Aug. 21, 1787		Hugh Vance			mr 83 *
Lippet, Michael m. Eack, Marg't	Apr. 9 1797	Jacob Hawk	David Young	1b107	cr 18	mr 1 *
Litten, Sener m. Sheets, Benjamin	Jan. 3, 1793		David Young		gc 7	*
Littenl, John m. Butt, Fanny	May 30, 1797	Edward Bessen		1b 15	gc 2	*
Little, Elis. m.Coffenberger, Geo.L.	Dec. 5, 1786		Hugh Vance			mr 43 *
Little, George m. Griffith, Ann	June 28, 1781		Daniel Sturges			mr 31 *
Little, James m. McConnell, Elis.	Feb. 9, 1810	William Tabb		3b136		mr 48 *
Little, John m. Quinn, Nancy	Nov. 29, 1825	Adam Sanaker	Jas. M. Brown	5b 28		mr 56 *
Little, Richard m. Wintermck,Carolin	Dec. 6, / Apr. 3, 1796		David Young		gc 5	
Littlejohn, Abr'm m. Shaffer, Sarah	Oct. 23, / Apr. 24, 1819	Edward Littlejohn	Nathan Young	4b121		
Littlejohn, Edward m. Colter, Betsy	Apr. 27, 1812	Corbin Colter		3b223		
Littlejohn, Joseph m. Clark, Mary	Oct. 7, 1809	John Clark		3b120		
Littlejohn, Mary Ann m. Davis, Joseph	June 14, / June 17, 1833	Francis R. Datton	Nathan Young	5b276		mr 66 *
Littlejohn, Sarah m. Dehaven, Job	Mar. 18, 1815	Edward Littlejohn		5b315		
Livingston, John m. Householder,Elis.	Oct. 30, / Nov. 4, 1832	Jon'm Householder	Nathan Young	5b245		mr 65 *
Livingston, Mary Ann m.Donacre, Jos.	Feb. 5, 1800	Geo. Livingston		2b 51		
Livingston, Susan m. McCartney, Jos.	Oct. 6, 1800	Henry Frank		2b 91		
Llake, Cath. m. Chenoweth, Arthur	Jan. 12, 1807	Jacob Weaver		3b 42		
Locke, Ann S. m. Orde, Hiram L. Jr.	Sept 17, 1835	Colin Peter		3b 57		
Locke, Cath. E. m.Snodgrass,Stephen	May 16, 1835	John Locke		6b 44		
Locke, J. m. Col. Boyd's negroes	Apr. 1814					*
Locke, Jacob L.m.Cummingham, Elinor	Oct. 13, 1845	Fran's Cummingham	Rev. Reebenack	7b 45		
Locke, Mary m. Harrison, John S.	Nov. 6, 1838	Harrison Waite		6b149		
Locke, Mervil m. Forrest, Sally D.	Sept 15, 1844	R.P. Bryarly	James Chisholm	7b 6		mr 75 *
*Little, George m. Rousch, Caroline	Jan. 31, 1797		David Young		gc 6	*

Name	(marriage)		(suretor)	(minister)	(bond)		
Locke, Meverell m. McCleary, Rosanna	Feb. 17,	1812	Robert Wilson		3b212		
Locke, Neal m. Merchant, Rachel	Aug. 7,	1809	Isaac Merchant		3b116		
Locke, Rose m. Davenport, Jacob Van	Jan. 8,	1845	Norman Miller	James Chisholm	7b 20		nr 76 *
Locke, Sarah Jane m.Dellinger, Fred.	June 23,	1852	Jacob VanDoren	D.Francis Spriggs	7b258		nr 85 *
Locke, Sophia m. Clise, John	Dec. 24,	1829		Nathan Young			nr 60 *
Locke, Thomas m. Hall, Cynthia	Dec. 27,	1809	Reuben Hall		3b131		
Lockery, Charles m. Crawford, Eliz.	Sept. 4,	1786					
Lockhart, Benj. m. Roberts, Marg't	Aug. 17,	1829	Jacob Ward	Hugh Vance	5b138		nr 43 *
Lockman, David m. Weaver, Jemimah	Dec. 9,	1829	Martin Houseman	Robert Cadden	5b146		nr 61 *
Lochman, David m. Pults, Nancy A.	Oct. 23,	1837	John Faris	Jacob Medtart	6b120		nr 63 *
Ledmew, Cath. m. Kestner, Henry	Nov. 9,	1792		J. Larken			
Loftus, Cath. m. Gary, Patrick W.	Dec. 26,	1839	Thomas Higgins	David Young	6b189	gc 2	
Loftus, Marg't m. Higgins, Thomas	Oct. 14,	1839	Michael Loftus		6b179		
Logan, Mary m. Long, Daniel	Aug. 15,	1850	Chas. Ridenour		7b193		
Lohr, Sarah Cath. m. Bradshaw,Harr'n	Feb. 17,	1847	Samuel Lohr	Henry Furlong	7b 86		nr 81 *
Lompa, Conrad m. Confar, Eliz.	Dec. 31,	1801	Jacob Wagoner		4b 28		
Lonass, John m. Davis, Mary	Nov. 3,	1817	*Dorothea Spahr	Nathan Young	2b146		nr 55 *
Lonekins, Tracy m. Vanaker, Geo.	June 8,	1794				gc 4	*
Long, Abr'm D. m. Hanna, Eliz.	May 22,	1817		David Young	4b108		nr 56 *
Long, Cath. m. Roberts, Robert	May 16,	1819	Martin Houseman	W.N.Scott	7b193		nr 81 *
Long, Daniel m. Logan, Mary	Aug. 15,	1850	Chas. Ridenour	Nathan Young			nr 32 *
Long, Elenor m. Colyer, William	Mar. 19,	1782	Wm. Cunningham	Henry Furlong			
Long, Eliz. m. Tabb, George	Oct. 7,	1835	William Long	Hugh Vance	6b 59		
Long, Elis. Mary m. Finley, Jas. W.	Oct. 14,	1830	John Hixon	Jas. M. Brown	5b177		nr 54 *
Long, Jane m. Johnston, John	Mar. 22,	1805	Wm. Long		2b257		
Long, Jane m. Stewart, John	June 12,	1806	John Strother		3b 23		
Long, Jane Mrs. m. Payne, Jesse	Apr. 12,	1824			4b261		
Long, Joanna m. Seckman(Sheoken)Dennis	Oct. 26,	1853	Jesse Wright				nr 88 *
Long, John m. Wright, Jane	June 26,	1817		A. Talty	4b 38		
Long, Lucinda m. Finley, Wm.Warner	May 8,	1833	William Long	W.N.Scott	5b273	cr 17	nr 22 *
Long, Nancy m. Cunningham, Wm.	Dec. 24,	1805	Charles Orrick	Moses Hoge	3b 6		nr 35 *
Long, Rebecca m. Seneker, Adam	Apr. 22,	1788		Moses Hoge			
Long, Robert m. Nicholas, Betsy	Feb. 24,	1806	Wm. Chenoweth		3b 12		
Long, Sarah m. Miller, Daniel	Oct. 2,	1797	John August	John Boyd	1b 53		nr 13 *
Long, Sarah A.C. m. Payne, Jos. E.	Apr. 10,	1837	Jesse Payne	John Allemong	6b105	cr 32	nr 69 *
Long, Susan m. Inbody, Lewis	Oct. 28,	1841	Wm. McDonald	John Hodges	6b250		nr 73 *
Long, Thomas m. Miller, Mary	Feb. 25,	1834	John Long		5b303		
Long, Wm. S. m. Bryan, Sarah R.	Nov. 14,	1840	John Strother		6b224		
Longbright, Eve m. Jones, George	Dec. 18,	1800?		Moses Hoge		cr 38	mr 20 *
Loran, Henry m. High, Esther	Aug. 22,	1815	Daniel High	Rev. Reebecnack	3b334	gc 15	
Lort, George m. Freshour, Susan	Aug. 15,	1792		David Young		gc 2	
Lot, Richard m. Gassaway, Hannah	Dec. 11,	1780		Daniel Sturges			no 31 *
Lott, Garrett V. m. Faulkner,Sally P	Oct. 4,	1853		A.H.Boyd			
Loudon, Sarah m. Clark, John	Aug. 7,	1794		Edward Tiffin		cr 25	mr 9 *

**Michael Byerly also was a suretor.

	(marriage)		(surety)	(minister)	(bond)		
London, Wm. m. Doyle, Eliz.	Oct. 2,	Oct. 12, 1797	John Clarke	Richard Swift	1b 51	cr 12	mr 14 *
Lountis, Samuel m. Cook, Peggy		Nov. 1, 1793		David Young		gc 3	*
?Lout, Betsy m. Strode, Edward		June 29, 1793		Moses Hoge		cr 22	mr 7 *
Love, John m. Cox, Ann		June 13, 1793		Edward Tiffin		cr 9	mr 8 *
Love, Mary m. Campbell, John	Mar. 18,	Mar. 18, 1797	Thos. Shepherd	Moses Hoge	1b 5	cr 36	mr 13 *
Love,Joy, John m. Kirby, Susannah E.	Mar. 13,	1797	Robert Boggess		1b 1		
Loveless, Sally m. Eversole, Henry	Aug. 15,	1821	Thomas Taffe		4b187		
?Lowe, Betsy m. Strode, Edward	Dec. 14,	June 29, 1793		Moses Hoge		cr 22	mr 7 *
Lowe, John m. Smith, Sarah	Dec. 14,	1807	Christ'r Olinger	Moses Hoge	3b 79		
Lowe, Mary m. Campbell, John	Mar. 18,	Mar. 18, 1797	Thomas Shepherd		1b 5	cr 26	mr 13 *
Lowe, Matty m. Smith, Joseph	Sept 14,	1820	John Lowe		4b161		
Love, Matty m. Smock, Henry	Dec. 20,	1809	John Lowe		3b128		
Lowe, Phebe m. Collins, Timothy	Sept 22,	1800	Richard Lowe	David Young	2b 88	gc 9	
Lower, Henry m. High, Esther	Aug. 15,	1815	Daniel High	Rev. Reebenack	3b334	gc 15	*
Lowery, Mary m. Stanley, Isaac	Feb. 8,	1837	John Lowry	Lewis F. Wilson	6b 95		*
Lowery, Susan m. McMaggin, Thomas		Jan. 14, 1797		David Young		gc 6	*
Lowman, Alex. m. Spillman, Charlotte	Jan. 24,	1825	Wm. Faris	Chas. P. Krauth	4b288		mr 48 *
Lowman, Daniel m. Leopard, Margaret	Feb. 14,	1837	Michael Leopard	Lewis F. Wilson	6b 96		
Lowman, Eliza M. Claycomb(Klay-)Fred.	June 3,	June 9, 1811?	John Burk	John B. Hoge	3b189	cr 14	mr 24 *
Lowman, Ephraim m. Row, Rebecca	May 12,	1788		Hugh Vance			mr 35 *
Lowman, Mary m. Murphy, Jacob	Apr. 20,	1814	Ephraim Lowman		3b295		
Lowman, Mary m. Pitzer, Elias		Aug. 4, 1789		Hugh Vance		cr 39	mr 4 *
Lowman, Nancy m. Snider, Jacob	Feb. 17,	1816	John Lowman	Rev. Reebenack	3b355	gc 15	*
Lowman, Philip m. Trout, Elinor		Nov. 2, 1785		Edward Tiffin		gc 38	mr 1 *
Lowman, Rachel m. Dowlan, Thomas	July 2,	1807	John Lee		3b 63		
Lown, Fanny m. McBride, John W.	Feb. 13,	1806	John Lown		3b 11		
Lowry, Fanny m. Samples, John W.		Jan. 30, 1794	Mathew Rippey	B. Page	1b 62		mr 40 *
Lowry, George m. Rippey(Ripley),Jane	Nov. 18,	Nov. 21, 1797	Joseph Hartsook	John Boyd	6b 70	cr 32	mr 13 *
Lowry, James M. m. Hartsook, Eliz.	Feb. 6,	1836	Samuel Kennedy		2b 53		
Lowry, Jane m. Kennedy, Dan'el	Feb. 10,	1800	Wm. Miller		3b100		
Lowry, John m. Miller, Peggy	Nov. 22,	1808			6b 95		*
Lowry, Mary H. m. Stanley, Isaac	Feb. 8,	Feb. 14, 1837	John Lowry	Lewis F. Wilson	3b320	gc 14	
Lowry, Samuel m. Miller, Eliz.	Apr. 27,	Apr. 27, 1815	Geo. Robinson	Rev. Reebenack	7b 21		mr 75 *
Lowry, Samuel S. m. Manor, Sarah C.	Jan. 16,	Jan. 16, 1845	David Gray	John Boggs	2b261		
Lowry, Wm. m. Miller, Mary	May 7,	1805	James Miller		6b 27		
Lowry, Wm. m. Sterret(Sta-), Lydia	Jan. 12,	Jan. 15, 1835	James Sterret	John Howell	5b263		mr 68 *
Loyd, James m. Kennedy, Eliz.		Apr. 10, 1788		?Hugh Vance			mr 34 *
Lucas, Basil m.Mussetter,Jane Aphes'	Mar. 23,	Mar. 28, 1833	John Mussetter	Nathan Young	4b 30		mr 66 *
Lucas, Dennis m. Eakins, Mary	Jan. 21,	Jan. 22, 1817	John Wright	W.N.Scott	6b 80		*
Lucas, Dennis m. Mussetter, Eliz.	May 25,	1836	John Mussetter				
Lucas, Eliz. m. Coontz(Coots),Abr'm		May 15, 1790		Moses Hoge		cr 4	mr 5 *
Lucas, Eliz. m. Hubbard, Jesse	Aug. 24,	1830	Barton Henshaw		5b173		
Lucas, Eliz. m. Manor, George	Sept 28,	1818	Henderson Lucas		4b 79		

Name	(marriage)	(suretor)	(minister)	(bond)	ref
Lucas, Ellen m. Carr, Thomas	Aug. 5, 6, 1829	Wm. McDonald	Nathan Young	9b135	mr 60 *
Lucas, Emily m. Throckmorton, John	Mar. 15, 1819	Henderson Lucas		4b102	
Lucas, Gabriel m. Gardiner, Sarah	Feb. 25, 1799	Samuel Gardiner		1b171	
Lucas, Henderson m. Buckles, Maria	May 12, 1831	Jacob Sumption		5b194	
Lucas, Jacob m. Butt, Ellen	Jan. 27, 1845	Stephen Mansfield		7b 24	
Lucas, Joseph m. Humphries, Hannah	Feb. 14, 1792		Moses Hoge		cr 8, mr 7 *
Lucas, Mary m. Wager, John	May 20, 1790		Moses Hoge		cr 4, mr 5 *
Lucas, Matilda m. Freize(-ize)Peter	Jan. 26, Jan. 24, 1849	George Swinley	James Chisholm	7b145	mr 78 *
Lucas, Rebecca m. Reed, Samuel	Oct. 30, Nov. 5, 1799	William Lucas	Moses Hoge	2b 32	cr 29, mr 17 *
Lucas, Susannah m. Buckles, Robert	May 20, 1793		William Hill	1b103	cr 30, mr 9 *
Luck, Jane m. Foreby, Wateman	Jan. 22, Aug. 25, 1798	Richard Blue	John Heitt(Hutt)		cr 37, mr 16 *
Luckett, Mary Eliz. m. Chapman, John	Nov. 20, 1832	Dan'l H. Conrad		5b247	
Lucky, George m. Wright, Sarah	Aug. 28, 1810	John Wright		3b159	
Ludwig, Geo. F. m. Butt, Matilda	Nov. 26, 1832	Harrison Waite		5b248	
Ludwig, Peggy m. Butt, Wm.	May 18, 1807	John Ludwig		3b 59	
Luke, Cath. m. Haslewood, Thomas	Oct. 7, Oct. 9, 1806	Thos. Haslewood		3b 32	or 28, mr 23 *
Luke, Jean m. Foreby, Wateman	Jan. 22, Aug. 25, 1798	Richard Blue	J. Bond	1b103	or 37, mr 16 *
Luke, Mary m. Finney, John	June 20, 1797	Wm. Gilbert	John Hutt(Heitt)	1b 22	
Lumon, Wm. m. Light, Eliz.	Jan. 14, 1801	Wmm Winship		2b110	*
Lupton, John W. m. Arnold, Eliz. Ann	Oct. 11, 1853		Joseph Baker		
Lupton, Marg't Ann m.McCormick.Prov'eApr.	Apr. 7, Apr. 12, 1832	Marg't Lupton Sr.	Jacob Medtart	5b224	or 10, mr 63 *
Lustre, Mary m. Armstrong, Thomas	Nov. 18, 1795		Moses Hoge		mr 11 *
Layers, Jacob m. Bowman, Mary	July 22, Oct. 30, 1798	John Bowman		1b 25	
Lydy, Samuel m. McKeever, Sarah	Oct. 30, Dec. 22, 1794	Robert Hastings	David Young	1b143	gc 8 *
Lydy, Susan m. Wilson, Joshua	Nov. 28, 1850	Wm. H. VanDoren	David Young		gc 4 *
Lyeth, Benj. S. m. Harden, Harriet S.	Sept 16, Nov. 27, 1812	John Lyle	D.Francis Sprigg	7b204	mr 82 *
Lyle, Anna m. Kennedy, John	Mar. 6, 1838	William Lyle		3b236	
Lyle, Emily m. Marker, Daniel	Nov. 14, 1815	William Lyle	James Watts	6b136	
Lyle, Emily m. Miller, David	Sept 17, Sept 19, 1816	Robert ?	W.N.Scott	3b347	mr 26 *
Lyle, Harriet m. Henshaw, Wm. Jr.	Dec. 19, Dec. 21, 1843	William Lyle	John B. Hoge	4b 13	
Lyle, Harriet Ann m. Miller, Smith	Dec. 23, 1784		Lewis F. Wilson	6b310	mr 74 *
Lyle, Hugh m. Creighton, Isabella	Nov. 27, Dec. 20, 1820	Levi Henshaw	Hugh Vance	4b167	mr 32 *
Lyle, Hugh M. m. Henshaw, Eleanor	Dec. 26, 1826	John F. Snodgrass		5b 58	
Lyle, Ignat's m. Tate, Marg't M.	Mar. 12, Mar. 14, 1811	Robert Wilson		3b179	or 14, mr 24 *
Lyle, Marg't H. m. Lyle, Robert	July 1, 1835	William Lyle	John B. Hoge	6b 48	
Lyle, Nancy m. Bell, Thomas	Mar. 4, 1796		John Boyd		or 10, mr 12 *
Lyle, Nancy m.Broy(Bray), Samuel	Sept 9, 1806	John Lyle		3b 29	
Lyle, Polly m. Campbell, James W.	Mar. 12, Mar. 14, 1811	Robert Wilson	John B. Hoge	3b179	
Lyle, Robert m. Lyle, Marg't H.	May 31, 1853		John O. Proctor		or 14, mr 24 *
Lyle, Robert Glenn m. Daniels, Sarah	Jan. 1, 1802	Hugh Lyle		2b156	
Lyle, Sally m. Chenoweth, Philemon	Feb. 21, 1805	James Campbell	Moses Hoge	2b255	
Lyle, Sarah m. Campbell,Dugal(DouglasFeb.	Jan. 10, 1805	Wm. H. VanDoren		7b193	or 17, mr 22 *
Lyle, Sarah M. m. Holiday, Geo. W.	Aug. 29, 1850				

Name	(marriage)	(suretor)	(minister)	(bond)		
Lyles, Ignat's P. m. Forman, Rebecca	Oct. 25, 1830	Archibald Oden		9b179		mr 86 *
Lynch, Johanna m. O'Conner, Timothy	Feb. 13, 1840	James Murphy		6b197		mr 76 *
Lynch, Marg't m. McCarthy, Charles	Feb. 20, 1841	James Lynch		6b234		
Lynch, Mary m. Colter, Mathew	Sept 18, 1839	James Lynch		6b176		
Lynch, Sarah m. Horner, Richard	Apr. 5, 1798	Corn's Thompson		1b105		*
Lynn, Edward m. Fritz, Cath.	May 4, 1801	Caty Fritz		2b126		*
Lynn, Elijah m. Bowman, Mary	Apr. 10, 1798	Joseph Vance		1b 97		mr 1 *
Lyon, John m. McCarty, Ellenor	May 14, 1806	George Gill		3b 19		

"Mc"

Name	(marriage)	(suretor)	(minister)	(bond)		
McAbee, Jas. B. m. Simmons, Ann M.	Apr. 8, 1852	John W. Blakeney	David Thomas	7b252		mr 44 *
McAllister, Ann S. m. Fleming, Jos.	May 8, 1845	Benj. McAllister	John Light	7b 33		
McAllister, Benj. m. Dugan, Marg't	Aug. 18, 1849	Michael Leopard		7b163		
McAllister, Benj. m. Evans, Eliz.	Nov. 24, 1801	Wm. Orrick		2b149		
McAllister, Christ'r m. Holm, Barbara	Dec. 13, 1810	Patrick Duffy	Rev. Reebensack	3b168	gc 11	
McAllister, Eliz. m. Faris, George	Dec. 2, 1813	Thos. C. Smith	Rev. Reebensack	2b278	gc 14	
McAllister, Marg't m. Irwin, John	Nov. 27, 1785	Edward Tiffin			cr 38	*
McAllister, Marg't m. Deck, Geo. Jr.	Aug. 8, 1836	Christ'r McAllister		6b 83		mr 1 *
McAllister, Mary m. Chambers, Robert	Jan. 17, 1788	Hugh Vance			cr 24	
McAllister, Mary m. Miller, John W.	May 22, 1844	Benj. McAllister	John Light	7b 1		mr 2 *
McAllister, Nancy m. Smith, Lewis	Dec. 25, 1794	John Boyd			cr 21	mr 76 *
McAllister, Rosella m. Pitzer, Philip	Dec. 4, 1849	Benj. McAllister	John Light	7b168		mr 8 *
McAlpin, John m. Garrety, Mary	Oct. 3, 1841	Bernard Fealy		6b248		mr 80 *
McAtee, Hannah m. Thompson, Elias	Aug. 24, 1810	Bernet Thompson		3b 58		
McBee, Rebecca m. High, Peter	Jan. 22, 1822	James McCoach		4b205		
McBride, Aaron m. Schrodes, Hester	Nov. 6, 1837	Jonathan Baker		6b123		
McBride, Eliz. m. Grubb, Adam	May 8, 1800	James Johnson	David Young	2b 69	gc 9	
McBride, James m. Martin, Sarah Ann	Oct. 28, 1844	James Martin	John Boggs	7b 10		mr 75 *
McBride, John m. Lown, Fanny	Feb. 13, 1806	John Lown		3b 11		
McBride, Katy m. Boyle, Patrick	Jan. 8, 1852	Jacob VanDoren	D. Thomas	7b242		mr 84 *
McBride, Mary Ann m. Ollinger, John	Jan. 13, 1835	John Shearer		6b 28		
McBride, Thomas m. John, Cath.	Sept 28, 1797	Robert Jones	David Young	1b 48	gc 7	
McBride, Vincent m. Martin, Jane	Apr. 16, 1842	James Martin		6b270		
McCabe, Cath. m. Maloney, John	May 3, 1853	J.H.Plunkett				mr 88 *
McCabe, Lawrence m. McLaughlin, Rosa	Oct. 16, 1841	Bernard Fealy		6b248		
McCannon, Wm. m. Campbell, Mary	Nov. 9, 1801	Robert Campbell		2b147		
McCany, Cath. m. Fanas, Patrick	Mar. 24, 1799					*
McCarthy, Chas. m. Lynch, Marg't	Feb. 20, 1841	James Lynch	David Young	6b234	gc 8	
McCarty, Ellenor m. Lyon, John	May 14, 1806	George Gill		3b 19		
McCarty, Florenz m. Miner, Ellen	Oct. 9, 1850	Michael Sullivan		7b199		

Name	Date	(marriage)	(surety)	(minister)	(bond)	
McCarty, Florens m. Morrison, Alen	Oct. 9,	Oct. 9, 1850	Michael Sullivan	Jos. Plunkett	7b199	mr 84 *
McCarty, James m. Young, Polly	Mar. 25,	Mar. 26, 1800	Joseph Young	John Hedtt(Hutt)	2b 59	or 33; mr 18 *
McCarty, Martin m. Quinn, Marg't	June 14,	Mar. 4, 1838	Harrison Waite		6b141	mr 54 *
McCarty, Peter m. Bishop, Eliza	Mar. 3,	Jan. 11, 1790	Zachariah Sanks	Nathan Young	3b286	or 3; mr 4 *
McCarty, Rachel m. Morgan, Morgan	Apr. 10,	1800		Moses Hoge		
McCarty, Savanna m. Howard, John		May 18, 1800	John How		2b 64	or 35; mr 19 *
McCarty, Susanna m. Hornb, John		1800		John Hedtt(Hutt)		
McCartney, Joseph m. Livingston, Susan	Oct. 6,	1805	Henry Frank		2b 91	
McCartney, Letitia m. Cahill, Dennis	Apr. 30,	1806	Cornelius Kelly		2b260	
McCartney, Marg't m. McIntdire, John	May 26,	1819	Robert Grimes		3b 20	
McCaughlin, Marg't m. Hooper, John	Dec. 2,	1821	John Gallaher	W.N.Scott	4b125	or 11; mr 40 *
McCausland, Fanny m. Cross, James	Mar. 7,	Nov. 26, 1796	John Porter	Nathan Young	4b174	gc 5; mr 57 *
McCausland, Francis m. Booth, Jane	Nov. 26,	Dec. 17, 1795		John Boyd		gc 6; mr 12 *
McCausland, Thomas m. Patton, Marg't	Dec. 17,	Sept 7, 1797		David Young		gc 7
McClain, John m. Carson, Marg't	Sept 6,	June 19, 1798	Chas. McGarran	David Young	1b 39	
McClane, John m. Williamson, Marg't	June 16,	Oct. 7, 1797	Abraham Coleman	David Young	1b117	
McClanahan, Wm. m. Griggs, Eliz.	Oct. 7,	1799	John Griggs	John Hedtt(Hutt)	1b 52	or 11; mr 14 *
McClay, Nancy m. Essex, Joseph	Aug. 31,	Feb. 6, 1834	James McClay		2b 24	
McClay, Wm. A. m. Nelson, Sarah M.	Feb. 4,	Dec. 24, 1834	James Nelson	Jas. M. Brown	5b302	mr 67 *
McClean, Agnes m. Sargeant, Edward		Mar. 25, 1784				mr 32 *
McCleary, Andrew m. Beatty, Amanda	Mar. 23,	1830	Jacob F. Light	Hugh Vance	5b159	mr 54 *
McCleary, Angelina m. Cookum, Peter	Apr. 9,	1832	Andrew McCleary	W. Monroe	5b225	
McCleary, Elis. m. Likens, Wm. R.	Mar. 28,	1833	Christian Wolff		5b264	
McCleary, Elis. m. Nichols, Samuel	Dec. 29,	Jan. 3, 1826	Andrew McCleary	Jas. M. Brown		mr 50 *
McCleary, Ephraim m. Johnston, Cath.	Apr. 23,	1833	Lemuel Johnston		5b 31	
McCleary, Jane m. Campbell, Robert	Oct. 29,	1808	Wm. McCannon		5b259	
McCleary, Jane m. Rochester, Sam'l	July 24,	1847	John McCleary		3b 99	
McCleary, John m. Austin, Mary	Oct. 18,	Oct. 1849	Jacob VanDoren	Lewis F. Wilson	7b102	mr 83 *
McCleary, John m. Pryatt, Eliz.		Jan. 1, 1789		Hugh Vance	7b166	mr 37 *
McCleary, John Jr. m. Showalter, Jane	Dec. 4,	Dec. 4, 1820	Merkle Locke	W.N.Scott	4b168	mr 41 *
McCleary, Mary m. Criswell, James	July 22,	1807	Robert Grimes		3b 63	
McCleary, Mary m. Kownslar, Randolph	Jan. 5,	1836	John Harrison Jr.		6b 68	
McCleary, Matilda m. Vametre, Robt.	Mar. 25,	Mar. 27, 1840	John McCleary	Lewis F. Wilson	6b 203	mr 71 *
McCleary, Rosanna m. Locke, Maverell	Feb. 17,	1812	Robert Wilson		3b212	
McCleland, Nancy m. Wilson, George	Jan. 18,	Jan. 19, 1800	Robert Shirley	John Hedtt(Hutt)	2b 48	or 33; mr 18 *
McClintock, Rebecca m. Boyle, Chas.	Oct. 23,	Aug. 11, 1782		Hugh Vance	7b235	or 9; mr 1 *
McClure, Sarah A. m. Shilling, Jacob		Oct. 23, 1794	John Zimmerman	D. Thomas	7b235	mr 85 *
McClure, Daniel m. Demoss, Elis.	Mar. 20,	Sept 13, 1851		Richard Swirt		mr 40 *
McClure, Isabella m. Lee, Anthony Jr	Sept 27,	Mar. 27, 1827		John Mathews	5b 64	mr 51 *
McClure, John m. Carson, Margaret	Jan. 23,	Sept 24, 1797	James McClure	David Young	1b 39	gc 6
McClure, Mary E. m. Barley, Nathaniel		Jan. 24, 1850	Chas. McGarrans	P. Lipscomb	7b176	mr 82 *
McClure, Richard m. Anderson, Mary	Oct. 4,	Oct. 5, 1821	Richard McClure	Nathan Young	4b193	mr 87 *
McClure, Sarah A. m. Shilling, Jacob	Oct. 23,	Oct. 23, 1851	Joseph McFeely; John Zimmerman	D. Thomas	7b235	mr 85 *

Name		(marriage)		(surety)	(minister)	(bond)		
McClure, Wm. m. Betty, Mary	Jan. 24,	Jan. 26, 1826		John Porterfield	Jas. M. Brown	3b 33		mr 50 *
McCluskin, James m. McMullen, Mary	Oct. 11,	1785			Hugh Vance			mr 34 *
McCoach, James m. Barnard, Eliz.Mrs.	Mar. 30,	Mar. 30, 1830		John Gallaher	Nathan Young	3b160		mr 60 *
McCollister, Eliz. m.Burk(Bush),Henry		Aug. 26, 1789			Hugh Vance		cr 40	mr 4 *
McCollister, Jane m. Richardson,John		May 12, 1792			Moses Hoge			mr 39 *
McCollister, Martha m. Kerney, Wm.		Dec. 31, 1791			Moses Hoge		cr 8	mr 7 *
McCollough, Joseph m. Darke(Duke)Reb.		Apr. 2, 1789			Hugh Vance		cr 20	mr 3 *
McCollough, John m. Morgan, Olivia		July 26, 1787			Hugh Vance		cr 18	mr 1 *
McCollough, Nancy m. Hess, Benj.		Jan. 6, 1795			David Young		go 4	
*McConnell, Eliz. m. Little, James	Feb. 9,	1810		William Tabb		3b136		
McConnell, Hannah m. Nelson, James	Jan. 2,	1826		James McConnell	John Winter	3b 31		mr 50 *
McConnell, Jane m. Hodge, John	Feb. 15,	1803		Wm. McConnell		2b194		
McConnell, Marg't M. m. Henshaw, Jas.	Nov. 23,	1818		Levi Henshaw		4b 90		
McConnell, Mary m. Henshaw, Hiram	Feb. 24,	1802		Wm. McConnell		2b162		
McConnell, Moses m. Fryatt, Sarah	Jan. 15,	1783			Hugh Vance		cr 9	mr 1 *
McConnell, Sarah m. McConnell, Wm.	Feb. 21,	1825		Hiram Henshaw	Jas. M. Brown	4b290		mr 48 *
McConnell, Wm. m. McConnell, Sarah	Feb. 21,	1825		Hiram Henshaw	Jas. M. Brown	4b290		mr 48 *
McCormick, Ann m. Wright, John	Dec. 13,	1780			Daniel Sturges			mr 31 *
McCormick, Bridget m. O'Brian, Thos.	Feb. 8,	1841		Michael Ryan		6b232		
McCormick, Edward m. Cochrane,Rachel	Feb. 9,	1799		Mathew Ramone		1b166		
McCormick, Eliz. m. Lightzer, Mathias	Nov. 14,	1803		Corn's McCormick		2b213		
McCormick, Ellen m. Baker, Otho	Dec. 15,	1841		Wm. McCormick	John Hedges	6b257		mr 73 *
McCormick, Isabella m. Howell, Chas.	Dec. 17,	1844		John M. Holmes		7b 16		
McCormick, Isabella m. Howell, Chas.	Dec. 13,	1841		Wm. McCormick		6b257		
McCormick, James m. Eaton, Eliz.	Feb. 28,	1801		Corn's McCormick		2b116		
McCormick, Jane m. Bennett, James	Dec. 30,	1785			Hugh Vance			mr 34 *
McCormick, Jane m. Gallaher, Sam'l	July 11,	July 1822		James McCormick	Chas. P. Krauth	4b219		mr 45 *
McCormick, Johanna m. Ryan,Patrick	Nov. 25,	1840		John Butt		6b226		
McCormick, Levi m. Grimes, Jane	Feb. 2,	Feb. 4, 1816		John Hawkins	Nathan Young	3b353		mr 55 *
McCormick, Lucinda m.Markel(-ikle)Wm	Jan. 8,	Jan. 10, 1828		Geo. M. Bowers	Jas. M. Brown	3b 87		mr 51 *
McCormick, Mary A. m.Patterson, Chas.	July 13,	1841		Ellis Ross		6b243		
McCormick, Mary Cath. m.Burke,James	Dec. 7,	Dec. 7, 1850		Wm. McCormick	F.C.Tebbs	7b205		mr 83 *
McCormick, Moses m. Evans, Elis.	Dec. 31,	Dec. 31, 1798		Elijah Williams	David Young	1b158		
McCormick, Nancy m. Kidinger, George	Nov. 1,	Nov. 1, 1814			Rev. Reebenack		go 14	*
McCormick, Patsy m. Edward, Abraham	May 28,	1807		Mathias Lightzer		3b 60		
McCormick,Prov.Jr. m. Lupton,Marg't	Apr. 7,	Apr. 12, 1832		Marg't Lupton Sr.	Jacob Medtart	5b224		mr 63 *
McCormick, Thos. m. Fisher, Cath.	Dec. 22,	Dec. 27, 1810		Peter Fisher	John B. Hoge	5b169	cr 14	mr 24 *
McCormick, Wm. m. Brady, Martha	Aug. 3,	1801		John Beavon		2b134		
McCormick, Wm. m. Montague, Mary		Nov. 10, 1853			J.H.Plunkett			mr 88 *
McCormick, Wm. m. Pyles, Jane	Mar. 8,	1820		John J. Willson		4b139		
McCoy, Elis. m. Spring, Richard	Aug. 10,	1795			Moses Hoge	3b100	or 10	mr 11 *
McCoy, John m. Ryan, Phebe	Oct. 31,	1808		David Rippey		7b181		
McCoy, Joseph m. Zeigler(Sigler)Elis.	Apr. 13,	Apr. 25, 1850		Wm. Sigler(Zeigler)	John Bauman	3b 18		
**McConnell, Anna m. Henshaw, Levi	Apr. 29,	1806		Wm. McConnell				mr 80 *

Names	(marriage)	(suretor)	(minister)	(bond)	
McCoy, Mary m. Fish(Fiste),John	Dec. 8, 1828	Henry Payne Jr.	W. Monroe	5b114	mr 53 *
McCoy, Mary m. Startzman, John	Dec. 22, 1853		G.W.Cooper		mr 11 *
McCoy, Milly m. Brown, David	June 5, 1796		Richard Swift	or 26	mr 30 *
McCoy, Moses m. Ellis, Rhuanna	Sept 23, 1819?	Geo. Peterman	W.N.Scott	4b114	mr 53 *
McCoy, Nancy m. Howard, James	Apr. 16, 1829	Robert Stewart	Wm. Monroe	5b127	mr 33 *
McCracken, Seneca m. Reynolds, Rebecca	May 3, 1785		Hugh Vance		
McCrary, Jane m. Shover, Thomas	Feb. 9, 1786		Hugh Vance		
McCrea, Wm. m. White, Hannah	Dec. 11, 1821	Thomas White	Geo. M. Frye	4b201	mr 44 *
McCrea, Eliz. m. White, John	Aug. 6, 1822	Moses McCrea	Nathan Young	4b220	mr 57 *
McCrea, Jane m. Shover, Thomas	Feb. 5, 1786		Hugh Vance		mr 33 *
McCrea, Wm. m. Shover, Maria Eliz.	Aug. 18, 1814	Robert Wilson	Nathan Young	3b300	mr 54 *
McCrea, Wm. m. White, Hannah	Dec. 11, 1821	Thomas White	George M. Fry	4b201	mr 44 *
McDade, Daniel m. Cooper, Mary	Sept 4, 1797	Richard Ransom	Daniel Sturges	1b 37	mr 42 *
McDade, John m. Cunningham, Ann	Oct. 16, 1781		David Young		go 5
McDade, Nancy m. Close, John	Aug. 12, 1795		Rev. Reebenack		go 12
McDaniel, Alex. m. Johnston, Mary	May 16, 1811	Daniel Gavin	John Winter	3b187	mr 77 *
McDaniel, Alex. m. Seibert, Barbary	Dec. 1, 1846	Vincent McBride	John Howell	7b 79	mr 68 *
McDaniel, Alice m. Fisher, Samuel	Feb. 17, 1836	Chas. McDonald	John Howell	6b 72	mr 56 *
McDaniel, Chas. m. White, Rebecca	Sept 2, 1818	Ellis Rees	Nathan Young	4b 79	
McDaniel, Eliz. m. Darrial, Sam'l	Jan. 27, 1800	Wm. McDaniel		2b 49	
McDaniel, Ellen m. Burkhouse, Chas.	Nov. 1, 1841	Alex. McDaniel	John Hedges	6b251	mr 73 *
McDaniel, Emily m. Eaton, James	Feb. 3, 1847	A. McDaniel	Wm. Love	7b 84	mr 78 *
McDaniel, Johnston P. m.Markle,Anabel	Sept 2, 1851	B.B.Hollis	David Thomas	7b230	mr 84 *
McDaniel, Lavina m. Payne, Mahlon	Mar. 27, 1848	Alex. McDaniel	J.B.Jennings	7b126	mr 82 *
McDaniel, Mary m. Miller, John	Nov. 10, 1846	Alex. McDaniel	John Winter	7b 77	mr 77 *
McDaniel, Mary m. Pitzer, Conrad	Sept 11, 1818	Alex. McDonald	W.N.Scott	4b 78	
McDaniel, Michael m. Hastings,Amanda	Sept 29, 1851	John Hastings	F.C.Tebbs	7b235	mr 85 *
McDaniel, Nelly m. Pitzer, Michael	July 8, 1822	Jacob McDaniel	Nathan Young	4b219	mr 57 *
McDermott, Cath. m. McMahon, Patr'k	Oct. 21, 1831	Corn's McDermott		5b207	
McDermott, James m. Eaty, Sarah	Jan. 2, 1834	Harrison White		5b298	
McDermott, Philip m.Markel, Rebecca	Sept 30, 1822	W. Markel		4b224	
McDonald, Allen m. Monroe, Agnes	July 17, 1783?		Hugh Vance		mr 32 *
McDonald, Alice m. Fisher, Samuel	Feb. 17, 1836	Chas. McDonald	John Howell	6b 72	mr 68 *
McDonald, Andrew m. Hair, Mary	Oct. 2, 1788		Moses Hoge		mr 36 *
McDonald, Angelina m. Miller, Jos. A.	Dec. 14, 1852		James Baker		mr 87 *
McDonald, Ann Eliz. m. Sandindiver,S	Sept 10, 1844	Sebastian McDonald		7b 6	
McDonald, Annie m. Throckmorton, T.L	Jan. 24, 1856		J.R.Graham		or 29
McDonald, Asa m. Shaler, Marg't	Mar. 1, 1795		Wm. Hill		mr 9 *
McDonald, Cath. m. Chambers, Jos. S.	Mar. 30, 1837	Gerard McDonald		6b103	
McDonald, Cleburg m. Crook, Sarah	Oct. 6, 1815	Edward Beeson Jr.		3b342	
McDonald, Eliz. m. Henshaw, Uriah S.	Sept 29, 1807	John McDonald		3b 72	
McDonald, Eliz. m. Perry, Thomas	June 2, 1801	James Conway		2b127	
McDonald, Ellen m.Backhouse(Bur)Chas.	Nov. 1, 1841	Alex. McDaniel	John Hedges	6b251	mr 73 *

Name		(marriage)	(suretor)	(minister)	(bond)	
McDonald, Enos m. Martin, Mary	Aug. 3,	Oct. 12, 1853	Chas. McDonald	A. Talty	5b278	mr 88 *
McDonald, Farber m. Sebastian,Chr'tn	Aug. 9,	1833	Jacob Fisher		5b299	
McDonald, Geo. W. m. Shoafstall,Nancy	Jan. 5,	1834				*
McDonald,Gerard m.Daily, Eliz.	Nov. 9,	Nov. 6, 1814	Robert Grimes	Rev. Reebenack	3b307	go 14
McDonald, Garard m.Hedronimus, Sarah	May 9,	1833	Michael Couchman		5b294	
McDonald, Harriet m. White, James	May 6,	1844	D. McDonald		6b322	
McDonald, Hugh m. Moore, Phebe	Feb. 11,	1799	John Conway		1b167	
McDonald, Isabella m. White, John M.	May 19,	May 20, 1845	Wm. McDonald	Lewis F. Wilson	7b 35	mr 77 *
McDonald, John m. Lee, Eliz.	Mar. 14,	Mar. 17, 1831	Anthony Lee Jr.	Nathan Young	5b187	mr 61 *
McDonald, John m. Silver, Jane	May 13,	May 14, 1812	Wm. Maxwell	Rev. Reebenack	3b224	go 12
McDonald, Mary m. Lemmen, George	Apr. 20,	Nov. 17, 1785		Hugh Vance	1b x	mr 34 *
McDonald, Mary m. Palin, John	Feb. 27,	Apr. , 1789	Henry Placker		6b198	
McDonald, Mary m. Snyder, George	Mar. 12,	Feb. 27, 1840	Jos. S. Chambers	James Reily	5b305	mr 70 *
McDonald, Mary Ellen m. Medtart,Jacob	Sept 11,	1834	Robert McDonald		4b 78	
McDonald, Mary Mrs. m. Pitzer, Conrad	Nov. 19,	Sept 15, 1818	Alex. McDonald	W.N.Scott	6b151	*
McDonald, Rebecca m. Dixor, Geo.	Mar. 15,	1838	Wm.G. Butler		5b219	
McDonald, Robert m. Barnett,Martha J	Aug. 23,	Mar. 15, 1832	Joseph Severns	Nathan Young	5b 20	mr 64 *
McDonald, Robert m. Campbell,Mary Mrs	Aug. 22,	Aug. 25, 1825	Thomas Miller	John Winter	3b 95	mr 50 *
McDonald, Robert m. Lewis, Priscilla	Aug. 3,	1808	David Lewis		5b278	
McDonald, Sarah m. Farber, Christ'n	Apr. 13,	Aug. 8, 1833	Chas. McDonald	W. Monroe	4b262	mr 67 *
McDonald, Wm. m. Miller, Marg't	Feb. 15,	1824	Harrison Waite		5b302	gc 2
McDonald, Wm. m. Sybole, Eleanor	Mar. 9,	1834	Ichabod Sybole		5b156	gc 8
McDonald, Wm. m. Varmetre, Marg't	Jan. 14,	Mar. 9, 1830	Isaac Varmetre			mr 63 *
McFadden, Eliz. m. Evans, John	Aug. 26,	Jan. 14, 1793		Jacob Medtart		cr 14
McFenn, David m. Fleece, Mary	Mar. 21,	Aug. 26, 1799		David Young		*
McFarland, Dugal m. Campbell, Marg't	Dec. 9,	Mar. 26, 1811	Robert Grimes	David Young	2b 22	mr 24 *
McFarland, Hannah m. Ferrel, John	Aug. 12,	Dec. 17, 1829	Wm. Campbell	John B. Hoge	3b181	mr 53 *
McFarland, John m. Bailey, Eliz.	Sept 19,	Aug. 13, 1815	John McFarland	Jacob Beecher	5b147	mr 55 *
McFee, James m. Milholland, Agnes	Mar. 5,	Jan. 1, 1795	John Dawson	Nathan Young	3b334	gc 4
McFeely, Joseph m. Ransome, Lucy	Jan. 2,	Sept 19, 1812		David Young	3b237	
McFeely, Mary Ann m. Lewis, Samuel	Sept 22,	1838	Robert Wilson		6b136	
McFallen, Hugh m. Games(Gaines),Anna	Jan. 26,	Jan. 4, 1800	Elij. Sendindiver		2b 45	
McGard, Andrew m. Buckles, Ann	Feb. 27,	Jan. 26, 1791	Mathew McGerry	John Hitt(Hedtt)	1b134	cr 33 mr 18 *
McGarrah, Robt. m. Dick, Mary	Aug. 3,	1798		Moses Hoge	5b 89	cr 6 mr 6 *
McGee, John m. Garber, Cath.	June 20,	Feb. 27, 1828	John Dick			cr 9 mr 59 *
McGee, Oliver m. West, Eliz.	Jan. 12,	Aug. 3, 1782	Christian Garber	Nathan Young		cr 35 mr 1 *
McGermon, Mary m. Johnson, John	Apr. 17,	June 21, 1800	John Conway	Hugh Vance	2b 73	
McGerry, Nancy m. Burr, James	Sept 24,	1799	Mathew McGerry	John Hitt(Hedtt)	1b162	mr 19 *
McGinnis, Felix m. Chovald, Agnes	Dec. 23,	Apr. 17, 1793				gc 3
McGlaughlin, Daniel m. McKenny,Nancy	May 18,	Sept 24, 1799	Philip McGowan	David Young	2b 28	gc 9
McGlaughlin, Geo. m. Huston, Marg't		Dec. 23, 1794		David Young		gc 4
McGlaughlin, Nancy m. King, James		1798	Israel Crow	David Young	1b111	
McGlinsey, Mary m. Graver, George		Dec. 17, 1818		John B. Hoge		mr 29 *

Name		(marriage)	(surety)	(minister)	(bond)			
McGonagle, Cath. m.Shone(Sione)Henry	Dec. 6,	Dec. 7, 1797	Patr'k McGonagle	David Young	1b 70	gc 7		*
McGonagle, Patr'k m. Boland, Eliz.	Oct. 13,	1798	John Mulhall		1b139			*
McGonagle, Sally m.Diffenderfer,Geo.	Feb. 11,	Feb. 12, 1818	John Doll	John B. Hoge	4b 60		mr 29	*
McGorian, Nicholas m.Rosenberger,Barb	Jan. 13,	1846	David Rosenberger		7b 55			
McGovrain, Chas. m. Kennedy,Eliz.T.	Dec. 19,	1797	Daniel Kennedy		1b 73			
McGowan, Ann E. m. Moore, Henry	Dec. 21,	1829	Thomas Smith		5b148			
McGowan, John m. Carothers, Jane	Aug. 5,	Aug. 8, 1799	John Ravenaugh	John Heitt(Hutt)	2b 16	cr 38		*
McGrane, Cath. m. Shield, Daniel	Feb. 8,	1840	Richard Whelan		6b196			
McGuire, Robert m. Fry, Cath.	Nov. 2,	1802	Conrad Fry		2b183			*
McGwiggin, Thomas m. Lowery, Susan								
McIlvena, Hannah m. Baker, Wm.	Jan. 14,	1797	James Sterrat	David Young	2b202	gc 6		*
McIlwaine, Marg't m. Bolln, Geo. W.	June 7,	Jan. 14, 1803	Harrison Waite		6b 40			
McIntire, Andrew m. Tabb, Eliza	Apr. 15,	1835	Seaton E. Tabb	Jas. M. Brown	6b 3		mr 68	*
McIntire, Eliz. m. Augustus, Enoch	Apr. 7,	1834	William Blue		1b133			
McIntire, Eliz. m. Brown(Bohm), Jas.	Sept 19,	1798	Andrew McIntire	James Chisholm	6b312		mr 75	*
McIntire, John m. McCartney,Marg't	Jan. 24,	Jan. 24, 1844	Robert Grimes		3b 20			
McIntire, John m. Wilson, Jane	May 26,	1806	James Wilson		2b 87			
McIntire, Marg't m. Levy, John Jr.	Sept 13,	1800	John McIntire		6b 14			
McIntire, Mary m. Blue, Wm.	June 26,	1834	John McIntire	Moses Hoge	5b192		mr 35	*
McIntire, Mary m. Hill, Moses	Apr. 13,	Mar. 15, 1831	Peter Innes		6b 83			
McIntire, Owen m. Cooney, Alice	July 21,	1836	Jacob Shaffer		5b268			
McIntire, Patrick m. Dick, Harriet	Apr. 22,	1833	Robert Grimes		3b190			
McIntire, Prudence m.Matton,Cornelius	June 28,	1811	Adam Stewart	Jas. M. Brown	5b177		mr 54	*
McIntire, Robert m. Bishop, Marg't	Apr. 12,	Oct. 12, 1830	Cornelius Kelly	W.N.Scott	4b152		mr 41	*
McIntire, Thomas m.Fullerton(To-)Jane	June 22,	June 22, 1820	John Emberson		1b 74			
McIntire, Wm. m. Scarlett, Elinor	Dec. 23,	1797	David Blue		2b159			
McKee, Alex. m. Blue, Eliz.	Feb. 2,	1802	Conrad Rousch	?	6b147			*
McKee, Hugh m. Rousch, Cath. Jane	Oct. 18,	Oct. 18, 1838	Boyd Roberts	John Winter	5b 21		mr 50	*
McKee, Robert m. Merchant, Mary	Aug. 30,	Sept 1825	Angus McKeever	Rev. Reebemack	3b239			
McKeever, Alex. m. Suffrance,Martha	Nov. 10,	Nov. 10, 1812	Daniel McKeever	Nathan Young	4b120	gc 13		*
McKeever, Jane m. Abernathy, Samuel	Oct. 16,	Oct. 17, 1819	Daniel McKeever	Nathan Young	4b170			*
McKeever, Mary m. Stack, Demarius	Jan. 22,	Jan. 23, 1821	Wm. McCausland		1b 35		mr 56	*
McKeever, Nancy m. Hastings, Robert	Aug. 24,	1797	Robert Hastings	David Young	1b143		mr 57	*
McKeever, Sarah m. Lydy, Samuel	Oct. 30,	1798		David Young	2b167			*
McKellop, John m. Armstrong, Cath.	Apr. 1,	1795		Hugh Vance	2b178			*
McKenan, Mary m. Lemmon, Robert	Aug. 25,	1788	Jonathan Pownall		2b 28	gc 8		*
McKenny, Eliz. m. Tate, Samuel	Sept 24,	1802	Daniel McKenny		2b 71	gc 5		*
McKenny, Marg't m. Hardshew,Adam S.	May 20,	1802	Philip McGowan		6b241	cr 24		*
McKenny, Nancy m. McGlaughlin, Dan'l	May 18,	Sept 24, 1799			3b151		mr 2	*
McKenny, Wm. m. Kiger, Eliz.	May 15,	May 21, 1800	George Kiger	David Young		gc 9		*
McKerney, Elderglrt m. Kilmer, Isaac		May 20, 1841	Thomas Patton	David Young		gc 9		*
McKewan, Cath. m. Dare, Henry		1810	Lewis B. Willis	Lewis F. Wilson			mr 72	*
McKewan, Mary m. Gray, Andrew		Nov. 20, 1787		Hugh Vance		cr 23	mr 2	*

Name	(marriage)		(suretor)	(minister)	(bond)		
McKewan, Mary m. Lemmon, Robert Sept 27,	Jan. 31,	1788		Hugh Vance	1b 47	cr 24	mr 2 *
McKewan, Mary m. Morrow, James		1797	Charles McKewan				
McKey, Mary m. Hayes, Thomas	Dec. 22,	1796		John Boyd		cr 11	mr 13 *
McKinney, Cath. m. Cage, Martin	Apr. 26,	1796		Moses Hoge		cr 36	mr 12 *
McKinney, James m. Houck, Christina	Aug. 31,	1820	Daniel McGlaughlin		4b159		
McKinney, Marg't m. King, Samuel	Dec. 8,	1800	Amos Tullice		2b101		
McKinney, Thos. m. Boxzell, Eliz.	Oct. 25,	1821	Cornelius Kelly	John B. Hoge	4b195		mr 44 *
McKinney, Wm. m. Kiger, Eliz.	May 21,	1800	George Kiger	David Young	2b 71	gc 9	
McKnight, Deborah m-Shissolen,Rich'd	Oct. 25,	1795		David Young		gc 5	
McKnight, Robert m. Fullerton, Ann	May 20,	1786		Hugh Vance			mr 33 *
McKown, Anna m. Mercer, Joshua	Aug. 15,	1799	James Sellers	Lewis F. Wilson	2b 21		mr 83 *
McKown, Evelina m. Busey, Samuel	Feb. 26,	1849	Samuel McKown	Joseph Baker	7b147		mr 87 *
McKown, F.S.S. m. Campbell, Mary R.	Feb. 1,	1853		Jas. M. Brown			mr 48 *
McKown, George m. Henshaw, Eveline	Apr. 8,	1825	Hiram Henshaw		4b288		
McKown, Hiram m. Campbell, Isabella	Feb. 8,	1851	Geo. W. Hoke		7b221		
McKown, Isabella m. Campbell, Lemuel	Jan. 7,	1847	Samuel McKown		7b 84		
McKown, Isabella M. m. Miller, Wm. S	June 7,	1851	John McKown	Lewis F. Wilson	7b210		mr 87 *
McKown, Jane m. Gold, Washington	Nov. 13,	1830			5b167		
McKown, John m. Demoss, Eloisa	Sept 28,	1830	George McKown	Jas. M. Brown	5b180		mr 54 *
McKown, John m. Hall, Marg't	Jan. 1,	1818	Wm. Wilson		4b 80		
McKown, Joseph m. Varmetre, Mary R.	Oct. 20,	1841	Morgan Morgan	Lewis F. Wilson	6b229		mr 72 *
McKown, Maria m. Hoke, George W.	Apr. 10,	1847	Wm. McDonald		7b109		
McKown, Morgan m. Varmetre, Rebecca	Apr. 11,	1849	Morgan McKown		7b15*		
McKown, Samuel m. Morgan, Sarah	Jan. 2,	1842	Wm. McDonald	Lewis F. Wilson	6b270		mr 73 *
McKown, Samuel m. Oak, Marg't Lucinda?	June 2,	1851	Jeptha Morgan	Lewis F. Wilson	7b214		mr 87 *
McKown, Warner m. Silver, Ann Amelia	Nov. 30,	1828	Mathew Hunter	J.E.Jackson	5b102		
McKoy, Isabella m. Chaffin,Solomon	May 30,	1803	Francis Silver		2b214		
McLanahan, Rebecca m. Orrick,Cromwell	Apr. 3,	1843	Daniel McKoy	Lewis F. Wilson	6b299		mr 74 *
McLaughlin, George m. Day, Jane	Mar. 5,	1839	James McSherry	David Young	6b165		
McLaughlin, James m. Gallaher, Eliz.	May 27,	1793	James Day	Hugh Vance		gc 2	
McLaughlin, James m. Morrison,Sarah	Dec. 2,	1788					mr 35 *
McLaughlin, Marg't m. Hooper, John P		1819	John Gallaher	W.N.Scott	4b125		mr 40 *
McLaughlin, Marg't m. Price, Ephraim		1789		D. Thomas			mr 37 *
McLaughlin, Rosa m. McCabe,Lawrence	Oct. 16,	1841	Bernard Feely		6b248		
McLaughlin, Susan m. Gallaher,Patr'k	June 6,	1848	Geo. McLaughlin		7b131		
McLean, John m. Butt, Nancy	Feb. 9,	1820	Barrack Butt		4b134		
McLean, John m. Williamson,Margaret	June 16,	1798	Abr'm Coleman	David Young	1b117	gc 7	
McLean, Robert m. Welsh, Mary	Nov. 22,	1796		John Boyd		cr 11	
McLinsey, Mary m. Graver, George	Dec. 17,	1818	John Doll	John B. Hoge	4b 94		mr 12 *
McMachon, Richard m. Hawker, Barbara	Feb. 27,	1787		Hugh Vance			mr 29 *
McMahon, Barrett m. Smith, Lydia	Apr. 18,	1844	Wm. Smith		6b319		mr 44 *
McMahon, Patr'k J. m.McDermott,Cath.	Oct. 21,	1831	Corn's McDermott		5b207		
McMakin, Lydia m. Miller, Jas. H.	Mar. 15,	1853		James Watts			
McKoy, Mary m. Hayes, Thomas	Dec. 22,	1796		John Boyd		cr 11	mr 13 *

Name	Date	(marriage)	(suretor)	(minister)	(bond)	Ref
McMams, Cath. m. Bodine, John	Aug. 21,	Aug. 22, 1816	John McMams	Rev. Reebenack	4b 6	gc 15 **
McMams, James m. Keesecker, Elis.	Dec. 10,	Feb. 8, 1853	Robert Hill	J.H.Plunkett	4b 93	mr 88 **
McMams, John m. Hill, Sally	Jan. 27,	Dec. 10, 1818	Luke McMams	W.N.Scott	3b 44	mr 30 **
McMams, Polly m. Harding, Richard	Dec. 30,	1807	James McMams		4b254	
McMams, Sarah m. Severs, Charles	Dec. 22,	1823	John McMerla		2b103	
McMerla, Wm. m. Gaff, Mary		1800				*
McMert, Daniel m. Kirkhart, Cath.	Nov. 24,	Dec. 27, 1791		David Young	3b101	gc 1 *
McMitt, John m. Syster, Susannah	Apr. 7,	1808	David Syster		1b x	
McMullen, Alex. m. Murphy, Elis.	Apr. 23,	1789	Zachariah Murphy		3b 87	
McMullen, Marg't m. Foster, Isaac		1808	George McMullen			mr 34 **
McMullen, Mary m. McCluskin, James	Nov. 25,	Oct. 11, 1785		Hugh Vance	5b291	mr 66 **
McMullen, Nimrod m. Fellers, Jane	Mar. 31,	Nov. 28, 1833	Henry Fellers	Nathan Young	5b223	
McMurran, James m. Vanorsdal, Mary	Dec. 4,	1832	Isaac Vanorsdal	John Mathews	4b230	mr 45 **
McMurran, Joseph m. Snodgrass, Eliz.	July 20,	Dec. 3, 1822	Wm. Snodgrass	Jas. M. Brown	5b134	mr 53 **
McMurran, Samuel m. Snodgrass, Ann S	Apr. 11,	July 21, 1829	Wm. Snodgrass		2b233	
McNeal, Eliz. m. Walker, John		1804	John McNeal	B. Reynolds		mr 52 **
McNeal, Jacob m. Davis, Mary Ann	May 10,	July 25, 1828			2b234	
McNeal, Marg't m. Small, James	Apr. 18,	1804	John McNeal	Rev. Reebenack	3b185	gc 12 **
McNeal, Martha m. Dunham(Dur-), Martha	Mar. 10,	Apr. 18, 1811	Jas. B. Small	James Redly	5b 19	mr 48 **
McNeal, Polly m. Cole, Wm.	May 12,	1825	Levi Austin		4b 35	
McNealy, Eliz. m. Chew, Joshua		1817	Robert Snodgrass			
McNett, John m. Soyster, Susan	Apr. 20,	Dec. 1, 1808	Thomas Green	Rev. Reebenack	1b 10	gc 10 **
McNutt, David m. Glass, Margaret		Apr. 22, 1797	Alex. Miller	Richard Swift		cr 27 **
McPhamon(McPherson), Ann m. Moore, Geo.	Mar. 28,	Aug. 10, 1791	Robert Wilson	Moses Hoge	2b229	cr 7 **
McPheerin, Thomas m. Spence, Eliz.	May 6,	1804	Michael Fiser		3b224	
McPheerin, Thomas m. Gaither, Sally	May 2,	May 6, 1812	Isaac Alstadt	Rev. Reebenack	2b 4	gc 12 *
McPherson, Amy m. Massey, John	Apr. 17,	1798	Hugh Black		1b 8	
McPherson, Daniel m. Alstadt, Susana	Mar. 16,	1797	Thomas Spencer		1b173	
McPherson, Marg't m. Fiser, Peter	Jan. 22,	1799	Thos. McQuilkin		4b287	
McQuade, Eliz. m. Yarder, John	Jan. 26,	1825	Abr'm V. Varmetre		6b182	
McQuilkin, Eliza m. Williamson, Jacob	Feb. 25,	1839	Thos. McQuilkin		6b 33	
McQuilkin, Jacob m. Tabb, Elis.	Jan. 18,	1835	Wm.T. McQuilkin		5b214	
McQuilkin, Nancy m. Schoppert, Jacob	Mar. 27,	Jan. 19, 1832	Jacob Williamson	Jacob Medtart	7b 62	mr 63 *
McQuilkin, Rebecca m. Rice, John	Feb. 3,	1846	William Rush		7b213	
McQuilkin, Sarah E. m. Dailey, John	May 21,	1851	Thos. McQuilan		2b235	
McQuilkin, Thos. m. Rush, Sarah	Nov. 8,	1804			5b 83	
McQuillan, Mary m. Varmetre, Thos.		Nov. 8, 1827		B. Reynolds		gc 1 *
McQuint, Esther m. Klein, Christian	May 20,	Nov. 22, 1791		David Young	5b102	mr 52 **
McSherry, Anastasia m. Nicholson, Edw	Apr. 21,	1828	Richard McSherry		6b 9	
McSherry, Cath. m. Doll, George	Feb. 23,	1834	Harrison Waite		3b311	
McSherry, Cath. m. Wolverton, George	Oct. 15,	Feb. 23, 1815	Benj. Thomas	Rev. Reebenack	7b 7	gc 14 *
McSherry, Eliza T. m. McSherry, Wm.	July 3,	1844	James McSherry		5b 72	
McSherry, Mary m. Byrne, Lawrence		1827	Richard McSherry			*

(name)	(marriage)	(suretor)	(minister)	(bond)	
McSherry, Polly m.Boyle(Boyer),Jas.	Jan. 29, 1799	Wm. Mackey Jr.	David Young	1b165	gc 8 *
McSherry, Sally Ann m.Gosnell,Jas.L.	Mar. 4, 1847	Mathew T. Gosnell	James Chisholm	7b 89	mr 77 *
McSherry, Wm. m. McSherry, Eliza T.	Oct. 15, 1844		James McSherry	7b 7	*
McVey, Bridget m. Angel, John	Aug. 10, 1784		Hugh Vance	4b176	mr 53 *
McWhorter, Robert m. Boyd, Mary	Mar. 12, 1821	Robert Boyd	John B. Hoge	4b176	mr 41 *
McWilliams, Geo. G. m. Couchman,Mary	Sept 18, 1851	William Rush	Geo. W. Harris	7b232	mr 85 *

"M"

(name)	(marriage)	(suretor)	(minister)	(bond)	
Mace, Francis m. Hhlett, Ann	Apr. 22, 1789	John Brady		1b x	*
MacGill, Carroll N. m. Clarke, Eliz.	May 11, 1829	Mathew J. Clarke		1b129	
Mackey, James m. Demoss, Jane	Sept 7, 1795		David Young		gc 5 *
Mackey, Sally m. Faulkner, Jas.	Sam'l Dec. 15, 1803	William Mackey	Richard Swift	2b216	cr 27 mr 21 *
Mackey, Wm. Jr. m. Cromwell, Ruth	Sept 6, 1798	James Faulkner	John Boyd	1b128	cr 32 mr 15 *
Mackmedy, Corn's m. Sullivan, Eliz.	May 2, 1840	Timothy Sullivan		6b207	
Macrocklin, James m. Moore, Anna	Aug. 6, 1796		John Boyd		cr 11 mr 12 *
Madden, Aquilla m. Hess, Mary	Mar. 20, 1844	Lorenzo Madden	James Chisholm	6b316	mr 75 *
Madden, Mary A. m. Sandindiver, John	Aug. 8, 9, 1832	Lorenzo Madden	Nathan Young	5b236	mr 64 *
Madden, Patrick m. Holden, Jane	Apr. 26, 1786		Hugh Vance		mr 42 *
Madden, Rachel m. Davis, Joseph	Oct. 19, 1793		Wm. Hill		cr 30 *
Maddock, Ann m. Underdunk, Henry	Dec. 31, 1796		David Young		gc 5 *
Maddox, Aquilla m. Hess, Mary	Mar. 24, 1844	Lorenzo Maddox	James Chisholm	6b316	mr 75 *
Maddox, Cath. m. Stump, Casper	Oct. 14, 1839	Lorenzo Maddox	M.G.Hamilton	6b180	mr 71 *
Maddox, John m. Sweney, Maria	Nov. 1, 1829	Jeremiah Sweney	W. Monroe	5b145	mr 54 *
*Maddox, Mary A. m. Sandindiver,John	Aug. 8, 1832	Lorenzo Maddox	Nathan Young	5b236	mr 64 *
Madison, Mary M. m. Warner, John	July 8, 1845	Wm. Madison		7b 38	*
Magdaline, Maria Mrs. m.Miller,Philip	Nov. 14, 1793				gc 3
Magee, Marg't m. Swisher, George	Dec. 3, 18 8	Michael Runner	David Young	5b213	
Magee, Maria m. Weggoner, John	Mar. 3, 1830	George Hauck		5b154	
Magill, Carroll N. m. Clark, Eliz. A	May 11, 1829	Mathew J. Clark		5b129	
Magill, Nelly m. Coulter, John	Oct. 22, 1806	James Eakin		3b 34	
Magimrds, John W. m. Beales, Marg't	Dec. 23, 1837	David Beales		6b127	
Magnus, Susannah m.Bennett, Thos.	Nov. 25, 1783		Hugh Vance		gc 3 *
Magowan, Wm. m. Davis, Polly	Oct. 10, 1799	Samuel Harrison		2b 30	mr 32 *
Magruder, Daniel m. Davenport, Elenor	Jan. 24, 1798	Hezekiah Young		1b 82	
Magruder, I.W.B. m. Bennett, Lurena	Apr. 5, 1842		Peyton Harrison	6b 87	mr 73 *
Magruder, Robert P. m. VanDoren,Aleta	Nov. 7, 1836	Jacob VanDoren	Peyton Harrison		mr 73 *
Magruder, Thos. P. m. Bennett,Lurena	Apr. 5, 1842	Jacob VanDoren	Peyton Harrison	6b268	*
Mahon, Jane m. Bramhall, James	Aug. 10, 1785		Edwin Tiffin		cr 38 mr 1 *
Mahoney, Cath. m. Rardin, Thomas	Feb. 11, 1839	John Mahoney		6b159	
Mahoney, Ellen m. Casey, Daniel	June 15, 1842	James McSherry		6b212	
Mahoney, Joanna m. Coughlan, Timothy	June 2, 1850	John Hess	Jos. Plunkett	5b218	mr 84 *
*Maddox, Lorenzo m. Hess, Maria	Mar. 3, 1832				

Name	(marriage)	(year)	(surety)	(minister)	(bond)		
Mahoney, Jos. E. m. Triggs, Sarah	Mar. 16,	1843	James McSherry		6b293		
Main, Cath. m. Kopp, Joseph	Dec. 8,	1799	George Grove		2b 38		
Main, Wm. m. Gorgas, Cath.	Aug. 17,	1825	Samuel Gorgas	James Redly	5b 19		mr 48 *
Mallick, Charlotte m. Henshaw, Wash'ton	Apr. 10,	1802	John Barkley		2b170		*
Mallenaux, Sarah m. Chapman, Jost		1794					*
Malone, Casey m. Harden, John	Apr. 14,	1803	Thomas Malone	David Young	2b200	gc 4	*
Malone, Cath. m. Irwin, Robert	Nov. 22,	1803	John Cunningham	David Young	2b214	gc 10	*
Malone, James m. Smith(Stutt), Betsy	Apr. 13,	1798	Chas. McGowan	David Young	1b 91	gc 10	*
Malone, Mary m. Spencer, Richard	Oct. 4,	1798		David Young		gc 7	*
Malone, Nelly m. Warden, Timothy	Aug. 10,	1794		David Young		gc 8	*
Malone, Polly m. Snowdeal, George	Dec. 31,	1811	John Harden	Rev. Reebenack	3b206	gc 12	*
Malonex, James m. Manor, Polly	Aug. 31,	1802	David Manor		2b179		
Maloney, John m. McCabe, Cath.	Mar. 3,	1853	Daniel Conkery	J.H.Plunkett	6b318		mr 88 *
Maloney, Wm. m. Dunavan, Mary	Apr. 11,	1844	Joseph Hoffman		6b260		
Manford, James m. Vorhees, Kesiah	Dec. 23,	1841	Wm. Wilson Jr.	John Hedges	9b306		mr 73 *
Manford, Jane m. Calvert, John A.	Mar. 13,	1834	Thomas Madden	Chas. P. Krauth	5b 43		
Manford, Leatha m. Dennison, Thos.	May 27,	1826	Peter Miller	Hugh Vance			mr 51 *
Manford, Wm. m. Boyd, Mary	Apr. 6,	1786					mr 33 *
Manford, Wm. m. Wilson, Nancy	Jan. 2,	1804	John Helferstay		2b228		
Mardon(Maxwell)Isabel m.Biddle, Geo.	Oct. 10,	1830		Nathan Young	5b176		mr 61 *
Manken, Mary m. Jones, John	Nov. 25,	1794		David Young		gc 4	
Menliky, John m. Mcmaline, Eliz.	June 15,	1794		David Young		gc 4	
Mann, Cath. m. Englatt, Joseph	Oct. 2,	1840	Andrew Mann	David Young	6b219		
Mamm, Marg't m. Englatt, Michael	Oct. 2,	1840	Andrew Mann	David Young	6b219		
Manning, A. m. Clapton, John		1796					*
Manning, Ann m. Price, Jacob	Oct. 19,	1796					
Manning, Jacob m. Rutherford, Mary	Dec. 11,	1798	Edward Christian	John Hett(hutt)	1b135		mr 16 *
Manning, James m. Bovey(Roney), Mary	Sept 25,	1797	Robert Stewart	David Young	7b207		mr 83 *
Manning, Sarah m. Brown, Dennis	Sept 6,	1850	Jonas Hedges		7b155	gc 6	
Manor, Benj. G. m. Hedges, Ruth	Dec. 23,	1849	John Clarke	F.C.Tebbs		gc 6	
Manor, David m. Martin, Jean	Apr. 21,	1805			2b251	cr 11	
Manor, Elenor C. m. Hedges, Samuel	Jan. 21,	1847	Wm. Hedges	E.L.Dulin	7b 83	gc 6	mr 77 *
Manor, Eliz. m. Dunham, Benjamin	Jan. 18,	1813	Samuel Dunham		3b299		
Manor, Eliz. m. Frazier, Thos.	Apr. 12,	1836	David Manor		6b 90		
Manor, Erid m. Beatty, David	Dec. 27,	1807	Benj. Manor		3b 50		
Manor, George m. Lucas, Eliz.	Mar. 10,	1818	Henderson Lucas		4b 79		
Manor, Horner m. Gilbert, Mary Ann	Sept 28,	1841	Samuel Manor	Lewis F. Wilson	7b 17		mr 72 *
Manor, Isabella S. m. O'rork, Jas. K.	Feb. 23,	1844	Fred. Gilbreth	John Reynoldson	4b117		mr 75 *
Manor, John m. Gilbreth, Hannah	Dec. 24,	1818	Samuel Manor	John Howell	6b 52		mr 68 *
Manor, Mary Ann m. Tate, David J.	Oct. 6,	1835	Samuel Lowry	W. Love	7b158		mr 80 *
Manor, Martha Jane m. Pine, John W.	Aug. 6,	1849	John Manor	Mayberry Goheen	6b283		mr 74 *
Manor, Mary Ann m. Hutzler, Joseph	Nov. 5,	1842					
Manor, Polly m. Malonex, James	Aug. 31,	1802	David Manor		2b179		

Name	(marriage)	(suretor)	(minister)	(bond)	ge/cr/gc	mr
Manor, Rosanna m. Dunham, Samuel	Oct. 22, 1846	Joseph Manor		7b 75		
Manor, Samuel m. Booth, Eliz.	Aug. 11, 1804	Caleb Booth		2b240		
Manor, Samuel m. Grimes, Jane	June 23, 1798	Wm. Grimes		1b119		
Manor, Sarah C. m. Lowry, Samuel S.	Jan. 16, 1845	David Gray	John Boggs	7b 21		mr 75 *
Manor, Warner m. Gilbert, Mary Ann	Feb. 23, 1841		Lewis F. Wilson			mr 72 *
Manor, Zebulon W. m. Gilbert, Mary A	Feb. 22, 1841	Edward Gilbert		6b235		
Mans, Susanna m. Miller, John	June 8, 1802	Frederick Mans		2b115		
Mansen, Eliz. m. Kruber, Christian	Feb. 6, 1800		Rev. Reebenack		ge 11	*
Mansen, George m. Schall, Catherine	Apr. 2, 1793		David Young		ge 2	*
Mansfield, Rose Ann m.Ridemour,Geo.	July 10, July 11, 1847	William Butt	James Chisholm	7b100		mr 78 *
Mansfield, Stephen m. Butt, Susanna	Mar. 15, 1822		Nathan Young			mr 57 *
Mansing, Sarah m. Brown, Dennis	Dec. 23, 1850	Robert Stewart	F.C.Tebbs	7b207		mr 83 *
Maple, Jacob m. Sagathy, Marg't	Oct. 11, 1796		David Young		ge 6	
Mapler, Mary m. Morlatt, Abraham	Dec. 2, 1795		Moses Hoge		cr 10	mr 11 *
March, Hannah m. Hollinger, John	Dec. 21, 1799	Henry March		2b 41		
March, Henry m. Hollinger, Mary	Apr. 5, 1800	John Hollinger		2b 62		
Marchant, Abr'm m. Ferby, Nancy	Jan. 13, 1812	Waltman Ferby		3b208		
Marchant, Frances m. Cameron, Joseph	June 23, 1798	Richard Marchant		1b119		
Marchant, Louisa m. Bishop, Elias	Jan. 6, 1818	James Marchant	Mathias Riser	4b 55		mr 29 *
Marchant, Nathan m. Lindsey, Mary	Nov. 18, 1805	David Rees		3b 3		
Marchant, Roady m. Gerrard, Justis	Sept 16, 1797	David Lewis		1b 42		
Mard, Stephen m. Forest, Hannah	Aug. 15, 1799		David Young		gc 8	*
Margrove, Sarah m. Tucker, John	May 29, 1806	Jacob Rees		3b 21		
Markle, Annabel m. McDaniel,Johnston	Sept 2, 1851	B.B.Hollis	David Thomas	7b230		mr 84 *
Markle, Eliz. m. Carper, John	Apr. 22, 1829	Wm. Markle	W. Monroe	5b127		mr 53 *
Markle, Isabel m. McDaniel, J.Porter	Sept 2, 1851	B.B.Hollis	David Thomas	7b230		mr 84 *
Markle, Kitty m. Hoffman, John W.	Jan. 16, 1819	Wm. Markle	Nathan Young	4b 97		mr 56 *
Markle, Mary m. Cresinger, John	Sept 22, 1810	Philip Wright		3b161		
Markle, Rebecca m. McDermott, Philip	Sept 30, 1822	Wm. Markle		4b224		
Markle, Rosanna m. Huttle, Henry	Dec. 27, 1826	Isaac Eversole	Benedict Reynolds	5b 59		mr 51 *
Markle, Wm. m. McCormick, Lucinda	Jan. 8, 1828	Geo. M. Bowers	Jas. M. Brown	5b 87		mr 51 *
Mark, Anna m. Baker, John	Mar. 29, 1799	Mathew Ranson	Moses Hoge	1b176	cr 29	mr 17 *
Mark, Sally m. Rutherford, Van(Wm)	Jan. 4, 1798	Mathew Ranson	Moses Hoge	1b 79	cr 36	mr 14 *
Marke, Sarah m. Rutherford, Van	Jan. 4, 1798	Mathew Ranson	Moses Hoge	1b 79	cr 36	mr 14 *
Marker, Daniel m. Grove, Susan	July 10, 1851	Wm. L. Seibert	David Thomas	7b228		mr 84 *
Marker, Daniel m. Lyle, Emily	Mar. 6, 1838	William Lyle	James Watts	6b136		
Marker, Daniel m. Morrow, Jane E.	Aug. 2, 1832	Harrison Waite	W. Monroe	5b235		mr 65 *
Marker, Eliz. m. Burns, Jacob	May 22, 1823	Daniel Marker	Chas. P. Krauth	4b240		mr 46 *
Marker, Leonard m.Fauber, Eliza	Mar. 15, 1798	Adam Fauber	David Young	1b 89	gc 7	*
Marker, Michael m. Starr, Susanna	Mar. 31, 1807	Fred. Starr		3b 53		
Markfine, John m. Walter, Mary	Dec. 24, 1795		David Young		gc 5	*
Markwood, John m. Dust, Rebecca	Nov. 27, 1797	Paul Dust	David Young	1b 64		*
Markwood,Marg. m. Randal(Reynold)John	Mar. 31, 1800	John Shober	David Young	2b 61	gc 9	*

*Markel (See Markle)

Name	(marriage)		(surety)	(minister)	(bond)		
Marlay, Francis m. Oller, Cath.	June 27,	1815	George Oller		3b329		
Marlay, Gracy m. Butt, John	Sept 16,	1815	John Marlay		3b340		
Marley, John m. Maymugh(Mayhew),Mary	Sept 9.	1806	John Maymugh	John Mathews	3b 28	cr 28	mr 23 *
Marlin, Ann m. Boyd, John		1791				go 1	*
Marlin, Eliz. m. Callahan, Thomas	Jan. 6,	1803	Harvey Boothe	David Young	2b189	go 9	*
Marmaduke, John m. Motter, Cath.	Dec. 17.	1816	John Motter	Lewis Mayer	4b 27		mr 42 *
Maroning, John m. Harris, Rebecca		1790		Moses Hoge		cr 3	mr 5 *
Marquart, Ann m. Kennedy(Kenny)Mathias	Aug. 11.	1805	Nicholas Marquart	John Bond	2b267	cr 28	mr 22 *
Marquart, Eliz. m.Snider(Snyder)Jacob	Dec. 24.	1806	Nicholas Marquart	John Mathews	3b 39	cr 13	mr 23 *
Marquart, Polly m. Chew, Joshua	Mar. 19.	1804	John Marquart		2b228		
Marquart, Sophia m. Ambrose, Daniel	Aug. 4.	1809	Nicholas Marquart	Rev. Reebenack	3b116	go 10	mr 36 *
Marlot, John m. Hageley, Margaret	Dec. 9.	1788		Moses Hoge			
*Marshall, Benj. m. Asenhurst, Eliz.	Sept 12.	1797	Oliver Asenhurst	John Mathews	1b 40		
Marshall, Jane m.Burns(Beems),Wm Jr.	Aug. 27.	1817	William Marshall		4b 44		
Marshall, John m. Payne, Sarah M.	Nov. 15.	1841	Joseph Payne		6b252		
Marshall, Martha m. Bushman, Isaac	Sept 23.	1845	George Roberts		7b 44	?	
Marshall, Martha m. Rosenberger,John	Sept 11.	1826	Thos. Marshall	John Winter	5p 52		mr 50 *
Marshall, Thomas m. Boggs, Ann	Mar. 17.	1823	Boyd Roberts	Chas. P. Krauth	4b234		mr 46 *
Martin, Eliza m. Williamson, Wm.	May 12.	1818	Jeptha Martin	John Mathews	4b 71		mr 44 *
Martin, Eliz. m. Bowers, Jacob	June 23.	1789		Hugh Vance			mr 3 *
Martin, Eliz. m. Callahan, Thomas	Jan. 6.	1803	Harvey Boothe	David Young	2b189	cr 39	
Martin, Ellen E. m. Woodall, Jas. Jos	Nov. 28.	1839	James Martin	John Light	6b184	go 9	mr 70 *
Martin, Jacob m. Sever, Fanny	July 20.	1816	Alex. McDonald		4b 2		
Martin, James m. Johnson, Rachel	Dec. 20.	1815	James Martin	Rev. Reebenack	3b351	ge 15	*
Martin, Jane m. McBride, Vincent	Apr. 16.	1842	James Martin		6b270		
Martin, Jean m. Manor, David	Jan. 21.	1805	John Clarke		2b251		
Martin, Jeptha m. Williamson, Ally	Sept 8.	1792		Moses Hoge			mr 39 *
Martin, John m. Seibert, Rachel Jane	Aug. 1.	1835	Christian Seibert		6b 51		
Martin, Julia m. Rankin, Simeon H.	Dec. 30.	1846	Vincent McBride	John Winter	7b 82	cr 29	mr 77 *
Martin, Kath. m. Eversole, Abr'm	July 10.	1794		W. Hill			mr 9 *
Martin, Levi m. Files, Mary	Aug. 4.	1819	John Files		4b112		
Martin, Levi m. Varmetre, Eliz.	Sept 12.	1798	Nathan Varmetre	Moses Hoge	1b132	cr 29	mr 14 *
Martin, Luther m. Miller, Cath.	Nov. 30.	1853		John Light			mr 86 *
Martin, Manning m. Huffman, Mary	Apr. 4.	1825	Levi Martin	John Mathews	5p 6		mr 50 *
Martin, Marg't m. Thornburg, Thomas	June 25.	1812	Charles Williams	David Young	3b228		mr 40 *
Martin, Mary m. Crook, Andrew	Jan. 25.	1793		A. Talty			
Martin, Mary m. McDonald, Enos	Oct. 12.	1853					
Martin, Mary m. Pitzer, Conrad	Jan. 8.	1838?	James Martin	Peyton Harrison	6b129	go 2	mr 88 *
Martin, Mary m. Tally, Ebenezer	Sept 30.	1845	James Martin	John Boggs	7b 45		mr 69 *
Martin, Peter m. Dun, Mary	Dec. 28.	1791		Moses Hoge			mr 75 *
Martin, Peter m. Eveline, Eliz.	Nov. 3,	1794		Moses Hoge		cr 8	mr 7 *
Martin, Sarah m. Wynkoop, Garret	Aug. 15.	1797	Jeptha Martin		1b 30		mr 9 *
Martin, Sarah Ann m. McBride, James	Oct. 28.	1844	James Martin	John Boggs	7b 10	cr 22	mr 75 *
Martin, Sarah m. Hammond, Chas.	Aug. 23.	1801	Magnus Tate Jr.		2b138		
*Warshall, Eliz. m. Comegys, John	Apr. 26.	1810	Wm. Marshall		3b149		

Name m. Spouse	(marriage)		(suretor)	(minister)	(bond)	ref
Martin, Squire Hacket m.Bowers,Rachel	Aug. 16,	1851	Samuel L. Rees		7b229	
Martin, Sullivan m. Wiler, Ann Maria	Nov. 24,	1842	William Wilen		6b284	
Martin, Wm. m. Winn, Polly	Jan. 7,	1813	Charles Young	Rev. Reebenack	3b246	ge 13 *
Masch, John Nich. m. Friiman,Adeline	May 20,	1846	Norman Miller		7b 66	
Mase, Francis m. Hulett, Ann	Apr. 22,	1789	John Brady		1b x	*
Maslin, Elis. m. Maslin, James L.	July 4,	1837	Harrison Waite	Lewis F. Wilson	6b109	*
Maslin, Hanson m. Tabb, Martha Jane	Feb. 14,	1842	Wm. Cunningham	Lewis F. Wilson	6b265	mr 73 * *
Maslin, James L. m. Maslin, Elis.	July 4,	1837	Harrison Waite	Lewis F. Wilson	6b109	*
Maslin, Joseph m. Lemon, Aura	Sept 4,	1809	George Lemon		3b117	
Maslin, Margaret m. Lemon, Wm.	May 22,	1781		Daniel Sturges	3b 94	mr 31 *
Maslin, Martha m. Bell, John	Mar. 20,	1828	John Griffith		3b300	
Maslin, Mary m. Stewart, John W.	Jan. 13,	1834	Wm. Maslin	Wm. Monroe	6b185	mr 67 *
Maslin, Wm. m. Russell, Elisa B.	Nov. 30,	1839	Thomas S. Page	Lewis F. Wilson	3b 47	mr 70 *
Mason, Alex. m. Strode, Eliz.	Feb. 16,	1807	James Foreman		7b198	
Mason, Bingley J. m. Mason, Edna	Oct. 2,	1850	James Mason	Geo. W. Harris	7b198	mr 83 *
Mason, Edna m. Mason, Bingley J.	Oct. 3,	1850	James Mason	Geo. W. Harris	3b189	mr 83 *
Mason, Elisa m. Rush, Jacob	Mar. 21,	1831	Newton Boley		3b287	
Mason, Elir. m. Mathews, Samuel	Oct. 15,	1833	John Cross		2b106	
Mason, Eliz. m. Perfelter, Philip	Dec. 29,	1800	John W. Wolff		6b291	
Mason, Enoch Geo. m.Purnell,Sarah A.	Mar. 6,	1843	James Mason		6b155	
Mason, Evelina m. Miller, Jacob	Jan. 4,	1839	Solomon Billmire		6b 77	
Mason, James m. Foreman, Nancy	Apr. 5,	1836	Wm. Rush	John Mathews	3b108	mr 23 *
Mason, James m. Rush, Mary	Feb. 20,	1809	John C. Small	B.M.Schmucker	7b211	mr 84 *
Mason, James m. Small, Ann Rebecca	Jan. 20,	1851	Isaac Childs		2b124	
Mason, Jeptha m. Childs, Eliz.	Apr. 28,	1801	Daniel Gehr	Lewis F. Wilson	6b175	mr 70 *
Mason, John m. Gehr, Susan	Sept 14,	1839	James Mason	Lewis F. Wilson	7b 9	
Mason, Mary m. Harrison, Dennis	Oct. 21,	1844	Jacob Miller	D F.Bragunier	7b223	mr 84 *
Mason, Mary Jane m. Houser, Isaac	Apr. 24,	1851	Robert Stephenson	Lewis F. Wilson	7b 16	
Mason, Nancy m. Stephenson, Joseph	Dec. 22,	1844	John Porterfield	Moses Hoge	2b180	cr 17
Mason, Patty m. Newkirk, George	Sept 6,	1802	James Small	Rev. Reebenack	3b101	mr 21 *
Mason, Polly m. Small, John	Nov. 24,	1808	Edward Mason	Moses Hoge	2b269	ge 10
Mason, Sarah m. Wright, Samuel(David)	Aug. 21,	1805	James Mason	W. Hawk	5b287	cr 17
Mason, Sarah A. m.Billmyer, Conrad	Oct. 14,	1833	Samuel Mathews		7b165	mr 22 *
Mason, Thornton W. m. Foreman, Ellen	Oct. 1,	1849	John Gregg	John B. Hoge	4b181	mr 65 *
Mason, Wm. m. Klinger, Sarah	Apr. 18,	1821	John Lockman	Moses Hoge	1b 95	mr 41 *
? Massey, Jesse m. Welsh, Eliz.	Mar. 31,	1798	Michael Fiser		2b 4	cr 36
Massey, John m. McPherson, Amy	May 2,	1798				mr 14 *
* Masters, Henry m. Bell, Rebecca	Apr. 24,	1785	Harrison Waite	Hugh Vance	6b202	mr 33 *
Mathews, Chas. H. m.Lodkins, Eliz.	Mar. 27,	1840	Jacob Poisal	Lewis F. Wilson	7b181	mr 71 *
Mathews, Daniel m. Poisal, Ann Maria	Apr. 16,	1850	John Alburtis	B.M.Schmucker	3b 35	mr 83 *
Mathews, Enoch m. Alburtis, J	Nov. 3,	1806	Harrison Waite		7b 64	
Mathews, George m. Gallaher, Ann R.	Apr. 4,	1846	Andrew Grubb	Wm. Tibbett	1b 15	cr 27
Mathews, John m. Grubb, Margaret	May 4,	1797	John Lockman	Moses Hoge	1b 95	cr 36
? Mason, Jesse m. Welsh, Eliz.	Mar. 31,	1798				mr 13 * / mr 14 *

Name	Date	(marriage)	(surety)	(minister)	(bond)	
Mathews, John m. Moles, Polly	Jan. 1,	Jan. 1, 1810	Zachariah Moles	Rev. Reebenack	3b132	gc 11 *
Mathews, John m. Wilson, Eliz. C.	Apr. 8,	Apr. 8, 1818	John B. Hoge	John B. Hoge	4b 68	mr 29 *
Mathews, Levi m. Butler, Sarah	Jan. 7,	Jan. 7, 1801	Corn's Vanorsdal	Moses Hoge	2b107	cr 38 *
Mathews, Marg't m. Foulk, John S.	Dec. 11,	Dec. 12, 1844	John Wysong	Lewis F. Wilson	7b 15	mr 20 *
Mathews, Maria W. m. Hunter, David	Nov. 18,	Dec. 18, 1835	Enoch Mathews		6b 64	
Mathews, Mary m. Hollis, Thos. P.	Feb. 25,	Feb. 26, 1850	Wm. Mathews	Henry Furlong	7b178	mr 79 *
Mathews, Matilda m. Snyder, John O.	July 6,	July 6, 1843	John Mathews	T.H.W.Monroe	6b302	mr 75 *
Mathews, Nancy m. Hess, Peter		Apr. 28, 1795		David Young		gc 4
Mathews, Samuel m. Mason, Eliz.	Oct. 15,	Oct. 15, 1833	Newton Boley		5b287	
Mathews, Wm. C. m. Hunter, Mary Susan	Aug. 23,	Aug. 23, 1831	Alex. Cooper		5b203	
Mathews, Wm. H. m. Snyder, Cath.	Mar. 7,	Mar. 7, 1833	Jacob Snyder	W. Monroe	5b261	mr 65 *
Mathias, James m. Miller, Margaret		Dec. 9, 1789		Hugh Vance		cr 25
Matlock, Marg't m. Bond, George	May 19,	May 19, 1823	Joel Reed		4b239	mr 4 *
Matlock, Mary m. Benegar, George	Aug. 6,	Aug. 8, 1816	Joel Reed	Nathan Young	4b 8	mr 55 *
Matson, Aury m. Rose, Samuel	Mar. 1,	Mar. 1, 1810	John Matson		3b138	
Matson, Daniel m. Conner, Sarah	Mar. 21,	Mar. 21, 1807	Abraham Howe		3b 51	
Matson, Nehemiah m. Dutton, Sarah	Jan. 30,	Jan. 30, 1807	Daniel Dutton		3b 45	
Matson, Sarah m. Miller, David	Oct. 8,	Oct. 8, 1801	James Kennedy		2b142	
Matton Cornel's m. McIntire, Prudence	June 28,	June 28, 1811	Robert Grimes		3b190	
Mattox, Lorenzo D. m. Hess, Maria	Mar. 3,	Mar. 3, 1832	John Hess		5b218	
Maxwell, Eliz. m. Bowman, Andrew	Aug. 23,	Aug. 23, 1820	John Strother	Henry Furlong	4b157	mr 79 *
Maxwell, Ellen m. Hooper, Edward B.	June 7,	June 7, 1849	Robert Maxwell	Nathan Young	7b160	mr 61 *
Maxwell, Isabella m. Biddle, George	Oct. 9,	Oct. 10, 1830	John Halferstay	David Young	5b176	mr 46 *
Maxwell, James m. Bentness, Mary		Oct. 4, 1794		Chas. P. Krauth		ge 4
Maxwell, James Jr. m. Chambers, Emily	May 8,	May 8, 1823	Seaman Gerard	Hugh Vance	4b238	cr 25
Maxwell, Jane m. Collins, Moses		Dec. 8, 1789				
Maxwell, John m. Fisher, Mary	Nov. 8,	Nov. 9, 1820	Peter Fisher	John B. Hoge	4b166	mr 4 *
Maxwell, John m. Walker, Elinor	Nov. 16,	Nov. 16, 1825	Washington Evans	Chas. P. Krauth	5b 28	mr 41 *
Maxwell, Maria m. Evans, Washington	July 20,	July 20, 1812	James Maxwell		3b230	mr 49 *
Maxwell, Mary m. Elliott, Patrick	May 8,	Mar. 6, 1785		Edward Tiffin		cr 38
Maxwell, Nancy m. Reed, Wm. H.		May 8, 1843	Anthony S. Chamber	T.H.W.Monroe	6b296	mr 1 *
Maxwell, Peggy m. Baley, Daniel	Nov. 19,	Nov. 19, 1795		David Young	5b149	mr 74 *
Maxwell, Susan m. Evans, John T.	Jan. 19,	Jan. 19, 1830	Washington Evans	Wm. Monroe	2b117	ge 5
May, George m. Chesmut, Eliz.	Mar. 9,	Mar. 9, 1801	John Chestnut		4b 42	mr 54 *
Mayburgh, Amos m. Hall, Lorenda	Aug. 5,	Aug. 5, 1817	Peter Kreps		6b109	
Mayers, Abraham m. Ebberts, Marg't	June 10,	June 10, 1794	Esom E. Mayhew	Nathan Young		cr 21
Mayers, Ann m. Park, Joseph		Dec. 23, 1813		John Boyd	3b244	mr 8 *
Mayers, Cath. m. Semaker, Adam	Dec. 28,	Jan. 7, 1814	Stephen Mayer	John Mathews		mr 25 *
Mayers, Eliz. m. Ritz, Samuel(Charles)		Nov. 13, 1793		Rev. Reebenack		ge 14
Mayers, George m. Kyster, Agnes		Nov. 14,		David Young	4b145	ge 3
Mayers, Jacob m. Kroh, Rebecca Marg.	Apr. 17,	Apr. 18, 1820	Henry Kroh	Lewis Mayer	3b196	mr 40 *
Mayers, Nancy m. Shirley(Th.), Wm.	Oct. 7,	Oct. 10, 1811	John Mayer	John B. Hoge	6b124	cr 14
Mayhew, Evan E. m. Sendind(ver), Amelia	Nov. 13,	Nov. 16, 1837	Martin Sendind(ver)	James Watts	5b221	mr 24 *
*Mathews, John T. m. Hedges, Ann Maria	Mar. 22,	Nov. 16, 1832	Anthony Chambers			

Name	(bond date)	(marriage)	(surety)	(minister)	(bond)		
Mayhew, Harriet A. m. Lewis, Walter	Sept 9,	Aug. 26, 1852	John Mayhew	David Thomas	3b 28	cr 28	mr 86 *
Mayhew, Mary W. m. Marley, John	Sept 11,	1806	Mathias Gossett	John Mathews	3b 67		mr 23 *
Mayhew, Percy m. Gossett, Betsy	Aug. 29,	1807	Exon Mayhew		6b103		
Mayhew, Rebecca m. Wilson, David	Apr. 4,	Apr. 6, 1837	Peter Kreps	James Watts	4b 42		mr 55 *
Mayhugh, Amos m. Hall, Lorenda	Aug. 5,	Aug. 7, 1817	Andrew J. Johnson	Nathan Young	7b 47		
Mayhugh, Rachel C. m. Hays, John F.	Nov. 3,	1845	Andrew Criswell		6b188		
Mayhugh, Warner m. Downs, Angelina	Dec. 19,	Dec. 24, 1839		John Light		cr 22	mr 70 *
Medley, Sarah m. Trigger, Clem		Sept 10, 1794		Moses Hoge	5b305		mr 9 *
Medtart, Jacob m. McDonald, Mary E.	Mar. 12,	1834	Robert McDonald		3b220		
Meek, Eliz. m. Barker, Elias	Apr. 13,	1812	John Robinson				
Meek, James m. Shaw, Agnes		July 8, 1789		Moses Hoge	3b104	cr 2	mr 3 *
Meeks, Phebe m. College, John	Dec. 26,	1806	Wm. Bell		6b274		
Megary, Ann m. Smith, Patrick	Aug. 6,	1842	John McNamee				
Megary, John m. Burr, Anna		1801					
Megary, m. White, Thomas	Sept 9,	June 17, 1800?		Moses Hoge	3b 28	cr 38	mr 20 *
Mehn, Mary W. m. Marley, John	May 20,	Dec. 25, 1806	John Mehn	Moses Hoge	4b148	cr 38	mr 20 *
Mehus, Stephen m. Fisher, Elis.		Sept 11, 1820	Andrew Tate	John Mathews		cr 28	mr 23 *
Melehall, Cath. m. Naild, Adam	Mar. 29,	Mar. 31, 1799		David Young		gc 8	
Melick, Fanny m. Miller, Isaac		Mar. 28, 1798	Absalom Miller	John Boyd	1b 92	cr 32	mr 15 *
Melick, Marg't m. Kennedy, George	Jan. 4,	1800	James Kennedy		2b 46		
Melix, David m. Foster, Rebecca	Oct. 12,	1798	Jonas Baldwin		1b138		
Mellenburg, Augustus m. Rice, Jennet	Dec. 13,	Dec. 16, 1838		John Light	6b154		mr 70 *
Mellon, Patrick m. Cooper, Marg't M	Mar. 22,	Feb. 22, 1823	Wm. McCoy		4b234		
Melvin, Eliz. m. Stall, Jesse	Apr. 2,	Apr. 26, 1796	Geo. McLaughklin	Moses Hoge		cr 36	mr 12 *
Melvin, John m. Burr(Burn)Jane	Aug. 30,	Aug. 2, 1791		Moses Hoge		cr 7	mr 6 *
Melvin, John m. Engle(Eagle),Mary	May 30,	June 4, 1799	John Engle	Moses Hoge	2b 8	cr 29	mr 17 *
Melvin, Joseph m. Vanacter, Phebe	Aug. 18,	1785		Hugh Vance			mr 34 *
Melvin, Mary m. Butler, Elsha	Dec. 24,	1793		Moses Hoge		cr 22	mr 8 *
Melvin, Samuel m. Osborne, Polly	Dec. 8,	Dec. 12, 1797	Wm. Osborne	Hugh Vance	1b 71	cr 36	mr 13 *
Melvin, Susannah m. Wright, Samuel		Sept 28, 1785		Moses Hoge			mr 34 *
Melvin, Thomas m. Sly, Mary		Mar. 2, 1792		Moses Hoge			mr 38 *
Mendinghall, Amos m. Dunn, Jane	Jan. 3,	1812	David Dunn		3b207		
Mendinghall, Ann m. Young, Nathan	Aug. 30,	1814	Amos Mendenhall		3b301		
Mendinghall, Elis. m. Baldwin, James	Feb. 21,	1810	Amos Mendenhall		3b137		
Menghind, Chas. L. m. Thomas, Mary	Feb. 20,	1838	Benj. Thomas		6b133		
Menghind, Joidal m. Barnet, James	May 23,	?	Thomas G. Flagg	Peyton Harrison	6b139		mr 69 *
Menser, George m. Black, Polly	Dec. 11,	Dec. 11, 1817	John Black	W.N.Scott	4b 52		
Menser, George m. Rhodes, Sarah	Nov. 22,	1832	Jacob Rhodes		5b248		
Menser, John C. m. Brady, Mary Ann	May 14,	May 14, 1840	Adam Shober	Peyton Harrison	6b209		mr 71 *
Menser, Sarah m. Beeson, George	Nov. 15,	1832	George Memser		5b246		
Meracle, Daniel m. Jackson, Rachel	Apr. 20,	Dec. 25, 1793		Moses Hoge	1b x	cr 22	mr 8 *
Mercer, John m. Barrett, Lydia	Aug. 15,	1789	Edward Mercer		2b 21		
Mercer, Joshua m. McKown, Anna		1799	James Sellers				
*Mesnor, Mary Ann m. Tate, David Jr.	Aug. 6,	Aug. 6, 1835	Samuel Mesnor	John Howell	6b 52		mr 68 *

Name	(marriage) date	year	(suretor)	(minister)	(bond)		
Mercer, Margaret m. Cox, Thomas	Jan. 16,	1786	John Stuart	Hugh Vance	1b101		mr 43 *
Mercer, Phoebe m. Grubb, Adam	July 22,	1798			5b170		mr 61 *
Merchant, Hannah m. Hays, David	July 22,	1830	Barnet Gilbert	Nathan Young	5b 50		
Merchant, Hiram m. Watson, Rachel	Sept 7,	1826	Boyd Roberts		5b 50	cr 30	mr 15 *
Merchant, Isaac m. Studman, Nancy	Nov. 5,	1798	Jonathan Gerrard	John Heitt(Hutt)	1b144		
Merchant, Isaac m. Thomas, Nelly	Feb. 28,	1811	Leonard Thomas		3b177		
Merchant, John m. Sumption, Mary	Feb. 15,	1841	Jacob Sumption		6b233		
Merchant, Justice m. Houseman, Rachel	Sept 2,	1808	Martin Houseman		3b 96		
Merchant, Leana m. Smoot, Joseph	Oct. 17,	1815	Jane Merchant		3b 343		
Merchant, Liddy m. Morgan, Rees	Jan. 30,	1805	Abr'm Merchant		2b253		
Merchant, Louisa m. Bishop, Elias	Jan. 6,	1818	James Merchant	Mathias Riser	4b 56		mr 29 *
Merchant, Mary m. McKee, Robert	Aug. 30,	1825	Boyd Roberts	John Winter	5b 21		mr 50 *
Merchant, Nancy m. Throckmorton, Phil	July 23,	1828	Thomas Horn		5b104		
Merchant, Priscilla m. Bacon, Burwell	Nov. 27,	1813	Wm. Merchant		3b277		
Merchant, Priscilla m. Burwell, Bacon	Nov. 27,	1813	Wm. Merchant		3b277		
Merchant, Rachel m. Locke, Neal	Aug. 7,	1809	Isaac Merchant		3b116		
Merchant, Rebecca m. Dunham, David	Apr. 25,	1808	Abr'm Merchant	Nathan Young	3b 88		mr 56 *
Merchant, Sarah m. Likens, Joseph	Apr. 18,	1818	Bacon Burwell		4b 69		
Merchant, Wm. m. Anderson, Hannah	Aug. 3,	1828	Benj. Custer		5b104		
Merchant, Wm. m. Jeans, Russey	Nov. 23,	1806	Richard Merchant		3b 36		
Merchant, Wm. P. m. Schoppert Rosanna	Sept 14,	1850	George Sedmley	D.F. Bragunier	7b195		mr 80 *
Merl, Kath. m. Shepherd, Richard	Aug. 14,	1781		Hugh Vance			mr 32 *
Mericle, Mary m. Britton, Wm.	Feb. 12,	1820	Wm. Mericle	Nathan Young	4b135		mr 57 *
Meskimen, Nelson m. Woke, Anna	Aug. 11,	1816		Mathias Riser			mr 26 *
Messor, Wm. m. Cruson, Eliz.	Nov. 16,	1786		Hugh Vance			mr 43 *
Metcalf, Amos m. Hyett, Milly	Aug. 3,	1793		Richard Swift			mr 38 *
Metcalf, Drusilla m. Earp, Wm.	Nov. 21,	1785		Hugh Vance			mr 34 *
Metcalf, Vatchel m. Green, Ann	Oct. 22,	1799		Richard Swift		cr 34	mr 16 *
Metz, Ann m. Voorhees, Aaron	Nov. 23,	1840	Joseph Hoffman	David Young	6b225		
Meyer, Cath. m. Bouny, Philip	Mar. 31,	1793		Moses Hoge			
Michael, Alex. m. Kearsly, Betsy	June 17,	1790	Mathias Nichols	David Young	1b178	gc 2	mr 5 *
Michael, Jacob m. Ox, Polly	Apr. 6,	1799	Daniel Ambrose		4b 31	cr 4	
Michael, Martha m. Caw, Isaac	Apr. 2,	1817	Peter Michael	Mathias Riser	3b353	gc 8	mr 26 *
Michael, Mary m. Dawson, Isaac	Jan. 15,	1816	Joseph Franceway	Mathias Riser	1b179		
Michael, Mary m. Riser, Mathias	May 9,	1799		Moses Hoge		cr 2	mr 2 *
Mickler, Michael m. Griffith, Mary	May 5,	1789	Phebe Copeland		3b 17		
Midanda, Francis m. Copeland, Sally	Apr. 28,	1806	Edward Arls		4b 27		
**Midcalf, Edward m. Arls, Sarah	Dec. 28,	1819	David Cushwa	W.N. Scott	5b154		mr 41 *
Middlekauf, John m. Cushwa, Cath.	Mar. 8,	1830	Joseph Henderson	Jas. M. Brown	1b 6		mr 54 *
Middleton, Aby m. Gano, Stephen	Apr. 30,	1797					
Middleton, Adam m. Fulton, Mary	Feb. 28,	1794		Wm. Hill		cr 29	mr 9 *
Middleton, Bethnel m. Gano, Naomy	Oct. 2,	1797	Stephen Gano		1b 51		
Middleton, James m. Mussetter, Ann	Mar. 5,	1827	John Mussetter	Nathan Young	5b 66		mr 59 *
**Metcalf, Edward m. Arls, Sarah	Dec. 28,	1819	Edward Arls	W.N. Scott	4b 27		mr 41 *
**Middlekauf, Ann m. Evans, Chas. H.	Mar. 15,	1854		D.F. Bragunier			

	(marriage)	(suretor)	(minister)	(bond)	
*Middleton, John m. Davis, Ann	Mar. 26, 1821	Bethuel Middleton	John Winter	4b178	mr 50 *
Middleton, John m. Mussetter, Susan	Apr. 10, Apr. 13, 1826	John Mussetter		2b192	mr 59 *
Middleton, Leonley m. Clawson, Okey	Feb. 5, 1803	Stephen Gano		5p 40	mr 59 *
Middleton, Mary m. Kitchen, Thos.	Oct. 31, Nov. 1, 1826	John Shober	Nathan Young	5p 54	mr 75 *
Milburn, Thos. m. Hartsook, Sarah	Oct. 22, Oct. 25, 1827	Enoch Hartsook	Nathan Young	5p 81	
Milburn, Eliz. m. Cronse, Charles	Feb. 18. Mar. 2, 1843	Jesse Gain	John Grove	6p290	mr 81 *
Milburn, Jas. Wn. m. Stuckey, Mary M.	July 3, July 5, 1848	Israel Robinson	P. Lipscomb	7b133	
Milburn, Jane M. Satterfield, James	May 29, June 1, 1848	Jacob VanDoren	P. Lipscomb	7b129	
Miles, Delilah m. Myers, Adam	June 1, 1816	Elijah Compton		4p 4	mr 86 '
Miles, Jacob m. Cox, Eliz.	Apr. 12, 1813	John Groves		3p28	
Miles, Jenny m. Myers, John	Jan. 4, 1808	John Miles		3p 81	
Miles, John m. Bowers, Susanna,Lurena	July 26, June 27, 1852	John Bowers	R.A.Fink	7b257	
Miles, John m. Eversole, Mary	Mar. 19, 1833	Isaac Eversole		5p262	
Miles, John m. Farrell, Mary	Oct. 21, 1800	Joseph Farrell		2p 94	
Miles, Margaret m. Earp, Burgess R.	June 18 June, 6, 1817	Jesse Turner	W.N.Scott	4p 37	mr 86 *
Miles, Marg't A. Shanks, Wn. H.	Jan. 20, 1853		J.M.Dennis		mr 65 *
Miles, Mary m. Cox, Henry	Dec. 25, Dec. 3, 1832	John Floyd	Wm. Hawk	5p251	
Miles, Thomas m. Burns, Mary	Aug. 12, 1841	Joseph Bowers		6b245	
Miles, Wm. m. Cole, Barbara	Oct. 10, 1806	Barney Cole		3p 33	
Miles, Wm. m. Eversole, Cath.	Dec. 23, 1835	Isaac Eversole		2p 48	
Miholland, Agnes m. McFee, James	July 27, Jan. 1, 1795		David Young		gc 4
Milbatton, Eliz. m. Letton, Wm.	Apr. 29, Dec. 26, 1792		David Young		gc 2
Miller, Abigail m. Job, Andrew	Jan. 31, 1786	Wm. Boden	Hugh Vance	4b111	
Miller, Abraham m. Dooly, Eliz.	July 27, 1819	Abraham Snider		4b183	mr 33 *
**Miller, Andrew m. Snider, Charlotte	Apr. 29, 1821	Jacob Miller		2b 86	
Miller, Ann m. Byerly(Bier-), Michael	Sept 6, Sept. 7, 1800	John Fuller	David Young	4b 31	gc 9
Miller, Ann m. Cook, Jacob	Feb. 19, Feb. 20, 1817		W.N.Scott		
Miller, Ann m. Keesecker. Eli	Feb. 14, 1854		John Light		
Miller, Ann m. Morlatt, Richard	Apr. 27, Apr. 29, 1813	John Porterfield	Rev. Reebenack	3b261	gc 13
Miller, Ann m. Vincenheler, John	Dec. 31, Jan. 1, 1803	Jacob Miller	David Young	2b188	gc 9
Miller, Anna M.m. Harris, Geo. W.	Aug. 17, Aug. 10, 1846	Samuel Miller	Joseph Baker	7p 71	
Miller, Ann Rebecca m.Wagely,Jacob W	Dec. 3, 1844	Vance Bell		7p 14	mr 77 *
Miller, Betsy m. Yost, Wm.	Mar. 14, 1812	Nicholas Henry		3b216	
Miller, Casper m. Rizer, Rachel	Dec. 12, 1818	Mathias Rizer		4p 93	
Miller, Cath. m. Andrews, James	Jan. 16, 1850	John Points		7b175	
Miller, Cath. m. Martin, Luther	Jan. 20, Nov. 30, 1853	John Strother	John Light	4b 98	mr 86 *
Miller, Cath. m. Snider, Abr'm	May 19, Jan. 21, 1819	John A. Miller	W.N.Scott	6b 13	mr 30 *
Miller, Cath. E. m. Gorrell, Abr'm V	Sept 13, 1834	Peter Shaffer		2b243	
Miller, Caty m.Paultsgrove, Henry	Aug. 5, 1804	Paul Taylor		4b 15	mr 26 *
Miller, Caty m. Streithoff, Francis	Dec. 20, Aug. 11, 1816	John Miller	Mathias Riser	3p 37	
Miller, Christina m. Weaver, John	Aug. 29, 1806	Conrad Miller		2b140	
Miller, Christian m. Catlett, Eliz.	Dec. 22, 1801	Wm. Davis		7b 81	mr 79 *
Miller, Christian m. Davis, Rebecca	Dec. 24, 1846		John Light		
*Middleton, Eliz. m. Grify, John	Mar. 17, 1791		David Young		
***Miller, Abraham m. Grove, Cath.	Feb. 25, 1814		Robt. V. Snodgrass	3b285	gc 1

	(marriage)		(suretor)	(minister)	(bond)			
Miller, Conrad m. Catlett, Sarah	Aug. 22,	1797	Wm. Catlett		1b 34			
Miller, Conrad m. Groves, Cath.	Feb. 25,	1814	Robt. Snodgrass		3b285			
Miller, Daniel m. Clark, Frances	Dec. 4,	1833	John Clark		5b292			
Miller, Daniel m. Johnson, Jane	Jan. 20,	1833	Harrison Waite		5b251	or 32		
Miller, Daniel m. Long, Sarah	Oct. 2,	1797	John August	John Boyd	1b 53		mr 13	*
Miller, David m. Daniel, Eliz.	Mar. 20,	1800	Wm. Seaman		2b 58			*
Miller, David m. Dennison, Eliz.	Feb. 21,	1815	?	Rev. Reebenack	3b312	gc 14		
Miller, David m. Lyle, Emily	Nov. 14,	1815	William Lyle	W.N.Scott	3b347			*
Miller, David m. Matson, Sarah	Oct. 8,	1801	James Kennedy		2b142		mr 26	*
Miller, David m. Mitchell, Marg't	Nov. 22,	1816	Samuel Mitchell	Lewis Mayer	4b 23		mr 42	*
Miller, David m. Ramsburg, Rebecca	Feb. 6,	1839	John Ramsburg	Lewis F. Wilson	6b159		mr 70	*
Miller, David m. Riser, Sarah Ann	Sept 19,	1846	George Riser		7b 73			
Miller, David m. Young, Mary	Mar. 18,	1820	Wm. Griffith		4b140			
Miller, David m. Daniel, Robert	Nov. 18,	1809	Wm. Miller		3b124			
Miller, Eliz. m. Eversole, Jacob	Apr. 26,	1834	Henry M. Miller		6b 10			
Miller, Eliz. m. Gary, Patrick F.	July 4,	1832	Wm. Showalter		5b233			
Miller, Eliz. m. Gibbons, Giles C.	Sept 30,	1839	Daniel Miller		6b177			
Miller, Eliz. m. Hewitt, Thomas	Sept 18,	1837	David Miller	Lewis F. Wilson	6b111		mr 79	*
Miller, Eliz. m. Hoffman, Wm.	Sept 21,	1846	Jacob Spero	John Light	7b 73			
Miller, Eliz. m. Hovermal, Christian	Sept 24,	1801	Jacob Miller		2b125			
Miller, Eliz. m. Job, Henry	May 14,	1807	Adam Miller		3b 58			
Miller, Eliz. m. Kane, James	Feb. 5,	1810	Henry Myers	Rev. Reebenack	5b135	gc 11		*
Miller, Eliz. m. Leopard, Daniel	Mar. 24,	1814	Wm. Miller	Rev. Reebenack	3b289	gc 14		*
Miller, Eliz. m. Lowry, Samuel	Apr. 27,	1815	Geo. Robinson	Rev. Reebenack	3b320	gc 14		*
Miller, Eliz. m. Miller, Jacob	Feb. 9,	1801	John Miller	John Boyd	2b115	cr 35	mr 19	*
Miller, Eliz. m. Shober, Wm.	Mar. 30,	1820	John Shober		4b142			
Miller, Eliz. m. Showalter, Wm.	Sept 5,	1828	Vincent Bell	Wm. Monroe	5b106		mr 53	*
Miller, Eliz. m. Tabler, Christian	Apr. 15,	1811	George Tabler	Rev. Reebenack	3b184	gc 12		*
Miller, Emanuel m. Turner, Sarah Ann	Nov. 10,	1845	James Turner		7b 48			
Miller, Ephraim m. Kiter, Easter	Feb. 19,	1818		Mathias Riser			mr 29	*
Miller, Evelina m. Haines, Henry	Apr. 26,	1833	Nancy Miller		5b271			
Miller, Fred. m. Snider, Polly	Feb. 20,	1798	Casper Snider		1b 86			
Miller, George m. Hammond, Mary	Dec. 5,	1808	Michael Hammond	Rev. Reebenack	3b102	gc 10		*
Miller, George m. Pitzer, Eliza	Dec. 26,	1839	Jacob Pitzer	Lewis F. Wilson	6b190		mr 70	*
Miller, George m. Raney, Charlotte	Jan. 22,	1839	Jacob Raney		6b156			
Miller, G.W. m. Davis, Mary Eliz.	Sept 13,	1851	Elias Baker	George M. Harris	7b231		mr 85	*
Miller, Harriet B. m. Taylor, Chas.	May 4,	1824	Wm. J. Miller	John Winter	4b264		mr 50	*
Miller, Harriet H. m. Pitzer, Henry	Feb. 16,	1841	David Miller	Lewis F. Wilson	6b234		mr 72	*
Miller, Harrison m. Horne, Emily	Mar. 8,	1851	Joshua Gallaher		7b217			
Miller, Henry m. Coons, Cath.	Aug. 30,	1798	Jacob Coons		1b127			
Miller, Henry m. French, Mary	Apr. 22,	1835	Wm. A. Donaldson		6b 42			
Miller, Henry m. Solster, Eliz.	Oct. 14,	1800	Jacob Miller		2b 92			
Miller, Henry m. Varmetre, Eliz.	Apr. 1,	1800	James Varmetre		2b 61			

Name	date	(marriage)	(surety)	(minister)	(bond)	
Miller, Henry m. Webster, Christina	Sept 30,	Oct. 12, 1820	Henry Snider	John B. Hoge	4b163	mr 41 *
Miller, Henry m. Welshans, Polly	Apr. 1,	1806	Abr'm Welshans		3b 14	
Miller, Henry M. m. Kerns, Sarah C.	Dec. 4,	Dec. 5, 1830	Jacob Kerns	Nathan Young	5b182	mr 61 *
Miller, Isaac m. Melick, Fanny	Mar. 29,	Mar. 28, 1798	Absalom Miller	John Boyd	1b 92	cr 32 · mr 15 *
Miller, Isaac m. Pearce, Cath.	Feb. 13,	1829	Abr'm Morlatt		5b119	
Miller, Isabella m.Thompson, James	Jan. 23,	Jan. 1823	Smith Miller	Chas. P. Krauth	4b232	mr 46 *
Miller, Jacob m. Bodine, Hannah	Dec. 23,	Dec. 28, 1809	John Bodine	Rev. Reebenack	5b129	gc 11 · gc 26
Miller, Jacob m. Filson, Jane		May 26, 1795		Richard Swift		gc 9
Miller, Jacob m. Ronymous, Cath.	Feb. 26,	Mar. 4, 1800	Conrad Ronymous	David Young	2b 55	mr 10 *
Miller, Jacob m. Johnston, Ruth	Sept 6,	1834	John H. Palmer		6b 18	
Miller, Jacob m. Leckner, Susan	Sept 30,	1816	John Mulhall	John B. Hoge	4b 10	
Miller, Jacob m. Leopard, Mary		June 11, 1789		Christian Streit		cr 15 · mr 4 *
Miller, Jacob m. Mason, Eveline	Jan. 4,	1839	James Mason		6b155	
Miller, Jacob m. Miller, Eliz.	Feb. 9,	Feb. 10, 1801	John Miller	John Boyd	2b115	cr 35 · mr 19 *
Miller, Jacob m. Moore, Mary	Apr. 20,	Apr. 20, 1802	James Moore	John Boyd	2b172	cr 8 · mr 20 *
Miller, Jacob m. Orndorff, Eliz.	Mar. 12,	1812	Christ'r Orndorff		2b165	
Miller, Jacob m. Waugh, Nancy	Jan. 16,		Singleton Waugh		3b209	
Miller, Jacob A. m. Trigg, Marg't	June 1,	June 2, 1831	Jeremiah Trigg	Nathan Young	5b196	mr 61 *
Miller, James D. m. Ramsburg, Eliza	Mar. 28,	Mar. 29, 1838	George Ramsburg	Lewis F. Wilson	6b137	
Miller, Jas. H. m. McMahon, Lydia		Mar. 15, 1855		James Watts		
Miller, Jacob R. m. Green, Mary Ann	Mar. 6,	Feb. 9, 1832	John Green	Jas. M. Brown	5b218	mr 64 *
Miller, James m. Rumsey, Mary		Oct. 18, 1796		John Boyd		cr 11 · mr 12 *
Miller, Jane m. Brabson, Thomas		Feb. 13, 1795		John Boyd		cr 33 · mr 10 *
Miller, Jane m. Park, John		Jan. 19, 1797		John Boyd		cr 32 · mr 13 *
*Miller, Jeremiah m. Potsal, Susan	Nov. 13,	Nov. 1, 1851	Jacob Potsal	D. Thomas	7b236	mr 85 *
Miller, John m. Bell, Hannah	Jan. 25,	Jan. 25, 1820	Wm. Bell		4b131	
Miller, John m. Frog, Ruby		May 8, 1794		David Young		gc 4
Miller, John m. Grove, Mary	Nov. 18,	Nov. 19, 1812	John Grove	Rev. Reebenack	3b241	gc 13
Miller, John m. McDaniel, Mary	Nov. 10,	Nov. 10, 1846	Alex. McDaniel	John Winter	7b 77	
Miller, John m. Mans, Susanna	June 8,	1802	Frederick Mans		2b115	mr 77
Miller, John m. Nicholson, Mary Maria	Sept 6,	Sept 7, 1809	John Meyers	Rev. Reebenack	3b118	
Miller, John m. Reed, Jane	May 10,	1800	Joseph Oalton		2b 69	gc 10
Miller, John m. Ropp, Mary	June 3,	1819	Solomon Ropp		4b109	
Miller, John m. Shockey, Eliz.	Sept 5,	1800	Christian Shockey		2b 85	
*Miller, John m. Sutton, Susanna		Oct. 3, 1788		Hugh Vance		
Miller, John m. Zimmerman, Cath. Mrs.	Oct. 18,	Oct. 19, 1828	George Hughes	B. Reynolds	5b109	mr 36 *
Miller, John A. m. Miller, Susanna		Mar. 24, 1842		Peyton Harrison		mr 52 *
Miller, John A. m. Trigg, Mary	June 2,	1831	Jeremiah Trigg	Nathan Young	5b197	mr 73 *
Miller, John A. m. Waller, Susanna	Mar. 23,	Mar. 24, 1842	George Weller	Peyton Harrison	6b267	mr 61 *
Miller, John W. m. McAllister, Mary	May 20,	May 22, 1844	Benj. McAllister	John Light	7b 1	mr 73 *
Miller, Joseph m. Devinney, Eliza A.	Oct. 18,	1826	*Edmund B. Hunter	Chas. P. Krauth	5b 54	mr 76 *
Miller, Joseph m. Hamilton, Marg't		1808	Alex. Miller		3b 99	mr 51 *
Miller, Joseph A. m.McDonald,Angelin	Dec. 14,	1852		James Baker		mr 87 *
*Miller, John m. Bailey, Ruth	Mar. 25,	1782		Daniel Sturges		mr 42 *

*John Shober also was a suretor.

Name	date	(marriage)	(surety)	(minister)	(bond)		
Miller, Joshua m. Crowl, Margaret	Oct. 28,	Oct. 31, 1799	Thomas Thompson	John Heitt(Hutt)	2b 32	cr 33	mr 17 *
Miller, Judith m. Fry, Jacob	Dec. 22,	1800	Thomas Sharp		2b103		
Miller, Julian m. Miller, Wm. J.	Feb. 19,	1820	Richard S. Head		4b136		
Miller, Kitty m. Smith, Joseph	Nov. 23,	Nov. 23, 1819	George Miller	W.N.Scott	4b124		mr 40 *
Miller, Lucy m. Gladden, Joseph	Oct. 23,	Oct. 23, 1828	John Miller Jr.	J.B. Reynolds	5b111		mr 52 *
Miller, Lucy m. Painter, John	Sept 19,	Sept 19, 1822	Jacob Hill	Chas. P. Kreuth	4b224		mr 45 *
Miller, Magdaline m. Sheets, Adam		Nov. 20, 1793		David Young		gc 3	
Miller, Margaret m. Hill, George	Dec. 20,	1817	John Miller		4b 53		
Miller, Margaret m. McDonald, Wm.	Apr. 13,	1824	Harrison Waite		4b262	cr 25	
Miller, Margaret m. Mathias , James	Feb. 12,	Dec. 9, 1789	John F. Strode	Hugh Vance	7b 27		mr 4 *
Miller, Margaret m. Otty, Wm.		Feb. 13, 1845		John Light		gc 4	mr 76 *
Miller, Maria m. Good, John	Oct. 29,	Dec. 16, 1794	Henry Miller	David Young	2b 95		
Miller, Mary m. Brown, Adam	May 30,	1800	Joshua Miller		3b327		
Miller, Mary m. Chamberlain, Joseph	Apr. 13,	June 1, 1815	Jonas Miller	Nathan Young	2b233		mr 55 *
Miller, Mary m. Hedges, Joshua	June 27,	1804	Henry S. Seibert		7b161		
Miller, Mary m. Hill, Job C.	Feb. 25,	1849	John Long		5b303		
Miller, Mary m. Long, Thomas	May 7,	1834	James Miller		2b261		
Miller, Mary m. Lowry, Wm.	May 22,	1805	Henry Job		3b 20		
Miller, Mary m. Shoppert, Jacob	Apr. 18,	1806	Jacob Miller		3b 56		
Miller, Mary m. Snider, Abraham	Dec. 11,	1807	Michael Miller		3b 79		
Miller, Mary m. Spitsmogle, Adam	Aug. 21,	1806	George Miller		4b 11		
Miller, Mary m. Starr, John		Aug. 22, 1816		Rev. Reebenack	5b121	gc 15	*
Miller, Mary m. Westenhaver, John	Mar. 3,	1829	Hezekiah Hedges		7b192		mr 83 *
Miller, Mary Ann m. Gorrell, G.W.	Aug. ?	Aug. ?, 1850	Wm. S. Miller	Lewis F. Wilson	7b 86		mr 79 *
Miller, Mary Ann m. Riser, John	Feb. 13,	Feb. 15, 1847	Henry M. Miller	John Light	6b 47		
Miller, Mary Jane m. Davis, Benj.	June 16,	1835	Thomas Miller		3b174		
Miller, Michael m. Eglestone, Ann	Feb. 13,	Feb. 14, 1811	John Porterfield	John B. Hoge	4b 86	cr 14	mr 24 *
Miller, Michael m. Morlatt, Lancy	Nov. 4,	Nov. 5, 1818	Abraham Morlatt	W.N.Scott	2b 40	gc 9	mr 30 *
Miller, Nancy m. Compton, Isaac		Dec. 19, 1799					
Miller, Nancy m. Johnstone, Robert	Dec. 19,	Mar. 12, 1810	Elijah Compton	David Young	3b140		
*Miller, Nancy m. King, Wm. B.	Mar. 12,	Feb. 20, 1806	James Miller	Moses Hoge	3b 12	cr 17	mr 22 *
Miller, Nancy m. Vermilion, Charles	Feb. 18,	May 14, 1811	Absalom Miller	Rev. Reebenack	3b186	gc 12	mr 54 *
Miller, Nancy m. Hensell, David	Apr. 29,	Apr. 21, 1814	Christian Miller	Nathan Young	3b295		
Miller, Nancy E. m. Henshaw, James W.	Apr. 20,	Dec. 8, 1837	Wm. D. Miller	Lewis F. Wilson	6b126		
Miller, Nancy E. m. Thatcher, John W.	Dec. 11,	Dec. 8, 1842	James H. Miller	Lewis F. Wilson	6b285		mr 73 *
Miller, Peggy m. Elliott, Thomas	Dec. 6,	1800	David Miller		2b 47		
Miller, Peggy m. Lowry, John	Jan. 6,	1808	Samuel Elliott		3b100		
Miller, Philip m. Magdaline,Maria Mrs	Nov. 22,		Wm. Miller				
Miller, Polly m. Chenoweth, Samuel		Nov. 14, 1793	Joseph Miller	David Young		gc 3	mr 16 *
Miller, Polly m. Showers, Segismund	Aug. 6,	Aug. 8, 1799	James Maxwell	John Boyd	2b 17	cr 34	mr 57 *
Miller, Rebecca m. Gallaher, Robert	Aug. 8,	Feb. 8, 1820	John Shober	Nathan Young	4b133		
Miller, Rebecca m. Westenhaver,Jacob	Aug. 8,	1826	Henry Polsgrove		5b 47		mr 22 *
*Miller, Rosanna m. Beall, Jeremiah	Oct. 9,	Oct. 13, 1805	James McSherry	John Bond	3b 1	cr 28	mr 75 *
*Miller, Nancy m. Gerrard, Wm.	Aug. 30,	Aug. 31, 1843	David Miller	T.H.W.Monroe	6b303		
**Miller, Rebecca m. Gorrell, John B.	May 23,	Dec. 5, 1854	Geo. W. Harris		3b 89		mr 88 *

Name	(marriage)		(suretor)	(minister)	(bond)	
Miller, Rosanna m. Houte, Peter	Nov. 21,	1786		Hugh Vance	4b 16	mr 43 *
Miller, Samuel m. Bedinger, Maria	Mar. 27,	1816	Henry Bedinger	Alex. Balmain	6b128	mr 26 *
Miller, Samuel m. Cross, Sarah	Dec. 27,	1837	Conrad Bilhaire		6b 34	
Miller, Samuel m. Powell, Marg't W.	Mar. 3,	1835	Harrison Waite			
Miller, Sarah m. Everhart, Christ'r		1785				mr 33 *
Miller, Sarah m. Silver, Joseph	June 1,	1813	James McDonald	Hugh Vance	3b260	gc 13
Miller, Sarah m. Young, Bernard	Apr. 20,	1822	Solomon Swisher	Rev. Reebomack	4b213	mr 45 *
Miller, Sarah E. m. Grove, Wm. I.	May 4,	1846	John Kearfott	Chas. P. Krauth	7b 74	mr 77 *
Miller, Smith m. Gray, Mary Ann	?		Thomas Miller	Joseph Baker	5b 2	mr 48 *
Miller, Smith m. Lyle, Harriett Ann	Mar. 1,	1825	Wm. Lyle	Jas. M. Brown		mr 74 *
Miller, Sophia m. Hill, Jacob	Dec. 19,	1843	John Miller	Lewis F. Wilson	6b310	mr 45 *
Miller, Susan m. Sheneberg, Michael	May 2,	1822		Chas. P. Krauth	4b212	
Miller, Susan E. m. Grove, Wm. I.	July 31,	1794		David Young		
Miller, Susannah m. Bowers, Wm.	Oct. 4,	1846	John P. Kearfott	Joseph Baker	7b 74	gc 4
Miller, Susanna m. Fisher, Fred.		1836	Samuel Miller		6b 84	
Miller, Susanna m. Miller, John A.	Sept 10,	1801	Mathew Ransome		2b123	
Miller, Thomas m. Chenoweth, Mary P.	Apr. 24,	1842	Joseph Chenoweth	Peyton Harrison	5b166	mr 73 *
Miller, Wm. m. Hensell, Selly	May 10,	1830	Henry Coutchman	Jas. M. Brown	3b170	mr 54 *
Miller, Wm. H. m. Price, Isabella Ann	Jan. 3,	1811	Wm. D. Wilson	John B. Hoge	5b289	cr 14 / mr 24 *
Miller, Wm. J. m. Wilson, Margaret	Dec. 10,	1846	John Likens		7b 80	mr 77 *
Miller, Wm. S. m. Miller, Julian	Feb. 8,	1820	Richard S. Head	John Winter	4b136	
Miller, Wm. S. m. McKown, Isabella M.	Jan. 9,	1851	John McKown	Lewis F. Wilson	7b210	mr 87 *
Miller, Zachariah m. Shimp, Cath.	Mar. 7,	1802	John Shimp		2b164	
Millholland, Daniel m. Starr, Cath.		1792		David Young		gc 2
Mills, Josiah m. Dutton, Nancy	Sept 17,	1821	David Dutton	George M. Frye	4b189	mr 44 *
Mills, Rebecca m. Gorrell, John B.	Nov. 17,	1854		George W. Harris		mr 88 *
Miner, Ellen m. Hamilton, Hannah	Dec. 5,	1793		Edward Tiffin		mr 8 *
Miner, Ellen m. McCarty, Flory	Apr. 26,	1850				cr 9
Hines, John m. Kearsley,Marg't(Peggy)	Oct. 9,	1799	Michael Sullivan	Moses Hoge	7b199	
Minghini, Hanna m. Faulkner, James	Apr. 23,	1825	John Kearsley		2b 2	cr 29
Minghini, Joidal m. Barnet, James	May 23,	1838	Cornelius Kelly	Peyton Harrison	5b 12	mr 17 *
Minghini, Mary R. m. Rites, Geo. M.	June 10,	1852	Thos. G. Flagg		6b139	mr 69 *
Mingle, Margaret m. Black, Samuel	Nov. 9,	1811	Henry C. Mathews	Rev. Reebomack	7b257	
Mingle, Polly m. Sprigg, Robert	Nov. 10,	1788	Robert Spriggs	Rev. Reebomack	3b200	gc 12
Minton, Sarah m. Vanjakel, Vermont	Dec. 22,	1859	Samuel Black	Moses Hoge	3b204	gc 12
Mirth, John m. Vent, Mary	Nov. 19,			R.A.Fink		mr 36 *
Mitchell, Cath. m. Ward, Adam	Mar. 30,	1799	Samuel Thompson		1b177	
Mitchell, David m. Bulger, Nancy	Dec. 11,	1838	John McCleary		6b153	
Mitchell, Eliz. m. Flgg, John	Mar. 13,	1792		Moses Hoge		cr 26
Mitchell, Hannah m. Keating, Wm.	Mar. 15,	1800	John Throckmorton		2b 68	mr 7 *
Mitchell, Marg't m. Miller, David	Apr. 23,	1816	Samuel Mitchell	Lewis Mayor	4b 23	mr 42 *
Mitchell, Samuel m. Hess, Maria	Nov. 14,	1825	Peter Hess	Chas. P. Krauth	5b 27	mr 49 *
Mitchell, Susannah m. Butt, Edward	Nov. 21,	1812	John Richason	Rev. Reebomack	3b243	gc 13

Name	(marriage)	(surety)	(minister)	(bond)		nr
Mitchell, Wm. m. Bane, Margaret	June 23, 1840	Jacob Gooten	James Redly	6b214	go 1	nr 72 *
Mixell, John m. Faschbdin, Metla	Jan. 25, 1791		David Young	4b263		nr 47 *
TMixell, Mary m. Gard, Elias	Apr. 29, 1824	Adam Mixell	J.L.Bromwell	4b263		nr 47 *
TMixell, Mary m. Gard, Eli	Apr. 29, 1824	Adam Mixell	J.L.Bromwell	4b117		nr 40 *
TThixell, Susan m. Ring, Wm.	Oct. 2, 1819	John Mixell	Charles P. Krauth	3b 26		*
Mock, Margaret m. Smith, Alex.	Oct. 23, 1806	Robert Jones			cr 22	nr 94 *
Mock, Peter m. Pennybaker, Susanna	Apr. 1, 1788		Hugh Vance			nr 8 *
Modley, Ella m. Fraser, Alex.	Oct. 22, 1793		Moses Hoge	2b264		*
Moffett, John m. Seaman, Elenor	June 4, 1805	Cornelius Seaman			gc 3	*
Moffett, Rachel m. Close, Joseph	Nov. 21, 1793		David Young		gc 3	*
Moffett, Wm. m. Cook, Elis.	Dec. 5, 1793		David Young		gc 7	*
Moixall, Adam m. Walters, Elis.	Jan. 2, 1798		David Young	1b 78	gc 4	*
Moixal, Cath. m. Rhor, Christian	May 9, 1795	Christian Rohr	David Young			nr 40 *
TThoixell, Susan m. Ring, Wm.	Oct. 2, 1819	John Mixell	Chas. P. Krauth	4b117		nr 36 *
Molding, Elis. m. Randolf, John	July 9, 1788		Moses Hoge		cr 4	nr 5 *
Moler, Adam m. Banks, Mary	May 25, 1790		Moses Hoge		cr 6	nr 6 *
Moler, John m. Griffith, Sarah	Mar. 8, 1791		Moses Hoge			
Moler, Robert m. Carroll, Mary M.	June 11, 1849	George A. Carroll		7b160		nr 26 *
Moles, Daniel m. Bowman, Cath.	Jan. 16, 1819	Peter Howard	W.N.Scott	4b 97		nr 81 *
Moles, Elis. m. Barnett, George	Dec. 12, 1815	Z. Moles		3b350		*
Moles, Elis. m. Crin(Crem), Henry	Apr. 25, 1850	Daniel Moles	Henry Furlong	7b183		*
Moles, Mary A. m. Eaton, John M.	Oct. 20, 1842	Daniel Moles		6b280		*
Moles, Polly m. Mathews, John	Jan. 1, 1810	Zachariah Moles	Rev. Reebemack	3b132		*
Moley, Patrick m. Waln, Susanna	Oct. 17, 1797	William Waln		1b 55	go 11	
Mcmaline, Elis. m. Manliky, John	June 15, 1794		David Young			
Momers, Henry m. Rob, Sarah	June 12, 1796		David Young			
Mong, Cath. m. Seibert, Jacob	Sept. 10, 1812	John Mong	Rev. Reebemack	3b236	gc 4	nr 42 *
Mong, Elis. m. Hawk, Michael	Sept. 19, 1816	John Mong	Lewis Mayer	4b 14	gc 5	
Mong, Elis. m. Winning, Thos. R.	Apr. 1, 1834	George Mong		6b 2	gc 13	nr 63 *
Mong, Eve m. Eachus, David	Aug. 20, 1828	Jacob Seibert	Jacob Medtart	5b106		
Mong, John m. Bender, Magdalena	Aug. 20, 1793		David Young		go 3	
Mong, Margaret m. Gladden, Wm.	Dec. 20, 1823	John Mong	Chas. P. Krauth	4b254		nr 46 *
Mong, Margaret m. Leman(Lemon), Wm.L	Mar. 10, 1842	Harrison Waite	Peyton Harrison	6b266		nr 73 *
Mong, Mary m. Seibert, Samuel	Jan. 7, 1819	John Mong	Lewis Mayer	4b108		nr 31 *
Mong, Nancy m. Diffenderfer, Philip	May 1, 1832	John Mong	Jacob Medtart	5b227		nr 64 *
Mong, Nancy m. Zorn, John	Apr. 5, 1823	George Mong	Chas. P. Krauth	4b237		nr 46 *
Mong, Sarah m. Small, John C.	Mar. 21, 1827	John Mong	Chas. P. Krauth	5b 65		nr 51 *
Mong, Susanna m. Stewart, David	Feb. 10, 1842	Wm. H. Mong	Lewis F. Wilson	6b263		nr 73 *
Mong, Wm. H. m. Seibert, Mary C.	Mar. 7, 1843	George Seibert		6b292		
Monmouth, Louisa m. Johnston, Samuel	Aug. 9, 1833	Wm. Wilson	Geo. W. Humphreys	5b279		nr 67 *
Monroe, Agnes m. McDonald, Allen	July 17, 1783?		Hugh Vance			nr 32 *
Montague, Mary m. McCormick, Wm.	Nov. 10, 1853		J.H.Plunkett			nr 88 *
Montgomery, George m. Gibson, Sarah	Aug. 7, 1794		Edward Tiffin		cr 25	nr 9 *

Name (marriage)	(marriage) date	surety	minister	(bond)	cross-ref
Montgomery, Robert m. Payne, Sally	Dec. 9, 1801	George Payne	Moses Hoge	2b151	mr 35 *
Moody, Philip m. Snyder, Eliz.	Mar. 28. 1833	Jacob Pultz		5b264	mr 61 *
Mooler, Henry m. Welsh, Mary	1788				
Moon(Moore), Geo. m. Eglestone, Hanna	Feb. 15, 1830	Henry Nichols	Nathan Young	5b172	
Moon, Hannah m. Arick, George	Aug. 5. 1823	John Helferstay		4b251	
Moon, Hiram m. Underdunk, Nancy	Oct. 30. 1839	Henry Underdunk	M.G.Hamilton	6b168	mr 71 *
Moon, Jacob m. Houseworth, Mary	May 4, 1847	Hiram Bowen	J. Boggs	7b105	mr 78 *
Moon, Jacob m. Rees, Leah	Sept 1. 1806	Daniel Rees		3b 16	
Moon, Jacob m. Underdunk, Sarah	Apr. 17, 1823	Henry Underdunk	J·Nathan Young	4b244	mr 58 *
Moon, James m. Pine, Eliz.	Aug. 4, 1800	Michael Brown		2b 54	
Moon, Jane m. Rees, Daniel	Feb. 25. 1823	Thomas Moon		3b 25	
Moon, Rees m. Young, Eliz.	Aug. 15. 1806	Nathan Young		3b159	
Moon, Thomas m. Job, Lydia	Sept 1. 1810	John Shober		3b 22	
Moon, Valentine m. Henshaw, Margaret	June 4, 1806	James Henshaw		7b201	
Mooney, Phebe m. Baldwin, Wm.	Nov. 4, 1850	Evan Rees		1b152	
Moore, Anna m. Macrocklin, James	Dec. 8. 1798		John Boyd		cr 11 mr 12 *
Moore, Charles m. Cross (Cra-),Marg.	Aug. 6, 1796		Richard Swift		gc 26 mr 10 *
* Moore, Eliz. m. Creamer, George	Sept 19, 1795	Johnson Moore	Rev. Reebenack	3b169	gc 11 mr 6 *
Moore, George m. McPhanon, Anna	Dec. 24. 1810		Moses Hoge		cr 7 mr 99 *
Moore, Gilman m. Vanorsdal, Ann	Aug. 10, 1791		Moses Hoge		
Moore, Henry m. McGowan, Ann C.	June 12. 1792	Thomas Smith		5b148	
Moore, James V. m. Voorhees, Phebe A	Dec. 21. 1829	Gamnet Voorhees		6b213	gc 9
Moore, James W. m. Whitson, Sarah R	June 13, 1840	Benj. T. Whitson		7b 57	
Moore, John m. Bishop, Eliz.	Feb. 10. 1846	John Bishop	David Young	2b 78	mr 56 *
Moore, John m. Knupp, Eliz.	July 25, 1800	Valentine Knupp	Nathan Young	4b 89	mr 36 *
Moore, Johnson m. Kitzmiller, Martha	Nov. 21. 1818		Hugh Vance		mr 55 *
Moore, Joseph m. Walters, Mary	July 27, 1788	Isaac Walters	Nathan Young	4b 11	
Moore, Julia m. Young, Nathan	Nov. 22, 1816	George Creamer		4b191	gc 10 mr 99 *
Moore, Margaret m. Hollingsworth, Wm.	Nov. 25, 1821	Jeremiah Jack	Rev. Reebenack	3b118	cr 8 mr 20 *
Moore, Martha m. Vanorsdal, Cornel's	Mar. 7. 1809		Moses Hoge		gc 6
Moore, Mary m. Miller, Jacob	Mar. 4, 1792	James Moore	John Boyd	2b172	
Moore, Nancy m. Bishop, George	Sept 25, 1802		David Young		
Moore, Nancy m. Butler, Wm.	Sept 8. 1800	Vincent Moore		2b 57	
Moore, Patsy m. Karinger, Jacob	Sept 10, 1806	Johnstone Moore		3b 36	
Moore, Peter m. Coyle, Mary	Dec. 27, 1797	Wm. Coyle		1b 49	
Moore, Phebe m. McDonald, Hugh	Apr. 20, 1799	John Conway		1b167	
Moore, Rachel m. Nigh, Jacob	Apr. 20. 1815			3b317	
Moore, Rebecca m. Siler, John	Feb. 28. 1822	Jonathan Moore	Rev. Reebenack	4b227	gc 14 *
Moore, Richard m. Bishop, Marg't	Mar. 17, 1797	George Creamer	David Young	1b 61	gc 7 mr 12 *
Moore, Sarah m. Davis, Thos. W.	Nov. 19, 1796	Valentine Grace	Moses Hoge		cr 36 mr 1 *
Moore, Sarah m. Linvil, Elisha	Sept 28. 1787		Hugh Vance		cr 18
Moore, Susan Jane m. Tabler, Ephraim	Jan. 27. 1846	James W. Moore		7b 56	
* Moore, Geo. m. Aclestone, Hannah	Aug. 4, 1830	Henry Nichols	Nathan Young	5b172	mr 61 *

Name	(marriage)		(surety)	(minister)	(bond)		
Moot, Cath. m. Schenck, Adolph	Mar. 21,	1846	Johanus Buffaim	D.F.Bragunier	7b 61		mr 78 *
Moot, Philip m. Reniche, Frederica	July 24,	1844	George Reniche		7b 4		mr 88 *
Moran, Daniel m. Greer, Cecelia	Dec. 22,	1852		J.H.Plunkett			
Morehead, Achsah m. Stanford, John	Nov. 24,	1798	George S. Harris		1b149		mr 84 *
Morehead, Eliz. m. Hardie, Geo. W.	Apr. 1,	1851	Samuel Morehead	B.M.Schmucker	7b220		
Morehead, Moses m. Patterson, Annie	Aug. 27,	1801	Moses Collins		2b139		
Morgan, Cath. m. Hedges, Josiah	Oct. 21,	1800	Morgan Morgan		2b 94		mr 49 *
Morgan, David m. Morrison, Susan	July 26,	1825	Richard Morrison	Benedict Reynolds	5b 16		
Morgan, David m. Foltz, Eve	Apr. 7,	1800	Jacob Gardiner		2b 63		
Morgan, Drusilla m. Thornburg,Azariah	June 15,	1798	William Lemen	Moses Hoge	1b116		mr 14 *
Morgan, Drusilla m. Williams, Chas.	May 2,	1815	? ?		3b322	cr 29	
Morgan, Elinor m. Selby, Walter B.	Dec. 27,	1797	M. Ranson		1b 75		mr 13 *
Morgan, Eliz. m. VanKirk, John	Dec. 24,	1797		Moses Hoge			mr 34 *
Morgan, Eliz. Ann m. Ross, Alfred	Dec. 29,	1785		Hugh Vance			mr 54 *
Morgan, Eliz.S. m. Chamberlain,Jos.B	Nov. 30,	1829	Wm. G. Morgan	Wm. Monroe	5b146		mr 76 *
Morgan, Humphrey m. Phillips, Susanna	May 10,	1845	Morgan Morgan	James Chisholm	7b 34		mr 30 *
Morgan, Isaac m. Roberts, Letitia	Oct. 5,	1819		Mathias Riser			mr 31 *
		1781		Daniel Sturges			
Morgan, James m. Walley, Maria	Apr. 11,	1814	Henry Packer	Rev. ReeBenack	3b292	go 14	mr 7 *
Morgan, John m. Torrence(Fau-)Rebecca	Apr. 8,	1793		Moses Hoge		cr 21	mr 30 *
Morgan, Joncy m. Johnson, Margaret	Nov. 21,	1819		Mathias Riser			
Morgan, Levi m. Ross, Lydia	June 23,	1835	Alfred Ross	J.E.Jackson	6b 48		mr 7 *
Morgan, Margaret m. Cox, John	May 20,	1835	Henry Miller	John Light	6b 44		mr 67 *
Morgan, Margaret m. Morgan, Zacheis	Apr. 15,	1790		Moses Hoge		cr 4	mr 5 *
Morgan, Maria m. Swinley, John	Nov. 29,	1831	Wm. G. Morgan	J.E.Jackson	5b210		
Morgan, Martha m. Cosgrove, Patrick	Dec. 16,	1844	Mathias Kyne		7b 15		
Morgan, Mary m. Lemen, Alex.	Aug. 24,	1793		Richard Swift			mr 39 *
Morgan, Mary m. Lewis, Thomas	Nov.	1789		D. Thomas			mr 37 *
Morgan, Mary m. Salehamer, John	Sept 2,	1835	Conrad Roush		6b 56		
Morgan Morgan m. Chamberlain, Mary	Nov. 17,	1819	Ellis Rees		4b123		
Morgan, Mary m. McCarty, Rachel		1790		Moses Hoge		cr 3	mr 4 *
Morgan, Olivia m. McCollough, John	Jan. 11,	1787		Hugh Vance		cr 18	mr 1 *
Morgan, Raleigh m. Swearingen, Liddy	July 26,	1790		Moses Hoge		cr 5	mr 5 *
Morgan, Rebecca m. Gardner, Peter	Dec. 5,	1798	Jacob Gardner		1b151		
Morgan, Rebecca m. Knox, James	Sept 16,	1837	John Faris	John Winter	6b111		mr 49 *
Morgan, Rebecca m. Swingle, Benoni	Nov. 17,	1823	Morgan Morgan		4b252		
Morgan, Rees m. Merchant, Liddy	Jan. 30,	1805	Abr'm Merchant		2b253		
Morgan, Sarah m. Comegys, Wm.	June 21,	1842	James Foreman		2b 74		
Morgan, Sarah m. McKown, Samuel	Apr. 11,	1835	Jeptha Morgan		6b270		
Morgan, Solomon m. Snyder, Eliza	Aug. 1,	1851	Joseph Merlatt	Richard Swift	6b 51	er 34	
Morgan, William m. Lemen, Ann Ward	Sept 18,	1829	George Lemon	Lewis F. Wilson	7b233		mr 18 *
Morgan, Wm. m. Rees, Phebe	Mar. 17,	1800	Ellis Rees	Lewis F. Wilson	5b123		mr 73 *
Morgan, Wm. m. Spurr, Sarah	Dec. 24,	1800	Solomon Offutt		2b105		mr 87 *
Morgan, Wm. G. m. Henshaw, Mary C.	Feb. 25,	1839	Hiram Henshaw	Lewis F. Wilson	6b161		mr 70 *

Name	(marriage)		(surator)	(minister)	(bond)		
Morgan, Wm. S. m. Baker, Ann R.	Feb. 28.	1833	Alex. Cooper		5b259	cr 4	mr 5 *
Morgan, Zacheis m. Morgan, Margaret		Apr. 15, 1790		Moses Hoge		gc 15	*
Morlatt, Abr'm m. Beller, Eliz.	Aug. 8.	Aug. 1, 1816	Henry Seibert	Rev. Reebenack	4b 7	cr 10	mr 34 *
Morlatt, Abr'm m. Linden, Ann		Aug. 2, 1785		Hugh Vance		cr 10	mr 11 *
Morlatt, Abr'm m. Mapler, Mary		Dec. 2, 1795		Moses Hoge			*
Morlatt, Abr'm m. Myers, Eliz.	Aug. 23,	1806	Adam Myers		3b 27		*
Morlatt, Bunn m. Morrison, Jane	Dec. 16,	Dec. 17, 1811	John Kyser	Rev. Reebenack	3b203	gc 12	
Morlatt, Elenor m. Morlatt, Jacob	Feb. 18,	1811	Abr'm Morlatt		3b176		*
Morlatt, Elinor m. Davis, Benj.	Mar. 30,	1818	Peter Morlatt	W.N.Scott	4b 67	gc 13	mr 19 *
Morlatt, Eliz. m. Lee, James	Mar. 13,	Mar. 14, 1813	Joseph Morlatt	Rev. Reebenack	3b256	gc 12	
Morlatt, Eliz. m. Smith, Jacob	Oct. 15,	Oct. 16, 1800	Philip Smith	Richard Swift	2b 93		
Morlatt, George m. Smith, Polly	Nov. 22,	Nov. 24, 1811	James Mason	Rev. Reebenack	3b201	gc 12	
Morlatt, Isaac m. Eglestone, Eliz.	Jan. 1,	Jan. 1, 1818	Richard Morlatt	W.N.Scott	3b176		
Morlatt, Jacob m. Morlatt, Elenor	Feb. 18,	1811	Abr'm Morlatt		3b305	gc 14	
Morlatt, Joseph m. Hoke, Nancy	Sept 28,	1814	Peter Hoke	Rev. Reebenack	4b 86		mr 30 *
Morlatt, Lancy m. Miller, Michael	Nov. 4,	Sept 29, 1818	Abr'm Morlatt	W.N.Scott	3b139		
Morlatt, Mary m. Covenhaver, Joseph	Mar. 6,	Nov. 5, 1810	Josiah Varmetre			cr 10	mr 11 *
Morlatt, Nancy m. Dunham, Abel		Dec. 24, 1795		Moses Hoge			
Morlatt, Rebecca m. Bodine, Wm.	Nov. 19,	Dec. 24, 1816	George Morlatt		4b 22		mr 44 *
Morlatt, Rhnanna m. Varmetre, Wm.	Feb. 16,	1822	John Morlatt	John B. Hoge	4b208		mr 33 *
Morlatt, Richard m. Beller, Lidy	Apr. 27,	Mar. 29, 1786		Hugh Vance			
Morlatt, Richard m. Miller, Ann	Oct. 16,	Apr. 29, 1813	John Porterfield	Rev. Reebenack	3b261	gc 13	
Morlatt, Sarah m. Shrader, Michael	Apr. 17,	Oct. 17, 1813	Abel Dunham	Rev. Reebenack	3b273	gc 13	
*Morlay, Margaret m. Green, Thomas	Apr. 22,	1812	John Morlay		3b221		
Morris, Ann m. Varmetre, Abisha	Sept 8,	Apr. 23, 1833	Abr'm Varmetre	Nathan Young	5b269		mr 66 *
Morris, Ann Amelia m. Smith, Jacob		1851	John Morris		7b230		mr 84 *
Morrison, Alen m. McCarthy, Florenz	Oct. 9,	Oct. 9, 1850	Michael Sullivan	Jos. Plunkett	7b199		mr 85 *
Morrison, Alfred m. Welshans, Ann Eliz	Sept 21,	Sept 21, 1851	Harrison Tabler	John Hanney	7b233		mr 53 *
Morrison, Ann Rebecca m. Bowers, Hiram	Dec. 18,	1828		W. Monroe			
Morrison, Cath. m. Seibert, Samuel	Jan. 15,	1836	Jacob Seibert		6b 69		mr 26 *
Morrison, Chas. m. Mortimore, Mary	Oct. 20,	Oct. 19, 1815	Timothy Mortimore	W.N.Scott	3b345		
Morrison, Daniel Jr. m. Porterf'ld, J.	May 21,	May 26, 1825	Wm. Porterfield	John Mathews	5b 10		mr 50 *
Morrison, Geo. P. m. Tabb, Eliz. B.	Dec. 4,	Dec. 6, 1849	James Ijams	Lewis F. Wilson	7b169		mr 83 *87
Morrison, Hannah C. m. Page, Thos. S	Dec. 22,	1835	Wm. Morrison		6b 67		
Morrison, James m. Baker, Mary E.	Dec. 30,	1839	Otho Baker		6b191		
Morrison, James m. Christian, Lucinda	Oct. 18,	Oct. 18, 1827		B. Reynolds		gc 12	mr 52 *?
Morrison, Jane m. Morlatt, Bunn	Dec. 16,	Dec. 17, 1811	John Kyser	Rev. Reebenack	3b203		
Morrison, Jean m. Newsom, John	Jan. 14,	1799	Hugh Morrison		1b162		mr 62 *
Morrison, John m. Anderson, Rebecca	Nov. 26,	Nov. 27, 1846	Colbert Anderson	Nathan Young	5b209		
Morrison, Mary m. Crim, John S.	June 8,	1831	John Faris		7b 69		
Morrison, Mary m. Riser, David	July 18,	1825	?		5b 15		
Morrison, Richard m. Kimble, Mary	Aug. 8.	1801	Richard Merchant		2b135		
Morrison, Sarah m. McLaughlin, James		Aug. 8, 1788		Hugh Vance			
*Morlay, Gracy m. Butt, John	Sept 16,	May 27, 1815	John Morlay	John Morlay	3b340		mr 35 *

Name (m. spouse)	(marriage)		(suretor)	(minister)	(bond)		
Morrison, Susan m. Morgan, David	July 26,	1825	Richard Morrison	Benedict Reynolds	5b 16		mr 49 *
Morrison, Wm. S. m. Baker, Virginia	Jan. 28,	1830	Wm. C. Compton	W. Monroe	5b150		mr 54 *
Morrow, Ann R. m. Bower, Hiram	Dec. 18,	1828	James Morrow	Wm. Monroe	5b115		mr 53 *
Morrow, James m. Christian, Lucinda	Oct. 18,	1827	Israel Hoge	B. Reynolds	5b 80		mr 52 *
Morrow, James m. McKewan, Mary	Sept 27,	1797	Chas. McKewan		1b 47		
Morrow, James m. Shoafstall, Deborah	Aug. 10,	1835	Harrison Waite		6b 54		
Morrow, Jane E. m. Marker, Daniel	Aug. 2,	1832	Harrison Waite	Wm. Monroe	5b235		mr 65 *
Morrow, John m. Peyton, Mary	July 6,	1781		Daniel Sturges			mr 31 *
Morrow, Mary m. Robinson, Leonard	Apr. 14,	1796		Moses Hoge			mr 11 *
Morrow, Wm. m.Risner(Reiner),Elis.	Mar. 4,	1805	James Morrow	John Bond	2b256	cr 36	mr 22 *
Mortal, Abr'm m. Clanson, Anna	Jan. 22,	1788		Moses Hoge		cr 28	mr 35 *
Mortal, Peter m. Colbert, Jean	Oct. 2,	1788		Moses Hoge			mr 36 *
Mortimore, Mary m. Morrison, Charles	Oct. 20,	1815	Timothy Mortimore	W.N.Scott	3b345		mr 26 *
Morton, Prudence m. Walker, Henry	Nov. 1,	1799	?	John Boyd	2b 33	cr 34	mr 17 *
Morton, Sarah m. Hammond, Chas.	Aug. 23,	1801	Magnus Tate Jr.		2b138		
Moss, Elis. m. Keith, Jacob	Mar. 30,	1793		Wm. Hill		cr 30	mr 10 *
Motter, Cath. m. Marmaduke, John	Sept 24,	1807	Elisha Boyd	Lewis Mayer	3b 71		
Motter, John m. ? Cath.	Dec. 17,	1816	John Motter		4b 27		mr 42 *
Motter, John m. Kontzman(Couch-)Cath.	Dec. 17,	1816	Presley Marmaduke		4b 26		
Mound, Wm. m. Senseman, Rebecca	May 19,	1795		David Young		go 4	*
Mound, Wm. m. Senseman, Rachel	Apr. 18,	1820		Lewis Mayer			*
Mound, Wm. m. Welsh, Mary T.	Feb. 5,	1794	Samuel C.P.Welsh	B. Page			mr 40 *
Mounts, Elis. m. Henshaw, Jonathan S	Aug. 27,	1838	Seth Duncan		6b145		
Mounts, George m. Hoffman, Mary	Feb. 18,	1799	Joseph Randall		1b169		
Mounts, Providence m.Vanmetre,Hannah	Jan. 25,	1843			6b288		
Mountz, Elis. m. Jackson, George	Sept 20,	1785	Alex. Eckhart	Hugh Vance	1b 84		mr 34 *
Mouser, Elis. m. Groover,Christian	Feb. 7,	1798	Jacob Mouser		3b136		
Howdes, Adam m. Hawkins, Rebecca	Feb. 16,	1810	Wm. McDaniel		1b129		
Muck, Caty m. Bentley, Jeremiah	July 22,	1792	William Jack	David Young	6b150	gc 2	*
Mudcap, Rebecca m. Ward, Archibald	Nov. 12,	1838	Jacob A. Shepherd		7b194		
Mudge, Wm. R. m. Brannon, Virginia H.	Sept 9,	1850		David Young		gc 6	*
Mulhall, John m. Harris, Jane	Dec. 30,	1796					
Munn, John B. m. Murphy, Elis.	July 9,	1847	Jos. M. Murphy	J.H.Jennings	7b 99	gc 5	*
Munn, John B. m. Murphy, Elis.	Aug. 28,	1849					
Muntz, Barbary m. Otuem, Peter	Apr. 12,	1796		David Young			
Murman, Michael m. Knadler, Mary M.	Sept 2,	1845	David Knadler		7b 42		mr 82 *
Murphy, Abr'm m. Compton, Cath.	Mar. 4,	1833	Ezekiel Compton	Nathan Young	5c260		mr 66 *
Murphy, Cath. m. Cashman, John	Oct. 13,	1819	Jacob Murphy	W.N.Scott	4b119		mr 30 *
Murphy, Cath. m. Schmier, Dennis	May 16,	1846	Michael Russell		7b 66		
Murphy, David m. Thatcher, Martha	July 28,	1806	Thomas Thatcher		3b 24		
Murphy, Dennis m. Trenton, Susan	Oct. 3,	1807	Wm. McCausland		3b 73		
Murphy, Elenor m. Dorney, Alex.	July 26,	1794		David Young		gc 4	*

Name	(marriage)	(suretor)	(minister)	(bond)			
Murphy, Eliza. m. Cunningham, Hugh	Dec. 20, 1833	William Faris	Jas. M. Brown	5b297		mr 67	*
Murphy, Eliza m.Johnson, Joseph	Aug. 16, 1813	Wm. Anderson	Rev. Reebenack	3b269	gc 13		*
Murphy, Eliz. m. McMullen, Alex.	Apr. 7, 1789	Zachariah Murphy		1b x			*
Murphy, Eliz. m. Munn, John B.	July 9, 1847	Jos. M. Murphy		7b 99			
Murphy, Eliz. m. Munn, John B.	Aug. 28, 1849		J.H.Jennings			mr 82	*
Murphy, Ephraim m. Varley, Susannah	Feb. 17, 1804	Thomas Varley		2b222			
Murphy, Geo. W. m. Kennedy, Jane	June 11, 1838	Samuel Roney		6b140			
Murphy, Hannah m. Berley, Thomas	Feb. 13, 1840	Daniel Mullins		6b196			
Murphy, Harrison. m. Kennedy, Eveline	Mar. 22, 1847	Geo.W. Murphy		7b 92			
Murphy, Jacob m. Lowman, Mary	Apr. 20, 1814	Ephraim Lowman		3b295			
Murphy, James m. Snodgrass, Eliz.	Nov. 14, 1803	Wm. Snodgrass		2b213			
Murphy, James m. Wallingsford, Phebe	Oct. 22, 1789		Hugh Vance	5b217	cr 25	mr 4	*
Murphy, John m. English, Mary	June 24, 1788		Moses Hoge	6b101		mr 35	*
Murphy, John m. France, Eliz.	Oct. 20, 1795		David Young	2b108	gc 5		
Murphy, John m. Winning, Jane	Feb. 21, 1832	Wm. Anderson		7b 98			*
Murphy, Lydia m. Anderson, John	Mar. 8, 1837	Geo. W. Hensel	Lewis F. Wilson	3b114			
Murphy, Lydia m. Dunn, Robert Jr.	Jan. 13, 1801	Ephraim Murphy	John Boyd	2b244	cr 35	mr 19	*
Murphy, Michael m. Helferstay, Lydia	June 7, 1847	Jacob VanDoren		7b 36			
Murphy, Nancy m. Anderson, Wm.	June 27, 1809	John Winning		6b118			
Murphy, Philip m. Clasby, Polly	Sept 6, 1804	Robert Grimes	John Bond	4b157	cr 13	mr 21	*
Murphy, Philip m. Johnson, Cath.	May 31, 1845	William Abel	Lewis F. Wilson	6b 35		mr 77	*
Murphy, Rebecca S. m. Rooney, James	May 16, 1838?	Harvey Hedges	Peyton Harrison	1b 20		mr 69	*
Murphy, Rose Ann m. Orr, John W.	Apr. 5, 1853		Geo. W. Cooper	2b212		mr 87	*
Murphy, Sally m. Garard, Caleb	Aug. 21, 1820	John Fearls		6b146			
Murphy, Samuel m. Johnson, Lydia	Mar. 6, 1835	Joseph Johnson		1b105			
Murphy, Wm. m. Hall, Susannah	June 10, 1799	Thomas Murphy		6b227			
Murphy, Wm. m. Kennedy, Jane	Nov. 8, 1803	Samuel Kennedy		4b261			
Murphy, Wm. m. Rutherford, Cath.	Sept 18, 1838	John Rutherford	James Watts	6b274		mr 69	*
Murphy, Wm. m. Sevt, Ann	Mar. 24, 1798	David Smedley		2b198			
Murray, Ann m. Sively, Patrick	Dec. 10, 1840	Michael Murray		2b168			
Murray, John m. Myers, Margaret	Apr. 2, 1824	Michael M. Fiser		1b 61			
Murray, Nimrod m. Wilson, Ann	Aug. 3, 1842	James McSherry		5b 66			
*Murray, Patrick m. Higgins, Margaret	Mar. 21, 1852	John Conwell	J.H.Plunkett	5b263	cr 27	mr 88	*
Murray, Wm. m. Conwell(Connell), Ann	Mar. 24, 1803	Samuel Davenport	Richard Swift	4b209	gc 7	mr 21	*
Murray, Zachariah m. Smith, Mary Mrs.	Apr. 3, 1802	Valentine Grase		6b 80			
Murrer, Richard m. Bishop, Margaret	Nov. 16, 1797		David Young	5b263		mr 99	*
Mussetter, Ann m. Middleton, James	Mar. 5, 1827	John Mussetter	Nathan Young	3b302		mr 66	*
Mussetter, Aphesiba m.Lucas,Basil Jr.	Mar. 28, 1833	John Mussetter	Nathan Young	4b245		mr 57	*
Mussetter, Barbara m.Rambaugh (Ru)Geo	Mar. 27, 1822	John Mussetter	Nathan Young				*
Mussetter, Eliz. m. Lucas, Dennis	May 25, 1836	John Mussetter					*
Mussetter, Jane A. m. Lucas, Basil	Mar. 28, 1833	John Mussetter	Nathan Young			mr 66	*
Mussetter, Margaret m. Shaffer, Geo.	Sept 8, 1814	Christ'n Mussetter	Lewis Mayers			mr 25	*
Mussetter, Mary m. Rumbaugh, Wm.	Aug. 24, 1823	John Mussetter	Nathan Young		gc 4	mr 58	*
*Murray, Sarah m. Harper, James	Nov. 13, 1794		David Young				

Name	(license)	(marriage)	(surety)	(minister)	(bond)	
Mussetter, Mary m. Rambaugh. Philip	Sept 13,	Aug. 24, 1823	Israel Robinson	Nathan Young	7b107	mr 58 *
Mussetter, Plummer m. Hedges, Mary E	May 12,	Sept 15, 1847	John Winter	John Winter	5b101	mr 78 *
Mussetter, Ruth m. Gano, James H.	May 13,	May 13, 1828	Nathan Young	Nathan Young	4b 88	mr 60 *
Mussetter, Sarah m. Stewart, Adam	Nov. 19,	Nov. 19, 1818	Christn Mussetter	W.N.Scott	5b 40	mr 30 *
Mussetter, Susanna m.Middleton,John	Apr. 10,	Apr. 13, 1826	John Mussetter	John Winter	4b213	mr 50 *
Myers, Aaron m. Hedges, Mary	May 14,	May , 1822	Josiah Hedges	Chas. P. Krauth	7b254	mr 45 *
Myers, Abr'm m. Crim, Deborah	May 24,	May , 1852	Richard M. Crim		4b 4	
Myers, Adam m. Miles, Delilah	June 1,	, 1816	Elijah Compton			*
Myers, Alfred m. Fellers, Mary Jane		Mar. 22, 1855	John Myers	J.L.Frary	7b 72	
Myers, Ann m. Wigle, John		Mar. 9, 1854				
Myers, Arch'd m. Myon, Sarah Ann		Oct. 29, 1835	Jacob Riner	John O. Proctor	6b 59	mr 68 *
Myers, Arch'd m. Riner, Rosannah		Mar. 3, 1836	Henry Fellows	John Howell	6b 73	mr 68 *
Myers, Benj. m. Fellows, Eliz.		Aug. 10, 1815	John Myers	John Howell	3b333	
Myers, Betsy m. Crowl, George		Mar. 27, 1819	John Myers		4b103	
Myers, Cath.m. Fiser, Michael		Feb. 20, 1837	Peter Myers Jr.	Lewis F. Wilson	6b 98	
Myers, Cath. m. Kislnger, James		Mar. 14, 1814	John Myers	Lewis F. Wilson	3b288	go 14
Myers, Cath. m. Seibert, Michael		Sept 13, 1830	Jacob Myers	Rev. Reebenack	5b174	
Myers, Cath. m. Sprinkle, Welcome		Mar. 22, 1795				
Myers, Cath. m. Wolff, George		Feb. 22, 1816	Peter Myers	David Young	3b356	go 4
Myers, Daniel m. Vincenheller,Nancy		Feb. 26, 1838	John Lemaster	W.N.Scott	6b133	mr 26 *
Myers, David m. Lemaster, Eliz. A.		Nov. 19, 1831	Henry Myers		5b208	
Myers, Eliz. m. Couchman, John G.		Feb. 8, 1847	Conrad Robbins	Jacob Medtart	7b 85	mr 63 *
Myers, Eliz. m. Guinn, John		Apr. 27, 1808	John Myers		3b 88	
Myers, Eliz. m. Hensell, Michael		Aug. 23, 1806	Adam Myers		3b 27	
Myers, Eliz. m. Morlatt, Abr'm		Dec. 28, 1791				
Myers, Eliz. m. Severs, Henry		Dec. 20, 1796				
Myers, Eliz. m. Short, Daniel		, 1821		David Young		gc 1 *
Myers, Eliz. m. Start, Govey		Nov. 25, 1846	John L. Myers	David Young	4b198	gc 6 *
Myers, Elvira m. Stewart, Samuel L		June , 1818	Aaron Myers		7b 77	
Myers, George m. Compton, Anna		Mar. , 1858	Exekiel Compton	James Chisholm	4b 73	mr 77 *
Myers, George m. Siler, Sarah		Mar. 27, 1849		Mathias Riser		mr 29 *
Myers, Harriet m. Herring, Wm. T.		Nov. 18, 1798	Jacob Myers	J.H.Jennings	7b149	
Myers, Henry m. Duffield, Rachel		Dec. 10, 1820	Peter Hedges	B.M.Schmucker	1b147	mr 79 * / gc 8
Myers, Henry m. Harris, Emily		Feb. 13, 1783	Samuel Hedges	David Young	4b169	mr 40 *
Myers, Henry m. Kaign, Susanna		Apr. 5, 1808		James Paynter		mr 32 *
Myers, Henry m. Sybert, Cath.		Oct. 21, 1842	Jacob Sybert	Hugh Vance	3b 84	
Myers, Henry m. Wilson, Maria		Sept 7, 1843	Benj. Comegys		6b279	
Myers, Henry W. m. Linton, Ann E.		Aug. 18, 1821	Zachariah Linton	Mayberry Goheen	6b304	mr 74 *
Myers, Isaac m. Hudson, Cath.		Jan. 5, 1854	John Brennan	T.H.W.Monroe	4b 187	mr 75 *
Myers, Isaballa m. Zorn, W.J.		Apr. 11, 1811		Nathan Young		mr 57 *
Myers, Jacob m. Claycomb, Barbara	Apr. 3,	Apr. 11, 1811	? Conrad Claycomb	James Watts	3b183	cr 14 / mr 24 *
Myers, Jacob m. Kroh, Margaret	Apr. 18,	Apr. 18, 1820	Henry Kroh	John B. Hoge	4b145	mr 40 *
Myers, Jacob m. Siler, Hannah	Mar. 17,	Mar. 20, 1832	Philip Siler	Lewis Mayer / Nathan Young	5b220	mr 64 *

Name	(marriage)		(surety)	(minister)	(bond)		
Myers, James m. Collins, Mary	Jan. 1,	Jan. 2, 1845	Joseph Collins	Lewis F. Wilson	7b 19		*
Myers, James m. Wilson, Maria	Oct. 19,	Oct. 21, 1842	Benjamin Comegys	Mayberry Goheen	6b279		mr 74 *
Myers, Jesse m. Grove, Eliz.	Apr. 22,	Apr. 1822	?	Chas. P. Krauth	4b211		mr 45 *
Myers, John m. Everhart, Cath.	Jan. 29,	1798	George Everhart		1b 83		*
Myers, John m. Fiser, Margaret	Mar. 13,	Mar. 16, 1813	Michael Fiser	Rev. Reebenack	3b255	gc 13	
Myers, John m. Miles, Jenny	Jan. 4,	1808	John Miles		3b 81		*
Myers, John m. Robinson, Martha	Dec. 17,	Dec. 18, 1798	Alex. Robinson	David Young	1b154	gc 8	
Myers, John m. Shober, Ann	Feb. 6,	Feb. 6, 1812	John Shober	Rev. Reebenack	3b211	gc 12	
Myers, John m. Snyder, Maria	Apr. 23,	Apr. 27, 1828	Abr'm Snyder	Nathan Young	5b 99		mr 60 *
Myers, John Jr. m. Claycomb, Mary	Dec. 8,	1801	Conrad Claycomb		2b151		
Myers, Lewis m. Line, Cath.	Nov. 5,	Nov. 5, 1809		Rev. Reebenack		gc 10	
Myers, Louisa m. Criswell, Joseph	Feb. 8,	Feb. 16, 1847	Aaron Myers	James Chisholm	7b 85		mr 77 *
Myers, Lydia m. Stine(Stein), Henry	Sept. 20,	Sept 20, 1849	John Myers	Jos. Plunkett	7b165		mr 84 *
Myers, Margaret m. Murray, John	Apr. 2,	1824	Michael Fiser		4b261		mr 47 *
Myers, Margaret m. Syster, Jacob	May 17,	May 20, 1824	Teter Myers Jr.	J.L.Bromwell	4b266		mr 74 *
Myers, Margt Ann m. Kyne(Kl-)Mathias	July 3,	July 4, 1843	Jacob Myers	Lewis F. Wilson	6b301		mr 83 *
Myers, Mary m. Alder, Thomas	Jan. 23,	Jan. 23, 1837	John Daily	R.T.Berry	7b212		mr 24 *
Myers, Mary m. Seibert, Jacob	Mar. 7,	Mar. 8, 1810	John Myers	Lewis Mayers	3b139	cr 14	mr 64 *
Myers, Mary m. Small, Adam	Mar. 26,	Mar. 29, 1832	Henry Myers	Jas. M. Brown	5b222		
Myers, Nancy m. Fiser, James	Aug. 28,	1815	John Myers		3b336		
Myers, Nancy m. Lee, James	Dec. 31,	Dec. 31, 1829	Isaac Myers	Nathan Young	5b 46		mr 60 *
Myers, Philip m. Hudson, Mary	Aug. 8,	Aug. 10, 1826	Adam Myers	Nathan Young	3b 9		mr 58 *
Myers, Polly m. Henry, George	Jan. 30,	1806	?		2b258		
Myers, Polly m. Silvers, Wm.	Mar. 23,	1805					
Myers, Prudence m. Kitchen, John J.	Feb. 19,	Feb. 19, 1844	Henry Kitchen	Nathan Young	6b314		mr 56 *
Myers, Sally m. Henry, Wm.	Mar. 19,	Mar. 22, 1818	Richard Henry		4b 66		
Myers, Samuel m. Richardson, Mary	Aug. 19,	Aug. 19, 1812	Thomas Richardson		3b233		
Myers, Sarah m. Barrack, Samuel M.	June 5,	June 5, 1838	Harrison Waite	James Watts	6b140		mr 69 *
Myers, Sarah m. French, John	Nov. 11,	Nov. 1822	Teter Myers	Chas. P. Krauth	4b227		mr 45 *
Myers, Sarah m. Thornburgh, Eli	Sept 6,	Sept 6, 1824	John L. Myers		4b271		
Myers, Sarah Ann m. Coffenberger, Sam.	Mar. 25,	May 16, 1858		J.H.Jennings	6b203		*
Myers, Sarah Ann m. Couchman, Henry	Dec. 2,	1840	Henry Myers	James Chisholm	7b115		mr 78 *
Myers, Sarah Ann m. Seibert, John N.	June 10,	Dec. 8, 1847	Aaron Myers	Jas. M. Brown	5b132		mr 53 *
Myers, Sarah m. Robbins, Levi K.	Jan. 16,	June 11, 1829	Teter Myers Jr.	Thomas Adams	3b 42	cr 16	mr 23 *
Myers, Susan (Sarah) m. Evans, Isaac	Dec. 3,	Jan. 18, 1807	Teter Myers	Henry Myers	6b185		mr 70 *
Myers, Susan m. Robbins(-bens)Conrad	Feb. 13,	Dec. 3, 1839	Henry Myers	Lewis F. Wilson	6b160		mr 70 *
Myers, Susan m. Robbins, George W.	Jan. 10,	Feb. 14, 1839	Garrett Wynkoop	Lewis F. Wilson	3b132	cr 14	mr 24 *
Myers, Susannah m. Nichols, John	Sept 18,	Jan. 11, 1810	Henry Myers	Lewis Mayer	2b181		
Myers, Teter Jr. m.Vincenheller,Cath.	Oct. 24,	1802	Jacob Swisher		1b141	cr 2	mr 3 *
Myers, Thomas m. Fips, Sarah	Dec. 8,	Dec. 9, 1789		Moses Hoge			
Myers, Thomas m. Stewart, Margaret	June 2,	1798	John Grantham	Nathan Young	5b210		mr 62 *
Myers, Wm. m. Hahn, Mary		Dec. 8, 1831	James Kidwell		4b 37		
Myles, Marg't m. Earp, Burgess R.		June 6, 1817	Jesse Turner	W.N.Scott			*

	(marriage)	(surety)	(minister)	(bond)	
Myon, Sarah m. Myers, Archibald	Mar. 9, 1854		John O. Proctor		*

"N"

Name	Marriage	Year	Surety	Minister	Bond	Ref
Nace, Mary m. Barnhart, Philip	Apr. 24,	1797	Henry Nace	John Winter	1b 11	mr 50 *
Nadenbousch, Eliza M. m. Gaw, Joseph	June 25,	1825	Vincent Bell	John Winter	5b 15	mr 25 *
Nadenbousch, Fred. m. Collins, Eleanor	Apr. 6,	1815	Ignat's O'Ferrall	John Mathews	3b218	mr 87 *
Nadenbousch, Marg't. m. Ling'r, W.H	Mar. 18,	1851	M.C.Nadenbousch	Lewis F. Wilson	7b219	mr 85 *
Nadenbousch, Moses m. Harris, Marg't A	Dec. 15,	1851	Thomas Harris	David Thomas	7b239	
Naff, Eliz. m. Turner, John	Mar. 15,	1321	John Naff		4b177	cr 40
Naff, George m. Covey, Mary	Sept. 8,	1789		Hugh Vance	5b145	mr 4 *
Naff, Jacob m. Clark, Margaret	Nov. 21,	1827	James Clark	Nathan Young	4b 61	mr 60 *
Naff, Jacob m. Painter, Sally	Feb. 13,	1818	Jacob Painter	John Keller	5b 94	mr 31 *
Naff, Michael m. Grimes, Mary	Mar. 26,	1828	Wm. Wolff		5b 1	
Naff, Polly m. Bowers, George	Feb. 23,	1825	John Naff	Chas. P. Krauth		mr 48 *
Nalid, Adam m. Melshall, Cath.	Jan. 10,	1799		David Young		
Nbbet, Eliz. m. Small, George	Oct. 14,	1793		David Young		
Neal, Eliz. m. Cordeary, John	Oct. 11,	1800	Basil Williamson	Moses Hoge	2b 47	gc 8
Neal, Polly m. Lee, Jesse	Apr. 16,	1822	Aaron Chaffin	Nathan Young	4b225	gc 2
Needler, Andrew m. Walters, Cath.	Aug. 12,	1808	Peter Needler		3b 98	or 29
Needler, Bastion m. Sanders, Peggy	Aug. 26,	1814	John Strothers		3b294	mr 19 *
Needler, George m. Wright, Rachel	Sept 15,	1810	James Wright		3b158	mr 58 *
Needler, Maria m. Conner, George	Aug. 14,	1831	George Biddle	Nathan Young	5b203	mr 62 *
Needler, Peter m. Butt, Cath.	Dec. 17,	1831	Jacob Eaty	Nathan Young	5b206	mr 62 *
Needler, Polly m. Smith, Philip	Apr. 3,	1816	Jacob Needler	W.N.Scott	4b 8	mr 66 *
Needler, Polly m. Tabler, Washington	Mar. 31,	1837	Benj. Conover	Nathan Young	5b295	mr 61 *
Neel, Hannah S. m. Talbott, Samuel	Dec. 24,	1831	John L. Neel	Nathan Young	5b190	
Neely, John H. m. Oth, John Mrs.	Mar. 5,	1855		J.W.N.Brown	7b248	mr 86 *
Neer, John W. m. Butler, Harriet M.	Apr. 20,	1852	Joel Fulton	David Thomas	1b 10	mr 13 *
Neet, David M. m. Glass, Margaret	Mar. 7,	1852	Thomas Green	Richard Swift	5b 63	cr 27
Neff, Susannah m. Grove, John	?	1797	John Neff	James Redley		mr 90 *
Negroes, Col. Boyd's m. Locke, J.(?)	Apr.	1827		Rev. Reebenack		gc 5
Neisle, Henry m. Fisher, Christina	Sept 1,	1814		David Young		
Nelson, James m. McConnell, Hannah	Jan. 2,	1795	James McConnell	John Winter	9b 31	mr 50 *
Nelson, James P. m. Tabb, Louisa F.	Apr. 26,	1826		Lewis F. Wilson	5b241	mr 87 *
Nelson, Mann P. m. Kownslar, Lydia A	Sept 25,	1853	Gideon Rupert	J. H. Jackson	1b129	cr 11
Nelson, Robert m. Whte(Wite)M.Mary	Sept 8,	1832	Jacob Dovenburger	John Heitt(Hatt)	9b302	mr 16 *
Nelson, Sarah M. m. McClay, Wm.	Feb. 4,	1798	James Nelson	Jas. M. Brown		mr 67 *
Nephins, John m. Quick, Frances	Jan. 21,	1834		Moses Hoge		cr 8
Nesbitt, Isaac m. Gregory, Jane	Oct. 15,	1792	Robert Gregory		5b244	mr 7 *

Name / Marriage	(marriage)		(suretor)	(minister)	(bond)			
Nemques, Amly(Abby) m. Kerney, Alex.	Jan. 2,	Aug. 18, 1791	John Farr	Moses Hoge	1b 78	cr 7	mr 6	*
Newcomb, George m. Farr, Mary	Jan. 25,	1798			6b294			
Newcomb, Louisa m. Touchstone, Wm.	Mar. 25,	1843	Morgan Morgan					
Newcomb, Wm. m. Constant, Jane		Jan. 12, 1790		Hugh Vance	7b 10		mr 38	*
Newcomer, Mary Ann m. Spencer, Wm.	S.Oct. 23,	1844	Jacob Newcomer		7b 41			
Newcomer, Sarah J. m. Wolff, Christn	Sept 2,	1845	Jacob Newcomer		1b 9			
Newell, Ann m. Wilson, Jacob Jr.	Apr. 18,	1797	Jacob Wilson Sr.		1b 9			
Newell, Wm. m. Cochran, Hannah	Oct. 2,	1799	Andrew Davis		2b 28	cr 29	mr 17	*
Newkirk, Eliz. m. Cunningham, James	Mar. 24,	1799	George Chrisman	Moses Hoge	6b102	cr 17	mr 21	*
Newkirk, George m. Mason, Patty	Sept 6,	1802	John Porterfield	Lewis F. Wilson	2b180			
Newkirk, Isaac m. Seibert, Ellen	Oct. 23,	1844	John Ellis	Moses Hoge	7b 9			
Newkirk, James m. Ford, Mary	Jan. 28,	1833	Wm. P. Hammond	Lewis F. Wilson	5b255			
Newkirk, James m. Porterfield, Patty	Jan. 7,	1815?	Robert Wilson	John Mathews	3b308		mr 25	*
Newkirk, Marg't M.m.Cunningham, Wm.C	Oct. 29,	1847	Archibald Oden	Lewis F. Wilson	7b11		mr 82	*
Newkirk, Marg't M. m.Hammond, Allen	Apr. 24,	1830	James M. Newkirk	Jas. M. Brown	5b164		mr 94	*
Newkirk, Reuben m. Kemp, Mary	Sept 25,	1797	Henry Kemp	Moses Hoge	1b 45	cr 36	mr 13	*
Newkirk, Ruris m. Hayes, Susannah	Apr. 8,	1801	Adam Hayes	John Boyd	2b120	cr 35	mr 19	*
Newlin, Mary m. Farr, Edward	Sept 27,	1797	John St. Clair	Richard Swift	1b 47	cr 28	mr 16	*
Newman, Eliz. m. Cline(Kline)Philip	?	May 12, 1799	Thomas Manldin		1b179			
Newsom, Abr'm m. Emberson, Mary	Apr. 19,	1834	Charles Ardinger		6b 8			
Newsom, John m. Morrison, Jean	Jan. 14,	1799	Hugh Morris		1b162			
Newsom, Rachel m. Pitzer, Mathias	Dec. 22,	1830	Francis Emerson	John Light	5b184		mr 62	*
Nicely, Robert J. m. Nipe, Mary	Jan. 14,	1840	Andrew McIntire	John Light	6b193		mr 71	*
Nicholas, Betsy m. Long, Robert	Feb. 24,	1806	Wm. Chenoweth		3b 12			
Nichols, Amos m. Rineberger, Mary	Sept 3,	1827	Jacob E. Light		5b 78	gc 6		*
Nichols, Christian m. Short(Schot Nan)	Sept 4,	1797	James Fleming	David Young	1b 38	cr 15	mr 62	*
Nichols, Dariel m. Rhineberger, Susan	Sept 24,	1831	Amos Nichols	John Light	5b206		mr 25	*
Nichols, Elinor m. Ford, Henry	Apr. 15,	1812	Amos Nichols	Lewis Mayer	3b221			
Nichols, Henry m. Lemaster, Marg't	Oct. 21,	1839	John H. Wilson	John Light	6b180		mr 70	*
Nichols, Isaac m. Palmer, Rachel	Oct. 21,	1797	John Palmer		1b 57			
Nichols, Jacob m. Ox, Polly	Apr. 6,	1799	Mathias Nichols	David Young	1b178	gc 8		*
Nichols, John m. Myers, Susannah	Jan. 10,	1810	Henry Myers	Lewis Mayer	3b132	cr 14	mr 24	*
Nichols, John m. Steele, Eliz.		1788		Hugh Vance	3b118		mr 35	*
7Nichols, Mary m. Miller, John	Sept 6,	1809	John Myers	Rev. Reebenack	2b112	gc 10	mr 19	*
Nichols, Mary m. Williamson, Peter	Jan. 24,	1801	Jacob Nichols	John Boyd	2b 34	cr 35	mr 17	*
Nichols, Robert m. Kain, Mary	Nov. 9,	1799	Henry Myers	John Boyd	5b 31	cr 34	mr 34	*
Nichols, Samuel m. McCleary, Eliz.	Dec. 29,	1826	Andrew McCleary	Jas. M. Brown	5b301		mr 50	*
Nichols, Susan m. Kislinger, Samuel H	Jan. 27,	1834	James Criswell		5b102			
Nicholson, Edward m. McSherry, Anas'e	May 20,	1828	Richard McSherry		3b118			
7Nicholson, Maria m. Miller, John	Sept 6,	1809	John Mayers	Rev. Reebenack	6b120	gc 10		*
Nicklin, Wm. m. Ward, Eliz. M.	Oct. 18,	1837	Nicholas Ward		5b266			
Nicodemus, Fred. m. Kessler, Mary A	Apr. 18,	1833	Harrison Waite		5b247			
Nicodemus, John m. Lewis, Susan	Nov. 20,	1832	Wm. Lewis					

	(marriage)	(suretor)	(minister)	(bond)		
Nigh, Jacob m. Moore, Rachel	Apr. 4,	Apr. 4, 1815	Jonathan Moore	Rev. Reebemack	3b317	gc 14 mr 44 *
Nigh, Peter m. McBee, Rebecca	Jan. 22,	Jan. 1822	James McCoach	Chas. P. Kreuth	4b205	mr 79 *
Nigh, George m. Haines, Sarah E.M.	Nov. 8,	Nov. 9, 1847	Henry Haines	John Light	7b11	*
Nipe, John N. m. Zimmerman,Jane E.	Nov. 16,	1836	Peter Gardner		6b 88	
Nipe, Martha m. Colbert, Fielding	May 17,	May 18, 1834	George Nipe	John Light	6b 12	mr 67 *
Nipe, Mary m. Nicely, Robert J.	Jan. 14,	Jan. 16, 1840	Andrew McIntire	John Light	6b193	mr 71 *
Nipe, Susan A. m. Winebrenner, Thos.	Jan. 1,	Jan. 1, 1846	Norman Miller	John Light	7b 52	mr 76 *
Noffsinger, Cath. m. Wingard, John	Mar. 24,	1798	John Stewart		1b104	
Noland, Burr P. m. Wilson, Susan C.	Nov. 11,	1845	Edmund Pendleton		7b 49	
*Noland, Hiram m. Young, Nancy		Feb. 11, 1784	John Williamson	John Bell	4b 9	cr 10 mr 1 *
**Noland, John m. Williamson, Mary	Aug. 21,	Aug. 22, 1816	Job Kitchen	John Mathews	3b248	mr 26 *
Noland, Lazarus m. Donaldson, Sally	Jan. 20,	1813	John Williamson		6b146	
Noland, Margaret m. Hanson, Thos.	Oct. 6,	1838	Thomas Noland		4b159	
Noland, Mary m. Beech, Alex.	Sept 2,	1820				
Noland, Mehitabel m.Russell,Moses		Jan. 23, 1785	John Williamson		6b 74	
Noland, Nancy m. Walker, Emod(Elmo)	Mar. 26,	Mar. 31, 1836	Alex. Beach	Hugh Vance	5b 73	mr 33 *
Noland, Obed m. Beach, Linda	July 31,	July 2, 1827	Robert Jones	W. Monroe	5b 53	mr 68 *
Noland, Obed m. Jones, Mary	Sept 23,	Aug. 24, 1826	John Strother	Nathan Young	4b133	mr 99 *
Noland, Priscilla m. Wolff, John	Feb. 1,	1820	Thomas Noland	Nathan Young	3b155	mr 58 *
Noland, Rachel m. Kitchen, Job	July 2,	1810	Christ'r Farber		5b109	
Noland, Thomas m. Farber, Eliz.	Oct. 18,	Oct. 23, 1828	John P. Walters	Wm. Monroe	7b240	mr 53 *
Noland, Wm. m. Crabb, Mary	Dec. 24,	Dec. 25, 1851	John Trigg	David Thomas	1b 50	mr 85 *
Noland, Wm. m. Fryer, Mary	Sept 28,	1797	John M. Small		7b167	
Noll, George m. Small, Barbara Ellen	Nov. 6,	Nov. 8, 1849	Harrison Waite	D.F.Bragunier	6b 38	mr 80 *
Noll, Jacob m. Hartsook, Eliz.	Mar. 27,	1835	George Noll		9b215	
Noll, Mary m. Cushaw, David W.	Jan. 30,	Jan. 31, 1832	Gotlieb Noll	Jas. M. Brown	6b239	mr 64 *
Noll, Mary Ann m. Rentch, Lawrence S	Apr. 7,	1841	Gotlieb Noll		7b114	
Noll, Susan Nicodemus m.Emert,Geo.C.	Nov. 23,	Nov. 25, 1847		D.F.Bragunier		mr 78 *
Nomal, Cath. m. Gramp, John		Jan. 25, 1793	Arch'd Butt	David Young	3b130	ge 2 *
Noncum, George m. Far, Mary	25,	Jan. 4, 1798	Thomas Sullivan	David Young	2b 48	ge 7 *
Noon, James D. m. Rinehart(Rig.),Elis.	Jan. 20,	Dec. 26, 1809		Rev. Reebemack		ge 11 *
Noose, Wm. m. Dye, Sarah		1800				
Norman, Basil m. Warner, Fanny A.	Dec. 12,	1796		David Young		ge 6 *
Norman, Cath. m. Wise, Andrew	Aug. 9,	1791		David Young		ge 1 *
Norman, Charley m. Applegate, James	Feb. 20,	1792	Christ'r Palmer	David Young		ge 1 *
Norrington, Israel m. Rumbaugh, Sarh	Mar. 18,	1814	Wm. Hinco		3b288	
Norrington, James m. Hinco, Mary C.	Aug. 19,	1848	Hugh Kennedy		7b134	
Norrington, John m. Kennedy, Eliz.	Mar. 20,	1849	Wm. H. Van Doren		7b148	
Norrington, Lavy m. Courtney, Geo.	H.May 31,	1852			7b255	
Norrington, Mary m. Johnston, John	Aug. 7,	Aug. 7, 1787	Jacob VanDoren	Hugh Vance		cr 18 mr 1 *
Norrington, Nancy m. Courtney, Jas.H	Nov. 14,	Nov. 14, 1851	Jonas Hedges		7b226	
Norrington, Wm. m. Hedges, Mary	Nov. 11,	Nov. 11, 1844		Lewis F. Wilson	7b 13	cr 29 mr 15 *
Norris, Elinor m. Thomas, Jeremiah	Dec. 4,	Dec. 4, 1798		Moses Hoge		
*Noland, Elis. m. Russell, Chas.	May	May 1791				
**Noland, Hiram m. Young, Nancy	Feb. 7,	Feb. 7, 1804	Peter Noland	David Young	2b222	gc 1

167

Name		(marriage)		(suretor)	(minister)	(bond)		
Norris, Sarah m. Roberts, Gersham		June 30,	1793		Edward Tiffin	5b125	cr 9	mr 8 *
North, Wm. D. m. Gill, Hannah	Apr. 13.	Apr. 14,	1829	Thomas Gill	J. E. Jackson		cr 11	mr 12 *
Norwood, Eliz. m. Hood, James		Oct. 13,	1796		John Boyd		cr 21	mr 8 *
Norwood, James m. Wilson, Sarah		Dec. 25,	1794		John Boyd			mr 39 *
Now, Abraham m. Grove, Cath.		Nov. 27,	1792		Moses Hoge			mr 37 *
Nowell, John m. Shambaugh, Kath.		Feb. 10,	1789		Hugh Vance			mr 26 *
Nowland, John m. Williamson, Mary		Aug. 22,	1816		John Mathews			mr 4 *
Nuef, George m. Covey, Mary		Sept 8,	1789		Hugh Vance		cr 40	
"O"								
Oak, Marg. Lucinda m. McKown, Samuel ?		Jan. 20,	1851	Mathew Hunter	Lewis F. Wilson	7b214		mr 87 *
Oak, Mary E. m. Hunter, Mathias	Feb. 29,	Mar. 3,	1840	Silas Oak	Lewis F. Wilson	6b199		mr 70 *
Oak, Silas m. Collins, Margaret	Nov. 13,	Nov. 15,	1835	Robert Wilson	John Mathews	3b347		mr 25 *
O'Brien, Anastasia m. O'Brien, Chas.	July 15,		1835	Patr'k Cunningham		6b 50		
O'Brien, Chas. m. O'Brien, Anastasia	July 15,		1835	Patr'k Cunningham		6b 50		
O'Brien, James m. Johnson, Daybrick		Nov. 21,	1819		Mathias Riser			mr 30 *
O'Brien, John m. Simmons, Susan	Feb. 6,		1845	Joseph Simmons		7b 25		
O'Brien, Sarah m. Strayer, Jacob S.	Dec. 17,		1834	Benj. C. Speck		6b 24		
O'Brien, Thomas m. McCormick,Bridget	Feb. 8,		1841	Michael Ryan		6b232		
Oburn, Daniel m. Kennedy, Sarah	Jan. 24,	Jan. 1,	1807	John Kennedy	John Mathews	3b 43	cr 13	mr 23 *
O'Connell, Dominick m. Gano, Cath.	July 16,		1838	John Gano		6b143		
O'Connell, Dominick m.Pryor,Mary Mrs	Jan. 23,		1844	James McSherry		6b311		
O'Connor, Hugh m. Fox, Sarah	Mar. 5,		1804	Wm. Patterson		2b225		
O'Connor, Timothy m. Lynch, Johanna	Feb. 13,		1840	James Murphy		6b197		
Oden, Alex. p. m. Porterfield,Martha	Aug. 8,	Aug. 8,	1831	Wm. Porterfield	Jas. M. Brown	5b201	cr 34	mr 62 *
Oden, Elias m. Shearer, Ann	Mar. 6,	June 6,	1799	Wm. Orrick	John Boyd	2b 1		mr 16 *
Oden, Martha m. Cunningham, Wm.	Oct. 20,	Oct. 15,	1840	George Tabb	Lewis F. Wilson	6b221		mr 71 *
Odenwald, George m. Brown, Mary	June 26,	June 27,	1819	John Wolff	John B. Hoge	4b110		mr 31 *
O'Ferrall, Cath. m. Graham, Samuel	July 27,		1813	Ignat's O'Ferrall		3b267		
O'Ferrall, Francis m. Kerney, Jane B.	Sept 15,		1829	Jacob VanDoren		5b141		
Offutt(-ord),Jos. m. Howard,Susannah	Dec. 26,	Dec. 26,	1799	John Moore	John Hedtt(Hutt)	2b 43	cr 33	mr 17 *
Offutt, Clarisse m. Jones, Edward		Nov. 4,	1790		Moses Hoge	1b 22	cr 5	mr 5 *
Offutt, Rachel m. Buckmaster, Alex.	June 20,		1797	Zachariah Buckmaster		4b105		
Ogelvie, David m. Everhart, Kitty	Apr. 12,		1819	Henry Everhart				
Oglin, James m. Clawson, Peggy		Feb. 22,	1791		Moses Hoge		cr 6	mr 6 *
Oldfield, Agnes Ann m. Berry, John	Feb. 24,		1818	Wm. Griffith		4b 62		
Oldfield, Eliz. m. Joy, Peter	Apr. 5,		1812	Joseph Haines		3b223		
Oldfield, Jonathan m.Plotner, Susan	Aug. 29,	Sept 24,	1812	Sarah Plotner	Rev. Reebenack	3b234	gc 13	*
Oldfield, Joseph m. Berryman, Polly	Dec. 21,		1801	Fred. Blue		2b153		
Oldfield, Mary Jane m. Pool, Fred.	Apr. 24,		1830	?		5b163		
Olinger, Christ'r m. Sprigg, Nancy	Dec. 7,	Dec. 12,	1833	John Bowers	Nathan Young	5b292		mr 66 *
Olinger, John m. McBride, Mary Ann	Jan. 13,		1835	John Shearer		6b 28		mr 88 *
*O'Conner, Eliz. m. Welsh, Thomas		Dec. 7,	1852		J.H.Plunkett			

		(marriage)	(suretor)	(minister)	(bond)		
* Olinger, Nancy m. Secrist, John B.	Feb. 23,	Feb. 22, 1846	John Olinger	J. H. Jennings	7b 59		mr 82 *
Olinger, Sarah m. Johnston, James	Oct. 19,	1836	Christ'r Olinger		6b 85		
Oliver, Agnes m. Davies, Ephraim		1789					
Oliver, Margaret m. Eckles, Richard		Dec. 24, 1789		Hugh Vance			mr 38 *
Ollebaugh, Amelia m. Phillps, Jason		July 17, 1787		Hugh Vance			mr 1 *
Oller, Cath. m. Morlay, Francis	Sept 25,	Sept 25, 1841	Curtis Vermilyea	John Hedges	6b247	cr 18	
Oller, Eliz. m. Barber, John	June 27,	1815	George Oller		3b329		mr 72 *
Oller, G. m. Ray, Wm. Jr.	Aug. 23,	Aug. 24, 1797	Jonathan Rust	David Young	1b 34	gc 6	
Oller, Polly m. Tabler, Henry	Nov. 26,	1816	William Ray Sr.		4b 24		*
O'Neal, Hannah m. Talbott, Samuel	Aug. 19,	Aug. 20, 1808	Peter Oller	Lewis Mayer	3b 94	cr 16	
O'Neal, John R. m. Hill, Mary E.	Mar. 31,	Apr. 3, 1831	John O'Neal	Nathan Young	5b190		mr 24 *
O'Neal, Joseph m. Faris, Rachel	May 25,	May 26, 1846	John Schaffer	John Winter	7b 67		mr 61 *
O'Neal, Robert m. Shaffer, Susannah	May 1,	May 15, 1826	Peter Hoke	Benedict Reynolds	5b 41	gc 12	
Opie, Hiram L. Jr. m. Locke, Ann S.	Mar. 5,	Mar. 5, 1812	Peter Shaffer	Rev. Reebenack	3b214		mr 76 *
Orendorff, Eliz. m. Miller, Jacob	Sept 17,	1835	Colin Peter		6b 57		mr 49 *
Orick, George m. Schonover, Mary	Mar. 12,	1802	Christ'r Orendorff		2b165		
Orick, James C. m. Pendleton, Susan	Feb. 28,	Feb. 18, 1840	Nicholas Orick		6b198		
Orick, Violet m. Beva, Charles	Feb. 18,	1835	Seaman Gerard	David Young	6b 31	gc 5	
O'Rorke, Felix m. Dowlan, Mary		Apr. 19, 1796	Bernard O'Rorke				*
Ororke, James m. Manor, Isabel S.	Aug. 21,	1816	James Manor	J.S.Reynoldson	4b 9		mr 75 *
Orr, James m. Vance, Jane	Dec. 23,	Dec. 24, 1844	William Orr		7b 17		
Orr, John W. m. Murphy, Rose Ann	July 4,	1822	James Orr	Geo. W. Cooper	4b218		mr 87 *
Orr, Mary Ann m. Evans, Tillotson F.	Mar. 8,	Apr. 5, 1853	Wm. Mitchell				
Orr, Sarah m. Hawkins, James	Oct. 15,	1848	Joseph Butt				
Orr, William m. Butt, Eliz.	Feb. 1,	1801	Nicholas Orrick		7b125		
Orrick, Betsy m. Gibbs, Edward A.	June 22,	1826	Geo. Porterfield		2b143		
Orrick, Chas. m. Campbell, Ann	June 11,	1813					
Orrick, Chas. m. Davenport, Kath.		1806	James McSherry	Hugh Vance	5b 35		mr 43 *
Orrick, Cromwell m.McLanahan, Rebecca	May 30,	Jan. 2, 1787	John Clawson	Lewis F. Wilson	3b265		mr 74 *
Orrick, John m. Clawson, Phebe	Nov. 12,	June 5, 1843	Charles Orrick	W.N.Scott	3b 22		mr 26 *
Orrick, Marg. m. Campbell, Barton	Feb. 5,	1810	Cromwell Orrick		6b299		mr 40 *
Orrick, Mary m. Elliott, Eli Wm.	Feb. 8,	Mar. 7, 1816	Charles Orrick	John Mathews	3b165		mr 45 *
Orrick, Mary m. Harlan, James	Mar. 11,	1815	James Orrick		4b 11		mr 2 *
Orrick, Sarah Ann m. Evans, Isaac W.	July 20,	mar. 12, 1812	Nicholas Orrick	Edw. R. Lippett	3b310		mr 19 *
Orrick, Susan m. Taylor, John B.	Mar. 8,	1836			3b215		mr 77 *
Osborn, Ann m. Buckles, James		Mar. 8, 1821	John Lafferty	Moses Hoge	6b 82		mr 64 *
Osborn, David Jr. m. Barnes, Ruth	Feb. 17,	Feb. 3, 1789	Aaron Buckles	Moses Hoge	4b175	cr 1	
Osborn, David m. Buckles, Phebe	Oct. 26,	Feb. 18, 1800	John C. Walper		2b 54	cr 29	
Osborn, David K. m. Perry, Angeline	Jan. 14,	1835	Harrison Waite	John Winter	6b 60		mr 13 *
Osborn, Horace m. Woodward, Francy	Sept 8,	Jan. 14, 1847	Wm. Osborn	Jacob Medtart	7b 83	cr 36	
Osborn, Polly m. Melvin, Samuel	Sept 9,	Sept 2, 1832	George Osborn	Moses Hoge	5b240		mr 25 *
Osborn, Polly m. Rymer, John	Dec. 8,	1797			1b 71		mr 3 *
Osborn, Polly(Patty) m.Taylor, John	Mar. 14,	Mar. 19, 1815		Lewis Mayer	3b315	cr 2	
Osborn, Sarah m. Lafferty, John	Sept. 6,	June 23, 1789	David Osborne	Moses Hoge	2b 86	cr 29	
*Olinger, Cath. m. Barnes, Jacob	Jan. 26,	Sept 10, 1800	Christian Olinger	Moses Hoge	6b 29		mr 19 *

	(marriage)	(suretor)	(minister)	(bond)	
Osborn, Wm. m. Buckles, Eliza	Dec. 23, 1833	Aaron Buckles	Jacob Medtart	5b297	mr 64 *
† Osmur, Horace m. Woodward, Francy	Sept 8, 1832	Harrison Waite	David Young	5b240	**
*Ostume, Joseph m. Richards, Mary	Sept 20, 1792				gc 2
*Ott, Eliz. m. Tharp, Wm.	Nov. 29, 1800	Edward Howe		2b100	*
Ott, John m. Helm, Mary	June 21, 1800	Mathew Ransone	David Young	2b 74	gc 9
Ott, Jacob m. Shough, ?	Sept 2, 1805	Joseph Shough		2b270	
Ott, John m. Kimble, Rebecca	Nov. 28, 1801	Jacob Kimble		2b150	
Ott, John H. m. Poisal, Ellen R.	Jan. 8, 1845	Jacob Poisal		7b 20	
Ott, Marg.Mary m. Poisal, Jacob	June 1, 1805	Jacob Ott	Christian Streit	2b263	cr 16 mr 22 *
Ott, Mary m. Siler, Philip	Sept 28, 1797	Benjamin Ott		1b 48	
Ott, Mary m. Snyder, Jacob	Aug. 6, 1807	John Ott		3b 65	
Ott, Michael m. Hooper, Mary	May 18, 1820	Jacob Poisal	W.N.Scott	4b147	mr 41 *
Otter, Eliz. m. Barber, John	Aug. 23, 1797	Jonathan Rust	David Young	1b 34	gc 6
Otter, Hannah m. Wollam, Benj.	Feb. 3, 1803	English P. Otter		2b192	
Otto, Ann m. Silver, Samuel	May 23, 1825	Rich. Richardson	Chas. P. Krauth	5b 11	mr 48 *
Otton, Sarah m. Anderson, Jacob	Sept 22, 1827	John Shober	B. Reynolds	5b 79	mr 52 *
Otty, Wm. m. Miller, Margaret	Feb. 13, 1845	John F. Strode	John light	7b 27	mr 76 *
Otuen, Peter m. Muntz, Barbara	Apr. 12, 1796		David Young		gc 5
Ovelchain, Nancy m. Wade, James	Sept 19, 1797	Reynolds Ovelchain	David Young	1b 42	gc 3
Overstake, Benj. m. Winekeart, Eliz.	July 21, 1793				*
Owen, Eliz. m. Roberts, Richard	Feb. 3, 1798	Joseph Roberts	David Young	1b 83	gc 3
Owings, Beall m. Butler, Henrietta	Mar. 13, 1810	Charles Orrick	Rev. Reebenack	3b141	gc 11
Ox, Frederick m. Painter, Margaret	Apr. 14, 1801	Jacob Painter		2b121	*
Ox, Polly m. Nichols(Michael),Jacob	Apr. 6, 1799	Mathias Nichols	David Young	1b178	gc 8
Oxenrider, Henry m. Everhart, Marg't	Aug. 23, 1825	John Walter	Chas. P. Krauth	5b 21	mr 49 *
*Oth, John Mrs. m. Neely, John H.	Dec. 24, 1855		J.M.Brown		**

"P"

	(marriage)	(suretor)	(minister)	(bond)	
Pabson, Caty m. Stipe, George	Apr. 23, 1789	Michael Shaver	Richard Swift	1b x	*
Packer, Mary m. Smith, James	Nov. 8, 1800	Henry Parker		2b 97	cr 31 mr 19 *
Packett, Jos. G. m. Fry, Isabella	Mar. 1, 1845	Moses S. Grantham		7b 28	*
Paden, Jacob m.Smart(Sweart)Tabitha	Oct. 22, 1828	Daniel Smart	B. Reynolds	5b111	mr 52 *
Paden, Nathaniel m. Wibly, Mary Marg.	Mar. 31, Apr. 5, 1831	Callender Wibly	Nathan Young	5b191	mr 61 *
Page, Eliz. m. Lashorn, Ralph	June 10, June 11, 1830	Adam Schoppert	Jacob Medtart	5b 167	mr 63 *
Page, James N. m. Friddle, Mary Jane	Aug. 25, 1853		John light		mr 86 *
Page, Mary m. Walters, Isaac W.	Oct. 23, 1839	Jacob Walters		6b181	
Page, Mary Ann m. Ragear(Roger)Magnus	June 5, June 5, 1839	Wm. Sperow	M.G.Hamilton	6b171	mr 71 *
Page, Nathaniel m. Conner, Ann	Sept 15, 1815	Joseph Conner		3b339	
Page, Thomas S. m. Morrison, Hannah	Dec. 22, 1835	Wm. Morrison		6b 67	
Page, Wm. m. Roberts, Eliz.	May 23, 1816	Samuel Roberts		4b 1	
Pagle, Mary m. Shriver, David	Oct. 17, 1805	Henry Shriver		3b 2	
Paine, Betsy m. Harris, Wm. H.	Apr. 1, 1809	Samuel B. Harris		3b110	
Paine, Eliz. m. Crawford, Augustine	Dec. 8, 1854		L.M.Colloway		gc 13
Paine, Sally m. Butt, William	Nov. 19, 1812		Rev. Reebenack		**

Name	date	(marriage)	(suretor)	(minister)	(bond)	
?Paine, Will m. Hedges, Agnes	Mar. 11	Mar. 12, 1811	Samuel Hedges	Rev. Reebenack	3b178	gc 11 *
Painter, Cath. m. Walter, John	Sept 11	1798	Jacob Painter		1b130	
Painter, Eliz. m. Bell, William	Apr. 13	1808	George Painter		3b 85	
Painter, Eliz. m. Helferstay, John	May 17	1810	Jacob Painter		3b152	
Painter, Eve m. Black, Jacob	Dec. 25	Dec. 26, 1813	Jacob Painter	Rev. Reebenack	3b280	gc 14 *
Painter, George m. Smith, Sarah	Apr. 10	1809	Valentine, Ale		3b111	
Painter, Jacob m. Shertle(Shorter)Sall	Dec. 15	Dec. 15, 1804	Jacob Shertle	Christian Streit	2b249	cr 16 *
Painter, John m. Miller, Lucy	Sept 19	Sept 1822	Jacob Hill	Chas. P. Krauth	4b224	mr 22 *
Painter, Marg't m. Ox, Frederick	Apr. 14	1801	Jacob Hill		2b121	mr 45 *
Painter, Mary m. Cole(Coal), Joseph	Apr. 16	Apr. 19, 1832	George Painter	Jacob Medtart	5b226	mr 64 *
Painter, Mary m. Horn, George	Dec. 23	1805	George Painter		3b 6	
Painter, Rachel m. David, Lewis	Dec. 14	Dec. 14, 1797	George Painter	David Young	1b 72	gc 7 *
Painter, Sally m. Naff, Jacob	Feb. 13	1818	Jacob Painter	John Kehler	4b 61	mr 31 *
Painter, Susanna m. Strickle, John	July 3	1802	George Painter		2b176	
?Pair, William m. Hedges, Agnes	Mar. 11	Mar. 12, 1811	Samuel Hedges	Rev. Reebenack	3b178	gc 11 *
Paise, Michael m. Sensler, Cath.	May 2	1798	Fred. Blue		1b110	
Palin, John m. McDonald, Mary	Apr. 20	1789	Henry Placker		1b x	
Palmer, Charlotte m. Burns, Mark	May 27	May 27, 1822	Thomas Patton	John B. Hoge	4b214	mr 44 *
Palmer, Charlotte m. Hooper, Edmund	June 23	June 23, 1843	William Palmer	W.F. Mercer	6b272	mr 74 *
Palmer, Chrisly m. Pinkerton, Anna	Oct. 1	1812	Robert Pinkerton		3b238	
Palmer, Eliz. m.Bragunier(Braz_)Jacob	June 7	June 7, 1798	James Harlan	David Young	1b114	gc 7 *
Palmer, Henry m. Crone, Mary M.	Oct. 28	Oct. 29, 1811	Samuel Cunningham	John B. Hoge	3b197	cr 14 *
Palmer, John m. Sanders(Souders),Eliz	Nov. 26	Dec. 24, 1799	Jas. Richardson	David Young	2b 36	mr 24 *
Palmer, John m. Winning, Sarah	Nov. 3	1835	Wm. Anderson		6b 61	
Palmer, Joseph m. Kimble, Marg't	Aug. 11	1801	Jacob Kimble		2b135	
Palmer, Melinda m. Church, Truman	Oct. 14	Oct. 14, 1851	Edward B. Hooper	D. Thomas	7b234	mr 85 *
Palmer, Martin m. Plotner, Sarah	Oct. 23	Oct. 1822	Daniel Plotner	Chas. P. Krauth	4b226	mr 45 *
Palmer, Mary m. Caskey, Wm.	Oct. 28	1843	George Dougherty		6b206	
Palmer, Polly m. Harrison, John	Sept 21	1812	Wm. Palmer		3b237	
Palmer, Rachel m. Harlan, James	Oct. 2	Oct. 2, 1793	John Palmer	David Young	1b 57	gc 3 *
Palmer, Rachel m. Nichols, Isaac	Oct. 21	Sept 28, 1828	Seaman Garard	B. Reynolds	5b107	mr 52 *
Palmer(Panner)Wm. m. Bowman,Julia Ann	Sept 27	Aug. 13, 1818	John Severns	Nathan Young	4b 76	mr 56 *
Panabaker, Adam m. Severns, Margaret	Aug. 10	Apr. 8, 1828	Edward Severns	Nathan Young	5b 96	mr 59 *
Panabaker,Christ'r m.Severns,Rebecca	Apr. 8	Feb. 10, 1825	Jacob Bromwell	Jacob L. Bromwell	4b289	mr 47 *
Panabaker, Wm. m. Snider, Hannah	Feb. 7	June 23, 1820	Fred. Gilbert	Nathan Young	4b152	mr 57 *
Pane, Hannah m. Booth, John	June 22			Richard Swift		
Pankey, John m. Smith, Eliz.	Jan. 23	Jan. 2, 1797		Edward Tiffin		cr 26
Panter, Benj. m. Baskett, Sarah	Dec. 4	Dec. 4, 1794		John Howell		cr 25
Paole, Mary J. Mrs. m. Crowl, Jacob	Sept 22	Sept 22, 1835	Harrison Waite	David Young	6b 58	mr 9 *
Parcels, John m. Terrell, Cath.	Dec. 24	Dec. 25, 1798	James Wilson	John Howell	1b156	mr 68 *
Park, Amos Ebenezer m. Compston, Mary	Mar. 23	Mar. 23, 1789		Hugh Vance		gc 8 / mr 3 *
Park, Jane m. Faris, Aaron	Dec. 23	Dec. 23, 1794		John Boyd		cr 20 / mr 8 *
Park, John m. Miller, Jane	Jan. 19	Jan. 19, 1797		John Boyd		cr 32 / mr 13 *
*Park, Joseph m. Mayers, Ann	Dec. 23	Dec. 23, 1794		John Boyd		cr 21 / mr 8 *
*Park, John m. Vance, Mary	Jan. 14	Jan. 14, 1788		Hugh Vance		cr 23 / mr 2 *

Name	(marriage)		(suretor)	(minister)	(bond)		
Park, Mary m. Wilson, Samuel K.	Apr. 6,	1819	John Park		4b105		
Park, Mary m. Wilson, Wm.	Feb. 2,	1786		Hugh Vance			mr 33 *
Parker, Ann m. Downs, Charles	Feb. 28,	1822		John B. Hoge			mr 44 *
Parker, Anna m. Hanna, James	Mar. 12,	1804	Wm. Hanna		2b226	gc 12	*
Parker, Barbara m. Bartleson, James	Mar. 31,	1812	John Poisal	Rev. Reebenack	3b218		
Parker, John m. Bright, Susanna	Mar. 30,	1804	Jeptha Martin		2b230		
Parker, John m. Harna, Eliz.	Apr. 12,	1808	Wallace Parker		3b 84		
Parker, Mary m. Smith, James	Nov. 25,	1800	Henry Parker	Richard Swift	2b 97	cr 31	mr 19 *
Parker, Nelly m. Basore, Jacob	Oct. 28,	1814	James Bartleson	Rev. Reebenack	3b306	gc 14	
Parker, Samuel m. Pitzer, Barbara	Dec. 26,	1786		Hugh Vance			mr 43 *
Parkinson, Mary Ann m. Fry, Newton H	Mar. 8,	1841	Wm. Parkinson	Lewis F. Wilson	6b236		mr 72 *
Parkinson, Wm. R. m. Dunham, Eliz.	Dec. 27,	1847	Benjamin Dunham		7b118		
Parks, Jane m. Boyd, Wm.	Nov. 10,	1796		John Boyd		cr 11	mr 12 *
Parr, John m. Hedges, Nancy	May 31,	1817	Peter Mayers	W.N.Scott	4b 36		
Parrott(Parral), Samuel m.Young,Mary	Oct. 26,	1822	Adam Young	Chas. P. Kranth	4b226		mr 45 *
Parrott, Wm. m. Turner, Susanna	Mar. 3,	1802	Thomas Turner	Richard Swift	2b163	cr 32	mr 20 *
Parson, Tobias m. Armbrester, Levina	Sept 30,	1834	Michael Armbrester		6b 20		
Paskell, Eliza m. Hollis, James J.	Mar. 17,	1831	John Hoglin	Nathan Young	5b188		mr 61 *
Paskell, Cath. m. Scorse, Wm.	Nov. 29,	1821	John Miller	Chas. P. Kranth	4b197		mr 42 *
Paskell, Eliza m. Hollis, James J.	Mar. 17,	1831	John Hoglin	Nathan Young	5b188		mr 61 *
Paskell, Isaac m. Barnhart, Sarah	Dec. 1,	1796		David Young		gc 6	
Paskell, Jerry m. Copeland, Phebe	Apr. 15,	1796		David Young		gc 5	
Patch, Margaret m. Douglas, John	Oct. 29,	1801	Isaac Patch		2b145		
Pate, Thomas m. Keys, Eliz.	May 10,	1813	John Keys		3b262		
Patrick, Mary F. m.Strickland,Henry	Apr. 21,	1808	John Gray		3b 86		
Patten, John m. Eakin, Esther	Jan. 6,	1818	Robert Eakin		4b 56		*
Patterson, Ann m. Crook, John	Feb. 18,	1794				gc 3	
Patterson, Annie m. Morehead, Moses	Aug. 27,	1801	Moses Collins	David Young	2b139		
Patterson, Chas. W. m. McCormick,Mary	July 13,	1841	Ellis Rees		6b243		
Patterson, Chas. W. m. Tucker,Emelin	June 20,	1833	Peter Gardner	W. Hawk	5b277		mr 65 *
Patterson, Eleanor m. Hayes, Justice	Mar. 2,	1802	Thomas Gill		2b163		
Patterson, Hannah m. Gill, Thomas	Dec. 10,	1795		John Boyd		cr 33	mr 11 *
Patterson, Hugh V. m. Christie, Eliz.	Oct. 19,	1803	Robert Christie	David Young	2b210	gc 10	mr 36 *
Patterson, James m. Shaw, Mary	Dec. 12,	1788		Hugh Vance			mr 12 *
Patterson, John m. Tabb, Anna	Mar. 7,	1807	George Tabb	John Boyd	3b 49	cr 11	mr 12 *
Patterson, Mary m. Quigley, John	Nov. 3,	1796	Robert Christy		5b217		
Patterson, Sarah Ann m. Stipp, John	Feb. 24,	1632	Israel Clawson		2b122		
Patterson, Thomas m. Billum, Sarah	Apr. 16,	1801					
Patton, David m. Cherry, Eliz.	Oct. 17,	1796	Robert Eaken	David Young	4b 56	gc 6	*
Patton, John m. Eakins, Easter	Jan. 8,	1818		W.N.Scott			*
Patton, Margaret m. McCausland, Thos.	Dec. 17,	1795	Robert Hedges	David Young	4b181	gc 5	*
Patton, Samuel m. Hedges, Jane	Apr. 19,	1821	Charles Ridenour	D.F.Braganier			mr 78 *
*Patterson, John m. Tabb, Alma	Jan. 26,	1807		John Mathews	7b121	cr 13	mr 23 *

	(marriage)	(suretor)	(minister)	(bond)	
Patton, Thomas m. Kerney, Eliz.	Apr. 28, 1820	John Strother	John B. Hoge	4b146	mr 31 *
Patton, Wm. m. Bishop, Polly	June 30, 1821	?	Chas. P. Krauth	4b185	mr 42 *
Paul, Hannah m. Booth, John	June 22, 1820	Fred. Gilbert	Nathan Young	4b152	mr 57 *
Paul, Hugh m. Small, Nancy	Apr. 10, 1816	Henry Small	W.N.Scott	4b 17	mr 26 *
Paul, Robert m. Tabler, Eliz.	June 13, 1815	Adam Tabler	John Mathews	3b328	mr 25 *
Paul, Sarah Ann m. Easterday, John	July 28, 1817	Robert Paul	John B. Hoge	4b 40	
Paul, Wm. m. Smith, Wm. A.	June 12, 1843	Adam Small	Lewis F. Wilson	6b300	mr 74 *
Paul, Wm. m. Jack, Anne	May 12, 1796		John Boyd		mr 12 *
					cr 11
Paulitsgrove, Henry m. Miller, Caty	Sept 13, 1804	Peter Shaffer		2b243	
Paulitsgrove, Nancy m. Schoppert,Mose	Mar. 29, 1830	Joseph Paulitsgrove	Jacob Medtart	5b160	mr 63 *
Paviner, Wm. m. Bowman, Julia Ann	1828	S. Gerrard	B.Reynolds	5b107	mr 52 *
Payne, Ann m. Payne, Thomas	Nov. 26, 1816	Wm. Payne	W.N.Scott	4b 23	
Payne, Ann Jane m. Light, Joseph	Jan. 30, 1839	Thomas Payne	Lewis F. Wilson	6b158	mr 70 *
Payne, Eliz.Mrs. m. Chapman, John	June 2, 1829	Jesse Payne		5b132	
Payne, Eliz. m. Crothers, Henry	Dec. 12, 1816	Thomas Payne	John B. Hoge	4b 26	**
Payne, Ellen Jane m. Zeigler,Jos. H.	Mar. 22, 1854		W.G.Eglestone		
Payne, Frances m. Grubb, Jefferson	Dec. 17, 1849	Hanson Payne		7b170	
Payne, George m. Grantham, Phebe	Aug. 27, 1798	Henry Payne		1b125	
Payne, Hannah m. Allemong, John	Jan. 17, 1823	John Payne		4b232	
Payne, Henry m. Boak, Marg't Jane	Feb. 9, 1829	Wm. Boak	Wm. Monroe	5b118	mr 53 *
Payne, Hanson m. Cage, Margaret	Aug. 5, 1834	Harrison Waite		6b 15	mr 61 *
Payne, Jane m. Wade, Wm.	Apr. 12, 1830	Jesse Payne	Robert Cadden	5b162	
Payne, Jesse m. Dunn, Martha	Jan. 8, 1799	George Payne		1b160	
Payne, Jesse m. Long, Jane Mrs	Apr. 12, 1824	John Strother		4b261	
Payne, John m. Cunningham, Mary D.	Oct. 11, 1830	Wm. Cunningham	John Allemong	5b176	mr 94 *
Payne, John B. m. Gary, Mary D.	Apr. 13, 1839	Jas. E. Payne		6b166	
Payne, Jos. E. m. Long, Sarah A.C.	Apr. 10, 1837	Jesse Payne	John Allemong	6b105	mr 69 *
Payne, Mahlon m. McDaniel, Lavina	Mar. 27, 1848	Alex. McDaniel	J.H.Jennings	7b126	mr 82 *
Payne, Marg't A. m. Hayes, Anthony R.	Dec. 2, 1853		D.Francis Sprigg		
Payne, Martha m. Gill, Wm.	Mar. 29, 1834	Jesse Payne		6b 1	
Payne, Mary m. Cunningham, Wm.	Aug. 10, 1844	Samuel D. Rees		7b 5	
Payne, Rachel m. Phelps, Elisha	Feb. 17, 1813	Henry Payne		3b251	
Payne, Sally m. Montgomery, Robert	Dec. 9, 1801	George Payne		2b151	
Payne, Sarah m. Hoggins, Richard	Oct. 22, 1816	Jacob Payne		4b 18	
Payne, Sarah m. Marshall, John	Nov. 15, 1841	Jos. E. Payne		6b232	
Payne, Thomas m. Payne, Annie	Nov. 26, 1816	Wm. Payne	W.N.Scott	4b 23	
Payne, Wm. m. Johnson, Abby	Mar. 3, 1789		Hugh Vance		cr 19 *
Peace, James m. Ryans, Frances	Sept 20, 1794		William Hill		cr 30 *
Pear, Nancy m. Kennedy, James	Apr. 9, 1833	Harrison Waite		5b266	
Pearce, Cath. m. Miller, Isaac	Feb. 13, 1829	Abraham Morlatt		5b119	mr 3 *
Pearce, John m. Thompson, Ann	Nov. 19, 1816	Benjamin Comegys	John Mathews	4b 22	mr 9 *
Pearce, Joseph m. Smith, Eliz.	Nov. 13, 1819	Mathew R. Gerrard	Nathan Young	4b122	mr 26 *
Pearce, Lewis B. m. Hoke, Cath.	Aug. 1, 1818	Joseph Morlatt		4b 76	mr 56 *

	(marriage)		(suretor)	(minister)	(bond)	
Pearl, Ann m. Spitznogle, Jacob	Apr. 7,	1842	James McSherry	John Light	6b259	mr 74 *
Pearson, Solomon m. Kidd, Elis.	May 11,	1826	Thomas Thornburg	James Redly	5b 42	mr 49 *
Peck, Nancy m. Strickler, Geo. W.	Sept 18,	1823	Seigismund Showers		4b249	
Peck, Sarah m. Bolton, Wm.	May 26,	1819	Joseph Snyder		4b107	
Peltz, Jos. M. m. Grove, Nancy	May 26,	1852	Michael Grove	A. Talty	7b255	mr 88 *
Penderbaugh, Daniel m. Stookey,Barb'a	Oct. 24,	1815	Jacob Stookey	Nathan Young	3b346	mr 55 *
?Pendez(Pendry,Mary m.Wilmouth, Thos.	Jan. 2,	1798	Ralph Pendez	David Young	1b 77	
Pendleton, Ann m. Kennedy, John	Oct. 2,	1794		John Boyd		gc 7
Pendleton, Ann E. m. Williamson,Amos	July 14,	1840	Wm.H.Pendleton		6b214	cr 21
Pendleton, Elenor m. Walker, James	Sept 26,	1814	Wm. Pendleton		3b304	
Pendleton, Eliz. m. Cunningham, John	Dec. 22,	1800	Wm. Pendleton		2b102	
Pendleton, Eliz. m. Hunter, David	Nov. 19,	1791		David Young		gc 1
Pendleton, Ellen m. Campbell, Nathan	Aug. 20,	1841	Wm. Pendleton		6b246	*
Pendleton, Fanny C. m. Campbell, Wm.	Feb. 28,	1811	Wm. Pendleton	John B. Hoge	3b177	cr 14
Pendleton, Maria W. m.Cooke, John R.	Nov. 17,	1813	Robert Wilson	John Mathews	3b276	mr 24 *
Pendleton, Nancy m. Porterfield,John	Mar. 27,	1802	Wm. Pendleton		2b166	mr 25 *
Pendleton, Phil.C. m. Boyd, Sarah A	Nov. 25,	1813	Elisha Boyd	John Mathews	3b277	mr 25 *
Pendleton, Sarah m. Dandridge,Adam S	Jan. 1,	1805	Philip C. Wilson	Moses Hoge	2b250	cr 17, mr 22 *
Pendleton, Susannah m.Wilson, Jas.	Feb. 11,	1781		Daniel Sturges		mr 31 *
Pendleton, Susan m. Orick, James C	Feb. 18,	1835	Seaman Garard		6b 31	
Pendleton, Wm. m. Brady, Hannah	Feb. 14,	1806	David Hunter	John Bond	3b 11	cr 28 *
Pendleton, Wm. m.Robinson,Elis. A.	June 22,	1840	Harrison Waite		6b213	mr 22 *
Pendleton, Wm. m. Snodgrass, Susan	Feb. 16,	1811	Robert Wilson		3b175	
Pendry, Elis. m. Kenter, Jacob	Oct. 22,	1804	James Shearer		2b246	
Pendry, Martha m. Riner, Adam	Feb. 23,	1805	Richard Pendry		2b255	
*Pendry, Robert m. Wolff, Mary	Jan. 5,	1813	Samuel Lion	Rev. Reebenack	3b245	gc 13
Penry, Robert m. Davis, Susannah	June 30,	1832	Henry Myers	Wm. Monroe	5b233	mr 65 *
Pendl, Basil m. Campbell, Polly	Nov. 25,	1797	John Campbell	John Heitt(hutt)	1b 64	cr 11 *
Pendl, Elis. m. Thornbury, Thos. S.	Aug. 10,	1829	John Pendl	Wm. Monroe	5b136	mr 14 *
Penn, Wm. m. Clark, Elis.	June 23,	1831	James Clark	Nathan Young	5b198	mr 53 *
Pennybaker, Elis. m. Snyder, Fred.	Jan. 25,	1785		Hugh Vance		mr 61 *
Pennybaker, Sarah m. Lane, Lewis	Nov. 18,	1788		Hugh Vance		mr 33 *
Pennybaker, Susannah m. Mock, Peter	Apr. 1,	1788		Hugh Vance		mr 36 *
Pennybaker, Wm. Jr. m. Snider,Hannah	Feb. 7,	1825	Jacob Bromwell	J.F.Bromwell	4b289	mr 34 *
Pentil, Cath. m. Grove, Jacob	Dec. 23,	1799	Johan Pensil		2b 42	mr 47 *
Penterbaugh, Daniel m.Stookey,Barbara	Oct. 24,	1815	Jacob Stookey	Nathan Young	3b346	
Pentony, Luke m.Ellenberger,Mary A.	June 29,	1816	John Ellenberger	Mathias Riser	4b 2	mr 55 *
Pentony, Nancy m. Zimm, Dariel	Sept 2,	1819	Henry Ronsch		4b115	
Pepper, Elis. m. Drinker, John	Apr. 12,	1797	Robert W. Wood		1b 7	
Pepper, Elis. D. m. Wright, Daniel	Dec. 22,	1832	Wm. Pepper	W. Monroe	5b250	mr 65 *
Pepper, Henry m. Tate, Rachel	Feb. 24,	1831	John Tate	Jas. M. Brown	5b187	mr 62 *
Pepper, Mary m. Shepherd, Abr'm	Aug. 18,	1789		Hugh Vance		cr 39
Perfelter, Philip m. Mason, Eliz.	Dec. 29,	1800	John Cross		2b106	mr 4 *
?*Pendry, Mary (SeePendez)						

	(date)	(marriage)	(surtor)	(minister)	(bond)		
Perkins, Mary m. Hedges, Enoch		June 10, 1793	James McSherry	Wm. Hill	6b269	cr 30	mr 10 *
Perrel, Ann m. Spitsmogle, Jacob	Apr. 7,	Apr. 7, 1842	John Campbell	John Hutt(Hedtt)	1b 64	cr 11	mr 74 *
Perrel, Basil m. Campbell, Polly	Nov. 25,	Nov. 25, 1797	Thomas Perrell	Peyton Harrison	6b273		mr 73 *
Perrel, Cath. m. Spitsmogle, John S	July 19,	July 21, 1842	John Perrell	W. Monroe	5b136		mr 53 *
Perrell, Eliza m. Thornberg, Thos. S	Aug. 10,	Aug. 13, 1829	Thomas Perrell	John Light	6b228		mr 72 *
Perrell, Emily m. Coontz, Samuel	Dec. 23,	Dec. 24, 1840	John McFarland	Jacob Beecher	5b147		mr 53 *
Perrell, John m. McFarland, Hannah	Dec. 9,	Dec. 17, 1829	Harrison Waite	Nathan Young	5b230		mr 64 *
Perrell, Mary m. Pitzer, Mary	May 28,	May 29, 1832	John Perrell	Wm. Monroe	5b224		mr 65 *
Perrell, Mary m. Horner, Dorsey	Apr. 3,	Apr. 5, 1832	James Pitzer	John Light	6b166		mr 70 *
Perrell, Thomas m. Eversole, Rosanna	Apr. 8,	Apr. 9, 1839	John C. Walper	John Winter	7b 83		mr 77 *
Perry, Angeline m. Osburn, David K.	Jan. 14,	Jan. 14, 1847	Peter Snowdeal	Rev. Reebenack	3b106	gc 10	
Perry, John m. Lehman(Le~),Charlotte	Jan. 12,	Jan. 12, 1809	?		5b 70		
Perry, Polly m. Hoffman, Abr'm	May 31,	1827			2b127		
Perry, Thomas m. McDonald, Eliz.	June 2,	1801	James Conway				mr 87 *
Peterman, Emily L. m. Simpson, W.H.		June 16, 1853		G.W.Cooper	4b 10		
Peterman, George m. Tabler, Mary	Sept 25,	Sept 26, 1816	Wm. Tabler	W.N.Scott	4b156		mr 41 *
Peterman, John m. Hammond, Susan	Aug. 17,	Aug. 17, 1820	?	W.N.Scott			mr 41 *
Peterman, John m. Harrison, Susan		Aug. 17, 1820		W.N.Scott			mr 35 *
Peters, Eliz. m. Fury, Henry		June 10, 1788	Conrad Fultz	Hugh Vance			
Peters, Isaac m. Clarke, Anna	Mar. 4,	1799	Jacob Stookey		1b171		mr 55 *
Peterbaugh,Daniel m. Stookey,Barbara	Oct. 24,	Oct. 26, 1815		Nathan Young	3b346		mr 31 *
Peyton, Mary m. Morrow, John		July 6, 1781	John Stead	Daniel Sturges	1b x		
Phelps, Elisha m. Hughes, Eliz.	Apr. 21,	1789	Henry Payne		3b251		
Phelps, Elisha m. Payne, Rachel	Feb. 17,	1813		Richard Swift			
Phelps, Mary m. Harlan, Stephen		June 11, 1795		Richard Swift			
Philes, John m. Cross, Eliz.		Jan. 14, 1795					
Philips, Cath. m. Dobbin, Samuel		Mar. 17, 1796	Wm. Hawke	Moses Hoge		cr 26	mr 10 *
Philips, Charity m. Clayton, John	July 27,	July 29, 1802		Richard Swift	2b177	cr 26	mr 10 *
Philips, Hannah m. Kroesen,Cornelius	Mar. 17,	Mar. 24, 1800	Isaac Kroesen	John Hedtt(Hutt)	2b 58	cr 35	mr 11 *
Philips, Jason m. Sheely, Hannah		Jan. 20, 1785	Curtis Vermilyea	Edward Tiffin		cr 33	mr 20 *
Philips, Robert m. Allebaugh, Amelia	Sept 25,	Sept 25, 1841	Abr'm Varmetre	John Hedges	6b247	cr 37	mr 18 *
Philips, Susanna m. Varmetre, Ruth	Nov. 17,	Nov. 18, 1798		David Young	1b148	gc 8	mr 1 *
Philips, Wm. m.Burches(Bencher),Cath.		Oct. 5, 1819	Nicholas Orrick	Mathias Riser			mr 72 *
Philpy, Elinor m. Morgan, Humphrey	July 27,	Aug. 1, 1797	Alex. Stephens	John Boyd	1b 26	cr 32	mr 30 *
Philpy, Henry m. Hedges, John	Dec. 1,	Dec. 2, 1824	Lewis Specht	Jacob L. Bromwell	4b279		mr 13 *
Philpy, Mary m. Specht, Nancy	Jan. 24,	Jan. 26, 1816	Isaac Kawke	Rev. Reebenack	3b309	gc 14	mr 47 *
Philson, Rachel m. Severe, Charles	Apr. 4,	Apr. 4, 1806	Edward D. Foreman	John Bond	3b 15	cr 28	mr 22 *
Pickens, Jacob m. Basore, David	Dec. 30,	Dec. 30, 1813	Norman Miller	Seely Bunn	3b280	cr 41	mr 25 *
Pierce, Eliz. m. Snowdian, Jane	Oct. 6,	1844			7b 7		
Pierce, James m. Dawson, John L.	Mar. 28,	Mar. 31, 1831	Thomas Spencer	Jas. M. Brown	5b189	gc 10	mr 62 *
Pierce, John m. Shaffer, Marg't	Oct. 19,	Oct. 19, 1809	Peter Shaffer	Rev. Reebenack	3b122		mr 26 *
Pierce, Joseph m. Thompson, Ann	Nov. 19,	Nov. 19, 1816	Benjamin Comegys	John Mathews	4b 22	cr 35	
Pierce, Joseph m. Taylor, Martha		Mar. 1, 1796		Moses Hoge			mr 11 *

Name	Date	Marriage	Year	(surety)	(minister)	(bond)		
Pierce, Jos. S.C. m. Smith, Eliz.	Nov. 13,	Nov. 14,	1819	Mathew R. Gerrard	Nathan Young	4b122		mr 56 *
Pierce, Wm. m. Ady, Jessimina	Sept 23,		1807	Thos. Blackburn		3b 71	gc 11	
Pifer, John m. Sergeant, Polly	Oct. 31,	Nov. 1,	1810	John Pitzer	Rev. Reebenack	3b165		mr 71 *
Pike, John m. Risner, Mary	Mar 4,	May 4,	1839	Benj. Darby	M.G.Hamilton	6b168	gc 4	
Palmer, Wm. m. Hale,Christiana B.		Feb. 11,	1795		David Young			
Pine, Eliz. m. Moon, James		Feb. 25,	1800	Michael Brown		2b 54		mr 82 *
Pine, Eliz. m. Grant, Chas. S.	Feb. 21,		1849	James Pine	P. Lipscomb	7b147		
Pine, James m. Hutsler, Mary	Feb. 22,		1847	Alfred Hutsler		7b 87		
Pine, John W. m. Manor, Martha Jane	May 24,		1849	Samuel S. Lowry	W. Love	7b158		mr 80 *
Pine, Lydia m. Zimmerman, John W.	Oct. 13,	Oct. 14,	1847	James Burkhart	P. Lipscomb	7b109		mr 81 *
Pinkerton, Anna m. Palmer, Chrisly	Oct. 1,		1812	Robert Pinkerton		3b238		*
Pinkerton, Cath. m. Henry, Michael	Apr. 13,			Robert Pinkerton		3b219		*
?Pinkerton, Mary m.Crumpton, Elijah	July 31,	Aug. 6,	1799	Robert Pinkerton	David Young	2b 13	gc 8	*
?Pinkerton, Mary m.Compton, Elijah	July 31,	Aug. 6,	1799	Robert Pinkerton	David Young	2b 13	gc 8	
Piper, Eliz. m. Pitzer, John	Mar. 18,	Mar. 21,	1809	Emanual Piper	Rev. Reebenack	3b109	gc 10	
Piper, Eve m. Pitzer, Andrew	June 5,		1801	Emanual Piper Jr.		2b128		
Piper, Lucy m. Cline, John	Dec. 20,	Dec. 24,	1834	?	John Howell	6b 25		mr 68 *
Pisel, Eve m. Clapper, Fred.	June 28,	June 30,	1805	Joseph Chambers	Christian Streit	2b266	cr 16	mr 22 *
Pisel, Jacob m. Ott, Margaret	June 1,	June 1,	1805	Jacob Ott	Christian Streit	2b263	cr 16	mr 22 *
Pisel, Jacob m. Smith, Nancy	Dec. 31,		1801	Peter Pisel		2b155		
Pisel, Susanna m. Roberts, Thomas	Nov. 24,	Nov. 24,	1803	Bastian Pisel	David Young	2b215	gc 10	
Pitlock, John m. Fisher, Mary	Feb. 15,		1791		Moses Hoge		cr 6	mr 6 *
Pitwick, Gersuy m. Braman, Wm.	Aug. 27,		1789		Moses Hoge		cr 2	mr 3 *
Pitzer, Alex. m. Ridenour, Eliz.	Dec. 7,	Dec. 9,	1841	Jacob Myers	John Light	6b256		mr 72 *
Pitzer, Andrew m. Piper, Eve	June 5,		1801	Emanuel Piper Jr.		2b128		
Pitzer, Barbara m. Parker, Samuel	Dec. 26,		1786		Hugh Vance			mr 43 *
Pitzer, Cath. m. Couchman, Wm.	Oct. 26,	Oct. 27,	1842	Jacob Pitzer	Lewis F. Wilson	6b282		mr 73 *
Pitzer, Cath. m. Emberson, Francis	Nov. 9,	Nov. 11,	1830	Mathias Pitzer	Nathan Young	5b180		mr 61 *
Pitzer, Conrad m. Courtney, Mary	Nov. 7,		1797	James Robinson		1b 60		
Pitzer, Conrad m. Curtis, Margaret	Dec. 12,		1797					
Pitzer, Conrad m. Martin, Mary	Jan. 8,		1838?	James Martin	Peyton Harrison	6b129	gc 7	mr 69 *
Pitzer, Conrad m.McDaniel(McDon)Mary	Sept 11,	Sept 15,	1818	Alex. McDonald	W.N.Scott	4b 78		
Pitzer, Elias m. Lowman, Mary	Aug. 4,		1789		Hugh Vance		cr 39	
Pitzer, Elias m. Gladden, Mary C.	Sept 6,		1842	Wm. Gladden		6b277		mr 4 *
Pitzer, Eliza m. Miller, Geo. D.	Dec. 23,	Dec. 26,	1839	Jacob Pitzer	Lewis F. Wilson	6b190		mr 70 *
Pitzer, Eliza B. m. Walker, James	Mar. 17,	Feb. 22,	1832	Martin Pitzer	Jas. M. Brown	5b221		mr 64 *
Pitzer, Eve m. Bowers, George	Nov. 2,	Nov. 4,	1824	Jacob Pitzer	J.L.Bromwell	4b276		mr 47 *
Pitzer, Hannah Ann m. Walker, John	Feb. 5,	Feb. 7,	1844	Chas. Ridenour	John Light	6b312		mr 76 *
Pitzer, Harriet A. m. Brady, Benj.F.	Oct. 15,	Oct. 16,	1849	Jacob Pitzer	W. Love	7b166		mr 80 *
Pitzer, Henry B. m. Miller, Harriet	Feb. 16,	Feb. 18,	1841	David Miller	Lewis F. Wilson	6b234		mr 72 *
Pitzer, Jacob m. Alter(Aller),Eve	Mar. 30,	Apr. 6,	1815	Jacob Houke	Rev. Reebenack	3b317	gc 14	
Pitzer, Jacob m. Ramsburger, Nancy	Jan. 19,		1819	Geo. Ramsburger		4b 98		
Pitzer, Jacob m. Specht, Cath.	Sept 8,	Sept	1823	John Pitzer	Chas. P. Krauth	4b248		mr 46 *

	(marriage)			(surator)	(minister)	(bond)		
Pitzer, James m. Bowman, Eliz.	June 25,		1822	Henry Burns	Chas. P. Krauth	4b218		mr 45 *
Pitzer, James m. Earp, Cath Ann	May 21,		1839	Burgess Earp	John Light	6b170		mr 70 *
Pitzer, James m. Shank, Ann E.	Dec. 24,		1844	John Shank	John Light	7b 18		mr 76 *
Pitzer, James S. m. Bender, Eliz.	Feb. 8,		1853		A.G.Chenoweth			mr 87 *
Pitzer, Jane m. Hill, Benjamin	Apr. 17,		1844	Michael Pitzer		6b319		*
Pitzer, John m. Keesecker, Mary	May 11,	May 12,	1799	Andrew Keesecker	David Young	1b180	gc 8	
Pitzer, John m. Piper, Eliz.	Mar. 18,	Mar. 21,	1809	Emanuel Piper	Rev. Reebenack	3b109	gc 10	
Pitzer, John m. Sergeant, Polly	Oct. 31,	Nov. 1,	1810	John Pitzer	Rev. Reebenack	3b165	gc 11	
Pitzer, John m. Switzer, Mary			1797	Mathias Pitzer		1b 21		
Pitzer, John W. m.Rosenberger,Susan	June 14,		1848	Anthony Rosenbergr		7b141		
Pitzer, Lydia m. Pitzer, Mathias	Dec. 11,		1821	John Pitzer		4b188		
Pitzer, Marg't m. Barnes, George	Aug. 30,		1852	John Jordan		7b246		
Pitzer, Marg't m. Quigley, Michael	Feb. 24,		1820	Conrad Pitzer	W.N.Scott	4b147		mr 41 *
Pitzer, Marg't m. Rector, Samuel	May 8,		1826	Jacob Pitzer	John Winter	50 50		? mr 50 *
Pitzer, Martin m. Bowers, Rachel	Sept 7,		1813	Henry Bowers,	Rev. Reebenack	3b274	gc 13	
Pitzer, Mary m. Hanna, James	Nov. 3,		1817	Martin Pitzer	Nathan Young	4b 31		mr 55 *
Pitzer, Mary m. Perrel, John	Mar. 22,	May 29,	1832	Harrison Waite	Nathan Young	5b230		mr 64 *
Pitzer, Mary m. Ulm, Andrew	Oct. 28,	Nov. 4,	1824	Michael Pitzer	J.L.Bromwell	4b275		mr 47 *
Pitzer, Mary Ann m. Butt, Geo. W.	Sept	Sept 16,	1847	Michael Pitzer	J.H.Jennings	7b106		mr 82 *
Pitzer, Mary Ann C. m.Couchman,Cor'ls	Dec. 26,	Dec. 27,	1832	Martin Pitzer	Wm. Monroe	5b251		mr 65 *
Pitzer, Mathias m. Newson, Rachel	Dec. 22,	Dec. 23,	1830	Francis Emerson	John Light	5b184		mr 62 *
Pitzer, Mathias m. Pitzer, Lydia	Aug. 30,		1821	John Pitzer		4b188		
Pitzer, Michael m. Creamer, Polly	Sept 3,		1810	George Creamer		3b160		mr 57 *
Pitzer, Michael m. McDaniel, Nelly	July 8,	July 10,	1822	Jacob McDaniel	Nathan Young	4b219		mr 46 *
Pitzer, Michael m. Solster, Marg't	Oct. 8,		1823	Jacob Solster	Chas. P. Krauth	4b250		
Pitzer, Michael m. White, Sarah	July 28,		1841	James White		6b244		
Pitzer, Nancy m. Cress, Philip	Aug. 8,		1808	Michael Pitzer	John Light	3b 93		mr 80 *
Pitzer, Philip m. McAlister,Rosella	Dec. 3,	Dec. 4,	1849	Benj. McAlister		7b168		
Pitzer, Rachel Susan m. Busey, Benj.	July 9,		1849	James Pitzer		7b159		
Pitzer, Rebecca m. Bender,Washington		May 24,	1853		Geo. M. Cooper			mr 87 *
Pitzer, Samuel m. Leighner, Mary	June 15,	June 17,	1817	Jacob Miller	W.N.Scott	4b 38		
Pitzer, Susan m.Kupler(Coogler),Benj.	Dec. 7,	Dec. 10,	1799	John Pitzer	David Young	2b 38	gc 9	mr 67 *
Pitzer, Wm m. Jordan, Hannah	Sept 23,	Sept 26,	1833	Thomas Silver	Jas. M. Brown	5b284		
Pitzer, Wm. m. Leighner, Nancy	Apr. 26,	Apr. 29,	1817	Elijah Wilson	W.N.Scott	4b 33		
Place, Mary m. Finch, David			1818		Mathias Riser			mr 29 *
Plotner, Benj. m. Ebert, Nancy	Oct. 13,		1825	John Sherrard	Chas. P. Krauth	5b 24		mr 45 *
Plotner, Cath. m. Palmer, Martin	Oct. 23,		1822	Daniel Plotner		4b226		
Plotner, Daniel m. Crowl, Sarah	May 11,		1807	Henry Crowl		3b 58		
Plotner, Eliz. m. Shepherd, Philip	Dec. 10,		1821	Teter Myers		4b200		
Plotner, Eve m. Hedges, Jonas	Apr. 4,		1799	Jesse Hedges	David Young	1b177	gc 8	
Plotner, Eve m. Rooney, Henry	Aug. 25,		1823	Daniel Plotner	Jacob L. Bromwell	4b246		mr 46 *
Plotner, Jane m. Rooney, Michael	Sept 19,		1820	Daniel Plotner		4b162		mr 41 *
Plotner, Nancy m. Sherrard, John	Jan. 28.		1820	John Myers	W.N.Scott	4b132		

Name	(marriage)		(suretor)	(minister)	(bond)		
Plotner, Sally m. Crowl, Henry	Dec. 22,	1809	Mamus Plotner	Chas. P. Krauth	3b129		mr 45 *
Plotner, Sarah m. Palmer, Martin	Oct. 23,	1822	Daniel Plotner	Rev. Reebenack	4b226		mr 42 *
Plotner, Susan m.Oldfield, Jonathan	Aug. 29,	1812	Sarah Plotner	Daniel Sturges	3b234	ge 13	mr 42 *
Plug,Nich's(Newlas) m.Shively, Marg't	Mar. 5,	1782		David Young			
Plumer, Tabitha m. Price, Thomas	Aug. 22,	1795	Wm. Robinson	Nathan Young	5b271	ge 5	mr 66 *
Poffenberger, Sarah m.Stephens, Henry	Apr. 25,	1833	John Zorn	Lewis F. Wilson	6b317		mr 83 *
Points, John m. Leopard, Mary E.	Mar. 23,	1844	Jacob Poisal	B.M.Schmucker	7b181		mr 42 *
Poisal, Ann M. m. Mathews, Daniel	Apr. 11,	1850	John Poisal	Chas. P. Krauth	4b194		
Poisal, Betsy m. Stevens, Thos.	Oct. 16,	1821	Peter Poisal		2b166		
Poisal, Cath. m. Armstrong, James	Mar. 26,	1802	Bastian Poisal	Rev. Reebenack	3b228	ge 13	
Poisal, Cath. m. Clark, John	June 20,	1812	Jacob Poisal	John Winter	7b 69		mr 76 *
Poisal, Cath. m. Helferstay, Wm.	June 18,	1846	Jacob Poisal	David Thomas	7b231		mr 84 *
Poisal, Charlotte m. Light, Jacob	Sept 11,	1851	Jacob Poisal	W. Monroe	5b115		mr 53 *
Poisal, Eliza m. Walker, John	Dec. 15,	1828	John Shober	Nathan Young	5b178		mr 61 *
*Poisal, Eliz.Mrs. m.Helferstin,Henry	Oct. 16,	1830	Jacob Poisal		7b 20		
Poisal, Ellen R. m. Ott, John H.	Jan. 8,	1845					
Poisal, Eve m. Bishop, Jacob		1794		David Young		gc 3	
Poisal, Eve m. Clapper, Fred.	June 25,	1805	Joseph Chambers	Christian Stredt	2b266	cr 16	mr 22 *
Poisal, George m. Burkett,Mary Ann	Apr. 22,	1835	Jacob Hamme		6b 42		
Poisal, Henry m. Hess, Mary	May 28,	1835	Wm. W. Walker		6b 45		
Poisal, Henry m. Trigg, Elinor	Apr. 20,	1825	Jeremiah Trigg	B. Reynolds	5b 9		mr 49 *
Poisal, Jacob m. Diffenderfer,Mary A	Nov. 8,	1827	Geo. Diffenderfer	Jacob Beecher	5b 84		mr 53 *
Poisal, Jacob m. Ott, Mary Marg.	June 1,	1805	Jacob Ott	Christian Stredt	2b263	cr 16	mr 22 *
Poisal, Jacob m. Whetstone, Eliz.	June 15,	1822	John Bowers		4b217		
Poisal, John m. Deal, Rosanna	July 3,	1796		David Young		gc 6	
Poisal, Marg't m. Keys, John	June 8,	1811	Jacob Poisal	Rev. Reebenack	3b189	gc 12	
Poisal, Mary m. Harris, Thos.	Apr. 19,	1832	Jacob Poisal	Wm. Monroe	5b227		mr 65 *
Poisal, Michael O. m. Watts, Eliz.	Mar. 1,	1838	James Watts		6b134		
Poisal, Peggy m. Armstrong, Geo.	Oct. 7,	1808	John Poisal		3b 98		
Poisal, Peter m. Cline, Eve(Isabella)	Aug. 25,	1824	David Cline	Chas. P. Krauth	4b270		mr 47 *
Poisal, Polly m. Burkett, John	Oct. 10,	1816	John Poisal	John B. Hoge	4b 19		
Poisal, Polly m. Strayer, Adam	Aug. 24,	1812	John Poisal	Rev. Reebenack	3b233	ge 13	
?Poisal, Rose m. Kenney, Samuel	Nov. 25,	1850	Jacob VanDoren	Lewis F. Wilson	7b203		mr 87 *
?Poisal, Rose m. Kinney, Samuel	Nov. 25,	1850	Jacob VanDoren	Lewis F. Wilson	7b203		mr 87 *
Poisal, Sebastian m. Hooper,Eveline	Dec. 14,	1837	Abr'm Hooper	James Watts	6b126		
Poisal, Sebastian m. Lashorn, Eliz.	Mar. 5,	1816	John Lashorn	Rev. Reebenack	4b 11	gc 15	
Poisal, Susan m. Miller, Jeremiah	Nov. 13,	1851	Jacob Poisal	David Thomas	7b236		mr 85 *
Poisal, Susan m. Roberts, Thomas	Nov. 24,	1803	Bastian Poisal	David Young	2b215	gc 10	
Poisal, Susannah m. Cocke, Peter	June 8,	1794		David Young		gc 4	
Poisal, Susan m. Shaffer, Christian	Jan. 16,	1840	Jacob Poisal	James Redly	6b194		mr 70 *
Poitler, Franz m. Harsch, Mary	Dec. 30,	1853		J.H. Plunkett			mr 88 *
Pollock, Alex. m. Campbell, Mary	Feb. 11,	1796		John Boyd		cr 10	mr 12 *
Pollock, Mary Ann m. Ware, Ralph	June 11,	1798	James Lane	Richard Swift	1b115	cr 31	mr 15 *
*Poisal, Eliz. m. Kyle, Mathew	Nov. 7,	1807	John Poisal		3b 76		

Name	(marriage)		(suretor)	(minister)	(bond)		
Pool, Eliz. m. Turner, Geo. W.	Jan. 9,	1845	Jacob Crowl		7b 21	cr 26	mr 10 *
Pool, Fred. m. Oldfield,Mary Jane	Apr. 24,	1830	?		5b163		mr 84 *
Pool, Henry m. Custck, Eliz.		1795					mr 68 *
Pool,Joseph m. Zimmerman, Mary L.	June 5,	1851	Francis Burkhart	Richard Swift	7b226		
Pool,Mary Jane Mrs. m. Crowl, Jacob	Sept 22,	1835	Harrison Waite	David Thomas	6b 58		
Porter, Elenor m. Hurley, Samuel	Nov. 23,	1840	John Porter	John Howell	6b224		
Porter, John m. Aulebaugh, Nancy	Feb. 20,	1835	Harrison Waite		6b 32		
Porter, John m. Kilhown, Eliz.	June 29,	1808	Collin Carroll		3b 92		
Porter, Robert m. Yoke, Martha	May 27,	1799	David Simpson		2b 8		
Porter, Sarah m. Taffe, Thomas	Aug. 27,	1829	John Murray		5b139		
Porter, John m. Howe, Eliz.	Mar. 21,	1799	John Howe	David Young	1b174	gc 8	
Porterfield, Abr'm W. m. Small, Luc.		1852		R.A.Fink			mr 86 *
Porterfield,Alex. m.Shearer(Shaver),E		1783		Hugh Vance			mr 32 *
Porterfield, Ann m. Snodgrass, M.T.	Nov. 27,	1843	Jacob VanDoren	Lewis F. Wilson	6b308		mr 74 *
Porterfield, Cath. m. Gregg, John	Apr. 11,	1809	John Porterfield	John Mathews	3b111	cr 17	mr 23 *
Porterfield, Eliz. m.Harrison,Jacob	Dec. 22,	1853		G.W.Cooper			
Porterfield, Eliz. m.Robinson, Alex.	Mar. 27,	1821	Geo. Porterfield	John B. Hoge	4b179		mr 41 *
Porterfield, Geo. m. Tabb, Mary E.	Sept 29,	1821	John Porterfield		4b193		
Porterfield, Geo. m. Vance, Rachel	Mar. 22,	1792		Moses Hoge			
Porterfield, James m. Jack, Ann R.	July 1,	1820	Arch'd Porterfield	John B. Hoge	4b154		mr 39 *
Porterfield, Jane m. Morrison, Dan'l	May 21,	1825	Wm. Porterfield	John B. Hoge	5b 10		mr 41 *
Porterf'd,John m.Pendleton, Nancy	Mar. 27,	1802	Wm. Pendleton		2b166		mr 50 *
Porterf'd,John S.m.Porterf'd,Julia A	Dec. 15,	1824	Wm. A. Porterf'd	Jas. M. Brown	4b281		mr 48 *
Porterf'd,Julia A m.Porterf'd,John S	Dec. 15,	1824	Wm. A. Porterf'd	Jas. M. Brown	4b281		mr 48 *
Porterf'd, June m. Morrison,Dan'l	May 21,	1825	Wm. A. Porterf'd	John Mathews	5b 10		mr 50 *
Porterf'd, Martha m.Oden, Alex. P.	Aug. 8,	1831	Wm. Porterf'd	Jas. M. Brown	5b201		mr 62 *
Porterf'd, Mary m. Harlan, Elijah	Sept 12,	1815	Mathew Porterf'd	John Mathews	3b339		mr 25 *
Porterf'd, Mary m. Tabb, George	Mar. 9,	1818	Geo. Porterf'd	John B. Hoge	4b 65		mr 29 *
Porterf'd m.Mary A. m. Burr,Moses Wm	Apr. 28,	1845	Abner Williamson		7b 33		
Porterf'd, Nancy m.Chrisman, Geo.	Aug. 10,	1829	Archibald Oden	Jas. M. Brown	5b136		mr 53 *
Porterf'd, Patty m.Newkirk, James	Jan. 7,	1815	Robert Wilson	John Mathews	3b308		mr 25 *
Porterf'd, Rachel m. Hill, Geo.	Mar. 10,	1829	John Shober	Jas. M. Brown	5b122		mr 53 *
Porterf'd,Sarah(Sally)m.Light, Jacob	Mar. 20,	1809	Arch'd Shearer	John Mathews	3b110	cr 17	mr 23 *
Porterf'd, Wm. m.Williamson, Mary	May 27,	1823	George Hill	Nathan Young	4b240		mr 58 *
Post, Lewis m. Quick, Jenny	Dec. 28,	1796		Moses Hoge		cr 5	
Postgale, Billy m. Ferguson, Rachel	Feb. 8,	1844		David Young		gc 5	
Potter, Drusilla m. Keesarre, Geo.	Oct. 16,	1821	John Risor	Nathan Young	7b 8		mr 57 *
Potter, Ralph m. Smeltzer, Peggy	Nov. 5,	1821	?		4b196		
Potts, Barbara m. Shazely, John	Feb. 14,	1798	Fred. Potts		1b 85		
Potts, Eliz. m. Bowman, George	Mar. 10,	1810	John Beckett	Lewis Mayer	3b140	cr 14	mr 24 *
Potts, Hannah m. Beckett, John	Mar. 27,	1794		Richard Swift			mr 40 *
Potts, John m. Hall, Eliz.	Oct. 15,	1800					
Potts, John m. Hibbans, Susan	Mar. 14,	1782	Robert McKnight	Daniel Sturges	2b 93		
*Porter, John m. Howe, Eliz.	Apr. 2,	1799	John Howe	David Young	1b174	gc 8	mr 42 *

	(marriage)		(surety)	(minister)	(bond)		
Potts, John m. Vestal, Mary	July 18.	Jan. 25, 1794	John Potts	William Hill	2b131	cr 29	mr 9 *
Potts, Nelly m. Coplin, James		July 28, 1801		Richard Swift		cr 31	mr 20 *
Potts, Peggy m. Siler, Daniel		June 18, 1795		John Boyd		cr 33	mr 11 *
Pottsgrove, Nancy m. Schoppert, Moses	Mar. 29,	Mar. 25, 1830	Thomas Friddle	Jacob Medtart	5b160		mr 63 *
Powell, Arch'd M. m. Fearman, Maria	Aug. 17,	1836	Joseph Paulsgrove		6b 84		mr 56 *
Powell, Cath. m. Coyle, John	Apr. 13,	Apr. 16, 1818	James Powell	Nathan Young	4b 68		mr 46 *
Powell, Humphrey B. m. Boyd, Anne R	Oct. 30,	Oct. 30, 1823	Phil. C. Pendleton	John Mathews	4b251		
Powell, John m. Clarke, Eliz.	Mar. 5,	1798	Robert Powell		1b 87		
Powell, Lydia m. Eversole, Isaac	Dec. 13,	Dec. 15, 1831	John McFarland	W. Monroe	9b211		mr 62 *
Powell, Marg't m. Miller, Samuel	Mar. 3,	1835	Harrison Waite		6b 34		
Powell, Martha m. Watson, Francis	Mar. 5,	1798	Robert Powell		1b 88		
Powell, Mary m. Steidley, John	June 20,	1808	Robert Powell		3b 91		
Powell, Samuel R. m.Linton,Henrietta	Sept 23,	Sept 24, 1850	Zachariah Linton	B.M.Schmucker	7b196		mr 84 *
Powell, Wm. m. Sperow, Rebecca	Feb. 17,	Feb. 20, 1845	William Sperow	Lewis F. Wilson	7b 27		
Powers, Thomas m. Smith, Gracy	Mar. 7,	1815	Christian Tabler		3b313		
Prather, Ady m. Glassford, Dennis	July 5,	July 4, 1848	Norman Miller	Wm Love	7b132		mr 80 *
Prather, Ann m. Cooper, Israel	Aug. 5,	Aug. 7, 1831	Nathan Davis	John Light	9b200		mr 62 *
Prather, Eliz. m. Cox, Isaac		Sept 18, 1790		Moses Hoge		cr 5	mr 5 *
Prather, Rhoda m.Williamson,Theodor	Sept 2,	Sept 3, 1800	Silas Prather	Richard Swift		cr 34	mr 18 *
Prather, Richard m. Covenhaver, Lydia		Aug. 3, 1782		Hugh Vance		cr 9	mr 1 *
Prather, Wm. m. Bell, Lucy		Feb. 5, 1797		Richard Swift	2b 84	cr 26	mr 13 *
Price, Annie m. Ray, Wm.	Oct. 5,	Oct. 8, 1820	Samuel Lyle	Nathan Young	4b164		mr 57 *
Price, Daniel m. Alexander, Mary	Feb. 23,	Feb. 24, 1828	John Stanley	Nathan Young	9b 91		mr 59 *
Price, Daniel m. Weller, Cath.	Jan. 6,	Jan. 11, 1838	George Weller	James Watts	6b116		
Price, Eliz. m. Dennis, Henry	Oct. 24,	1818	George Powell		4b 84		
Price, Ephraim m. McLaughlin, Marg't		1789					
Price, George m. Hummeldorf, Cath.	Apr. 8,	Apr. 8, 1847	Jacob VanDoren Jr.	John Winter	7b 93		mr 37 *
Price, Geo. L. m. Bowers, Mary	Nov. 30,	1840	John Bowers		6b226		mr 77 *
Price, Isabella m. Smith, Thos. C.	July 27,	1824	Alex. Cooper		4b268		
Price, Isabella A. m. Miller, Wm.	Oct. 19,	1833	Wm. D. Wilson		9b289		
Price, Jacob m. Huntsburg, Emeline	July 19,	1845	George Price		7b 38		
Price, Jacob m. Manning, Ann		Dec. 11, 1796	Isaac Crabb	David Young	3b197	go 6	*
Price, Jane m. Clarke, Isaac	Oct. 31,	1811					
Price, Mary m. Daugh, Michael		1789		D. Thomas			
Price, Susanna m. Errick(En-), John	Jan. 5,	Jan. 10, 1803	James Walker	John Mines	2b189	cr 27	mr 37 *
Price, Thomas m. Plumer, Tabitha		Aug. 22, 1795		David Young		gc 5	mr 21 *
Prill, Phebe m. Johnson, John	Nov. 23,	Nov. 23, 1818	John Robinson		4b 89		
Proctor, Ann m. Cooper, Israel	Aug. 5,	Aug. 7, 1831	Nathan Davis	John Light	6b200		mr 62 *
Proctor, Robert m. French, Mary	Mar. 14,	Mar. 23, 1831	John French	Jas. M. Brown	9b188		mr 62 *
Pryor, Mary Mrs. m.O'Connell,Dominic	Jan. 23,	1844	James McSherry		6b311		
Puffenberger, Henry m. Strode, Maria	Dec. 2,	Dec. 30, 1830	John Puffenberger	J.E.Jackson	9b182		
Puffenberger, Maria m. Fiser, Jacob	Feb. 11,	1837	Wm. Robinson		6b 97		
Puffenberger, Sarah m. Stephen, Henry	Apr. 25,	Apr. 28, 1833	Wm. Robinson	Nathan Young	9b271		mr 66 *

Name		(marriage)	(surety)	(minister)	(bond)			*
Pugh(Pugle),Samuel m.Grove,Barbara	Oct. 21	Oct. 20, 1803	Christian Grove	David Young	2b221	ge 10		*
Pulse, Cath. m. Boltz, George	Oct. 10,	1806	John Pulse		3b 32			
Pulse, George m. Shall, Mary	Apr. 21,	1810	Nicholas Shall		3b148			
Pulse, Joseph m. Cole(Coal),Elenor A.	Nov. 3,	Nov. 8, 1832	Samuel Cole	Nathan Young	5b245		mr 65	*
Pulse, Levi m. Thompson, Mary Jane	Oct. 29,	1844	Wesley Ellis		7b 11			
Pulse, Lewis m. Sharp, Jane	Feb. 28,	Feb. 28. 1820	Daniel McKeever	Nathan Young	4b137		mr 57	*
Pulse, Mary m. Faris, John	Dec. 23,	1824	George I. Boltz		4b281			
Pultz, Eliz. m. Gilbert, Henry	Aug. 8,	1797	Peter Pultz		1b 27			
Pultz, Eliz. m. Haslett, Robert	Nov. ?	1833	Jacob Shaull		5b290			
Pultz, Eliz. m. Rutherford, Thomas	Dec. 25,	Dec. 25, 1806	John Pultz	John Mathews	3b 39	or 13	mr 23	*
Pultz, Eve m. Morgan, David	Apr. 7,	1800	Jacob Gardiner		2b 63			
Pultz, Frances m. Woodward, Thos.	July 24,	July 25, 1819	John Kemp	Nathan Young	4b111		mr 56	*
Pultz, Henry m. Rutherford,Frances	Sept 4,	1834	Jacob M. Gardiner		5b296			
Pultz, Jacob m. Roberts, Rhoda	Dec. 16,	1833	Boyd Roberts		6b120			
Pultz, Nancy Ann m.Seckman(Lock)David	Oct. 23,	Oct. 25, 1837	John Faris	J. Larken	5b155			*
Pultz, Susanna m. Smith, John F.	Mar. 8,	1830	George S. Boltz	David Young	1b156	ge 8		*
Purcell, John m. Terrell, Cath.	Dec. 24,	Dec. 25, 1798	James Wilson	John Boyd	1b 95	or 32	mr 15	*
Purcell, John m. Wilkinson, Eliz.	Feb. 13,	Feb. 15, 1798	Thomas Beard	David Young		or 3	mr 13	*
Purcell, Susanna m. Burtze, Andrew		Aug. 6, 1793		David Young		or 26		*
Purkey, John m. Smith, Eliz.		Jan. 3, 1797		Richard Swift				
Purnell, Sarah Ann m.Mason,Enoch Geo.	Mar. 6,	1843	John W. Wolff		6b291			
Putman, Cath. m. Cox, Samuel		Jan. 16, 1816		Mathias Riser			mr 26	*
Puy, Margaret m. Right, Josias	Aug. 24,	Aug. 24, 1793		David Young		ge 3		*
Pyle,Milton(Miflin) m.Rigsby,Susan	June 17,	June 17, 1841	John R. O'Neal	John Hedges	6b242		mr 72	*
Pyles, Jane m. McCormick, Wm.	Mar. 8,	Mar. 8, 1820	John J. Wilson	Hugh Vance	4b139		mr 36	*
Pysle, Rebecca m.Helphingston,Henry		Dec. 11, 1788						

"Q"

Name		(marriage)	(surety)	(minister)	(bond)			*
Quaid, Anna m. Clark, Anthony	Jan. 10,	Jan. 10, 1813	John Harrison		3b246			
Quick, Frances m. Nephins, John		Jan. 21, 1792		Moses Hoge		ge 8	mr 7	*
Quick, James m. Gorrell, Hannah	Sept 23,	1789	Wm. Maslin	Hugh Vance		or 40	mr 4	*
Quick, James m. Jennings, Sarah	Oct. 17,	Oct. 17, 1807		Moses Hoge	3b 74			
Quick, Jenny m. Post, Lewis	Dec. 28,	Dec. 28, 1790	John Clawson			or 5	mr 5	*
Quick, John m. Clawson, Phebe	Nov. 12,	Nov. 12, 1810		Hugh Vance	3b165			
Quick, Leanah m. Roberts, Phebe	Feb. 15,	Feb. 15, 1785	James Quick				mr 33	*
Quick, Polly m. Seabourne,Theodorus	Nov. 25,	Nov. 25, 1809		Hugh Vance	3b125			
Quick, Tunis m. Gorrell, Ruth		Feb. 22, 1786		Hugh Vance			mr 33	*
Quigley, Cath. m. French, Harrison	July 21,	July 21, 1847	Michael Quigley	Jas. H. Jennings	7b101		mr 82	*
Quigley, Jane m. Hay, Gabriel	Sept 24,	Sept 24, 1789		Hugh Vance		or 40	mr 4	*

Name	(lic.)	(marriage)	(suretor)	(minister)	(bond)		
Qudgley, John m. Patterson, Mary	Aug. 30,	Nov. 3, 1796	John French	John Boyd	3b194	cr 11	mr 12 *
Qudgley, John m. Stripe, Betsy	May 8,	Sept 1, 1811	Conrad Pitzer	John B. Hoge	4b147	cr 14	mr 24 *
Qudgley, Michael m. Pitzer, Marg't		May 9, 1820		W.N.Scott			mr 41 *
Qudgley, Sarah m. Davis, John		Sept 22, 1789		Hugh Vance		cr 40	mr 4 *
Quinby, Ann m. Warrel, Elijah		Sept 22, 1793		William Hill		cr 30	mr 9 *
Qudnn, Bridget m. Conner, Patrick	Jan. 11,	1840	Nicholas Dunfee		6b192		
Qudnn, Marg't m. McCarty, Martin	June 14,	1838	Harrison Waite		6b141		
Qudnn, Nancy m. Little, John	Nov. 29,	Dec. 6, 1838	Adam Sanaker	Jas. M. Brown	5b 28		mr 48 *
Qudnn, Sarah Ann m. Strayer, Geo. W.	Nov. 4,	1844	Jeremiah Quinn		7b 12		
*Qudnn, Jeremiah m. Bare, Eliz.	Feb. 17,	1840	William Hedges		6b197		

"R"

Name	(lic.)	(marriage)	(suretor)	(minister)	(bond)		
Rafferty, Wm. B. m. Downey, Susanna	Aug. 28,	1838	Joseph Bell	M.G.Hamilton	6b145		
Ragear, Magnus m. Page, Mary Ann	June 5,	1839	Wm. Sperow		6b171		mr 71 *
Raimer, Cath. m. Duffey, John W.	Apr. 17,	1837	Fred. Raimer		6b105		
Raimer, Christian m. Raimer, Dolly	Dec. 24,	Dec. 31, 1798	Jonathan Tricle	David Young	7b 1	ge 8	
Raimer, George m. Small, Cath. B.	May 18,	1844	Wm. Bowers		1b155	ge 8	
Raimer, Dolly m. Raimer, Christian	Dec. 24,	Dec. 31, 1798	Jonathan Tricle	David Young	1b155		*
Raimer, Sarah m. Houseworth, Isaac	Apr. 25,	1831	Fred. Raimer	Jacob Medtart	5b193		mr 63 *
Radney, Eliz. m. Barrett, Wm.	Aug. 1,	1825	Samiel Rainey	Nathan Young	5b 17		mr 58 *
Radney, Eliz. m. Stilwell, Stephen	Jan. 19,	1802	Ignat's O'Ferrall		2b158		
Radney, Jacob m. Butt, Mary	Mar. 23,	1842	Elisha Butt	Peyton Harrison	6b268		mr 73 *
Adney, James m. Syler, Martha	Dec. 25,	1816	Jonathan Thatcher		4b 28		
Radney, John m. Tharp, Kitty	Oct. 26,	1819	William Tharp	John B. Hoge	4b121		mr 31 *
Radney, Polly m. Kennedy, Robert	Sept 22,	1797	John Rainey Jr.		3b272		
Radney, Presley m. Throckmorton, Mary	Oct. 16,	1797	Thos. Throckmorton		1b 54		
Radney, Wm. m. Booth, Hannah	Mar. 22,	1821	Caleb Booth		4b178		
Ralphsnder, Christena m. Snider, Jacob	Feb. 2,	1804	Aaron Refsnider	David Young	2b221		
Ralphsnder, Leonard m. Bonawitz, July	Apr. 7,	1800	Jacob Bonawitz	Lewis Mayer	2b 63	gc 9	mr 24 *
Ralphsnder(Ref-Mary m. Achey, Michael	Aug. 14,	1809	Aron Ralphsnider	Nathan Young	3b119	cr 16	mr 60 *
Ralphsnder, Rebecca m. Robinson, Jas.	Dec. 21,	1829	Seaman Garard		5b148		
Rambaugh, George m. Dust, Eliz.	Mar. 19,	1798	John Dust		1b 90		
Rambaugh, Philip m. Mussetter, Mary	Aug. 24,	1823		Nathan Young	5b 14		mr 58 *
†Rambaugh, Susanna m. Hudson, James	June 13,	1825	Wm. Grantham	Nathan Young			mr 58 *
*Ramety, John m. Doyle, Eliz.	Oct. 12,	1797		Richard Swift		cr 26	mr 13 *
**Ramety, Fred. m. Jack, Ann	Jan. 10,	1797		Richard Swift			
Ramsburg, Barbara m. Ramsburg, Ezra	Apr. 9,	1834	John Ramsburg	Jas. M. Brown	6b 4		mr 67 *
Ramsburg, Cath. m. Fisher, James	Jan. 25,	1830	John Ramsburg	W. Monroe	5b150		mr 54 *
Ramsburg, Cath. m. Worly, Silas	Mar. 11,	1829	Wm. Tabler		5b122		
Ramsburg, Eliza m. Miller, Jas. D.	Mar. 28,	1838	George Ramsburg	Lewis F. Wilson	6b137	cr 12	mr 36 *
*Ramer, Hezekiah m. Gray, Lilly	June 24,	1788		Moses Hoge			
**Ramety, John m. Swift, Cath.	Aug. 15,	1797		Richard Swift			mr 14 *

Name		(marriage)	(suretor)	(minister)	(bond)		
Ramsburg, Ezra m. Ramsburg, Barbara	Apr. 9,	Apr. 10, 1834	John Ramsburg	Jas. M. Brown	6b 4		mr 67 *
Ramsburg, Ezra m. Waggoner,Mary Jane	Sept 1,	Sept. 4, 1849	John Waggoner	Henry Furlong	7b164		mr 79 *
Ramsburg, George m. Dust, Eliz.	Mar. 19,	1798	John Dust		1b 90		
Ramsburg, John m. Kerney, Julia Ann	Dec. 23,	Dec. 24, 1839	James Chenoweth	Lewis F. Wilson	6b190		mr 70 *
Ramsburg, Nancy m. Pitzer, Jacob	Jan. 19,	1819	Geo. Ramsburg		4b 98		
Ramsburg, Rebecca m. Miller, David H.	Feb. 6,	Feb. 7, 1839	John Ramsburg	Lewis F. Wilson	6b159		mr 70 *
*Randall, Adrian W. m. Shaffer, Eliz.	Oct. 1,	Oct. 1823	Peter Shafer	Chas. P. Krauth	4b250		mr 46 *
Randall, Benj. m. Williamson, Alley	Oct. 23,	Oct. 25, 1797	Peter Williamson	Richard Swift	1b 58	cr 12	mr 14 *
Randall, Elenor m. Strode, Joseph	Jan. 13,	1819	Edmund Randall		4b 96		
Randall, Eliz. m. Hill, Jacob	Oct. 30,	1839	John Waite		6b182		
Randall, Eliz. B. m. Crowl, John F.	Aug. 17,	Aug. 17, 1842	Geo. S. Randall	John Light	6b275		mr 74 *
Randall, Ellen m. Eversole, John	Mar. 5,	1851	John F. Crowl		7b217		
Randall, Geo. m. Wynkoop, Mary	Apr. 9,	1827	Garret Wynkoop		5b 67		
Randall, John m. Markwood, Marg't	Mar. 31,	1800	John Shober	David Young	2b 61	gc 9	*
Randall, Nicholas m. Snowdeal, Cath.	Oct. 23,	Oct. 26, 1813	Peter Snowdeal	Rev. Reebenack	3b273	gc 13	*
Randall, Sarah m. Roush, Conrad	Mar. 7,	Mar. 8, 1814	George Randall	Rev. Reebenack	3b287	gc 14	*
Randall, Susannah m. Jones, Francis	May 13,	1811	John Randall		3b186		
Randolf, John m. Molding, Eliz.		July 9, 1788					
Raney, Agnes m. Collins, Joseph	Aug. 20,	1840	Wm. Barret	Moses Hoge	6b216		mr 36 *
Raney, Charlotte m. Miller, Geo.	Jan. 22,	1839	Jacob Raney		6b156		
Raney, Eliz. m. Right, Robert		Mar. 31, 1791		Moses Hoge		cr 7	mr 6 *
Raney, Eve m. Keyes, John	Oct.	1843	Samuel Raney		6b305		
Raney, Marg't Ann m. Snyder, Daniel	Dec. 29,	1834	Samuel Raney	B.M.Schmucker	6b 26		
Raney, Maria m. Carper, Jacob	Aug. 11,	Aug. 14, 1849	Mr. Collins	Rev. Reebenack	7b162	gc 11	mr 79 *
Raney, Martha m. Brown, Robert		Oct. 25, 1810					
Raney, Samuel m. Hess, Charlotte	July 30,	Nov. 19, 1804	Luke Pentony	E.L.Dulin	2b239		mr 77 *
Raney, Samuel W. m. Ridenour, Mary E	Nov. 3,	June 24, 1846	John Ridenour	Moses Hoge	7b 79		mr 36 *
Ranier, Hezekiah m. Gray, Lilly	June 17,	1800	Wm. Murphy		2b 72		
Rankin, Abigail m. Johnson, James	Dec. 31,	Dec. 31, 1797	William Downs	John Hill	1b 76	cr 37	mr 14 *
Rankin, Frances m. Bloys(Blogs),Wm.	Feb. 2,	1799	Jas. Abernathy		1b166		
Rankin, Samuel m. Abernathy, Ann	Mar. 30,	1804	Wm. McCoughtry		2b230		
Rankin, Samuel m. Brady, Rebecca	Dec. 30,	Dec. 31, 1846	Vincent McBride	John Winter	7b 82		mr 77 *
Rankin, Simeon H. m. Martin, Julia	Sept 9,	1815	John Thompson		3b338		
Rankin, Wm. m. Thompson, Marg't	May 23,	1831	Mathew Ranson		5b196		
Ranson, Ann Eliz. m. Davis, Thomas	Sept 23,	June 24 1788		Moses Hoge			
Ranson, Hezekiah m. Gray, Lilly	Sept 19,	1812	Robert Wilson	Moses Hoge	3b237		mr 36 *
Ranson, Lucy m. McFeely, Joseph	Jan. 14,	1790				cr 3	mr 5 *
Rash, Mary m. Williamson, Peter		1839					
Rardin, Thomas m. Mahoney, Cath.	Feb. 11,	1807?	John Mahoney	John Mathews	6b159	cr 13	mr 23 *
Raving, Joshua m. Sellers, Rachel	May 27,	1794	Bolzer Sellers	David Young	3b 59	gc 4	
Rawlings, Hanna m. Clawson, Thomas	Oct. 27,	1794		Hugh Vance			
?Ray, Ann m. Eccles, William	Aug. 12,	1783					mr 32 *
Ray, Ann m. Turner, John	Sept 15,	1833	Jacob Sperow	John Light	5b283		mr 67 *
?*Ramsburg, Ruth m. Turner, John	Aug. 12,	1783		Hugh Vance			mr 32 *

Name	(marriage) date	Year	(surety)	(minister)	(bond)	
Ray, Delilah m. Butt, Richard	Nov. 8,	1811	Swearingen Ray		3b200	mr 36 *
Ray, Eliz. m. Ellison, Jacob	May 13,	1815	Swearingen Ray		3b323	
Ray, Eliz. m. Kerns, Michael	Sept 3,	1815	Abraham Levy	Rev. Reebenack	3b337	ge 15 *
Ray, Hazel m. Kroesen, Eliz.	Oct. 21,	1834	John Hedges		6b 21	
Ray, James m. Riffle, Marg't	Dec. 19,	1801	Conrad Riffle		2b153	
Ray, Joseph m. Crow, Cath.	Mar. 15,	1830	John Crow		5b158	
Ray, Luke m. Souther, Nancy	Nov. 27,	1788		Moses Hoge	6b143	
Ray, Margaret m. Holland, Joseph	Aug. 7,	1838	Harvey E. Foreman		2b159	
Ray, Mildred m. Hoover, Henry	Feb. 2,	1802	Robert Filson		3b154	
Ray, Nancy m. Butt, Charles	July 16,	1810	Wm. Butt	Rev. Reebenack	3b157	ge 11 *
Ray, Nelly m. Butt, Henry	Aug. 8,	1810	Robert Collins	Rev. Reebenack	3b127	ge 11 *
Ray, Nicholas m. Coupe, Cath.	Dec. 5,	1809	Andrew Shewinder	Rev. Reebenack	6b250	ge 10 *
Ray, Priscilla m. Short, George		1793				
Ray, Priscilla m. Walters, Fred.	Oct. 27,	1841	Wm. Myers	David Young	4b162	ge 2 *
Ray, Robert m. Bradford, Mary	Apr. 11,	1793		Christian Stredt	2b106	cr 15
Ray, Swearingen m. Butt(Batt),Cath.	Sept 23,	1820	John Batt	Nathan Young	4b155	mr 8 *
Ray, Thomas m. Short, Mary Ann	Jan. 1,	1801	George Short	Richard Swift	4b222	cr 31
Ray, Van m. Kay, Anne	Aug. 14,	1820	Jacob Kay		4b 24	
Ray, Wm. m. Crow, Sophia	Aug. 27,	1822	Jacob Crow		4b164	
Ray, Wm. m. Oller, G___	Nov. 26,	1816	William Ray Sr.		5b243	
Ray, Wm. m. Price, Anna	Oct. 8,	1820	Samuel Lyle	Nathan Young	4b121	mr 57 *
Ray, Wm. m. Stewart, Sally	Oct. 14,	1832	George Oller	Nathan Young	1b 19	mr 19 *
Reaney, John m. Tharp, Kitty	Oct. 28,	1819	Wm. Tharp	John B. Hoge		mr 57 *
Reckhart, Michael m. Shindler, Eliz.	June 2,	1797	John Waters			
Recob, Joseph m. Jones, Ann	Jan. 6,	1795		David Young	5b 50	mr 65 *
Rector, Samuel m. Pitzer, Margaret	Sept 6,	1826	Jacob Pitzer	John Winter	2b 57	mr 31 *
Redfern, Nancy m. Sprinkle, Peter	Mar. 16,	1800	John Rohr	David Young	1b107	ge 4 *
Redgrave, Henrietta m. Leckron, Mich'l	Jan. 22,	1849		B.M.Schmucker	3b250	mr 50 *
Reece, Jane m. Kennedy, Stephen	Apr. 9,	1798	Wm. Snodgrass	Richard Swift	7b141	ge 9 *
Reed, Eliza m. Baker, Samuel Jr.	Feb. 9,	1813	Cyrus Murray		3b108	
Reed, Emily m. Chambers, John M.	Dec. 4,	1848	Wm. Reed	P. Lipscomb	3b 78	mr 79 *
Reed, Frances m. Irvine, John	Aug. 18,	1785		Hugh Vance	6b300	cr 31
Reed, Isaac m. Hill, Jane	Feb. 27,	1809	John Hill		1b107	mr 15 *
Reed, James m. Runner, Christina	Nov. 26,	1807	Wm. Runner		2b 69	mr 82 *
Reed, James F. m. Snyder, Ann	June 15,	1843	John R. Snyder	T.H.W.Monroe		mr 34 *
Reed, Jane m. Kennedy, Stephen	Apr. 9,	1798	Wm. Snodgrass	Richard Swift		mr 75 *
Reed, Jane m. Miller, John	May 10,	1800	Joseph Colton			mr 15 *
Reed, John m. Hutchinson, Jane		1789		D. Thomas		cr 31
Reed, Marg't m. Sanders(Saun-),Fred.	Aug. 6,	1807	Wm. Reed	John Mathews	3b 65	mr 37 *
Reed, Marg't K. m. Brown, James	Jan. 13,	1812	Taif'ro Stribling		3b208	mr 23 *
Reed, Maria K. m. Cooper, Alex.	Nov. 21,	1805	David Hunter		3b 3	cr 13
Reed, Samuel m. Burr(Rurr), Eliz.	Jan. 23,	1797		Moses Hoge		cr 29 mr 13 *
Reed, Samuel m. Lucas, Rebecca	Oct. 30,	1799	Wm. Lucas	Moses Hoge	2b 32	mr 17 *

Name	(marriage)	(suretor)	minister)	(bond)		
Reed, Samuel m. Run, Eliz.	Jan. 23, 1797	David Soister	Moses Hoge	3b222	cr 36	mr 13 *
Reed, Samuel m. Siler, Kath.	Apr. 21, 1812				gc 6	*
Reed, Sarah m. Kanifer, John	Feb. 17, 1797	David Young		4b 85		
Reed, Sarah m. White, John	Oct. 30, 1818	John Evans		6b298		mr 74 *
Reed, Sarah E. m. Sayles, John	May 18, 1843	William Reed	T.H.W.Monroe	1b153	cr 29	mr 17 *
Reed, Sarah m. Blue, Ezekiel	Dec. 11, 1799	James Watson	Moses Hoge			mr 32 *
Reed, Wm.(Wallace) m. Snodgrass,Kath.	Feb. 12, 1782		Hugh Vance	3b161		mr 40 *
Reed, Wm. Jr. m. Hedges, Sarah	Sept 5, 1810	Wm. Reed Sr.	John Mathews	6b296		mr 74 *
Reed, Wm. H. m. Maxwell, Nancy	May 5, 1843	Anthony S.Chamber	T.H.W.Monroe	7b198		mr 88 *
Reedy, Hannah m. Connell, Patrick	Mar. 25, 1851	Michael Connell	J.H.Plunkett			
Reef, David m. Snider, Cath.	Dec. 21, 1794		David Young		gc 4	
Reel, Peter m. Folk, Eliz.	Jan. 12, 1801	Christ'r Folk		2b108		mr 38 *
Rees, Daniel m. Moon, Jane	Aug. 15, 1806	Thomas Moon		3b 25		mr 50 *
Rees, David m. Daniel, Susannah	Mar. 4, 1807	John Daniel		3b 49		mr 87 *
Rees, Davidson m. Lewis, Ann	Sept 5, 1797	Thomas Lewis		1b 39		
Rees, Eliz. m. Jett, Wm.	Oct. 8, 1800	John Rees		2b 91		
Rees, Hannah m. Todhunter, Joshua	1789					
Rees, Jane m. Smith, Elisha	Feb. 26, 1825	Jesse Holliday	D. Thomas	5b 2		mr 66 *
Rees, John E. m. Evans, Isabella J.	Feb. 27, 1853		John Winter			
Rees, Leah m. Moon, Jacob	Feb. 10, 1806		R.G.Chenoweth			
Rees, Mary m. Cromley, Henry	Apr. 17, 1801	Samiel Rees		3b 16		
Rees, Nancy m. Sellers, James	Aug. 30, 1804	Evan Rees		2b140		
Rees, Phebe m. Morgan, Wm.	Dec. 22, 1829	Rees Branson		2b250		
Rees, Rachel m. Larken, Joseph	Mar. 17, 1801	Ellis Rees		5b123		
Rees, Rebecca m. Simmons, Samuel	May 20, 1822	Jacob Rees		2b126		
Rees, Ruth m. Fryer, Mathew	Dec. 23, 1847	Ellis Rees		4b231		
Rees, Samuel D. m. Ward, Margaret	Aug. 22, 1833	Wm. Gilbert		2b138		
Rees, Simon m. Steddley(Ste-,Mary	Mar. 5, 1821	Alfred Ross		7b 90		
Refsneider, Aron m. Clise, Rebecca	Sept 16, 1818 A.Sept 19,	John Steddley	Nathan Young	5b284		mr 66 *
Refsneider, Rachel m. Cline, Jacob	Aug. 2, 1821			4b186		
Refsneider, Susannah m.Brennan, Fred.	Sept 30, 1824	Aaron Refsneider		4b 81		
Refsnyder, Eliz. m. Gusman, Abraham	Mar. 10, 1795	Aaron Refsneider		4b175		mr 42 *
Reichard, Cath. Mrs. m.Cochran, Geo.	Aug. 2, 1788		Chas. P. Krauth		gc 5	mr 47 *
Reichert, Eve m. Houseman, Christian	July 8, 1783	George Hoe	David Young	4b268	gc 5	mr 36 *
Reikart, Adam m. Fisher, Kath.	1789		Chas. P. Krauth			mr 32 *
Reily, John m. Caslett, Mary	June 11, 1792		David Young		cr 25	mr 4 *
Reily, Mary m. Kennedy, James	June 24, 1805		Moses Hoge		gc 1	
Reiner(Riner),Cath. m.Schneider, Jos.	Feb. 25, 1830		Hugh Vance		cr 28	mr 22 *
Reiner(Riner),Eliz. m.Morrow, Wm.	Mar. 16, 1853	James Morrow	Hugh Vance			mr 63 *
Reitzell, Jacob m. Hughes, Rebecca	Mar. 4, 1789	Christian Conrad	David Young			mr 88 *
Relvey, John m. Thomas, Eve	Mar. 9, 1853		John Bond	2b256		
Reney, John m. Snodgrass, Cath.	Dec. 20, 1789		Jacob Medtart	5b156	cr 19	
*Rentch,Lawrence S. m.Noll, Mary Ann	Apr. 7, 1841	Godlieb Noll	J.H.Plunkett	6b239		
*Rentche, Frederica m. Moot, Philip	July 24, 1844	George Rentche	Hugh Vance	7b 4		mr 3

	(marriage)	(suretor)	(minister)	(bond)		
Replovel, Henry m. Stottlemyer, Libby	Aug. 5, 1815	Jacob Garinger	Moses Hoge	3b331	cr 29	mr 14 *
Reppy, Joseph m. Davis, Eliz.	Sept 1, 1798	David Gerrard	Jacob Medtart	1b127	cr 12	mr 63 *
Retzell, Jacob m. Hughes, Rebecca	Mar. 8 1830	Christian Conrad	Richard Swift	5b156	ge 9	mr 14 *
Reynolds, John m. Lemon, Jane	Oct. 15, 1797	Alex. Lemon	David Young	1b 54		
Reynolds, John m. Markwood, Marg't	Mar. 31, 1800	John Shober	Hugh Vance	2b 61		mr 33 *
Reynolds, Rebecca m. McCracken,Samuel	May 3. 1785					
Rheinstine, Eliz.m.Cunningham,Jas.L	Mar. 24, 1837	George Chrisman		6b102	gc 2	
Rheiske, Will m. Thornberry, Ann	Feb. 7, 1793		David Young	5b206	ge 11	mr 62 *
*Rhineberger, Susan m. Nichols, Dan'l.	Sept 24, 1831	Amos Nichols	John Light			
Rhodes, Cath. m. Connelly, Benj. V.	Feb. 21, 1811		Rev. Reebenack			
Rhodes, Jacob m. Cook, Cath.	Aug. 23, 1834	Peter Cook		6b 16		
Rhodes, Kitty m. Connell, Benj.	Feb. 20, 1811	Jacob Rhodes		3b176		
Rhodes, Mary m. Kiger, Daniel	Jan. 12, 1815	Jacob Rhodes		3b308		
Rhodes, Sarah m. Menser, George	Nov. 22, 1832	Jacob Rhodes		5b248		
Rhodes, Susannah m. Hogelan, John	Mar. 29, 1834	Benj. Connelly		6b 2		
Rhomind, Reuben m. Smallwood, Lydia	Mar. 21, 1789	Hebron Smallwood		1b x		
Rhore, Christian m. Moixal, Cath.	May 9, 1795		David Young		ge 4	mr 81 *
Rice, Henry m. Seibert, Harriet	Oct. 9, 1848	Martin Pitzer	P. Lipscomb	7b136		mr 70 *
Rice, Jennett m. Mellenburg, Augustus	Dec. 13, 1838	Wm. McCoy	John Light	6b154		
Rice, John m. McQuilkin, Rebecca R.	Mar. 27, 1846	Wm.T. McQuilkin		7b 62		
Rice, Samuel m. Turner, Eliza	Mar. 25, 1839	Wm. Turner	John Light	6b164		mr 70 *
Richards, Abr'm m. Short, Cloe	Aug. 19, 1790		Moses Hoge		cr 5	mr 5 *
Richards, Cath. m. Cochran, George	Aug. 2, 1824	George Hoe	Chas. P. Krauth	4b268		mr 47 *
Richards, Daniel m. Smithers, Sally	May 4, 1792		Moses Hoge			mr 39 *
Richards, Emma Jane m. Zorn, Joseph	Apr. 16. 1853		Jas. H. Jennings			mr 87 *
Richards, Fred. m. Hoe, Cath.	1822	George Hoe				
Richards, Jane m.Cunningham, George	Dec. 20, 1813	Levi Cunningham		4b210	go 2	mr 60 *
Richards, Mary m. Ostume, Joseph	1792			3b279		
Richards, Thomas m. Kitchen, Julia	Mar. 10, 1830	Henry G. Kitchen	David Young	5b157	ge 13	mr 43 *
Richardson, James m. Souder, Eliz.	Jan. 24, 1787		Nathan Young			
Richardson, John m. Butt, Jemima	Mar. 23, 1813	Wm. Butt	Hugh Vance	3b257		mr 39 *
Richardson, John m.McCollister,Jane	May 1792		Rev. Reebenack			
Richardson, Mary m. Myers, Samuel	Aug. 19, 1812	Thomas Richardson	Moses Hoge	3b233		
Richardson, M.cka Ann m.Cramer, John	Sept 2, 1812	Jos. Richardson		3b235		
Richardson, Thos. m. Southerland,Kisy	July 26, 1810	Thomas Walley	Rev. Reebenack	3b154	gc 11	
Richardson, Thos. m. Swim, Mary	Mar. 6, 1787		Hugh Vance			mr 44 *
Rickard, Wm. m. Robinson, Dolly S.	Mar. 24, 1849	Richard Ijams		7b149		
Rickard, Wm. m. Robinson, Jane	1849		Lewis F. Wilson			
Rickers, Rake m. Kimberling, Fred.	May 19, 1851	?	David Thomas	7b225		mr 83 *
Riddle, A. Eliz. w. Stribling,Corn's	Sept 15, 1853	Wm. M. Riddle	W.B.Dutton			mr 84 *
Riddle, John R. m. Tabb, Susan	Mar. 6, 1828			5b 92		
Riddle, Joseph m. Keersley, Sally	Sept 12, 1789	Leonard Goodnaugh	Moses Hoge			
Ridenour, Cath. m. Fernow, Daniel	Sept 28, 1811	John Snyder		3b195	cr 2	mr 3 *
*Rhinestine, Cath. m. Walters,Michael	Mar. 15, 1837			6b102		

Name	Date	(marriage)	(suretor)	(minister)	(bond)			
Ridenour, Elisa m. Badly, Richard	June 21,	1830	George Ridenour		5b169			
Ridenour, Elis. m. Claycomb, Conrad	June 9,	1802	John Ridenour		2b115			
*Ridenour, Elis. m. Rousch, John	Nov. 15,	1834	Jacob Myers		6b 23			
Ridenour, Elis. m. Rynely, John	Aug. 11,	1816	William Butt	Mathias Riser	7b100		mr 78	*
Ridenour, George m.Mansfield,Rose A	July 10,	1847	John Ridenour	James Chisholm	7b 76		mr 77	*
Ridenour, Mary Elis. m.Raney, Sem'l	Nov. 19,	1846	Henry Rohrer	E.L.Dalin	5b195			*
Ridenour, Sarah Karns m.Elliot,James	May 19,	1831						*
Rider, Elis. m. Runner, John Wm.	Oct. 3,	1853	Thos. Vananda	Jacob Rinehart	4b 34			*
Ridgely, Charlotte m.Seer(Seem),Alex.	Apr. 29,	1817		W.N.Scott		cr 29		
Ridgeway, Ann m. Sheely, John	Feb. 14,	1782		Daniel Sturges			mr 42	*
Ridgeway, Elir. m. Byrnes, Thomas	Feb. 10,	1794		Wm. Hll			mr 9	*
Ridgeway, Jonas J. m. Lewis, Mary	Nov. 25,	1853		D.Francis Sprigg			mr 86	*
Ridgeway, Josiah m. Likam, Ann	Apr. 13,	1789	Jonas Likam		1b x			
Ridgeway, Strother m. Rousch,Ann M.	May 17,	1836	Conrad Rousch	Nathan Young	6b 79		mr 62	*
Riding, Joseph m. Roush, Rosanna	Nov. 5,	1831	Conrad Rousch		5b208			
Rieniche, Fredericka m.Moot,Philip	July 24,	1844	George Rieniche		7b 4			
Rife, Deborah m. Brome, James	Apr. 26,	1797	Conrad Rife		1b 13			*
Rife, Elis. m. Brown, John	Mar. 31,	1796		David Young	2b 77	gc 5		*
Rife, Hannah m. Shuler, Conrad	July 19,	1800	Conrad Rife	David Young		gc 1		*
Rife, Magdaline m. Leckner, John	Jan. 11,	1791	Conrad Rife		2b247	cr 13	mr 21	*
Rife, Polly m. Andrews, James	Nov. 7,	1804	Conrad Rife	John Bond	3b342		mr 26	*
Rife, Susannah m.Bixalar(Bes-), Geo.	Oct. 5,	1815	Conrad Riffle	W.N.Scott	2b153			*
Riffle, Margaret m. Ray, James	Dec. 19,	1801	Arch'd Butts			gc 11		
?Rig, Elis. m. Dnoon(D.Noon), Sally	Dec. 26,	1809?	David Bowman	Rev. Reebenack	3b130	gc 14		
Riger, Samuel m. Bowman, Sally	June 15,	1815		Rev. Reebenack	3b328	gc 3		
Right, Josias m. Puy, Margaret	Aug. 24,	1793		David Young		cr 7	mr 6	*
Right, Robert m. Raney, Elis.	Mar. 31,	1791		Moses Hoge				
Rightstine, Adam m. Hessey, Mary	May 11,	1837	Abr'm Harris	John Mathews	6b186			
Rightstine, Wm. m. Stevens, Cath.	Sept 20,	1837	A. Oden		6b112			
Rigaby, Ann M. m. Calhoun, Wm.	Aug. 23,	1845	John A. Boyer	Richard Swift	7b 40		mr 25	*
Rigaby, David m. Biddle, Margaret	Nov. 23,	1813	Patrick Duffy	John Hedges	3b276		mr 21	*
Rigaby, Henrietta m. Ingman, Henry	Dec. 14,	1802	Wm. Rigsby	David Thomas	2b186	cr 32	mr 72	*
Rigaby, Susan E. m.Pyle,Milton Mifflin	June 17,	1841	John R. O'Neal	Nathan Young	6b242		mr 84	*
Riker Kate m. Kimberling, Fred.	May 19,	1851	?		7b225		mr 55	*
Riley, Alex. m. Houseworth, Nancy	Dec. 6,	1815	Isaac Houseworth	Rev. Reebenack	3b349	gc 10		
Riley, Denny m. Siler, Esther	May 25,	1811	Conrad Starry	Moses Hoge	3b187	cr 8	mr 7	*
Riley, Elis. m. Zimmerman, Henry	Dec. 24,	1808	Richard Bodley	David Young	3b304	gc 5		
Riley, George m. Baker, Elis.	Dec. 29,	1792						
Riley, John m. Blade, Martha	Feb. 7,	1796	Henry Siler		5b163			
Riley, Lany m. Robinson, James	June 14,	1830	Amos Mendenhall		2b188			
Riley, Martha Mrs. m.Whitalook,Jas.	Apr. 14,	1802	Nicholas Howard		2b160			
Riley, Thomas m.Applegate,Hannah	Dec. 24,	1802						
Rimley, John m. Smith, Cath.	Feb. 10,	1797	Fred. Bower	Richard Swift	1b 28	cr 12		
*Rldenour, Elis. m. Pixter, Alex.	Aug. 12,	1841		John Light				
**Rife, Mary m. Kibler, John	Dec. 7,	1796	Jacob Myers	David Young	6b256	gc 5	mr 72	*

187

Name	date	(marriage)	(suretor)	(minister)	(bond)		ref
Rhne, John m. Wood, Charlotte	Sept 3,	Feb. 26, 1793	Jacob Light	Richard Swift	9b 78		mr 38 *
Rineberger, Mary m. Nichols, Amos	Dec. 25,	Dec. 26, 1827	Arch'd Butt	Rev. Reebemack	3b130	go 11	*
?Rinehart, Eliz. m. Noon, Jas. D.	Feb. 23,	1809?	Richard Pendry		2b255		
Rinehart, Adam m. Pendry, Martha	Mar. 9,	1805	Jacob Riner		6b266		
Riner, Andrew m. Everhart, Hester	Mar. 22,	Mar. 25, 1842	Peter Riner	Lewis F. Wilson	6b238		mr 72 *
Riner, Cath. m. Ropp, Jacob	Apr. 23,	Apr. 23, 1841	Joseph Blinco	John Boggs	7b 32		mr 75 *
Riner, Daniel m. Blinco, Ann	Mar. 21,	1845	Nathan Roberts		3b181		
Riner, Daniel m. Roberts, Hannah	Dec. 28,	Dec. 29, 1811	Daniel Starry	Nathan Young	9b 59		mr 99 *
Riner, Daniel m. Starry, Polly	Dec. 4,	Dec. 12, 1826	John M. Flagg	P. Lipscomb	7b140		mr 82 *
Riner, David m. Flagg, Mary Marg't	Jan. 24,	1848	Henry Riner		2b112		
Riner, Eliz. m. Ellis, Abraham	May 11,	May 14, 1801	Daniel Riner	Nathan Young	9b 42		mr 98 *
Riner, Eliz. m. Keesecker, George	Oct. 20,	1826	Peter Riner		5b110		
Riner, Eliz. m. Sperow, George	Feb. 6,	Feb. 8, 1829	William Myers	Nathan Young	5b118		mr 98 *
Riner, Hannah m. Kees, Peter	Sept 4,	1810	Henry Riner		3b160		
Riner, Hannah m. Stookey, Simon	Apr. 19,	1828	Henry J.Coutchman		6b 78		
Riner, Henry m. Contchman, Eliz.	Mar. 6,	Mar. 9, 1836	Nathan Everhart	Lewis F. Wilson	6b100		mr 60 *
Riner, Jacob m. Everhart, Mary	Jan. 26,	1837	Henry Riner		3b 43		
Riner, John m. Huffman, Cath.	July 14,	1807	John Harden		3b299		
Riner, Kitty m. Cooper, Joseph	Sept 27,	Sept 27, 1814	Daniel Riner	James Paynter	4b163		mr 40 *
Riner, Margaret m. Grubb, John	Mar. 2,	1820	Henry Riner		3b304		
Riner, Margaret m. Kearns, Henry	Dec. 16,	1814	Henry Riner		3b213		
Riner, Mary m. Brouse, Lewis	Dec. 5,	1812	Henry Riner		3b127		
Riner, Nancy m. Swingley, Michael	Oct. 17,	1809	Jonathan Gushwa		4b 51		
Riner, Peter m.Lingamfelter, Mary	Apr. 23,	Oct. 29, 1817	Jacob Riner	Lewis Mayer	6b 59		mr 68 *
Riner, Rosannah m. Myers, Arch'd	Dec. 21,	1835	Henry Riner	John Howell	3b222		*
Riner, Sally m. Walsh, John	Aug. 15,	1812	Jacob Riner		6b259		
Riner, Sarah m. Kearns, James	Aug. 25,	1841	Jacob Riner		6b 54		
Riner, Susan m. Yost, Wm.	Oct. 2,	Aug. 20, 1835	Henry Riner	John Howell	1b 35		mr 68 *
Riner, Susannah m. Baysore, John		1797	John Mixell		4b117		
Ring, William m.Motxell(Mixe-),Susan		Oct. 23, 1819					
Rion, Cloe m. Boggis, Robert		1788					
?Rion, John m. Talbott, Sarah		Sept 23, 1792					
?Rion, Jollice m. Talbutt, Sarah		Aug. 9, 1792					
Rion, Thomas m. Dawson, Elenor	Apr. 27,	Apr. 27, 1798	Timothy Collins	Chas. P. Krauth	1b 99	gc 7	mr 40 *
?Ripley, Jane m. Lowry, George	Nov. 18,	Nov. 21, 1797	Mathew Rippey	Moses Hoge	1b 62	cr 32	mr 36 *
Rippey, David m. Vance, Eliz.	Mar. 10,	1806	Mathew Rippey	Moses Hoge	3b 13		mr 39 *
Rippey, David m. Yeates, Elenor	?	1798	Andrew Yeates	Moses Hoge	1b 93		mr 39 *
Rippey, Eliz. m. Hoge, John	June 1,	1808	Mathew Rippey	David Young	3b 90		mr 13 *
?Rippey, Jane m. Lowry, George	Nov. 18,	Nov. 21, 1797	Mathew Rippey	John Boyd	1b 62	cr 32	mr 13 *
*Rippey, Joseph m. Davis, Eliz.	Sept 1,	Sept 11, 1798	David Gerrard	John Boyd	1b 127	cr 29	mr 14 *
Rippey, Nancy m. Sanks, Zachariah	Aug. 17,	1813	Mathew Rippey	Moses Hoge	3b270		
Ripple, John m. Lewis, Nancy	Jan. 9,	1838	Joseph Lewis		6b116		
Rise, Mary m. Slain, Daniel		Feb. 20, 1817		Mathias Riser			
*Rippey, Mary m. Reed, John		Feb. 5, 1789		Hugh Vance			mr 37 *

Entry	(marriage)	(surety)	(minister)	(bond)	ref
Riser, David m. Morrison, Mary	July 18, 1825		Christian Streit	5b 15	cr 15 mr 4 *
Riser, George m. Ambrose, Margaret	Dec. 1, 1789		John Light	7b 86	gc 12 mr 79 *
Riser, John m. Miller, Mary Ann	Feb. 13, 1847	Henry M. Miller	Rev. Reebenack	1b179	*
Riser, Maria m. Bauman, David	Nov. 4, 1811			7b171	
Riser, Mathias m. Michael, Mary	May 9, 1799	Joseph Franceway		7b 73	
Riser, Samuel m. Strouse, Mary Cath.	Dec. 19, 1849	Isaiah Strouse		2b256	gc 3 mr 22 *
Riser, Sarah Ann m. Miller, David C.	Sept 19, 1846	George Riser	David Young	6b168	cr 28 mr 71 *
*Risert, Cath. m. Houseman, Peter	1794		John Bond	7b257	gc 14 *
Risner, Eliz. m. Morrow, Wm.	Mar. 4, 1805	James Morrow	M.G.Hamilton		
Risner, Mary m. Pike, John	May 4, 1839	Benj. Darby			
Rites, Geo. M. m. Minghird, Mary R.	June 10, 1852	Henry C. Mathews	Rev. Reebenack	4b 26	mr 44 *
Ritz, Samuel(Chas.) m. Mayer, Eliz.	Nov. 13, 1814	John Strother			gc 14
Riser, Anna m. Ambrose, Daniel	Dec. 7, 1819		Hugh Vance		
Rizer, Anthony m. Hays, Sarah	Mar. 29, 1787				mr 85 *
Rizer, Mary m. Bowman, David	Nov. 2, 1811	Magdalina Riser		3b199	
Rizer, Mary m. Widmeyer, Jacob	June 2, 1802	Mathias Riser		2b174	
Rizer, Rachel m. Miller, Casper	Dec. 12, 1818	Mathias Riser		4b 93	
Rizer, Samuel m. Bowman, Sally	June 12, 1815	David Bowman	Rev. Reebenack	3b328	
Roach, Edward m. Cook, Sarah Ann	Dec. 27, 1851	George A. Smith	J.W.Ernest	7b240	gc 5
Roach, James m. Dunham, Rosanna	Mar. 2, 1825	Samuel Dunham		5b 3	
Rob, Sarah m. Momers, Henry	June 12, 1796		David Young		
Robbins, Conrad m. Myers, Susan	Dec. 3, 1839	Henry Myers	Lewis F. Wilson	6b185	mr 70 *
Robbins, Geo. W. m. Evans, Mary S.	Sept 13, 1853		D. Francis Sprigg		
Robbins, Geo. W. m. Myers, Susan	Feb. 14, 1806	Garret Wynkoop	Lewis F. Wilson	6b160	mr 70 *
Robbins, Job m. Claycomb, Cath.	Sept 13, 1806	Conrad Claycomb		3b 29	
Robbins, John K. m. Criswell, Elvira	Feb. 27, 1843	Samuel Hedges	James Chisholm	6b291	mr 75 *
Robbins, Levi K. m. Myers, Sarah K.	June 11, 1829	Tater Myers Jr.	Jas. M. Brown	5b132	mr 53 *
Robbins,A.D. Dr. m. Belle, Fanny	Dec. 6, 1805	Wm. Belle	Moses Hoge	3b 5	mr 22 *
Roberts, Agnes m. Criswell(Chr–)ohn	Mar. 12, 1795		Moses Hoge		mr 11 *
Roberts, Boyd m. Cunningham, Lydia	Dec. 12, 1808	Levi Cunningham	Moses Hoge	3b103	cr 17
Roberts, Charity m. Anderson, Jacob	Oct. 3, 1808	James Orrick		3b 97	cr 10
Roberts, Daniel m. Cunningham, Nancy	Dec. 4, 1802	Wm. Cunningham		2b184	
Roberts, Eliza m. VanCleve, Samuel	Jan. 27, 1841	John J. Henshaw	Moses Hoge	6b231	cr 17 mr 21 *
Roberts, Eliz. m. Beeson, Lewis R.	Dec. 16, 1899	Boyd Roberts		6b187	
Roberts, Eliz. m. Bell, John	Dec. 21, 1841	Benj. Loekhart		6b299	cr 10
Roberts, Eliz. m. Page, Wm.	May 23, 1816	Samuel Roberts		4b 1	
Roberts, Eliz. Ann m. Seibert, Harr'n	Mar. 22, 1843	Wm. H. Roberts		6b294	
Roberts, Frances m. Seibert, Joseph	Dec. 29, 1851	Harr'n J. Seibert		7b241	
Roberts, Gersham m. Norris, Sarah	June 30, 1793	Nathan Roberts	Edward Tiffin	3b181	cr 9 mr 8 *
Roberts, Hannah m. Riner, Daniel	Mar. 21, 1811				
Roberts, Hannah m. Smith, Christ'r	Nov. 4, 1788	Samuel Roberts	Hugh Vance	3b 54	mr 36 *
Roberts, James L. m. Wilson, Jane	Apr. 1, 1807	Isaac V. Burns		6b 53	
Roberts, Jas. L. m. Bell, Mary R.	Aug. 7, 1835				
*Risley, John m. Blake, Patty	Apr. 29, 1794		David Young		gc 4

Name	(marriage)		(surety)	(minister)	(bond)	ref.
Roberts, Jane m. Billings, Newman	Oct. 1,	1802	Daniel Roberts		2b182	
Roberts, John m. Baker, Cath.	June 27,	1805	John Baker		2b265	
Roberts, John m. Bell, Polly	Apr. 7,	1798	John Bell		1b 96	
Roberts, Jonathan m. Ward, Margaret	Jan. 11,	1816	Joel Ward	Nathan Young	3b352	mr 55 *
Roberts, Joseph m. Spur, Nancy	Dec. 26,	1812	James Gardner		3b244	
Roberts, Josiah m. Burn, Mary	May 22,	1822	John Burns Jr.		4b214	
Roberts, Letitia m. Morgan, Isaac	Aug. 20,	1781		Daniel Sturges		mr 31 *
Roberts, Lidy m. Edwards, Joseph	Aug. 9,	1813	Levi Cunningham		3b268	
Roberts, Marg't m. Lockhart, Benj.	Aug. 17,	1829	Jacob Ward	Robert Cadden	5b138	mr 61 *
Roberts, Mary m. Bushman, Isaac	Jan. 2,	1832	Boyd Roberts	Jacob Medtart	5b213	mr 63 *
Roberts, Mary m. Crem, Samuel	Aug. 23,	1787		Hugh Vance		cr 18; mr 1 *
Roberts, Mary m. Tool, Joseph	Mar. 5,	1795		Moses Hoge		cr 10; mr 11 *
Roberts, Nemd m. Bushman, Isaac	Jan. 2,	1832	Samuel Roberts	Jacob Medtart	5b212	mr 63 *
Roberts, Nemd m. Varmetre, Abr'm	Aug. 8,	1816	David Stewart		4b 7	
Roberts, Nathan m. Haslett, Elis.	Oct. 17,	1803	Robert Roberts		2b210	
Roberts, Polly m. Bull, Thomas	June 7,	1839		John B. Boge		cr 10; *
Roberts, Prudence M. m. Hite, John	Dec. 16,	1833	Samuel Roberts	Lewis F. Wilson	6b171	cr 11; mr 70 *
Roberts, Rhoda m. Pclts, Jacob	Feb. 3,	1798	Boyd Roberts		9b296	
Roberts, Richard m. Owen, Elis.	May 15,	1819	Joseph Roberts	Nathan Young	1b 83	mr 56 *
Roberts, Robert m. Long, Cath.	Sept 17,	1839	Martin Houseman	Moses Hoge	4b108	mr 11 *
Roberts, Samuel m. Butler, Rachel A.	Jan. 13,	1836	Thos. White	John Boyd	6b176	mr 12 *
Roberts, Samuel m. Varmetre, Marg't	Nov. 22,	1795	Harrison Waite		6b 63	
Roberts, Samuel m. Whitenaught, Hanna	Aug. 26,	1796	Harrison Waite		6b307	
Roberts, Samuel Jr. m.Varmetre, Nacony	Oct. 15,	1843	Bastian Poisal		2b215	
Roberts, Sarah m. Sutton, John Jr.	Nov. 24,	1789		Hugh Vance	2b215	or 25; mr 4 *
Roberts, Thomas m. Edleman, Caty	Nov. 24,	1803	Bastian Pizel	David Young	2b215	gc 10; *
Roberts, Thomas m. Pclsal, Susan	Mar. 8,	1803	Bastian Pizel	Hugh Vance	2b164	*
Roberts, Thomas m. Pisel, Susannah	Feb. 15,	1802	James Chenoweth			
Roberts, Wm. m. Dodd, Rachel	Apr. 9,	1785				
Roberts, Wm. m. Quick, Leanah	Nov. 24,	1785				
Roberts, Wm. H. m.Schoppert, Nancy	Apr. 9,	1842	Nicholas Schoppert	Moses Hoge	6b269	mr 33 *
Roberts, Wm. J. m. Bell, Lavina Eliza	Dec. 4,	1845	Alfred Ross		7b 49	
*Roberts, Daniel m.Cunningham, Nancy	Dec. 8,	1802	Wm. Cunningham	David Young	2b184	cr 17; mr 21 *
Robinson, Abr'm m. Hedges, Rebecca	Mar. 27,	1793	Wm. Cunningham		4b257	
Robinson, Alex. m.Cunningham,Dolly	Mar. 2,	1824		Chas. P. Krauth		gc 3; *
Robinson, Alex. m. Hedges, Anna	Mar. 24,	1785		Hugh Vance		cr 17; mr 47 *
Robinson, Alex. m.Porterfield, Eliz.	Mar. 27,	1821	Geo. Porterfield	John B. Hoge	4b179	mr 33 *
Robinson, Alex m.Robinson, Hannah	June 20,	1832	Hezekiah Hedges	Jas. M. Brown	5b231	mr 41 *
Robinson, Ann m. Shields, John	Feb. 11,	1809	Thos. Robinson		3b107	
Robinson, Ann m. Wilson, James	Dec. 12,	1850				
Robinson, Ann E. m. Harley, Thos. J.	May 16,	1843	Jas. H. Robinson		6b297	mr 64 *
Robinson, Ann E. m. Wilson, Jas. M.	Oct. 5,	1847	Alex. Robinson	Jas. H. Jennings	7b108	mr 82 *
Robinson, Christina M. m. Kennedy,Sam	Sept 27,	1830	Josiah Hedges		5b175	
*Robertson, Susanne m. Clarke, Wm.	Apr. 17,	1782		Daniel Sturges		mr 42 *

	(marriage)	(suretor)	(minister)	(bond)		
Robinson, Dolly S. m. Rickard, Wm. H.	Mar. 24, 1849	Richard Ijams	W.N.Scott	7b149		*
Robinson, Eliz. m. Garard, John	July 28, 1817	Thos. Robinson		4b 40		
Robinson, Eliz. m. Hedges, John	Nov. 11, 1812	John Robinson		3b240		
Robinson, Eliz. m. Jennings, Jas. H.	Jan. 2, 1848	B.M.Kitchen	Lewis F. Wilson	7b144		mr 83 *
Robinson, Eliz. m. Syler, Philip	Apr. 2, 1840	Garret Wynkoop	Lewis F. Wilson	6b204		mr 71 *
Robinson, Eliz. A. m.Pendleton, Wm.	June 22, 1840	Harrison Waite		6b213		
Robinson, Amelia m. Bell, Wm.	Nov. 19, 1807	John Robinson		3b 77		
Robinson, Geo. W. m. Hedges, Mary E.	Feb. 1, 1843	Badley Hedges	James Chisholm	6b289		*
Robinson, Hannah m. Cunningham, John	Sept 17, 1795		John Boyd	4b234	cr 33	mr 75 *
Robinson, Hannah m. Garber(Gru-)Jacob	Mar. 17, 1823	Abr'm Robinson	Chas. P. Krauth	4b234		mr 11 *
Robinson, Hannah m. Robinson, Alex.	June 20, 1832	Hezekiah Hedges	Jas. M. Brown	5b231		mr 46 *
Robinson, Hannah m.Vincenhaller,John	May 21, 1812	Jas. Robinson	Rev. Reebenack	3b225	gc 13	mr 64 *
Robinson, Israel m.Callahan, Sarah	Nov. 24, 1853		G.W.Cooper			*
Robinson, Israel m. Shellor, Jenny	Apr. 18, 1800	Wm. Shellor		2b 67		*
Robinson, Israel m. Snodgrass, Cath.	Sept 4, 1841	Geo. W. Robinson	Lewis F. Wilson	6b246		mr 72 *
Robinson, James m. Dennison, Jane	Sept 18, 1821	Samuel Cummingham		4b190		
Robinson, James m. Hedges, Ruth	Sept 28, 1814	Hezekiah Hedges		3b305		
Robinson, James m. Ralphsmider,Rab'ca	Dec. 24, 1829	Seaman Garard	Nathan Young	5b148		mr 60 *
Robinson, James m. Riley, Lany	Apr. 14, 1830	Henry Siler		5b163		
Robinson, James m. Wigle, Mary	Sept 5, 1826	John Wigle		5b 49		
Robinson, Jane m. Hedges, Enoch G.	Apr. 9, 1840	Bailey Hedges	Lewis F. Wilson	6b205		mr 71 *
Robinson, Jane m. Hensel, Jacob	Dec. 9, 1850	G.W.Hensel		7b205		
Robinson, Jane m. Kerns, George	Mar. 21, 1811	John Robinson	Rev. Reebenack	3b180	gc 12	*
Robinson, Jane m. Rickard, Wm.	Jan.		Lewis F. Wilson			mr 83 *
Robinson, Joseph m. Hart, Marg't	June 13, 1798	Thomas Hart		1b116		
Robinson, Joseph m. Rumner, Eve	Jan. 25, 1808	John Robinson		3b 82		
Robinson, Leonard m. Morrow, Mary	Apr. 14, 1796		Moses Hoge			*
Robinson, Lydia m. Satterfield, Thos.	June 19, 1820	James Robinson		4b151		mr 11 *
Robinson, Lydia m. Stinson, James	Dec. 28, 1808	James Robinson		3b105		
Robinson, Martha m. Blue, Ezekiel	June 12, 1798	Nathan Kennedy		1b115		
Robinson, Martha m. Myers, John	Dec. 17, 1832	Alex. Robinson	David Young	1b154	gc 8	*
Robinson, Nancy m. Robinson, Robert	Aug. 13, 1832	James Robinson	Jas. M. Brown	5b237		mr 64 *
Robinson, Polly m. Blue, Peter	Jan. 27, 1802	Fred. Blue		2b158		
Robinson, Rebecca m. Robinson, Wm.	Dec. 11, 1838	Alex. Robinson	Lewis F. Wilson	6b153		mr 70 *
Robinson, Robert K. m. Robinson,Nancy	Aug. 13, 1832	James Robinson	Jas. M. Brown	5b237		mr 64 *
Robinson, Samuel m. Alexander, Rebecca	Jan. 27, 1840	Alex. Robinson		6b195		
Robinson, Sarah m. Hew, John	Jan. 2, 1806	Thomas Smart		3b 8		
Robinson, Sarah m. Hunter, John	Dec. 10, 1821	John G. Wilson	Edw. R. Lippett	4b200		mr 45 *
Robinson, Sarah m.Hensell, Geo. W.	Jan. 31, 1837	Aaron Chaffin		6b 94		mr 42 *
Robinson, Susanna m. Clarke, Wm.	Apr. 17, 1782		Daniel Sturges			*
Robinson, Susan m. Cox, James	Dec. 22, 1819	James Robinson	Hugh Vance	4b127		mr 37 *
Robinson, Susan m. Hedges, Josiah	Nov. 28, 1831	John Stevens		5b239		mr 82 *
Robinson, Thomas m. Kennedy, Ruth	Jan. 8, 1789		Hugh Vance			
*Robinson, Jane m. Ferrall, Jacob	Dec. 12, 1850		Jas. H. Jennings			

Name	(marriage)		(suretor)	(minister)	(bond)		
Robinson, Thomas m. Snow, Mary	Aug. 28,	1798	Daniel Fitzpatrick	G.W.Cooper	1b126		*
Robinson, Wm. m. Kisner, Susan D.	Sept 15,	1853					*
Robinson, Wm. m. Robinson, Rebecca	Dec. 11,	1838	Alex. Robinson	Lewis F. Wilson	6b153		mr 70 *
Rochester, Samuel S. m. McCleary,Jane	July 24,	1847	John McCleary		7b102		*
Rockwell, Nancy m.Curts(Carts),Jacob	Dec. 7,	1818	Jesse Rockwell	Mathias Riser	4b 91		mr 29*
Roderick, Elis. m. Wood, Wm.	Oct. 13,	1798	Robert Roderick	John Hedt(Hutt)	1b139	cr 11	mr 16 *
Rodes, Polly m. Gelger, Daniel	Jan. 12,	1815		Rev. Reebemack		gc 14	*
Rodgers, Marg't m. Keyes, Thos.	Jan. 23,	1796	George North		1b 82		*
Rodgers, Martha m. Wadkevin, John	June 5,	1792		David Young		gc 2	*
Rodgers, Mary m. Campbell, John	Apr. 18,	1794		David Young		gc 3	*
Rodgers, Susannah m. Vestal, John		1801					
Roe, James m. Crab, Phebe	Mar. 11,	1810	John Conway		2b117		*
Roe, James m. Hunter, Elis. Ann	Dec. 19,	1833	Isaac Crab	Wm. Monroe	3b168		mr 65 *
Rosss, Mary m. Winning, James	Feb. 16,	1833	John Gallaher		3b237		
Rogers, Hester A. m. Cunningham,John	Sept 1,	1797	James Anderson		1b 36		mr 81 *
Rogers, Jenny m. Grimes, John	June 8,	1786	Ephraim Barlett		7b 98		mr 43 *
Rogers, John m. Blue, Mary	July 4,	1786		Hugh Vance			mr 3 *
Rogers, Magnus m. Page, Mary A.	Apr. 9,	1789		Hugh Vance		cr 20	*
Roher, Maria m. Barnes, Joseph D.	June 5,	1839	Wm. Sperow	M.G.Hamilton	6b171		mr 71 *
Roland, Samuel J. m. Hott, Jane	Dec. 26,	1849	Martin Roher	John light	7b172		mr 80 *
Rollins, Mary m. Ball, Nathan	Dec. 3,	1846	Jacob Hott	John Winter	7b 78		mr 77 *
Rombaugh, Wm. m. Mussetter, Mary	Dec. 20,	1792		Moses Hoge			mr 39 *
Rembo, Wm. m. Coffenberger, Mary	Aug. 24,	1823	John Mussetter	Nathan Young	4b245		mr 58 *
Rorymons, Cath. m. Miller, Jacob	Apr. 13,	1789		Christian Streit		cr 15	mr 4 *
Roney, James m. Smith, Rhoda	Mar. 4,	1800	Conrad Ronymous	David Young	2b 55	gc 9	*
Roney, Maria m. Carper, Jacob	Feb. 26,	1811	Zachariah Murray		3b182		
Roney, Michael Jr. m. Plotner, Jane	Mar. 26,	1849	Mister Collins	B.W.Schmucker	7b162		mr 79 *
Ronk, Valentine m. Strayer, Elis.	Aug. 11,	1820	Danial Plotner	W.W.Scott	4b162		mr 41 *
Rooney, George m. Clayton, Polly	Sept 19,	1820	Harvey A Hedges	James Watts	6b108		
Rooney, Henry m. Plotner, Eve	June 20,	1837	Isaac Bacon	Wm. N. Scott	4b144		mr 41 *
Rooney, James m. Murphy, Rebecca S.	Apr. 12,	1820	Danial Plotner	Jacob M. Bromwell	4b246		mr 46 *
Rooney, Mary m. Ryner, Henry	Aug. 26,	1823	Harvey Hedges	Peyton Harrison	6b118		mr 69 *
Rooney, Michael m. Ensminger, Martha	May 16,	183?	Henry Rooney		4b196		
Rooney, Milly m. Light, Peter	Nov. 13,	1821	Cornelius Keely		4b 25		
Ropp, Cath. m.Lingamfelter, Jacob	Nov. 27,	1816	James Sanders		4b119		
Ropp, Daniel m. Small(Smith),Nancy	Oct. 16,	1819					
Ropp, Elis. m. Cox, Jacob	May 26,	1829	Solomon Ropp	Jas. M. Brown	5b130		mr 53 *
Ropp, Hannah m. Hoffman, David	Apr. 4,	1831	Jacob Small	Jacob Medtart	5b192		mr 63 *
Ropp, Jacob m. Riner, Cath.	Oct. 6,	1824	Solomon Ropp	J.L.Bromwell	4b274		mr 47 *
Ropp, Mary't m. Hedges, Benj.	Mar. 3,	1847	Danial Ropp	D.F.Bragunder	7b 88		mr 78 *
Ropp, Mary m. Miller, John	Mar. 22,	1841	Peter Riner	Lewis F. Wilson	6b238		mr 72 *
Ropp, Solomon m. Folk, Mary Ann	Oct. 1,	1840	Jacob Ropp		6b217		
	June 3,	1819	Solomon Ropp		4b109		
Ropp, Solomon m. Folk, Mary Ann	May 11,	1840	Daniel Lefevre	Lewis F. Wilson	6b207		mr 71 *
Rorke, Barney m. Conner, Anna	Dec. 19,	1799	William Reed	David Young	2b 40	gc 9	*

Entry	(marriage)	(surety)	(minister)	(bond)	
Ross, Samuel m. Matson, Aury	Mar. 1, 1810	John Matson		3b138	
Rosenberger, Barbara m.McCorlan,Nich.	Jan. 13, 1846	David Rosenberger		7b 55	
Rosenberger,Cath. m. Burkhart,Franci	Dec. 11, 1829	Anthony Rosenberg	Jacob Medtart	5b147	mr 63 *
Rosenberger,Fred. m.Shall, Cath.	June 13, 1811				gc 12
Rosenberger, John m. Marshall,Martha	Sept 14, 1826	Thomas Marshall	John Winter	5b 52	? mr 50 *
Rosenberger, John m. Shall, Cath.	Mar. 28, 1815	Nicholas Shall	Lewis Mayer	3b314	mr 25 *
Rosenberger, John m. Shall, Cath.	June 13, 1811		Rev. Reebenack		
Rosenberger, Marg't m. Watson, Wm.	Dec. 3, 1822	Anthony Rosemb'r		4b230	*
Rosenberger, Susan m. Pilter, John W	Dec. 11, 1848	Anthony Rosemb'r		7b141	
Rostmeier, Susan m. Harris, Michael			David Young		
Ross, Alfred m. Morgan, Elis. Ann	Nov. 30, 1795	Wm. G. Morgan	Wm. Monroe	5b146	mr 54 *
Ross, Lydia m. Gein, Christian	Jan. 19, 1829	John A. Wolff		6b 92	
Ross, Lydia m. Morgan, Levy	June 23, 1837	Alfred Ross	J.E.Jackson	6b 48	
Ross, Margaret m. Bailey, David	Apr. 14, 1835	Nathan Ross	B. Reynolds	4b237	mr 49 *
Ross, Mary m. Brotherton, Wm.	May 11, 1823	Nathan Ross		4b212	
Ross, Mary m. Green, Johnson	Mar. 5, 1822	Enoch Ross		3b 13	
Ross, Nathan m. ?	Aug. 19, 1806	Archelaus Stanley		2b 21	
Rothwell, Thomas m. Clawson, Sarah	Oct. 10, 1799	Brant Clawson		1b 53	
*Rousch, Ann M. m. Ridgeway, Strother	May 17, 1836	Conrad Rousch		6b 79	
Rousch, Caroline m. Little, Geo.	Jan. 31, 1797	David Young		4b139	gc 6
Rousch, Cath. m. Faris, Wm.	Mar. 9, 1820	Henry Rousch	David Young	6b147	mr 31 *
Rousch, Cath. Jane m. McKee, Hugh	Oct. 18, 1838	Conrad Rousch	John B. Hoge	3b287	*
Rousch, Conrad m. Randall, Sarah	Mar. 7, 1814	George Randall	?	6b188	gc 14
Rousch, Dorothy F m. Walters,Jacob	Dec. 18, 1839	Martin Rousch	Rev. Reebenack	3b296	*
Rousch, Elis. m. Line, Daniel	Apr. 28, 1814	Nicholas Rousch Jr	Rev. Reebenack	5b144	gc 14
Rousch, Elis. m. Wright, Jesse	Oct. 24, 1829	?	Nathan Young	6b 92	mr 60 *
Rousch, Elis. D. m. Pryatt, James	Jan. 26, 1837	Conrad Rousch		6b 85	
Rousch, George m. Walters, Margaret	Oct. 18, 1836	Conrad Rousch		5b175	
Rousch, John m. Jackson, Margaret	Sept 28, 1830	John Grove	Nathan Young	6b 23	mr 61 *
Rousch, John m. Ridenour, Eliz.	Nov. 15, 1834	Jacob Myers		4b 43	
Rousch, Mary Mrs. m. Busey, Benj.	Aug. 14, 1817	John Strother		5b208	
Rousch, Rosanna m. Ridings, Joseph	Nov. 5, 1831	Conrad Rousch	Nathan Young	2b180	mr 62 *
Rousch, Rosanna m. Young, Adam	Sept 6, 1802	John Rhinefelt			
Row, Rebecca m. Lowman, Ephraim	May 12, 1788	Hugh Vance		4b 83	mr 35 *
Rowe, Nancy m. Courtney, Jacob	Oct. 22, 1818	Jacob Murphy		5b124	
Rowen, Marg't K. m. Kerney,Uriah B.	Mar. 21, 1829	Wm. S. Kerney		7b 78	
Rowland, Samuel Jas. m. Hott, Jane	Dec. 1, 1846	Jacob Hott	John Winter	7b135	mr 77 *
Royer, Samuel m. Bolls, Nancy	Oct. 2, 1848	Saml. P. Henshaw		6b262	
Ro , Elis. m. Hunter, Wm.	Jan. 27, 1842	Patrick Cummingham			
Rukart, Adam m. Fisher, Kath.	June 24, 1788				
Romans, Thomas m.Strowbridge,Martha	Jan. 30, 1849	Lewis Strowbridge	Moses Hoge	7b146	mr 36 *
Rumbaugh, George m. Mussetter,Barbara	Mar. 27, 1822	John Mussetter	Nathan Young	4b209	mr 57 *
Rumbaugh, Nicholas m. Hudson, Elis.	July 31, 1826	Isaac Myers	Nathan Young	5b 45	mr 58 *
*Rousch, Andrew m. Seibert, Emily	Oct. 22, 1845	John P. Walters	Nathan Young	7b 46	

193

Name	(marriage)	(suretor)	(minister)	(bond)	ref.
Rumbaugh, Sarah m. Norrington, Israel	Mar. 18, 1814	Chrst'r Palmer	Nathan Young	3b288	mr 58 *
Rumbaugh, Susannah m. Hudson, James	June 13, 1825	Wm. Grantham	Nathan Young	5b 14	mr 58 *
Rumbaugh, Wm. m. Mussetter, Mary	Aug. 20, 1823	John Mussetter		4b245	cr 21 mr 8 *
Rumbo, Cath. m. Kees, Daniel	May 7, 1816	John Kees		4b 3	
Rumbo, Mary m. Russell, Wm.	Nov. 25, 1794		John Boyd		
Rumbo. Susan m. Coffenberger, George	Dec. 25, 1793		David Young		gc 3
Ramsey, Mary m. Miller, James	Oct. 18, 1796		John Boyd		cr 11 mr 12 *
Ramsey, Susanna m. Freely, Adam	July 11, 1794		Moses Hoge		cr 22 mr 9 *
Ron, Elis. m. Reed, Samuel	Jan. 23, 1797		Moses Hoge		cr 36 mr 13 *
Runner, Christena m. Reed, James	Nov. 26, 1807	Wm. Runner		3b 78	
Runner, Eve m. Robinson, Joseph	Jan. 25, 1808	John Robinson		3b 82	
Runner, John Wm. m. Rider, Elis.					*
Rupel, James m. Scott, Ungaletta	Oct. 3, 1853		Jacob Rinehart		cr 35 mr 11 *
Rupel, Jas. B. m. Varmetre, Eliza	Jan. 7, 1796		Moses Hoge		mr 62 *
Rupert, Oldeon H. m. Kownslar, Eliza	Jan. 25, 1831	Wm. N. Thompson	James M. Brown	5b185	
Rurr, Klis. m. Reed, Samuel	Oct. 1, 1828	Thomas Walker	J.E.Jackson	5b107	
Rush, Ann m. Beller, Jacob	Jan. 23, 1797		Moses Hoge		cr 36 mr 13 *
Rush, Elenor m. Grantham, Joseph	Mar. 29, 1790		Moses Hoge		cr 3 mr 5 *
Rush, Isabella m. Varmetre, Thomas	Apr. 14, 1817	William Rush	W.N.Scott	4b 32	
Rush, Jacob m. Mason, Eliza	Feb. 22, 1820	Philip Carmino		4b137	
Rush, Jane m. Turner, Robert E.	Mar. 21, 1831	James Mason		5b189	
Rush, Mary m. Mason, James	Feb. 5, 1816	Wm. Rush		3b354	
Rush, Mary m. Williamson, Peter	Feb. 20, 1809			3b108	
Rush, Nancy m. Turner, Thos. Jr.	Jan. 14, 1790	Wm. Rush			cr 17 mr 26 *
Rush, Rebecca m. Canine, Philip	May 23, 1814		John Mathews		cr 3 mr 23 *
Rush, Sarah m. McQuilkin, Thos.	May 21, 1791		John Mathews		cr 3 mr 5 *
Rush, Susan m. Couchman, George	May 8, 1804	Wm. Rush	Moses Hoge	3b298	cr 7 mr 6 *
Rush, Susana m. Hill, George	Oct. 19, 1832	Jacob Rush		2b235	
Rush, Wm. m. Canine, Sarah		Samuel Hill	Jacob Medtart	5b229	cr 7 mr 64 *
Rusler, Sarah m. Hill, John W.	Mar. 22, 1815		Nathan Young	3b344	mr 55 *
Russell, Charles m. Noland, Eliz.	Nov. 2, 1791	John L. Rusler	Moses Hoge	6b183	mr 6 *
Russell, Eliza m. Russell, Thomas	May 4, 1839		David Young		gc 1
Russell, Eliza B. m. Maslin, Wm.	Jan. 15, 1817	James Russell		4b 29	
Russell, Kliz. m. Hommas, Wm.	Nov. 30, 1839	Thomas S. Page	Lewis F. Wilson	6b185	gc 1
Russell, George m. Griffith, Ann	June 13, 1791	Samuel K. Wilson	David Young	4b 91	
Russell, James m. Scott, Ungaletta	Nov. 30, 1818				cr 35 mr 11 *
Russell, Jas. B. m. Varmetre, Eliza	Jan. 7, 1796		Moses Hoge	5b185	mr 62 *
Russell, John m. Ellis, Ann	Jan. 24, 1831	Wm. N. Thompson	Jas. M. Brown	2b231	
Russell, John m. Houte. Eliz.	Apr. 3, 1804	Thos. Crothers		4b126	cr 40 *
Russell, Moses m. Noland, Mehitabel	Dec. 22, 1819	Michael Houte	Chas. P. Krauth		mr 33 *
Russell, Thomas m. Russell, Eliza	Jan. 23, 1785		Hugh Vance		
Russell, Wm. m. Rumbo, Mary	Jan. 15, 1817			4b 29	cr 21 mr 8 *
Russell, Wm. m. Sevel, Jane	Nov. 25, 1794	James Russell	John Boyd		cr 4 mr 5 *
*Rusler, John m. Houte, Eliz.	June 21, 1790		Moses Hoge		mr 40 *
	Dec. 22, 1819	Michael Houte	Chas. P. Krauth	4b126	

Name	(date)	(marriage)	(suretor)	(minister)	(bond)	ref
Russler, John m. Houte, Eliz.	Dec. 22,	Dec. 22, 1819	Michael Houte	Chas. P. Krauth	4b126	mr 40 *
Rust, Robert B. m. Burkhart,Susan D	May 7.	May 7. 1833	Daniel Burkhart		5b273	*
Ruth(Rutherford),Maria m. Tabler, Wm.		1794				*
Rutherford, Arch'd m. Tabler, Mary	Jan. 27,	Jan. 27, 1801	Wm. Tabler	David Young	2b136	cr 31 mr 20 *
Rutherford, Cath. m. Murphy, Wm.	Aug. 17,	July 20, 1838	John Rutherford	Richard Swift	6b146	mr 69 *
Rutherford, Cath. m. Sperow, John	Sept 18,	Sept 18, 1827	Arch'd Rutherford	James Watts	5b 75	mr 99 *
Rutherford, Elinor m. Brown, James	Aug. 9.	July 10, 1799		Nathan Young	6b 17	cr 12 mr 18 *
Rutherford, Francy m. Pultz, Henry	Sept 4,	Feb. 5, 1834	Jacob M. Gardner	John Hedtt(Hatt)	3b166	gc 11 *
Rutherford, George m. Cline, Peggy	Nov. 14,	Sept 4, 1810	Jacob Snowdeal		6b321	mr 59 *
Rutherford, George F. m.Vanmetre,Mary	May 2,	Nov. 15, 1844	Asahel Varmetre			mr 73 *
Rutherford, Henry m. Vanmetre, Ruth	May 9,	Nov. 2, 1827	Abr'm Varmetre	Rev. Reebeneack	5b 69	cr 11 mr 16 *
Rutherford, Jas. M. m.Stilwell,Ann E	Jan. 4,	May 10, 1838	Elisha Butt		6b128	cr 15 mr 7 *
Rutherford, John W. m.Shaffer, Sarah	Feb. 22,	Jan. 4, 1842	James Fryatt		6b265	cr 13 mr 23 *
Rutherford, Mary m. Manning, Jacob	Sept 25,	Feb. 22, 1798	Edward Christian	Nathan Young	1b135	cr 36 mr 14 *
Rutherford, Thomas m. Darke, Mary	Nov. 30,	Sept 25, 1792		James Watts		mr 52 *
Rutherford, Thomas m. Pultz, Eliz.	Dec. 25,	Nov. 30, 1806	John Pultz	Peyton Harrison	3b 39	mr 9 *
Rutherford, Van m.Mark, Sarah(Sally)	Jan. 25,	Dec. 25, 1798	Mathew Ranson	John Hedtt(Hatt)	1b 79	cr 30 mr 29 *
Rutherford, Wm. m. Brown, Sarah	Jan. 31,	Jan. 25, 1828	John Brown	Christian Streit	5b 90	
Ryan, Frances m. Peace, James	Sept 20,	Jan. 31, 1794		John Mathews		
?Ryan, Harriet m. Dawson, Isaac	Feb. 23,	Sept 20, 1818	Samuel Hill	Moses Hoge	4b 62	mr 29 *
Ryan, James m. Holloway, Ann	Dec. 19,	Mar. 1. 1823	Seaman Garard	B. Reynolds	4b253	mr 84 *
Ryan, Patrick m.McCormick, Johanna	Nov. 25,	1840	John Butt	Wm. Hill	6b226	
Ryan, Phebe m. McCoy, John	Oct. 31.	1808	David Rippy		3b100	
?Ryne, Harriet m. Dawson, Isaac	?	1818				
Ryneal, Everhart m. Shaffer, Susan	May 27,	May 29, 1850	John Shaffer	Mathias Riser	7b187	mr 59 *
Rynberger, Nancy m. Souper, Thomas	Nov. 14,	1819	Stephen Foreman	B.M.Schmucker	4b 92	
Rynely, John m. Eldenour, Eliz.	Aug. 11,	Aug. 11, 1816				
Ryner, Dariel m. Starry, Polly	Dec. 28,	Dec. 29, 1826	Daniel Starry	Mathias Riser	5b 59	
Ryner, Henry m. Rooney, Mary	Nov. 13,	1821	Henry Rooney	Nathan Young	4b196	
Ryner, John m. Osbourn, Polly	Mar. 14,	Mar. 19, 1815	George Oebourn	Lewis Mayer	3b315	mr 25 *
Ryner, Margaret m. Grubb, John	Sept 27,	Sept 20, 1820	Daniel Ryner	James Paynter	4b163	mr 40 *
Ryner, David m. Smart, Eliza	Aug. 21,	Aug. 21, 1833	Zachariah Smart	Nathan Young	5b280	mr 66 *

"S"

Name	(date)	(marriage)	(suretor)	(minister)	(bond)	ref
Sack, Isabel m. Flleon, George	Aug. 17,	Apr. 29, 1795	Charles Keel	Richard Swift	3b232	cr 26 mr 10 *
Sackman, Polly m. Lewis, Lewis	Aug. 27,	Aug. 28, 1812	Benedict Rush	Richard Swift	2b179	cr 32 mr 21 *
Saal, Mordecai m. Short, Sarah		1802	Thos. Hetherington			
Saffall, Jesse m.Hetherington,Lydia	Sept 23,	1797		David Young	1b 43	gc 3 *
Sagathy, Cath. m. Baller, Jacob		Mar. 13, 1794				

Name	(date)	(marriage)	(surator)	(minister)	(bond)		
Sagathy, Elis. m. Toole, Joseph		Mar. 21, 1786		Hugh Vance			mr 33 *
Sagathy, Emelia m. Beller, Peter		Nov. 8, 1786		Hugh Vance			mr 43 *
Sagathy, Isabella m. Conoway,Jas.	Feb. 1,	Feb. 6, 1812	Peter Sagathy	Rev. Reebenack	3b210	gc 12	*
Sagathy, Jacob m. Beller, Naomi	Oct. 9,	Oct. 11, 1798	Jacob Beller	David Young	1b137	gc 8	*
Sagathy, Margaret m. Maple, Jacob		Oct. 11, 1796		David Young		gc 6	*
Sagathy, Sarah m. Foy, Patrick	Nov. 24,						
Sagathy, Peter m. Demoss, Jane		Sept 16, 1788	George Mason	Hugh Vance	1b149		mr 35 *
Salehamer, Eliz. m. Custer, Isaiah	June 2,	June 5, 1825	George Kmp	B. Reynolds	5b 13		mr 49 *
Salehamer, John m. Morgan, Mary	Sept 2,	Sept 2, 1835	Conrad Rousch	James Watts	6b 56		*
Salehamer, Julia Ann m. Siler,Jacob	Oct. 24,	Oct. 26, 1837	Jacob Hoke	M.G.Hamilton	6b121		mr 71 *
Salehamer, Phebe m. Hooper, Alfred	Apr. 18,	Apr. 18, 1839	John M. Wolff	John Howell	6b167		mr 68 *
Salehamer, Sarah m. Butt, Arch'd	May 8,	May 11, 1834	Geo. Swinley	B. Page	6b 11		mr 40 *
Samples, John W. m. Lowry, Fanny		Jan. 30, 1794	Harrison Waite				
Sampson, Jane m. Wolbley, Callender	Sept 26,	Sept 26, 1835		G.W.Cooper	6b 58		*
Sampson, Mary I. m. Lashorn, Jas. H.		Jan. 3, 1854	Jacob Poisal	J.L.Bromwell	4b272	gc 2	mr 47 *
Sampson, Wm. m. Flagg, Frances C.	Sept 22,	Sept 22, 1824		David Young			
Sanders, Christian m. Doddardck.Molly	Nov. 26,	Dec. 16, 1792		David Young	2b 36		*
Sanders, Elis. m. Palmer, John		Dec. 24, 1799	James Richardson	David Young	3b 65		mr 23 *
Sanders, Fred. m. Reed, Margaret	Aug. 6,	Aug. 6, 1807	Wm. Reed	John Mathews	2b 60	cr 13	mr 18 *
Sanders, John m. Sanders, Margaret	Mar. 27,	Mar. 30, 1800	Wm. Davis	John Hett(Hutt)	6b249	cr 33	mr 73 *
Sanders, John m. Wallis, Rebecca	Oct. 23,	Oct. 23, 1841	Adam Spitznogle	John Hedges	2b 60		mr 18 *
Sanders, Margaret m. Sanders, John	Mar. 27,	Mar. 30, 1800	Wm. Davis	John Hett(Hutt)		cr 33	mr 42 *
Sanders, Moses m. Sheely, Rachel		Jan. 1, 1782		Daniel Sturges	3b294		
Sanderson, Peggy m. Needler, Bastion	Apr. 16,	Apr. 16, 1814	John Strother				mr 39 *
Sanderson, Alex. m. Kearsley, Jane		Feb. 1, 1793		Moses Hoge	1b 58	gc 7	*
Sanderson, Elenor m. Lewis, Nicholas	Oct. 25,	Nov. 30, 1797	Thos. Armstrong	David Young		cr 17	mr 20 *
Sandiss, John m. Banks, Rhuanna		Sept 3, 1801		Moses Hoge			mr 86 *
Sandker, Elis. m.Brillhart, Jesse		Sept 16, 1852		David Thomas			
Sanks, Joshua m. Dardel, Lavina	Jan. 28,	Jan. 28, 1812	Morgan Morgan		3b209		
Sanks, Joshua m. Dunlap, Sarah	Mar. 20,	Mar. 20, 1804	Robert Dunlap		2b229		
Sanks, Zachariah m. Rippy, Nancy	Aug. 17,	Aug. 17, 1813	Mathew Rippy		3b270		
Santman, Jos. H. m. Barnett, Susan	Oct. 11,	Sept 30, 1840	James Mathews	James Relly	6b218		mr 72 *
Sappington,Wm. m.Emberson, Cath.	Nov. 12,	Nov. 12, 1818	Leonard Emberson	W.N.Scott	4b 87		mr 30 *
Sargeant, Sarah m. Hawk, Jesse(Isaac)	Sept 23,	Sept 25, 1800	John Shaffer	David Young	2b 89	gc 9	*
?Sargeant, Sarah Ann m. Joy, Stephen		Aug. 28, 1831		John Light			mr 62 *
Satterfield, Benj. m. Grovine,Mary	Sept 2,	Feb. 19, 1789	Joseph Dillon	Moses Hoge	1b 37		mr 2 *
Satterfield, Eliz. m. Haslip, John		Sept 2, 1797				cr 1	
Satterfield, James m. Copas, Mary		Sept 8, 1793		Wm. Hill	7b129	cr 30	mr 10 *
Satterfield, James m. Milburn, Jane	May 29,	June 1, 1848	Jacob VanDoren	P. Lipscomb	6b321		mr 81 *
Satterfield, Sarah Ann m. Everhart,P.	May 29,	May 18, 1844	Harrison Waite	James Chisholm	4b151		mr 75 *
Satterfield, Thomas m. Robinson,Lydia	June 19,	May 29, 1820	James Robinson		5b178		
Saunders,Dorothy m. Hardshew, Hiram	Oct. 18,	Oct. 21, 1830	John Payne				mr 61 *
Saunders, Elinor m. Devers, Benj.	Mar. 8,	Mar. 8, 1824	Ellis Rees	Wm. Monroe	4b258		

Name	(marriage)	(suretor)	(minister)	(bond)	Refs
Saunders, Fred. m. Reed, Margaret	Aug. 6, 1807	Wm. Reed	John Mathews	3b 65 / 4b 29	cr 13; mr 23 *
Saunders, James m. Foreman,Priscilla	Jan. 1. 1817	Joseph Foreman			mr 47 *
Saunders, Jas. W. m. Greenwell, Jane	Aug. 5, 1824		J.L.Bromwell	3b13	*
Saunders, John m. Davis, Phebe Mrs.	Apr. 20. 1809	George Payne	David Young		gc 4; *
Saveley, Cath. m. Letman, John	Jan. 13. 1795			3b 68	*
Saveley, Christina m. Wilson, James	Sept 3, 1807	George Saveley		3b332	*
Saveley, Jacob m. Siler(2iler), Eliz.	Aug. 8. 1815	Jas. Thompson	Rev. Reebenack		gc 14; mr 4 *
Saveley, Molly m. French, George	Oct. 10. 1789		Hugh Vance		cr 25; mr 43 *
Saveley, Rosanna m. Fareacre, James	Jan. 16. 1787		Hugh Vance		mr 38 *
Savor, Wm. m. Taylor, Eliza C.	? 1789		David Thomas		*
Sayher, Rachel m. Dunn, John	Jan. 14. 1801	George Baker	John Boyd	2b109	or 35; mr 19 *
Sayles, John m. Reed, Sarah E.	May 18. 1843	Wm. Reed	T.H.W.Monroe	6b298	mr 74 *
Scanlyn, Barbara m. Jones,Jonathan	Jan. 14. 1799	Jacob Etty	Richard Swift	1b163	cr 28; mr 16 *
Scarlett, Elinor m. McIntire, Wm.	Dec. 23, 1797	John Emberson		1b 74	
Schaffer, Marg't m. Hooper, Thos. B.	Nov. 28. 1846	Everhart Runnell	John Winter	7b 76	mr 77 *
Schaffer, Mary m. Handler, Wentworth	Mar. 9. 1821	Daniel Schaffer		4b179	*
Schaffer, Wm. M. m. Swingle,Mary Va.	Apr. 2. 1849	Benord Swingle	B.M.Schmucker	7b153	mr 79 *
Schall, Cath. m. Mansen, George	Apr. 26. 2793		David Young		gc 2; *
Schall, Mary m. Boltz, George	Feb. 1810		Rev. Reebenack		gc 11; *
Schall, Michael m. Seidner, Rosanna	Mar. 21. 1791		David Young		gc 1; *
Schenck, Adolph m. Moot, Cath.	Mar. 28. 1846	Johanns Buffaim	D.F.Bragunier	7b 61	mr 78 *
Schickles,Hesekiah m.Hebrigle, Crese	Mar. 31, 1799	Richard Gartwell	Davıd Young	1b175	*
Schmal, Eliz. m. Strocker, Dariel	Mar. 9. 1815		Rev. Reebenack		gc 8; *
Schneider, John m. Siler, Mary	Apr. 26. 1792		David Young		gc 14; *
Schneider, Jos. m. Reiner, Cath.	Mar. 16. 1792		David Young		gc 1; *
Schneider, Regina m. Strucker, Simeon	Aug. 6, 1793		David Young		gc 1; *
Schonover, Mary m. Orick, George	Feb. 28. 1840	Nicholas Orick		6b198	gc 3; mr 22 *
Schoppert, Cath. m. Hooper, Thos.	Mar. 4. 1833	Adam Schoppert		5b260	cr 16; *
Schoppert,Christina m.Anderson, Jas.	Apr. 6. 1805	Nicholas Schoppert		2b259	gc 1; *
Schoppert, Eliz. m. Ward, Joel	Apr. 7, 1791		Christian Streit		*
Schoppert, Geo. A. m. Colvin, Sarah	Oct. 23, 1848	John M. Colvin	David Young	7b120	mr 81 *
Schoppert, Jacob m.McQuilkin,Nancy	Jan. 26. 1832	Thos. McQuilkin	P. Lipscomb	5b214	mr 63 *
Schoppert,Moses m. Paulsgrove, Nancy	Jan. 18. 1830	Joseph Paulsgrove	Jacob Medtart	5b160	mr 63 *
Schoppert, Nancy m. Roberts, Wm. H.	Mar. 29. 1842	Mich's Schoppert	Jacob Medtart	6b269	*
Schoppert, Rosanna m. Merchant, Wm.P	Apr. 9. 1850	George Swinley		7b195	mr 80 *
Schoppert, Samuel m. Beard, Sarah G.	Sept 14, 1841	James Beard	D.F.Bragunier	6b238	mr 72 *
Schot, Nancy m. Nichols, Christian	Mar. 22. 1797	James Flemming	John Hedges	1b 38	gc 6; *
Schouer, Margaret m. Baker, John	Sept 1, 1799	Michael Cress	David Young	2b 23	gc 9; *
Schrodes, Hester m. McBride, Aaron	Aug. 30. 1837	Jonathan Baker	David Young	6b123	*
Schrodes, Mary J. m. Baker, Jonathan	Nov. 6, 1835	Wm. Schrodes		6b 47	*
Schuher, Dennis m. Murphy, Cath.	June 28, 1846	Michael Russell	J.E.Baker	7b 66	*
Schwartz, Fredericka m. Fuss,John G.	May 16. 1839	Mathias Schwartz	Peyton Harrison	6b167	mr 71 *
Scorse, Wm. m. Paskill, Cath.	Apr. 17. 1821	John Miller	Chas. P. Krauth	4b197	mr 42 *
**Schoppert, Mary m. Varmetre, Abram	Nov. 29. 1845	Nicholas Schoppert		7b 48	*
**Schoppert, Mary m. Wyland, Wm.	Nov. 10. 1842	Jacob Schoppert		6b278	*

Name	(marriage)	(surety)	(minister)	(bond)			
Scott, John Dennis m. Violett, Eliz.	Oct. 11, 1795		David Young		gc 5	mr 11	*
Scott, Ungaletta m. Russel(Rupel), Jas.	Jan. 7, 1796		Moses Hoge		cr 35	mr 21	*
Scott, Wm. m. Hanns, Mary	Dec. 15, 1802	Wm. Hanns	Moses Hoge	2b216	cr 17		
Seaborn, Daniel m. Snider, Mary	Dec. 14, 1807	Theo. Seaborn		3b 61			
Seaborn, David m. Degroot, Sophia	Mar. 22, 1792	David Seaborn	Richard Swift	2b 53	cr 34	mr 39	*
Seaborn, Mary m. Cross, Basil	Feb. 13, 1800	George Seaborn	Richard Swift	2b207	cr 27	mr 18	*
Seaborn, Nelly m. Vanmetre, John	Aug. 11, 1803	?		3b357		mr 21	*
Seaborn, Peter m. Smith, Sally	Apr. 1812	Peter Seaborn	Moses Hoge	3b294	cr 19	mr 9	*
Seaborn, Wm. m. Stip, Mary	Dec. 30, 1794	Daniel Seaborne		1b157			
Seaborn, Ely m. Wilson, Lambert	Apr. 16, 1814						
Seaborn, Olive m. Fleming, Henry	Dec. 25, 1798	George North		3b125			
Seaborn, Theodorus m. Quick, Polly	Nov. 25, 1809	James Quick		1b 65			
Seabright, Sarah m. Stern, James	Nov. 27, 1797			2b264			
Seaman, Eleor m. Moffett, John	June 4, 1805	Cornelius Seaman	D. Thomas	2b168		mr 37	*
Seaman, Elinor m. Buckler, Wm.	1789	Mathias Urick					
Seaman, Jonas m. Downey, Jane	? 1802						
Seaman, Joseph m. Shaffer, Mary	Oct. 29, 1818	Peter Shaffer	W.N.Scott	4b 85		mr 71	*
Seaman, Nancy D. m. Curtis, Isaiah	Mar. 20, 1840	Richard Seaman	Lewis F. Wilson	6b201		mr 51	*
Seaman, Richard m. Tate, Rosanna	Aug. 18, 1828	Robert Stewart	Jas. M. Brown	5b105			
Seckman, Charles m. Custer, Mary	Mar. 15, 1830	Benj. Custer	J. Larkin	5b158		mr 88	*
Seckman, David m. Polts, Nancy Ann	Oct. 25, 1837	John Faris	A. Talty	6b120		mr 86	*
Seckman, Dennis m. Long, Joanna	Oct. 26, 1853		D. Francis Sprigg			mr 82	*
Seckman, Mary Ann m. Light, Fred.	Feb. 10, 1853		J.H.Jennings				
Secrist, John B. m. Olinger, Nancy	Feb. 22, 1846	John Olinger	W.N.Scott	7b 99			
Seere(Seem), Alex. m. Ridgely, Charlott	Apr. 29, 1817	Thomas Vananda		4b 34			
Seery, Bridget m. Halpin, Thomas	May 24, 1848	Corn's McDermott		7b129			
Seery, Mary m. Warner, Samuel	Apr. 6, 1797	Edward Mason	Moses Hoge	1b 4	cr 36	mr 13	*
Seever, Rebecca m. Panabaker, Christ'r	Apr. 8, 1828	Edward Severns	Nathan Young	5b 96	cr 31	mr 39	*
Segar, David m. Spry, Ann	Oct. 12, 1798	David Sugar	Richard Swift	1b138	cr 34	mr 15	*
Segar, Wm. m. Walter, Sarah	Oct. 28, 1799	John Walter	Richard Swift	2b 31		mr 16	*
Seibert, Amelia A. m. Thornburg, Sol'n	Jan. 8, 1855	Vincent McBride	John O. Proctor	7b 79		mr 77	*
Seibert, Barbara J. m. McDaniel, Alex.	Dec. 3, 1846	Peter Zuber	John Winter	4b 90	gc 11		
Seibert, Cath. m. Arachen, Jacob	Mar. 20, 1810	Michael Seibert	Rev. Reebenack	7b140			
Seibert, Cath. m. Weidman, Solomon	Nov. 26, 1818	Thomas Patton	Nathan Young	5b156		mr 56	*
Seibert, Cath. Elvira m. Butler, Thos.	Dec. 2, 1848	David Seibert		7b249			
Seibert, David m. Kerney, Eliza	Mar. 11, 1830	Michael Seibert	J.M.Brown	5b190			
Seibert, Eldergert m. Vanmetre, Thos. T.	Mar. 22, 1852	John Seibert	Lewis F. Wilson	5b 35			
Seibert, Eliz. m. Small, Henry C.	Mar. 31, 1831	Michael Seibert	Jacob Mediart	6b 99		mr 54	*
Seibert, Eliz. m. Hoffman, Valentine	Feb. 2, 1826	Jacob Seibert	John Winter	3b225		mr 87	*
Seibert, Eliz. m. Hill, Jacob	Mar. 7, 1837	Jacob Seibert	Lewis F. Wilson	5b 72		mr 63	*
Seibert, Eliz. m. Seibert, Michael	May 19, 1812	John Ellis	Rev. Reebenack	7b 9		mr 50	*
Seibert, Eliz. m. Smith, David	June 16, 1827	Chas. McDonald		5b278	gc 12		
Seibert, Ellen m. Newkirk, Isaac	Oct. 24, 1844	Charles Keel	Lewis F. Wilson	3b232			
*Sebastian, Christian m. McDonald, Parb'g. 3, 1833							*
**Seckman, Polly m. Lewis, Lewis	Aug. 17, 1812						*

Name	(marriage)	(surety)	(minister)	(bond)		
Seibert, Emily Ann m. Rousch, Andrew	Oct. 22, 1845	John P. Walters	Lewis Mayer	7b 46		mr 31 *
Seibert, George m. Gushwa, Eliz.	Mar. 7, 1820	Jonathan Gushwa		4b138		mr 49 *
Seibert, George m. Walters, Polly	May 31, 1825	John Walters	Chas. P. Kreuth	5b 13		
Seibert, Harriet m. Holliday,Geo. W.	Sept 8, 1831	Jacob F. Seibert		5b205		
Seibert, Harriet m. Rice, Henry	Oct. 9, 1848	Martin Pitser	P. Lipscomb	7b136		mr 81 *
Seibert, Harriet A. m.Griffith,Elijah	Aug. 20, 1831	John F. Smith	Wm. Monroe	5b202		mr 62 *
Seibert, Harrison m. Roberts, Eliz A	Mar. 22, 1843	Wm. H. Roberts		6b294		
Seibert, Harrison S. m.Hedges,Cath.V	Feb. 7, 1848	Wm. L. Seibert	James Chisholm	7b122		mr 78 *
Seibert, Henry m. Hoffman, Susan	June 17, 1800	Wendle Seibert	David Young	2b 73	gc 9	
Seibert, Henry J. m. Small, Peggy	June 3, 1822	Jacob Small	Chas. P. Kreuth	4b215		mr 45 *
Seibert, Henry J. m.Seibert,Marg't	Jan. 1, 1851	John D. Cushwa		7b208		
Seibert, Jacob m. Ellis, Ellen	May 12, 1837	Ellis Ellis		6b107		
Seibert, Jacob m. Kirney, Ann	Dec. 1, 1835	Harrison Waite		6b 65		
Seibert, Jacob m. Mong, Cath.	Sept 8, 1812	John Mong	Rev. Reebenack	3b236	gc 13	
Seibert, Jacob m. Myers, Mary	Mar. 7, 1810	John Myers	Lewis Mayer	3b139	cr 14	mr 24 *
Seibert, Jacob M. m.Beatty, Maria	Mar. 25, 1840	Wm. Pendleton	John Light	6b202		mr 71 *
Seibert, John m. Bowers, Cath.	Dec. 31, 1806	Henry Bowers		3b 40		
Seibert, John m. Small, Ruth Cath.	Feb. 4, 1824	Jacob Small	Chas. P. Kreuth	4b256		mr 46 *
Seibert, John N. m. Myers, Sarah Ann	Dec. 2, 1847	Aaron Myers	James Chisholm	7b115		mr 78 *
Seibert, John S. m. Grantham, Eliza	May 4, 1829	Wm. Grantham	Nathan Young	5b129		mr 60 *
Seibert, Joseph m. Roberts, Frances	Dec. 29, 1851	Harrison Seibert		7b241		
Seibert, Marg't A. m. Showers,Philip	Nov. 15, 1843	George Seibert		6b307		
Seibert, Marg't E. m.Seibert,Henry J	Jan. 1, 1851	John D. Cushwa		7b208		
Seibert, Martha m. Seibert, Otho W.	Mar. 7, 1849	John P. Walter	B.M.Schmucker	7b148		mr 79 *
Seibert, Mary m. Criswell, James	Feb. 13, 1837	Jacob Seibert	Lewis F. Wilson	6b 95		
Seibert, Mary A. m. Speck, Benj.	Oct. 26, 1835	Michael Seibert		6b 60		
Seibert, Mary C. m. Mong, Wm. H.	Mar. 7, 1843	George Seibert		6b292		
Seibert, Michael m. Myers, Cath.	Mar. 17, 1814	John Myers	Rev. Reebenack	3b288	gc 14	
Seibert, Michael m. Seibert, Eliz.	May 19, 1812	Jacob Seibert	Rev. Reebenack	3b225	gc 12	
Seibert, Michael m. Tice, Polly	Nov. 5, 1811	Fred. Sybert	Rev. Reebenack	3b198	gc 12	
Seibert, Otho W. m. Seibert,Martha	Mar. 7, 1849	John P. Walter	B.M.Schmucker	7b148		mr 79 *
Seibert, Peggy m. Craiglo., George	Mar. 4, 1814	Jacob Seibert	Rev. Reebenack	3b286	gc 14	
Seibert, Rachel E. m. Boak, Wm. L.	May 6, 1830	Jacob F. Seibert	Wm. Monroe	5b165		mr 94 *
Seibert, Rachel J. m. Martin, John	Aug. 1, 1835	Christian Seibert		6b 51		
Seibert, Samuel m. Mong, Mary	Jan. 7, 1819	John Mong	Lewis Mayer	4b108		mr 31 *
Seibert, Samuel m. Morrison, Cath.	May 31, 1836	Jacob Seibert		6b 69		
Seibert, Susannah m. Cushwa, John D.	Jan. 15, 1835	Michael Seibert		6b 39		
Seibert, Susannah m. Suber, Peter	Mar. 30, 1811	Jacob Ballmyer	Rev. Reebenack	3b182	gc 12	
Seibert, Wm.Luther m. Wolff,Mary C.	Mar. 26, 1849	John M. Wolff	John W. Wolff	7b168		mr 79 *
Seibert, Wm. T. m. Fryatt, Marg't A.	Nov. 22, 1843	Jas. H. Schwartz		6b293		
Seidner, Rosarna m. Schall, Michael	Feb. 1, 1791	Jeptha Hensell	David Young		gc 1	
Sedgler, Wm. m. Howe, Marg't Jane	Nov. 6, 1848		B.M.Schmucker	7b139		mr 79 *
Sedler, Peter m. Hovermale, Eliz.	Oct. 29, 1799		David Young		gc 9	

Name	date	(marriage)	(surety)	(minister)	(bond)			
Selby, Solomon m. Stephens, Mary Ann	Aug. 3,	Aug. 3, 1799	Thomas Walters	David Young	2b 16	gc 8		*
Selby, Walter B. m. Morgan, Elinor	Dec. 27,	Dec. 24, 1797	M. Ranson	Moses Hoge	1b 75		mr 13	*
Sellers, Allana m. Stover, Fred.	Nov. 1,	Nov. 5, 1809	John Kysinger	Lewis Mayers	3b123	cr 16	mr 24	*
Sellers, Bolzer m. Job, Sarah	Jan. 29,	1807	Daniel Rees		3b 44			
Sellers, Cath. m. Berry, Peter	Oct. 21,	Oct. 1822	John Sellers	Chas. P. Krauth	4b225		mr 45	*
Sellers, Eliz. m. Boerkapp, Adam		May 5, 1788		Hugh Vance			nr 94	*
Sellers, George m. Emberson, Eliz.	June 1,	June 2, 1829	Daniel Emberson	Nathan Young	5b131		nr 60	*
Sellers, Jacob m. Hoff, Eliz. Elinor	Nov. 13,	Nov. 1822	John Sellers	Chas. P. Krauth	4b228		nr 45	*
Sellers, James m. Rees, Nancy	Dec. 22,	1804	Rees Branson		2b250			
Sellers, Mary m. Davis, Richard	July 2,	1804	Bolzer Sellers		2b238			
Sellers, Rachel m. Raving, Joshua	May 26,	May 27, 1807?	Bolzer Sellers	John Mathews	3b 59	cr 13	nr 23	*
Sellers, Samuel m. Criswell, Eliz.	Feb. 14,	Feb. 16, 1842	Wm. D. Wilson	John Light	6b264		nr 74	*
Sellers, Wm. m. Ashley, Mary		Sept 19, 1781		Daniel Sturges			nr 32	*
Sellers, Wm. m. Knave(Kane), Nancy	July 29,	July 31, 1831	Jacob Smith	John Light	5b199		nr 62	*
Sendindiver, Amelia m. Mayhew, Evan	Nov. 13,	Nov. 16, 1837	Martin Sendindiver	James Watts	6b124			
Sendindiver, Cath. C. m. Crim, Geo.W	Nov. 13,	1850	Martin Sendindiver		7b202			
Sendindiver, Elisha m. Lewis, Eliz.	Jan. 10,	Jan. 10, 1833	Lewis Lewis	Nathan Young	5b253		nr 66	*
Sendindiver, Jacob m.Boltz,Eliz., Ann	Dec. 13,	1833	Harrison Waite		5b295			
Sendindiver, John m. Madden(-ox),Mary	Aug. 8,	Aug. 9, 1832	Lorenzo Maddox	Nathan Young	5b236		nr 64	*
Sendindiver, Lydia m. Crim, John W.	Mar. 8,	Mar. 11, 1847	Martin Sendindiver	Richard T. Brown	7b 90		nr 77	*
Sendindiver, Lydia m. Stump, Ephraim	Nov. 9,	1818	Louis Sendindiver	John Kehler	4b 86		nr 31	*
Sendindiver,Marg't A. m.Johnson Isaac	Dec. 23,	Dec. 1850	Martin Sendindiver	F.C.Tebbs	7b206		nr 83	*
Sendindiver, Martin m.Stump, Margaret	June 15,	1818	Louis Sendindiver	John Kehler	4b 74		nr 30	*
Sendindiver, Samuel m.McDonald,Ann E	Sept 10,	1844	Sebast'n McDonald		7b 6			
Seneker, Adam m. Mayers, Cath.	Dec. 28,	Jan. 7, 1813	Stephen Mayer	John Mathews	3b244		nr 25	*
Seneker, Adam m. Long, Rebecca		Apr. 22, 1788		Moses Hoge			nr 35	*
?Seneker, Cath. m. Bear, Michael		May 2, 1798		David Young		gc 7		
Senele, Nancy m. Snider, Conrad		Aug. 19, 1797		David Young		gc 6		
*Senseman, Rachel m. Mound, Wm.		Feb. 5, 1794		B. Page			nr 40	*
?Seneler, Cath. m. Paise, Michael	May 2,	Feb. 1798	Fred. Blue		1b110			
Seppy, Joseph m. Johnson, Lucretia		Feb. 20, 1787		Hugh Vance			nr 43	*
Sergeant, Edw. m. McClean, Agnes		Dec. 24, 1784		Hugh Vance			nr 32	*
Sergeant, Nathan m. Coplin, Mary		Feb. 25, 1788		Moses Hoge			nr 35	*
Sergeant, Polly m. Pitzer(Pifer),John	Oct. 31,	Nov. 1, 1810	John Pitzer	Rev. Reebenack	3b165	gc 11	nr 36	*
Servimon, John m. Wilson, Mary		Dec. 29, 1788		Hugh Vance				
?Sesler, Mary m. Strayer, Adam	Aug. 12,	Aug. 12, 1813	Patrick Duffy	Rev. Reebenack	3b269	gc 13		
?Sesler, Maria m. Strother, Adam								
Sett, Ann m. Murphy, Wm.	Mar. 24,	1798	Davis Smedley	Rev. Reebenack	1b105			
Sett, Anthony m. Cross, Cath.	Apr. 12,	Apr. 13, 1800	George Boston	John Helt(Hutt)	2b 64	cr 33	nr 18	*
Sever, Charles m. McManus, Sarah	Dec. 30,	1823	James McManus		4b254			
Sever, Charles m. Philipy, Mary	Apr. 4,	Apr. 4, 1806	Isaac Hawke	John Bond	3b 15	or 28	nr 22	*
**Sever, Fanny m. Martin, Jacob	July 2,	1816	Michajah Beeson		4b 2			
Sever, Henry m. Myers, Eliz.		Dec. 28, 1791		David Young		gc 1		
Senseman, Rebecca m. Mound, Wm.		Apr. 18, 1820		Lewis Mayer				*
**Sever(Si.), Eliz. m. Howe, Andrew		Dec. 27, 1793		David Young		gc 3		*

Genealogical marriage index (surnames Severns – Shaffer). Entries read: name (bride/groom) · marriage date · (surety) · (minister) · (bond) reference · record code · marriage reference.

Name	(marriage)	(surety)	(minister)	(bond)		
Severns, Eliz. m. Henderson, James	Jan. 27, Jan. 30, 1823	Richard Severns	James Samson	4b233		mr 45 *
Severns, Joseph m. Duffey, Cath.	Mar. 12, Mar. 15, 1832	Robert McDonald	Nathan Young	9c219		mr 64 **
Severns, Marg't m. Panabaker, Adam	Aug. 10, Aug. 13, 1818	John Severns	Nathan Young	4b 76		mr 56 **
Severns, Rebecca m. Panabaker,Christ'r	Feb. 26, Apr. 8, 1828	Edward Severns	Nathan Young	5b 96		mr 59 *
Severns, Susan m. Stinchcomb, Levi	Apr. 3, 1824	Joseph Turner		4b256		
Sewell, Aaron m. Hendricks, Rebecca	Apr. 3, 1798	John Ingle		1b 96		
Sewell, Abigail m.Can-Con-Cunklin,JhnMay	May 20, 1798	James Burr		1b112	cr 36	mr 14 *
Sewell, Ann m. Joslin, Jeremiah	Jan. 31, 1786		Moses Hoge			mr 33 *
Sewell, Hannah m. Burr, Peter	Feb. 9, 1790		Hugh Vance		cr 3	mr 5 *
Sewell, Ilscena m. Burr, Peter	Feb. 9, 1790		Moses Hoge		cr 3	mr 5 *
Sewell, Jane m. Russell, Wm.	June 22, 1790		Moses Hoge		cr 4	mr 5 *
Sewell, John m. Hendricks,Priscilla	Apr. 22, 1790		Moses Hoge		cr 21	mr 7 *
Sewell, Mordecai m. Short, Sarah	Aug. 27, Aug. 28, 1802	Benedict Rush	Richard Swift	2b179	cr 32	mr 21 **
Sewell, Sarah m. Blackford, Ebenezer	Feb. 24, 1791		Moses Hoge		cr 6	mr 6 *
Sewen, Mary m. Smith, Joseph	June 15, Dec. 15, 1795		Moses Hoge		ge 5	mr 6 **
Seybert, Cath. m. Strayer, Jacob	Mar. 17, 1816	Jacob Seybert	Mathias Riser	3b142		mr 26 *
Shade, Jacob m. Crouse, Cath.	Jan. 6, 1836	Peter Caw		6b 66		
Shade, Jacob m. Sprigg, Eliz.	Mar. 5, 1836		James Watts	6b135		
?Shafer, Geo. m. Wareham, Cath.	Mar. 26, 1846	John T. Hilliard		6b 75		
Shafer, John F. m. Gallaher, Mary	Mar. 30, 1846	Charles Downs	John Winter	7b 62		mr 76 *
Shafer, Ann E. m. Davis, John L.	Dec. 2, 1846	George Shaffer		4b 24		
Shafer, Aaron m. Shaffer, Eliz.	Dec. 13, 1816	John Fry		3b167	ge 11	
Shafer, Cath. m. Inbody, Jacob	Dec. 11, 1810	Jacob Shaffer	Rev. Reebemack		ge 7	
Shafer, Christian m. Ward, Hannah	Oct. 31, 1797		David Young			**
Shaffer, Eliz. m. Polsal, Susan	Jan. 16, 1840	Jacob Polsal	James Reily	6b194		mr 70 *
Shaffer, Eliz. m. Hedges, Solomon	Apr. 20, 1820	Henry Shaffer	John B. Hoge	4b145		mr 31 *
*Shaffer, Eliz. m. Throckmorton, Job	Apr. 5, 1826	Stephen Shaffer	Nathan Young	5b 38		mr 58 *
Shaffer, Geo. m. Mussetter, Marg't	Sept. 8, 1814	Christ. Mussetter	Lewis Mayor	3b302		mr 25 *
?Shaffer, Geo. m. Wareham, Cath.	Mar. 5, 1838	John T. Hilliard	James Watts	6b135		
Shaffer, Henry m. Heck, Cath.	May 1, 1798	George Doll	David Young	1b 99	gc 7	
Shaffer, Jacob m. Snowdeal, Eliz.	Nov. 4, 1840	Jacob Pickings		6b223		
Shaffer, John m. Davis, Cath.	July 24, 1821	Daniel Shaffer		4b186		
Shaffer, Marg't m. Pierce, James	Oct. 19, 1809	Peter Shaffer		3b122	ge 10	mr 77 **
Shaffer, Marg't L. m. Hooper, Thos.B	Nov. 7, 1846	Everhart Rummall		7b 76	ge 3	
Shaffer, Maria m. Biter, Michael	Mar. 11, 1794					
Shaffer, Maria m. Daniel, Joseph H.	June 13, 1837	George Shaffer	John Light	6b108		mr 86 *
Shaffer, Martha m.Arriba,Josiah Isaiah	Mar. 12, 1851	Robert Mcely	David Young	7b219		
Shaffer, Martin m. Keesecker, Cath.	Sept. 17, 1795		Rev. Reebemack			**
Shaffer, Mary m. Keller, George	Sept. 18, 1813	Peter Kress		3b271	ge 5	
Shaffer, Mary m. Seaman, Joseph	Oct. 29, 1818	Peter Shaffer	W.N.Scott	4b 85	ge 13	
Shaffer, Peter m. Butt, Sally	Dec. 28, 1843	Henry Stephens		6b311		
Shaffer, Sarah m. Littlejohn,Abr'm	Oct. 23, 1819	Edward Littlejohn	Nathan Young	4b121		mr 56 *
Shaffer, Eliz. m. Randall, Adrian W.	Oct. 1, 1823	Peter Shaffer	Chas. P. Krauth	4b250		mr 46 *

	(marriage)		(surety)	(minister)	(bond)		
Shaffer, Sarah m. Rutherford, John W	Feb. 22,	1842	James Fryatt	Peyton Harrison	6b265		mr 73 *
Shaffer, Susannah m. O'Neal, Robert	Mar. 5,	1812	Peter Shaffer	Rev. Reebenack	3b214	ge 12	mr 84 *
Shaffer, Susan m. Ryneal, Everhart	May 27,	1850	John Shaffer	B.M.Schmucker	7b187		mr 79 *
Shaffer, Wm. M. m. Swingle, Mary Va.	Apr. 9,	1849	Benard Swingle	B.M.Schmucker	7b153		mr 9 *
Shaler, Marg't m. McDonald, Asa	Mar. 14,	1795		W. Hill		cr 29	mr 9 *
Shall, Cath. m. Rosenberger, John	Mar. 28,	1815	Nicholas Shall	Lewis Mayer	3b314		mr 25 *
Shall, Jacob m. Rosenberger, John Fred.	June 13,	1811		Rev. Reebenack		ge 12	
Shall, Jacob m. Bolts, Susannah	Jan. 19,	1809		Rev. Reebenack		ge 10	
Shall, Marg't m. Stoltz (Stubbs), Jacob	Jan. 7,	1799	Barth'w Shall	David Young	1b160	ge 8	
Shall, Mary m. Pulse, George	Apr. 21,	1810	Nicholas Shall		3b148		
Shambaugh, Kath. m. Nowell, John							mr 37 *
Shane, Fanny m. Bain(Bane), Charles	Oct. 25,	1821		Hugh Vance	4b104		mr 45 *
Shane, Frank m. Kitchcart, Jane	?	1789		S.S.Robertson			mr 38 *
Shane, James m. Snode, Cath.	Apr. 15,	1809	John Booth	David Thomas	3b112		
Shane, Marg't A. m. Lemon, Edwin M.	June 6,	1834	James Shane		6b 13		
Shane, Mary m. Hayes, Nathan	May 1,	1802	Joseph Sander		2b173		
Shane, Sarah m. Johnston, Robert	Feb. 15,	1821	John Bowning		4b172		
Shank, Ann E. m. Pitzer, James	Dec. 24,	1844	John Shank	John Light	7b 18		mr 76 *
Shank, Cath. m. Walker, James	Apr. 5,	1818		Mathias Riser			mr 29 *
Shank, John m. Hoke, Susan	Dec. 13,	1841	Peter Crowl	John Light	6b258		mr 72 *
Shank, Michael m. Cleon, Martha B.	Sept 20,	1821	John Strother		4b191		
Shank, Wm. H. m. Miles, Marg't A.	Jan. 20,	1853		J.M.Dennis			mr 86 *
Sharff, Henry m. Hess, Sarah Ann	Jan. 8,	1846	Norman Miller	Lewis F. Wilson	7b 53		mr 77 *
Sharff, Peter m. Huffman, Susanna	Dec. 15,	1830	Philip Carper	Nathan Young	5b183		mr 61 *
Sharff, Sarah m. Sprace, Jacob	Oct. 24,	1817		Mathias Riser			
Sharp, Eliza m. Gano, Amos	Mar. 18,	1830	James Gano	Jas. M. Brown	5b159		mr 54 *
Sharp, Eliz. m. Keef, John	Aug. 13,	1822	Isaac Crab	Nathan Young	4b221		mr 58 *
Sharp, Henry m. Hess, Sarah A.	Jan. 8,	1846	Norman Miller	Lewis F. Wilson	7b 53		mr 77 *
Sharp, Horatio m. Sloan, Evelina	Aug. 15,	1826	James Sloan	John Winter	5b 48	?	mr 50 *
Sharp, Jane m. Curtis, Edward	May 1,	1789		Hugh Vance			mr 3 *
Sharp, Jane m. Pulse, Lewis	Feb. 28,	1820	Daniel McKeever	Nathan Young	4b137	cr 20	mr 57 *
Sharp, John m. Sloan, Maria	June 22,	1824	?	John Winter	4b267		mr 50 *
?Sharp, Mary m. Clawson, Iram(Isaac)	Dec. 9,	1817	Thomas Sharp	Nathan Young	4b126		mr 56 *
Sharp, Rebecca m. Abernathy, Clark	Nov. 6,	1817	John Sharp	Nathan Young	4b 49		mr 55 *
?Sharpe, Mary m. Clawson, Isaac(Iram)	Dec. 9,	1819	Thomas Sharp	Nathan Young	4b126		mr 56 *
Shartel, Sally m. Painter, Jacob	Dec. 15,	1804	Jacob Shertel	Christian Stredt	3b235	cr 16	mr 22 *
Shartel, Jacob m. Burnes, Alsy	Aug. 29,	1812	John Whitenack		3b 8		
Shaul, George m. Kindpp, Cath.	Jan. 13,	1806	George Boltz		1b 59		
Shaver, Christian m. Ware, Hannah	Oct. 30,	1797	Wm. Steele				
Shaver, Eliz. m. Porterfield, Alex.	June 11,	1783		Hugh Vance			mr 32 *
Shaver, Jacob m. Wigle, Mary	June 16,	1788 ?		Hugh Vance			mr 35 *
Shaw, Agnes m. Meek, James	July 8,	1789		Moses Hoge		cr 2	mr 3 *
Shaw, Ann m. Gallagher, John	Apr. 30,	1819 ? John Strother	John B. Hoge	4b106		mr 29 *

Name	Marriage	Year	Suretor	Minister	Bond	cr/gc	mr
Shaw, Eliz. m. Taylor, Caleb	Feb. 17,	1813	Stephen Shaw	Hugh Vance	3b251		mr 36
Shaw, Joseph m. Baker, Ruth	Oct. 3,	1820	Reiser Hudgel	John Boyd	4b164		mr 10
Shaw, Mary m. Patterson, James		1788				cr 33	mr 40
Shaw, Mary m. Small, Samuel	Apr. 7,	1795				cr 14	mr 24
Shawhan, David m. Hedges, Mary O.	Jan. 15,	1810	Jonas Hedges	John Mathews	3b134	cr 34	mr 16
Shawhan, Mary m. Foreman, John	Mar. 11,	1811	Fred. Shawhan	John B. Hoge	3b178		mr 32
Shazely, John m. Potts, Barbara	Feb. 14,	1798	Fred. Potts	John Boyd	1b 85	gc 9	mr 67
Shearer, Ann m. Oden, Elias	May 4,	1799	Wm. Orrick	Hugh Vance	2b 1		mr 11
Shearer, Eliz. m. Porterfield, Alex.	June 6,	1783					mr 55
Shearer, Marg't m. Baker, John	June 11,	1799	Michael Cress	David Young	2b 23	cr 33	mr 88
Shearer, Mary m. Kepler, John Rev'd.	Sept 1,	1834	Arch'd Shearer	Samuel Keppler	6b 3	cr 22	mr 8
Shearer, Patty m. Towson, Jacob	Aug. 30,	1795		John Boyd			mr 1
Shearer, Sarah m. Catlett, Strother	Apr. 4,	1815	Fred.Householder	Nathan Young	3b341	gc 8	mr 42
Sheckem, Dennis m. Long, Joannah	Apr. 8,	1853		A. Talty			mr 5
Sheckles, Eliz. m. Gatrel, Richard	Sept 3,	1793	Richard Gartrell	Moses Hoge	1b175	cr 37	mr 42
Sheckles, Hezediah m. Hebrigle, Cress	Sept 30,	1799	Adam Stewart	David Young	6b152	cr 3	mr 19
Sheeler, John m. Stewart, Maria C.	Oct. 1,	1838		Edward Tiffin		cr 35	mr 10
Sheeley, Hannah m. Phillips, James	Oct. 26,	1785		Daniel Sturges		cr 30	mr 14
Sheeley, John m. Ridgeway, Ann	Oct. 19,	1782		Moses Hoge			
Sheeley, Margaret m. Hibbon, Wm.	Mar. 28,	1790		Daniel Sturges		gc 3	
Sheeley, Rachel m. Sanders, Moses	Mar. 31,	1782		John Hutt(Hectt)		gc 2	
Sheeley, Samuel m. Ashfield, Phebe	Nov. 26,	1800	Benj. Sheeley	Wm. Hill	2b 75	cr 37	
Sheeley, Wm. m. Hardy(Hanly), Mary	Jan. 20,	1793		David Young			
Sheets, Adam m. Miller, Magdaline	Feb. 14,	1793		David Young			
Sheets, Benj. m. Litten, Sener	Feb. 4,	1793		John Potts			
Sheets, Cath. m. Simmons, Jonas	Jan. 1,	1798	George Sheets		1b109		
Sheets, Daniel m. Kibler, Eliz.	July 12,	1800	Gabriel Hayes		2b 50		
Sheets, Eliz. m. Woibly, Alex.	Feb. 1,	1817	Mathias Kanay		4b 41		
Sheets, Geo. W. m.Beales(Bales),Eliz.	Sept 23,	1847	David Beales	P. Lipscomb	7b107	go 6	mr 81
Sheets, Julia m. Eckhart, Henry	Jan. 3,	1797	Michael Yearley	David Young	1b 7		
Sheets, Wm. m. Edwards, Mary	Apr. 19,	1845	Joseph Edwards	John Boggs	7b 30	go 2	mr 75
Shdick, Adolph m. Moot, Cath.	Apr. 18,	1846	Johanns Buffaim	D.F.Bragunier	7b 61	go 4	mr 78
Shedlor, Jenny m. Robinson, Israel	Jan. 28,	1800	Wm. Shedlor		2b 67		
Shelby, Sarah m. Young, George		1792					
Sheldon, James m. Wright, Jane	Jan. 24,	1804	Samuel Wright	Moses Hoge	2b220	cr 17	
Shell, Jacob m. Biddle(Bittle), Mary	Apr. 27,	1815	Francis Bittle	Moses Hoge	3b321	gc 14	
Shell, Susannah m. Hiveley, Abr'm	Oct. 8,	1799	James Lane	Rev. Reebenack	2b 30		
!Shelley, Wm. m. Hogan, Bridget	Aug. 10,	1853		J.H.Plunkett			
Shenenberg, Jacob m. Weise, Marg't	Feb. 5,	1793		David Young			mr 39
Shenenberg, Michael m. Miller, Susan	July 31,	1794		David Young			mr 21
Shennebere, George m. Heath, Hannah	Dec. 23,	1788		Hugh Vance			mr 88
Shepherd, Abr'm m. Peppers, Mary	Aug. 18,	1789		Hugh Vance			mr 36
Shepherd, Abr'm m. Strode, Rhianna	Dec. 27,	1780		Daniel Sturges		cr 39	mr 31
!*Shelby, Wm. m. Hogan, Bridget	Aug. 10,	1853		J.H.Plunkett			mr 88

Name	(marriage)	(surety)	(minister)	(bond)	ref
Shepherd, Cath. m. Courtney, Michael	Jan. 20, 1836	Henry Swisher		6b 70	
Shepherd, Elis. m. Zombro, Jacob Jr.	July 27, 1825	James Shepherd		5b 17	
Shepherd, Geo. A. m. Light, Elis. M.	June 24, 1850	Jacob F. Light		7b189	
Shepherd, Gideon m. Grantham, Marg't	June 13, 1826	James Grantham		5b 43	
Shepherd, Lydia m. Huffman, Henry	Mar. 19, 1805	David Rees		2b257	
Shepherd, Marg't m. Acres, George	May 23, 1825	John Shepherd		5b 12	
Shepherd, Marg't m. Hazelett, Robert	Oct. 12, 1837	Lewis Beeson		6b119	
Shepherd, Mathew m. Leckner, Peggy	Aug. 26, 1812	John Leckner	Rev. Reebenack	3b234	gc 13 *
Shepherd, Philip m. Plotner, Eliz.	Dec. 10, 1821	Peter Myers		4b200	
Shepherd, Polly m. Coltman, Joseph	Jan. 11, 1816	James Shepherd	Rev. Reebenack	3b352	gc 15 *
Shepherd, Richard m. Merel, Kath.	Jan. 14, 1781		Hugh Vance		mr 32 **
Shepherd, Mathew m. Leckner, Peggy	Aug. 27, 1812	John Leckner	Rev. Reebenack	3b234	gc 13 **
Sherer, John m. Johnston, Sarah	Feb. 16, 1847	John Sherard		7b 87	
Sherrard, John m. Gilbert, Lany	Feb. 26, 1812	Hezekiah Johnston		6b 33	
Sherrard, John m. Plotner, Nancy	Oct. 20, 1835	John Gray		3b 75	
Sherrard, Joseph m. Seibert, Eliz.	Jan. 28, 1807	John Myers		4b132	
Sherrard, Joseph m. Zuber, Eliz.	Aug. 14, 1820	John Seibert		4b113	
?Sherrard, Robert m. Wilson, Eliz. P.	Apr. 26, 1819	John Zuber		4b113	
Shertle, Sally m. Painter, Jacob	Dec. 15, 1804	Wm. Wilson	Christian Streit	3b260	cr 16 * mr 22 *
Shertle, Eliz. m. Wibely, Alex.	July 31, 1817	Jacob Shertle	W.N.Scott	2b249	cr 30 * mr 15 *
Shervin, Wm. m. Downs, Ann Rebecca	Jan. 28, 1845	Christ'r Downs		7b 24	
Sheuman, Nancy m. Merchant, Isaac	Nov. 5, 1798	Jonathan Gerrard		1b144	
Shields, Charity m. Hedges, Samuel	Mar. 30, 1807	John Shields	John Hutt(Hedtt)	3b 52	cr 11 * mr 12 *
Shields, Charity m. Cunningham, Sam'l	Dec. 1, 1796	Richard Whelan	John Boyd	6b196	cr 17 * mr 23 *
Shields, Dardel m. McGrane, Cath.	Feb. 8, 1840	Wm. Cunningham		3b 86	mr 60 **
Shields, David m. Cunningham, Mary	Apr. 20, 1808	Alex. Robinson	John Mathews	5b100	cr 17 * mr 21 *
Shields, Eliz. m. Harper, Joseph	May 6, 1828	Samuel Wright	Nathan Young	2b220	cr 17 * mr 21 *
Shields, James m. Wright, Jane	Jan. 24, 1804	Thos. Robinson	Moses Hoge	3b107	cr 30 * mr 9 *
Shields, John m. Robinson, Ann	Feb. 11, 1809				
?Shields, John m. Wright, Jane	Jan. 26, 1804	Wm. Shields	Moses Hoge	3b258	
Shields, Nancy m. Yates, John	Apr. 10, 1813				
Shisly, James m. Strodeman, Susannah	May 12, 1794	Joshua Robinson	Wm. Hill	4b 71	
Shiderly, Dardel m. Flinn, Nancy	May 31, 1818	John W. Zimmerman	Mathias Riser	7b235	
Shilling, Jacob m. McClune, Sarah A.	Oct. 23, 1851	Jonas Shimp	D. Thomas	7b115	
Shimp, Barbara m. Hedges, Jonas K.	Dec. 6, 1847				
Shimp, Cath. m. Miller, Zachariah	Mar. 6, 1802	John Shimp	James Paynter	2b164	
Shimp, Jacob m. Harper, Meazy	Aug. 26, 1820	Jacob Curtis	F.C.Tebbs	4b158	
Shimp, Jemima C. m. Wilson, John W.	Dec. 9, 1850				
Shimp, Jonas m. Kerns, Eliz.	Sept 20, 1813	Jacob Kerns		3b272	mr 29 **
Shimp, Salome m. Albright, Peter	Mar. 3, 1820	John Shimp		4b138	mr 85 **
Shimp, Sarah A. m. Griffith, Zebulon	Mar. 31, 1849	Benj. G. Manor		7b152	mr 40 *
Shindler, Eliz. m. Reckhart, Michael	June 2, 1797	John Waters		1b 19	mr 83 **
*Shilly, Darvis m. Fisher, Peter	June 2, 1788		Moses Hoge		mr 35 *
** Shimp, Eliz. R. m. Johnson, Andrew	Nov. 22, 1841	Casper Shimp	John Hedges	6b294	mr 73 **

Genealogical marriage index — column headers: (marriage), (surety), (minister), (bond)

Name	(marriage)	(surety)	(minister)	(bond)	ref
Shindler, Richard m. Avis, Mary	Aug. 26, 1833	James Shane	Nathan Young	5b280, 1b 44	mr 66 *
Shine, Phebe m. Hunt, Wm.	Sept 23, 1797	John Heaton			*
Shink, Eliz. m. Hedronemous, Geo.	Apr. 9, 1793				mr 19 *
Shirmafelt, Wm. m. Jeffries, Rebecca	Apr. 2, 1801	Peter Williamson	David Young	2b19	gc 3, mr 20 *
Shipe, Hannah m. Jones, John	Aug. 3, 1801	John Brakefield	Richard Swift	2b139	cr 31, mr 29 *
Shipman, Stephen m. Gassaway, Nancy	May 26, 1801	Benj. Palmer	Richard Swift	2b127	cr 32, mr 39 *
Shirley, Daniel m. Flinn, Nancy	May 31, 1818	Joshua Robinson	Mathias Riser	4b 71	mr 10 *
Shirley, Eliz. m. Johnston, Wm.	May 2, 1792		Moses Hoge		cr 30, mr 1 *
Shirley, James m. Frier, Ruth	May 5, 1793		Wm. Hill		*
Shirley, John m. Smithey, Ann	Mar. 5, 1793		Edward Tiffin		cr 30 *
Shirley, Walter m. Stanford, Eliz.	Feb. 7, 1785		Wm. Hill		mr 9 *
Shirley, Wm. m. Godman, Charlotte	Dec. 30, 1801	Zachariah Godman	John B. Hoge	2b155	gc 14 *
Shirley, Wm. m. Mayers, Nancy	Oct. 7, 1811	John Mayer	David Young	3b196	gc 9, mr 24 *
Shrok, Maria m. Barnhart, Henry	May 1, 1797	Simon Shunk	David Young	1b 14	gc 5 *
Shissolen, Richard m. McKnight, Debora	Dec. 15, 1795		Daniel Sturges		*
Shively, Marg't m. Plug, Nicholas	Mar. 5, 1782				mr 42 *
Shoafstall, Ann m. Caskey, Wm.	Jan. 3, 1822	Joseph Chambers	Robert Cadden	4b203	mr 61 *
Shoafstall, David m. Fryatt, Deborah	Apr. 25, 1830	John Gallaher		5b164	
Shoafstall, Deborah m. Morrow, James	Aug. 10, 1835	Harrison Waite		6b 54	
Shoafstall, Elenor m. Fisher, Jacob	Nov. 26, 1835	Anthony Chambers		6b 64	
Shoafstall, Eli m. Cage, Elenor	Oct. 4, 1832	Anthony Chambers	Jacob Medtart	5b241	mr 64 *
Shoafstall, Eliz. m. Blakeney, Andrew	Dec. 2, 1826	Seth Shoafstall	John Mathews	5b 53	mr 50 *
Shoafstall, Eliza Ann m. Graves, Chas.	Apr. 24, 1849	William Graves		7b156	
Shoafstall, Geo. m. Aver, Elira Ann	June 5, 1845	Christian Aver		7b 36	
Shoafstall, Isaac m. Evans, Eliz.	Jan. 4, 1804	*Ephraim Evans		2b217	
Shoafstall, Marg't m. Cage, Joseph E	Apr. 2, 1836	Michael Grover		6b 77	
Shoafstall, Marg't m. Blue, John	Jan. 10, 1832	Morgan VanCleve		5b213	
Shoafstall, Mary m. Blakeney, Edw. P.	Jan. 15, 1825	Seth Shoafstall		4b285	
Shoafstall, Mary m. James, Reuben	Jan. 18, 1825	Abr'm Strayer	Chas. P. Krauth	4b286	mr 48 *
Shoafstall, Nancy m. McDonald, Geo. W	Jan. 9, 1834	Jacob Fisher		5b299	
Shoafstall, Priscilla m. Grove, Mich	Apr. 27, 1822	Seth Shoafstall		4b211	
Shoafstall, Sally m. Friese, Peter (Mich	May 29, 1820	Solomon Shrode	W.N.Scott	4b149	
Shoafstall, Sophia m. Turner, James	July 1, 1820	Seth Shoafstall	James Redmond	4b153	
Shoas, Jane m. Curtis, Edward	May 1, 1789	Peter Potsal		6b216	cr 20
Shober, Adam m. Geiger, Nancy	Aug. 20, 1840	John Shober	Hugh Vance		
Shober, Ann m. Myers, John	Feb. 6, 1812	John Shober	Rev. Reebenack	3b211	gc 12, mr 41 *
Shober, Cath m. Brady, James	May 8, 1813	John Shober	Rev. Reebenack	3b261	gc 13, mr 31 *
Shober, Henry m. Miller, Eliz.	Mar. 30, 1820	Adam Shober		4b142	mr 3 *
Shober, Mary Ann m. Haddox, John P.	Apr. 16, 1840	John Shober		6b206	gc 14
?Shober, Susannah m. Bales, David	May 20, 1815		Rev. Reebenack	3b325	*
?Shober, Susannah m. Baler, Joseph	May 21, 1815		Rev. Reebenack		*
Shockey, David m. Hoyle, Rachel	Mar. 30, 1797	Mathias Riser		1b 3	
Shockey, Eliz. m. Miller, John	Sept 5, 1800	Christian Shockey		2b 85	*

*John Shoafstall also was a suretor.

Name	(marriage)	(suretor)	(minister)	(bond)	ref.
Shockey, John m. Crabb, Priscilla	Aug. 23, 1789	John Shockey	David Thomas	3b194	mr 37 *
Shockey, Susannah m. Crouse, Christ'n	Feb. 3, 1811	James Steidman		2b113	*
Shoebridge, John m. Steidman, Margt	1801	Patrick McGonagle		1b 70	gc 7 *
Shone, Henry m. McGonagle, Cath.	Dec. 7, 1797	John R. Turner	David Young	7b252	
Shook, Andrew m. Turner, Sarah A.	Apr. 7, 1852	Thos. Henshaw		5b 18	
Shook, Jacob m. Frye, Cath.	Apr. 8, 1825	John Pitzer Jr.		4b 39	**
Shook, John m. Keesecker, Rachel	June 30, 1817		W.N.Scott	3b253	**
Shoop, Daniel m. Lindsey, Ann(Fanny)	Feb. 24, 1813	John Lindsey		2b259	gc 13
Shoppert, Christina m.Anderson, Jas.	Apr. 6, 1805	Nicholas Shoppert	Rev. Reebenack	3b 20	mr 22 *
Shoppert, Jacob m. Miller, Mary	May 22, 1806	Henry Job	Christian Streit		
Shoppert, George m. Waters, Cath.	Dec. 25, 1792				gc 2
Short, Cloe m. Richards, Abr'm	Aug. 19, 1790		David Young		cr 5 mr 5 *
Short, Daniel m. Myers, Eliz.	Dec. 20, 1796		Moses Hoge		gc 6
Short, George m. Horner(Hamer),Eliz.	Oct. 2, 1802	Andrew Yates	David Young	2b183	cr 32 mr 21 *
Short, George m. Ray. Priscilla	Feb. 28, 1793		Richard Swift		gc 2 mr 20 *
Short, James m. Slaughter, Eliz.	Sept. 1, 1801	Robert Filson	David Young	2b141	cr 31
Short, Mary Ann m. Ray, Thomas	Oct. 28, 1791		Richard Swift	2b106	gc 1 mr 19 *
Short, Nancy m. Nichols, Christian	Dec. 29, 1801	George Short	David Young	1b 38	cr 31 mr 21 *
Short, Sarah m. Sewel(Sue,Sael)Word	Sept. 4, 1797	James Flemming	Richard Swift	2b179	gc 6
Shorter, Sally m. Painter, Jacob	Aug. 27, 1802	Benedict Rush	Richard Swift	2b249	cr 32 mr 22 *
Shortz, Cath. m. Harden, Christian	Dec. 15, 1804	Jacob Shertle	Christian Streit	5b 3	cr 16 mr 48 *
Shortz, Julia m. Eckhart, Henry	Apr. 17, 1797	Andrew Ullum(Ulm)	Chas. P. Krauth	1b 7	gc 6
Shough, ? m. Ott, Jacob	Sept. 2, 1805	Michael Yearly	David Young	2b270	
Shover, John m. Bowers, Susannah	Dec. 22, 1785	Joseph Shough	Hugh Vance		mr 34 *
Shover, Thomas m. McCrary(McCrea)Jane	Feb. 9, 1786		Hugh Vance		mr 33 *
Showalter, Ann Rebecca m. Kelly,Thos	Oct. 22, 1834			6b 22	
Showalter, Eliza m. Fishburn, John	Dec. 11, 1815	John McCleary		3b350	cr 26 mr 51 *
Showalter, Harriet m. Wysong, Lewis	Dec. 4, 1820	Joseph Showalter		5b 36	cr 36 mr 41 *
Showalter, Jane m. McCleary,John Jr.	Feb. 14, 1826	John McCleary Jr.	W.N.Scott	4b168	cr 51 mr 51 *
Showalter, Joseph Jr. m.Kownslar,Elnr	Nov. 13, 1826	Mericle Locke	Chas. P. Krauth	5b 56	cr 53 mr 53 *
Showalter, Wm. m. Miller, Eliz.	Sept. 5, 1828	John Shober	W.N.Scott	5b106	
Showers, Jacob m. Small, Mary G.	Aug. 27, 1834	Vincent Bell	John Winter	6b 16	mr 34 *
Showers, John m. Bowers, Susannah	Dec. 22, 1785	Jacob A. Grove	Wm. Monroe		mr 68 *
Showers, Maria E. m. Doll, Bernard	Apr. 10, 1834	Ezekiel Showers		6b 4	mr 54 *
Showers, Maria Eliz. m. McCrea, Wm.	Aug. 18, 1814	Robert Wilson	Hugh Vance	3b300	
Showers, Mary E. m. Gardner, Abr'm	Oct. 8, 1832	Ezekiel Showers	John Howell	5b242	
Showers, Naomi m. Fouke, Joseph	Dec. 13, 1824	Segismund Showers	Nathan Young	4b280	mr 47 *
Showers, Philip m. Seibert, Margt A.	Nov. 15, 1843	George Maxwell	J.L.Bromwell	6b307	
Showers, Segismund m.Miller, Polly	Feb. 8, 1820	James Maxwell		4b133	mr 57 *
Showers, Susan M. m. Alburtis, Samuel	Mar. 13, 1847	Ezekiel Showers	Nathan Young	7b 91	mr 77 *
Shrader, Michael m. Morlatt, Sarah	Oct. 16, 1813	Abel Dunham	John Winters	3b273	
Shriver, David m. Pagle, Mary	Oct. 17, 1805	Henry Shriver	Rev. Reebenack	3b 2	gc 13
*Short, Cath. m. Harden, Christian	Mar. 1, 1825	Andrew Ulm	Chas. P. Krauth	5b 3	mr 48 *

(name / marriage)	(marriage date)			(surety)	(minister)	(bond)		
Shriver, Eliz. m. Baker, George	Feb. 8,	1800		Michael Bryerly	David Young	2b 52 / 6b 3	gc 9	mr 67 *
Shriver, Mary m. Keppler,John Rev'd	Apr. 4,	1834		Arch'd Shearer	Samuel Keppler	6b 61		*
Shroad, Wm. m. Baker. Eliz.	Oct. 31,	1835		Jonathan Baker	Samuel Keppler	3b254		*
Shrode, David m. Copelan, Sarah Sally	Mar. 1,	1813		Wm. Copelan	Rev. Reebenack	3b125	gc 13	*
Shrode, George m. Booth, Nancy	Nov. 22,	1809		Jonathan Booth	Rev. Reebenack	3b264 / 6b 47	gc 10	mr 54 *
Shrode, Hannah m. Frees, John	Apr. 31,	1813		Solomon Shrode	Nathan Young	4b271 / 2b104		
Shrode, Mary Jane m. Baker, Jonathan	June 22,	1835		William Strode	J.E. Jackson			
Shrode, Solomon m. Whitelock,Rosanna	Sept 4,	1824		Edward Southwood		7b 60		mr 77 *
Shrode, Susannah m. Crim, Peter	Dec. 22,	1800		Solomon Shrode		7b123		
Shuart, George m. Swinley, Mary E.	Mar. 2,	1846		John Swinley	Richard Brown		gc 14	**
Shuart, Wm. m. Thornburg, Mary S.	Feb. 14,	1848		Thos. Thornburg			gc 8	*
Shuck, Isaac m. Werbel, Eliz.	June 11,	1815			Rev. Reebenack	4b 39		
Shuck, John m. Keesecker, Rachel	Nov. 12,	1817		John Pitzer Jr.	W.N.Scott	1b146		
Shuh, Jacob m. Copenhaver, Cath.	Feb. 23,	1798		Charles Myers	David Young	5b257		mr 68 *
Shuh, Barbara m. Bower, Wm.	Mar. 2,	1833		Solomon Shuh		5b259		mr 78 *
Shuh, Henry m. Keesecker, Rosannah	July 19,	1833		Eli Flemming		2b 77	cr 33	mr 11 *
Shuler, Conrad m. Rife, Hannah	Apr. 21,	1800		Conrad Rife	John Howell	6b 9	gc 6	*
Shull, Mary Ann m. Kern, Wm.	July 28,	1834		John Shull	John Winter	7b102	gc 13	*
Shull, Mary Va. m. Franceway, Bennet	Mar. 6,	1847		David Shull		2b256	gc 9	mr 59 *
Shull, ? m. Carr, (Carey),Robert		1805		John Shull				
Shulton, Eliz. m. Curry(Carey),John	July 31,	1795			John Boyd	1b 14		mr 74 *
Shunk, Mary m. Barnhart, Henry	May 2,	1797		Simon Shunk	David Young	3b253		mr 83 *
Shupe, Daniel m. Lindsey, Ann(Fanny)	Feb. 24,	1813		John lindsey	Rev. Reebenack	5b 77	cr 14	mr 24 *
Shy, Rachel m. Wilson, Danial	Aug. 30,	1827		Seaman Garard	Nathan Young	2b 73		mr 34 *
Sibert, Henry m. Hoffman, Susannah	June 17,	1800		Wendle Sibert	David Young	6b284	cr 15	mr 7 *
Sibole, Ebeneser m. Swingle, Eliz.	Nov. 19,	1842		Michael Coleman		6b281		mr 80 *
Sibole, James m. Hooper, Mary E.	Oct. 22,	1842		Wm. McDonald	Mayberry Goheen	7b142		mr 80 *
Sibole, Morgan m. Vance, Harriet	Dec. 20,	1849		Wm. Smart	Lewis F. Wilson	6b132		mr 79 *
Sibole, Presley B. m. Higgins, Eliz.	Feb. 19,	1838		John Shull	James Watts	5b157		
Sickafoos, Sarah Ann m.Williams,Dav.	Mar. 11,	1830		John Sickafoos		3b188		
Sigler, Martin m. Bowersmith, Mary	May 29,	1811		James Harrison	John B. Hoge		cr 14	mr 24 *
Siddelman, Rosy m. Young, Anthony	July 28,	1785			Hugh Vance			mr 34 *
Sidmor, Philip m. Banner, Mary	Oct. 2,	1791			Christian Stredt		cr 15	mr 7 *
Sigler, Eliz. m. McCoy, Joseph	Apr. 13,	1850		Wm. Sigler	John Bauman	7b181		mr 80 *
Sigler, Rhuanna m. Hoffman, Michael	July 20,	1850		Mathew Spear	D.F.Bragunier	7b189		mr 80 *
Sigler, Wm. m. Horn (Howe),Marg. Jane	Nov. 6,	1848		Jeptha Hensel	B.M.Schmucker	7b139		mr 79 *
Sigmund, Cath. m. Baird, Samuel	Dec. 1,	1791			David Young		gc 1	
Siler, Barbara m. Yost, John	Apr. 22,	1829		Henry Siler				
Siler, Bennet m. Wigle, Sarah	June 20,	1837		John Wigle		5b128		
Siler, Cath. m. Snyder, Jacob	Dec. 12,	1825		Philip Siler	Nathan Young	6b109		mr 58 *
Siler, Cath. m. Thompson, James	Apr. 28,	1806		Jacob Siler		5b 29		
Siler, Charity m. Fraise, John	Jan. 16,	1787			Hugh Vance	3b 17	cr 33	mr 43 *
Siler, Daniel m. Potts, Peggy	June 18,	1795			John Boyd			mr 11 *

Name	(marriage)	(surety)	(minister)	(bond)	
Siler, Elis. m. Chiles, John	Oct. 12, 1818	Philip Siler		4b 82	gc 14 *
Siler, Elis. m. Saveley, Jacob	Aug. 8, 1815	James Thompson	Rev. Reebenack	3b332	*
Siler, Esther m. Riley, Dennis	May 25, 1811	Conrad Starry		3b187	*
Siler, George m. Borer, Anna	Mar. 12, 1812	Jacob Borer		3b216	*
Siler, Hannah m. Myers, Jacob	Mar. 17, 1832	Philip Siler	Nathan Long	9b220	mr 64 *
Siler, Hannah m. Stookey, Samuel	Feb. 8, 1819	James Thompson	W.N.Scott	4b 99	mr 30 *
Siler, Henry m. Siler, Mary	Jan. 5, 1833	Philip Siler	Nathan Young	9b252	mr 65 *
Siler, Jacob m. Canby, Beulah Marg't	Oct. 12, 1843	Philip Siler	Lewis F. Wilson	6b306	mr 74 *
Siler, Jacob m. Castle, Elis.	Apr. 12, 1830	Elias Siler	Nathan Young	5b161	mr 60 *
?Siler, Jacob m. Salehamer, Julia A.	Oct. 24, 1837	John Castle	James Watts	6b121	
Siler, John m. Moore, Rebecca	Oct. 26, 1822	Jacob Hoke		4b227	
Siler, John m. Thompson, Susannah	Mar. 17, 1804	George Crammer		2b227	
Siler, Kath. m. Reed, Samuel	Apr. 21, 1812	Bennet Thompson		3b222	
Siler, Margt m. Tabler, Wm. Levi	Apr. 23, 1849	David Soister		7b155	
Siler, Mary m. Schneider, John	Apr. 26, 1792	Mathias Kne	David Young		gc 1 *
Siler, Mary m. Siler, Henry	Jan. 5, 1833	Philip Siler	Nathan Young	9b252	mr 65 *
Siler, Mary m. Snider, Martin	Dec. , 1824	Launcelot Cofflan	Chas. P. Krauth	4b280	mr 47 *
Siler, Philip m. Ott, Mary	Sept. 28, 1797	Benj. Ott		1b 48	
Siler, Ruth m. Bacon, Isaac	Jan. 16, 1801	Jacob Siler	John Boyd	2b111	cr 35 mr 19 *
Siler, Sarah m. Everhart, Nathan	Aug. 1, 1816	Philip Siler	Rev. Reebenack	4b 15	gc 15 mr 22 *
Siler, Sarah m. Myers, George	July 30, 1858				
Siling, Mildred m. Clodinger, Philip	May 30, 1805	Henry Clodinger	J.H.Jennings	2b262	
Silver, Ann Amelia m.McKown, Warner	June 2, 1828	Francis Silver	John Bond	5b102	cr 28 *
Silver, Francis m. Beall, Anna	Sept. 21, 1802	Zephaniah Beall	J.E.Jackson	2b182	mr 72 *
Silver, Harriet m. Jacques, Arthur	Feb. 26, 1841	John Miles	John Light	6b235	
?Silver, Jacob m. Salehamer, Julia A.	Oct. 26, 1837	Wm. Maxwell	James Watts	3b224	*
Silver, Jane m. McDonald, John	May 13, 1812	James McDonald	Rev. Reebenack	3b260	gc 12 *
Silver, Joseph m. Miller, Sarah	Apr. 20, 1813	John Faris	Rev. Reebenack	5b185	gc 13 *
Silver, Lydia m. Evans, Isaac W.	Jan. 20, 1831	Zephaniah Silver		5b 68	
Silver, Nancy m. Edwards, Joseph	Apr. 30, 1827	Rich. A. Richardson	J.E.Jackson	5b 11	mr 48 *
Silver, Samuel m. Otto, Ann	May 3, 1825	Thomas Jordan	Chas. P. Krauth	6b134	
Silver, Thomas m. Jordan, Ann E.	May , 1838	?			
Silver, Wm. m. Myers, Polly	Feb. 27, 1805			2b258	
Silver, Zephaniah m=Henshaw,Martha J	Apr. 17, 1834	Hiram Henshaw	Jas. M. Brown	6b 6	mr 68 *
Simmerman, Rachel m. Mound, Wm.	Feb. 5, 1794		B. Page		mr 40 *
Simmons, Ann m. Bennett, Rees	Apr. 14, 1800	Jonas Chamberlain		2b 75	
Simmons, Ann Maria m. McAbee, Jas. B	July 3, 1852	John W. Blakeney	David Thomas	7b252	cr 37 mr 86 *
Simmons, Jonas m. Sheets, Cath.	Apr. 8, 1798	George Sheets	John Potts	1b109	mr 14 *
Simmons, Rachel m. Bane, Abner	Apr. 18, 1789		D. Thomas		mr 37 *
Simmons, Samuel m. Rees, Rebecca	Dec. 23, 1822	Ellis Rees		4b231	
Simmons, Susan m. O'Brien, John	Feb. 6, 1845			7b 25	
Simpson, Joseph m. Lewis, Sally	Mar. 19, 1810	Joseph Simpson		3b143	
Simpson, W.H. m. Peterman, Emily L.	June 16, 1853	Jacob Simpson	G. W. Cooper		mr 87 *

Name	(marriage)		(surety)	(minister)	(bond)			
Singer, John m. Stinson, Eliz.	July 1,	1803	M. Morgan		2b205			
Sipe, Michael m. Collember, Patty	Mar. 9,	1812	James Callahan		3b214			
Sirbaugh, Henry m. Hardy, Rebecca J	Sept 10,	1845	Jos. L. Hardy		7b 43			*
Sivers, Eliz. m. Howe, Andrew								*
Sively, Patrick m. Murray, Ann	Dec. 10,	1840	Michael Murray	David Young	6b227	gc 3		*
Slain, Daniel m. Rise, Mary	Feb. 20,	1817		Mathias Riser			mr 4	*
Slaine, Peter m. Freshour, Barbara	Sept 1,	1789		Hugh Vance		cr 40	mr 4	*
Slater, James m. Hlue, Nancy	Jan. 7,	1807	Fred. Hlue		3b 46			
Slater, Mary m. Harper, Alex.	Oct. 30,	1794		John Boyd	4b207	cr 21	mr 8	*
Slaughter, Amelia m.Eichelberger,Dav.	Jan. 31,	1822	James Sterrett	George M. Frye	1b170		mr 44	*
Slaughter, Cath. m. Aiken, Wm.	Feb. 22,	1799	William Askew		2b141	cr 31	mr 20	*
Slaughter, Eliz. n. Short, James	Sept 1,	1801	Robert Filson	Richard Swift	1b122			
Slaughter, Wm. Jr. m. Ward, Margt.	July 25,	1798	Joel Ward		3b 77			
Slenck, Cath. m. Ward, Aaron	Nov. 14,	1807	John Basore		5b 48		fmr 50	*
Sloan, Evelina m. Sharp, Horatio	Aug. 15,	1826	James Sloan	John Winter	4b267		mr 50	*
Sloan, Maria m. Sharp, John	June 22,	1824	?	John Winter				*
Slocum, Betsy m. Heath, James	May 11,	1803		David Young		gc 10		*
Slomacre, Cath. m. Hedt, Peter	Apr. 16,	1795		David Young		gc 4		*
Slonaker, Mary m. Files, Jacob	Feb. 7,	1854		John O. Proctor				, *
Slone, Henry m. McGonagle, Cath.	Dec. 6,	1797	Patrick McGonagle	David Young	1b 70	gc 7	mr 4	*
Slough, Sarah m. Baker, Christian	Feb. 20,	1789	David Boyer	Christian Streit	7b184	cr 15	mr 81	*
Sluser(Sluper),Sara m.Gaither, Rich.	Apr. 28,	1850	Mathias Sly	Henry Furlong	1b130			
Sly, Cath. m. Ager, John	Sept 8,	1798						
Sly, Mary m. Melvin, Thomas	Mar. 2,	1792		Moses Hoge			mr 38	*
Sly, Rachel m. Wilson, Daniel	Aug. 30,	1827	Seaman Garard	Nathan Young	5b 77		mr 99	*
Small, Adam m. Myers, Mary	Mar. 26,	1832	Henry Myers	J.M.Brown	5b222		mr 64	*
Small, Ann Rebecca m. Mason, James	Jan. 20,	1851	John C. Small	B.M.Schmucker	7b211		mr 84	*
Small, Barbara Ellen m. Noll, Geo.M.	Nov. 6,	1849	John M. Small	D.F.Bragunier	7b167		mr 80	*
Small, Cath. m. Ramer, George	May 18,	1844	Wm. Bowers		7b 1			
Small, Cath. m. Swindle, George	Feb. 7,	1852	Henry Riner	Lewis F. Wilson	7b244		mr 87	*
Small, Eliz. m. Stayer, Daniel	Mar. 8,	1815	Jacob Small		3b313			
Small, Ellen m. Brown,Benj. N. Rev'd	Oct. 4,	1837	John M. Wolff	E.P.Phelps	6b113		mr 69	*
Small, George m. Grove, Mary	May 29,	1822	Peter Grove	Chas. P. Krauth	4b215		mr 45	*
Small, George m. Nobst(Ubbet), Eliz.	Jan. 10,	1793		David Young		gc 2		*
Small, Henry m. Carson, Elinor	June 9,	1795		John Boyd		cr 33		*
Small, Henry C. m. Seibert, Eliza	Mar. 30,	1831	Michael Seibert	Jacob Medtart	5b190		mr 10	*
Small, Henry m. Smith, Mary	Mar. 14,	1826	John Strother	Hugh Vance	5b 37		mr 63	*
Small, Jacob A. m. Cushwa, Mary	Apr. 28,	1789	David Hill		6b206		mr 37	*
Small, Jacob A. m. Hill, Ann	May 10,	1840	John McNeal		2b234		mr 51	*
Small, James m. McNeal, Margaret	Mar. 28,	1804	David Kilner		5b 5			
Small, John m. Kilner, Eliz.	Nov. 24,	1825	James Small	Chas. P. Krauth	3b101	gc 10	mr 48	*
Small, John m. Mason, Polly	Nov. 24,	1808		Rev. Reebenack				
Small, John C. m. Mong, Sarah	Mar. 21,	1827	John Mong	Chas. P. Krauth	5b 65		mr 51	*
*Sippey, Joseph m. Johnson, Lucretia	Feb. 20,	1787		Hugh Vance			mr 43	*

209

Name	(marriage)	(surety)	(minister)	(bond)	
Small, Lucinda m. Porterfield, Abr'm	Dec. 2, 1852	Samuel Williamson	R.A.Fink	5b151	mr 86 *
Small, Margt m. Dugan, Thomas T. Mrs.	Feb. 4, 1830	Wm. Small	Jas. M. Brown	5b114	mr 54 *
Small, Mary m. Couchman, Michael	Dec. 4, 1828	John C. Small	Jacob Medtart	7b117	mr 63 *
Small, Mary Ellen m. Couchman, Benj.	Dec. 27, 1847	Jacob A. Grove		6b 16	
Small, Mary G. m. Showers, Jacob	Aug. 27, 1834	Samuel Williamson	James M. Brown	5b151	mr 54 *
Small, Margt Mrs. m. Dugan, Thos. T.	Feb. 4, 1830	Henry Small	W.N.Scott	4b 17	mr 26 *
Small, Nancy m. Paul, Hugh	Apr. 11, 1816	Jacob Small	Jacob Medtart	5b192	mr 63 *
Small, Nancy m. Ropp, Daniel	Apr. 5, 1831	Robert Small	John B. Hoge	4b 72	mr 29 *
Small, Nancy m. Windle, John	June 9, 1818	Jacob Small	Chas. P. Krauth	4b215	mr 45 *
Small, Peggy m. Seibert, Henry I.	June 3, 1822	Jacob Small	Rev. Reebenack	3b113	ge 10
Small, Polly m. Folk(-sul,-al), Jacob	May 18, 1809	Jacob Small	Chas. P. Krauth	4b256	mr 46 *
Small, Ruth Cath. m. Seibert, John	Feb. 4, 1824	John Boyd			cr 33
Small, Samuel m. Shaw, Mary	Apr. 7, 1795			4b183	mr 10 *
Small, Samuel m. Williamson, Margt.	May 8, 1821	Samuel Williamson	John B. Hoge	5b 5	mr 42 *
Small, Wm. m. Couchman, Polly	Mar. 23, 1825	George Couchman	Chas. P. Krauth	7b215	mr 48 *
Small, Wm. C. m. Couchman, Ann	Feb. 25, 1851	John Couchman	B.M.Schumucker	6b210	mr 84 *
Small, Wm. C. m. Williamson, Margt.	May 23, 1840	John Williamson			
Smallwood, Lydia m. Rhondirl. Reuben	Mar. 21, 1789	Hebron Smallwood		1b x	
Smallwood, Nancy m. Strain, Samuel	July 27, 1800	George Smallwood	Moses Hoge	2b 78	mr 19 *
Smart, Amelia m. Kyser, John	Apr. 29, 1825	Daniel Smart		5b 9	cr 29
Smart, Elisa m. Kyser (Ky-,Ky-,David	Aug. 21, 1833	Zachariah Smart	Nathan Young	5b280	mr 66 *
Smart, Sarah Ann m. Castle, Elijah	Nov. 14, 1826	Sarah Smart	Nathan Young		mr 99 *
Smart, Tabitha m. Castle, Elijah	Nov. 13, 1826	Daniel Smart		5b 55	
Smart, Tabitha m. Paden, Jacob	Oct. 22, 1828	John Strother	Benedict Reynolds	5b111	mr 52 *
Smeltzer, Leonard m. Waltinger, Tracy	Jan. 1, 1820			4b129	
Smeltzer, Mary m. Smith, Zachary	Apr. 15, 1816	Charles Butt			
Smeltzer, Michael m. Butt, Dorcas Ann	May 23, 1835	?	Rev. Reebenack	6b 45	gc 15
Smeltzer, Peggy m. Potter, Ralph	Nov. 5, 1821	Benjamin Butt	Elisha Gardner	4b196	mr 68 *
Smith, Aaron m. Butt, Mary	Oct. 9, 1843	Robert Jones	Nathan Young	6b305	mr 57 *
Smith, Alex. m. Mock, Margt.	Aug. 23, 1806			3b 26	
Smith, Andrew m. Holderman, Cath.	Oct. 7, 1792	John Strother			ge 2
Smith, Ann m. Hunter, Philip P.	June 26, 1823	Wm. H. VanDoren	David Young	4b242	mr 46 *
Smith, Ann E. m. Callahan, Joshua S.	Mar. 25, 1852		John Mathews	7b250	
Smith, Ann Elisa m. Gallaher, Joshua	Mar. 13, 1852				
Smith, Barbara m. Aris(Earis), Edward	Aug. 1, 1799	Philip Smith		2b 13	mr 86 *
Smith, Basil m. Wolfe, Elis.	Dec. 27, 1809	Philip Wolfe	David Thomas	3b131	cr 34
Smith, Betsy m. Malone, James	Mar. 26, 1798	Chas. McGowan	Richard Swift	1b 91	ge 11
Smith, Cath. m. Esldant, Charles	Aug. 20, 1827	John Murray	Rev. Reebenack	5b 75	ge 7
Smith, Cath. m. Leiby, Jonathan	Mar. 4, 1818	Jacob Waggoner	David Young	4b 65	mr 16 *
Smith, Cath. m. Rimley, John	Aug. 15, 1797	Fred. Bower	B. Reynolds		
Smith, Charles m. Burke, Mary	Aug. 13, 1802	David Garard Jr.		1b 28	cr 12
Smith, Charles m. England, Elis.	Jan. 13, 1810	Jacob England	Richard Swift	2b157	mr 51 *
Smith, Christ'r m. Roberts, Hannah	Jan. 24, 1788		Hugh Vance	3b134	mr 36 *

	(marriage)	(surety)	(minister)	(bond)	
Smith, Conrad m. Griffith, Frances	Oct. 11, 1850	Nicholas Smith	Henry Furlong	7b200	mr 81 *
Smith, Daniel m. Burr, Mary	June 29, 1784		Hugh Vance		mr 52 *
Smith, David m. Seibert, Eliz.	June 16, 1827	Jacob Seibert		5b 72	*
Smith, Eli m. Gill, Sarah R.	Dec. 20, 1834	John Gill	J.E.Jackson	6b 25	*
Smith, Elisha m. Rees, Jane	Feb. 26, 1825	Jesse Holliday	John Winter	5b 2	mr 50 *
Smith, Eliz. m. Bishop, Michael	Oct. 12, 1793		David Young		go 2
Smith, Eliz. m.Blume(Bloomer),Philip	Sept 3, 1819	John Lowe	W.N.Scott	4b118	mr 30 *
Smith, Eliz. m. Bockins,Daniel David	June 26, 1823	?	Chas. P. Krauth	4b247	mr 46 *
Smith, Eliz. m. Brakefield, John	Oct. 27, 1821	Jacob Zimmerman		4b185	*
Smith, Eliz. m. Charinger, David	Jan. 3, 1795		David Young		*
Smith, Eliz. m.Purkey(Pankey), John	Nov. 14, 1797		Richard Swift		go 5
Smith, Eliz. m. Pierce(Pea-),Jos-S.C.	Apr. 13, 1819	Mathew R.Gerrard	Nathan Young	4b122	cr 26
Smith, Eliz. m. Unger, David Daniel	Oct. 30, 1818	George Snowdeal	Mathias Riser	4b 69	mr 13 *
Smith, George A. m. Cook, Susan	Mar. 7, 1838	Jacob Cook		6b148	mr 56 *
Smith, Gracy m. Powers, Thomas	Oct. 16, 1815	Christian Tabler		3b313	mr 29 *
Smith, Hannah m. Starry, Daniel	Nov. 29, 1798	Alex. Smith	David Young	1b140	go 8
Smith, Harrison . m. Waggoner,Susan	May 19, 1843	Andrew Waggoner		6b308	*
Smith, Henry m. Fricker, Rebecca			Christian Streit		cr 15 mr 4 *
Smith, Jacob m. Beatty, Margt.	May 23, 1789	Anthony Rosenbg'r	Chas. P. Krauth	4b239	mr 46 *
Smith, Jacob m. Keesecker, Fanny Mrs.	Nov. 23, 1828	?		5b105	*
Smith, Jacob m. Miller, Kitty	Oct. 15, 1819	George Miller.	W.N.Scott	4b124	mr 40 *
Smith, Jacob m. Morlatt, Eliz.	Sept 8, 1851	Philip Smith	Richard Swift	2b 93	mr 19 *
Smith, Jacob m. Morris, Ann Amelia	Apr. 23, 1800	John Morris		7b230	cr 31
Smith, James m. Hume, Beersheba	Nov. 8, 1799	Hubbard Hume		2b 3	*
Smith, James m. Parker(Packer),Mary	Dec. 27, 1800	Henry Parker	Richard Swift	2b 97	mr 19 *
Smith, James m. Stout, Cath.	Oct. 30, 1814	Edward Aris		3b307	cr 31
Smith, Jane m. Boarland, Alex.	Oct. 6, 1797	Robert Gallaher	David Young	1b 59	go 7
Smith, Jean m. Brown, Andrew	May 10, 1797	Henry Small	David Young	1b 52	go 7
Smith, Jeremiah m. Snyder, Eliz.	Feb. 11, 1832	Jacob Snyder	Wm. Monroe	5b229	*
Smith, John m. Bull, Usomen	Nov. 29, 1781		Daniel Sturges		mr 65 *
Smith, John F. m. Crim, Susan	Jan. 10, 1826	John Sencindiver	Chas. P. Krauth	5b 57	mr 31 *
Smith, John H. m. Light, Rebecca	Mar. 8, 1825	Peter Light	Chas. P. Krauth	4b284	mr 51 *
Smith, John F. m. Pultz, Susannah	Nov. 23, 1830	George S. Boltz		5b155	mr 48 *
Smith, John Rufus m. Brewer, Mary E,	Feb. 17, 1853	Harrison Waite	G. Stephenson		mr 88 *
Smith, Jonas m. Fredze, Hannah	Sept 12, 1836	Wm. Tabler	Moses Hoge	6b 71	cr 38 *
Smith, Jonas m. Harden, Susannah	July 21, 1818		(a run away match)/	4b 78	mr 20 *
Smith, Jonathan m. Ault, Barbara	June 18, 1801	Isaac Hawxer	Moses Hoge	1b118	*
Smith, Joseph m. Barkman, Cath.	July 27, 1798	Philip Siler	Lewis F. Wilson	6b302	mr 74 *
Smith, Joseph m. Compton, Eliz.	Mar. 8, 1843	Joseph Thomas	Moses Hoge	1b 88	mr 14 *
Smith, Joseph m. Hutchcraft, Ann	Mar. 4, 1798	John Lowe		4b161	cr 36 *
Smith, Joseph m. Lowe, Matty	Dec. 15, 1820		David Young		go 5
Smith, Joseph m. Seaver, Mary	Dec. 25, 1795		John Boyd		cr 21 mr 8 *
Smith, Lewis m. McAlister, Nancy	Sept 14, 1794				

Name	(marriage)		(surety)	(minister)	(bond)	ref
Smith, Lydia m. McMahon, Barrett	Apr. 18	1844	Wm. Smith	David Young	6b319	gc 7 *
Smith, Margt. m. Byers, Joseph	Apr. 6,	1798	Jacob Tinsell	John Light	1b106	mr 76 *
1Smith, Margt. A. m.Burket, Parker	Sept 4,	1845	Jacob Smith	John Light	7b 42	mr 76 *
1Smith, Martha A. m.Burket(Bec-)ParkerSept 3	Nov. 6,	1795	Jacob Smith	Richard Swift	7b 42	cr 26 mr 10 *
Smith, Mary m. Bingan, Nicholas	Oct. 22,	1804	Zachary Murray	Hugh Vance	2b245	
Smith, Mary m. Bumgardner, John	Nov. 1,	1827	Joseph Henderson		5b 83	
Smith, Mary m. Burch, Barnet	Jan. 15,	1789		Hugh Vance		mr 37 *
Smith, Mary m. Small, Henry	June 15,	1848	John R. Crook	Wm. Love	7b132	mr 80 *
Smith, Mary m. Woolard, John	June 15,	1811	James Harrison	John B. Hoge	3b188	cr 14 mr 24 *
Smith, Mary Bower m.Zeigler, Martin	May 29,	1802	Samuel Davenport		2b168	
Smith, Mary Mrs. m.Murray, Zachariah	Apr. 3.	1815		Rev. Reebenack		gc 15 *
Smith, Moses m. Gilbert, Elinor	Sept 1,	1815	Joseph Coltman	John B. Hoge	4b104	mr 29 *
Smith, Nancy m. Clarke, Henry	Apr. 8.	1789	Wm. Stribling		1b x	
Smith, Nancy m. Jackson, Thomas	Apr. 2,	1801	Peter Poisal		2b155	
Smith, Nancy m. Poisal(Pisal),Jacob	Apr. 23,	1801	Robert Gallaher		2b145	
Smith, Nelly m. Tiser, John Clark	Dec. 31,	1848	Jacob Gapman		7b128	
Smith, Nicholas m. Hess, Polly	Oct. 21,	1804	Wm. Smith		2b224	
Smith, Olly m. Grubb, Wm.	May 16,	1842	John McManee		6b274	
Smith, Patrick m. Negary, Ann	Feb. 27,	1816	Jacob Needler		4b 8	mr 26 *
Smith, Philip m. Needler, Polly	Aug. 6,	1811	James Mason	W.N.Scott	3b201	gc 12 **
Smith, Polly m. Morlatt, George	Aug. 14,	1811	Zachariah Murray	Rev. Reebenack	3b182	
Smith, Rhoda m. Roney, James	Nov. 22,	1812	?		3b357	
Smith, Sally m. Seaborn, Peter	Mar. 26.	1818	Joseph Smith	John B. Hoge	4b103	gc 10 ne 29 *
Smith, Sally m. Zimmerman, Jacob	Apr. 2,	1809	Jesse Smith	Rev. Reebenack	4b165	
Smith, Sarah m. Bemden George	Oct. 17,	1820	Christ'r Olinger		3b 79	
Smith, Sarah m. Keller, Samuel	Dec. 14,	1807	Valentine Ale		3b111	
Smith, Sarah m. Low, John	Apr. 10,	1809	Edward Aris	Rev. Reebenack	3b226	gc 13 *
Smith, Sarah m. Painter, George	May 21,	1812		Hugh Vance		cr 39 *
Smith, Sarah m. Stout(Aout),Philip	Aug. 10,	1789		A.G. Chenoweth		mr 4 *
Smith, Sarah E. m. Wilcox, Robert	Dec. 6,	1852				mr 87 *
Smith, Sarah E. m. Bender, Samuel	Apr. 18,	1800	Benj. Boley		2b 66	
Smith, Seth m. Boley, Eliz.	Feb. 9,	1842	James McSherry		6b263	
Smith, Thomas m. Snyder, Cath.	Nov. 25,	1819	James Stephenson	John B. Hoge	4b124	mr 31 *
Smith, Thos. C. m. Cooper, Jane	July 27.	1824	Alex. Cooper		4b268	
Smith, Thos. C. m. Price, Isabella	?	1797	Cath. Campbell	David Young	1b 40	gc 7 *
Smith, Wm. m. Campbell, Sarah	Sept 16,	1843	Adam Small	Lewis F. Wilson	6b300	mr 74 *
Smith, Wm. A. m. Paull, Sarah Ann	June 12,	1816	Wm. Palmer		4b 3	
Smith, Zachariah m. Gerickson, Mary	Apr. 15,	1816				gc 15 *
Smith, Zachary m. Smeltzer, Mary	Apr. 15,	1792		Rev. Reebenack		mr 39 *
Smithers, Sally m. Richards, Daniel	May 4,	1785		Moses Hoge		mr 1 *
Smithey, Ann m. Shirley(Thirley)John	Feb. 7,	1828	Philip Seckman	Edward Tiffin	9b113	
Smithey, James m. Cram, Rosanna	Nov. 25,					
Snock, Henry m. Love, Matty	Dec. 20,	1809	John Lowe		3b128	

(name)	(marriage)		(suretor)	(minister)	(bond)			
Smock, Mary m. Toole, Joseph	Mar. 5,	1803	Mathias Smock		2b197			
Smock, Wm. m. Kyle, Mary	Nov. 11,	1809	John Kyle	Rev. Reebemack	3b123	gc 10		*
Smoot, Joseph m. Merchant, Leana	Oct. 17,	1815	Jane Merchant		3b343			
Snickers, Eliz. F. m. Brown, Chas.	H.Feb. 17,	1835	Robert T. Brown		6b 31			
Snider, Abr'm m. Miller, Cath.	Jan. 20,	1819	John Strother	W.N.Scott	4b 98		mr 30	*
Snider, Abr'm m. Miller, Mary	Apr. 18,	1807	Jacob Miller		3b 56			
Snider, Barbara m. Wood, Hugh	May 3,	1798	John Bowman	John Boyd	1b110	cr 32	mr 15	* *
Snider, Cath. m. Reef, David	May 10,	1794		David Young		ge 4		* *
Snider, Charlotte m. Miller, Andrew	Apr. 29,	1821	Abr'm Snider		4b183			
Snider, Christina m. Weaver, Peter	Apr. 7,	1789	Henry Snider		1b x			
Snider, Conrad m. Semele, Nancy	Aug. 19,	1797		David Young		ge 6		*
Snider, Eliz. m. Crout, Daniel	Apr. 28,	1797	Jacob Snider		1b 13			
Snider, Eliz. m. Jeffries, Jervis	Mar. 9,	1790		Hugh Vance			mr 38	*
Snider, Eliz. m. Lewis, David	Apr. 10,	1802	John Grantham		2b170		mr 47	* *
Snider, Hannah m. Panabaker, Wm.	Feb. 7,	1825	Jacob Bromwell	J.L.Bromwell	4b289	gc 1		* *
Snider, Henry m. Benner, Christmas	Jan. 6,	1791		David Young				* *
Snider, Jacob m. Butt, Adah	Feb. 17,	1823	Benjamin Thomas	Nathan Young	4b231	gc 15	mr 58	*
Snider, Jacob m. Lowman, Nancy	Dec. 24,	1816	John Lowman	Rev. Reebemack	3b355	cr 13	mr 23	*
Snider, Jacob m. Marquart, Eliz.	Feb 2,	1806	Nicholas Marquart	John Mathews	3b 39	cr 13	mr 23	*
Snider, Jacob m. Ralphsnider,Christ'a	Apr. 22,	1804	Aaron Refender		2b221			
?Snider, John m. Coons, Eliz.	Apr. 22,	1807	David Coons	John Mathews	3b 57	cr 13	mr 23	*
?Snider, John m. Cedans(Credons),Eliz	Apr. 23,	1807 ?		John Mathews		cr 13	mr 23	*
Snider, Maria m. Myers, John	Dec. 13,	1828	Abraham Snider	Nathan Young	5b 99		mr 60	*
Snider, Martin m. Siler, Mary	Jan. 24,	1824	Launcelot Cofflan	Chas. P. Krauth	4b280		mr 47	*
Snider, Mary m. Fist, Charles	Feb. 25,	1825	Martin Snider		4b287			
Snider, Mary m. Lemaster, Daniel	June 16,	1818	W. Snider		4b 63			
Snider, Mary m. Seaborn, Daniel		1807	Theo. Seaborn		3b 61			
Snider, Mary m. Williamson,Jonathan	Feb. 28,	1850		John Light	5b 86		mr 80	*
Snider, Mary m. Wolfe, Jacob	June 29,	1798		David Young	4b267	gc 8		* *
Snider, Nelly m. Chambers, Joseph	Feb. 6,	1789		Hugh Vance			mr 38	*
Snider, Polly m. Miller, Fred.	Sept 11,	1798	Casper Snider		3b 45			
Snider, Sarah m. Ansain, Fred.	Dec. 23,	1824	Samuel Seibert	Chas. P. Krauth	1b131		mr 47	*
Snider, Sarah m. Walgamott, David	Sept 10,	1807	Thomas Butler	John Mathews	3b130	cr 13	mr 23	*
Snider, Uley m. Wolfe, Jacob	Apr. 15,	1798	Hugh Wood		3b 69			
Snider, Wm. m. Hiveley, Susannah		1809	Solomon Shrodes	Rev. Reebemack	3b112	gc 11		*
Snideley, Mary, Mary m. Line, Henry		1807	Jacob Snyder					
Snede, Cath. m. Shane, James		1809	John Booth					
Snodgrass, Ann m. Evans, Joseph	Jan. 2,	1786		Hugh Vance			mr 34	*
Snodgrass, Ann S. m.McFurran, Samuel	July 20,	1829	Wm. Snodgrass	Jas. M. Brown	5b134		mr 55	*
Snodgrass, Andrê m. Henshaw, Levi	July 21, Dec. 16,	1851	Robt. V. Snodgrass	Jas. H. Jennings	7b238		mr 85	*
Snodgrass, Cath. m. Reney, John	Mar. 12,	1789		Hugh Vance			mr 3	*
Snodgrass, Cath.E. m. Robinson,Israel	Sept 17,	1841	Geo. W. Robinson	Lewis F. Wilson	6b246	or 19	mr 72	*
Snodgrass, Eliz. m. Duncan, Thomas	Feb. 12,	1782		Hugh Vance			mr 32	*

Name	(marriage)	(suretor)	(minister)	(bond)	
Snodgrass, Els. m. Hedges, Hesekiah Nov. 20,	1824	Seaman Gerard	John Mathews	4b278	mr 45 *
Snodgrass, Els. m. McMurran, Joseph Dec. 4,	1822	Wm. Snodgrass		4b230	mr 32 *
Snodgrass, Els. m. Murphy, James Nov. 14,	1803	Wm. Snodgrass		2b213	mr 64 *
Snodgrass, Kath. m. Reed, Wallace Wm Feb. 12,	1782		Hugh Vance		mr 32 *
Snodgrass, Levina m. Evans, Wash't'n Oct. 15,	1832	Stephen Snodgrass	Jas. M. Brown	5b244	mr 62 *
Snodgrass, Lucinda m. Hedges, Morgan Dec. 8,	1831	Paul V. Snodgrass	Nathan Young	5b211	mr 83 *
Snodgrass, Lucinda Va. m.Tabb, Ellio Feb. 24,	1848	Robt V. Snodgrass	J.H.Jennings	7b124	mr 74 *
?Snodgrass, Magnus m.Porterfield, Ann Nov. 28,	1843	Jacob VanDoren	Lewis F. Wilson	6b308	mr 74 *
?Snodgrass, M. T. m. Porterfield, Ann Nov. 27,	1843	Jacob VanDoren	Lewis F. Wilson	6b308	mr 10 *
Snodgrass, Mary m. Vardier, James Apr. 23,	1795		John Boyd		cr 33
Snodgrass,Mary Thos. m. Evans,Jeff'n Dec. 26,	1828	Chas. J. Faulkner	Jas. M. Brown	5b 85	mr 51 *
Snodgrass, Priscilla m. Foreman, Edw.Apr. 9,	1898	Wm. Snodgrass	Richard Swift	1b 97	cr 31 mr 15 *
Snodgrass, Robert m. Evans, Kitty Feb. 10,	1806	Jas. Faulkner		3b 10	mr 42 *
Snodgrass, Robert m.Snodgrass,Sarah May 25,	1821	Seaman Gerrard	John Boggs	4b184	mr 32 *
Snodgrass, Sarah m. Eaken, Wm. May 29,	1821		Hugh Vance		mr 43 *
Snodgrass, Sarah m. Vardier, Paul Feb. 6,	1781		Hugh Vance		mr 85 *
Snodgrass, S. Anna m. Henshaw,Levi Dec. 11,	1851	Robt. Snodgrass	J.H.Jennings	7b238	mr 42 *
Snodgrass, Sarah Ann m.Snodgrass,Rbt May 25,	1821	S. Gerrard	John Boggs	4b184	
Snodgrass, Stephen m. Locke, Cath.E. May 16,	1835	John Locke		6b 44	
Snodgrass, Stephen m. Vardier, Els. Mar. 19,	1789		Hugh Vance	3b175	cr 19 mr 3 *
Snodgrass, Susan m. Pendleton, Wm. Feb. 16,	1811	Robert Wilson			
Snodgrass, Susan P. m. Thomas, Jacob Feb. 28,	1854		John Proctor		*
Snodgrass, Susan R. m. Henshaw,Th't'n Apr. 26,	1844	Wm. T. Snodgrass	Lewis F. Wilson	6b320	*
Snodgrass, Wm. m Fryatt, Nancy July 7,	1798	Robert Snodgrass	John Boyd	1b113	cr 32 mr 15 *
Snodgrass, Wm.Tyler m. Tabb, Anabel Jan. 21,	1845	John T. Tabb	Lewis F. Wilson	7b 22	
Snook, Els. m. VanCleve,Nathaniel July 9,	1851	Wm. P. Shipman		7b228	
Snow, Mary m. Robinson, Chas.	1798	Daniel Fitzpatr'k		1b126	
Snowdeal, Cath. m.Bockey,John Peter Aug. 21,	1817	Henry Rousch	W.N.Scott	4b 44	*
Snowdeal, Cath. m. Randall, Nicholas Oct. 23,	1813	Peter Snowdeal	Rev. Reebenack	3b273	gc 13
Snowdeal, Els. m. Shaffer, Jacob Nov. 4,	1840	Jacob Picking		6b223	*
Snowdeal, George m. Malone, Polly Dec. 31,	1811	John Harden	Rev. Reebenack	3b206	gc 12
Snowdeal, Jacob m. Cline,Cath.(Kitty)Dec.23,	1811	James Brady	Rev. Reebenack	3b204	gc 12
Snowdeal, Nicholas m. Buck, Margt. Feb. 9,	1819	Peter Snodgrass		4b100	go 12
Snowdian, Jane m. Pickens, Jacob Oct. 6,	1844	Norman Miller		7b 7	go 12
Snyder, Abr'm m. Chidester, Sarah June 10,	1797	Elip't't Chidester		1b 21	
Snyder, Ann m. Reed, James F. June 15,	1843	John R. Snyder	T.H.W.Monroe	6b300	mr 75 *
Snyder, Barbara m. Woods, Hugh May 10,	1798	John Bowman	John Boyd	1b110	cr 32 mr 15 *
Snyder, Cath. m. Bashore, Samuel May 3,	1839	Thomas Powell		6b163	
Snyder, Cath. m. Mathers, Wm. H. Mar. 18,	1833	Jacob Snyder	W. Monroe	5b261	mr 65 *
Snyder, Cath. m. Smith, Thos. Mar. 7,	1842	James McSherry		6b263	
Snyder, Cath. m. Swinley, Jacob Feb. 9,	1804	George Pulse		2b237	
Snyder, Conrad m. Lindle, Nancy June 23,	1797	Jervis Jeffries		1b 32	
Snyder, Daniel m. Raney, Margt. Ann Aug. 19, Dec. 29,	1834	Samuel Raney		6b 26	

Name	(marriage)	(surety)	(minister)	(bond)		
Snyder, Eliza m. Morgan, Solomon	Aug. 1, 1835	Joseph Morlatt	Wm. Monroe	6b 51		mr 65 *
Snyder, Eliz. m. Moody, Philip	Mar. 28, 1833	Jacob Pultz	Wm. Monroe	5b264		mr 65 *
Snyder, Eliz. m. Smith, Jeremiah	May 10, 1832	Jacob Snyder	Wm. Monroe	5b229		mr 65 *
Snyder, Eliz. m. Smith, Jeremiah	May 10, 1832					mr 33 *
Snyder, Fred. m. Pennybaker, Eliz.	Jan. 25, 1785		Hugh Vance			
Snyder, Gasper m. Deberry, Rachel	June 15, 1805	Richard Morrison		2b265		
Snyder, George m. Everhart, Barbara	Jan. 1, 1849	Peter Everhart	J.H.Jennings	7b143		mr 82 *
Snyder, George m. McDonald, Mary	Feb. 27, 1840	Jos. S. Chambers	James Reily	6b198		mr 70 *
Snyder, Geo. V. m. Croney, Maria	July 10, 1838	John P. Strayer		6b142		
Snyder, Hannah m. Everhart, Peter (Pe-	May 21, 1850	Jacob Kees	J.H.Jennings	7b185		mr 82 *
Snyder, Jacob m. Butt, Adah	Jan. 6, 1823	Benj. Thomas	Nathan Young	4b231		mr 58 *
Snyder, Jacob m. Marquart, Eliz.	Dec. 24, 1806	Nicholas Marquart	John Mathews	3b 39	cr 13	mr 23 *
Snyder, Jacob m. Ott, Mary	Aug. 6, 1807	John Ott		3b 65		
Snyder, Jacob m. Siler, Cath.	Dec. 12, 1825	Philip Siler	Nathan Young	5b 29		mr 58 *
Snyder, Jenny m. Cameron, Joseph	Oct. 12, 1807	Levi Cunningham		3b 74		
Snyder, John O. m. Mathews, Matilda	July 6, 1843	John Mathews	T.H.W.Monroe	6b302		mr 75 *
Snyder, Margt. m. Ingles, Samuel P.	Feb. 17, 1838	Wm. Karley		6b132		
Snyder, Maria m. Myers, John	Apr. 23, 1828	Abr'm Snyder	Nathan Young	5b 99		mr 60 *
Snyder, Martha m. Stilwell, Enoch	Aug. 12, 1811	Daniel Seaborn		3b193		
Snyder, Mary m. Williams, Jonathan	Aug. 10, 1850	Jacob VanDoren	John Light	7b192		mr 80 *
Snyder, Rosanna m. Wilson, James Jr.	Oct. 10, 1842	Harrison Waite		6b279		
Snyder, Samuel m. Legg, Mary A.	Sept 24, 1850	Jacob VanDoren	Henry Furlong	7b197		mr 81 *
Snyder, Sarah m. Copelan, Wm.	Mar. 1, 1813	David Shrode	Rev. Reebenack	3b254	gc 13	
Snyder, Susanna m. Fist(Fish), James	Feb. 1, 1827	Reginal Butt	B. Reynolds	5b 61		mr 51 *
Snyder, Wm. m. Butt, Hannah	Apr. 2, 1846	Charles Butt	J.H.Jennings	7b 63		mr 82 *
Snyder, Wm. m. Farber, Cath.	Mar. 31, 1819		Mathias Riser			mr 30 *
Snyder, Wm. m. Hveley, Susannah	Dec. 23, 1809	Solomon Shrode	Rev. Reebenack	3b130	gc 11	
Snyder, Wm. m. Miller, Henry	Oct. 14, 1800	Jacob Miller		2b 92		
Soister, Eliz. m. Lefevre, Henry	Jan. 15, 1822	Henry Lefevre	John B. Hoge	4b204		mr 44 *
Soister, John m. Pitzer, Michael	Oct. 8, 1823	Jacob Soister	Chas. P. Krauth	4b250		mr 46 *
Soister, Margt. m. ?	Oct. 21, 1788		Hugh Vance			
Sellins, Solomon m. ?	Aug. 10, 1852		D. Francis Sprigg			mr 86 *
Sommers, Ann M. m. Burkhart, Wm. David	June 24, 1833	Ezekiel Showers		5b277		
Sommerville, Eliz. A. m. Edwards, Wm.	Nov. 1, 1842	Edmund Pendleton	James Chisholm	6b282		
Sommerville, Robt. A. m. Waite, Mary	Dec. 23, 1808	David Hunter	Rev. Reebenack	3b103	gc 10	mr 75 *
Sommerville, Wm. m. Brown, Marg Peggy	Sept 19, 1806	Robert Owen	Hugh Vance	3b 30		
Soper, Eliz. m. Beatty, Wm.	Mar. 11, 1815	Wm. Beatty		3b314		
Soper, Eliz. m. Light, David	June 28, 1838	Thomas Soper		6b142		
Soper, Eliz. m. Tabler, Ephraim	Nov. 18, 1817					
Soper, Ruth m. Light, Jacob		Thomas Soper		4b 50		
Souder, Christ'r m. Butt, Sally	Dec. 16, 1788		Moses Hoge			mr 1 *
Souders, Eliz. m. Palmer, John	Nov. 26, 1799	James Richardson	David Young	2b 36		mr 1 *
Souder, Eliz. m. Richardson, James	Jan. 24, 1787					
Souper, Thomas m. Ryneberger, Nancy	Nov. 14, 1819	Stephen W. Foreman	Hugh Vance	4b 92		mr 43 *

Name	(marriage)		(suretor) Christ'r Souther	(minister)	(bond) 3b147			
Souther, Ellender m. Butt, Van S.	Apr. 20,	1810	Christ'r Souther	Moses Hoge	3b147			
Souther, Nancy m. Ray, Luke	Nov. 27,	1788						
Southerland, Diana m.Beatty(-lly)John	Feb. 14,	1799	George Southerland	John Hett(Hutt)	1b166	cr 12	mr 96	*
Southerland, Kissy m. Richardson, ino.	July 26,	1810	Thomas Walley	Rev. Reebenack	3b154	gc 11	mr 18	*
Southern, Sarah m. Butt, Arch'd	Jan. 20,	1789		Moses Hoge		cr 1	mr 2	*
Southwood, Frances m. Burns, John	Dec. 25,	1794		Moses Hoge		cr 19	mr 9	*
Southwood, Margt. m. Bell, Benj.	Sept 2,	1799	John Roberts		2b 24			
Southwood, Ruth m. Hedges, Joshua	June 11,	1804	Edward Southwood		2b236			
*Sowman, Susannah m. Hite, Samuel	Dec. 13,	1802	George Sedther	John Hines	2b186	cr 27	mr 20	*
Sowman, Eliza m. Claycomb, Fred.	June 9,	1811	John Burk	John B. Hoge	3b189	cr 14	mr 24	*
Soyster, Susan m. McNett, John	Dec. 1,	1808		Rev. Reebenack		gc 10		*
Spangler, Eliz. m. Denhifer, John	Aug. 8,	1799		David Young		gc 8		*
Spangler, Mathias m. Bedeman, Eve	May 20,	1789		Hugh Vance		gc 39		*
Spatts, John H. m. Bane, Nancy	June 1,	1840	Jacob Lemaster	Samuel Sedth	6b221		mr 3	*
Spear, Wm. m. Farr, Mary	June 5,	1804	Henry Fulton		2b249		mr 71	*
	Jan. 8,	1805	Benson Lecky		2b251			
Specht, Cath. m. Pitzer, Jacob	Sept 8,	1823	John Pitzer	Chas. P. Krauth	4b248		mr 46	*
Specht, George m. Seisher, Mary	Feb. 10,	1827	Henry Swisher	Nathan Young	5b 62		mr 59	*
Specht, Nancy m. Philippy, Henry	Jan. 24,	1815	Lewis Specht	Rev. Reebenack	3b309	gc 14		
Speck,Benj. m. Seibert, Mary Ann	Oct. 26,	1835	Michael Seibert		6b 60			
Speck, David m. Beatty, Melissa C.	Jan. 18,	1845	Wm. Pendleton	Lewis F. Wilson	7b 22			
Speck, Eliz. m. Kisinger, Otho	Feb. 15,	1831	Jonathan Cushwa	Jas. M. Brown	5b186		mr 62	*
*Speck, Geo. F. m. Hollenberger, Cath.	June 15,	1811	Jonathan Hoover	John B. Hoge	3b190	cr 14	mr 24	*
Speck, Margt. m. Lefevre, Danial	Nov. 20,	1844	John M. Speck	Lewis F. Wilson	7b 14			
Speer, Mathew m. Gldia, Cath. E.	Jan. 3,	1846	Norman Miller		7b 53			
Spellman, Solomon m.Fenensdal,Cath.	Dec. 10,	1816						
Spellman, Charlotte m. Lowman,Alex.	Jan. 24,	1825	William Faris	Mathias Riser	4b288		mr 48	*
Spence, Eliz. m. McPheely, Isaac	Mar. 28,	1804	Alex. Miller	Chas. P. Krauth	2b229			
Spence, Wm. m. Hamilton, Sarah	Mar. 27,	1833	David H. Brummer	Jas. M. Brown	5b263		mr 67	*
Spence, Wm. m. Williams, Sophia	July 27,	1810	Jonas Seaman		3b155			
Spencer, Henry m. Dawson, Nelly	Sept 11,	1820	Thomas Spencer		4b160			
Spencer, John m. Butt, Mary	Aug. 12,	1826		Nathan Young			mr 58	*
Spencer, Martha C. m.Barleson,Elijah	Apr. 27,	1852	Jacob VanDoren	John Light	7b253	or 33	mr 86	*
Spencer, Mary m. Goldberg, Teddy	Feb. 13,	1800		John Hett(Hutt)			mr 18	*
Spencer, Nancy m. Hearse, Philip	Jan. 22,	1805	Thomas Spencer		2b252			
Spencer, Richard m. Malone, Mary	Oct. 4,	1798		David Young		gc 8		*
Spencer, Sally m. Duncan, James	Jan. 6,	1818	Peter Hess		4b 57			
Spencer, Susanna m. Kearns, Joseph	Apr. 28,	1802	Thomas Spencer		2b172			
Spencer, Thomas m. Dawson, Nancy	Aug. 9,	1815	Samuel Christy	Rev. Reebenack	3b333	gc 14		
Spencer, Wm. S. m.Newcomer, Mary Ann	Oct. 23,	1844	Jacob Newcomer		7b 10			
Spero, Jacob m. Westenhaver, Eliz.	Sept 14,	1833	Joseph Turner		5b283			
Spero, Maria m. Lefevre, Jacob	Aug. 27,	1827	George Sperow	Jas. M. Brown	5b 76		mr 51	*
Spero, Sarah m. Trammel, Philip	Apr. 11,	1837	Jacob Spero	Lewis F. Wilson	6b104		mr 44	*
**Sowers, Henry m. Kraunk, Philip	Mar. 20,	1787		Hugh Vance			mr 24	*
!**Speck, Geo. F. m. Kellenberger,Cath	June 15,	1811	Jonathan Hoover	John B. Hoge	3b190	cr 14		

Name	(marriage)	(suretor)	(minister)	(bond)		
Sperow, George m. Riner, Eliz.	Oct. 20, 1828	Peter Riner	Nathan Young	5b110		mr 59 *
Sperow, John m. Rutherford, Cath.	Aug. 9, 1827	Arch'd Rutherford	Lewis F. Wilson	5b 75	cr 20	
Sperow, Rebecca m. Powell, Wm. V.	Feb. 17, 1845	Wm. Sperow		7b 27		*
Sperow, Wm. m. Dubble, Rebecca	Aug. 10, 1835	Jacob Dubble		6b 53		*
Sprbling, Fanny m.Cove(Cou,Core)Chr'n	Mar. 31, 1789		Hugh Vance			mr 3 *
Spilman, Charlotte m. Lowman, Alex.	Jan. 24, 1825	Wm. Faris	Chas. P. Krauth	4b288	cr 33	mr 48 *
Spinner, Mary m. Goldberg, Teddy	Feb. 13, 1800		John Heitt(Hutt)		cr 20	mr 18 *
?Spirling, Fanny m.Cove(Cou,Core)Chr'n	Mar. 31, 1789		Hugh Vance			mr 3 *
Spitsmogle, Adam m. Miller, Mary	Dec. 11, 1807	Michael Miller		3b 79		
Spitsmogle, Adam m. Wallick,Mary A.	Mar. 11, 1839	Levi Spitsmogle		6b162		
Spitsmogle, Jacob m.Perrell(Pearl)Ann	Apr. 7, 1842	James McSherry	John Light	6b269		mr 74 *
Spitsmogle, John m. Perrell, Cath.	July 19, 1842	Thomas Perrell	Peyton Harrison	6b273		mr 73 *
Spitsmogle, Michael m. Haines, Sarah	Apr. 8, 1835	Harrison Waite		6b 40		
Spong, David m. Kyser, Eliz.	July 20, 1811	Patrick Duffy	Rev. Reebenack	3b191	gc 12	
Sporr, Cath. m. Gosner, John	Mar. 25, 1799	Thomas Stilwell	Samuel Smith	1b175		mr 71 *
Spotts, John H. m. Bane, Nancy	June 1, 1840	Jacob Lemaster	Mathias Riser	6b211		
Sprace, Jacob m. Sharff, Sarah	1817					
Sprigg, Eliz. m. Shade, Jacob	Jan. 6, 1836	Peter Caw		6b 66		mr 66 *
Sprigg, James M. m. Castle, Mary Ann	Sept 8, 1834	John Castle		6b 18		mr 58 *
Sprigg, Mary Ann m. Cook, Benj.	Dec. 26, 1845	Robert Sprigg		7b 41		mr 79 *
Sprigg, Nancy m. Olinger, Christ'r	Dec. 7, 1833	John Bowers	Nathan Young	5b292	gc 12	
Sprigg, Robert m. Allebaugh, Mary	Mar. 23, 1826	James Beggs	Nathan Young	5b 38	gc 12	
Sprigg, Robert m. Connelly, Cath.	Mar. 31, 1849	John E.Hogeland	Henry Furlong	7b151		
Sprigg, Robert m. Mingle, Polly	Dec. 21, 1811	Samuel Black	Rev. Reebenack	3b204	cr 10	mr 11 *
Sprigg, Thomas m. Chambers, Eliz.	Dec. 25, 1811	Jacob Zimmerman	Rev. Reebenack	3b205	cr 15	mr 4 *
Spring, Richard m. McCoy, Eliz.	Aug. 10, 1795		Moses Hoge	2b 17		mr 39 *
Sprinckle, Mary m. Walper, Casper	June 3, 1789	Casper Walper	Christian Streit	2b 57		
Sprinkle, Eliz. m. Becket, Wm.	Oct. 8, 1792		Moses Hoge	2b105		
Sprinkle, Eliz. m. Darnhafer, John	Aug. 6, 1799	John Rohr		2b187		
Sprinkle, Peter m. Redfern, Nancy	Mar. 16, 1800	Jacob Myers		2b185		
Sprinkle, Welcome E. m. Myers, Cath.	Sept 13, 1830	Samuel Rippey	David Young	5b174	gc 9	*
Sprowl, Wm. m. Vance, Mary	Mar. 31, 1807			3b 53		
Spry, Ann m. Segar(Sugar),David(Wm.)	Oct. 12, 1798	David Sugar	Richard Swift	1b138	cr 31	mr 15 *
Spurr, John m. Batt, Mary	Sept 9, 1826	Eliz. Batt		5b 51		
Spurr, Nancy m. Roberts, Joseph	Dec. 26, 1812	James Gardner		3b244		
Spurr, Sarah m. Morgan, Wm.	Dec. 24, 1800	Solomon Offutt				
Stacey, Sarah m. French, John	Dec. 14, 1802	Conrad Keesecker	Richard Swift			mr 21 *
Stacey, Thomas m. Bonner, Mary	Dec. 11, 1802	Samuel Hedges	Nathan Young			mr 57 **
Stacks, Demarius m. McKeever, Mary	Jan. 22, 1821	Daniel McKeever	David Young	4b170	cr 32	
Stagner, Peter m. Bishop, Mary	Aug. 28, 1798	Henry Bishop		1b126	gc 8	
Staley, Cath. m. Hain, Thomas R.	Aug. 23, 1811	Jacob Staley		3b205		
Staley, Emanuel m. Tabler, Ann R.	Apr. 19, 1847	Adam Tabler	D.F.Bragunier	7b 94		mr 78 *
Staley, Solomon m. Williams, Isabel	June 4, 1832	John Williams	Wm. Hawk	5b231		mr 65

Name		(marriage)	(suretor)	(minister)	(bond)		
Staley, Susan m. Gwilliam, Henry	Feb. 6.	Feb. 9, 1832	Solomon Staley	Wm. Monroe	5b216	cr 36	mr 62 *
Stall, Jesse m. Melvin, Eliz.		Apr. 26, 1796		Moses Hoge		gc 1	mr 12 *
Standley, Joseph m. Bailey, Eliz.		Mar. 1, 1792		David Young			
Stane, Christiana m. Harrison, Alex.	Sept 8,	Sept 8, 1811	Fred. Starr	John Bond	3b302	cr 41	mr 25 *
Staner, Eliz. m. Cushwa, Wm. A.	Mar. 21,	Mar. 21, 1842	Wm. Seibert		6b267		
Stanford, John m. Shirley, Walter	Sept 4,	May 10, 1794	John Crasmuck	Wm. Hill	2b 85	cr 30	mr 9 *
Stanford, John m. Cooper, Margt.	Nov. 24,	Sept 7, 1800	George S. Harris	John Heitt(Hutt)	1b149	cr 35	mr 19 *
Stanford, John m. Morehead, Achsah	Nov. 7,	1798	John Curry		2b 76		
Stanford, Wm. m. Curry, Margt.		1800	John Cushman				
?Stang, Nicholas m. Cushman(Ca-),Marg.	June 26.	June 29, 1823	Isaac Stanley	Nathan Young	4b242		mr 58 *
??Stanley, Archelaus m. Hudson, Mahala	Jan. 10,	Jan. 14, 1838	John Brannon	James Watts	6b130		
Stanley, Archibald m. Brannon, Mary	Jan. 18,	1803	Isaac Stanley		2b190		
??Stanley, Archelaus m. Hudson, Mahala	Jan. 10,	Jan. 14, 1838	Isaac Stanley	James Watts	6b130		*
Stanley, Isaac m. Lowery, Mary	Feb. 8,	Jan. 14, 1837	John Lowry	Lewis F. Wilson	6b 95	cr 41	mr 68 *
Stanley, Joseph m. Steidley, Abilonia	Feb. 16,	Feb. 19, 1835	John Steidley	Elisha Gardner	6b 30	gc 12	mr 66 *
Stapleton, Clayton N.m. Grove, Eliza	June 12,	June 13, 1833	Abr'm Grove	Nathan Young	5b276	gc 6	mr 25 *
Star, Christiana m. Harrison, Alex.	Sept 8,	Sept 8, 1814	Fred. Starr	John Bond	3b302		
Star, Christina m. Coons, Philip	Jan. 29,	Jan. 30, 1812	Fred. Starr	Rev. Reebenack	3b210		
Starkely, Cath. m. Cotter, John		Nov. 17, 1786		David Young		gc 2	mr 43 *
Starne, John m. Bonner, Kath.		July 18, 1786		Hugh Vance		gc 15	
Starr, Cath. m. Milholland, Daniel		June 22, 1792		David Young			
Starr, John m. Miller, Mary	Aug. 21,	Aug. 22, 1816	George Miller	Rev. Reebenack	4b 11		
Starr, Susanna m. Marker, Michael	Mar. 31,	1807	Fred. Starr		3b 53		
Starrett, Elis. m. Swaney, Jeremiah	Jan. 26,	Jan. 15, 1831	Joseph Starrett	Robert Cadden	5b186		mr 61 *
Starrett, Lydia m. Lowery, Wm.	Jan. 12,	Jan. 15, 1835	James Starrett	John Howell	6b 27		mr 68 *
Starry, Barbara m. Gertman, Christ'r		Sept 26, 1795		David Young		gc 5	
Starry, Conrad m. Grantham, Jemima	Mar. 24,	1814	Wm. Grantham		3b290		
Starry, Daniel m. Smith, Hannah	Oct. 16,	Oct. 25, 1798	Alex. Smith	David Young	1b140	gc 8	
Starry, Eliz. m. Ditzler, Jacob		Sept 6, 1796		David Young		gc 6	
?Starry, Nicholas m.Cashman(Cu-),Marg.	June 26.	June 29, 1823	John Cashman	Nathan Young	4b242		mr 58 *
Starry, Polly m. Riner, Daniel	Dec. 28,	Dec. 29, 1826	Daniel Starry	Nathan Young	5b 59		mr 59 *
Start, Govey m. Myers, Eliz.	Nov. 30,	1821	John L. Myers		4b198		
Start, Solomon m. Harmon, Eliz.	May 16,	1815	Michael Harmon		3b324		
Startzman, John m. McCoy, Mary		Dec. 22, 1853		G.W.Cooper			*
Staub, Laura M. m. Tegmeyer,John H.		June 21, 1853		D.F.Bragunier			
Staub, Leonora P. m. Gruber,John G.	Jan. 15,	Jan. 16, 1850	Andrew Bowman	John Light	7b173		mr 80 *
Stauber, T.Justin m.Burwell,Margt. A.		Oct. 26, 1854		G.W.Cooper			
Stayer, Daniel m. Small, Eliz.	Mar. 8,	1815	Jacob Small		3b313	gc 6	*
Steck, Maria m. Grove, Abr'm		Aug. 11, 1796		David Young			
Stedley, Eliz. m. Hartcook, Elijah	May 27,	May 29, 1820	Solomon Steidley	David Young	4b149		mr 57 *
Stedley, Mary Ann m. Rees, Simon	Sept 16,	Sept 19, 1833	John Stedley	Nathan Young	4b284		mr 66 *
Stedman, Lowry m. Lemon, Harriet	Mar. 29,	1823	John V. Lemon	Chas. P. Krauth	4b236		mr 46 *
Steed, Jesse m. Ceny, Eva Rose		?		David Thomas			mr 37 *

Name	(marriage)	(surety)	(minister)	(bond)		
Steel, B. F. m. Johnston, Frances A.	Apr. 15, 1851	Johnston W. Lamon	F.C.Tebbs	7b222		mr 84 *
Steel, James m. White, Mary	Sept 5, 1820	Charles McDaniel	Nathan Young	4b160		mr 57 *
Steel, Jane m. Gano, George	Aug. 24, 1824	George Jones	John Winter	4b270		mr 50 *
Steel, John m. Clouse(Clouds). Eliz.	Aug. 30, 1806	John Clouse	John Bond	3b 27	cr 28	mr 23 *
Steel, John m. Thruston, Eliz.	Apr. 19, 1796	John Thruston	John Boyd		cr 10	mr 12 *
Steel, Joseph m. Thruston, Nancy	Dec. 2, 1797	Robert Hastings	David Young	1b 68	ge 7	
Steel, Mary m. Bare, Jacob	Sept 16, 1799	John Thruston	John Boyd	2b 26	cr 34	mr 17 *
Steel, Wm. m. Billingsly, Eliz.	Dec. 15, 1798	John Thruston	David Young	1b154	ge 8	
Steele, Eliz.m. Nichols, John	Sept 16, 1788	David Baldwin	Hugh Vance	1b 62		mr 35 *
Steele, George m. Baldwin, Amey	Nov. 20, 1797	John Clouse		3b 27		
?Steele, John m. Clouse(Clouds),Eliz.	Aug. 30, 1806	Elisha Boyd	John Bond	2b 20	cr 28	mr 23 *
Steele, John m. Farrell, Peggy	Aug. 14, 1799	Robert Hastings	John Boyd	2b 26	cr 34	
Steele, Mary m. Bare, Jacob	Sept 16, 1799	John Gilbert	John Hedtt(Rutt)	7b162	cr 38	mr 17 *
Steen, Hannah m. Welsh, Zachariah	Apr. 5, 1799	Cyrus Sanders		2b104		mr 18 *
Steen, Mary m. Delly, Daniel M.	Aug. 9, 1849	Aaron Dunham		5b 34		
Steen, Mary m. Welsh, Jacob	Dec. 23, 1800	Jas. W. Gray	Nathan Young	6b 24		mr 53 *
Steen, Sarah m. Hair, Henry	Jan. 31, 1826	Martin Myers	Jas. M. Brown	2b204		mr 68 *
Steen, Stephen m. Foster, Mary	Dec. 13, 1834	John Steidley	Christian Streit	6b 30		mr 6 *
Steetz, Margt. m. Haines, John	Jan. 6, 1790	Jacob Hott	Richard Swift	6b15		mr 21 *
Stegler, Christiana m.Wilmouth,John	June 21, 1803	John Steidley	Elisha Gardner	5b 65	cr 15	mr 68 *
Staidley, Ablonia m. Stanley,Jos.	Feb. 19, 1835	Solomon Steidley	Nathan Young	4b149	cr 27	
Staidley, Amos m. Hott, Cath.	Oct. 9, 1837	Solomon Steidley	Nathan Young	5b143		mr 59 *
Staidley, Cath. m. Henderson, John	Mar. 27, 1827	John Steidley	Nathan Young	5b284		mr 57 *
Staidley, Eliz. m. Hartsook, Elijah	May 27, 1820	James Steidman	Nathan Young	2b113		mr 60 *
Staidley, Hannah m. Henderson, David	Oct. 6, 1829	John Myers		7b165		mr 66 *
Staidley, Mary Ann m. Rees, Simon	Sept 16, 1801					
Steidman, Margt. m. Shoebridge, John	Feb. 3, 1833		Jos. Plunkett			mr 84 *
Stein, Henry m. Myers, Lydia	Sept 20, 1849		Moses Hoge			mr 20 *
Step, Eliz. m. Taylor, Samuel	Mar. 5, 1801					
Stephens, Albert m. Hamme(Hanna)Lydia	July 5, 1810	Jacob Hamme Jr.	Rev. Reebenack	3b153	cr 38	mr 23 *
Stephens, Alec. m. Chenoweth, Julia	Dec. 20, 1809	Robert Wilson	Christian Streit	3b128	ge 11	
Stephens, Benj. m. Leonard, Sarah	Oct. 30, 1844	John Gallaher		7b 11	cr 16	
Stephens, Charlotte B. m. Hughes,Jas.	R.Dec.Apr. 23, 1851	T.D.Scott		7b223		
Stephens, Dennis m. Bell, Rachel	Feb. 25, 1791		Moses Hoge			mr 6 *
Stephens, Henry m. Puffenberger,Sarah	Apr. 25, 1833	Wm. Robinson	Nathan Young	5b271	cr 6	mr 66 *
Stephens, Mary Ann m. Selby,Solomon	Aug. 3, 1799	Thomas Waters	David Young	2b 16	ge 8	
Stephens, Mary Jane m.Fellers,Geo.	R.Dec. 23, 1844	Benj. Stephens		7b 17		mr 7 *
Stephens, Robert m. Johnson, Ann	Apr. 15, 1792	John Hall	Christian Streit	1b 2	cr 15	
Stephens, Sophia m. Hall, Thomas	Mar. 27, 1797	John Poisal		4b194		mr 42 *
Stephens, Thomas m. Poisal, Betsy	Oct. 16, 1821	Benj. Stephenson	Chas. P. Krauth	2b209		
Stephenson, Isabella m. Boyd, John	Oct. 10, 1803	Benj. Stephenson	David Young			
Stephenson, James m.Cunningham, Ann	May 17, 1792		David Young		ge 1	
Stephenson, Joseph m. Mason, Nancy	Dec. 21, 1849	Robert Stephenson	Lewis F. Wilson	7b 16		

Name	(marriage)	(surety)	(minister)	(bond)		
Stephenson, Maria m. Boyd, Samuel	Nov. 1, 1798	James Kennedy	John Boyd	1b142	cr 37	mr 16 *
Stephenson, Sarah m. Kennedy, James	Dec. 29, 1792	Aaron Faris	David Young	2b194	gc 2	*
Stern, Alex. m. Faris, Nancy	Oct. 26, 1803	George North		1b 65		
Stern, James m. Seabright, Sarah	Feb. 21, 1797	James Stern		1b 76		
Stern, Mary m. Buckhannon, James	Nov. 27, 1797	James W. Gray		6b 24		
Stern, Stephen m. Foster, Mary	Dec. 13, 1834	Joseph Sterrett		5b186		
Sterrett, Eliz. m. Swaney, Jeremiah	Dec. 13, 1831	James Sterrett	Jas. M. Brown	6b 27		mr 68 *
Sterrett, Lydia m. Lowry, Wm.	Jan. 26, 1835	James Sterrett	Robert Cadden	4b265		mr 61 *
Sterrett, Nancy m. Gwinn, James	Jan. 12, 1824	Wm. Creighton	John Howell	1b167		mr 68 *
Sterrett, Wm. M. m. Creighton, Polly	May 3, 1799	A. Oden	John Boyd	6b112	cr 34	mr 16 *
Stevens, Cath. m. Rightstine, Wm.	Feb. 14, 1837	Richard W. Buckle		6b137		
Stevens, Thomas m. Bricker, Mary E.	Sept. 20, 1837	John Poisal	Peyton Harrison	4b194		mr 69 *
Stevens, Thomas m. Poisal, Betsy	Mar. 21, 1821	Robert Stephenson	Chas. P. Krauth	7b 16		mr 42 *
Stevenson, Joseph m. Mason, Nancy	Oct. 16, 1844	Ch'tin Mussetter		4b 88		
Stewart, Adam m. Mussetter, Sarah	Dec. 21, 1818	Harrison Waite	Lewis F. Wilson	6b 76		mr 30 *
Stewart, Ann. E. m. Burkhart, Francis	Nov. 19, 1836	Wm. H. Mong	W.N. Scott	6b263		
Stewart, David m. Mong, Susan A.	Apr. 1, 1842	Thomas Hite	Lewis F. Wilson	6b 17		mr 73 *
Stewart, Eliz. m. Duffield, John W.	Feb. 7, 1834	John Swinley		7b 60		
Stewart, George m. Swinley, Mary E.	Sept. 4, 1846	Adam Shober	Richard F. Brown	6b 19		mr 77 *
Stewart, Jacob m. Armstrong, Eliz.	Mar. 2, 1834	Wm. H. Dugan		6b 49		
Stewart, James m. Jack, Cath.	Sept. 13, 1838	Abner. Mendenhall		6b320		
Stewart, John m. Curtis, Jane	Sept. 20, 1844		Lewis F. Wilson			*
Stewart, John m. Long, Jane	Apr. 22, 1806	Wm. Long		3b 23		
Stewart, John W. m. Maslin, Mary	Jan. 16, 1834	Wm. Maslin	Wm. Monroe	5b300		mr 67 *
Stewart, John W. m. Taylor, Martha A	Jan. 13, 1841	Thomas Hughes		6b230		
Stewart, Margt. m. Myers, Thomas	Jan. 9, 1798	John Granthan		1b141		
Stewart, Maria C. m. Sheeler, John	Oct. 24, 1838	Adam Stewart		6b152		
Stewart, Rachel m. Strayer, John	Nov. 26, 1819	Robert Stewart		4b118		
Stewart, Robert m. line, D. Elis.	Oct. 6, 1829	Wm. Faris	Jacob Medtart	5b140		mr 63 *
Stewart, Robert m. Ward, Harriet E.	Sept. 10, 1846	Alfred Ross	Lewis F. Wilson	7b 58		mr 77 *
Stewart, Sally m. Ray, Wm.	Feb. 13, 1832	George Oller	Nathan Young	5b243		mr 65 *
Stewart, Samuel m. Sumption, Ruth	Oct. 10, 1803	Joseph Sumption		2b199		
Stewart, Samuel L. m. Myers, Elvira	Mar. 26, 1846	Aaron Myers	James Chisholm	7b 77		mr 77 *
Stewart, Susan m. Hawk, Wm.	Nov. 24, 1804	Isaac Hawk		2b235		
Stewart, Thos. W. m. Heck, Sarah	May 11, 1844					*
Stidley, Wm. m. Crumley, Rebecca	Oct. 28, 1813	Thomas Wright	D. Francis Sprigg	3b274	ge 13	*
Stidley, Cath. m. Henderson, John	Mar. 27, 1827	John Stidley	Rev. Reebenack	5b 65		mr 59 *
Stidley, John m. Powell, Mary	June 20, 1808	Robert Powell	James Watts	3b 91		
Stigler, Christiana m. Wilmouth, John	June 27, 1803	Martin Myers	Richard Swift	2b204		mr 21 *
Stilwell, Ann E. m. Rutherford, Jas.	Jan. 2, 1838	Elisha Butt		6b128		
Stilwell, Enoch m. Snyder, Martha	Aug. 12, 1811	Daniel Seaborn		3b193		
Stilwell, Epha m. Buren, Nicholas	Sept. 22, 1803	Thomas Stilwell		2b209		
Stilwell, Jane m. Gano, Joseph	Jan. 24, 1841	Harrison Waite	Lewis F. Wilson	6b231		mr 71 *

Name		(marriage)	(suretor)	(minister)	(bond)	
Stilwell, John H. m. Carper, Mary A.	Sept 9,	Sept 17, 1839	Jonas Carper	Lewis F. Wilson	6b174	mr 70 *
Stilwell, Nancy m. Boggs, Thomas	Sept 27,	1815	Levi Cunningham		3b341	mr 73 *
Stilwell, Sarah m. Butt, Charles	Nov. 25,	Nov. 29, 1841	Swearingen Butt	Peyton Harrison	6b254	mr 61 *
Stilwell, Sarah m. Butt, Elisha	Aug. 2,	Aug. 5, 1830	Cornelius Stilwell	Nathan Young	5b171	*
Stilwell, Stephen m. Rainey, Eliz.	Jan. 19,	Jan. 1802	Ignatius O'Ferrall		2b158	mr 36 *
Stilwell, Stephen m. Toogood, Mary		Aug. 13, 1788				
Stilwell, Thomas m. Hill, Polly	Jan. 1,	Jan. 1, 1811	Thomas Sharp	Moses Hoge	3b171	
Stimmel, Peter m. Grimes, Sarah	Aug. 31,	1846	Wm. Grimes		7b 72	
Stinchcomb, Levi m. Severns, Susan	Feb. 26,	1824	Joseph Turner		4b256	
Stine, Henry m. Myers, Lydia	Sept 20,	1849	John Myers	Joseph Plunkett	7b165	mr 84 *
Stine, Susan m. Wigginton, Geo. W.	Sept 11,	1853		G.W.Cooper		*
Stinecley, Amos m. Holt, Cath.	Oct. 10,	1837		Elisha Gardner		*
Stinitt, Wm. M. m. Creighton, Polly	Feb. 14,	1799	Wm. Creighton	John Boyd	1b167	cr 34 mr 16 *
Stinson, Eliz. m. Singers, John	July 1,	1803	M. Morgan		2b205	
Stinson, James m. Robinson, Lydia	Dec. 28,	1808	James Robinson		3b105	
Stinson, Samuel m. Courtney, Barbara	Mar. 4,	1809	Enoch Mathers		3b109	
Stip, Eliz. m. Couchman, James	May 30,	May 31, 1838	Jas. Hutchinson	Lewis F. Wilson	6b140	mr 69 *
Stip, Mary m. Barket, Michael	Feb. 2,	1796		David Young		gc 5 mr 9 *
Stip, Mary m. Seaborn, Wm.	Dec. 30,	1794		Moses Hoge		cr 19 mr 79 *
Stipe, Benj. m. Landerkin, Mary E.	Mar. 29,	1849	Wm. Creighton	John Winter	7b150	mr 58 *
Stipe, George m. Pabson, Cathy	Apr. 23,	1789	Michael Shaver		1b x	mr 52 *
Stipp, Fanny m. Hutchinson, James	Feb. 11,	Feb. 16, 1823	Abr'm Stipp		4b233	*
Stipp, Fred. m. Coffenberry, Frances	June 22,	1784		Hugh Vance		*
Stipp, John m. Patterson, Sarah Ann	Feb. 24,	1832	Robert Christy	John Boyd	5b217	cr 34
Stirritt, Wm. M. m. Creighton, Polly	Feb. 14,	1799	Wm. Creighton	Rev. Reebenack	1b167	gc 12 mr 16 *
Stoddart, James m. Brosius, Eliz.	Oct. 25,	1813	John Powell	Rev. Reebenack	3b196	gc 14 *
Stoffer, Alfred L. m. Bower, Mary A	Oct. 28,	1847	Hiram Bower	John Boyd	7b110	mr 81 *
Stoltz, Jacob m. Shall, Margt.	Jan. 2,	1799	Bartholomew Shall	David Young	1b160	gc 8 *
*Stone, Polly m. Burkmaxon, Zachariah	Apr. 8,	Apr. 6, 1800	Vincent Moore	John Hedtt(futt)	2b 62	gc 33 mr 18 *
Stonebraker, Jane m. Dugan, Robinson	Apr. 8,	1837	John Stonebraker		6b104	
Stookey, Barbara m. Penterbaugh, Dan'l	Oct. 24,	Oct. 26, 1815	Jacob Stookey	Nathan Young	3b346	mr 55 *
Stookey, John m. Kerns, Barbara	June 13,	June 13, 1816	Jacob Kerns	W.N.Scott	4b 5	mr 26 *
Stookey, Margt. m. Bishop, Josephus	Mar. 28,	Mar. 29, 1832	Henry J. Seibert	Nathan Young	5b223	mr 64 *
Stookey, Mary m. Fry, John	Nov. 19,	1836?	John Stuckey	Peyton Harrison	6b151	mr 69 *
Stookey, Samuel m. Siler, Hannah	Feb. 8,	Feb. 11, 1819	James Thompson	W.N.Scott	4b 99	mr 30 *
Stookey, Sarah m. Graves, Wm.	Nov. 22,	Nov. 27, 1851	Daniel K. Stuckey	Jas. H. Jennings	7b237	mr 85 *
Stookey, Sarah m. Lee, Alfred	Oct. 15,	Oct. 16, 1832	Jacob Stookey	W. Monroe	5b243	mr 65 *
Stookey, Simon m. Riner, Hannah	Sept 4,	Sept 1810	Henry Riner		3b160	
Stool, Wm. m. Billingsly, Eliz.	Dec. 15,	Dec. 18, 1798	John Thruston	David Young	1b154	gc 8
Stottlemire, Libby m. Replovel, Henry	Aug. 5,	1815	Jacob Garinger		7b331	*
Stottlemeyer, Mary A. m. Lida, James		1817		Mathias Riser		
Stout, Cath. m. Smith, James	Dec. 27,	Dec. 2, 1814	Edward Arls	David Young	3b307	gc 8
?*Buchmaster, Zach'h m. Stone, Polly	Apr. 2,	Apr. 6, 1800	Vincent Moore	John Hedtt(futt)	2b 62	cr 33 mr 18 *

Name	(marriage)		(suretor)	(minister)	(bond)			
Stout, Elis. m. Tederick, George	July 28,	1801	Michael Wolfe		2b129			*
Stout, Mary m. Wolfe, Michael	July 23,	1801	Philip Stout		2b130			
Stout, Philip m. Crowl, Cath.	Feb. 17,	1815	Robert Wilson		3b311			*
Stout, Philip m. Smith, Sarah	May 21,	1812	Edward Aris	Rev. Reebenack	3b226	gc 13		*
Stout, Rebecca m. Anderson, John	Mar. 9,	1804	Philip Stout		2b226			*
Stout, Sally m. Tederick, Peter	June 23,	1803	Philip Stout	David Young	2b204	gc 10		*
Stover, Frances m.Legler(Zed-Martin	May 5,	1803	Robert Filson	Richard Swift	2b201	cr 27	mr 21	*
Stover, Fred. m. Sellers, Allana	Nov. 5,	1809	John Kydinger	Lewis Mayer	3b123	cr 16	mr 24	*
Stow, Christina m. Coons, Philip	Jan. 30,	1812	Fred. Starr	Rev. Reebenack	3b210	gc 12		*
Stowers, Mary m. Banks, John	Dec. 3,	1795		Moses Hoge		cr 10	mr 11	*
Strack, Alex. m. Hunter, Mary	Jan. 22,	1793		Moses Hoge			mr 39	*
Straith, Samuel m. Smallwood, Nancy	July 27,	1800	George Smallwood	Moses Hoge	2b 78	cr 29		*
Strayer, Adam m. Potsal, Polly	Jan. 22,	1793		Moses Hoge			mr 19	*
Strayer, Adam m. Seeler, Mary	Aug. 24,	1812	John Poisal	Rev. Reebenack	3b233	gc 13	mr 39	*
Strayer, Cath. m. Barnes, Michael	Aug. 12,	1813	Patrick Duffy		3b269			
Strayer, Elis. m. Gaseman, John	Apr. 4,	1844	Geo. W. Strayer	Lewis F. Wilson	6b317			*
Strayer, Elis. m. Ronk, Valentine	Jan. 26,	1814	George Shaffer		3b283			
Strayer, Geo. W. m. Quinn, Sarah Ann	June 17,	1837	Harvey A. Hedges	James Watts	6b108			*
Strayer, Jacob m. Seybert, Cath.	Nov. 4,	1844	Jeremiah Quinn		7b 12			
Strayer, Jacob S. m. O'Brien, Sarah	Mar. 17,	1810	Jacob Seybert		3b142			
Strayer, John m. Stewart, Rachel	Dec. 17,	1834	Benj. C. Speck		6b 24			
Strayer, John m. Wood, Priscilla	Oct. 6,	1819	Robert Stewart		4b118			
Strayer, Kitty m. Weaver, George	Jan. 9,	1798	Daniel Buckles	Moses Hoge	1b 80		mr 14	*
Strayer, Mary m. Kreglow, Adam	May 9,	1810	John Strayer		3b150			
Strayer, Nicholas m. Whiteneck,Rebes	Feb. 10,	1838	Addison McKee		6b131			
Strayer, Susannah m.Conchman, George	June 7,	1813	John Whiteneck		3b264			
Streeter, Samuel W. m.Varmetre,Mary	Oct. 17,	1797	John Davis	David Young	1b 55	gc 7		*
Strehers, Cath. m. Weaver, George	Jan. 25,	1848	Abraham VanMetre	P. Lipscomb	7b119	gc 11	mr 81	*
Stredthoff, Francis m.Klaycomb, Cath.	May 10,	1810		David Young		gc 6		*
Stredthoff, Francis m. Miller, Caty	Aug. 5,	1816	Paul Taylor	Rev. Reebenack	4b 15			*
Stribling, Cornelius m. Riddle, Elis.	Sept 15,	1853	John Strother	Mathias Riser	4b 46			*
Stribling, Dulcebella W. m.Beeson,Edw.	Sept 17,	1817	Robert Wilson	W.B.Dutton	3b281			*
Stribling,Thilafero m.Tate, Polly	Jan. 17,	1814	Arch'd Magill	John B. Hoge	1b x		mr 26	*
Stribling, Wm. m. Humphrey, Sally	Apr. 23,	1789	John Grey		3b 86			
Strickland, Henry m. Patrick,Mary F.	Apr. 21,	1808	Abr'm Ellis		3b 31			
Strickle, Jacob m. Ellis, Ann	Sept 27,	1806	George Painter		2b176			
Strickle, John m. Painter, Susanna	July 3,	1802	Segismund Showers		4b249			
Strickler, Geo. W. m. Peck, Nancy	Sept 18,	1823						
Strider, Elis. m. Faulk, Charles	Apr. 3,	1791	Asahel Varmetre	Moses Hoge	5b 91	cr 7	mr 6	*
Strider, Isaac m. Varmetre, Elis.	Mar. 2,	1828	Wm. Dellia	B. Reynolds	1b155		mr 52	*
Strider, Jacob m. Young, Polly	Dec. 19,	1798		Moses Hoge		cr 29	mr 15	*
Strider, John H. m. Varmetre, Naomi	Dec. 13,	1847	Israel Varmetre	James Baker	7b116		mr 78	*

Name	(marriage)	(suretor)	(minister)	(bond)		
Strider, Samuel m. Varmetre, Mary M.	Jan. 25, 1848	Abr'm P. Varmetre	P. Lipscomb	7b119		mr 81 *
Strider, Sarah m. Eaty, Jacob	Feb. 15, 1799	Michael Bente		1b168		
Strider, Sarah m. Harris, George S.	Dec. 23, 1799	Henry Harris		2b 43		
Strigler, Geo. m.Breckfield,Barbara	Oct. 28, 1818	John Breckfield		4b 84		
Stripe, Betsy m. Quigley, John	Sept. 1, 1811	John French	John B. Hoge	3b194	cr 14	mr 24 *
Stripe, Hannah m. Ensminger, David	Apr. 1, 1810	Mathias Kessacre	Rev. Reebenack	3b144	gc 11	
Stripe, Hannah Mrs. m.Jones, John	Aug. 29, 1801	John Brakefield	Richard Swift	2b139	cr 32	mr 20 *
Stritehofer, Francis m. Miller, Cath.	Aug. 11, 1816	Paul Taylor	Mathias Riser	4b 15	gc 14	mr 26 *
Strooker, Dan'l m. Schmal, Eliz.	Mar. 9, 1815		Rev. Reebenack		go 14	
Strode, Edward m.Low(Lout), Betsy	June 29, 1793		Moses Hoge		cr 22	mr 7 *
Strode, Eliz. m. Mason, Alex.	Feb. 16, 1807	James Foreman		3b 47		
Strode, George m. Foreman, Mary	Aug. 23, 1791		Moses Hoge		cr 7	mr 6 *
Strode, Hannah m. Trees, John	May 1, 1813		Nathan Young			mr 44 *
Strode, James m. Chenoweth, Chloe	Mar. 29, 1787		Hugh Vance			
Strode, Jeremiah m. Athe, Eliz.	Feb. 6, 1796		Richard Swift		cr 26	mr 11 *
Strode, John m. Foreman. Eliz.	Oct. 24, 1795		Richard Swift		cr 26	mr 10 *
Strode, Joseph m. Randall, Elenora	Jan. 13, 1819	Edmund Randall		4b 96		
Strode, Maria m. Puffenberger,Henry	Dec. 30, 1830	John Puffenberger	J.E.Jackson	5b182		
Strode, Mary E.F. m.Lemaster, Jacob	May 31, 1853		John Light			
Strode, Nancy m. Light, John	May 15, 1786		Hugh Vance			mr 88 *
Strode, Priscilla m. Turner, Ehud	Feb. 11, 1818	Alex. Mason		4b 61		mr 43 *
Strode, Rachel m. Bedinger, Henry	Dec. 22, 1784		Hugh Vance		cr 33	mr 32 *
Strode, Rhuanna m. Shepherd, Abr'm	Dec. 27, 1780		Dan'el Sturges		cr 31	mr 31 *
Strode, Sarah m. Harris, George	Dec. 26, 1799		John Hedtt(Hutt)			mr 17 *
Strode, Wm. m. Foreman, Ruth	Nov. 3, 1798	Joseph Foreman	Chas. P. Krauth	1b145	go 30	mr 15 *
Strodeman, Lowery m. Lemon, Harriet	Nov. 6, 1823	John V. Lemon	Wm. Hill	4b236	gc 14	mr 46 *
Strodeman, Susannah m. Shiely, James	Mar. 29, 1794		Rev. Reebenack		gc 13	mr 9 *
Storm, Eliz. m. Guseman, John	May 12, 1813		Rev. Reebenack		go 14	
Strother, Adam m. Sesler, Maria	Aug. 12, 1849					
Strother,David H. m. Wolff,Ann Doyne	June 15, 1849	A.W.Vanorsdale	Lewis F. Wilson	7b157		mr 83 *
Strother, John m. Hunter, Eliz.	Sept 7, 1815	Robert Wilson	John Mathews	3b337		
Strouse, David m. Wolly(Walley),Ann	May 7, 1815	Jacob French	Rev. Reebenack	3b327		mr 25 *
Strouse, Eliz. m. French, Jacob	Oct. 12, 1839	Thos. G. Evans		6b179		
Strouse, Isaiah m. French, Mary Ann	Oct. 3, 1848	Conrad Crumbaugh		7b136		
Strouse, Lydia m. Brannon, Thomas	Feb. 5, 1852	Jacob VanDoren		7b244		
Strouse, Mary Cath. m. Riser, Samuel	Dec. 19, 1849	Isaiah Strouse		7b171		
Strouse, Sarah E. m. French, John	Mar. 16, 1850	Isaiah Strouse		7b179		
Strowbridge, Martha m. Rumans, Thos.	Jan. 30, 1849	Lewis Strowbridge		7b146	go 3	
Strmcker, Simeon m. Schneider, Regina	Aug. 6, 1793		David Young			
Stryder, Jacob m. Young, Polly	Dec. 19, 1798	Wm. Dollie	Moses Hoge	1b155	cr 29	mr 15 *
Stubbs, Jacob m. Shall, Margt.	Jan. 7, 1799	Bartholomew Shall	David Young	1b160	gc 8	
!Stuckey, Daniel m. Grantham, Eliz.	Nov. 16, 1850	Lewis Grantham		7b202		
!Stuckey, David m. Grantham, Eliz.	Apr. 9, 1851		Lewis F. Wilson			mr 87 *

Name	(date)	(marriage)	(surety)	(minister)	(bond)	cr/gc	mr
Stuckey, David m. Grantham, Susan	Feb. 10,	Feb. 13, 1845	Lewis Grantham	James Chisholm	7b 26		mr 76 *
Stuckey, Eliz. m. Bear, John C.	July 27,	July 30, 1846	Samuel Stuckey	J.H.Jennings	7b 70		mr 82 *
Stuckey, Hannah m. Barney, Wm. Jr.		Oct. 13, 1852		J.H.Jennings			mr 86 *
Stuckey, Jacob m. Grove, Maria	Oct. 26,	1837	Wm. C. Grove		6b122		
Stuckey, Jacob m. Wilson, Nancy	June 11,	June 13, 1850	James Wilson	J.H.Jennings	7b187		mr 82 *
Stuckey, Jacob S. m. Ferrell, Effy	Mar. 19,	1844	Benj. Ferrell		6b316		
Stuckey, John m. Bishop, Mary Ellen		Feb. 14, 1854		John O. Proctor			
Stuckey, Mary M.m. Milburn, Jas.Wm.	July 3,	July 5, 1848	Israel Robinson	P.D.Lipscomb	7b133		mr 81 *
Stuckey, Margt. Ann m. Ferrell, John	Nov. 30,	Dec. 3, 1846	Charles Stuckey	James Chisholm	7b 78		mr 77 *
Stuckey, Mary m. Fry, John	Nov. 19,	1833	John Stuckey	Peyton Harrison	6b151		mr 69 *
Stuckey, Mary m. Keefer, Joseph	Sept 14,	1822	Jacob Stuckey	Chas. P. Krauth	4b223		mr 45 *
Stuckey, Mary m. Milburn, Jas. W.	July 5,	1845	Israel Robinson	P. Lipscomb	7b133		mr 81 *
Stuckey, Mary Eliz. m. Bear, John C.	July 27,	July 30, 1846	Samuel Stuckey	J.H.Jennings	7b 70		mr 82 *
Stuckey, Samuel m. Siler, Hannah	July 8,	Feb. 11, 1819	Jesse Thompson	W.N.Scott	4b 99		mr 30 *
Stuckey, Sarah m. Graves, Wm.	Nov. 22,	Nov. 27, 1851	Daniel K. Stuckey	James H. Jennings	7b237		mr 85 *
Stuckey, Susan m. Syler, Elias	Apr. 6,	Apr. 14, 1840	Israel Robinson	Lewis F. Wilson	6b205		mr 71 *
Studman, Nancy m. Merchant, Isaac	Nov. 24,	1798	Jonathan Gerrard	John Heitt(Hutt)	1b144	cr 30	mr 15 *
Stump, Casper m. Maddox, Cath. E.	Oct. 14,	1839	Lorenzo Maddox	M.G.Hamilton	6b180		mr 71 *
Stump, Eliz. Rachel m.Johnson,Andrew	Nov. 22,	1841	Casper Stump	John Hedges	6b254		mr 73 *
Stump, Ephraim m. Sendindiver, Lydia	Nov. 9,	?	Louis Sencindiver	John Kehler	4b 86		mr 31 *
Stump, Jemima Cath. m. Wilson, John	Dec. 9,	1850	Esom Mayhew	F.C. Tebbs	7b206		mr 83 *
Stump, Margt. m.Sendindiver, Martin	June 15,	1818	*John Stump	John Kehler	4b 74		mr 30 *
Stump, Polly m.Fitzsimmons,Nicholas	Mar. 4,	1800	Henry Small		2b 56		
Sturme, John m. Bonner, Kath.	July 18,	July 18, 1786		Hugh Vance			mr 43 *
Stutsman, Sarah Ann m. Bowman,Jona'n	Nov. 27,	1807	John Stutsman		3b 78	gc 7	
Stutt, Betsy m. Malone, James	Mar. 26,	Apr. 13, 1798	Chas. McGowan	David Young	1b 91	cr 15	
Stuts, Margt. m. Haines, John		Jan. 1790		Christian Streit			
Suber, Eliz. m. Houseworth,Valentine	Sept 28,	Oct. 1, 1829	Robert Daniel	Jas. M. Brown	5b143		mr 6 *
Suber, Mary m. Eck, John T.	Jan. 15,	Jan. 17, 1850	Solomon Weidman	Richard Brown	7b173		mr 53 *
Suber, Peter m. Sybert, Susanna Mrs.	Mar. 26,	Mar. 28, 1811	Jacob Billmyre	Rev. Reebenack	3b182	gc 12	mr 79 *
Suel, Mordecai m. Short, Sarah	Aug. 27,	Aug. 28, 1802	Benedict Rush	Richard Swift	2b179	gc 32	
Suffrance, Martha m. McKeever, Alex.	Nov. 10,	Nov. 10, 1812	Angus McKeever	Rev. Reebenack	3b239	gc 13	mr 21 *
Sugar, Benj. m. Davidson, Ann	Oct. 12,	Feb. 4, 1790	David Sugar	Hugh Vance			mr 38 *
Sugar, Wm. m. Spry, Ann		Oct. 16, 1798		Richard Swift	1b138		mr 15 *
Suhaim, Jacob B.F. m. Gilbert, Eliz.		Dec. 1, 1853		G.W.Cooper			
Sullivan, Eliz. m. Macknady,Cornel's	May 2,	1840	Timothy Sullivan		6b207	cr 31	
Sullivan, Ellen m. Goheen, Michael	Feb. 8,	1851	John Sullivan	Andrew Talty	7b214		mr 84 *
Sullivan, Hartley m. Butt, Charlotte	May 1,	1817	?		4b 34		
Sullivan, Hartley m.Tarlton, Eliz.	May 30,	June 5, 1800	Daniel Sullivan	John Heitt(Hutt)	2b 72	cr 35	mr 19 *
Sullivan, Johanna m. Tierney, Martin		Sept 11, 1852		J.H.Plunkett			mr 88 *
Sullivan, Thomas m. Ault, Mary		July 26, 1788		Moses Hoge			mr 36 *
Summers, Wm. m. Williamson, Susannah	Mar. 19,	Mar. 27, 1827	John Shober	John Mathews	5b 64		mr 51 *
Summers, Abr'm m. Kuntz, Sarah	Nov. 1,	1791		David Young		gc 1	
Summers, John m. Wilson, Mary	Dec. 29,	1788	*Lewis Sencindiver	Hugh Vance			mr 36 *

Name	(marriage)	Year	(suretor)	(minister)	(bond)	cr/gc	mr
Summers, John m. Elkins, Lucy H.	June 8,	1812	Jacob Fenner		3b227		
Sumption, Franklin m. Hawk, Harriet	Oct. 17,	1844	Wm. H. Mong		7b 8		
Sumption, Jacob m. Dysert, Libby	July 18,	1809	Jabez Anderson		3b115		
Sumption, John W. m. Grimes, Tizzy A	Mar. 3,	1848	Wm. M. Grimes		7b125		
†Sumption, Joseph m. Lewis, Polly	May 22,	1810		Rev. Reebenack		gc 11 *	
Sumption, Mary m. Merchant, John	Feb. 15,	1841	Jacob Sumption		6b233		
Sumption, Ruth m. Stewart, Samuel	Mar. 26,	1803	Joseph Sumption		2b199		
Sunsford, Nicholas m. House, Sarah	Nov. 10,	1800	Henry Vollum		2b 98		
Suter, Wm. m. Wilan, Melinda	Oct. 7,	1839	Andrew Bowman		6b178		
Sutherland, Diana m. Beally, John	Feb. 14,	1799	Geo. Sutherland	John Hutt(Hedtt)	1b168	cr 12 *	
Sutton, Amy m. Hedges, John	Feb. 9,	1799		Hugh Vance			
Sutton, Daniel m. Alburtis, Mary Ann	Jan. 16,	1790		W. Love			mr 18 *
Sutton, John Jr. m. Roberts, Sarah	Jan. 17,	1850	G.W.Miller		7b175		mr 38 *
Sutton, Susannah m. Claycomb, Conrad	Nov. 20,	1843	Harrison Waite		6b307		mr 80 *
Sutton, Susanna m. Miller, John	Mar. 6,	1839	Harvey A. Hedges		6b162		
Swaim, Eliz. m. Holliday, Thomas	Oct. 3,	1788		Hugh Vance			mr 36 *
Swan, Hannah m. Crabb, Jacob	Feb. 5,	1801	John Swaim		2b114		
Swaney, Jeremiah m. Sterrett, Eliz.	Aug. 12,	1819	John Strother	Nathan Young	4b112		mr 56 *
Swanigan, Liddy m. Morgan, Raleigh	Jan. 26,	1831	Joseph Sterrett	Robert Cadden	5b186		mr 61 *
Swanigan, Priscilla m. Alder, Marcus	Sept 18,	1790		Moses Hoge		cr 5	mr 5 *
Swartz, Frederica m. Fuss, J.G.	Jan. 20,	1791		Moses Hoge		cr 5	mr 6 *
Swartz, Geo. W. m. Billmire, Rosanna	Apr. 17,	1839	Mathias Schwartz	Peyton Harrison	6b167		mr 71 *
Swartz, John F. m. Bowers, Ann A.	Oct. 1,	1840	Wm. Billmire		6b218		
Swartz, John T. m. Chambers, Ann R.	May 27,	1844	Ephraim Alburtis		7b 2		
Sweaney, Maria m. Maddox, John	July 13,	1837	Anthony S.Chambers		6b110		
Swearingen, Benoni m. Goding, Hester	Oct. 31,	1829	Jeremiah Sweney	W. Monroe	5b145		mr 54 *
Swearingen, Hezekiah m. Henshaw,Isabel	Nov. 1,	1793		Moses Hoge			mr 39 *
?Swearingen, James m. Darb(-ky)Marg.	Jan. 24,	1836					mr 73 *
?Swearingen, James m. Dailey, Margt.	Feb. 15,	1841	Bailey Tabb	John Hedges	6b 71		mr 73 *
Swearingen, James S. m. Bedinger, Nan	July 12,	1841	Benj. Dailey	John Hedges	6b243	cr 14	mr 24 *
Swearingen, Julia A. m. Beeson, Jesse	July 12,	1811	Benj. Dailey	John B. Hoge	6b243	cr 15	mr 7 *
Swearingen, Lydia m. Morgan, Raleigh	Nov. 2,	1791	Henry Bedinger	Christian Streit	3b198	cr 5	mr 5 *
Swearingen, Margt. m. Turner, Anthony	Dec. 31,	1790		Moses Hoge			
Swearingen, Mary m. Graham, Edmund	Sept 18,	1812	Van Brashier		3b232		mr 37 *
Swearingen, Nancy m. Graham, James	July 28,	1789		Hugh Vance			mr 43 *
Swearingen, Peggy m. Fenke, Christian	Jan. 8,	1786		Hugh Vance			
Swearingen, Sarah m. Blackford, John	July 27,	1799	Marcus Alder		2b 33		mr 52 *
Sweart, Tabitha m. Paden, Jacob	Nov. 2,	1828	John Gooding		1b 29		
Sweany, John B. m. Wilson, Mary Ann	Aug. 17,	1836	Daniel Smart	B. Reynolds	5011		mr 54 *
**Swift, Maria m. Maddox, John	Oct. 22,	1829	Wm. Wageley	Wm. Monroe	6b 80	cr 21	mr 7 *
**Swift, Richard m. Willis, Martha	May 25,	1793	Jeremiah Sweney	Moses Hoge	5b145	cr 38	mr 20 *
Swift, Jonathan m. Ault, Barbara	Oct. 31,	1801		Moses Hoge			mr 44 *
Swim, Mary m. Richardson, Thos.	Mar. 28,	1787		Hugh Vance			
†*Sumption, Joseph m. Lewis, Sally	Mar. 19,	1810	Jacob Sumption	Richard Swift	3b143	cr 12	mr 14 *
**Swift, Cath. m. Ramety, John	Aug. 15,	1797					

Name		Date	Year (marriage)	(suretor)	(minister)	(bond)	Ref.
Swinley, Cath. m. Thomas, Arch'd	Nov. 26,		1811	Jacob Swinley	John Winter	3b201	mr 50 *
Swinley, Dorothy m. Hazlett, Wm.	Feb. 10,	Feb. 17,	1825	John Swinley	John Howell	4b289	mr 68 *
Swinley, George m. Ward, Hester	Aug. 6,	Aug. 11,	1835	Boyd Roberts		6b 52	
Swinley, Henry m. Hazlett, Mary	Oct. 16,		1834	John Swinley		6b 14	
Swinley, Jacob m. Snyder, Cath.	June 23,		1804	George Pulse		2b237	
Swinley, John m. Hazlett(Has-)Hannah	Mar. 14,	Mar. 16,	1820	John Hazlett	Nathan Young	4b140	mr 57 *
Swinley, John m. Morgan, Maria	Nov. 29,	Dec. 1,	1831	Wm. G. Morgan	J.E.Jackson	5b210	
Swinley, Mary E. m. Stewart(Shu-)Geo.	Mar. 2,	Mar. 5,	1846	John Swinley	Richard F. Brown	7b 60	mr 77 *
Swingle, Benond m. Morgan, Rebecca	Nov. 17,	Nov. 20,	1823	Morgan Morgan	John Winter	4b252	mr 49 *
Swingle, Cath. m. Bower, Adam	Oct. 25,		1830	?		5b179	
Swingle, Eliz. m. Sibole, Ebenezer	Nov. 19,		1842	Michael Coleman		6b284	
Swingle, George m. Small, Cath. L.	Feb. 7,	Feb. 7,	1852	Henry Riner	Lewis F. Wilson	7b244	mr 87 *
Swingle, Maria B. m. Thornburg.Thos.	Oct. 6,		1828	Zebulun Bell		5b108	
Swingle, Mary m. Coleman, Michael	Aug. 20,	Aug. 22,	1838	Jas. L. Maslin	Lewis F. Wilson	6b144	mr 69 *
Swingle, Mary Va. m. Shaffer, Wm. M.	Apr. 9,	Apr. 12,	1849	Benond Swingle	B.M.Schmucker	7b153	mr 79 *
Swingley,Cath. m. Kindar, John	Apr. 24,		1799	John Bashore		2b 22	
Swingley, Michael m. Riner, Nancy	Dec. 16,		1809	Henry Riner		3b127	
Swingley, Rachel m. Bell, Zebulun	Sept 20,		1821	Benj. Swingley		4b190	
Swiser, Maria m. Leopard, Abr'm.		May 16,	1796		David Young		gc 5 *
Swisher, Ann m. Bowers, Samuel	June 11,	June 14,	1838	George Swisher	James Watts	6b117	gc 69 *
Swisher, George m. Banscott, Polly	Oct. 5,	Dec. 5,	1793		David Young		gc 3 *
Swisher, George m. Cloninger, Mary A	Oct. 3,	Oct. 5,	1839	John Clark	M.G.Hamilton	6b178	mr 71 *
Swisher, George m. Magee, Margt.	Dec. 1,		1828	Michael Runner		5b13	
Swisher, Henry m. Barnes, Eliz.	Oct. 7,		1837	John Helferstay		6b114	
Swisher, Henry m. Gilpin, Agnes	Aug. 1,	Aug. 2,	1798	James Robinson	David Young	1b124	gc 7 *
Swisher, Jacob m. Bonner, Cath.	Aug. 13,		1801	John Dupp		2b136	
Swisher, Jacob m. Cumpton, Evelina	Jan. 13,	Jan. 16,	1825	Exekiel Cumpton	Nathan Young	4b285	mr 58 *
Swisher, Mary m. Specht, George	Feb. 10,	Feb. 11,	1827	Henry Swisher	Nathan Young	5b 62	mr 59 *
Swisher, Rachel m.Dupp(Dunn), John	Jan. 14,	Jan. 15,	1801	George Baker	John Boyd	2b109	cr 35 mr 19 *
Swisher, Solomon m. Bonner, Elz.	Nov. 5,	Nov. 9,	1811	Fred. Shawhan	John B. Hoge	3b199	cr 14 mr 24 *
Switzer, Mary m. Pitzer, John	June 14,		1797	Mathias Pitzer		1b 21	
Switzer, Sally m. Hunt, Stewart	Mar. 18,		1807	Jacob Switzer		3b 51	
Sybert, Cath. m. Myers, Henry	Apr. 5,		1808	Jacob Sybert		3b 84	
Sybert, Jacob m. Mong, Cath.	Sept 8,	Sept 10,	1812	John Mong	Rev. Reebenack	3b236	gc 13 *
Sybert, Jacob m. Myers, Mary	Mar. 7,	Mar. 8,	1810	John Myers	Lewis Mayer	3b139	cr 14 mr 24 *
Sybert, Jacob F. m. Lemon, Rhuanna	Nov. 17,		1813	George Holliday		3b275	
Sybert, Michael m. Tice, Polly	Nov. 1,	Nov. 26,	1811	Fred. Sybert	Rev. Reebenack	3b198	gc 12 *
Sybert, Susanna Mrs. m. Suber, Peter	Mar. 26,	Mar. 28,	1811	Jacob Billmyer	Rev. Reebenack	3b182	gc 12 *
Sybole, Elenor m. McDonald, Wm.	Feb. 15,		1834	Ichabod Sybole		5b302	
Sybole, James m. Hooper, Mary E.	Oct. 22,	Oct. 24,	1842	Wm. McDonald	Mayberry Goheen	6b281	mr 74 *
Sybole, Presley B. m. Higgins, Eliz.	Feb. 19,	Feb. 22,	1838	John Shull	James Watts	6b132	
Syers, Alex. m. Hill, Christiana	Sept 4,		1797	Christ'r Hill		1b 38	
Syester, Jacob m. Crown, Belinda	July 30,	Aug. 2,	1832	Andrew McIntire	Wm. Monroe	5b234	mr 65 *

Name	Date	(marriage)	(surety)	(minister)	(bond)	Ref
Syester, Jacob m. Myers, Margt.	May 17,	May 20, 1824	Peter Myers Jr.	J.L.Bromwell	4b266	mr 47 *
Syester, Susanna m. McWitt, John	Nov. 24,	Nov. 24, 1808	David Syester		3b101	mr 60 *
Syler, David m. Garber(Guber), Eliza	June 1,	June 2, 1829	John Garber	Nathan Young	5b130	mr 71 *
Syler, Elias m. Stuckey, Susan	Apr.	Apr. 14, 1840	Israel Robinson	Lewis F. Wilson	6b205	mr 74 *
Syler, Jacob m. Canby, Margt.	Oct. 31,	Nov. 4, 1843	Elias Siler	Lewis F. Wilson	6b306	
Syler, Martha m. Rainey, James	Dec. 25,	1816	Jonathan Thatcher		4b 28	
Syler, Philip m. Robinson, Eliz.	Apr. 2,	Apr. 13, 1840	Garret Wynkoop	Lewis F. Wilson	6b204	mr 71 *

"T"

Name	Date	(marriage)	(surety)	(minister)	(bond)	Ref
Tabb, Alma m. Patterson, John	Mar. 7,	Feb. 12, 1807	George Tabb	John Mathews	3b 49	cr 13
Tabb, Anna m. Patterson, John	Feb. 2,	1807	Jacob V. Gerrard		6b 30	
Tabb, Ann V. m. Boley, Tolemiah	Feb. 14,	1835	Wm. Cunningham		6b264	mr 23 *
Tabb, Ann W. m. Light, Samuel H.	Jan. 20,	Feb. 17, 1842	John T.N.Tabb	Lewis F. Wilson	7b 22	
Tabb, Anabella E. m. Snodgrass, W.T.	Mar. 16,	Jan. 21, 1845	Douglas Campbell	Lewis F. Wilson	5b 4	mr 73 *
Tabb, Bailey m. Campbell, Sarah Ann	Dec. 4,	Mar. 17, 1825	George P. Morrison	Jas. M. Brown	7b169	mr 48 *
Tabb, Dorcas S. m. Ijams, James	Feb. 6,	Dec. 6, 1849	Edward Tabb Sr.	Lewis F. Wilson	2b254	cr 28 mr 83 * 87
Tabb, Edward Jr. m. Turner, Elithy	Mar. 8,	Feb. 7, 1805	Wm. Cunningham	John Bond	5b155	mr 22 *
Tabb, Edward F. m. Cunningham, Kitty	Apr. 7,	Mar. 8, 1830	Seaton E. Tabb	Jas. M. Brown	6b 3	mr 54 *
Tabb, Eliza m. McIntire, Andrew	Feb. 25,	Apr. 10, 1834	Abr'm Varmetre	Jas. M. Brown	6b 33	mr 68 *
Tabb, Eliz. m. McQuilkin, Jacob	Dec. 4,	1835	James Ijams		7b169	mr 83 *87
Tabb, Eliz. m. Morrison, George	Feb. 24,	Dec. 6, 1849		Lewis F. Wilson	7b124	mr 83 *
Tabb, Elliott R. m.Snodgrass,Lucinda		Feb. 29, 1848	Robert V.Snodgrass	J.H.Jennings		mr 7 *
Tabb, Frances m. Turner, Anthony		Mar. 14, 1793		Moses Hoge		mr 12 *
Tabb, George m. Eliason, Anna		Jan. 7, 1796		John Boyd		cr 21
Tabb, George m. Long, Eliz.	Oct. 7,	1835	Wm. Cunningham		6b 99	cr 10
Tabb, George m.Porterfield, Mary	Mar. 9,	Mar. 11, 1818	George Porterfield	John B. Hoge	4b 65	mr 29 *
Tabb, Geo. W. m. Wilson, Mary C.	Oct. 6,	Oct. 10, 1840	Seaton E. Tabb	Lewis F. Wilson	6b220	mr 71 *
Tabb, Harriet m. Wilson,Lewis F.	Rev.Apr.	1838?	Seaton E. Tabb	Peyton Harrison	6b138	mr 69 *
Tabb, Isaballa m.Varmetre, Abr'm	Sept 2,	Sept 17, 1817	John Strother	John Mathews	4b 45	
Tabb, John m. Turner, Arabella	Dec. 27,	Jan. 5, 1807?	Edward Tabb	John Mathews	3b 40	cr 13
Tabb, Louisa F. m. Nelson, Jas. P.		Apr. 26, 1852		Lewis F. Wilson		mr 23 *
Tabb, Lucinda m. Harrison, John F.		Nov. 6, 1852		Lewis F. Wilson		mr 87 *
Tabb, Martha J. m. Maslim, Hanson	Feb. 14,	Feb. 17, 1831	Wm. Cunningham	Lewis F. Wilson	6b265	mr 87 *
Tabb, Mary Mrs. m. Gorrell, Jacob V.	Sept 13,	Sept 15, 1831	John Shober	Nathan Young	5b205	mr 73 *
Tabb, Mary m. Hedges, Samuel		June 26, 1783		Hugh Vance		mr 62 *
Tabb, Mary E. m.Porterfield, George	Sept 29,	1821	John Porterfield		4b193	mr 32 *
Tabb, Mary Eveline m. Janney, Israel	May 19,	1831	Wm. Long		5b195	
Tabb, Susan m. Riddle, John R.	Mar. 6,	1828	Wm. Riddle		5b 92	
Tabb, Thomas m. Varmetre, Polly	Dec. 4,	Dec. 3, 1812	Nathan Varmetre	John Mathews	3b242	mr 25 *

	Date	(marriage)	(suretor)	(minister)	(bond)		
Tabb, Thomas m. Varmetre, Eliz.	Dec. 13,	Dec. 29, 1796	Asahel Varmetre	Moses Hoge	7b116	cr 36	mr 12 *
Tabler, Adam m. Varmetre,Isabella G.	Dec. 4,	Dec. 10, 1847		J. Baker	4b LL		mr 78 *
Tabler, Adam m. Worley, Piety	Apr. 19,	Dec. 6, 1818	Silas Worley	Nathan Young	7b 94		mr 56 *
Tabler, Ann Rebecca m.Staley,Emanuel	June 5,	Apr. 22, 1847	Adam Tabler	D.F.Bragunier	4b 5		mr 78 *
Tabler, Cath. m. Klaycomb, Fred.	Apr. 15,	June 6, 1816	Adam Tabler	W.N.Scott	3b184	ge 12	mr 26 *
Tabler, Christian m. Miller, Eliz.	June 2,	Apr. 16, 1811	George Tabler	Rev. Reebenack	6b242		mr 72 *
Tabler, Eliza m. Barns, Wm. E.	Jan. 5,	June 5, 1841	Christian Tabler	Lewis F. Wilson	5b253		mr 65 *
Tabler, Eliza m. Kneedler,Joseph	June 13,	Jan. 5, 1833	John Hudgel	Nathan Young	3b328		mr 25 *
Tabler, Eliz. m. Paul, Robert	June 28,	June 15, 1815	Adam Tabler	John Mathews	6b142		
Tabler, Ephraim m. Soper, Eliz.	Jan. 27,	June 28, 1838	Thomas Soper		7b 56		
Tabler, Ephraim G. m.Moore, Susan J.	Dec. 1,	Jan. 27, 1846	Jas. W. Moore	John Light	6b255		mr 72 *
Tabler, Harriet E. m. Tabler, Joshua	Aug. 19,	Dec. 1, 1841	Christian Tabler	Lewis Mayer	3b 94	cr 16	mr 24 *
Tabler, Henry m. Oller, Polly	Dec. 1,	Aug. 20, 1808	Peter Oller	John Light	6b255		mr 72 *
Tabler, Joshua m. Tabler, Harriet E.	Sept 25,	Dec. 1, 1841	Christian Tabler	W.N.Scott	4b 10		
Tabler, Mary m. Peterman, George	Mar. 28,	Sept 26, 1816	Wm. Tabler	Jacob Medtart	5b123		mr 63 *
Tabler, Mary m. Tabler, Wm.	Mar. 28,	Mar. 11, 1829	Adam Tabler	Chas. P. Krauth	5b 66		mr 51 *
Tabler, Mary A. m. Welehans,Ephraim	Aug. 17,	Mar. 28, 1827	Henry Tabler	Richard Swift	2b136		mr 20 *
Tabler, Mary A. m. Rutherford, Archd	May 21,	July 20, 1801	Wm. Tabler		7b157	cr 31	
Tabler, Mary E. m. Thompson, Mathias	Apr. 18,	Apr. 20, 1843	Abr'm Taylor	John Light	6b295		mr 74 *
Tabler, Peter O. m. Thomas, Jane	Mar. 19,	Mar. 19, 1808	John Lemaster		3b 83		
Tabler, Phebe m. Barnes, Michael	Sept 25,	Sept 26, 1818	Adam Tabler	W.N.Scott	4b 10		
Tabler, Polly m. Peterman, George	Feb. 15,	Feb. 16, 1841	William Tabler	John Light	6b233		mr 72 *
Tabler, Rhuana m. Lemaster, John	Mar. 28,	Feb. 28, 1835	Joshua Tabler		6b 38		
Tabler, Rosannah m. French, Wm.	Feb. 15,	Feb. 16, 1841	Wash't'n Tabler	John Light	6b233		mr 72 *
Tabler, Rhuanna m. Lemaster, John	Sept 25,	Dec. 25, 1833	Joshua Tabler		5b298		
Tabler, Sarah Ann m. Chambers, Jacob	Sept 3,	Sept 4, 1832	Seaman Stewart	Jacob Medtart	5b239		mr 64 *
Tabler, Susan m. Helferstay, John	Dec. 13,	Dec. 17, 1833	Adam Stewart	Nathan Young	5b295		mr 66 *
Tabler, Wash't'n m. Needler, Polly	Jan. 27,	Jan. 27, 1794	Benj. Conover	David Young	5b123		
Tabler, Will m. Rutherford, Maria	Mar. 18,	Mar. 11, 1829	Adam Tabler	Jacob Medtart	7b123		mr 63 *
Tabler, Wm. m. Tabler, Mary	Feb. 23,	Feb. 25, 1848	Samuel Cole	P. Lipscomb	3b319		mr 81 *
Tabler, Wm. m. Wilson, Susan	Apr. 11,	Apr. 13, 1815		Nathan Young	7b155		mr 55 *
Tabler, Wm. Jr. m. Worley, Prudence	Apr. 23,	1849	Brice Worley				
Tabler, Wm. m. Sler, Marg't.	Oct. 23,	Oct. 23, 1839	Mathias Kine				
Tabler, Wm. W. m. Kreglo, Eliz.	Sept 17,	Sept 17, 1817	George Kreglo				
?Taffe, Isabella m. Varmetre, Abr'm		1829	John Murray	John Mathews	6b181		*
Taffe, Thomas m. Porter, Sarah	Aug. 27,	Aug. 27, 1829	Wm. P. Shipman		5b139		mr 85 *
Talbott, Mary Eliz. m.Wolff,Armst'd	May 31,	June 3, 1851	John L. Neel	F.C.Tebbs	7b225		mr 61 *
Talbott, Samuel m. O'Neal, Hannah S.	Mar. 31,	Apr. 3, 1831		Nathan Young	5b190		mr 39 *
Talbott, Sarah m. Rion, John	Aug. 9,	Aug. 9, 1792		Moses Hoge			
Talbott, Wm. m. Boydstone, Anne	Dec. 5,	Dec. 16, 1797	Presley Boydstone	Richard Swift	1b 69	cr 12	mr 14 *
Tallis, John m. Cornwell, Elinor	Apr. 25,	May 16, 1799	John Bull	John Hedtt(Hutt)	2b 4	cr 13	mr 18 *
Tallis, Wm. m. Teards, Tabitha	May 22,	May 22, 1793		Wm. Hill		cr 3	mr 10 *
Tally, Ebenezer m. Martin, Mary	Sept 30,	Sept 30, 1845	James Martin	John Boggs	7b 45		mr 75 *

?Taffe here means Tabb

Name	(marriage)		(surety)	(minster)	(bond)			
Talman, Hannah m. Crabb, John	Sept 23,	1800	Edward Crabb		2b 89		mr 10	*
Talor, Mary m. Bell(Beall), John	May 21,	1795		Richard Swift		cr 26	mr 13	*
Tamel, Eliz. m. Truelock, Parker	Nov. 2,	1797		John Boyd		cr 32	mr 2	*
Tannihill, Rebecca m. Young, Wm.	Dec. 13,	1787		Hugh Vance		cr 23	mr 7	*
Tapscott, James m. Wood, Susannah	Apr. 30,	1793		Moses Hoge		cr 21		
Tapscott, Wm. Baylor, Cath.	Mar. 12,	1801	Richard Baylor		2b102			
Tarlney, Peter m. Dunham, Sarah	Feb. 21,	1798		Moses Hoge		cr 36	mr 14	*
Tarlton, Eliz. m. Sullivan, Hartley	May 30,	1800	Daniel Sullivan	John Butt(Rett)	2b 72	cr 35	mr 19	*
Tate, Andrew m. James(Jones), Eliz.	Mar. 28,	1818	Solomon Offutt	Nathan Young	4b 66		mr 56	*
Tate, David J. m. Meanor, Mary Ann	Aug. 6,	1835	Samuel Meanor	John Howell	6b 52		mr 68	*
Tate, Eliz. m. Evans, John	June 11,	1822	John Porterfield		4b216			
Tate, John m. Boothe, Hannah	Aug. 1,	1805	Samuel Meanor		2b266			
Tate, Lucinda M. m. Thomas, George	Apr. 4,	1837	Erasmus S. Tate		6b104			
Tate, Margt. M. m. Lyle, Ignatius P.	Dec. 26,	1826	John F. Snodgrass		5b 58		mr 42	*
Tate, Mary m. Edmondson, Thos.	Mar. 27,	1782		Daniel Sturges				
Tate, Polly m. Stribling, Taliafero	Jan. 17,	1814	Robert Wilson		3b281			
Tate, Rachel m. Pepper, Henry	Feb. 23,	1831	John Tate	Jas. M. Brown	5b187		mr 62	*
Tate, Rosanna m. Seaman, Richard D.	Aug. 16,	1828	Robert Stewart	Jas. M. Brown	5b105		mr 51	*
Tate, Rosannah m. Good, Alex. C.	May 6,	1833	Steph. Snodgrass		5b272			
Tate, Samuel m. McKimney, Eliz.	Apr. 1,	1802	Jonathan Powell		2b167			
Tate, Rosannah m. Seaman, Richard D.	Aug. 16,	1828	Robert Stewart	Jas. M. Brown	5b105		mr 51	*
Taylor, Ann m. Turner, Wm.	Jan. 16,	1827	Samuel Taylor		5b 60			
Taylor, Anne m. Boswell, George	Jan. 2,	1787		Hugh Vance			mr 43	*
Taylor, Caleb m. Shaw, Eliz.	Feb. 17,	1813	Stephen Shaw		3b251			
Taylor, Cath. m. Alburtis, John	Dec. 31,	1805	Chet D. Wilson	Moses Hoge	3b 7	cr 17	mr 22	*
Taylor, Chas. W. m. Miller, Harriet	May 4,	1824	Wm. J. Miller	John Winter	4b264		mr 50	*
Taylor, Eliza C. m. Savor, Wm.	?	1789		D. Thomas			mr 38	*
Taylor, Eliz. m. Alburtis, John	Dec. 31,	1805	Chet D. Wilson	Moses Hoge	5b181	cr 17	mr 22	*
Taylor, Eliz. m. Hudgel, John	Nov. 17,	1830	Jonas Smith	Nathan Young	3b 97		mr 61	*
Taylor, George m. Bready, Nancy	Oct. 3,	1808	David Morrison		7b221			
Taylor, Isaiah C. m. Comegys, Mary E.	Apr. 2,	1851	Benj. Comegys					
Taylor, Jane m. Taylor, Richard	May 22,	1781		Daniel Sturges			mr 31	*
Taylor, John m. Osborn, Patty	June 23,	1789		Moses Hoge		cr 2	mr 3	*
Taylor, John B. m. Orrick, Susan	Mar. 8,	1821	Nicholas Orrick	Edw. R. Lippett	4b175		mr 45	*
Taylor, Kath. m. Gaither, Ephraim	Feb. 2,	1792		Moses Hoge		cr 8	mr 7	*
Taylor, Lewis m. Lafferty, Esther	Jan. 1,	1794		Richard Swift			mr 40	*
Taylor, Martha m. Pierce, Joseph	Mar. 1,	1796		Moses Hoge		cr 35	mr 11	*
Taylor, Martha A. m. Stewart,John W.	Jan. 9,	1841	Thomas Hughes		6b230			
Taylor, Polly m. Violet, John	Oct. 13,	1791		Moses Hoge		cr 7	mr 6	*
Taylor, Rachel m. Levick, Caleb	Jan. 13,	1793		Christian Streit		cr 15	mr 8	*
Taylor, Rebecca m. Johnston, Robert	Oct. 3,	1825	Jesse Payne		5b 23			
Taylor, Richard m. Taylor, Jane	May 22,	1781		Daniel Sturges			mr 31	*
Taylor, Samuel m. Cross, Elinor	Sept 30,	1818	Basil Cross		4b 81			
Taylor, Samuel m. Stip, Eliz.	Mar. 5,	1801		Moses Hoge		cr 38	mr 20	*
Taylor, Mary m. Beall, John	May 21,	1795		Richard Swift		cr 26	mr 10	*
							229	

	(marriage)	(suretor)	(minister)	(bond)		
Taylor, Samuel m. Lay, Lydia	Aug. 23, 1823	Resen Hudgel	Richard Swift	4b246		
Taylor, Sophia m. Bedinger, Christ'n	Mar. 12, 1798	John Beall	John Bauman	1b 89	cr 31	mr 15 *
Taylor, Susan M. m. Lemaster, James	Sept 3, 1850	Samuel Taylor	John Boyd	7b194		mr 80 *
Taylor, Thomas m. Cromwell, Hannah	Oct. 8, 1798	Nicholas Orrick	Nathan Young	1b136	cr 32	mr 15 *
Taylor, Wm. m. Adams, Sarah	Nov. 8, 1818		Richard Swift			mr 56 *
Taylor, Wm. m. Lafferty, Esther	Jan. 7, 1794					mr 40 *
Taylor, Zachariah m. Irvin, Sarah	Nov. 13, 1799	Jonathan Tritt	John Boyd	2b 35	cr 34	mr 17 *
Tearis, Tabitha m. Tallis(Tullis),Wm.	Nov. 14, 1799		Wm. Hill		cr 34	mr 10 *
Tearney, John m. Kershner, Laura C.	May 22, 1845	Robert Lewis		7b 23		
Tederick, Charlotte m. Barns, Jacob	Jan. 28, 1799	Jacob Tederick	John Boyd	1b172	cr 34	mr 16 *
Tederick, George m. Stout, Elis.	Mar. 9, 1801	Michael Wolff		2b129		
Tederick, Jane m. Barns, John	July 28, 1798	Robert Jones	John Boyd	1b103	cr 32	mr 15 *
Tederick, Jane m. Tramhouse, Leonard	Jan. 19, 1795					
Tederick, John m. Hartman, Elis.	Feb. 4, 1806	Christian Hartman	David Young	3b 10	gc 5	*
Tederick, Peter m. Stout, Sally	June 20, 1803	Philip Stout	David Young	2b204	ge 10	
Teel, Wm. m. Johnson, Rosanna	Jan. 8, 1838	Hezekiah Hedges	David Young	6b129		
Tegmeyer, John H. m. Staub, Laura	June 21, 1853	D.F.Bragunier		1b156	gc 8	**
Terrell, Cath. m. Purcell(Paro), John	Dec. 25, 1853	David Young		1b 57	gc 8	**
Tharp, Abigail m. Everhart, Henry	Oct. 21, 1798					
Tharp, Hannah m. Thatcher, Jonathan	Aug. 2, 1797	Wm. Tharp		2b 15		
Tharp, Kitty m. Rainey(Reaney),John	Oct. 26, 1799					
Tharp, Mary m. Everhart, John	Oct. 19, 1819	Nathaniel Tharp	John B. Hoge	4b121		
Tharp, Wm. m. Ott, Eliz.	Nov. 29, 1801	Edward Howe		2b137		mr 31 *
Tat, Simon m. Grantham, Margt.	Feb. 20, 1789			2b100		
Thatcher, Absalom m. Hedges, Isabell	Feb. 20, 1828	Henry Myers	D. Thomas	5b 90		mr 37 *
Thatcher, Evans m. Brannon, Rachel	Sept 13, 1817	Stephen Gano	Nathan Young	4b 46		mr 99 *
Thatcher, Hester m. Kesler, Wm.	Oct. 27, 1838	Jonathan Thatcher	James Watts	6b148		mr 69 *
Thatcher, Hezekiah m. Kitchen, Alena	Feb. 26, 1829	Henry G. Kitchen	Jas. M. Brown	5b120		mr 53 *
Thatcher, Isaac m. Gano, Mary	Apr. 29, 1801	Bethuel Middleton		2b124		
Thatcher, John W. m. Miller, Nancy E	Dec. 8, 1842	David Miller	Lewis F. Wilson	6b285		mr 73 *
Thatcher, Jonathan m. Tharp, Hannah	Aug. 2, 1799	Wm. Tharp		2b 15		
Thatcher, Jonathan W. m. Miller, Nancy	Dec. 8, 1842	David Miller	Lewis F. Wilson	6b285		mr 73 *
Thatcher, Margt(Abigail m.Hoke,Jacob	Oct. 3, 1825	Jonathan Thatcher	James Redley	5b 23		mr 49 *
Thatcher, Martha m. Murphy, David	July 28, 1806	Thomas Thatcher		3b 24		
Thatcher, Mary m. Dunham, Aaron	Mar. 18, 1819	John Strother		4b102		
Thatcher, Mary m. Flemming, Wm.	July 27, 1807	Samuel Dunham		3b 64		
Thatcher, Nancy m. Conoway, Joseph	Aug. 27, 1827	Wash't'n Boling	Nathan Young	5b 76		mr 99 *
Thatcher, Sally m. Walter(Watten)John	Mar. 22, 1821	Gottleb Noll	Nathan Young	4b177		mr 57 *
Thatcher, Sylvester m. Dark(Dusk)Mary	Nov. 4, 1797	Isaac Allstadt		1b 60		
Thatcher, Thomas m. Thornburg, Margt.	Dec. 19, 1796		David Young		ge 6	
Theeby, Samuel m. Ashfield, Phebe	July 11, 1800	Benjamin Sheely	John Heitt(Hutt)	2b 75	cr 35	mr 19 *
Thelford, Nancy m. Hagerty, John	July 20, 1784		Hugh Vance			mr 53 *
Thirley, John m. Smithey, Ann	Feb. 7, 1785		Edward Tiffin			mr 1 *

Name	Date	(Marriage)	(surety)	(minister)	(bond)		
Thirlay, Wm. m. Mayers, Nancy	Oct. 7,	Oct. 10, 1811	John Mayer	John B. Hoge	5b196	cr 14	mr 24 *
Thirston, Wm. m. Bartleson, Virginia	Apr. 24,	Apr. 25, 1850	Elijah Bartleson	John Light	7b183		mr 80 *
Thistle, Arch'd m. Graham, Juliana	Dec. 22,	Dec. 22, 1818	Edmund Graham	W.N.Scott	4b 95		mr 30 *
Thistle, Cath. m. Todd, Miles	Dec. 27,	1799	John Thistle		2b 44		
Thistle, Arch'd m. Swinley, Cath.	Nov. 26,	1811	Jacob Swinley		3b201		
Thomas, Eliz. m. Dailey, Levi	Jan. 23,	Jan. 13, 1843	Jacob Thomas	Mayberry Goheen	6b288		mr 74 *
Thomas, Eve m. Relvey, John	Dec. 20,	Dec. 20, 1853		J.H.Plunkett			mr 88 *
Thomas, George m. Tate, Lucinda M.	Apr. 4,	Apr. 4, 1837	Erasmus S. Tate	John B. Hoge	6b104		
Thomas, Isaac m. Conoway, Eliza	Mar. 23,	Mar. 23, 1820	Samuel Conoway	John B. Hoge	4b141		mr 31 *
Thomas, Jacob m. Snodgrass,Susan P.	Feb. 28,	1854		John Proctor			
Thomas, James m. Barber, Cath.	Jan. 22,	1827	Wm. Ray		4b205		
Thomas, Jane m. Tabler, Peter O.	Apr. 18,	Apr. 20, 1843	John Lemaster	John Light	6b295	cr 29	mr 74 *
Thomas, Jeremiah m. Norris, Elinor		Dec. 4, 1798		Moses Hoge		cr 18	mr 15 *
Thomas, John m. Collins, Cath.		Sept 13, 1787		Hugh Vance			mr 2 *
Thomas, John m. Conway, Eliza	Mar. 23,	Mar. 23, 1820	Samuel Conway	John B. Hoge	4b141		mr 31 *
Thomas, John m. Deal, Susannah	Nov. 28,	1816	Robert Cockburn Jr.		4b 20		
Thomas, John H. m. Colston, Mary I.	Oct. 5,	1809	Rawleigh Colston		3b121		
Thomas, Joseph m. Howard, Sarah	May 22,	1797	Martin Howard		1b 17		
Thomas, Mary m. Conwell, Wm.	Feb. 6,	1803	Evan Rees		2b193		
Thomas,Mary m. Evans, Joseph	?	1789					mr 37 *
Thomas, Mary m. Menghini, Chas. L.	Feb. 20,	1838	Benj. Thomas	D. Thomas	6b133		
Thomas, Nelly m. Merchant, Isaac	Feb. 28,	1811	Leonard Thomas		3b177		
Thomas, Rosanna m. Caw, Peter	Oct. 26,	1833	John Beach		5b288		
Thomas, Thomas m. Fryatt, Sarah	Dec. 23,	1806	Arthur Chenoweth		3b 38		
Thompson, Ann m. Pierce(Pearce)John	Nov. 19,	Nov. 19, 1816	Benj. Comegys	John Mathews	4b 22		mr 26 *
Thompson, Bennett m. Curtis, Rhianna	Feb. 10,	1814	David Curtis		3b284		
Thompson, C. m. Couchman, Magdalena	Apr. 8,	Apr. 30, 1792		David Young	3b183	gc 1	
Thompson, Demaris m. Comegys, Benj.	Aug. 24,	Apr. 8, 1811	John Thompson	John Mathews	3b158		mr 40 *
Thompson, Elias m. McAtee, Hannah	Nov. 20,	Aug. 24, 1810	Bennett Thompson		2b248		
Thompson, Elias Edw. m. Wilmoth,Polly		Nov. 20, 1804	George Wilmooth				
Thompson, Eliz. m. Lettel, Henry	Nov. 19,	Sept 19, 1795		David Young		gc 5	
Thompson, James m. Brown, Mary	Jan. 23,	Nov. 21, 1816	Joseph Thompson	David Young	4b 21		mr 55 *
Thompson, James m. Miller, Isabella	Apr. 28,	Jan. 1823	Smith Miller	Nathan Young	4b232		mr 46 *
Thompson, James m. Siler, Cath.	Sept 8,	1806	Jacob Siler	Chas. P. Krauth	3b 17		
Thompson, Jane m. Inbody, John	Sept 9,	Sept 10, 1814	Joseph Thompson	Nathan Young	3b303		mr 55 *
Thompson, John m. Throckmorton, Lucy	Mar. 17,	1801	James Wood		2b142		
Thompson, Kitty m. Hazlewood, Jesse	Dec. 24,	1807	Abr'm Howe		3b 50		
Thompson, Samuel m. Wright, Mary	Feb. 21,	Dec. 24, 1798	Charles Wright	David Young	1b156	gc 8	
Thompson, Margt. m. Kern, Jacob	Sept 9,	Feb. 21, 1803	John Thompson	David Young	2b196	gc 10	
Thompson, Margt. m. Rankin, Wm.	June 24,	Sept 9, 1815	John Thompson		3b338		
Thompson, Martha m. Brooks, Benj.	Apr. 11,	June 26, 1817	Jacob R. Ripley	Mathias Riser	4b 39		
Thompson, Mary m. Delgard, John W.		Apr. 11, 1814	Joseph Thompson		3b291		

Name	(marriage)	(suretor)	(minister)	(bond)		
Thompson, Mary m. Kerns, Jacob	Feb. 21, 1803	John Thompson	David Young	2b196	gc 10	*
Thompson, Mary m. Kyger, John	July 27, 1810	Penny Thompson		3b155		
Thompson, Mary J. m. Pulse, Levi	Oct. 29, 1844	Wesley Ellis		7b 11		
Thompson, Mathias m. Tabler, Mary E.	May 21, 1849	Abr'm Tabler		7b157		
Thompson, Nancy m. Armstrong, Jacob	Apr. 10, 1832	Adam Stewart	Jacob Hedtart	5b226		mr 63 *
Thompson, Nancy m. Burke, Thomas	Apr. 12, 1832		David Young		gc 6	
Thompson, Nancy m. Deigarn, Stephen	Feb. 23, 1797	Joseph Thompson	Nathan Young	4b 41		mr 55 *
Thompson, Nancy m. Walker, James	July 28, 1817	James Thompson		2b 96		
Thompson, Philip m. Hill, Louisa	Nov. 5, 1800		John Hedtt(hutt)			
Thompson, Polly m. Laign, John	Oct. 29, 1799	Peter Williamson		2b 80	cr 33	mr 17 *
Thompson, Rachel m. Hardy, John C.	Aug. 9, 1800	John Ramsburg	Jas. M. Brown	5b305		mr 67 *
Thompson, Rebecca m. Ellis, Wesley	Mar. 12, 1834	Thos. Thompson	Lewis F. Wilson	6b200		mr 71 *
Thompson, Rhuan m. Clayton, John	Mar. 9, 1840	David Gerrard		2b241		
Thompson, Samuel m. Wright, Mary	Aug. 22, 1804	Chas. Wright	David Young	1b156	gc 8	mr 74 *
Thompson, Sarah m. Carver(Carri-)Geo.	Dec. 24, 1798	Jacob Armstrong	Mayberry Goheen	6b271		
Thompson, Susanna m. Siler, John	May 28, 1842	Ben't Thompson		2b227		
Thompson, Thos. m. Everhart, Clara	Mar. 17, 1804	Henry Miller	Nathan Young	5b215		mr 64 *
Thompson, Wm. m. Collis, Hannah	Feb. 1, 1832	John Strother		4b130		
Thompson, Wm. m. Demoss, Sarah	Jan. 10, 1820	Daniel Collis		6b106		
Thompson, Wm.N. m. Varmetre, Isabel	May 2, 1837	Wm. Seaman		2b 12		
?Thornberry, Polly m.Jackson, Charles	July 29, 1799	Van Varmetre		5b149		
?Thornberry, Polly m.Jackson, Charles	Aug. 22, 1797	Joseph Light	John Boyd	1b 33	cr 32	mr 13 *
Thornberry, Will m. Light, Ann	Feb. 6, 1800	Wm. Orrick	David Young	2b 51	gc 9	*
Thornberry, Ann m. Rhelske, Will	Feb. 7, 1793		David Young		gc 2	*
Thornburg, Asariah m. Morgan, Drusilla	June 15, 1798	Wm. Lemen	Moses Hoge	1b116	cr 29	mr 14 *
Thornburg, Eli m. Forbes, Eliz.	Oct. 4, 1824	James Forbes	Nathan Young	4b273		mr 58 *
Thornburg, Eli m. Myers, Sarah	Sept 6, 1824	John L. Myers		4b271		
Thornburg, Hannah m. Griffith, John	Nov. 6, 1794		John Boyd		cr 21	
Thornburg, Margt. m. Thatcher, Thos.	Dec. 19, 1796		David Young		gc 6	
Thornburg, Mary Shepherd m.Shuart,Wm.	Feb. 14, 1848	Thos. Thornburg		7b123		
Thornburg, Phoebe m. Eachus, Robert	? 1789		D, Thomas			
?Thornburg, Polly m. Jackson, Chas.	Aug. 23, 1797		John Boyd			
Thornburg, Rebecca m. Hollis, John J.	Oct. 27, 1845	Jos. M. Hollis	John O. Proctor	7b 46	cr 32	mr 37 *
Thornburg, Solomon m. Sedbert, Amelia	Jan. 8, 1855		Hugh Vance			mr 13 *
Thornburg, Susanna m. Leddy, Valent.	Apr. 7, 1789					
Thornburg, Thos. m. Ellis, Sarah	May 28, 1806	Amos Hoff	John Bond	3b 21	cr 20	mr 3 *
Thornburg, Thos. m. Martin, Margt.	June 25, 1812	Chas. Williams	John Mathews	3b228	cr 28	mr 22 *
Thornburg, Thos. m. Swingle, Maria	Oct. 6, 1828	Zebulun Bell		5b108		mr 40 *
Thornburg, Thos. m. Williamson, Sarah	Nov. 11, 1826	Thos. Lemen	John Mathews	5b 55		mr 50 *
Thornburg, Thos. m.Perrel(Peril)Eliza	Aug. 13, 1829	John Perrl	W. Monroe	5b136		mr 53 *
Thornton, Nancy m. Chalfin, June	June 26, 1797	Aaron Chalfin		1b 24		
Thrasher, Susanna m. Daylong, George	Apr. 6, 1798	Christ'r Thrasher		1b106		
Throckmorton, David m. White,Deborah	Oct. 14, 1833	Thomas White	Nathan Young	5b286		mr 66 *

Name	(marriage)	(surety)	(minister)	(bond)		
Throckmorton, Eliz. m.Thr'km'rton,P.	Jan. 21, 1789	Thomas Young	Hugh Vance	3b249	cr 19	mr 3 *
Throckmorton, Jas. E. m.Gustin,Mary	Aug. 29, 1813	Thomas Demoss		1b 36		
Thr'km'rton, Jean m. Demoss, Lewis	May 18, 1797	John Lee		5b194		mr 61 *
Thr'km'ton, Job m. Lee, Leah H.	May 19, 1831	Stephen Shaffer	Nathan Young	5b 38		mr 58 *
Thr'km'ton, Job m. Shaffer, Eliz.	Apr. 6, 1826	Henderson Lucas	Nathan Young	4b102		
Thr'km'ton, John m. Lucas, Emily	Mar. 15, 1819	James Wood		2b142		
Thr'km'ton, Lucy D. m.Thompson, John	Sept 9, 1801					mr 37 *
Thr'km'ton, Mary m. Bayley, Tarply	Oct. 16, 1789	Thos. Thr'km'ton	Hugh Vance	1b 54		
Thr'km'ton, Mary m. Rainey, Presley	Mar. 2, 1797				cr 19	mr 3 *
Thr'km'ton, Peter m. Thr'km'ton, Eliz	Mar. 3, 1789	Thomas Horn	Hugh Vance	5b104		
Thr'km'ton, Philip m.Merehant, Nancy	July 23, 1828		Rev. Reebenack		go 15	mr 44 *
Thr'km'ton, Rich'd m.Clemons,Margt.	Dec. 18, 1816		Geo. M. Frye	4b202		*
Thr'km'ton, Sarah m. Dunn, Seth	May 7, 1821	Jacob Cline	J.R.Graham			
Thr'km'ton, T.L. m. McDonald, Annie E	Dec. 18, 1856		John Boyd			
Thruston, Eliz. m. Steel, John	Jan. 24, 1796				cr 10	mr 12 *
Thruston, Hannah m. Ward, Stephen	Apr. 19, 1799	John Thruston		2b 19		
Thruston, Joseph m. Billingsly,Nancy	Aug. 13, 1794		David Young	1b 68	gc 3	
Thruston, Nancy m. Steel, Joseph	Dec. 2, 1797	John Thruston	David Young		ge 7	
Thurston, Wm. m. Bartleson, Virginia	Apr. 24, 1850	Elijah Bartleson	John Light	7b183		mr 80 *
Tice, Polly m. Sybert, Michael	Nov. 1, 1811	Fred. Sybert	Rev. Reebenack	3b198	gc 12	
Tierney, Martin m. Sullivan, Johanna	Sept 11, 1852		J.H.Plunkett			mr 88 *
Tiffin, Peggy m. Gardner, Joseph	Nov. 30, 1797	Edward Tiffin	John Potts	1b 67	cr 37	mr 14 *
Timmons, Mary P. m. Weller, Daniel	Sept 19, 1839	John Timmons		6b177		
Tingle, Jane m. Dunlap, Joseph	July 20, 1785		Hugh Vance			mr 34 *
Tiser, John Clark m.Smith,Nelly	Oct. 21, 1801	Robert Gallaher		2b145		
Todd, Miles m. Thistle, Cath.	Dec. 27, 1799	John Thistle		2b 44		
Todd, Reese m. Watson, Rebecca	Nov. 5, 1798	Hewey Watson		1b143		
Todhunter, Joshua m. Rees, Hannah	? 1789					
Toland, David m. Barrett(-ott),Delia	Jan. 5, 1828	John Shober	D. Thomas	5b 87		mr 38 *
Tollerton, Jane Mrs. m. McIntire,Thos	June 22, 1820	Cornelius Kelly	B. Reynolds	4b152		mr 52 *
Toogood, Mary m. Roberts, Mary	Aug. 13, 1788		Wm. N. Scott			mr 41 *
Tool, Joseph m. Stilwell,Stephen	Mar. 5, 1795		Moses Hoge			mr 36 *
Tool, Joseph m. Smock, Mary	Mar. 5, 1803	Mathias Smock	Moses Hoge	2b197	cr 10	mr 11 *
Tool, Moore m. Demoss, Margt.	Apr. 1, 1790				or 4	mr 5 *
Tool, Moore m. Warren, Jemima	Oct. 4, 1794		Moses Hoge			mr 40 *
Tool, Rosanna m. Brown, Jesse	Feb. 24, 1810	Magnus Tate	Richard Swift	3b137	go 11	mr 33 *
Toole, Joseph m. Sagathy, Eliz.	Mar. 21, 1786		Rev. Reebenack			
Torrence, Rebecca m. Morgan, John	Apr. 8, 1793		Hugh Vance		cr 21	mr 7 *
Touchstone, Wm m. Newcomb, Louisa	Mar. 25, 1843	Morgan Morgan	Moses Hoge	6b294		
Toup, Eliz. m. Kern, Ezra	July 14, 1820	?		4b154		
Toup, Evelina m.Backenstos,Jacob H.	Nov. 2, 1831	?	Jacob Medtart	5b207		mr 63 *
Towson, Jacob m. Shearer, Patty	Nov. 3, 1795	Jas. S. Boyd	John Boyd		or 33	mr 11 *
Towson, Wm. m. Hamme, Louisa	Oct. 4, 1824	Jacob Hamme		4b273		mr 47 *
*Tolman, Hannah m. Crabb, John	Sept 23, 1800	Edward Crabb	Chas. P. Krauth	2b 89		

233

Name	(marriage)	(suretor)	(minister)	(bond)		
Tracey, Mary m. Davies, Walter	June 11, 1785		Hugh Vance	6b104	gc 5	mr 33 *
Tramhouse, Leonard m. Tederick, Jane	Dec. 11, 1795		David Young			*
Trammell, Philip m. Spero, Sarah	Apr. 11, 1837	Jacob Spero	Lewis F. Wilson			*
Trees, John m. Strode, Hannah	May 1, 1813		Nathan Young			*
Trenton, Susan m. Murphy, Dennis	Oct. 3, 1807	Wm. McCausland		3b 73		
Trigg, Elinor m. Podsal, Henry	Apr. 20, 1825	Jeremiah Trigg	B. Reynolds	5b 9		mr 49 *
Trigg, Marg. m. Miller, Jacob A.	June 1, 1831	Jeremiah Trigg	Nathan Young	5b196		mr 61 *
Trigg, Mary m. Miller, John A.	June 2, 1831	Jeremiah Trigg	Nathan Young	5b197		mr 61 *
Trigg, Samuel m. Bareford, Jenny	Nov. 13, 1800	Horatio Hobbs		2b 99	cr 21	mr 7 *
Trigg, Samuel m. Blue, Rebecca	Feb. 17, 1793		Moses Hoge			mr 66 *
Trigg, Samuel m. Hess, Eliza	Apr. 18, 1833	Charlotte Hess	Nathan Young	5b267	cr 22	mr 9 *
Trigg, Sarah E. m. Mahoney, Jos. E.	Mar. 16, 1843	James McSherry		6b293		mr 66 *
Trigg, Sarah E. m. Hess, Solomon	Jan. 25, 1859		G.W.Cooper			*
Trigger, Clem m. Medley, Sarah	Sept. 10, 1794		Moses Hoge			
Tripp, Solomon m. Butt, Sally	June 8, 1833	Peter Gardner	Nathan Young	5b275	cr 22	mr 9 *
Tripp, Samuel m. Bryan, Sarah	Dec. 8, 1790		Moses Hoge			mr 66 *
Tritch, Wm. m. Chambers, Eliz.	Nov. 1, 1827			5b 82		
Tritapoe(Tritch)Marg. m.Waugh, Jas.	Dec. 29, 1818	James Maxwell Jr.	Mathias Riser	4b 55	cr 38	mr 1 *
Trout, Dorcas m. Kearfott, George	Jan. 1, 1846	Thos. Tritapoe		7b 52		
Trout, Elinor m. Lozman, Philip	Nov. 2, 1785	David Seibert	Edward Tiffin		cr 38	mr 1 *
Trowbridge, We. m. Adams, Cath. Mrs.	Feb. 23, 1854		John Grove			mr 69 *
Troxwell, Eliz. m.Anderson,Cornel's	May 26, 1838	Robert McIntire	James Watts	6b139	cr 32	mr 13 *
Truelock, Charlotte m. Jack, Robert	Nov. 1, 1797	Parker Truelock	John Boyd	1b100	cr 32	mr 13 *
Truelock, Parker m.Tunnel(Farral)Eliz.	Nov. 2, 1797		John Boyd			mr 65 *
Tucker, Emaline m.Patterson, Chas.W.	June 23, 1833	Peter Gardner	W. Hawk	5b277	cr 12	mr 52 *
Tucker, Henry St.G. m.Hunter, Evelina	Sept. 23, 1806	Philip Wilson		3b 31		mr 14 *
Tucker, John m. Margrove, Sarah	May 29, 1806	Jacob Rees		3b 21		mr 10 *
Tucker, Susan m. Anderson, Horace	Mar. 15, 1827	John Shober		5b 63		
Tullis(Tw-),John m. Cornwell, Elinor	May 16, 1799	Presley Boydstone	B. Reynolds	1b 69	cr 12	mr 52 *
Tullis(Tw-),Wm. m.Tearis,Mary Tabitha	Apr. 25, 1793		Richard Swift			mr 14 *
Tully, Isaac m. Hastings, Frances	June 1, 1843	John Hastings	Wm. Hill	6b299		mr 10 *
Tully, John m. Hollowbaugh, John	May 27, 1797	Walter Shirley		1b 1B		
Tully, Mary. m. Helferetay, George	Mar. 31, 1821	Samuel Blake		4b180		
Turner, Alex. m. Cardine, Margt.	Dec. 22, 1838?					mr 69 *
Turner, Ann m. Clark, Peter	June 16, 1845	Henry Deck	John Howell	6b155	cr 21	mr 7 *
Turner, Anthony m.Swearingen, Marg.	July 28, 1812	Michael Grove		7b 37	cr 13	mr 23 *
Turner, Anthony m. Tabb, Frances	Mar. 14, 1793	Van Brashires		3b232		
Turner, Arabella m. Tabb, John	Jan. 5, 1807?		Moses Hoge			
Turner, Ehud m. Strode, Priscilla	Dec. 27, 1818	Edward Tabb	John Mathews	3b 40	cr 28	mr 22 *
Turner, Elitha m. Tabb, Edward Jr.	Feb. 11, 1818	Alex. Mason		4b 61		mr 70 *
Turner, Eliza m. Rice, Samuel	Feb. 6, 1805	Edward Tabb Sr.	John Bond	2b254	cr 28	mr 22 *
Turner, Eliz. m. Hedges, John	Mar. 27, 1839	William Turner	John Light	6b164		mr 70 *
Turner, Geo. W. m. Pool, Eliz.	Nov. 29, 1821	Wm. Burns	John B. Hoge	4b198		mr 44 *
Turner, James m. Shoafstall, Sophia	July 1, 1820	Jacob Crowl		7b 21		
Turner, James H. m.Bowers, Ellen E.	Dec. 23, 1844	Bennett Franceway	James Redmond	4b153 / 7b 18		mr 31 *

Name		(marriage)	(suretor)	(minister)	(bond)	
Turner, Jesse m. Kimble(Ke-), Mima	Oct. 6,	Oct. 9, 1817	John Ferrel	W.N.Scott	4b 48	*
Turner, John m. Bronco, Ann		Mar. 2, 1790				mr 38 *
Turner, John m. Naff, Eliz.	Mar. 15,	1821	John Naff	Hugh Vance	4b177	
Turner, John m.Rawlings(Ramsburg)Ruth	Aug. 12,	1783		Hugh Vance		mr 32 *
Turner, John m. Ziler, Elis.	Aug. 10,	1825	George Ziler	Hugh Vance	5b 18	mr 48 *
Turner, John T. m. Ward, Mary	Feb. 12,	1827	Joseph Ward	Chas. P. Krauth	5b 62	mr 51 *
Turner, Joseph m. Keller, Eliz.	Sept 14,	1833	Jacob Spero		5b282	
Turner, Lucinda m. Boyd, James	Dec. 27,	1845	Wm. Turner		7b 51	
Turner, Lucinda m. Doyle, James		Dec. 30, 1845		John Light		mr 76 *
Turner, Martha m. White, John	July 20,	1850	David Cunningham		7b190	
Turner, Mary m. Carr, John	Nov. 13,	1828	Van Brashear		5b112	
Turner, Mary m. Evans, Jeremiah	Aug. 14,	Aug. 15, 1802	Charles Orrick	Richard Swift	2b177	cr 32 mr 20 *
Turner, Mary Eliz. m.Kensel, John S.	Jan. 30,	1850	John D. Turner		7b176	
Turner, Robert E. m. Rush, Jane	Feb. 5,	Feb. 8, 1816	James Mason	John Mathews	3b354	mr 26 *
Turner, Sarah A. m. Shook, Andrew	Apr. 7,	1852	John R. Turner		7b252	
Turner, Sarah Ann m. Miller, Emanuel	Nov. 10,	1845	James Turner		7b 48	
Turner, Susan m. Hasselt, Thomas	Nov. 12,	1838	Wm. Turner		6b150	
Turner, Susanna m. Parrott, Wm.	Mar. 3,	Mar. 4, 1802	Thomas Turner	Richard Swift	2b163	cr 32 mr 20 *
Turner, Thos. Jr. m. Rush, Nancy	May 23,	1814	Wm. Rush		3b298	
Turner, Walter m. Wilcox, Sophia	June 8,	May 9, 1803	Robert Wilcox	David Young	2b202	gc 10 *
Turner, Wm. m. Taylor, Ann	Jan. 16,	1827	Samuel Taylor		5b 60	
Tweggers, Anna m. Sewel, Moses	Feb. 24,	1791		Moses Hoge		cr 6 mr 6 *
Twiggs, Eliz. m. Williams, Dailey	Apr. 21,	1782				mr 42 *
Tyson, Basil E. m. White, Mary A.	Dec. 23,	1847	James M. Gano	Daniel Sturges	7b118	
Tyson, Belinda m. Crouse, Jacob	Jan. 17,	1837	John Waite	P. Lipscomb	6b 94	mr 81 *
Tyson, Peggy m. Hedrick, George	Oct. 8,	1809		Rev. Reebenack		gc 10 *
Tyson, Wm. m. Dunham, Maria	Dec. 24,	Dec. 26, 1844	Samuel Dunham	John Grove	7b 19	mr 75 *

"U"

Name		(marriage)	(suretor)	(minister)	(bond)	
Ubbet, Eliz. m. Small, George						*
Ulm(Ullum),Andrew m.Elliott,Verlinda	Mar. 16,	Jan. 10, 1793	Thomas Powell	David Young	6b 37	gc 2
Ulm, Andrew m. Pitzer, Mary	Oct. 28,	Nov. 4, 1835	Michael Pitzer	J.L.Bromwell	4b275	mr 47 *
Umphers, Minta m. Williams, Benj.		Jan. 20, 1824		Richard Swift		mr 38 *
Underdunk, Henry m. Beller, Julianna	Aug. 1,	Jan. 20, 1793	Wm. Coffenberger	Chas. P. Krauth	5b 45	mr 51 *
Underdunk, Henry m. Maddock, Ann	Dec. 31,	1826		David Young		gc 5
Underdunk, Maria m. Coffenberger,Wm.	?	1796	Henry Underdunk	John Kahler	4b 83	mr 31 *
Underdunk, Nancy m. Moon, Hiram B.	Oct. 20,	1818	Henry Underdunk	M.G.Hamilton	6b168	mr 71 *
Underdunk, Sarah m. Moon, Jacob	May 4,	1839	Henry Underdunk	Nathan Young	4b244	mr 58 *
Unger, Dariel m. Brannon, Melinda	Aug. 4,	1823	John W. Wolf	Nathan Young	5b265	mr 66 *
Unger,Dariel(David) m. Smith, Eliz.	Mar. 30,	Apr. 4, 1833	George Snowdeal	Nathan Young	4b 69	mr 29 *
Unger, George m. Bailey, Eliz.	Apr. 13,	Apr. 19, 1818	Thomas Bailey	Mathias Riser	4b 53	
Upsalom, Hannah m. Barrick, Micholas	Dec. 25,	1817		Mathias Riser		
Urick, Mathias m. Downey, Lydia	Dec. 20,	Aug. 16, 1792	Jesse Brown	David Young	2b 70	gc 2
	May 19,	1800				*

235

Name	(wgs)	(marriage)	(surety)	(minister)	(bond)			
*Vanaker, George m. Couchman,Rebecca	June 16,	1830	Henry Couchman	David Young	5b168	ge 4		*
Vanaker, George m. Lonakins,Tracy	June 3,	June 6, 1794		W. Love	7b130		mr 80	**
Vanarsdal, Andrew m. Wolff,Mary E.		June 6, 1848	Norman Miller				mr 43	**
Vanarsdal, James m. Bean,Eliz.	Nov. 11,	Nov. 20, 1766		Hugh Vance	2b 99	ge 9		
Vance, Alex. m. Kim,Eliz.	Mar. 10,	Nov. 11, 1800	Stephen Heard	David Young	3b 13			
Vance, Eliz. m. Rippy,David	Dec. 20,	Dec. 23, 1806	Mathew Rippy	Lewis F. Wilson	7b142		mr 83	**
Vance, Harriet m. Sibole,Morgan	Sept 11,	1849	Wm. Stuart	David Young	1b131	ge 8		
Vance, Jane m. Bostick,James		Sept 11, 1798	James Vance	Hugh Vance			mr 32	*
Vance, Jane m. Burke,John		Jan. 10, 1782						
Vance, Jane m. Orr,James	July 4,	1822	William Orr		4b218			
Vance, John m. Crosen,Mary		June 16, 1789		Hugh Vance		cr 39	mr 3	*
Vance, John m. Kinn,Diana		Oct. 20, 1793		Moses Hoge		cr 22	mr 8	*
Vance, Mary m. Park,John		Jan. 14, 1788		Hugh Vance		cr 23	mr 2	*
Vance, Mary m. Sprowl,Wm.	Mar. 31,	1807	Samuel Rippey		3b 53			
Vance, Mary m. Hanna,David	Sept 24,	1800	Harry Craighill		2b 90			
Vance, Rachel m. Porterfield,George	Sept 16,	Mar. 22, 1792	William Orr	Moses Hoge	4b161		mr 39	*
Vance, Rebecca m. Lane,Martin	Mar. 18,	1820	John Vance		2b165			
Vance, Sarah m. Harlan,George		1802						
VanCellor,Ferd. m. Fisher,Mary	June 14,	1792	Wm. Gorrell	Moses Hoge	5b 74		mr 39	*
VanCleve, Morgan m. Gorrell,Isabel	Aug. 7,	Aug. 9, 1827	Wm. P. Shipman	Nathan Young	7b228		mr 99	**
VanCleve, Nathaniel H. m. Snook,Eliz.	9,	1851	John J. Henshaw		6b231			
VanCleve, Samuel m. Roberts,Eliza V.	27,	1841	Jacob VanDoren		6b 87			
VanDoren, Aleta E. m. Magruder,Robt.	Nov. 7,	1836	Alex. Kerney	Moses Hoge	1b128	cr 29	mr 14	*
VanDoren, Christian m. Vanorsdal,P.	Sept 4,	Sept 13, 1798	Jacob VanDoren		7b153			
VanDoren, Jacob W. m. English,Henry	Apr. 9,	1849	Norman Miller	James Chisholm	7b 20		mr 76	**
VanDoren, Jacob m. Locke,Rose	Jan. 8,	Jan. 8, 1845		Geo. W. Harris			mr 88	**
VanDoren, John P. m. Davis,Susan A.		Jan. 5, 1854		Moses Hoge		or 38	mr 20	**
VanDoren, Katy m. Kerney,Wm.		Feb. 4, 1801		Moses Hoge		or 38	mr 20	**
VanDoren, Phebe m. Bennett,Van	Apr. 22,	Apr. 30, 1801	Thos. Swearingen	Hugh Vance	2b122		mr 36	**
VanJakel, Vermont m. Hinton,Sarah		Nov. 19, 1788		Moses Hoge			mr 34	*
VanKirk, John m. Morgan,Eliz.		Dec. 29, 1785		Nathan Young			mr 66	**
VanMetre, Abisha m. Morris,Ann	Apr. 22,	Apr. 23, 1791	Abr'm VanMetre	David Young	5b269	ge 1		
VanMetre, Abr'm m. Burns,Hannah	Jan. 2,	Nov. 24,	Samuel Roberts		5b212			
VanMetre, Abr'm m. Roberts,Naomi	Sept 2,	1832	John Strother	John Mathews	4b 45	cr 17	mr 22	*
VanMetre, Abr'm m. Tabb(-fre)Isabel	Aug. 14,	Sept 17, 1817	Isaac VanMetre	Moses Hoge	2b267	cr 19		
VanMetre, Abr'm m. VanMetre,Nancy		Aug. 15, 1805		Hugh Vance			mr 3	*
VanMetre, Abr'm m. VanMetre,Priscilla	Nov. 10,	Mar. 21, 1789	Nicholas Schoppert		7b 48			
VanMetre, Abr'm B. m.Schoppert,Mary	Apr. 22,	1845	Abr'm VanMetre	Nathan Young	5b269		mr 66	*
VanMetre, Atisha m. Morris,Ann	June 8,	Apr. 23, 1833	Abr'm VanMetre		6b212			
VanMetre, Ann E. m.Daugherty,George	Aug. 1,	1840	Colbert Anderson	R.T.Berry	7b191		mr 83	**
VanMetre, Ann S. m. Callahan,Jas. M.	May 14,	Aug. 1, 1850	Thomas Tabb		3b 89			
VanMetre, Asahel m. Burney,Polly	Jan. 27,	1808	Abr'm VanMetre	John Boggs	7b 23		mr 75	*
VanMetre, Asahel m. Wilhelm,Mary M.	July 30,	Jan. 27, 1845	Johnson Moore		1b 26			
Vacley, Thomas m. Hedton,Rachel		1797						
**Vanacter, Phebe m. Malin,Joseph		Aug. 18, 1785		Hugh Vance			mr 34	**

Name	(marriage)	(suretor)	(minister)	(bond)		
VanMetre, Daniel m. Harp, Ruth Apr. 8,	Apr. 17, 1793	Abr'm VanMetre	Moses Hoge	5b 97	cr 21	mr 7 *
VanMetre, Eliza m. Files, John Jr. Jan. 24,	Jan. 25, 1828	Wm. N. Thompson	Jas. M. Brown	5b185		mr 62 *
VanMetre, Eliza m. Russell, James B. Jan. 10,	1831	Abr'm VanMetre		6b119		
VanMetre, Eliza m. Deck, Fred. D. Oct. 10,	1837				cr 8	mr 7 *
VanMetre, Eliz. m. Gorrell, Abr'm	Jan. 5, 1792	Nathan VanMetre	Moses Hoge	1b132	cr 29	mr 14 *
VanMetre, Eliz. m. Martin, Levi Sept 12,	Sept 20, 1798	James VanMetre	Moses Hoge	2b 61		
VanMetre, Eliz. m. Miller, Henry Apr. 1,	1800	Asahel VanMetre	B. Reynolds	5b 91	cr 36	mr 52 *
VanMetre, Eliz. m. Strider, Isaac Feb. 29,	Mar. 2, 1828		Moses Hoge			mr 12 *
VanMetre, Eliz. m. Tabb, Thomas	Dec. 29, 1796	Abr'm VanMetre		3b324		mr 50 *
VanMetre, Eliz. m. VanMetre, John E. May 19,	Apr. 13, 1815	Abr'm VanMetre	John Mathews	5b 39		mr 34 *
VanMetre, Eliz. m. Wynkoop, Wm. Apr. 10,	Sept 20, 1785	Josiah VanMetre	Hugh Vance			mr 71 *
VanMetre, Hannah m. Mounts,Providence	Mar. 4, 1847		John Winter	7b 89	gc 2	
VanMetre, Henry S. m. Whitson,Mary E.Mar. 3,	Jan. 19, 1793	Benj. J. Whitson	David Young			
VanMetre, Isaac m. Evans, Polly Mar. 10,	1819	Morgan VanMetre		4b101		
VanMetre, Isaac m. VanMetre, Mary Mar. 17,	1823	Wash'ton Evans		4b235		
VanMetre, Isaballa m.Chenoweth, John Mar. Jan. 9,	1830	Van VanMetre	Nathan Young	5b149		mr 66 *
VanMetre, Isaballa m.Thompson, Wm.N. Jan. 9,	1833	Abr'm VanMetre	J. Baker	5b268		mr 78 *
VanMetre, Isabel Ann m.Anderson,Colb Apr. 22,	Apr. 23, 1847	Asahel VanMetre	Nathan Young	7b116		mr 60 *
VanMetre, Isabel G. m. Tabler, Adam Dec. 13,	Dec. 10, 1829	Colbert Anderson	R.A.Fink	5b144		mr 88 *
VanMetre, James m. Anderson, Amelia Oct. 28,	Oct. 29, 1851					mr 46 *
VanMetre, James W. m.Coffenberg,Ellen	1824	John Alburtis	Chas. P. Krauth	4b255		mr 21 *
VanMetre, John m. Gorrell, Mary Feb. 2,	Mar.	George Seaborn	Richard Swift	2b207	cr 27	
VanMetre, John m. Seaborn, Nelly Aug 9,	Aug. 11, 1803	Abr'm VanMetre		3b324		
VanMetre, John E. m. VanMetre, Eliz. May 19,	1815	John Alburtis		4b204		
VanMetre, John E. m. VanMetre,Josina Jan. 21,	1822	John McIver		2b182		
VanMetre, Joseph m. Evans, Nancy Sept 18,	1802	John McKeever		2b 82	go 9	
VanMetre, Joseph m. Whitsack,Mary M Aug 16,	Aug. 17, 1800	Wm. Covenhaver	David Young	2b196	go 10	
VanMetre, Josiah m.Covenhaver, Lydia Feb. 26,	Mar. 1, 1803	John Alburtis	David Young	4b204		
VanMetre, Josina m. VanMetre, John E.Jan. 9,	1822	Isaac VanMetre		5b156		**
VanMetre, Margt. m. McDonald, Wm. Mar. 9,	Mar. 9, 1830	Harrison Waite	Jacob Medtart	6b 63		mr 63 *
VanMetre, Margt. m. Roberts, Samuel Jan. 13,	1836	Wm. McDonald		7b237		
VanMetre,Marg'ta m. Berlin, George Nov. 24,	Nov. 25, 1851		Joseph Baker		cr 36	mr 85 *
VanMetre, Mary m. Evans, John	Jan. 26, 1797	Morgan VanMetre	Moses Hoge	4b101		mr 13 *
VanMetre, Mary m. VanMetre, Isaac Mar. 10,	1819	Asahel VanMetre		6b251		
VanMetre, Mary B. m.Gorrell,David H. Nov. 3,	1841	Wm. Maslin		7b177		mr 81 *
VanMetre, Mary E. m. Campbell, Hugh Feb. 11,	1850	Asahel VanMetre		6b321		
VanMetre, Mary M.m.Rutherford,Geo.F May 2,	1844	Abr'm VanMetre	P.Lipscomb	7b119		mr 72 *
VanMetre, Mary M. m. Strider,Saml. W.Jan. 25,	Jan. 25, 1848	Wm. McDonald	Lewis F. Wilson	6b229		mr 87 *
VanMetre, Mary R. m. McKown, Joseph Jan. 1,	Jan. 5, 1841		R.A. Fink			
VanMetre, Mary S. m. VanMetre, Warner	Aug. 11, 1853					
VanMetre, Nancy m. Alburtis, John Feb. 7,	Feb. 7, 1809	Robert Wilson	John Mathews	3b107	cr 17	mr 23 *
VanMetre, Nancy m. VanMetre, Abr'm Aug. 14,	Aug. 15, 1805	Isaac VanMetre	Moses Hoge	2b267	cr 17	mr 22 *
VanMetre, Naomi m. Strider, John H Dec. 13,	Dec. 10, 1847	Israel VanMetre	James Baker	7b116		nt 78 *

(entry)	(marriage)	(surety)	(minister)	(bond)		
VanMetre, Naoul m. Roberts, Samuel Jr.	Aug. 26, 1796	Nathan VanMetre	John Boyd	3b242	cr 11	mr 12 *
VanMetre, Polly m. Tabb, Thomas Dec. 4,	Dec. 3, 1812		John Mathews		cr 19	mr 25 *
VanMetre, Priscilla m.VanMetre, Abr'm	Mar. 21, 1789		Hugh Vance			mr 3 *
VanMetre, Rachel I.B.m. Flies, Thos.	Oct. 15, 1833		G.W.Cooper			
VanMetre, Rebecca m. McKown, Margt. Apr. 10,	1849	Wm. McDonald		7b154		mr 71 *
VanMetre, Robert T.m.McCleary,Matilda Mar. 25,	Mar. 27, 1840	John McCleary	Lewis F. Wilson	6b203	cr 29	mr 17 *
VanMetre, Ruth m. Gorrell, Joseph Aug. 8,	Aug. 8, 1799	Isaac VanMetre	Moses Hoge	2b 18	gc 8	
VanMetre, Ruth m. Philips, Robert Nov. 17,	Nov. 18, 1798	Abr'm VanMetre	David Young	1b148		mr 99 *
VanMetre, Ruth m.Rutherford, Henry May 9,	May 10, 1827	Abr'm VanMetre	Nathan Young	5b 69		
VanMetre, Sarah A. m. Walters, Geo.P.	Nov. 8, 1853		R.A. Fink	5b 83		mr 52 *
VanMetre, Thos. m. McQuillan, Mary Nov. 8,	Nov. 8, 1827	Thos. McQuilton	B. Reynolds	4b137		
VanMetre, Thos. m. Rush, Isabella Feb. 22,	Feb. 22, 1820	Philip Carnino		7b249		mr 87 *
VanMetre, Thos. T. m.Seibert,Eldeg't Mar. 22,	Mar. 22, 1852	David Seibert	Lewis F. Wilson	7b 28		
VanMetre, Vincent H. m.Whitney,Margt Mar. 5,	Mar. 5, 1845	Henry Campbell				
VanMetre, Warner m. VanMetre,Mary S.	Aug. 11, 1853		R.A.Fink	4b208		mr 87 *
VanMetre, Wm. m.Morlatt, Rhianna Feb. 16,	Feb. 17, 1822	John Morlatt	John B. Hoge			mr 44 *
VanMacter, Phebe m. Melvin, Joseph	Aug. 18, 1785		Hugh Vance			mr 34 *
Vanorsdal, Ann m. Moore, Gilman	June 12, 1792		Moses Hoge			mr 39 *
Vanorsdal, Andrew M. m. Wolf, Mary June 3,	1848		William Love	7b130		mr 80 *
Vanorsdal, Cornelius m. Moore,Martha	Dec. 27, 1792	Norman Miller	Moses Hoge			mr 99 *
Vanorsdal, Mary m. McMurran, James Mar. 31,	Sept 13, 1832	Isaac Vanorsdal	Moses Hoge	5b223	cr 29	mr 14 *
Vanorsdal, Phebe m. VanDoren, Christ.Sept 4,	Mar. 4, 1798	Alex. Kerney		1b128		
VanPelt, Anna m. Fearman, Henry Jr. Nov. 28,	Nov. 29, 1815	Jacob VanPelt	John Bond	3b348	cr 28	mr 22 *
VanZant, Jacob A. m. Godman, Nancy Mar. 27,	Mar. 28, 1805	Wm. Godman	John Light	2b259	cr 19	mr 62 *
VanZant, Sarah A. m. Joy, Stephen Aug. 27,	Apr. 19, 1831	Thomas Powell	Hugh Vance	5b204	cr 33	mr 3 *
Varder, Els. m. Snodgrass, Stephen	Apr. 23, 1789		John Boyd			mr 10 *
Varder, James m. Snodgrass, Mary	Feb. 8, 1795					
Varley, Susannah m. Murphy, Ephraim Feb. 17,	Aug. 8, 1804	Thomas Varley	David Young	2b222	gc 6	*
Varley, Thomas m. Heaton, Rachel	Oct. 19, 1797					
Varnes, Els. m. Conoway, John Apr. 24,	Sept 15, 1799	Wm. Harris	John Bond	2b 3	cr 13	mr 21 *
*Veal, Sarah m. Andrews, Robert Oct. 16,	?	Wm. F. Campbell		2b245		
Veal, Wm. m. Devine, Mary Sept 15,	Dec. 22, 1804	James R. Dugan		6b 57		
Vent, Mary m. Mirth, John	Feb. 6, 1835		R.A.Fink			*
Verdier, Jane m. Bridenhart, Christ'r	May 14, 1857		Moses Hoge			mr 39 *
Verdier, Paul m. Snodgrass, Sarah Apr. 29,	Jan. 28, 1792	Christian Miller	Hugh Vance	3b186	gc 12	mr 43 *
Vermillion, Chas. m. Miller, Nancy	Aug. 3, 1787		Rev. Reebenack		gc 13	
Vermillion, Curtis D. m. Flery,Bridgt	Jan. 1, 1811	John Lown	James Watts	3b266		*
Vermillion, Susan m. Ford(-it)Joseph July 24,	Jan. 25, 1855	John Conoway	Rev. Reebenack	2b117		*
Vestal, John m. Rodgers, Susannah Mar. 11,	Aug. 3, 1813					*
Vestal, Mary m. Potts, John	Jan. 25, 1801		Wm. Hill		cr 29	mr 9 *
Vincenheller,Cath. m. Myers, Peter Sept 18,	1794	Jacob Swisher	David Young	2b181	gc 9	*
Vincenheller,John m. Miller, Ann Dec. 31,	1803	Jacob Miller	David Young	2b188	gc 13	*
Vincenheller,John m. Robinson,Hanna May 20,	1812	James Robinson	Rev. Reebenack	3b225	gc 2	*
*Veal, Samuel m. Botere, Eliz.	Apr. 2, 1793		David Young			

Name		(marriage)	(suretor)	(minister)	(bond)		
Vincenheller,Nancy m.Myers,Daniel	Feb. 21,	Feb. 22, 1816	Peter Myers	W.N.Scott	3b356		mr 26 *
Vincenheller,Sarah m.Hedges,Solomon		July 28, 1789		Hugh Vance		cr 39	mr 3 *
Vincenheller,Thomas m. Kennedy, Kath.		Jan. 8, 1789		Hugh Vance			mr 37 *
Vincent, Robert m. Hedges, Phebe	Jan. 17,	Jan. 1825	Hezekiah Hedges	Chas. P. Krauth	4b286		mr 48 *
Violet, Edward m. Hite, Eliz.	Dec. 29,	Jan. 9, 1799?	Joseph Hite	John Heit(Hutt.)	1b158	cr 12	mr 18 *
Violet, Eliz. m. Scott, John Dennis		Oct. 11, 1795		David Young		gc 5	
Violet, James m. Violet, Sarah		Aug. 22, 1788		Hugh Vance			mr 35 *
Violet, John m. Taylor, Polly		Oct. 13, 1791		Moses Hoge		cr 7	mr 6 *
Violet, Sarah m. Violet, James		Aug. 22, 1788		Hugh Vance			mr 35 *
Violet, Sarah m. Young, Samuel	Jan. 29,	1811	Edward Violet	David Young	3b173		*
Voigal, Magda m. King, Samuel	Aug. 5,	1800					
Voke, Martha m. Porter, Robert	May 27,	1799	David Simpson		2b 8		
Voorhees, Aaron m. Metz, Ann	Nov. 23,	1840	Joseph Hoffman		6b225		
Vorhees, Kesiah m. Manford, James M.	Dec. 23,	1841	Joseph Hoffman	John Hedges	6b260		mr 73 *
Vorhees, Kitty m. Checks, George	Sept 26,	1821	?	E.R.Lippett	4b192		mr 45 *
Vorhees, Maria m. Billmire, Conrad	Sept 7,	1839	Ganet Vorhees		6b174		
Vorhees, Matilda m. Gorman, Edward	Mar. 29,	1849	David Hoffman		7b150		
Vorhees, Phebe Ann m.Moore,Jas. V.	June 13,	1840	Ganet Vorhees	John Winter	6b213		mr 79 *

Name		(marriage)	(suretor)	(minister)	(bond)		
Wade, Wm. m. Payne, Jane	Apr. 12,	Apr. 12, 1830	Jesse Payne	Robert Cadden	5b162		mr 61 *
Wageley, David m. Kirkhart, Margt.	Mar. 29,	Mar. 29, 1828	John Kirkhart	B. Reynolds	5b 95		mr 52 *
Wageley, Eliz. m. Kirkhart, John	Apr. 16,	Apr. 1828	Wm. Wageley	Benedict Reynolds	5b 98		mr 52 *
Wageley, Jacob W. m.Miller, Ann R.	Dec. 3,	1844	Vance Bell		7b 14		
Wageley, Maria L. m. Wilhelm,John P.		June 12, 1853		R.A.Fink			mr 87 *
Wageley, Mary m. Zacharias, Jacob	Aug. 7,	Aug. 9, 1832	Wm. Wageley	W. Monroe	5b236		mr 65 *
Wager, John Jr. m. Batte, Cath.	June 4,	1799	James Ferguson		2b 9		
Wager, John m. Lucas, Mary		May 20, 1790		Moses Hoge		cr 4	mr 5 *
Wager, Margt. m.Williamson, Barret	Jan. 9,	1798	Alex. Williamson	Richard Swift	1b 80	cr 12	mr 16 *
Waggoner, Daniel m. Brook, Eliz.	Jan. 8,	1818	George Brook		4b 75		
Waggoner, Mary m. Williamson, Basil	June 25,	1819	Daniel Waggoner		4b128		
Waggoner, Jacob m. Welch, Kitty	Dec. 30,	1810	Edmund Waggoner	John B. Hoge	3b170	cr 14	mr 24 *
Waggoner, James m. Beall, Lucy	Dec. 27,	1849	John Waggoner	Henry Furlong	7b164		mr 79 *
Twaggoner, Jane m. Ramsburg, Ezra	Sept 1,	1830	George Houck		5b154		
Waggoner, John m. Magee, Maria	Mar. 3,	1849	John Waggoner	Henry Furlong	7b164		mr 79 *
Twaggoner,Margt. J. m.Ramsburg, Ezra	Sept 4,	1830	John Waggoner		2b148		
Waggoner, Rebecca m. Dyer, Zebulon	Nov. 17,	1801	Elisha Boyd				
Waggoner, Sally m. Davis, Samuel Y.	Jan. 4,	1847	Isaac V. Burns		7b 82		
Waggoner, Sally m. Henry, George	Feb. 1,	1812	Nicholas Henry		3b211		

Name	(marriage)		(surator)	(minister)	(bond)		
Waggoner, Susan m. Duckwall, Lewis	Oct. 26,	1798	Jonas Grove	David Young	1bl41		
Waggoner, Susannah m. Smith, Abr'm Harrison	Nov. 29,	1843	Andrew Waggoner		6b308		
*Waid, Mary m. Waid, Abr'm	Jan. 4,	1798			6b908		
Twaight, Eliz. m. Bowman, John	Jan. 4,	1799	John Ellis	John Boyd	1bl59	ge 8	mr 16 *
Twaite, Eliz. m. Brown, John	Jan. 4,	1799	John Ellis	John Boyd	1bl59	cr 34	mr 16 *
Twaite, Harrison m. Harrison, Sarah A	Oct. 31,	1837	Phil.C. Pendleton		6bl23	cr 34	
Waite, John M. m. McDonald, Isabel	May 19,	1845	Wm. McDonald	Lewis F. Wilson	7b 35		mr 77 *
Waite, Mary A. m. Somerville,Robert	Nov. 1,	1842	Edmund Pendleton	James Chisholm	6b282		mr 75 *
Waldeck, John m. Cage, Sarah	July 28,	1823	Andrew Cage	Chas. P. Krauth	4b243		mr 46 *
Wales, George m. Bryant, Jane	Oct. 19,	1792		Moses Hoge			mr 39 *
Walgamott,David m. Snider, Sarah	Feb. 6,	1807	Thomas Butler	John Mathews	3b 45	cr 13	mr 23 *
Walgamott, Mary E. m. Hill, John	Apr. 19,	1846	Thos. S. Hooper		7b 65		*
Walgamott, Susanna m. Davis, Thomas	June 30,	1799	Jonathan Settle	David Young	2b 10	ge 8	
Walker, Ann B. m.Chenoweth, Jas. W.	Nov. 7,	1832	James Walker	Jas. M. Brown	5b246		mr 64 *
Walker, Cath. m.Blue, Nathanial	Apr. 18,	1834	John Calvert		6b 8		*
Walker, Enud m. Noland, Nancy	Mar. 26,	1836	John Williamson	W. Monroe	6b 74		mr 68 *
Walker, Eli m. Wilson, Eliz.	Aug. 22,	1849	Jacob VanDoren	Chas. P. Krauth	7bl64		mr 49 *
Walker, Elinor m. Maxwell, John	Nov. 16,	1825	Wash'ton Evans	John Hedges	3b 28		mr 73 *
Walker, Eliza m. Evans, Jacob V.	Dec. 7,	1841	Jacob Potsal		6b256		mr 68 *
Walker, Elmo m. Noland, Nancy	Mar. 26,	1836	John Williamson	Wm. Monroe	6b 74	cr 34	mr 17 *
Walker, Henry m. Morton, Prudence	Nov. 1,	1799	?	John Boyd	2b 33		
Walker, James m. Foster, Magdalena	May 1,	1797	Jacob Foster		1b 14		
Walker, James m. Pendleton, Elenor	Sept 26,	1814	Wm. Pendleton		3b304		
Walker, James m. Shank, Cath.	Apr. 5,	1818		Mathias Riser			mr 29 *
Walker, James m. Thompson, Nancy	Nov. 5,	1800	James Thompson		2b 96		
Walker, Jas. H. Kilmer, Mary E.	Mar. 13,	1852	John Kilmer		7b249		
Walker, Jas. J. m. Pitzer, Eliza B.	Feb. 22,	1832	Martin Pitzer	Jas. M. Brown	5b221	cr 1	mr 64 *
Walker, John m. Bramble, Sarah	Mar. 23,	1789		Moses Hoge			
Walker, John m. Potsal, Eliza	Dec. 15,	1828	Jacob Potsal		5bl15		mr 2 *
Walker, John m. McNeal, Eliza	Apr. 11,	1804	John McNeal	W. Monroe	2b233		mr 53 *
Walker, John W. m. Pitzer, Hannah A.	Feb. 5,	1844	Chas. Ridenour	John Light	6b312		mr 76 *
Walker, Margt. m. Linton, Jas. F.	Nov. 7,	1850	Jacob Potsal	F.C. Tebbs	7b201		mr 83 *
Walker, Prudence m. Bryan, Joseph	Jan. 17,	1806	Robert Grimes		3b 9		
Walker, Wm. m. Bowers, Eliz.	Nov. 6,	1824	Henry Bowers		4b276		
Walker, Wm. m. Fitch, Jane	Mar. 21,	1789?	Anthony Turner	Wm. Talbott	1bl73	cr 24	mr 18 *
Walkins, James m. Canby, Anna	Dec. 10,	1789		Hugh Vance			mr 38 *
Walley, Ann m. Strouse, David	May 7,	1815	Jacob French	Rev. Reebenack	3b327	gc 14	*
Walley, Maria m. Morgan, James	Apr. 11,	1814	Henry Packer	Rev. Reebenack	3b292	gc 14	*
Walleck, Mary A. m.Spitsmogle, Adam	Mar. 11,	1839	Levi Spitsmogle		6bl62		
Wallig, Rebecca m. Sanders, John	Oct. 23,	1841	Adam Spitsmogle	John Hedges	6b249		mr 73 *
Wallingsford, Eliz. m.Buckles, Abr'm	Jan. 31,	1801	Mich.Wallingsf'd		2bl13		
Wallingsford,Frances m.Buckles,John	Mar. 7,	1797		Moses Hoge		cr 36	
Wallingsford,Margt m.Blue,John S.	May 7,	1789		Hugh Vance		gc 20	mr 13 *
*Waid, Abraham m. Waid, Mary	Dec. 4,	1798		David Young		gc 8	mr 3 *

	(marriage)	(suretor)	(minister)	(bond)		
Wallingsford,Nich's m. Williams,Phebe	Sept 21, 1800	Mark Wallingsf'd	David Young	2b 88	gc 9	mr 4 *
Wallingsford,Phebe m.Murphy,Jas.	Oct. 22, 1789		Hugh Vanee		cr 25	mr 7 *
Wallingsford,Rich. m.Beckett,Eliz.	June 25, 1793		Moses Hoge		cr 22	mr 8 *
Wallingsford,Susan m.Walters,Isaac	July 30, 1793		Moses Hoge		cr 22	mr 30 *
Waln, Joseph m. Deck, Elenor	Oct. 19, 1819		Mathias Riser			
Waln, Susanna m.Moley, Patrick	Oct. 17, 1797	Wm. Waln		1b 55	cr 15	mr 4 *
Walper, Casper m. Sprinkle, Mary	June 3, 1789		Christian Streit			
Walters, Cath. m. Kilmer, John	Apr. 3, 1830	John Walters		5b161		
Walters, Cath. m. Needler, Andrew	Oct. 11, 1808	Peter Needler		3b 98		
Walters, Cath. m. Young, Nathan C.	Oct. 24, 1837	Michael Walters		6b121		
Walters, Eliza m. Hitson, John	May 7, 1834	Jas. W. Walters		6b 11		
Walters, Eliz. m. Mckrell, Adam	Jan. 2, 1798	Christian Rohr	David Young	1b 78	gc 7	
Walters, Eliz. E. m. Fryatt, James	Oct. 20, 1842	Phil. Diffenderfer		6b280		
Walters, Eve m. Carper, Philip	Apr. 19, 1822	John Walters	Chas. P. Krauth	4b210		mr 45 *
Walters, Fred. m. Ray, Priscilla	Oct. 27, 1841	Wm. Myers		6b250		
Walters, Geo. P. m.VanMetre, Sarah A	Nov. 10, 1853		R.A.Fink			*
Walters, Harrison W. m.Kilmer,Nancy	Dec. 2, 1851	Isaac Kilmer		7b238		
Walters, Isaac m.Wallingsf'd,Susan	July 30, 1793		Moses Hoge		cr 22	mr 8 *
Walters, Isaac W m. Page, Mary	Oct. 23, 1839	Jacob Walters		6b181		
Walters, Jacob m. Greenwell, Rebecca	May 16, 1816	John Strider	W.N.Scott	4b 1		mr 26 *
Walters, Jacob D. m. Rousch, Dorothy	Dec. 18, 1839	Martin Rousch		6b188		
Walters, John m. Bender, Cath.	Sept 11, 1798	Jacob Painter	David Young	1b130	gc 8	
Walters, John m. Painter, Cath.	Mar. 20, 1821	Gottlieb Noll	Nathan Young	4b177		mr 57 *
Walters, John m. Thatcher, Sally	Mar. 15, 1841	Isaac Kilmer		6b237		
Walters, John P. m. Kilmer, Mary	Apr. 27, 1826	Jeremiah Lee	B. Reynolds	5b 40		mr 49 *
Walters, Jonathan m. Lee, Eliz.	Mar. 22, 1796	Conrad Rousch	David Young		gc 5	
Walters, Leah m. Zumbro, Jacob	Oct. 18, 1836				gc 5	
Walters, Margt m. Rousch, George	Dec. 24, 1795					
Walters, Mary m. Markfline, John	Mar. 7, 1816	Isaac Walters	David Young	6b 85		
Walters, Mary m. Moore, Joseph	Mar. 15, 1837	John Snyder	Nathan Young	4b 11		mr 55 *
Walters, Michael m. Rhinestine, Cath.	May 31, 1825	John Walters		6b102		
Walters, Polly m. Selbert, George	Mar. 7, 1837	Michael Walters	Chas. P. Krauth	5b 13		mr 49 *
Walters, Sarah m. Diffenderfer,Phil.	Oct. 28, 1799	John Walter		6b101		
Walters, Sarah m. Segar, Wm.	Nov. 17, 1842	John Burke	Richard Swift	2b 31	cr 34	mr 16 *
Wandle, John m. Curtis, Eliz.	June 2, 1847	James Cox	Lewis F. Wilson	6b253		mr 73 *
Wandling, Geo. I. m. Cox,Frances E.	Dec. 28, 1824		James Chisholm	7b 97		mr 78 *
Wandling, Jonathan m. Harper, Polly	Nov. 14, 1807		John L. Bromwell	4b282		mr 47 *
Ward, Aaron m. Slenck, Cath.	Dec. 4, 1798	John Basore		3b 77		
Ward, Abr'm m. Ward, Mary	Mar. 30, 1799	Dan'el Ward	David Young	1b150	gc 8	
Ward, Adam m. Mitchell, Cath.	Mar. 25, 1842	Samuel Thompson		1b177		
Ward, Arch'd m. Chaston, Sarah	Oct. 12, 1838	James Barton		6b281		
Ward, Arch'd m. Mudcap, Rebecca	May 1, 1824	Wm. Jack		6b150		
Ward, Eliz. m. Lamen, George Jr.	Nov. 25, 1841	Jacob Ward	John Winter	4b264		mr 49 *
*Walters, Wm. m. Lashorn, Harriet		Jos. M. Higgins	Stephen Roznell	6b255		mr 73 *

Name	(marriage)	(suretor)	(minister)	(bond)	
Ward, Eliz. m. Nicklin, Wm.	Oct. 18, 1837	Nich's Ward		6b120	go 12 *
Ward, Esther m. Dougherty, John Jr.	Jan. 4, 1812	John Dougherty Sr	Rev. Reebenack	3b207	*
Ward, Hannah m. Cox, Samuel	Feb. 5, 1833	Wm. Ward	John Light	5b256	*
Ward, Hannah m. Shaffer, Christian	Oct. 31, 1797		David Young		go 7 *
Ward, Harriet E. m. Stewart, Robert	Feb. 13, 1846	Alfred Ross	Lewis F. Wilson	7b 98	mr 77 *
Ward, Hester m. Swinley, George	Aug. 6, 1835	Boyd Roberts	John Howell	6b 52	mr 68 *
Ward, Jacob m. Wendling, Mary Ann	Apr. 20, 1842	Samuel Cox		6b271	
Ward, James m. Cain, Carry	Jan. 24, 1801	Matthew Mahue		2b11	
Ward, Jas. T. m. Light, Cath. Ann	May 19, 1845	Jacob F. Light	John Light	7b 35	mr 76 *
Ward, Joel m. Schoppert, Eliz.	May 21, 1791		David Young		go 1 *
Ward, Joseph m. Fleming, Mary	Oct. 23, 1834	Jacob Harrison	John Light	5b300	mr 67 *
Ward, Joseph m. Lawyer, Mary	Jan. 21, 1801	Stephen Ward		2b137	
Ward, Joshua m. Harrison, Jane	Aug. 24, 1815	Jacob Harrison		5b335	
Ward, Margt m. Ross, Samuel D.	Aug. 22, 1847	Alfred Ross	Rev. Reebenack	7b 90	go 15 *
Ward, Margt m. Roberts, Jonathan	Mar. 5, 1816	Joel Ward	Nathan Young	5b352	mr 55 *
Ward, Margt m. Slaughter, Wm. Jr.	Jan. 8, 1798	Joel Ward		1b122	
Ward, Mary m. Turner, John T.	July 25, 1827	Joseph Ward	Chas. P. Krauth	5b 62	mr 51 *
Ward, Mary m. Ward, Abr'm	Feb. 12, 1798	Daniel Ward	David Young	1b150	go 8 *
Ward, Nancy m. Holmes, Christian	Dec. 4, 1810	Jacob Hamme		3b144	
Ward, Nich's m. Holliday, Rachel	Mar. 28, 1818	George Holliday		4b 59	
Ward, Rachel m. Barton, James	Feb. 3, 1822	Joshua Ward		4b209	
Ward, Stephen m. Thruston, Hannah	Mar. 26, 1799	John Thruston		2b 19	
Warden, Timothy m. Malome, Nelly	Aug. 13, 1794		David Young		go 4 *
Ware, Hannah m. Shaver, Christian	Oct. 30, 1797	Wm. Steele		1b 59	
Ware, James m. Young, Sarah	Dec. 3, 1808	Nathan Young		3b102	
Ware, Nancy m. Watts, Wm.	Aug. 19, 1797	Ralph Ware		1b 29	
Ware, Ralph m. Pollock, Mary Ann	June 11, 1798	James Lane		1b115	mr 15 *
Wareham, Cath. m. Shaffer, George	June 12, 1838	John T. Hilliard	Richard Swift	6b115	cr 31 *
Wareham, Mary Ann m. Bowers, John	Mar. 8, 1838	John Ebberts	James Watts	6b135	mr 53 *
Wares, Andrew m. Faris, Rebecca	Aug. 10, 1829		W. Monroe	5b137	mr 38 *
Warm, Alex. m. Kain, Eliz.	Nov. 2, 1793		Richard Swift		mr 9 *
Warner, Hannah m. Gooding, John	Jan. 2, 1800		David Young		
Warner, John m. Madison, Mary M.	July 8, 1845	Wm. Madison	Moses Hoge	7b 38	cr 22 *
Warner, Mary m. Fitch, Peter	Dec. 22, 1785		Hugh Vance		mr 34 *
Warner, Samuel m. Seever, Mary	Apr. 6, 1797	Edward Mason	Moses Hoge	1b 4	cr 36 *
Warner, Wm. m. Comegrs, Hannah	Mar. 23, 1810	Benj. Comegrs		3b143	mr 13 *
Warner, Zebulon m. Fulton, Mary	June 12, 1792		Moses Hoge		
Warrel, Elijah m. Quinby, Ann	Sept 22, 1793		Wm. Hill		mr 39 *
Warren, Jemima m. Tool, Moore	Oct. 14, 1794				mr 9 *
Washington, Jas. M. m. Jones, Mary	Dec. 19, 1839	Warner W. Mayhugh	Richard Swift	6b189	cr 30 mr 40 *
Washington, John m. Baylor, Frances	Dec. 17, 1799	John Dixon	Lewis F. Wilson	1b163	mr 70 *
Washington, Mildred m. Hammond, Thos.	Apr. 19, 1797	Joseph Crane		1b 9	
Wasson, Cath. m. Kennedford, John	Dec. 29, 1819	Thos. Simpson	Nathan Young	4b128	mr 56 *

Name	(marriage)	(suretor)	(minister)	(bond)	
Waters, Cath. m. Shoppert, George	Dec. 25, 1792		David Young		gc 2 *
Waters, Elinor m. Brashore, Reason	Mar. 15, 1792		Moses Hoge		mr 39 *
Waters, Wm. m. Law, Ann	Nov. 16, 1794		David Young		gc 4 *
*Watkins, Henry m. Wilson, Sally	Sept 13, / Sept 16, 1819	H. Waite	Nathan Young	4b116	mr 54 *
Watkins, Creasy m. Watson, Thomas	Jan. 18, 1787		Hugh Vance		mr 43 *
Watson, Eliz. m. Chenoweth, Thomas	Mar. 22, 1801	Henry Watson	James Chisholm	2b118	
Watson, Ellen S. m. Hivens, Thos. E.	Mar. 19, 1845	Norman Miller		7b 29	mr 76 *
Watson, Francis m. Powell, Martha	Mar. 5, 1798	Robert Powell		1b 88	
Watson, Henry m. Goodwin, Tabitha	Oct. 17, 1801	Gabriel Goodwin		2b143	
Watson, John m. Brown, Mary	Feb. 5, 1798	Richard Ransome		1b 94	
Watson, John m. Haw, Eliz.	Feb. 13, 1788		Hugh Vance		cr 24 *
Watson, Mary m. Watson, Samuel	Jan. 18, 1787		Hugh Vance		mr 43 *
Watson, Mary Ann m. Bell(Bee-), John	Feb. 23, 1839	Daniel Watson	Lewis F. Wilson	6b160	mr 70 *
Watson, Rachel m. Merchant, Hiram	Sept 7, 1826	Boyd Roberts		5b 50	mr 8 *
Watson, Rebecca m. Fulton(Fu-), Sam'l	Sept 8, 1794		John Boyd	1b143	cr 21 *
Watson, Rebecca m. Todd, Reese	Nov. 5, 1798	Hewey Watson	Hugh Vance		mr 43 *
Watson, Samuel m. Watson, Mary	Jan. 1, 1787	Joseph Bell		1b 81	
Watson, Thomas m. Hiele, Rebecca	1798		Moses Hoge		cr 6 *
Watson, Thomas m. Kern(Keen),Sarah	Feb. 1, 1791		Hugh Vance		mr 43 *
Watson, Thomas m. Watson, Creasy	Jan. 18, 1787			1b 72	
Watson, Wm. m. Dunham, Hannah	Dec. 15, 1797	Samuel Dunham		4b230	
Watson, Wm. m. Rosenberger, Margt.	Dec. 3, 1822	Anthony Rosenb'g'r			mr 12 *
Watten, John m. Thatcher, Sally	Mar. 22, 1820		Nathan Young		cr 36 *
Watts, Chas. m. Heson, Christina	Oct. 20, 1796		Moses Hoge		
Watts, Eliz. m. Podsal, Michael	Mar. 1, 1838	James Watts		6b134	
Watts, John m. Cook, Mary	May 29, 1821	John Hildt		4b184	
Watts, Samuel m. Davis, Ann	Aug. 20, 1816	Wm. Davis Jr.	W.N.Scott	4b 6	mr 26 *
Watts, Wm. m. Jeffries, Sally	Dec. 28, 1808	James Catlett		3b105	
Watts, Wm. m. Ware, Nancy	Aug. 19, 1797	Ralph Ware		1b 29	
Waugh, Cath. m. Buck, Isaiah	June 1, 1819	James Waugh	Mathias Riser	4b109	mr 30 *
Waugh, Elinor m. Hager, George	May 21, 1814	James Waugh	Rev. Reebenack	3b298	gc 14 *
Waugh, James m. Tritapoe, Margt.	Dec. 29, 1818	Thomas Tritapoe	Mathias Riser	4b 55	mr 29 *
Waugh, Maria m. Ambrose, David	Jan. 24, 1818	Wm. Waugh	Mathias Riser	4b 58	mr 29 *
Waugh, Nancy m. Miller, Jacob	Jan. 16, 1812	Singleton Waugh		3b209	
Waver, Andrew m. Faris, Rebecca	Mar. 26, 1793		Richard Swift		mr 38 *
Wawr, Cath m. Buck, Isaiah	June 1, 1819	James Waugh	David Young	4b109	mr 30 *
Wawner, Fanny A. m. Norman, Basil	Dec. 12, 1796		Mathias Riser		
Weaver, Barbara m. Houck(Hauk), Geo.	Feb. 14, 1811	Jonathan Thatcher	David Young	3b174	gc 6 *
Weaver, Cath. m. Irwin, John	Apr. 20, 1797	Wm. Irwin	Rev. Reebenack	1b 10	gc 11 *
Weaver, Eliz. m. Burckhart, Henry	May 17, 1827	Jacob Billmire	Nathan Young	5b 70	gc 6 *
Weaver, George m. Strehers, Cath.	May 10, 1810	John Strayer	Rev, Reebenack	3b150	gc 11 *
Weaver, George m. Strayer, Kitty	May 9, 1810		Hugh Vance		mr 99 *
*Watkins, James m. Canby, Anna	Dec. 10, 1789		Hugh Vance		mr 38 *

Name	(date)	(marriage)	(suretor)	(minister)	(bond)		
Weaver, Jemima m.Zeckman(Lockman)Ben.	Dec. 9,	Dec. 10, 1829	Martin Houseman	Jacob Medtart	5b146		mr 63 *
Weaver, John m. Grantham, Jemima	Mar. 14,	Mar. 1825	George Boltz	Chas. P. Krauth	5b 4		mr 48 *
Weaver, John m. Miller, Christina	Dec. 20,	1807	John Miller		3b 37		
Weaver, Peter m. Snider, Christina	Apr. 7.	1789	Henry Snider		1b x		
Weaver, Susan m. Kerns, Wm.	Mar. 17,	Mar. 18, 1813	Robert Wilson	Rev. Reebenack	3b256	gc 13	mr 65 *
Weaver, Wm. m. Eversole, Nancy	Jan. 5,	Jan. 8, 1833	Samuel Middlekauf	Wm. Monroe	5b252		mr 51 *
Webb, Elinor m. Colliflower, John	Aug. 7,	Aug. 1826	Wm. Webb	Chas. P. Krauth	5b 46		mr 41 *
Webster, Christina m. Miller, Henry	Sept 30,	Oct. 12, 1820	Henry Snider	John B. Hoge	4b163		
Weddle, Cath. m. Light, B.B.	Jan. 18.	1848	George Weddle		7b119		
Weddle, D.G.m. Wilhelm, Ruth E.		1841	Philip Wilhelm	John Light	6b241		mr 72 *
Weddle, Michael m.Coffenberger,Mary	Mar. 30,	Apr. 4, 1816	Geo. Coffenberger	Rev. Reebenack	4b16	gc 15	mr 72 *
Tweddle, Daniel G. m.Wilhelm,Ruth E.	May 26,	May 27, 1841	Philip Wilhelm	John Light	6b241		mr 72 *
Weddle, George m. Lee, Hannah	Aug. 27,	Aug. 16, 1846	Jacob Coffenberger	John Winter	7b 64		mr 76 *
Weddle, Jacob m.Coffenberger,Cath.	Aug. 24,	Feb. 25, 1813	George Coffenberger	Rev. Reebenack	3b253	gc 13	
Weddle, Jacob m.Coffenberger, Caty	Feb. 24,	Feb. 25, 1813	Geo. Coffenberger	Rev. Reebenack	3b253	gc 13	
Weddle, Mary m. Buxton, Basil	Nov. 30,	Dec. 1, 1847	John M. Wolff	John Winter	7b114		mr 78 *
Weddle, Susannah m. Canby, David	Nov. 14,	1835	Jacob Weddle		6b 62		
Weddman, Mary m. Calvin, Robert T.	Feb. 20,	1822	?		4b208		
Weddman, Solomon m. Eck, John T.	Jan. 15,	1850	?		7b173		
Weidman, Solomon m. Seibert, Cath.	Nov. 23,	Nov. 26, 1818	Mary Suber	Nathan Young	4b 90		mr 56 *
Weikevin, John m. Rodgers, Martha		June 5, 1792	Peter Zuber	David Young		gc 2	
Weise, Margt. m. Sheneberg, Jacob		Feb. 5, 1793		David Young		gc 2	
Weisenbargh, Jacob m. Kiner, Polly		Oct. 29, 1805		Lewis Duckwall		cr 17	mr 22 *
Weisgerben, John m. Bauer, Cath.		Apr. 1, 1792		David Young		gc 1	
Welch, Kitty m. Wagner, Jacob	Dec. 30,	Dec. 30, 1819	Daniel Wagner		4b128		
Wales, Margt. m. Fuller, Nathaniel	Mar. 27,	Mar. 27, 1797	Robert Grimes	David Young	1b 1	gc 6	
Weller, Cath. m. Price, Daniel	Jan. 6,	Jan. 11, 1838	George Weller	James Watts	6b116		
Weller, Eve Ann m. Hedges, Wm.	Apr. 19,	Apr. 19, 1841	Geo. Weller	John Hedges	6b240		mr 72 *
Weller, Daniel m. Timmons, Mary P.	Sept 19,	1839	John T. Timmons		6b177		
Weller, Geo. B. m.Kennedy(Sara	May 27,	May 30, 1850	John T. Kerney	Henry Furlong	7b186		mr 81 *
Weller, Jacob m. Zimmerman,Susannah		Nov. 1, 1789		Christian Stredt		cr 15	mr 4 *
Weller, Mary Ann m. Ambrouse, Wm.	Apr. 24,	Apr. 24, 1833	Harrison Waite	Peyton Harrison	5b270		mr 73 *
Weller, Susanna m. Miller, John A.	Mar. 23,	Mar. 24, 1842	George Weller	Nathan Young	6b267		mr 64 *
Wells, Harriet m. Johnson, John	May 5,	May 10, 1832	Daniel Price	Nathan Young	5b228		mr 64 *
Wells, Harriet m. Joy, Stephen		May 10, 1832		Nathan Young			
Welsh, Margt. m. Fuller, Nathaniel	Mar. 27,	Mar. 27, 1797	Robert Grimes	David Young	1b 1	gc 6	
Welsh, Ann J. m.Keesecker, Aaron W.	Apr. 19,	Apr. 19, 1855		James Watts			
Welsh, Benj. m. Barnett, Drusilla	Dec. 7,	Dec. 7, 1797	George Emmers	Richard Swift	1b 71	cr 12	mr 14 *
Welsh, Eliz. m. Mason(Massey), Eliz.	Mar. 31,	Mar. 31, 1798	John Lockman	Moses Hoge	1b 95	cr 36	mr 14 *
Welsh, Jacob m. Steen, Mary	Dec. 23,	1800	Cyrus Sanders		2b104		
Welsh, James m. Fisher, Nancy	Dec. 2,	Dec. 5, 1799	Wm. Aikens		2b 36	cr 33	
Welsh, John m. Riner, Sally	Apr. 23,	Apr. 23, 1812	Henry Riner	John Hutt(Hett)	3b222		mr 17 *
Welsh, John J. m. Hudgel, Eliz.	July 4,	July 5, 1836	Harrison Waite	Wm. Monroe	6b 81		mr 68 *

Name	(marriage) license date	(marriage) date	Surety	Minister	(bond)	Ref.	Ref.
Welsh, Margt. m. Emery, George	Feb. 10.	Nov. 5, 1794	Maxwell Welsh	Richard Swift	7b 26		mr 40 *
Welsh, Margt Ann m.Craiglow,Geo.		Feb. 12, 1845		Lewis F. Wilson		cr 11	mr 12 *
Welsh, Mary m. McLean, Robert		Nov. 22, 1796		John Boyd			mr 35 *
Welsh, Mary m. Mooler, Henry		Feb. 15, 1788		Moses Hoge			
Welsh, Mary T. m. Mound, Wm.	Aug. 27,	1838	Sam'l C.P.Welsh		6b145		mr 76 *
Welsh, Maxwell m. Bear(Bare),Cath.	Feb. 1,	Feb. 4, 1845	Jeremiah Quinn	James Chisholm	7b 25	cr 31	mr 15 *
Welsh, Samuel I. m. Darke, Nancy	Mar. 29.	Mar. 29, 1798	Edward Bennett	Richard Swift	1b 93		mr 88 *
Welsh, Thomas m. O'Connor, Eliz.		Dec. 7, 1852		J.H.Plunkett			mr 35 *
Welsh, Wm. m. Koughlyn, Hannah		Feb. 12, 1788		Moses Hoge			mr 18 *
Welsh, Zachariah m. Steen, Hannah		Apr. 5, 1799		John Heitt(Hutt)			mr 85 *
Welshans, Ann Eliz. m.Morrison,Alfred	Sept 20,	Sept 21, 1851	Harrison Tabler	John Hanney	7b233	cr 38	mr 51
Welshans, Ephraim m. Tabler, Mary Ann	Mar. 28.	1827	Henry Tabler	Chas. P. Krauth	5b 66		
Welshans, Daniel Jr. m. Errick, Eliz.	Nov. 10.	1807	*George Errick		3b 76		
Welshans. Fred. m. Hiser, Cath.	July 6,	1793		David Young	2b114	gc 3	*
Welshans, Henry m. Copenhaver, Eliz.	Jan. 4,	1808	Daniel Welshans		2b150		
Welshans, Magdalina m. Hoover,Jonas	Dec. 1,	1801	Daniel Welshans		3b 14		
Welshans, Polly m. Miller, Henry	Apr. 1,	1806	Abr'm Welshans		1b135		
Welshans, Jacob m. Yearley, Sarah	Sept 28,	1798	Nicholas Rousch		4b129		
Weltinger, Tracy m. Smeltzer, Leon'd		1820	John Strother				
Wench(Welsh),Eliz.m.Kroesen, Richard	Nov. 9,	Nov. 9, 1803	John Welsh	David Young	2b212	go 10	mr 62 *
Wendell, Nancy m. Wolff, John	Aug. 16,	Aug. 18, 1831	Archibald Oden	Jas. M. Brown	5b202		mr 47 *
Wendling, Jonathan m.Harper, Polly	Dec. 27,	Dec. 28, 1824	?	J.L.Bromwell	4b282		
Wendling, Mary Ann m. Ward, Jacob	Apr. 20,	1842	Samuel Cox		6b271		
Werbel, Eliz. m. Shuck, Isaac	June 11,	1815			2b 7	gc 14	*
West, Eliz. m. McGee, Oliver	Aug. 3,	1782	Thos. Swearingen	Rev. Reebenack	5b283	cr 9	mr 1 *
West, John m. Hays, Elenor	June 3,	June 4, 1799	Joseph Turner	Hugh Vance	3b 1	cr 34	mr 16 *
Westenhaver, Eliz. m. Spero, Jacob	Sept 14,	1833	Henry Paulsgrove	Richard Swift	3b 1		
Westenhaver, Jacob m. Miller, Rebecca	Oct. 9,	Oct. 13, 1805	Henry Paulsgrove	John Bond	3b 73	cr 28	mr 22 *
Westenhaver, Jesse m. Miller, Rebecca	Oct. 9,	1807	Christ'r Faulk		5b121		
Westenhaver, John m. Faulk, Cath.	Sept 30,	Oct. 1, 1829	Hezekiah Hedges	John Mathews	6b 67	cr 13	mr 23 *
Westenhaver, John m. Miller, Mary	Mar. 3,	1835	Jacob Sherrard		7b 95		
Westenhaver, Mary m. Basore, Michael	Dec. 23,	1847	John Quinn		4b 75		*
Westenhaver, Sophia m. Kreglow, Fred.	May 17,	1818	Wm. Brown	John Winter			
Whaley, Benj. m. Hayes, Sally	June 25,	Mar. 7, 1789		W.N.Scott		cr 19	mr 78 *
Whealand, Mary m. Haley, Thomas		Apr. 3, 1825		Hugh Vance			mr 3 *
Wheatly, Nancy n. Bridgeman, Uriah	Apr. 2,	1806	John Wheatly	J.L.Bromwell	5b 6		mr 3 *
Wheeler, Wm. m. Agent, Cath.	Apr. 10,	1829	Abr'm Agent		3b 16		mr 47 *
Wherritt, George m. Fisher,Margt.	Sept 21,	Sept 23, 1838	John Shober	Jacob Medtart	5b142		mr 63 *
Whets, John m. Fitzgerald, Mary	June 28,	June 28, 1822	Phil. Fitzgerald	James Watts	6b141		mr 69 *
Whetstone, Eliz. m. Poisal, Jacob	June 15,	Jan. 20, 1829	John Bowers	Jacob Medtart	4b217		
Whetstone, Sarah m.Helferstay,Henry	Jan. 20,	1851	Isaac Whisler	Jacob Medtart	5b117		mr 63 *
Whigdon, Rich. B. m. Hammell, Elenor	Sept 1,	Sept 3, 1851	George E. Hammell	Lewis F. Wilson	7b229		mr 87 *
Whisler, Eliz. m. Horn, Jesse	Mar. 1,	Mar. 1, 1821	Isaac Whisler	W.N.Scott	4b174		mr 41 *

*Daniel Welshans Sr. also was a suretor.

Name	Date	(marriage)	(suretor)	(minister)	(bond)	ref
Whips, Nancy m. Brown, Michael	Apr. 7,	1802	James Wright		2b169	
Whisler, Cath. m. Hill, Samuel	Apr. 24,	1821	Isaac Whisler		4b182	
Whisler, Eliza m. Horn, Jesse	Mar. 1,	Mar. 1, 1821	Isaac Whisler	Wm. N. Scott	4b174	mr 41 *
White, Isaac m. Armstrong, Cath.	Mar. 15,	1824	David Hunter		4b265	
White, Bateley m. Hare, Hannah	Feb. 22,	1814	Joseph Hare		3b284	
White, Daniel m. Davis, Sarah		1788		Moses Hoge		
White, Daniel S. m. Doll, Eliz. C.	Apr. 9,	Mar. 6, 1845	C.W.Doll	Moses Hoge	7b 31	mr 35 *
White, Deborah m. Throckmorton, D.W.	Oct. 14,	Apr. 14, 1833	Thomas White	D.F.Bragunier	5b286	mr 78 *
White, Eliz. m. Williams, James	June 23,	Oct. 17, 1798	Abr'm Morlatt	Nathan Young	1b18	mr 66 *
White, Hannah m. McCrea(McCray), Wm.	Dec. 11,	1821	Thomas White	George M. Frye	4b201	mr 44 *
White, James m. McDonald, Harriet	May 6,	Dec. 11, 1844	D. McDonald		6b322	
White, John m. Faris, Charity	Aug. 5,	May 21, 1786	Moses McCrea	Hugh Vance	4b220	mr 43 *
White, John m. McCrea, Eliz.	Oct. 30,	Aug. 6, 1822	John Evans	Nathan Young	4b 85	mr 57 *
White, John m. Reed, Sarah	July 20,	1818	David Cunningham		7b190	
White, Mary m. Turner, Martha	Sept 8,	1850	Jacob Dovenbarger	John Heitt(Hutt)	1b129	cr 11 mr 16 *
White, Mary m. Nelson, Robert	Sept 5,	1798	Charles McDaniel	Nathan Young	4b160	mr 57 *
White, Mary m. Steel, James	Dec. 21,	1820	James M. Gano	P. Lipscomb	7b118	mr 81 *
White, Mary Ann m. Tyson, Basil E.	Sept 2,	1847	Ellis Rees	Nathan Young	4b 79	mr 56 *
White, Rebecca m. McDaniel, Charles	July 28,	1818	James White		6b244	
White, Sarah m. Pitzer, Michael	Apr. 10,	Apr. 4, 1848	George W. Burns	Jas. H. Jennings	7b127	mr 82 *
White, Susan R. m.Coffenberger, John		Apr. 12, 1827	Jacob Keebler	John Winter	5b 67	mr 51 *
White, Thomas m. Keebler(Ki-?), Eliz.		Dec. 25, 1800?		Moses Hoge		mr 20 *
White, Thomas m. Megary, ?	Dec. 20,	1799	Moses Smith		2b 42	cr 38
Whitelock, Uriah m. Grantham, Hannah	Dec. 24,	1802	Amos Mendenhall		2b188	
Whitelock,Jas. m.Riley,Martha Mrs.	Feb. 20,	Feb. 23, 1813	Joshua Hodges	Rev. Reebennack	3b252	gc 13 *
Whitelock,Polly(Patty)m.Wilson,John	Sept 4,	1824	Edward Southwood		4b271	
Whitelock,Rosanna m. Shrode,Solomon		1795				
Whitenaugh, Hannah m. Roberts, Sam'l	Mar. 5,	Mar. 20, 1823	Wm. G. Burns	Moses Hoge	4b249	cr 10 mr 11 *
Whitenaugh,John B. m.Carroll,Mary A.	Sept 17,	Sept 20, 1800	John McKeever	B. Reynolds	2b 82	mr 49 *
Whiteneck, Mary m. VanMetre, Jos.	Aug. 16,	Aug. 17, 1800	John McKeever	David Young	2b 82	gc 9
Whiteneck, Mary m. VanMetre, Joseph	Aug. 16,	Aug. 17, 1813	John Whiteneck	David Young	3b264	gc 9 *
Whiteneck, Rebecca m. Strayer, Mich.	June 7,	1817	John Whiteneck		4b 37	
Whiteneck, Sarah m. Campbell, Robert	June 6,	June 8, 1845	Henry Campbell	Nathan Young	7b 28	mr 55 *
Whiteney, Margt. A. m.VanMetre,Vinc.	Mar. 5,	Aug. 25, 1798	Joseph Gardner	John Heitt(Hutt)	1b121	cr 37 mr 16 *
Whiting, Judith m.Jefferson,Hamilton	June 22,	Jan. 2, 1851	Joseph Gardner	D.Francis Sprigg	7b209	mr 83 *
Whiting, Sarah m. Williams, Edward O.	Jan. 2,	1793	Jacob VanDoren	Edward Tiffin		mr 8 *
Whiting, Susan m. Jefferson, John	Apr. 4,	1847		John Winter	7b 89	cr 9 mr 71 *
Whitson, Mary E. m.VanMetre,Henry S	Mar. 3,	1846	Benj. J. Whitson		7b 57	
Whitson, Sarah R. m. Moore, Jas. W.	Feb. 10,	Aug. 6, 1829	Benj. T. Whitson	W. Monroe	5b135	mr 53 *
Whittington, Richard m.Hays, Sarah	Aug. 5,	July 31,1817	Joseph Hays	W.N.Scott		
Wibly, Alex. m. Shertz, Eliz.		Apr. 5, 1831	Calendar Wbly	Nathan Young	5b191	mr 61 *
Wibly, Mary M. m. Paden, Nathaniel	Mar. 31,	Nov. 26, 1822	Samuel Swingley	James Samson	4b229	mr 45 *
Wickersham, Maria m. Evans, James	Nov. 26,					

Name	(marriage)	(surety)	(minister)	(bond)		
Wickham, Kitty, m. Bansle, Jacob	May 5, 1810	Jonas Hoover	David Young	3b150	gc 5	*
Widows, Eliz. m. Edwards, John	May 7, 1796	Reynolds Ovelchain		1b 42		*
Wide, James m. Ovelchain, Nancy	Sept 19, 1797	Mathias Rizer		2b174		
Widmeyer, Jacob m. Rizer, Mary	June 2, 1802	Wm. Widmire		2b197		
Widmire, Christiana m. Hobdy, Wm.	Mar. 15, 1803	Wm. Widmeyer		2b176		
Widmire, Eliz. m. Bohrer, Abr'm	June 26, 1802	Christ'r Widmire		3b293		
Widmire, Eliz. m. Clawson, Wm. H.	Apr. 12, 1814	Geo. H. Hammell	Lewis F. Wilson	7b229		mr 87 *
Wigdon, Richard B. m. Hammell, Ellen	Sept 1, 1851		G.W.Cooper			*
Wigginton, Geo. W. m. Stine, Susan	Sept 11, 1853					**
Wigle, Cath. m. Kerns, Jacob	Dec. 26, 1840	John Wigle	John Bond	6b228		
Wigle, Christina m. Bitts, John	Sept 17, 1804	Philip Wigle	Hugh Vance	2b243	cr 13	mr 21 *
Wigle, Eliz. m. Hedges, Benj.	Jan. 7, 1784					mr 32 *
Wigle, John m. Myers, Ann	Aug. 27, 1846	John Myers		7b 72		
Wigle, Margt. m. King, Samuel	Aug. 4, 1800	Philip Wigle	David Young	2b 79	gc 9	*
Wigle, Mary m. Robinson, James	Sept 5, 1826	John Wigle		5b 49		
Wigle, Mary m. Shaver, Jacob	June 16, 1788?		Hugh Vance	6b109		mr 35 *
Wigle, Sarah m. Siler, Bennett	June 20, 1837	John Wigle		6b178		
Wilan, Melinda m. Suter, Wm.	Oct. 7, 1839	Andrew Bowman		2b237		
Wilcox, Robert m. Campbell, Mary	June 25, 1804	Walter Turner		2b202	cr 39	mr 4 *
Wilcox, Robert m. Smith, Sarah	Aug. 10, 1789	Robert Wilcox		5b 48	gc 10	**
Wilcox, Sophia m. Turner, Walter	May 9, 1803	Thos. Dennison		6b284		
Wilease, Camilla m.Diffenderfer,Geo.	June 8, 1826	Wm. Wilen	B.M.Schmucker	7b210		mr 84 *
Wilen, Ann Maria m. Martin,Sullivan	Aug. 12, 1842	Wm. Wilson		6b164		
Wilen, Margt. m. Cutting, Nathaniel	Nov. 24, 1851	Benord Swingle		6b 93		
Wiley, James m. Abbott, Eliz. C.	Jan. 8, 1839	Philip Wilhelm				
Wilhelm, Eliza A. m. Kneedler,David	Apr. 7, 1837		R.A.Fink			
Wilhelm, John P. m. Wageley,Maria L.	Aug. 7, 1853	Abr'm VanMetre	John Boggs	7b 23		mr 87 *
Wilhelm, Mary M. m.VanMetre, Asahel	June 12, 1845	Philip Wilhelm	John Light	6b241		mr 75 *
Wilhelm, Ruth Ellen m.Weddle,Daniel	Jan. 27, 1841	Abraham VanMetre	John Boggs	7b 23		mr 72 *
Wilhelm, Mary M. m.VanMetre, Asahel	May 26, 1845	Benj. Harrison	Chas. P. Krauth	4b260		mr 75 *
Wilkinson, Beverly m. Craghill,Julia	Jan. 27, 1824	Thomas Beard	John Boyd	1b 95		mr 47 *
Wilkinson, Eliz. m. Purcell, John	Mar. 31, 1798	John Auten	Richard Swift		cr 32	mr 15 *
Wilkinson, John m. Dunham, Jane	Feb. 13, 1798				cr 31	mr 15 *
Wilkinson, John m. Dundem, Jean	Nov. 9, 1796	Jacob Hott	John Boyd	1b145		
Wilkinson, Mary B. m.Beard, Thomas	May 10, 1851	?		7b236	cr 11	mr 12 *
Willett, David m. Hott, Mary Ann	Oct. 29,					
Willett, James m. Lennor, Eliz.	Nov. 21, 1785	Hugh Vance	Hugh Vance			mr 34 *
Willett, Nancy m. Willett, Richard	Feb. 26, 1785		Edward Tiffin		cr 37	mr 1 *
Willett, Richard m. Willett, Nancy	Feb. 26, 1785		Edward Tiffin		cr 37	mr 1 *
Williams, Ann m. Lewis, William	Mar. 16, 1790		Moses Hoge		cr 3	mr 5 *
Williams, Benj. m. Umphers, Minta	Jan. 20, 1793	?	Richard Swift			
Williams, Chas. m. Morgan, Drusilla	May 2, 1815	George Holiday	Nathan Young	3b322		mr 38 *
Williams, David m. Holiday, Amelia	Aug. 5, 1822		David Young	4b220	gc 4	mr 57 *
*Wigle, Cath m. Bedinger, Adam	Nov. 11, 1794					

Name	(marriage)		(suretor)	(minister)	(bond)	
**Williams, David C. m.Sickafoos,Sarah	Mar. 11,	1830	John Sickafoos		5b157	
Williams, Elenor m.Griffth,Camelius	Apr. 26,	1814	Robt. Mandeville	D. Francis Sprigg	3b296	mr 83 *
Williams, Edward O. m. Whiting, Sarah	Jan. 2,	1851	Jacob Mandeville	David Young	7b209	**
Williams, Elijah m. Evans, Margt.	Jan. 12,	1797	John Strother	John Mathews		**
Williams, Eliza m. Aydelot, Benj.	Dec. 9,	1817	Jamew Wright		4b 52	ge 6
Williams, Eliz. m. Catrow, Samuel	Jan. 2,	1835	John Williams		6b 27	
Williams, Eliz. m. Cox, Wm.	Dec. 26,	1800	John Williams	Richard Swift	2b 44	mr 18 *
Williams, Eliz. m. Cox, Wm.	Mar. 9,	1799	John Williams		1b172	cr 34
Williams, Eliz. m. Hartley, John		1819				
Williams, Isabella m.Staley,Solomon	June 4,	1832	Levi Brannon	Mathias Riser	5b231	mr 30 *
Williams, James m. Brannon, Rebecca	Dec. 31,	1821		William Hawk	4b203	mr 65 *
Williams, James m. Brewer, Sally	Aug. 15,	1814	Wm. Spence	Rev. Reebenack	3b300	ge 14
Williams, James m. White, Eliz.	June 23,	1798	Abr'm Morlatt		1b118	*
Williams, Jane C. m. Foster, Seth B.	Apr. 16,	1834	Christian D. Wolf		6b 7	
Williams, John m. Cline, Barbara	June 13,	1803	John Cline	Richard Swift	2b203	mr 21 *
Williams, John m. Greenwell, Jane A.	Aug. 4,	1824	John M. Cleary Jr.		4b269	cr 27
Williams, John m. Wright, Jane E.	Dec. 17,	1833	James Wright	Jas. M. Brown	5b296	mr 67 *
Williams, John B. m. Gregg, Cath. S.	June 1,	1848	Henry K. Gregg	W. Love	7b130	mr 80 *
Williams, Jonathan . m.Snyder,Mary	Aug. 10,	1850	Jacob VanDoren	John Light	7b192	mr 80 *
Williams, Kath. m. Cockburn, Robert	Feb. 7,	1785		Hugh Vance		mr 33 *
Williams, Margt. m.Biggerstaff, Wm.	Apr. 18,	1819		Mathias Riser		mr 30 *
Williams, Margt. m. Lenor, James	July 29,	1788		Moses Hoge		mr 36 *
Williams, Mary m. Noland, John	Aug. 22,	1816		John Mathews	4b 9	mr 26 *
Williams, Patrick m. Eversole, Eliz.	Aug. 20,	1793	John Williamson	Wm. Hill		mr 9 *
Williams, Phebe m. Wallingsford,Mich.	Sept 20,	1800	Mark Wallingsford	David Young	2b 88	cr 30
Williams, Polly m.Jenkin(linkin),Wm.	Oct. 11,	1799	George Verraka	John Hoitt(Hutt)	2b 31	ge 9
Williams, Priscilla m.Friddle,Nimrod	July 20,	1846	Thos. S. Friddle		7b 70	cr 33
Williams, R.A. m. Colston, Eliz. M.	May 16,	1849	Edward Colston		7b158	mr 17 *
Williams, Samuel m. Beals, Elenor	Nov. 16,	1818	Moses Beal	Wm. N. Scott	4b 87	mr 30 *
Williams, Sophia m. Spence, Wm.	July 27,	1810	Jonas Seaman		3b155	mr 86 *
Williams, W.F. m. Anderson, Mary A.		1852				
Williams, Wm. m. Freshour, Sophia	Aug. 17,	1797	Alex. Catlett	Moses Hoge	1b 31	mr 39 *
Williamson, Ally m.Martin,Jeptha		1792				mr 14 *
Williamson, Amos m.Pendleton, Ann E.	Oct. 23,	1797	Peter Williamson	Richard Swift	1b 58	cr 12
Williamson, Ann A. m.Kershner, Sam'l	July 14,	1840	Wm.H.Pendleton		6b214	mr 76 *
Williamson, Arch'd m. Burke, Rebecca	Jan. 10,	1846	James Burke	John Light	7b 54	cr 12
Williamson, Barat(Basil) m.Wager,Margt	Dec. 22,	1806			3b 38	mr 16 *
*Williamson, David m. Ellis, Maria B.	Mar. 23,	1798	John Ellis	Richard Swift	6b239	mr 72 *
Williamson, Eliz. m. Jones, Mathew	Jan. 6,	1841	Robert Wilson	Lewis F. Wilson	3b245	mr 25 *
Williamson, Isabel m. Kershner, Eliz.	Jan. 10,	1813	Wm. Cole	John Mathews	7b 54	mr 76 *
Williamson, Jacob m. McQuilkin, Eliz.	Oct. 26,	1846	Thos. McQuilkin	John Light	6b182	mr 80 *
Williamson, Jonathan m. Snider, Mary		1839		John Light		mr 80 *
*Williams, Dailey m. Wager, Mary	Jan. 8,	1850			1b 80	
**Williamson, Basil m. Twiggs, Eliz.	Apr. 21,	1782	Alex. Williamson	Daniel Sturges		mr 42 *

Name	Date	(marriage)	(suretor)	(minister)	Bond)	Ref.
Williamson, Leonard m. Cross, Margt.	Nov. 1,	1824	John Files	John Mathews	4b275	mr 50 *
Williamson, Margt. m. Briscoe, John	Jan. 10,	1793		Moses Hoge		mr 99 *
Williamson, Margt. m. McClane, John	June 16,	1798	Abr'm Coleman	David Young	1b117	gc 7
Williamson, Margt. m. Small, Samuel	May 8,	1821	Samuel Williamson	John B. Hoge	4b183	mr 42 *
Williamson, Margt. m. Small, Wm. C.	May 23,	1840	John Williamson		6b210	
Williamson, Mary m. Noland, John	Aug. 27,	1816		John Mathews	4b240	mr 26 *
Williamson, Mary m. Porterfield, Wm.	May 28,	1823	George Hill	Nathan Young	6b229	mr 98 *
Williamson, Mary m. Minebrener, Lew.	Dec. 28,	1840	John Williamson		4b170	
Williamson, Nancy m. Burns, Jonathan	Jan. 8,	1821	John Williamson	John Mathews		mr 44 *
Williamson, Olly m. Kerney, Edward	July 6,	1792		Moses Hoge		mr 39 *
Williamson, Peter m. Nichols, Mary	Jan. 29,	1801	Jacob Nichols	John Boyd	2b12	cr 35 / mr 19 *
Williamson, Peter m. Rush(Rash), Mary	Jan. 24,	1790		Moses Hoge		cr 3 / mr 5 *
Williamson, Samuel m. John, Anne	Apr. 18,	1808	David John		3b 85	mr 90 *
Williamson, Sarah m. Thornburg, Thos.	Nov. 11,	1826	Thomas Lemen	John Mathews	5b 55	mr 61 *
Williamson, Sidney m. Burns, Caleb	Nov. 15,	1830	John Williamson	W. Monroe	5b181	mr 63 *
Williamson, Sidney m. Deck, Henry	Apr. 22,	1829	Wm. Rush	Jacob Medtart	5b128	mr 46 *
Williamson, Sophia m. Billmyre, Conrad	Aug. 11,	1823	John Williamson	John Mathews	4b244	mr 51 *
Williamson, Susannah m. Summers, Wm.	Mar. 19,	1827	John Shober	John Mathews	5b 64	mr 18 *
Williamson, Theodorus m. Prather, Rhoda	Sept 2,	1800	Silas Prather	Richard Swift	2b 84	cr 34 / mr 44 *
Williamson, Wm. m. Martin, Eliza.	May 12,	1818	Jeptha Martin	John Mathews	4b 71	cr 12 / mr 16 *
Willis, Carver m. Hite, Frances M.	Dec. 10,	1798	Richard Willis	John Hett(Hutt)	1b153	
Willis, John m. Demoss, Ann	Mar. 21,	1815	Morris Rees		3b316	
*Willis, Richard m. Gray, Eliz.	May 24,	1798	John Craghill	David Young	1b12 / 1b 50 / 2b 65	gc 7 *
Wilson, Zachariah m. Chenoweth, Susan	Sept 29,	1797	Edward Chenoweth		2b204	
Wilmouth, George m. Brown, Sarah	Apr. 15,	1800	Joseph H. Brown		2b248	
Wilmouth, John m. Stegler, Christina	June 27,	1803	Martin Myers	Richard Swift	1b 77	cr 27 / mr 21 *
Wilmouth, Joseph m. Kelly, Eliz.	Dec. 28,	1793		Wm. Hill	2b 36	cr 30 / mr 9 *
Wilmouth, Polly m. Thompson, Elias E.	Nov. 20,	1804	Geo. Wilmouth		4b144	
Wilmouth, Thos. m. Pendex(Pendry) Mary	Jan. 9,	1798	Ralph Pendes	David Young	6b274	gc 7
Wisk, James m. Fisher, Nancy	Dec. 5,	1799	Wm. Aikens	John Hett(Hutt)	3b166	cr 33 / mr 17 *
Wilson, Abigail m. Cline, Jacob	Apr. 12,	1820	Wm. Wilson	Nathan Young	7b139	mr 57 *
Wilson, Ann m. Murray, Nimrod	Aug. 2,	1842	James McSherry			
Wilson, Ann m. Yeates, David	Dec. 8,	1810	John G. Wilson			
Wilson, Anna C. m. Hoge, John Blair	Nov. 1,	1848	David H. Strother	Wm. Love	7b139	mr 80 *
Wilson, Daniel m. Sly(Shy), Rachel	Aug. 30,	1827	Seaman Garard	Nathan Young	5b 77	mr 99 *
Wilson, David m. Hoyle, Mary E.	Dec. 23,	1830	Samuel Mainor	Jas. M. Brown	5b183	mr 54 *
Wilson, David S. m. Mayhew, Rebecca	Apr. 6,	1837	Esom Mayhew	James Watts	6b103	mr 47 *
Wilson, Eliza m. Boyd, James S.	Oct. 21,	1824	John K. Wilson	Chas. P. Krauth	4b274	cr 10 / mr 11 *
Wilson, Eliz. m. Baldwin, Joseph	Feb. 10,	1795	Adam Leopard	John Boyd	6b 22	
Wilson, Eliz. m. Castle, Elijah	Nov. 8,	1834	Jacob VanDoren		7b164	
Wilson, Eliz. m. Walker, El	Aug. 22,	1849	John B. Hoge		4b 68	mr 29 *
Wilson, Eliz. m. Mathews, John	Apr. 8,	1818	Wm. Wilson	John B. Hoge		
Wilson, Eliz. P. m. Hoffman, Joseph	?	1836?	John B. Hoge	Peyton Harrison	6b130	mr 69 *
*Willis, Martha m. Swift, Richard	Mar. 28,	1793	Wm. Wilson	Moses Hoge		cr 21 / mr 7 *

	(marriage)		(surety)	(minister)	(bond)		
Wilson, Els. P. m. Sherrard, Robert	Apr. 26,	1813	Wm. Wilson	John Heitt(Hutt)	3b260		mr 18 *
Wilson, George m. McCleland, Nancy	Jan. 18,	1800	Robert Shirley	Nathan Young	2b 48	cr 33	mr 58 *
Wilson, Geo. M. Kerns, Susan	Apr. 5,	1826	Samuel Lowry	David Young	5b 39	gc 7	
Wilson, Hannah m. Davis, Henry	Aug. 23,	1798		B. Reynolds			
Wilson, Hannah m. Dick, Wm.	Jan. 10,	1826	Samuel Manor	Nathan Young	5b 32		mr 49 *
Wilson, Isabel m. Hill, Samuel	Feb. 24,	1818	John P.Porterfield	Nathan Young	4b 63		mr 56 *
Wilson, Jacob m. King, Margt.		1801		Moses Hoge		cr 38	mr 20 *
Wilson, Jacob Jr. m. Newell, Ann	Apr. 18,	1797	Jacob Wilson Sr.		1b 9		
Wilson, James m. Baldwin, Jane	Aug. 1,	1789		Hugh Vance		cr 39	mr 4 *
Wilson, James m. Bramhall, Margt.	Aug. 3,	1785		Edward Tiffin		cr 38	mr 1 *
Wilson, James m. Buckhannon, Mary	Oct. 7,	1783?		Hugh Vance			mr 32 *
Wilson, James m. Flack, Cath.	Aug. 5,	1794		John Boyd		cr 21	mr 8 *
Wilson, James m. Pendleton, Susan	Feb. 11,	1781		Daniel Sturges			mr 31 *
Wilson, James m. Saveley, Christina	Sept 3,	1807	George Saveley		3b 68		
Wilson, James m. Robinson, Ann	Dec. 12,	1850		James H. Jennings			mr 82 *
Wilson, James Jr. m. Snyder, Rosanna	Oct. 10,	1842	Harrison Waite		6b279		
Wilson, James M. m. Robinson, Ann E.	Oct. 5,	1847	Alex. Robinson		7b108		
Wilson, Jane m. McIntire, John	Sept 13,	1800	James Wilson		2b 87		
Wilson, Jane m. Roberts, James	Apr. 1,	1807	Samuel Roberts		3b 54		
Wilson, Jesse m. Goldsburg, Mary	June 9,	1785	Esom Mayhew	Edward Tiffin	7b206	cr 38	mr 1 *
Wilson, John m. Stump, Jemima Cath.	Dec. 9,	1850	Joshua Hedges	F.C. Tebbs	3b252	gc 13	mr 83 *
Wilson, John m. Whitelock, Polly	Feb. 20,	1813	Chas. D. Stewart	Rev. Reebenack	5b 44		mr 50 *
Wilson, John K. m.Anderson, Anabella	June 20,	1826		John Mathews			mr 83 *
Wilson, John W. m. Shimp,Jemima Cath.	Dec. 9,	1850		F.C. Tebbs		gc 4	
Wilson, Joshua m. Lyvly, Susan	Dec. 22,	1794		David Young			
Wilson, Lambert m. Seaborn, Ellen	Apr. 16,	1814	Peter Seaborn	Peyton Harrison	3b294		mr 69 *
Wilson, Lew. F. Revr. m.Tabb,Harriet	Apr. 6,	1838?	Seaton E. Tabb		6b138	gc 3	
Wilson, Margt. m. Brown, David	?	1794		David Young			
Wilson, Margt. m. Miller, Wm. H.	Feb. 14,	1846	John H. Likens	John Winter	7b 80		mr 77 *
Wilson, Margt. C. m. Cutting, Nathanian	Jan. 7,	1851	Wm. Wilson	B.M.Schmucker	7b210		mr 84 *
Wilson, Maria m. Myers,Jas. Henry	Oct. 19,	1842	Benj. Comegys	Mayberry Goheen	6b279		mr 74 *
Wilson, Mary m. Chenoweth, Edward	Sept 23,	1797	Zachariah Wilson		1b 44		
Wilson, Mary m. Forster, Christian		1792		David Young			
Wilson, Mary m. Hardy, Lewis	Feb. 21,	1826?	William Orr	James Redly	5b 32	gc 1	
Wilson, Mary m. Serrimon(Summers)John	Jan. 20,	1788		Hugh Vance			mr 49 *
Wilson, Mary Ann m. Sweney, John B.	Dec. 29,	1836	Wm. Wageley		6b 80		mr 36 *
Wilson, Mary C. m. Tabb, George W.	May 25,	1840	Seaton E. Tabb	Lewis F. Wilson	6b220		
Wilson, Mary M. m. Coe, Ebenezer	Oct. 6,	1824	Samuel K. Wilson		4b277		mr 71 *
Wilson, Nancy m. Mumford, Wm.	Nov. 2,	1804	Peter Miller		2b218		
Wilson, Nancy m. Stuckey, Jacob	Jan. 1,	1850	James Wilson	J.H.Jennings	7b187		mr 82 *
Wilson, Nancy m. Wilson, Wm.	June 11,	1829	Robert Johnston	Nathan Young	5b133		mr 60 *
Wilson, Nancy M. m. Stuckey, Jacob	June 13,	1850	James Wilson	J.H.Jennings	7b187		mr 82 *
Wilson, Polly M. m. Christy, Peter	Feb. 9,	1804	James Wilson		2b221		

Marriage index (surnames Wilson – Winning, Windle)

Name	(marriage)	(suretor)	(minister)	(bond)		
Wilson, Rachel m. Young, Israel	Nov. 25, 1834	?	Richard Swift	6b 23	cr 27	mr 21 *
Wilson, Richard m. Butt, Priscilla	July 20, 1803	John Butt		2b206		mr 54 *
Wilson, Robert m. Chenoweth,Henrieta	Oct. 23, 1810	Wm. Long		3b164		
Wilson, Robert m. Light, Elenor	May 29, 1815	Peter Light Jr.		3b326		
Wilson, Sally m. Watkins, Henry	Sept 16, 1819	Harrison Waite	Nathan Young	4b116		mr 75 *
Wilson, Sarah m. Cole, Samuel	Jan. 26, 1820	Jacob Kroesen		4b132		mr 34 *
Wilson, Samuel K. m. Park, Mary	Apr. 6, 1819	John Park		4b105		mr 11 *
Wilson, Sarah m. Donaldson, Geo. F.	Apr. 10, 1845	James Wilson	John Boggs	7b 31		mr 22 *
Wilson, Sarah m. Gilkrist, Henry	Sept 1, 1785		Hugh Vance		cr 33	mr 8 *
Wilson, Sarah m. Gray, James	June, 1795		John Boyd		cr 28	
Wilson, Sarah m. Kroesen, Isaac	May 10, 1806	Chas. Orrick	John Bond	3b 19	cr 21	
Wilson, Sarah m. Norwood, James	Dec. 25, 1794		John Boyd		cr 3	
Wilson, Sarah Ann m.Albright, Peter	July 15, 1847	Geo. M. Wilson		7b100		mr 3 *
Wilson,Sav'na(Susanna)m.Butt,Bazell	Dec. 24, 1789		Moses Hoge	7b123		mr 81 *
Wilson, Susan m. Tabler, Wm.	Feb. 25, 1848	Samuel Cole	P. Lipscomb	7b 49		mr 41 *
Wilson, Susan C. m. Noland, Burr P.	Feb. 23, 1845	Edmund Pendleton	John B. Hoge	4b155		mr 49 *
Wilson, Wm. m. Davidson, Mary	July 27, 1820	Phil. P. Hunter	B. Reynolds	5b 37		mr 33 *
Wilson, William m.Ducker, Cath.	Mar. 15, 1826	Wm. Ducker	Hugh Vance			mr 60 *
Wilson, Wm. m. Parks, Mary	Feb. 2, 1786		Nathan Young	5b133		mr 67 *
Wilson, Wm. m. Wilson, Nancy	June 13, 1829	Robert Johnston	John Light	5b294		mr 14 *
Wilson, Wm. D. m. Keesacre, Jane	Dec. 9, 1833	James Griswell,	David Young		gc 1	mr 73 *
*Wimilton, Wm. m. Short, Mary	Oct. 28, 1791		John Hill	1b 66	cr 37	mr 14 *
Wimmer, Mary m. Dunn, Richard	Nov. 27, 1797	Jonathan Moore	John Hedges	6b253		mr 29 *
Windham, Alfred H. m. Johnson, Nancy	Nov. 15, 1841	John D. Jones	John B. Hoge	4b 72		mr 60 *
Windle, John m. Small, Nancy	June 2, 1818	Robert Small	Nathan Young	5b133		mr 72 *
**Windoms, Nicholas m.Hillyard, Cath.	June 14, 1829	John Shober	John Light	6b260		
Winebrener, Ellen m. Hill, Wm.	Dec. 30, 1841	Israel Cooper		6b229		
Winebrener, Lewis m. Williamson,Mary	Dec. 28, 1840	John Williamson	John Light	7b 52		
Winebremer, Thos. S. m.Mips, Susan	Jan. 1, 1846	Norman Miller		3b146		
Winecoop, Hannah m. Lemen, Wm. M.	Apr. 14, 1810	James Lemen	David Young	4b 32	gc 3	mr 76 *
Winekeart, Elis. m. Overstake, Benj.	July 21, 1793			1b104		*
Winfield, Lawrence m. Chambers, Sally	Mar. 27, 1817	Abr'm Hooper	John Hill	1b 66		
Wingard, John m.Noffdinger, Cath.	Mar. 24, 1798	John Stewart		1b 23	cr 37	mr 14 *
Winmere, Mary m. Dunn, Richard	Nov. 29, 1797	Jonathan Moore		3b246		
Winn, Elis. m. Amey, George	June 24, 1797	Henry Fiser	Rev. Reebemack	1b120		
Winn, Polly m. Martin, Wm.	Jan. 7, 1813	Charles Young	David Young	4b141	gc 13	mr 41 *
Winning, Agnes m.Cummingham, Robert	June 25, 1798	James Cumningham	W.N.Scott	6b 35	gc 7	
Winning, Edward m. Grantham, Cath.	Mar. 30, 1820	Wm. Grantham		4b150		
Winning, Israel m. Castle, Melinda	Mar. 9, 1835	John Castle	David Young	1b 36		
Winning, James m. Davenport, Susan	Mar. 16, 1792		W.N.Scott	5b217	gc 1	mr 41 **
Winning, James m. Kennedy, Cath.	June 8, 1820	Edward Kennedy		1b 50		
Winning, James m. Roesz, Mary	June 6, 1797	James Anderson				
Winning, Jane m. Murphy, John	Sept 1, 1832	Wm. Anderson				
**Wilson, Zachariah m. Chenoweth,Susan	Feb. 21, 1797	Edward Chenoweth				
***Windle(Wem-),Nancy m- Wolf, John	Aug. 16, 1831	Arch'd Oden	Jas. M. Brown	5b202		mr 62 *

251

Name	Date	(marriage)	(surety)	(minister)	(bond)	
Winning, John m. Anderson, Phebe	June 2,	1812	Wm. Anderson	Rev. Reebenack	3b227	gc 13 *
Winning, Margt. m.Cunningham, James	Sept 22,	1797	Wm. Cunningham	John Boyd	1b 43	cr 32 mr 13 *
Winning, Sarah m. Palmer, John	Nov. 3,	1835	Wm. Anderson		6b 61	
Winning, Thos. R. m. Mong, Eliz.	Apr. 1,	1834	George Mong		6b 2	*
Wintermuck, Caroline m.Little, Rich'd	Apr. 3,	1796		David Young		ge 5 *
Wintermuth, Chas. m. Gallaher, Nancy	Dec. 31,	1810	Robert Gallaher		3b171	*
Wintermuth, Peggy m. Ardinger, John	Mar. 17,	1804	Horatio Wintermu'h		2b228	*
Wise, Andrew m. Norman, Cath.	Aug. 9,	1791		David Young		ge 1 *
Wise, Jacob m. Boyer, Kath.	Feb. 27,	1787		Hugh Vance		mr 44 *
Wisenberger, Eliz. m. Higgins, Jos.	Apr. 5,	1810	Stephen Gano		3b149	*
Wisenbergh, Jacob m. Kiner,Polly	Oct. 29,	1805	Harrison Waite	Lewis Duckwall		cr 17 mr 22 *
Withrow, Joseph m. Ewert, Margt.	May 7,	1832	Jacob Dovenburger	Jas. M. Brown	3b228	mr 64 *
Witle, Mary m. Nelson, Robert	Sept 8,	1798	Mathias Kenny	John Butt(Hedtt)	1b129	cr 11 mr 16 *
Wobley, Alex. m. Sheetz, Eliz.	July 31,	1817	Harrison Waite		4b 41	
Wobley, Calendar m. Sampson, Jane	Sept 26,	1835			6b 58	
Woke, Anna m. Meskimen, Nelson	Aug. 11,	1816		Mathias Riser		mr 26 *
Woke, David m. Ford, Ann	Feb. 24,	1816		Mathias Riser		mr 26 *
Woke, Thomas m. Goodman, Vemelia	Aug. 28,	1794		David Young		*
Wolfe, Eliz. m. Smith, Basil	Dec. 27,	1809	Philip Wolfe	Rev. Reebenack	3b131	ge 4 *
Wolfe, Jacob m. Snider, Uley	Sept 11,	1798	Hugh Wood		1b131	ge 11 *
Wolfe, John m. Windle, Nancy	Aug. 18,	1831		Jas. M. Brown		mr 62 *
Wolfe, Michael m. Stout, Mary	July 23,	1801	Philip Stout		2b130	*
Wolfe, Jacob m. Snider, Mary	Sept 11,	1798		David Young		ge 8 *
Wolff, Amos m. Harrison, Mary Jane	Dec. 25,	1848	Wm.Lew.Buzzard		7b142	*
Wolff, Ann Doyne m.Strother,Dav.Hunter	May 15,	1849	A.W.Vanoredel	Lewis F. Wilson	7b157	mr 83 *
Wolff, Bernard m. Doll, John	Apr. 6,	1820	Bernard Wolff	Lewis Mayrer	4b143	mr 40 *
Wolff, Armstead m. Talbott, Mary E.	May 31,	1851	Wm. P. Shipman	F.C.Tebbs	7b225	mr 85 *
Wolff, Cath. m. Doll, Daniel H.	Feb. 25,	1833	George Wolff		5b258	*
Wolff, Christian m. Newcomer, Sarah	Sept 2,	1845	Jacob Newcomer		7b 41	*
Wolff, Eliz. m. Smith, Basil	Sept 27,	1809	Philip Wolfe	Rev. Reebenack	3b131	*
Wolff, George m. Myers, Cath.	Dec. 28,	1795	John Strother	David Young		ge 11 *
Wolff, Henry m. Jameson, Martha	Mar. 22,	1796		David Young		ge 4 *
Wolff, John m. Noland, Priscilla	Aug. 9,	1820		David Young		ge 6 *
Wolff, John m. Wendell, Nancy	Feb. 1,	1831	John Strother		4b133	*
Wolff, Joseph m. Buckins, Mary Ann	Aug. 16,	1831	Arch'd Oden	James M. Brown	5b202	mr 62 *
Wolff, Mary m. Pendry, Robert	Sept 25,	1815	John Polsal	Rev. Reebenack	3b340	ge 15 *
Wolff, Mary Cath. m. Seibert,Wm. L.	Jan. 5,	1813	Samuel Lion	Rev. Reebenack	3b245	ge 13 *
Wolff, Mary E.m. Vanorsdal, Andrew	Nov. 22,	1849	John M. Wolff	John W. Wolff	7b168	mr 79 *
Wolff, Sarah Ann m. Ledghner, Philip	June 3,	1848	Norman Miller	W. Love	7b130	mr 80 *
Wolford, Eliz. m. Burns, Ely	Mar. 25,	1834	James Criswell	Jas. M. Brown	6b 1	cr 15 mr 67 *
Wolford, Martin m.Crim(-en)Polly(Mary)	Nov. 1,	1789		Christian Streit		mr 4 *
Wolford, Wm. m. Kerns, Susan	Aug. 3,	1815	John Crim	Nathan Young	3b331	mr 55 *
Wolford, Martin m. ...	Aug. 4,	1831	Abr'm Hooper	Nathan Young	5b199	mr 62 *
Wolgamott, David m. Snider, Sarah	Feb. 6,	1807	Thomas Butler	John Mathews	3b 45	cr 13 mr 23 *

Name	date	(marriage)	(suretor)	(minister)	(bond)			
Wolgamott, Susan m. Davis, Thomas	June 29,	June 30, 1799	Jonathan Sattle	David Young	2b 10	gc 8		*
Wolham, Eliz. m. Bough, Henry	Sept 28,	Sept 28, 1797	Baker Wolham		1b 49	gc 10		*
Wolick, Eliz. m. Kroessen, Richard	Nov. 6,	Nov. 9, 1803	John Welsh	David Young	2b212			
Wollam, Benj. m. Otter, Hannah	Feb. 3,	1803	English P. Otter		2b192			
Wollam, Henry m. Bough, Mary	Dec. 14,	1801	Henry Bough Jr.		2b152			
Wollam, John m. Duffield, Sarah	Apr. 24,	1797	Peter Hedges	David Young	1b 12	gc 6		*
Wollam, Joseph m. Flickinger, Magda	Dec. 10,	Dec. 12, 1799	Michael Flickinger	David Young	2b 39	gc 9		*
Wolly, Ann m. Strouse, David	May 7,	June 8, 1815	Jacob French	Rev. Reebenack	3b327	gc 14		*
Wolverton, George m. McSherry, Cath.	Feb. 23,	Feb. 23, 1815	Benj. Thomas	Rev. Reebenack	3b311	gc 14		*
Womeldorf, John m. Hout, Cath.	Sept 22,	Sept 23, 1800	Michael Hout	Rev. Reebenack	3b162	gc 11		*
Wood, Charlotte m. Rine, John		Feb. 26, 1793		Richard Swift			mr 38	*
Wood, Edgar Rev. m. Baker, Maria B.		Sept 7, 1853		R.T.Berry			mr 15	*
Wood, Hugh m. Snider, Barbara	May 3,	May 10, 1798	John Bowman	John Boyd	1b110	cr 32	mr 42	*
Wood, John m. Baker, Susanna		Oct. 8, 1781		Daniel Sturges				*
Wood, Mary m. Coffenberger, John	Dec. 26,	1834	Robert Wood	Richard Swift	6b 26	cr 26	mr 10	*
*Wood, Nancy m. Harris(Hannis),David	Jan. 9,	July 28, 1795		Moses Hoge			mr 14	*
Wood, Priscilla m. Strayer, John	Apr. 2,	Jan. 11, 1798	Daniel Buckles		1b 80		mr 18	*
Wood, Robert m. Johnson, Cath.	Feb. 19,	1838	Thos. C. Harper	John Heitt(Hutt)	6b138		mr 2	*
Wood, Samuel m. Hall, Eliz.		Mar. 7, 1799	Wm. Hall	Moses Hoge	1b170	cr 13	mr 7	*
Wood, Sarah m. Ebert, George		Feb. 8, 1789		Moses Hoge		cr 1		*
Wood, Susannah m. Tapscott, James		Apr. 30, 1793				cr 21		*
Wood, Thomas m. Yerkey, Priscilla	Dec. 3,	1806	Josiah Yerkey	John Heitt(Hutt)	3b 37		mr 17	*
Wood, Wm. m. Harris, Nancy	Aug. 2,	Aug. 8, 1799	Jacob Croesen	John Heitt(Hutt)	2b 15	cr 38	mr 16	*
Wood, Wm. m. Roderick, Eliz.	Oct. 13,	Oct. 13, 1798	Robert Roderick	John Light	1b 139	cr 11	mr 70	*
Woodall, James m. Martin, Ellen E.	Nov. 28,	Nov. 28, 1839	James Martin	John Light	6b184		mr 70	*
Woodall, Joseph m. Martin, Ellen		Nov. 28, 1839						*
Woodring, John m. Johnston, Mary	Feb. 19,	Feb. 13, 1802	Henry Claycomb	Richard Swift	2b161	cr 32	mr 20	*
Woods, Hugh m. Snyder, Barbara	May 3,	May 10, 1798	John Bowman	John Boyd	1b110	cr 32	mr 15	*
Woods, Mary m. Dunphy, Nicholas	Aug. 20,	1838	Bartholomew Garney		6b144			*
Woodward, Francey m.Osborn(Osmur),H.	Sept 8,	Sept 9, 1832	Harrison Waite	Jacob Medtart	5b240		mr 64	*
Woodward, Thos. m. Pultz, Frances	July 24,	July 25, 1819	John Kemp	Nathan Young	4b111		mr 56	*
Woolard, John m. Smith, Mary	June 15,	June 15, 1848	John R. Crook	W. Love	7b132		mr 80	*
Worley, Plety m. Tabler, Adam	Dec. 4,	Dec. 6, 1818	Silas Worley	Nathan Young	4b 11		mr 56	*
Worley, Prudence m. Tabler, Wm. Jr.	Apr. 11,	Apr. 15, 1815	Brice Worley	Nathan Young	3b319		mr 55	*
Worley, Walling m. Bell(Bea-),Elenor	Aug. 21,	Aug. 24, 1815	Jeremiah Beall	Nathan Young	3b335		mr 55	*
Worley, Silas m. Kildow, Eliz.	Nov. 7,	1816	Jacob Kildow		4b 18			
Worley, Silas m. Ramsburg, Cath.	Mar. 11,	1829	Wm. Tabler		5b122			
Worrell, John m. Eaton, Sarah	Nov. 26,	1804	John Eaton		2b248			
Worthington, Eppy m.Brackenridge,Tho.	Dec. 4,	1799	Richard Ransome		2b 37			
Worthington, Samuel m. Ewings, Ann	July 30,	July 30, 1807	John Gray		3b 64			
Wright, Ann m. Edwards, John	Mar. 13,	Mar. 16, 1843	Levi Henshaw	Leeds F. Wilson	6b292		mr 74	*
Wright, Daniel m. Pepper, Eliz.D.	Dec. 22,	Dec. 23, 1832	Wm. Pepper	W. Monroe	5b250		mr 65	*
Wright, David m. Mason, Sarah	Aug. 21,	Aug. 22, 1805	Edward Mason	Moses Hoge	2b269	cr 17	mr 22	*
*Wood, Phebe m. Wright, James		1789		D. Thomas			mr 38	*

Name	(marriage)		(surety)	(minister)	(bond)		
Wright, James m.Baley(Boley),Peggy	Nov. 14,	Nov. 15, 1812	Wm. Wright	Lewis Mayer	3b241	cr 15	mr 25 *
Wright, James m. Wood, Phebe		1789		D. Thomas	7b 68		mr 38 *
Wright, James Rev. m. Gorrell, Eliz.	June 6.	June 9, 1846	Benj. F. Burns	John Winter	4b 38		mr 76 *
Wright, Jane m. Long, John	June 24,	June 26, 1817	Jesse Wright	W.N.Scott	2b220	cr 17	mr 21 *
Wright, Jane m.Sheldon(Shields),Jas.	June 24,	Jan. 26, 1804	Samuel Wright	Moses Hoge	5b296		mr 67 *
Wright, Jane E. m. Williams, John	Jan. 24,	Dec. 19, 1833	James Wright	Jas. M. Brown	5b144		mr 60 *
Wright, Jesse m. Rousch, Eliz.	Dec. 17,	Oct. 25, 1829	?	Nathan Young			mr 31 *
Wright, John m. McCormick, Ann	Oct. 24,	Dec. 13, 1780	James Sterrett	Daniel Sturges	2b199		
Wright, Margt. m. Hett, Peter	Apr. 1,	Apr. 1, 1803	Levi Henshaw Jr.	Lewis F. Wilson	6b292		mr 74 *
Wright, Margt. Ann m. Edwards, John	Mar. 13,	Mar. 16, 1843	Charles Wright	David Young	1b156	go 4	
Wright, Mary m. Goth, James		Aug. 25, 1794	John Wright	David Young	3b516	gc 8	
Wright, Mary m. Thompson,Samuel L.	Dec. 24,	Dec. 24, 1798	John Wright	John Mathews			mr 25 *
Wright, Nancy m. Bowman, James	Mar. 29,	Mar. 30, 1815	James Wright	Moses Hoge	3b357	cr 2	mr 2 *
Wright, Peggy m. Hendricks, Tobias	May 13,	Feb. 29, 1789	Edward Mason	W.N.Scott	3b158		mr 26 *
Wright, Polly m.Colvin(Calvin), John	Feb. 29,	Feb. 29, 1816	John Wright				
Wright, Rachel m. Needler, George	Aug. 12,	Aug. 12, 1810	Jacob Kroesen	Moses Hoge	2b269	cr 7	mr 6 *
Wright, Rebecca m. Keath,Zachariah	Apr. 7,	Apr. 7, 1791	Jacob Schoppert	Moses Hoge		cr 17	mr 22 *
Wright, Samuel m. Mason, Sarah	Aug. 22,	Aug. 22, 1805	Jeptha Martin	Hugh Vance			mr 34 *
Wright, Samuel m. Melvin, Susannah	Sept 28,	Sept 28, 1785			3b159		
Wright, Sarah m. Lucky, George	Aug. 28,	Aug. 28, 1810	John Wright	John Hett(Hutt)	2b 39	cr 33	mr 17 *
Wyoff,Cornelius m.Inge(Ledge),Eliz.	Dec. 8,	Dec. 12, 1799	Jacob Kroesen		6b278		
Wyland, Wm. m. Schoppert, Mary	Sept 21,	Sept 21, 1842	Jacob Schoppert		1b 30		
*Wynkoop, Garret m. Martin, Sarah	Aug. 15,	Aug. 15, 1797	Jeptha Martin	John Mathews	4b176		mr 44 *
Wynkoop, Margt. m. Hendricks, Nathan	Mar. 12,	Mar. 15, 1821	Adrian Wynkoop		5b 67		
Wynkoop, Mary m. Randall, George	Apr. 2,	Apr. 2, 1827	Garret Wynkoop	Richard Swift	2b156	cr 32	mr 20 *
Wynkoop, Susannah m. Jones, Francis	Jan. 2,	Jan. 2, 1802?	Adrian Wynkoop	John Mathews	5b 39		mr 50 *
Wynkoop, Wm. W. m.VanWetre, Eliz.	Apr. 10,	Apr. 13, 1826	Josiah VanWetre	Chas. P. Kreuth	5b 36		mr 51 *
Wysong, Lewis B. m.Showalter,Harriet	Feb. 14,	Feb. 1826	John M. McCleary		7b 47		
Wysong, Mary D. m. Ball, Dabney	Oct. 29,	Oct. 29, 1845	Richard McGlathery				
*Wynkoop, Hannah m. Lemin, Wm.	Apr. 14,	Apr. 14, 1810 "T"	James Lemin		3b146		
Yaoban, Patrick m. Fenster, Ellen	Aug. 12,	1841	Domin'k O'Connell		6b245		
Yarder, John m. McQuade, Eliz.	Jan. 22,	1825	Thomas Spencer		4b287		
Yarnall, Joseph m.Howe, Mary	July 26,	July 1813	Abr'm Bell	Nathan Young	3b266		mr 54 *
Yates, Eliz. m. Covert, John	Dec. 23,	1797	Peter Morlatt		1b 73		
Yates, John m. Shields, Nancy	Apr. 10,	1813	Wm. Shields		3b258		
Yeardly, Phebe m. Brown, Benj.	Jan. 2,	1807	Peter Gardner		3b 41		
Yearly, Sarah m. Welehans,Jacob	Sept 28,	1798	Nicholas Rousch		1b135		
Yeates, David m. Wilson, Ann	Dec. 8,	1810	John G. Wilson		3b166		
Yeates, Eleanor m. Rippy, David	?	1798	Andrew Yeates		1b 93		
Yeates, Mary m. Finley, David	May 19,	1796		John Boyd			
Yeates, Joshua Jr. m. Eleade, Eliz.	Nov. 19,	1801	Martha Riley		2b149	cr 11	mr 12 *

	(marriage)	(suretor)	(minister)	(bond)	
Yerky, Mary m. Conklin(Can—), Jacob	Jan. 7, 1796		Moses Hoge		cr 35 mr 11 *
Yerky, Peggy m. Blue, Jesse(Jake)	Nov. 19, 1796		Moses Hoge	3b 37	cr 36 mr 12 *
Yerky, Rachel m. Irwin, Francis	Dec. 3, 1806	Josiah Terkey	Moses Hoge	2b180	cr 35 mr 11 *
Young, Adam m. Ronsch, Rosanna	Sept. 6, 1796	John Rhinafelt			
Young, Anthony m. Siddleman, Rosy	July 28, 1785		Hugh Vance	4b213	mr 34 *
Young, Bernard m. Miller, Sarah	May 17, 1822	Solomon Swisher	Chas. P. Krauth	6b170	mr 45 *
Young, Caroline m. Blondel, John H.	May 29, 1839	Adam Young	Henry Furlong	7b182	
Young, Eliz T. m.Dawes(Doure),Isaac	Apr. 23, 1850	John Young	Hugh Vance		mr 81 *
Young, Eliz. m. Bowers, Henry Jr.	Dec. 13, 1787		David Young	2b 9	cr 23 mr 2 *
Young, Eliz. m.Brandinger, Andrew	June 22, 1799	Peter Zinn	Chas. P. Krauth	4b206	ge 8
Young, Eliz. m. Dunham, James C.	Jan. 24, 1822	Adam Young	John Hedtt(futt)	2b 18	mr 45 *
Young, Eliz. m.Hagler(Hagly),John Jos	Aug. 10, 1799	John Cooke		3b159	cr 38 mr 17 *
Young, Eliz. m. Moon, Rees	Sept 1, 1810	Nathan Young	G.W.Cooper		*
Young, Eliz. S. m. Kinsey, Samuel	Jan. 19, 1854		Moses Hoge		nr 39 *
Young, George m. Shelby, Sarah	Oct. 19, 1792		Mathias Riser		nr 30 *
Young, Hannah m. Faris, Aaron	Jan. 14, 1819				
Young, Hannah m.Gelsendorff, G.W.	Mar. 12, 1834	George Young	David Thomas	5b304	
Young, Israel m. Wilson, Rachel	Nov. 25, 1834	?		6b 23	nr 84 *
Young, John R. m. Cage, Lucy Margt.	June 30, 1851	George Young		7b227	
Young, Julia Ann m. Gingerick, Mich'l	Mar. 28, 1836	Wm. L. Boak		6b 76	
Young, Lydia m. Kercheval, Samuel	Feb. 25, 1812	Nathan Young	Jacob Medtart	3b212	
Young, Margt. m.Gelsendorff, Jacob C.	Feb. 16, 1832	Nathan Young		5b216	mr 63 *
Young, Mary m. Hill, Robert	June 13, 1836	Michael Rooney		6b 81	
Young, Mary m. Miller, David	Mar. 18, 1820	Wm. Griffith	Chas. P. Krauth	4b140	
Young, Mary m. Parrott, Samuel	Oct. 26, 1822	Adam Young		4b226	mr 45 *
Young, Nancy m. Noland, Hiram	Feb. 7, 1804	Peter Nolard	John Bell	2b222	
Young, Nancy m. Noland, Hiram	Feb. 11, 1784				cr 10 mr 1 *
Young, Nathan m. Mendenhall, Ann	Aug. 30, 1814	Amos Mendenhall		3b301	
Young, Nathan m. Moore, Julia	Sept 25, 1821	George Creamer		4b191	
Young, Nathan m. Walters, Cath.	Oct. 24, 1837	Michael Walters		6b121	
Young, Peter m.Hollinback, Cath.	July 27, 1801	George Leps	Richard Swift	2b132	
Young, Polly m. Kerney, Wm.	May 14, 1795	Joseph Young	John Hedtt(futt)	2b 59	cr 26 mr 10 *
Young, Polly m. McCarty, James	Mar. 25, 1800	Wm. Dallia	Moses Hoge	1b155	cr 33 mr 18 *
Young, Polly m. Strider, Jacob	Dec. 19, 1798	Stephen Gano		2b191	cr 29 mr 15 *
Young, Rhesa m. Ganoe, Eliz.	Jan. 22, 1803	Adam Young	Jacob Medtart	3b137	
Young, Rosanna m. Faidley, Arch'd	Aug. 13, 1829	Edward Violet		5b173	mr 63 *
Young, Samuel m. Violet, Sarah	June 29, 1811	Nathan Young		3b102	
Young, Sarah m. Ware, James	Dec. 3, 1808	Nathan Young	John Howell	3b 77	
Young, Susan m. Davis, Jeremiah	Aug. 28, 1827	Jacob Riner	Hugh Vance	5b 54	cr 23 mr 68 *
Yost, Wm. W. m. Riner, Susan	Aug. 13, 1835		David Young	6b 54	ge 6
Young, Wm. m. Tannehill, Rebecca	Dec. 13, 1787	Jacob Entler		1b 16	mr 2 *
Yost, John m. Entler, Mary	May 14, 1797				

Name		(marriage)	(suretor)	(minister)	(bond)	
Yost, John m. Siler, Barbara	Apr. 22,	1829	Henry Siler		5b128	
Yost, Peter m. Bohrer, Cath.	June 3,	1799	George Bohrer		2b 7	
Yost, Polly m. Farber, Henry	Sept 23,	1799	Wm. Yost		2b 27	
Yost, Sarah m. Hite, Wm.	Aug. 14,	1812	Nicholas Henry		3b216	
Yost, Wm. m. Miller, Betsy	Aug. 15,	1835	Jacob Riner	John Howell	6b 54	mr 68 *
Youtz, John m. Entler, Mary	May 13,	1797	Jacob Entler		1b 16	
"Z"						
Zacharias, Jacob m. Wageley, Mary	Aug. 7,	1832	Wm. Wageley	W. Monroe	5b236	mr 65 *
Zeckman, Benj. m. Weaver, Jemimah	Dec. 9,	1829	Martin Houseman	Jacob Medtart	5b146	mr 63 *
Zeckman, Samuel m.Rydenrich, Fanny	Sept 13,	1824	Ebenezer Rydenrich	Chas. P. Krauth	4b272	mr 47 *
Zeckman, Sarah m. Hite, Wm.	Aug. 20,	1818	Abr'm Weldman		4b 77	mr 80 *
Zedgler, Elis. m. McCoy, Joseph	Apr. 13,	1850	William Zedgler	John Bauman	7b181	
Zedgler, Joseph H. m. Payne, Ellen J	Mar. 29,	1854		W.G.Eglestone		cr 14
Zedgler, Martin m.Bowerman4th, Mary	May 29,	1811	James Harrison	John B. Hoge	3b188	cr 27
Zedgler, Martin m. Stover,Fanny Fran	May 3,	1803	Robert Filson	Richard Swift	2b201	gc 14
Ziler, Eliz. m. Savelly, Jacob	Aug. 8,	1815	James Thompson	Rev. Reebenack	3b332	
Ziler, Elis. m. Turner, John	Aug. 10,	1825	George Ziler	James Redly	5b 18	
Zimmerman, Cath. Mrs. m.Miller, John	Oct. 18,	1828	George Hughes	B. Reynolds	5b109	gc 14
†Zimmerman, Daniel m. Haman, Cath.	Feb. 22,	1814	George Peterman	Rev. Reebenack	3b285	gc 14
†Zimmerman, David m. Haman, Cath.	Feb. 22,	1814	George Peterman	Rev. Reebenack	3b285	
Zimmerman, Elis. m. Agent, Abr'm	Nov. 9,	1805	Wm. Wheeler		3b 2	
Zimmerman, Henry m. Riley, Elis. Mrs.	Dec. 29,	1808	Richard Hodley	Rev. Reebenack	3b104	gc 10
Zimmerman, Jacob m. Blackeney,Juliet	Nov. 28,	1811	Andrew Blakeney	Rev. Reebenack	3b202	gc 12
Zimmerman, Jacob m. Smith, Sally	Apr. 2,	1818	Joseph Smith	John B. Hoge	4b103	
Zimmerman, James m. Dowden, Nancy	Mar. 11,	1811	Wm. Mound		3b179	
Zimmerman, Jane E. m. Nipe, John N.	Nov. 16,	1836	Peter Gardner		6b 88	mr 29 **
Zimmerman, John W. m.Pine, Lydia E.	Oct. 13,	1847	Jas. M. Barkhart	P. Lipscomb	7b109	mr 81 **
Zimmerman, Mary Louisa m.Pool, Jos.	June 5,	1851	Francis M. Burkh't	David Thomas	7b226	mr 84 **
Zimmerman,Savanah Susan m. Weller,Job	Nov. 1,	1789		Christian Streit		mr 4 *
Zinn, Daniel m. Graham, Ann Swear'n	June 30,	1812	Robert Wilson		3b230	
Zinn, Daniel m. Pentony, Nancy	Sept 2,	1819	Henry Rousch		4b115	
Zombro, Jacob Jr. m.Shepherd, Eliz.	July 27,	1825	James Shepherd		5b 17	
Zorn, Cath. m. Hull, Henry	Jan. 22,	1851	John Zorn	Jas. H. Jennings	7b212	mr 83 **
Zorn, Harriet A. m. Hensel, Jas. W.	Oct. 9,	1850	John Zorn	Henry Furlong	7b200	mr 81 **
Zorn, John m. Mong, Nancy	Apr. 5,	1823	George Mong	Chas. P. Krauth	4b237	mr 46 **
Zorn, Joseph m. Richards, Emma Jane	Apr. 16,	1853		Jas. H. Jennings		mr 87 **
Zorn, W.J. m. Myers, Isabella	Jan. 5,	1854		James Watts		
Zuber, Eliz. m. Sherrard, John	Aug. 14,	1819	John Zuber		4b113	
Zumbro, Jacob m. Walter, Leah	Mar. 22,	1796		David Young		gc 5
Zumbro, Jacob Jr.-m. Shepherd, Elis.	July 27,	1825	James Shepherd		5b 17	*